The Wealth of Networks

The Wealth of Networks

How Social Production

Transforms Markets and

Freedom

Yochai Benkler

Yale University Press

New Haven and London

Printed in the United States of America.

The Library of Congress has cataloged the hardcover edition as follows:

Benkler, Yochai.
  The wealth of networks : how social production transforms markets and
freedom / Yochai Benkler.
    p. cm.
  Includes bibliographical references and index.
  ISBN-13: 978-0-300-11056-2 (alk. paper)
  ISBN-10: 0-300-11056-1 (alk. paper)
    1. Information society. 2. Information networks. 3. Computer
networks—Social aspects. 4. Computer networks—Economic aspects.
I. Title.
  HM851.B457   2006
  303.48'33—dc22   2005028316

ISBN 978-0-300-12577-1 (pbk. : alk. paper)

A catalogue record for this book is available from the British Library.

The paper in this book meets the guidelines for permanence and durability of
the Committee on Production Guidelines for Book Longevity of the Council on
Library Resources.

10 9 8 7 6 5 4 3 2 1

For Deb, Noam, and Ari

"Human nature is not a machine to be built after a model, and set to do exactly the work prescribed for it, but a tree, which requires to grow and develop itself on all sides, according to the tendency of the inward forces which make it a living thing."

"Such are the differences among human beings in their sources of pleasure, their susceptibilities of pain, and the operation on them of different physical and moral agencies, that unless there is a corresponding diversity in their modes of life, they neither obtain their fair share of happiness, nor grow up to the mental, moral, and aesthetic stature of which their nature is capable."
John Stuart Mill, On Liberty *(1859)*

Contents

Acknowledgments

Reading this manuscript was an act of heroic generosity. I owe my gratitude to those who did and who therefore helped me to avoid at least some of the errors that I would have made without their assistance. Bruce Ackerman spent countless hours listening, and reading and challenging both this book and its precursor bits and pieces since 2001. I owe much of its present conception and form to his friendship. Jack Balkin not only read the manuscript, but in an act of great generosity taught it to his seminar, imposed it on the fellows of Yale's Information Society Project, and then spent hours with me working through the limitations and pitfalls they found. Marvin Ammori, Ady Barkan, Elazar Barkan, Becky Bolin, Eszter Hargittai, Niva Elkin Koren, Amy Kapczynski, Eddan Katz, Zac Katz, Nimrod Koslovski, Orly Lobel, Katherine McDaniel, and Siva Vaidhyanathan all read the manuscript and provided valuable thoughts and insights. Michael O'Malley from Yale University Press deserves special thanks for helping me decide to write the book that I really wanted to write, not something else, and then stay the course.

This book has been more than a decade in the making. Its roots go back to 1993–1994: long nights of conversations, as only graduate students can have, with Niva Elkin Koren about democracy in cyberspace; a series of formative conversations with Mitch Kapor; a couple of madly imaginative sessions with Charlie Nesson; and a moment of true understanding with Eben Moglen. Equally central from around that time, but at an angle, were a paper under Terry Fisher's guidance on nineteenth-century homesteading and the radical republicans, and a series of classes and papers with Frank Michelman, Duncan Kennedy, Mort Horwitz, Roberto Unger, and the late David Charny, which led me to think quite fundamentally about the role of property and economic organization in the construction of human freedom. It was Frank Michelman who taught me that the hard trick was to do so as a liberal.

Since then, I have been fortunate in many and diverse intellectual friendships and encounters, from people in different fields and foci, who shed light on various aspects of this project. I met Larry Lessig for (almost) the first time in 1998. By the end of a two-hour conversation, we had formed a friendship and intellectual conversation that has been central to my work ever since. He has, over the past few years, played a pivotal role in changing the public understanding of control, freedom, and creativity in the digital environment. Over the course of these years, I spent many hours learning from Jamie Boyle, Terry Fisher, and Eben Moglen. In different ways and styles, each of them has had significant influence on my work. There was a moment, sometime between the conference Boyle organized at Yale in 1999 and the one he organized at Duke in 2001, when a range of people who had been doing similar things, pushing against the wind with varying degrees of interconnection, seemed to cohere into a single intellectual movement, centered on the importance of the commons to information production and creativity generally, and to the digitally networked environment in particular. In various contexts, both before this period and since, I have learned much from Julie Cohen, Becky Eisenberg, Bernt Hugenholtz, David Johnson, David Lange, Jessica Litman, Neil Netanel, Helen Nissenbaum, Peggy Radin, Arti Rai, David Post, Jerry Reichman, Pam Samuelson, Jon Zittrain, and Diane Zimmerman. One of the great pleasures of this field is the time I have been able to spend with technologists, economists, sociologists, and others who don't quite fit into any of these categories. Many have been very patient with me and taught me much. In particular, I owe thanks to Sam Bowles, Dave Clark, Dewayne Hendricks, Richard Jefferson, Natalie Jeremijenko, Tara Lemmey, Josh Lerner, Andy Lippman, David Reed, Chuck Sabel, Jerry Saltzer, Tim Shepard, Clay Shirky, and Eric von Hippel. In constitutional law and political theory, I benefited early and consistently from the insights of Ed Baker, with whom I spent many hours puzzling through practically every problem of political theory that I tackle in this book; Chris Eisgruber, Dick Fallon, Larry Kramer, Burt Neuborne, Larry Sager, and Kathleen Sullivan all helped in constructing various components of the argument.

Much of the early work in this project was done at New York University, whose law school offered me an intellectually engaging and institutionally safe environment to explore some quite unorthodox views. A friend, visiting when I gave a brown-bag workshop there in 1998, pointed out that at very few law schools could I have presented "The Commons as a Neglected Factor of Information Policy" as an untenured member of the faculty, to a room full of law and economics scholars, without jeopardizing my career. Mark Geistfeld, in particular, helped me work though the economics of sharing—as we shared many a pleasant afternoon on the beach, watching our boys playing in the waves. I benefited from the generosity of Al Engelberg, who funded the Engelberg Center on Innovation Law and Policy and through it students and fellows, from whose work I learned so much; and Arthur Penn, who funded the Information Law Institute and through it that amazing intellectual moment, the 2000 conference on "A Free Information Ecology in the Digital Environment," and the series of workshops that became the Open Spectrum Project. During that period, I was fortunate enough to have had wonderful students and fellows with whom I worked in various ways that later informed this book, in particular Gaia Bernstein, Mike Burstein, John Kuzin, Greg Pomerantz, Steve Snyder, and Alan Toner.

Since 2001, first as a visitor and now as a member, I have had the remarkable pleasure of being part of the intellectual community that is Yale Law School. The book in its present form, structure, and emphasis is a direct reflection of my immersion in this wonderful community. Practically every single one of my colleagues has read articles I have written over this period, attended workshops where I presented my work, provided comments that helped to improve the articles—and through them, this book, as well. I owe each and every one of them thanks, not least to Tony Kronman, who made me see that it would be so. To list them all would be redundant. To list some would inevitably underrepresent the various contributions they have made. Still, I will try to say a few of the special thanks, owing much yet to those I will not name. Working out the economics was a precondition of being able to make the core political claims. Bob Ellickson, Dan Kahan, and Carol Rose all engaged deeply with questions of reciprocity and commons-based production, while Jim Whitman kept my feet to the fire on the relationship to the anthropology of the gift. Ian Ayres, Ron Daniels during his visit, Al Klevorick, George Priest, Susan Rose-Ackerman, and Alan Schwartz provided much-needed mixtures of skepticism and help in constructing the arguments that would allay it. Akhil Amar, Owen Fiss, Jerry Mashaw, Robert Post, Jed Rubenfeld, Reva Siegal, and Kenji Yoshino helped me work on the normative and constitutional questions. The turn I took to focusing on global development as the core aspect of the implications for justice, as it is in chapter 9, resulted from an invitation from Harold Koh and Oona Hathaway to speak at their seminar on globalization, and their thoughtful comments to my paper. The greatest influence on that turn has been Amy Kapczynski's work as a fellow at Yale, and with her, the students who invited me to work with them on university licensing policy, in particular, Sam Chaifetz.

Oddly enough, I have never had the proper context in which to give two more basic thanks. My father, who was swept up in the resistance to British colonialism and later in Israel's War of Independence, dropped out of high school. He was left with a passionate intellectual hunger and a voracious appetite for reading. He died too young to even imagine sitting, as I do today with my own sons, with the greatest library in human history right there, at the dinner table, with us. But he would have loved it. Another great debt is to David Grais, who spent many hours mentoring me in my first law job, bought me my first copy of Strunk and White, and, for all practical purposes, taught me how to write in English; as he reads these words, he will be mortified, I fear, to be associated with a work of authorship as undisciplined as this, with so many excessively long sentences, replete with dependent clauses and unnecessarily complex formulations of quite simple ideas.

Finally, to my best friend and tag-team partner in this tussle we call life, Deborah Schrag, with whom I have shared nicely more or less everything since we were barely adults.

Chapter 1 Introduction: A Moment of Opportunity and Challenge

Information, knowledge, and culture are central to human freedom and human development. How they are produced and exchanged in our society critically affects the way we see the state of the world as it is and might be; who decides these questions; and how we, as societies and polities, come to understand what can and ought to be done. For more than 150 years, modern complex democracies have depended in large measure on an industrial information economy for these basic functions. In the past decade and a half, we have begun to see a radical change in the organization of information production. Enabled by technological change, we are beginning to see a series of economic, social, and cultural adaptations that make possible a radical transformation of how we make the information environment we occupy as autonomous individuals, citizens, and members of cultural and social groups. It seems passé today to speak of "the Internet revolution." In some academic circles, it is positively naïve. But it should not be. The change brought about by the networked information environment is deep. It is structural. It goes to the very foundations of how liberal markets and liberal democracies have coevolved for almost two centuries.

A series of changes in the technologies, economic organization, and social practices of production in this environment has created new opportunities for how we make and exchange information, knowledge, and culture. These changes have increased the role of nonmarket and nonproprietary production, both by individuals alone and by cooperative efforts in a wide range of loosely or tightly woven collaborations. These newly emerging practices have seen remarkable success in areas as diverse as software development and investigative reporting, avant-garde video and multiplayer online games. Together, they hint at the emergence of a new information environment, one in which individuals are free to take a more active role than was possible in the industrial information economy of the twentieth century. This new freedom holds great practical promise: as a dimension of individual freedom; as a platform for better democratic participation; as a medium to foster a more critical and self-reflective culture; and, in an increasingly information-dependent global economy, as a mechanism to achieve improvements in human development everywhere.

The rise of greater scope for individual and cooperative nonmarket production of information and culture, however, threatens the incumbents of the industrial information economy. At the beginning of the twenty-first century, we find ourselves in the midst of a battle over the institutional ecology of the digital environment. A wide range of laws and institutions— from broad areas like telecommunications, copyright, or international trade regulation, to minutiae like the rules for registering domain names or whether digital television receivers will be required by law to recognize a particular code—are being tugged and warped in efforts to tilt the playing field toward one way of doing things or the other. How these battles turn out over the next decade or so will likely have a significant effect on how we come to know what is going on in the world we occupy, and to what extent and in what forms we will be able—as autonomous individuals, as citizens, and as participants in cultures and communities—to affect how we and others see the world as it is and as it might be.

THE EMERGENCE OF THE NETWORKED
INFORMATION ECONOMY

The most advanced economies in the world today have made two parallel shifts that, paradoxically, make possible a significant attenuation of the limitations that market-based production places on the pursuit of the political values central to liberal societies. The first move, in the making for more than a century, is to an economy centered on information (financial services, accounting, software, science) and cultural (films, music) production, and the manipulation of symbols (from making sneakers to branding them and manufacturing the cultural significance of the Swoosh). The second is the move to a communications environment built on cheap processors with high computation capabilities, interconnected in a pervasive network—the phenomenon we associate with the Internet. It is this second shift that allows for an increasing role for nonmarket production in the information and cultural production sector, organized in a radically more decentralized pattern than was true of this sector in the twentieth century. The first shift means that these new patterns of production—nonmarket and radically decentralized—will emerge, if permitted, at the core, rather than the periphery of the most advanced economies. It promises to enable social production and exchange to play a much larger role, alongside property- and market-based production, than they ever have in modern democracies.

The first part of this book is dedicated to establishing a number of basic economic observations. Its overarching claim is that we are seeing the emergence of a new stage in the information economy, which I call the "networked information economy." It is displacing the industrial information economy that typified information production from about the second half of the nineteenth century and throughout the twentieth century. What characterizes the networked information economy is that decentralized individual action—specifically, new and important cooperative and coordinate action carried out through radically distributed, nonmarket mechanisms that do not depend on proprietary strategies—plays a much greater role than it did, or could have, in the industrial information economy. The catalyst for this change is the happenstance of the fabrication technology of computation, and its ripple effects throughout the technologies of communication and storage. The declining price of computation, communication, and storage have, as a practical matter, placed the material means of information and cultural production in the hands of a significant fraction of the world's population—on the order of a billion people around the globe. The core distinguishing feature of communications, information, and cultural production since the mid-nineteenth century was that effective communication spanning the ever-larger societies and geographies that came to make up the relevant political and economic units of the day required ever-larger investments of physical capital. Large-circulation mechanical presses, the telegraph system, powerful radio and later television transmitters, cable and satellite, and the mainframe computer became necessary to make information and communicate it on scales that went beyond the very local. Wanting to communicate with others was not a sufficient condition to being able to do so. As a result, information and cultural production took on, over the course of this period, a more industrial model than the economics of information itself would have required. The rise of the networked, computer-mediated communications environment has changed this basic fact. The material requirements for effective information production and communication are now owned by numbers of individuals several orders of magnitude larger than the number of owners of the basic means of information production and exchange a mere two decades ago.

The removal of the physical constraints on effective information production has made human creativity and the economics of information itself the core structuring facts in the new networked information economy. These have quite different characteristics than coal, steel, and manual human labor, which characterized the industrial economy and structured our basic thinking about economic production for the past century. They lead to three observations about the emerging information production system. First, nonproprietary strategies have always been more important in information production than they were in the production of steel or automobiles, even when the economics of communication weighed in favor of industrial models. Education, arts and sciences, political debate, and theological disputation have always been much more importantly infused with nonmarket motivations and actors than, say, the automobile industry. As the material barrier that ultimately nonetheless drove much of our information environment to be funneled through the proprietary, market-based strategies is removed, these basic nonmarket, nonproprietary, motivations and organizational forms should in principle become even more important to the information production system.

Second, we have in fact seen the rise of nonmarket production to much greater importance. Individuals can reach and inform or edify millions around the world. Such a reach was simply unavailable to diversely motivated individuals before, unless they funneled their efforts through either market organizations or philanthropically or state-funded efforts. The fact that every such effort is available to anyone connected to the network, from anywhere, has led to the emergence of coordinate effects, where the aggregate effect of individual action, even when it is not self-consciously cooperative, produces the coordinate effect of a new and rich information environment. One needs only to run a Google search on any subject of interest to see how the "information good" that is the response to one's query is produced by the coordinate effects of the uncoordinated actions of a wide and diverse range of individuals and organizations acting on a wide range of motivations— both market and nonmarket, state-based and nonstate.

Third, and likely most radical, new, and difficult for observers to believe, is the rise of effective, large-scale cooperative efforts—peer production of information, knowledge, and culture. These are typified by the emergence of free and open-source software. We are beginning to see the expansion of this model not only to our core software platforms, but beyond them into every domain of information and cultural production—and this book visits these in many different domains—from peer production of encyclopedias, to news and commentary, to immersive entertainment.

It is easy to miss these changes. They run against the grain of some of our most basic Economics 101 intuitions, intuitions honed in the industrial economy at a time when the only serious alternative seen was state Communism—an alternative almost universally considered unattractive today. The undeniable economic success of free software has prompted some leading-edge economists to try to understand why many thousands of loosely networked free software developers can compete with Microsoft at its own game and produce a massive operating system—GNU/Linux. That growing literature, consistent with its own goals, has focused on software and the particulars of the free and open-source software development communities, although Eric von Hippel's notion of "user-driven innovation" has begun to expand that focus to thinking about how individual need and creativity drive innovation at the individual level, and its diffusion through networks of like-minded individuals. The political implications of free software have been central to the free software movement and its founder, Richard Stallman, and were developed provocatively and with great insight by Eben Moglen. Free software is but one salient example of a much broader phenomenon. Why can fifty thousand volunteers successfully coauthor *Wikipedia,* the most serious online alternative to the *Encyclopedia Britannica*, and then turn around and give it away for free? Why do 4.5 million volunteers contribute their leftover computer cycles to create the most powerful supercomputer on Earth, SETI@Home? Without a broadly accepted analytic model to explain these phenomena, we tend to treat them as curiosities, perhaps transient fads, possibly of significance in one market segment or another. We should try instead to see them for what they are: a new mode of production emerging in the middle of the most advanced economies in the world—those that are the most fully computer networked and for which information goods and services have come to occupy the highest-valued roles.

Human beings are, and always have been, diversely motivated beings. We act instrumentally, but also noninstrumentally. We act for material gain, but also for psychological well-being and gratification, and for social connectedness. There is nothing new or earth-shattering about this, except perhaps to some economists. In the industrial economy in general, and the industrial information economy as well, most opportunities to make things that were valuable and important to many people were constrained by the physical capital requirements of making them. From the steam engine to the assembly line, from the double-rotary printing press to the communications satellite, the capital constraints on action were such that simply wanting to do something was rarely a sufficient condition to enable one to do it. Financing the necessary physical capital, in turn, oriented the necessarily capital-intensive projects toward a production and organizational strategy that could justify the investments. In market economies, that meant orienting toward market production. In state-run economies, that meant orienting production toward the goals of the state bureaucracy. In either case, the practical individual freedom to cooperate with others in making things of value was limited by the extent of the capital requirements of production.

In the networked information economy, the physical capital required for production is broadly distributed throughout society. Personal computers and network connections are ubiquitous. This does not mean that they cannot be used for markets, or that individuals cease to seek market opportunities. It does mean, however, that whenever someone, somewhere, among the billion connected human beings, and ultimately among all those who will be connected, wants to make something that requires human creativity, a computer, and a network connection, he or she can do so—alone, or in cooperation with others. He or she already has the capital capacity necessary to do so; if not alone, then at least in cooperation with other individuals acting for complementary reasons. The result is that a good deal more that human beings value can now be done by individuals, who interact with each other socially, as human beings and as social beings, rather than as market actors through the price system. Sometimes, under conditions I specify in some detail, these nonmarket collaborations can be better at motivating effort and can allow creative people to work on information projects more efficiently than would traditional market mechanisms and corporations. The result is a flourishing nonmarket sector of information, knowledge, and cultural production, based in the networked environment, and applied to anything that the many individuals connected to it can imagine. Its outputs, in turn, are not treated as exclusive property. They are instead subject to an increasingly robust ethic of open sharing, open for all others to build on, extend, and make their own.

Because the presence and importance of nonmarket production has become so counterintuitive to people living in market-based economies at the end of the twentieth century, part I of this volume is fairly detailed and technical; overcoming what we intuitively "know" requires disciplined analysis. Readers who are not inclined toward economic analysis should at least read the introduction to part I, the segments entitled "When Information Production Meets the Computer Network" and "Diversity of Strategies in our Current Production System" in chapter 2, and the case studies in chapter 3. These should provide enough of an intuitive feel for what I mean by the diversity of production strategies for information and the emergence of nonmarket individual and cooperative production, to serve as the basis for the more normatively oriented parts of the book. Readers who are genuinely skeptical of the possibility that nonmarket production is sustainable and effective, and in many cases is an efficient strategy for information, knowledge, and cultural production, should take the time to read part I in its entirety. The emergence of precisely this possibility and practice lies at the very heart of my claims about the ways in which liberal commitments are translated into lived experiences in the networked environment, and forms the factual foundation of the political-theoretical and the institutional-legal discussion that occupies the remainder of the book.

NETWORKED INFORMATION ECONOMY AND
LIBERAL, DEMOCRATIC SOCIETIES

How we make information, how we get it, how we speak to others, and how others speak to us are core components of the shape of freedom in any society. Part II of this book provides a detailed look at how the changes in the technological, economic, and social affordances of the networked information environment affect a series of core commitments of a wide range of liberal democracies. The basic claim is that the diversity of ways of organizing information production and use opens a range of possibilities for pursuing the core political values of liberal societies—individual freedom, a more genuinely participatory political system, a critical culture, and social justice. These values provide the vectors of political morality along which the shape and dimensions of any liberal society can be plotted. Because their practical policy implications are often contradictory, rather than complementary, the pursuit of each places certain limits on how we pursue the others, leading different liberal societies to respect them in different patterns. How much a society constrains the democratic decision-making powers of the majority in favor of individual freedom, or to what extent it pursues social justice, have always been attributes that define the political contours and nature of that society. But the economics of industrial production, and our pursuit of productivity and growth, have imposed a limit on how we can pursue any mix of arrangements to implement our commitments to freedom and justice. Singapore is commonly trotted out as an extreme example of the trade-off of freedom for welfare, but all democracies with advanced capitalist economies have made some such trade-off. Predictions of how well we will be able to feed ourselves are always an important consideration in thinking about whether, for example, to democratize wheat production or make it more egalitarian. Efforts to push workplace democracy have also often foundered on the shoals—real or imagined—of these limits, as have many plans for redistribution in the name of social justice. Market-based, proprietary production has often seemed simply too productive to tinker with. The emergence of the networked information economy promises to expand the horizons of the feasible in political imagination. Different liberal polities can pursue different mixtures of respect for different liberal commitments. However, the overarching constraint represented by the seeming necessity of the industrial model of information and cultural production has significantly shifted as an effective constraint on the pursuit of liberal commitments.

Enhanced Autonomy

The networked information economy improves the practical capacities of individuals along three dimensions: (1) it improves their capacity to do more for and by themselves; (2) it enhances their capacity to do more in loose commonality with others, without being constrained to organize their relationship through a price system or in traditional hierarchical models of social and economic organization; and (3) it improves the capacity of individuals to do more in formal organizations that operate outside the market sphere. This enhanced autonomy is at the core of all the other improvements I describe. Individuals are using their newly expanded practical freedom to act and cooperate with others in ways that improve the practiced experience of democracy, justice and development, a critical culture, and community.

I begin, therefore, with an analysis of the effects of networked information economy on individual autonomy. First, individuals can do more for themselves independently of the permission or cooperation of others. They can create their own expressions, and they can seek out the information they need, with substantially less dependence on the commercial mass media of the twentieth century. Second, and no less importantly, individuals can do more in loose affiliation with others, rather than requiring stable, long-term relations, like coworker relations or participation in formal organizations, to underwrite effective cooperation. Very few individuals living in the industrial information economy could, in any realistic sense, decide to build a new Library of Alexandria of global reach, or to start an encyclopedia. As collaboration among far-flung individuals becomes more common, the idea of doing things that require cooperation with others becomes much more attainable, and the range of projects individuals can choose as their own therefore qualitatively increases. The very fluidity and low commitment required of any given cooperative relationship increases the range and diversity of cooperative relations people can enter, and therefore of collaborative projects they can conceive of as open to them.

These ways in which autonomy is enhanced require a fairly substantive and rich conception of autonomy as a practical lived experience, rather than the formal conception preferred by many who think of autonomy as a philosophical concept. But even from a narrower perspective, which spans a broader range of conceptions of autonomy, at a minimum we can say that individuals are less susceptible to manipulation by a legally defined class of others—the owners of communications infrastructure and media. The networked information economy provides varied alternative platforms for communication, so that it moderates the power of the traditional mass-media model, where ownership of the means of communication enables an owner to select what others view, and thereby to affect their perceptions of what they can and cannot do. Moreover, the diversity of perspectives on the way the world is and the way it could be for any given individual is qualitatively increased. This gives individuals a significantly greater role in authoring their own lives, by enabling them to perceive a broader range of possibilities, and by providing them a richer baseline against which to measure the choices they in fact make.

Democracy: The Networked Public Sphere

The second major implication of the networked information economy is the shift it enables from the mass-mediated public sphere to a networked public sphere. This shift is also based on the increasing freedom individuals enjoy to participate in creating information and knowledge, and the possibilities it presents for a new public sphere to emerge alongside the commercial, mass-media markets. The idea that the Internet democratizes is hardly new. It has been a staple of writing about the Internet since the early 1990s. The relatively simple first-generation claims about the liberating effects of the Internet, summarized in the U.S. Supreme Court's celebration of its potential to make everyone a pamphleteer, came under a variety of criticisms and attacks over the course of the past half decade or so. Here, I offer a detailed analysis of how the emergence of a networked information economy in particular, as an alternative to mass media, improves the political public sphere. The first-generation critique of the democratizing effect of the Internet was based on various implications of the problem of information overload, or the Babel objection. According to the Babel objection, when everyone can speak, no one can be heard, and we devolve either to a cacophony or to the reemergence of money as the distinguishing factor between statements that are heard and those that wallow in obscurity. The second-generation critique was that the Internet is not as decentralized as we thought in the 1990s. The emerging patterns of Internet use show that very few sites capture an exceedingly large amount of attention, and millions of sites go unnoticed. In this world, the Babel objection is perhaps avoided, but only at the expense of the very promise of the Internet as a democratic medium.

In chapters 6 and 7, I offer a detailed and updated analysis of this, perhaps the best-known and most contentious claim about the Internet's liberalizing effects. First, it is important to understand that any consideration of the democratizing effects of the Internet must measure its effects as compared to the commercial, mass-media-based public sphere, not as compared to an idealized utopia that we embraced a decade ago of how the Internet might be. Commercial mass media that have dominated the public spheres of all modern democracies have been studied extensively. They have been shown in extensive literature to exhibit a series of failures as platforms for public discourse. First, they provide a relatively limited intake basin—that is, too many observations and concerns of too many people in complex modern societies are left unobserved and unattended to by the small cadre of commercial journalists charged with perceiving the range of issues of public concern in any given society. Second, particularly where the market is concentrated, they give their owners inordinate power to shape opinion and information. This power they can either use themselves or sell to the highest bidder. And third, whenever the owners of commercial media choose not to exercise their power in this way, they then tend to program toward the inane and soothing, rather than toward that which will be politically engaging, and they tend to oversimplify complex public discussions. On the background of these limitations of the mass media, I suggest that the networked public sphere enables many more individuals to communicate their observations and their viewpoints to many others, and to do so in a way that cannot be controlled by media owners and is not as easily corruptible by money as were the mass media.

The empirical and theoretical literature about network topology and use provides answers to all the major critiques of the claim that the Internet improves the structure of the public sphere. In particular, I show how a wide range of mechanisms—starting from the simple mailing list, through static Web pages, the emergence of writable Web capabilities, and mobility—are being embedded in a social system for the collection of politically salient information, observations, and comments, and provide a platform for discourse. These platforms solve some of the basic limitations of the commercial, concentrated mass media as the core platform of the public sphere in contemporary complex democracies. They enable anyone, anywhere, to go through his or her practical life, observing the social environment through new eyes—the eyes of someone who could actually inject a thought, a criticism, or a concern into the public debate. Individuals become less passive, and thus more engaged observers of social spaces that could potentially become subjects for political conversation; they become more engaged participants in the debates about their observations. The various formats of the networked public sphere provide anyone with an outlet to speak, to inquire, to investigate, without need to access the resources of a major media organization. We are seeing the emergence of new, decentralized approaches to fulfilling the watchdog function and to engaging in political debate and organization. These are being undertaken in a distinctly nonmarket form, in ways that would have been much more difficult to pursue effectively, as a standard part of the construction of the public sphere, before the networked information environment. Working through detailed examples, I try to render the optimism about the democratic advantages of the networked public sphere a fully specified argument.

The networked public sphere has also begun to respond to the information overload problem, but without re-creating the power of mass media at the points of filtering and accreditation. There are two core elements to these developments: First, we are beginning to see the emergence of non-market, peer-produced alternative sources of filtration and accreditation in place of the market-based alternatives. Relevance and accreditation are themselves information goods, just like software or an encyclopedia. What we are seeing on the network is that filtering for both relevance and accreditation has become the object of widespread practices of mutual pointing, of peer review, of pointing to original sources of claims, and its complement, the social practice that those who have some ability to evaluate the claims in fact do comment on them. The second element is a contingent but empirically confirmed observation of how users actually use the network. As a descriptive matter, information flow in the network is much more ordered than a simple random walk in the cacophony of information flow would suggest, and significantly less centralized than the mass media environment was. Some sites are much more visible and widely read than others. This is true both when one looks at the Web as a whole, and when one looks at smaller clusters of similar sites or users who tend to cluster. Most commentators who have looked at this pattern have interpreted it as a reemergence of mass media—the dominance of the few visible sites. But a full consideration of the various elements of the network topology literature supports a very different interpretation, in which order emerges in the networked environment without re-creating the failures of the mass-media-dominated public sphere. Sites cluster around communities of interest: Australian fire brigades tend to link to other Australian fire brigades, conservative political blogs (Web logs or online journals) in the United States to other conservative political blogs in the United States, and to a lesser but still significant extent, to liberal political blogs. In each of these clusters, the pattern of some high visibility nodes continues, but as the clusters become small enough, many more of the sites are moderately linked to each other in the cluster. Through this pattern, the network seems to be forming into an attention backbone. "Local" clusters—communities of interest—can provide initial vetting and "peer-review-like" qualities to individual contributions made within an interest cluster. Observations that are seen as significant within a community of interest make their way to the relatively visible sites in that cluster, from where they become visible to people in larger ("regional") clusters. This continues until an observation makes its way to the "superstar" sites that hundreds of thousands of people might read and use. This path is complemented by the practice of relatively easy commenting and posting directly to many of the superstar sites, which creates shortcuts to wide attention. It is fairly simple to grasp intuitively why these patterns might emerge. Users tend to treat other people's choices about what to link to and to read as good indicators of what is worthwhile for them. They are not slavish in this, though; they apply some judgment of their own as to whether certain types of users—say, political junkies of a particular stripe, or fans of a specific television program—are the best predictors of what will be interesting for them. The result is that attention in the networked environment is more dependent on being interesting to an engaged group of people than it is in the mass-media environment, where moderate interest to large numbers of weakly engaged viewers is preferable. Because of the redundancy of clusters and links, and because many clusters are based on mutual interest, not on capital investment, it is more difficult to buy attention on the Internet than it is in mass media outlets, and harder still to use money to squelch an opposing view. These characteristics save the networked environment from the Babel objection without reintroducing excessive power in any single party or small cluster of them, and without causing a resurgence in the role of money as a precondition to the ability to speak publicly.

Justice and Human Development

Information, knowledge, and information-rich goods and tools play a significant role in economic opportunity and human development. While the networked information economy cannot solve global hunger and disease, its emergence does open reasonably well-defined new avenues for addressing and constructing some of the basic requirements of justice and human development. Because the outputs of the networked information economy are usually nonproprietary, it provides free access to a set of the basic instrumentalities of economic opportunity and the basic outputs of the information economy. From a liberal perspective concerned with justice, at a minimum, these outputs become more readily available as "finished goods" to those who are least well off. More importantly, the availability of free information resources makes participating in the economy less dependent on surmounting access barriers to financing and social-transactional networks that made working out of poverty difficult in industrial economies. These resources and tools thus improve equality of opportunity.

From a more substantive and global perspective focused on human development, the freedom to use basic resources and capabilities allows improved participation in the production of information and information-dependent components of human development. First, and currently most advanced, the emergence of a broad range of free software utilities makes it easier for poor and middle-income countries to obtain core software capabilities. More importantly, free software enables the emergence of local capabilities to provide software services, both for national uses and as a basis for participating in a global software services industry, without need to rely on permission from multinational software companies. Scientific publication is beginning to use commons-based strategies to publish important sources of information in a way that makes the outputs freely available in poorer countries. More ambitiously, we begin to see in agricultural research a combined effort of public, nonprofit, and open-source-like efforts being developed and applied to problems of agricultural innovation. The ultimate purpose is to develop a set of basic capabilities that would allow collaboration among farmers and scientists, in both poor countries and around the globe, to develop better, more nutritious crops to improve food security throughout the poorer regions of the world. Equally ambitious, but less operationally advanced, we are beginning to see early efforts to translate this system of innovation to health-related products.

All these efforts are aimed at solving one of the most glaring problems of poverty and poor human development in the global information economy: Even as opulence increases in the wealthier economies—as information and innovation offer longer and healthier lives that are enriched by better access to information, knowledge, and culture—in many places, life expectancy is decreasing, morbidity is increasing, and illiteracy remains rampant. Some, although by no means all, of this global injustice is due to the fact that we have come to rely ever-more exclusively on proprietary business models of the industrial economy to provide some of the most basic information components of human development. As the networked information economy develops new ways of producing information, whose outputs are not treated as proprietary and exclusive but can be made available freely to everyone, it offers modest but meaningful opportunities for improving human development everywhere. We are seeing early signs of the emergence of an innovation ecosystem made of public funding, traditional nonprofits, and the newly emerging sector of peer production that is making it possible to advance human development through cooperative efforts in both rich countries and poor.

A Critical Culture and Networked Social Relations

The networked information economy also allows for the emergence of a more critical and self-reflective culture. In the past decade, a number of legal scholars—Niva Elkin Koren, Terry Fisher, Larry Lessig, and Jack Balkin—have begun to examine how the Internet democratizes culture. Following this work and rooted in the deliberative strand of democratic theory, I suggest that the networked information environment offers us a more attractive cultural production system in two distinct ways: (1) it makes culture more transparent, and (2) it makes culture more malleable. Together, these mean that we are seeing the emergence of a new folk culture—a practice that has been largely suppressed in the industrial era of cultural production—where many more of us participate actively in making cultural moves and finding meaning in the world around us. These practices make their practitioners better "readers" of their own culture and more self-reflective and critical of the culture they occupy, thereby enabling them to become more self-reflective participants in conversations within that culture. This also allows individuals much greater freedom to participate in tugging and pulling at the cultural creations of others, "glomming on" to them, as Balkin puts it, and making the culture they occupy more their own than was possible with mass-media culture. In these senses, we can say that culture is becoming more democratic: self-reflective and participatory.

Throughout much of this book, I underscore the increased capabilities of individuals as the core driving social force behind the networked information economy. This heightened individual capacity has raised concerns by many that the Internet further fragments community, continuing the long trend of industrialization. A substantial body of empirical literature suggests, however, that we are in fact using the Internet largely at the expense of television, and that this exchange is a good one from the perspective of social ties. We use the Internet to keep in touch with family and intimate friends, both geographically proximate and distant. To the extent we do see a shift in social ties, it is because, in addition to strengthening our strong bonds, we are also increasing the range and diversity of weaker connections. Following

Manuel Castells and Barry Wellman, I suggest that we have become more adept at filling some of the same emotional and context-generating functions that have traditionally been associated with the importance of community with a network of overlapping social ties that are limited in duration or intensity.

FOUR METHODOLOGICAL COMMENTS

There are four methodological choices represented by the thesis that I have outlined up to this point, and therefore in this book as a whole, which require explication and defense. The first is that I assign a very significant role to technology. The second is that I offer an explanation centered on social relations, but operating in the domain of economics, rather than sociology. The third and fourth are more internal to liberal political theory. The third is that I am offering a liberal political theory, but taking a path that has usually been resisted in that literature—considering economic structure and the limits of the market and its supporting institutions from the perspective of freedom, rather than accepting the market as it is, and defending or criticizing adjustments through the lens of distributive justice. Fourth, my approach heavily emphasizes individual action in nonmarket relations. Much of the discussion revolves around the choice between markets and nonmarket social behavior. In much of it, the state plays no role, or is perceived as playing a primarily negative role, in a way that is alien to the progressive branches of liberal political thought. In this, it seems more of a libertarian or an anarchistic thesis than a liberal one. I do not completely discount the state, as I will explain. But I do suggest that what is special about our moment is the rising efficacy of individuals and loose, nonmarket affiliations as agents of political economy. Just like the market, the state will have to adjust to this new emerging modality of human action. Liberal political theory must first recognize and understand it before it can begin to renegotiate its agenda for the liberal state, progressive or otherwise.

The Role of Technology in Human Affairs

The first methodological choice concerns how one should treat the role of technology in the development of human affairs. The kind of technological determinism that typified Lewis Mumford, or, specifically in the area of communications, Marshall McLuhan, is widely perceived in academia today as being too deterministic, though perhaps not so in popular culture. The contemporary effort to offer more nuanced, institution-based, and political-choice-based explanations is perhaps best typified by Paul Starr's recent and excellent work on the creation of the media. While these contemporary efforts are indeed powerful, one should not confuse a work like Elizabeth Eisenstein's carefully argued and detailed *The Printing Press as an Agent of Change*, with McLuhan's determinism. Assuming that technologies are just tools that happen, more or less, to be there, and are employed in any given society in a pattern that depends only on what that society and culture makes of them is too constrained. A society that has no wheel and no writing has certain limits on what it can do. Barry Wellman has imported into sociology a term borrowed from engineering—affordances.[1] Langdon Winner called these the "political properties" of technologies.[2] An earlier version of this idea is Harold Innis's concept of "the bias of communications."[3] In Internet law and policy debates this approach has become widely adopted through the influential work of Lawrence Lessig, who characterized it as "code is law."[4]

The idea is simple to explain, and distinct from a naïve determinism. Different technologies make different kinds of human action and interaction easier or harder to perform. All other things being equal, things that are easier to do are more likely to be done, and things that are harder to do are less likely to be done. All other things are never equal. That is why technological determinism in the strict sense—if you have technology "t," you should expect social structure or relation "s" to emerge—is false. Ocean navigation had a different adoption and use when introduced in states whose land empire ambitions were effectively countered by strong neighbors—like Spain and Portugal—than in nations that were focused on building a vast inland empire, like China. Print had different effects on literacy in countries where religion encouraged individual reading—like Prussia, Scotland, England, and New England—than where religion discouraged individual, unmediated interaction with texts, like France and Spain. This form of understanding the role of technology is adopted here. Neither deterministic nor wholly malleable, technology sets some parameters of individual and social action. It can make some actions, relationships, organizations, and institutions easier to pursue, and others harder. In a challenging environment—be the challenges natural or human—it can make some behaviors obsolete by increasing the efficacy of directly competitive strategies. However, within the realm of the feasible—uses not rendered impossible by the adoption or rejection of a technology—different patterns of adoption and use can result in very different social relations that emerge around a technology. Unless these patterns are in competition, or unless even in competition they are not catastrophically less effective at meeting the challenges, different societies can persist with different patterns of use over long periods. It is the feasibility of long-term sustainability of different patterns of use that makes this book relevant to policy, not purely to theory. The same technologies of networked computers can be adopted in very different patterns. There is no guarantee that networked information technology will lead to the improvements in innovation, freedom, and justice that I suggest are possible. That is a choice we face as a society. The way we develop will, in significant measure, depend on choices we make in the next decade or so.

The Role of Economic Analysis and Methodological Individualism

It should be emphasized, as the second point, that this book has a descriptive methodology that is distinctly individualist and economic in orientation, which is hardly the only way to approach this problem. Manuel Castells's magisterial treatment of the networked society[5] locates its central characteristic in the shift from groups and hierarchies to networks as social and organizational models—looser, flexible arrangements of human affairs. Castells develops this theory as he describes a wide range of changes, from transportation networks to globalization and industrialization. In his work, the Internet fits into this trend, enabling better coordination and cooperation in these sorts of loosely affiliated networks. My own emphasis is on the specific relative roles of market and nonmarket sectors, and how that change anchors the radical decentralization that he too observes, as a matter of sociological observation. I place at the core of the shift the technical and economic characteristics of computer networks and information. These provide the pivot for the shift toward radical decentralization of production. They underlie the shift from an information environment dominated by proprietary, market-oriented action, to a world in which nonproprietary, nonmarket transactional frameworks play a large role alongside market production. This newly emerging, nonproprietary sector affects to a substantial degree the entire information environment in which individuals and societies live their lives. If there is one lesson we can learn from globalization and the ever-increasing reach of the market, it is that the logic of the market exerts enormous pressure on existing social structures. If we are indeed seeing the emergence of a substantial component of nonmarket production at the very core of our economic engine—the production and exchange of information, and through it of information-based goods, tools, services, and capabilities—then this change suggests a genuine limit on the extent of the market. Such a limit, growing from within the very market that it limits, in its most advanced loci, would represent a genuine shift in direction for what appeared to be the ever-increasing global reach of the market economy and society in the past half century.

Economic Structure in Liberal Political Theory

The third point has to do with the role of economic structure in liberal political theory. My analysis in this regard is practical and human centric. By this, I mean to say two things: First, I am concerned with human beings, with individuals as the bearers of moral claims regarding the structure of the political and economic systems they inhabit. Within the liberal tradition, the position I take is humanistic and general, as opposed to political and particular. It is concerned first and foremost with the claims of human beings as human beings, rather than with the requirements of democracy or the entitlements of citizenship or membership in a legitimate or meaningfully self-governed political community. There are diverse ways of respecting the basic claims of human freedom, dignity, and well-being. Different liberal polities do so with different mixes of constitutional and policy practices. The rise of global information economic structures and relationships affects human beings everywhere. In some places, it complements democratic traditions. In others, it destabilizes constraints on liberty. An understanding of how we can think of this moment in terms of human freedom and development must transcend the particular traditions, both liberal and illiberal, of any single nation. The actual practice of freedom that we see emerging from the networked environment allows people to reach across national or social boundaries, across space and political division. It allows people to solve problems together in new associations that are outside the boundaries of formal, legal-political association. In this fluid social economic environment, the individual's claims provide a moral anchor for considering the structures of power and opportunity, of freedom and well-being. Furthermore, while it is often convenient and widely accepted to treat organizations or communities as legal entities, as "persons," they are not moral agents. Their role in an analysis of freedom and justice is derivative from their role—both enabling and constraining—as structuring context in which human beings, the actual moral agents of political economy, find themselves. In this regard, my positions here are decidedly "liberal," as opposed to either communitarian or critical.

Second, I am concerned with actual human beings in actual historical settings, not with representations of human beings abstracted from their settings. These commitments mean that freedom and justice for historically situated individuals are measured from a first-person, practical perspective. No constraints on individual freedom and no sources of inequality are categorically exempt from review, nor are any considered privileged under this view. Neither economy nor cultural heritage is given independent moral weight. A person whose life and relations are fully regimented by external forces is unfree, no matter whether the source of regimentation can be understood as market-based, authoritarian, or traditional community values. This does not entail a radical anarchism or libertarianism. Organizations, communities, and other external structures are pervasively necessary for human beings to flourish and to act freely and effectively. This does mean, however, that I think of these structures only from the perspective of their effects on human beings. Their value is purely derivative from their importance to the actual human beings that inhabit them and are structured—for better or worse—by them. As a practical matter, this places concern with market structure and economic organization much closer to the core of questions of freedom than liberal theory usually is willing to do. Liberals have tended to leave the basic structure of property and markets either to libertarians—who, like Friedrich Hayek, accepted its present contours as "natural," and a core constituent element of freedom—or to Marxists and neo-Marxists. I treat property and markets as just one domain of human action, with affordances and limitations. Their presence enhances freedom along some dimensions, but their institutional requirements can become sources of constraint when they squelch freedom of action in nonmarket contexts. Calibrating the reach of the market, then, becomes central not only to the shape of justice or welfare in a society, but also to freedom.

Whither the State?

The fourth and last point emerges in various places throughout this book, but deserves explicit note here. What I find new and interesting about the networked information economy is the rise of individual practical capabilities, and the role that these new capabilities play in increasing the relative salience of nonproprietary, often nonmarket individual and social behavior.

In my discussion of autonomy and democracy, of justice and a critical culture, I emphasize the rise of individual and cooperative private action and the relative decrease in the dominance of market-based and proprietary action. Where in all this is the state? For the most part, as you will see particularly in chapter 11, the state in both the United States and Europe has played a role in supporting the market-based industrial incumbents of the twentieth-century information production system at the expense of the individuals who make up the emerging networked information economy. Most state interventions have been in the form of either captured legislation catering to incumbents, or, at best, well-intentioned but wrongheaded efforts to optimize the institutional ecology for outdated modes of information and cultural production. In the traditional mapping of political theory, a position such as the one I present here—that freedom and justice can and should best be achieved by a combination of market action and private, voluntary (not to say charitable) nonmarket action, and that the state is a relatively suspect actor—is libertarian. Perhaps, given that I subject to similar criticism rules styled by their proponents as "property"—like "intellectual property" or "spectrum property rights"—it is anarchist, focused on the role of mutual aid and highly skeptical of the state. (It is quite fashionable nowadays to be libertarian, as it has been for a few decades, and more fashionable to be anarchist than it has been in a century.)

The more modest truth is that my position is not rooted in a theoretical skepticism about the state, but in a practical diagnosis of opportunities, barriers, and strategies for achieving improvements in human freedom and development given the actual conditions of technology, economy, and politics. I have no objection in principle to an effective, liberal state pursuing one of a range of liberal projects and commitments. Here and there throughout this book you will encounter instances where I suggest that the state could play constructive roles, if it stopped listening to incumbents for long enough to realize this. These include, for example, municipal funding of neutral broadband networks, state funding of basic research, and possible strategic regulatory interventions to negate monopoly control over essential resources in the digital environment. However, the necessity for the state's affirmative role is muted because of my diagnosis of the particular trajectory of markets, on the one hand, and individual and social action, on the other hand, in the digitally networked information environment. The particular economics of computation and communications; the particular economics of information, knowledge, and cultural production; and the relative role of information in contemporary, advanced economies have coalesced to make nonmarket individual and social action the most important domain of action in the furtherance of the core liberal commitments. Given these particular characteristics, there is more freedom to be found through opening up institutional spaces for voluntary individual and cooperative action than there is in intentional public action through the state. Nevertheless, I offer no particular reasons to resist many of the roles traditionally played by the liberal state. I offer no reason to think that, for example, education should stop being primarily a state-funded, public activity and a core responsibility of the liberal state, or that public health should not be so. I have every reason to think that the rise of nonmarket production enhances, rather than decreases, the justifiability of state funding for basic science and research, as the spillover effects of publicly funded information production can now be much greater and more effectively disseminated and used to enhance the general welfare.

The important new fact about the networked environment, however, is the efficacy and centrality of individual and collective social action. In most domains, freedom of action for individuals, alone and in loose cooperation with others, can achieve much of the liberal desiderata I consider throughout this book. From a global perspective, enabling individuals to act in this way also extends the benefits of liberalization across borders, increasing the capacities of individuals in nonliberal states to grab greater freedom than those who control their political systems would like. By contrast, as long as states in the most advanced market-based economies continue to try to optimize their institutional frameworks to support the incumbents of the industrial information economy, they tend to threaten rather than support liberal commitments. Once the networked information economy has stabilized and we come to understand the relative importance of voluntary private action outside of markets, the state can begin to adjust its policies to facilitate nonmarket action and to take advantage of its outputs to improve its own support for core liberal commitments.

THE STAKES OF IT ALL: THE BATTLE OVER THE INSTITUTIONAL ECOLOGY OF THE DIGITAL ENVIRONMENT

No benevolent historical force will inexorably lead this technological-economic moment to develop toward an open, diverse, liberal equilibrium.

If the transformation I describe as possible occurs, it will lead to substantial redistribution of power and money from the twentieth-century industrial producers of information, culture, and communications—like Hollywood, the recording industry, and perhaps the broadcasters and some of the tele-communications services giants—to a combination of widely diffuse populations around the globe, and the market actors that will build the tools that make this population better able to produce its own information environment rather than buying it ready-made. None of the industrial giants of yore are taking this reallocation lying down. The technology will not overcome their resistance through an insurmountable progressive impulse. The reorganization of production and the advances it can bring in freedom and justice will emerge, therefore, only as a result of social and political action aimed at protecting the new social patterns from the incumbents' assaults. It is precisely to develop an understanding of what is at stake and why it is worth fighting for that I write this book. I offer no reassurances, however, that any of this will in fact come to pass.

The battle over the relative salience of the proprietary, industrial models of information production and exchange and the emerging networked information economy is being carried out in the domain of the institutional ecology of the digital environment. In a wide range of contexts, a similar set of institutional questions is being contested: To what extent will resources necessary for information production and exchange be governed as a commons, free for all to use and biased in their availability in favor of none? To what extent will these resources be entirely proprietary, and available only to those functioning within the market or within traditional forms of well-funded nonmarket action like the state and organized philanthropy? We see this battle played out at all layers of the information environment: the physical devices and network channels necessary to communicate; the existing information and cultural resources out of which new statements must be made; and the logical resources—the software and standards—necessary to translate what human beings want to say to each other into signals that machines can process and transmit. Its central question is whether there will, or will not, be a core common infrastructure that is governed as a commons and therefore available to anyone who wishes to participate in the networked information environment outside of the market-based, proprietary framework.

This is not to say that property is in some sense inherently bad. Property, together with contract, is the core institutional component of markets, and a core institutional element of liberal societies. It is what enables sellers to extract prices from buyers, and buyers to know that when they pay, they will be secure in their ability to use what they bought. It underlies our capacity to plan actions that require use of resources that, without exclusivity, would be unavailable for us to use. But property also constrains action. The rules of property are circumscribed and intended to elicit a particular datum—willingness and ability to pay for exclusive control over a resource. They constrain what one person or another can do with regard to a resource; that is, use it in some ways but not others, reveal or hide information with regard to it, and so forth. These constraints are necessary so that people must transact with each other through markets, rather than through force or social networks, but they do so at the expense of constraining action outside of the market to the extent that it depends on access to these resources.

Commons are another core institutional component of freedom of action in free societies, but they are structured to enable action that is not based on exclusive control over the resources necessary for action. For example, I can plan an outdoor party with some degree of certainty by renting a private garden or beach, through the property system. Alternatively, I can plan to meet my friends on a public beach or at Sheep's Meadow in Central Park. I can buy an easement from my neighbor to reach a nearby river, or I can walk around her property using the public road that makes up our transportation commons. Each institutional framework—property and commons—allows for a certain freedom of action and a certain degree of predictability of access to resources. Their complementary coexistence and relative salience as institutional frameworks for action determine the relative reach of the market and the domain of nonmarket action, both individual and social, in the resources they govern and the activities that depend on access to those resources. Now that material conditions have enabled the emergence of greater scope for nonmarket action, the scope and existence of a core common infrastructure that includes the basic resources necessary to produce and exchange information will shape the degree to which individuals will be able to act in all the ways that I describe as central to the emergence of a networked information economy and the freedoms it makes possible.

At the physical layer, the transition to broadband has been accompanied by a more concentrated market structure for physical wires and connections, and less regulation of the degree to which owners can control the flow of information on their networks. The emergence of open wireless networks, based on "spectrum commons," counteracts this trend to some extent, as does the current apparent business practice of broadband owners not to use their ownership to control the flow of information over their networks. Efforts to overcome the broadband market concentration through the development of municipal broadband networks are currently highly contested in legislation and courts. The single most threatening development at the physical layer has been an effort driven primarily by Hollywood, over the past few years, to require the manufacturers of computation devices to design their systems so as to enforce the copyright claims and permissions imposed by the owners of digital copyrighted works. Should this effort succeed, the core characteristic of computers—that they are general-purpose devices whose abilities can be configured and changed over time by their owners as uses and preferences change—will be abandoned in favor of machines that can be trusted to perform according to factory specifications, irrespective of what their owners wish. The primary reason that these laws have not yet passed, and are unlikely to pass, is that the computer hardware and software, and electronics and telecommunications industries all understand that such a law would undermine their innovation and creativity. At the logical layer, we are seeing a concerted effort, again headed primarily by Hollywood and the recording industry, to shape the software and standards to make sure that digitally encoded cultural products can continue to be sold as packaged goods. The Digital Millennium Copyright Act and the assault on peer-to-peer technologies are the most obvious in this regard.

More generally information, knowledge, and culture are being subjected to a second enclosure movement, as James Boyle has recently explored in depth. The freedom of action for individuals who wish to produce information, knowledge, and culture is being systematically curtailed in order to secure the economic returns demanded by the manufacturers of the industrial information economy. A rich literature in law has developed in response to this increasing enclosure over the past twenty years. It started with David Lange's evocative exploration of the public domain and Pamela Samuelson's prescient critique of the application of copyright to computer programs and digital materials, and continued through Jessica Litman's work on the public domain and digital copyright and Boyle's exploration of the basic romantic assumptions underlying our emerging "intellectual property" construct and the need for an environmentalist framework for preserving the public domain. It reached its most eloquent expression in Lawrence Lessig's arguments for the centrality of free exchange of ideas and information to our most creative endeavors, and his diagnoses of the destructive effects of the present enclosure movement. This growing skepticism among legal academics has been matched by a long-standing skepticism among economists (to which I devote much discussion in chapter 2). The lack of either analytic or empirical foundation for the regulatory drive toward ever-stronger proprietary rights has not, however, resulted in a transformed politics of the regulation of intellectual production. Only recently have we begun to see a politics of information policy and "intellectual property" emerge from a combination of popular politics among computer engineers, college students, and activists concerned with the global poor; a reorientation of traditional media advocates; and a very gradual realization by high-technology firms that rules pushed by Hollywood can impede the growth of computer-based businesses. This political countermovement is tied to quite basic characteristics of the technology of computer communications, and to the persistent and growing social practices of sharing—some, like p2p (peer-to-peer) file sharing, in direct opposition to proprietary claims; others, increasingly, are instances of the emerging practices of making information on nonproprietary models and of individuals sharing what they themselves made in social, rather than market patterns. These economic and social forces are pushing at each other in opposite directions, and each is trying to mold the legal environment to better accommodate its requirements. We still stand at a point where information production could be regulated so that, for most users, it will be forced back into the industrial model, squelching the emerging model of individual, radically decentralized, and nonmarket production and its attendant improvements in freedom and justice.

Social and economic organization is not infinitely malleable. Neither is it always equally open to affirmative design. The actual practices of human interaction with information, knowledge, and culture and with production and consumption are the consequence of a feedback effect between social practices, economic organization, technological affordances, and formal constraints on behavior through law and similar institutional forms. These components of the constraints and affordances of human behavior tend to adapt dynamically to each other, so that the tension between the technological affordances, the social and economic practices, and the law are often not too great. During periods of stability, these components of the structure within which human beings live are mostly aligned and mutually reinforce each other, but the stability is subject to shock at any one of these dimensions. Sometimes shock can come in the form of economic crisis, as it did in the United States during the Great Depression. Often it can come from an external physical threat to social institutions, like a war. Sometimes, though probably rarely, it can come from law, as, some would argue, it came from the desegregation decision in *Brown v. Board of Education*. Sometimes it can come from technology; the introduction of print was such a perturbation, as was, surely, the steam engine. The introduction of the high-capacity mechanical presses and telegraph ushered in the era of mass media. The introduction of radio created a similar perturbation, which for a brief moment destabilized the mass-media model, but quickly converged to it. In each case, the period of perturbation offered more opportunities and greater risks than the periods of relative stability. During periods of perturbation, more of the ways in which society organizes itself are up for grabs; more can be renegotiated, as the various other components of human stability adjust to the changes. To borrow Stephen Jay Gould's term from evolutionary theory, human societies exist in a series of punctuated equilibria. The periods of disequilibrium are not necessarily long. A mere twenty-five years passed between the invention of radio and its adaptation to the mass-media model. A similar period passed between the introduction of telephony and its adoption of the monopoly utility form that enabled only one-to-one limited communications. In each of these periods, various paths could have been taken. Radio showed us even within the past century how, in some societies, different paths were in fact taken and then sustained over decades. After a period of instability, however, the various elements of human behavioral constraint and affordances settled on a new stable alignment. During periods of stability, we can probably hope for little more than tinkering at the edges of the human condition.

This book is offered, then, as a challenge to contemporary liberal democracies. We are in the midst of a technological, economic, and organizational transformation that allows us to renegotiate the terms of freedom, justice, and productivity in the information society. How we shall live in this new environment will in some significant measure depend on policy choices that we make over the next decade or so. To be able to understand these choices, to be able to make them well, we must recognize that they are part of what is fundamentally a social and political choice—a choice about how to be free, equal, productive human beings under a new set of technological and economic conditions. As economic policy, allowing yesterday's winners to dictate the terms of tomorrow's economic competition would be disastrous. As social policy, missing an opportunity to enrich democracy, freedom, and justice in our society while maintaining or even enhancing our productivity would be unforgivable.

Part One The Networked Information Economy

For more than 150 years, new communications technologies have tended to concentrate and commercialize the production and exchange of information, while extending the geographic and social reach of information distribution networks. High-volume mechanical presses and the telegraph combined with new business practices to change newspapers from small-circulation local efforts into mass media. Newspapers became means of communications intended to reach ever-larger and more dispersed audiences, and their management required substantial capital investment. As the size of the audience and its geographic and social dispersion increased, public discourse developed an increasingly one-way model. Information and opinion that was widely known and formed the shared basis for political conversation and broad social relations flowed from ever more capital-intensive commercial and professional producers to passive, undifferentiated consumers. It was a model easily adopted and amplified by radio, television, and later cable and satellite communications. This trend did not cover all forms of communication and culture. Telephones and personal interactions, most importantly, and small-scale distributions, like mimeographed handbills, were obvious alternatives. Yet the growth of efficient transportation and effective large-scale managerial and administrative structures meant that the sources of effective political and economic power extended over larger geographic areas and required reaching a larger and more geographically dispersed population. The economics of long-distance mass distribution systems necessary to reach this constantly increasing and more dispersed relevant population were typified by high up-front costs and low marginal costs of distribution. These cost characteristics drove cultural production toward delivery to ever-wider audiences of increasingly high production-value goods, whose fixed costs could be spread over ever-larger audiences—like television series, recorded music, and movies. Because of these economic characteristics, the mass-media model of information and cultural production and transmission became the dominant form of public communication in the twentieth century.

The Internet presents the possibility of a radical reversal of this long trend. It is the first modern communications medium that expands its reach by decentralizing the capital structure of production and distribution of information, culture, and knowledge. Much of the physical capital that embeds most of the intelligence in the network is widely diffused and owned by end users. Network routers and servers are not qualitatively different from the computers that end users own, unlike broadcast stations or cable systems, which are radically different in economic and technical terms from the televisions that receive their signals. This basic change in the material conditions of information and cultural production and distribution have substantial effects on how we come to know the world we occupy and the alternative courses of action open to us as individuals and as social actors. Through these effects, the emerging networked environment structures how we perceive and pursue core values in modern liberal societies.

Technology alone does not, however, determine social structure. The introduction of print in China and Korea did not induce the kind of profound religious and political reformation that followed the printed Bible and disputations in Europe. But technology is not irrelevant, either. Luther's were not the first disputations nailed to a church door. Print, however, made it practically feasible for more than 300,000 copies of Luther's publications to be circulated between 1517 and 1520 in a way that earlier disputations could not have been.[1] Vernacular reading of the Bible became a feasible form of religious self-direction only when printing these Bibles and making them available to individual households became economically feasible, and not when all copyists were either monks or otherwise dependent on the church. Technology creates feasibility spaces for social practice. Some things become easier and cheaper, others harder and more expensive to do or to prevent under different technological conditions. The interaction between these technological-economic feasibility spaces, and the social responses to these changes—both in terms of institutional changes, like law and regulation, and in terms of changing social practices—define the qualities of a period. The way life is actually lived by people within a given set of interlocking technological, economic, institutional, and social practices is what makes a society attractive or unattractive, what renders its practices laudable or lamentable.

A particular confluence of technical and economic changes is now altering the way we produce and exchange information, knowledge, and culture in ways that could redefine basic practices, first in the most advanced economies, and eventually around the globe. The potential break from the past 150 years is masked by the somewhat liberal use of the term "information economy" in various permutations since the 1970s. The term has been used widely to signify the dramatic increase in the importance of usable information as a means of controlling production and the flow of inputs, outputs, and services. While often evoked as parallel to the "postindustrial" stage, in fact, the information economy was tightly linked throughout the twentieth century with controlling the processes of the industrial economy. This is clearest in the case of accounting firms and financial markets, but is true of the industrial modalities of organizing cultural production as well. Hollywood, the broadcast networks, and the recording industry were built around a physical production model. Once the cultural utterances, the songs or movies, were initially produced and fixed in some means of storage and transmission, the economics of production and distribution of these physical goods took over. Making the initial utterances and the physical goods that embodied them required high capital investment up front. Making many copies was not much more expensive than making few copies, and very much cheaper on a per-copy basis. These industries therefore organized themselves to invest large sums in making a small number of high production-value cultural "artifacts," which were then either replicated and stamped onto many low-cost copies of each artifact, or broadcast or distributed through high-cost systems for low marginal cost ephemeral consumption on screens and with receivers. This required an effort to manage demand for those products that were in fact recorded and replicated or distributed, so as to make sure that the producers could sell many units of a small number of cultural utterances at a low per-unit cost, rather than few units each of many cultural utterances at higher per-unit costs. Because of its focus around capital-intensive production and distribution techniques, this first stage might best be thought of as the "industrial information economy."

Radical decentralization of intelligence in our communications network and the centrality of information, knowledge, culture, and ideas to advanced economic activity are leading to a new stage of the information economy— the networked information economy. In this new stage, we can harness many more of the diverse paths and mechanisms for cultural transmission that were muted by the economies of scale that led to the rise of the concentrated, controlled form of mass media, whether commercial or state-run. The most important aspect of the networked information economy is the possibility it opens for reversing the control focus of the industrial information economy. In particular, it holds out the possibility of reversing two trends in cultural production central to the project of control: concentration and commercialization.

Two fundamental facts have changed in the economic ecology in which the industrial information enterprises have arisen. First, the basic output that has become dominant in the most advanced economies is human meaning and communication. Second, the basic physical capital necessary to express and communicate human meaning is the connected personal computer. The core functionalities of processing, storage, and communications are widely owned throughout the population of users. Together, these changes destabilize the industrial stage of the information economy. Both the capacity to make meaning—to encode and decode humanly meaningful statements— and the capacity to communicate one's meaning around the world, are held by, or readily available to, at least many hundreds of millions of users around the globe. Any person who has information can connect with any other person who wants it, and anyone who wants to make it mean something in some context, can do so. The high capital costs that were a prerequisite to gathering, working, and communicating information, knowledge, and culture, have now been widely distributed in the society. The entry barrier they posed no longer offers a condensation point for the large organizations that once dominated the information environment. Instead, emerging models of information and cultural production, radically decentralized and based on emergent patterns of cooperation and sharing, but also of simple coordinate coexistence, are beginning to take on an ever-larger role in how we produce meaning—information, knowledge, and culture—in the networked information economy.

A Google response to a query, which returns dozens or more sites with answers to an information question you may have, is an example of coordinate coexistence producing information. As Jessica Litman demonstrated in *Sharing and Stealing*, hundreds of independent producers of information, acting for reasons ranging from hobby and fun to work and sales, produce information, independently and at widely varying costs, related to what you were looking for. They all coexist without knowing of each other, most of them without thinking or planning on serving you in particular, or even a class of user like you. Yet the sheer volume and diversity of interests and sources allows their distributed, unrelated efforts to be coordinated— through the Google algorithm in this case, but also through many others— into a picture that has meaning and provides the answer to your question. Other, more deeply engaged and cooperative enterprises are also emerging on the Internet. Wikipedia, a multilingual encyclopedia coauthored by fifty thousand volunteers, is one particularly effective example of many such enterprises.

The technical conditions of communication and information processing are enabling the emergence of new social and economic practices of information and knowledge production. Eisenstein carefully documented how print loosened the power of the church over information and knowledge production in Europe, and enabled, particularly in the Protestant North, the emergence of early modern capitalist enterprises in the form of print shops. These printers were able to use their market revenues to become independent of the church or the princes, as copyists never were, and to form the economic and social basis of a liberal, market-based freedom of thought and communication. Over the past century and a half, these early printers turned into the commercial mass media: A particular type of market-based production—concentrated, largely homogenous, and highly commercialized—that came to dominate our information environment by the end of the twentieth century. On the background of that dominant role, the possibility that a radically different form of information production will emerge—decentralized; socially, no less than commercially, driven; and as diverse as human thought itself—offers the promise of a deep change in how we see the world around us, how we come to know about it and evaluate it, and how we are capable of communicating with others about what we know, believe, and plan.

This part of the book is dedicated to explaining the technological-economic transformation that is making these practices possible. Not because economics drives all; not because technology determines the way society or communication go; but because it is the technological shock, combined with the economic sustainability of the emerging social practices, that creates the new set of social and political opportunities that are the subject of this book. By working out the economics of these practices, we can understand the economic parameters within which practical political imagination and fulfillment can operate in the digitally networked environment. I describe sustained productive enterprises that take the form of decentralized and nonmarket-based production, and explain why productivity and growth are consistent with a shift toward such modes of production. What I describe is not an exercise in pastoral utopianism. It is not a vision of a return to production in a preindustrial world. It is a practical possibility that directly results from our economic understanding of information and culture as objects of production. It flows from fairly standard economic analysis applied to a very nonstandard economic reality: one in which all the means of producing and exchanging information and culture are placed in the hands of hundreds of millions, and eventually billions, of people around the world, available for them to work with not only when they are functioning in the market to keep body and soul together, but also, and with equal efficacy, when they are functioning in society and alone, trying to give meaning to their lives as individuals and as social beings.

Chapter 2 Some Basic Economics of Information Production and Innovation

There are no noncommercial automobile manufacturers. There are no volunteer steel foundries. You would never choose to have your primary source of bread depend on voluntary contributions from others. Nevertheless, scientists working at noncommercial research institutes funded by nonprofit educational institutions and government grants produce most of our basic science. Widespread cooperative networks of volunteers write the software and standards that run most of the Internet and enable what we do with it. Many people turn to National Public Radio or the BBC as a reliable source of news. What is it about information that explains this difference? Why do we rely almost exclusively on markets and commercial firms to produce cars, steel, and wheat, but much less so for the most critical information our advanced societies depend on? Is this a historical contingency, or is there something about information as an object of production that makes nonmarket production attractive?

The technical economic answer is that certain characteristics of information and culture lead us to understand them as "public goods," rather than as "pure private goods" or standard "economic goods." When economists speak of information, they usually say that it is "nonrival." We consider a good to be nonrival when its consumption by one person does not make it any less available for consumption by another. Once such a good is produced, no more social resources need be invested in creating more of it to satisfy the next consumer. Apples are rival. If I eat this apple, you cannot eat it. If you nonetheless want to eat an apple, more resources (trees, labor) need to be diverted from, say, building chairs, to growing apples, to satisfy you. The social cost of your consuming the second apple is the cost of not using the resources needed to grow the second apple (the wood from the tree) in their next best use. In other words, it is the cost to society of not having the additional chairs that could have been made from the tree. Information is nonrival. Once a scientist has established a fact, or once Tolstoy has written *War and Peace*, neither the scientist nor Tolstoy need spend a single second on producing additional *War and Peace* manu-scripts or studies for the one-hundredth, one-thousandth, or one-millionth user of what they wrote. The physical paper for the book or journal costs something, but the information itself need only be created once. Economists call such goods "public" because a market will not produce them if priced at their marginal cost—zero. In order to provide Tolstoy or the scientist with income, we regulate publishing: We pass laws that enable their publishers to prevent competitors from entering the market. Because no competitors are permitted into the market for copies of *War and Peace*, the publishers can price the contents of the book or journal at above their actual marginal cost of zero. They can then turn some of that excess revenue over to Tolstoy. Even if these laws are therefore necessary to create the incentives for publi-cation, the market that develops based on them will, from the technical economic perspective, systematically be inefficient. As Kenneth Arrow put it in 1962, "precisely to the extent that [property] is effective, there is un-derutilization of the information."[1] Because welfare economics defines a mar-ket as producing a good efficiently only when it is pricing the good at its marginal cost, a good like information (and culture and knowledge are, for purposes of economics, forms of information), which can never be sold both at a positive (greater than zero) price and at its marginal cost, is fundamen-tally a candidate for substantial nonmarket production.

This widely held explanation of the economics of information production has led to an understanding that markets based on patents or copyrights involve a trade-off between static and dynamic efficiency. That is, looking at the state of the world on any given day, it is inefficient that people and firms sell the information they possess. From the perspective of a society's overall welfare, the most efficient thing would be for those who possess information to give it away for free—or rather, for the cost of communicating it and no more. On any given day, enforcing copyright law leads to inefficient underutilization of copyrighted information. However, looking at the problem of information production over time, the standard defense of exclusive rights like copyright expects firms and people not to produce if they know that their products will be available for anyone to take for free. In order to harness the efforts of individuals and firms that want to make money, we are willing to trade off some static inefficiency to achieve dynamic efficiency. That is, we are willing to have some inefficient lack of access to information every day, in exchange for getting more people involved in information production over time. Authors and inventors or, more commonly, companies that contract with musicians and filmmakers, scientists, and engineers, will invest in research and create cultural goods because they expect to sell their information products. Over time, this incentive effect will give us more innovation and creativity, which will outweigh the inefficiency at any given moment caused by selling the information at above its marginal cost. This defense of exclusive rights is limited by the extent to which it correctly describes the motivations of information producers and the business models open to them to appropriate the benefits of their investments. If some information producers do not need to capture the economic benefits of their particular information outputs, or if some businesses can capture the economic value of their information production by means other than exclusive control over their products, then the justification for regulating access by granting copyrights or patents is weakened. As I will discuss in detail, both of these limits on the standard defense are in fact the case.

Nonrivalry, moreover, is not the only quirky characteristic of information production as an economic phenomenon. The other crucial quirkiness is that information is both input and output of its own production process. In order to write today's academic or news article, I need access to yesterday's articles and reports. In order to write today's novel, movie, or song, I need to use and rework existing cultural forms, such as story lines and twists. This characteristic is known to economists as the "on the shoulders of giants" effect, recalling a statement attributed to Isaac Newton: "If I have seen farther it is because I stand on the shoulders of giants."[2] This second quirkiness of information as a production good makes property-like exclusive rights less appealing as the dominant institutional arrangement for information and cultural production than it would have been had the sole quirky characteristic of information been its nonrivalry. The reason is that if any new information good or innovation builds on existing information, then strengthening intellectual property rights increases the prices that those who invest in producing information today must pay to those who did so yesterday, in addition to increasing the rewards an information producer can get tomorrow. Given the nonrivalry, those payments made today for yesterday's information are all inefficiently too high, from today's perspective. They are all above the marginal cost—zero. Today's users of information are not only today's readers and consumers. They are also today's producers and tomorrow's innovators. Their net benefit from a strengthened patent or copyright regime, given not only increased potential revenues but also the increased costs, may be negative. If we pass a law that regulates information production too strictly, allowing its beneficiaries to impose prices that are too high on today's innovators, then we will have not only too little consumption of information today, but also too little production of new information for tomorrow.

Perhaps the most amazing document of the consensus among economists today that, because of the combination of nonrivalry and the "on the shoulders of giants" effect, excessive expansion of "intellectual property" protection is economically detrimental, was the economists' brief filed in the Supreme Court case of *Eldred v. Ashcroft*.[3] The case challenged a law that extended the term of copyright protection from lasting for the life of the author plus fifty years, to life of the author plus seventy years, or from seventy-five years to ninety-five years for copyrights owned by corporations. If information were like land or iron, the ideal length of property rights would be infinite from the economists' perspective. In this case, however, where the "property right" was copyright, more than two dozen leading economists volunteered to sign a brief opposing the law, counting among their number five Nobel laureates, including that well-known market skeptic, Milton Friedman.

The efficiency of regulating information, knowledge, and cultural production through strong copyright and patent is not only theoretically ambiguous, it also lacks empirical basis. The empirical work trying to assess the impact of intellectual property on innovation has focused to date on patents. The evidence provides little basis to support stronger and increasing exclusive rights of the type we saw in the last two and a half decades of the twentieth century. Practically no studies show a clear-cut benefit to stronger or longer patents.[4] In perhaps one of the most startling papers on the economics of innovation published in the past few years, Josh Lerner looked at changes in intellectual property law in sixty countries over a period of 150 years. He studied close to three hundred policy changes, and found that, both in developing countries and in economically advanced countries that already have patent law, patenting both at home and abroad by domestic firms of the country that made the policy change, a proxy for their investment in research and development, decreases slightly when patent law is strengthened![5] The implication is that when a country—either one that already has a significant patent system, or a developing nation—increases its patent protection, it slightly decreases the level of investment in innovation by local firms. Going on intuitions alone, without understanding the background theory, this seems implausible—why would inventors or companies innovate less when they get more protection? Once you understand the interaction of nonrivalry and the "on the shoulders of giants" effect, the findings are entirely consistent with theory. Increasing patent protection, both in developing nations that are net importers of existing technology and science, and in developed nations that already have a degree of patent protection, and therefore some nontrivial protection for inventors, increases the costs that current innovators have to pay on existing knowledge more than it increases their ability to appropriate the value of their own contributions. When one cuts through the rent-seeking politics of intellectual property lobbies like the pharmaceutical companies or Hollywood and the recording industry; when one overcomes the honestly erroneous, but nonetheless conscience-soothing beliefs of lawyers who defend the copyright and patent-dependent industries and the judges they later become, the reality of both theory and empirics in the economics of intellectual property is that both in theory and as far as empirical evidence shows, there is remarkably little support in economics for regulating information, knowledge, and cultural production through the tools of intellectual property law.

Where does innovation and information production come from, then, if it does not come as much from intellectual-property-based market actors, as many generally believe? The answer is that it comes mostly from a mixture of (1) nonmarket sources—both state and nonstate—and (2) market actors whose business models do not depend on the regulatory framework of intellectual property. The former type of producer is the expected answer, within mainstream economics, for a public goods problem like information production. The National Institutes of Health, the National Science Foundation, and the Defense Department are major sources of funding for research in the United States, as are government agencies in Europe, at the national and European level, Japan, and other major industrialized nations. The latter type—that is, the presence and importance of market-based producers whose business models do not require and do not depend on intellectual property protection—is not theoretically predicted by that model, but is entirely obvious once you begin to think about it.

Consider a daily newspaper. Normally, we think of newspapers as dependent on copyrights. In fact, however, that would be a mistake. No daily newspaper would survive if it depended for its business on waiting until a competitor came out with an edition, then copied the stories, and reproduced them in a competing edition. Daily newspapers earn their revenue from a combination of low-priced newsstand sales or subscriptions together with advertising revenues. Neither of those is copyright dependent once we understand that consumers will not wait half a day until the competitor's paper comes out to save a nickel or a quarter on the price of the newspaper. If all copyright on newspapers were abolished, the revenues of newspapers would be little affected.[6] Take, for example, the 2003 annual reports of a few of the leading newspaper companies in the United States. The New York Times Company receives a little more than $3 billion a year from advertising and circulation revenues, and a little more than $200 million a year in revenues from all other sources. Even if the entire amount of "other sources" were from syndication of stories and photos—which likely overstates the role of these copyright-dependent sources—it would account for little more than 6 percent of total revenues. The net operating revenues for the Gannett Company were more than $5.6 billion in newspaper advertising and circulation revenue, relative to about $380 million in all other revenues. As with the *New York Times*, at most a little more than 6 percent of revenues could be attributed to copyright-dependent activities. For Knight Ridder, the 2003 numbers were $2.8 billion and $100 million, respectively, or a maximum of about 3.5 percent from copyrights. Given these numbers, it is safe to say that daily newspapers are not a copyright-dependent industry, although they are clearly a market-based information production industry.

As it turns out, repeated survey studies since 1981 have shown that in all industrial sectors except for very few—most notably pharmaceuticals—firm managers do not see patents as the most important way they capture the benefits of their research and developments.[7] They rank the advantages that strong research and development gives them in lowering the cost or improving the quality of manufacture, being the first in the market, or developing strong marketing relationships as more important than patents. The term "intellectual property" has high cultural visibility today. Hollywood, the recording industry, and pharmaceuticals occupy center stage on the national and international policy agenda for information policy. However, in the overall mix of our information, knowledge, and cultural production system, the total weight of these exclusivity-based market actors is surprisingly small relative to the combination of nonmarket sectors, government and nonprofit, and market-based actors whose business models do not depend on proprietary exclusion from their information outputs.

The upshot of the mainstream economic analysis of information production today is that the widely held intuition that markets are more or less the best way to produce goods, that property rights and contracts are efficient ways of organizing production decisions, and that subsidies distort production decisions, is only very ambiguously applicable to information. While exclusive rights-based production can partially solve the problem of how information will be produced in our society, a comprehensive regulatory system that tries to mimic property in this area—such as both the United States and the European Union have tried to implement internally and through international agreements—simply cannot work perfectly, even in an ideal market posited by the most abstract economics models. Instead, we find the majority of businesses in most sectors reporting that they do not rely on intellectual property as a primary mechanism for appropriating the benefits of their research and development investments. In addition, we find mainstream economists believing that there is a substantial role for government funding; that nonprofit research can be more efficient than for-profit research; and, otherwise, that nonproprietary production can play an important role in our information production system.

THE DIVERSITY OF STRATEGIES IN
OUR CURRENT INFORMATION
PRODUCTION SYSTEM

The actual universe of information production in the economy then, is not as dependent on property rights and markets in information goods as the last quarter century's increasing obsession with "intellectual property" might suggest. Instead, what we see both from empirical work and theoretical work is that individuals and firms in the economy produce information using a wide range of strategies. Some of these strategies indeed rely on exclusive rights like patents or copyrights, and aim at selling information as a good into an information market. Many, however, do not. In order to provide some texture to what these models look like, we can outline a series of ideal-type "business" strategies for producing information. The point here is not to provide an exhaustive map of the empirical business literature. It is, instead, to offer a simple analytic framework within which to understand the mix of strategies available for firms and individuals to appropriate the benefits of their investments—of time, money, or both, in activities that result in the production of information, knowledge, and culture. The differentiating parameters are simple: cost minimization and benefit maximization. Any of these strategies could use inputs that are already owned—such as existing lyrics for a song or a patented invention to improve on—by buying a license from the owner of the exclusive rights for the existing information. Cost minimization here refers purely to ideal-type strategies for obtaining as many of the information inputs as possible at their marginal cost of zero, instead of buying licenses to inputs at a positive market price. It can be pursued by using materials from the public domain, by using materials the producer itself owns, or by sharing/bartering for information inputs owned by others in exchange for one's own information inputs. Benefits can be obtained either in reliance on asserting one's exclusive rights, or by following a non-exclusive strategy, using some other mechanism that improves the position of the information producer because they invested in producing the information. Nonexclusive strategies for benefit maximization can be pursued both by market actors and by nonmarket actors. Table 2.1 maps nine ideal-type strategies characterized by these components.

The ideal-type strategy that underlies patents and copyrights can be thought of as the "Romantic Maximizer." It conceives of the information producer as a single author or inventor laboring creatively—hence romantic—but in expectation of royalties, rather than immortality, beauty, or truth. An individual or small start-up firm that sells software it developed to a larger firm, or an author selling rights to a book or a film typify this model. The second ideal type that arises within exclusive-rights based industries, "Mickey," is a larger firm that already owns an inventory of exclusive rights, some through in-house development, some by buying from Romantic Max-

Table 2.1: Ideal-Type Information Production Strategies

Cost Minimization/ Benefit Acquisition	Public Domain	Intrafirm	Barter/Sharing
Rights-based exclusion (make money by exercising exclusive rights—licensing or blocking competition)	*Romantic Maximizers* (authors, composers; sell to publishers; sometimes sell to Mickeys)	*Mickey* (Disney reuses inventory for derivative works; buy outputs of Romantic Maximizers)	*RCA* (small number of companies hold blocking patents; they create patent pools to build valuable goods)
Nonexclusion-Market (make money from information production but not by exercising the exclusive rights)	*Scholarly Lawyers* (write articles to get clients; other examples include bands that give music out for free as advertisements for touring and charge money for performance; software developers who develop software and make money from customizing it to a particular client, on-site management, advice and training, not from licensing)	*Know-How* (firms that have cheaper or better production processes because of their research, lower their costs or improve the quality of other goods or services; lawyer offices that build on existing forms)	*Learning Networks* (share information with similar organizations—make money from early access to information. For example, newspapers join together to create a wire service; firms where engineers and scientists from different firms attend professional societies to diffuse knowledge)
Nonexclusion-Nonmarket	*Joe Einstein* (give away information for free in return for status, benefits to reputation, value of the innovation to themselves; wide range of motivations. Includes members of amateur choirs who perform for free, academics who write articles for fame, people who write op-eds, contribute to mailing lists; many free software developers and free software generally for most uses)	*Los Alamos* (share in-house information, rely on in-house inputs to produce valuable public goods used to secure additional government funding and status)	*Limited sharing networks* (release paper to small number of colleagues to get comments so you can improve it before publication. Make use of time delay to gain relative advantage later on using Joe Einstein strategy. Share one's information on formal condition of reciprocity: like "copyleft" conditions on derivative works for distribution)

imizers. A defining cost-reduction mechanism for Mickey is that it applies creative people to work on its own inventory, for which it need not pay above marginal cost prices in the market. This strategy is the most advantageous in an environment of very strong exclusive rights protection for a number of reasons. First, the ability to extract higher rents from the existing inventory of information goods is greatest for firms that (a) have an inventory and (b) rely on asserting exclusive rights as their mode of extracting value. Second, the increased costs of production associated with strong exclusive rights are cushioned by the ability of such firms to rework their existing inventory, rather than trying to work with materials from an ever-shrinking public domain or paying for every source of inspiration and element of a new composition. The coarsest version of this strategy might be found if Disney were to produce a "winter sports" thirty-minute television program by tying together scenes from existing cartoons, say, one in which Goofy plays hockey followed by a snippet of Donald Duck ice skating, and so on. More subtle, and representative of the type of reuse relevant to the analysis here, would be the case where Disney buys the rights to Winnie-the-Pooh, and, after producing an animated version of stories from the original books, then continues to work with the same characters and relationships to create a new film, say, *Winnie-the-Pooh—Frankenpooh* (or *Beauty and the Beast—Enchanted Christmas*; or *The Little Mermaid—Stormy the Wild Seahorse*). The third exclusive-rights-based strategy, which I call "RCA," is barter among the owners of inventories. Patent pools, cross-licensing, and market-sharing agreements among the radio patents holders in 1920–1921, which I describe in chapter 6, are a perfect example. RCA, GE, AT&T, and Westinghouse held blocking patents that prevented each other and anyone else from manufacturing the best radios possible given technology at that time. The four companies entered an agreement to combine their patents and divide the radio equipment and services markets, which they used throughout the 1920s to exclude competitors and to capture precisely the postinnovation monopoly rents sought to be created by patents.

Exclusive-rights-based business models, however, represent only a fraction of our information production system. There are both market-based and nonmarket models to sustain and organize information production. Together, these account for a substantial portion of our information output. Indeed, industry surveys concerned with patents have shown that the vast majority of industrial R&D is pursued with strategies that do not rely primarily on patents. This does not mean that most or any of the firms that pursue these strategies possess or seek no exclusive rights in their information products. It simply means that their production strategy does not depend on asserting these rights through exclusion. One such cluster of strategies, which I call "Scholarly Lawyers," relies on demand–side effects of access to the information the producer distributes. It relies on the fact that sometimes using an information good that one has produced makes its users seek out a relationship with the author. The author then charges for the relationship, not for the information. Doctors or lawyers who publish in trade journals, become known, and get business as a result are an instance of this strategy. An enormously creative industry, much of which operates on this model, is software. About two-thirds of industry revenues in software development come from activities that the Economic Census describes as: (1) writing, modifying, testing, and supporting software to meet the needs of a particular customer; (2) planning and designing computer systems that integrate computer hardware, software, and communication technologies; (3) on-site management and operation of clients' computer systems and/or data processing facilities; and (4) other professional and technical computer-related advice and services, systems consultants, and computer training. "Software publishing," by contrast, the business model that relies on sales based on copyright, accounts for a little more than one-third of the industry's revenues.[8] Interestingly, this is the model of appropriation that more than a decade ago, Esther Dyson and John Perry Barlow heralded as the future of music and musicians. They argued in the early 1990s for more or less free access to copies of recordings distributed online, which would lead to greater attendance at live gigs. Revenue from performances, rather than recording, would pay artists.

The most common models of industrial R&D outside of pharmaceuticals, however, depend on supply–side effects of information production. One central reason to pursue research is its effects on firm-specific advantages, like production know-how, which permit the firm to produce more efficiently than competitors and sell better or cheaper competing products. Daily newspapers collectively fund news agencies, and individually fund reporters, because their ability to find information and report it is a necessary input into their product—timely news. As I have already suggested, they do not need copyright to protect their revenues. Those are protected by the short half-life of dailies. The investments come in order to be able to play in the market for daily newspapers. Similarly, the learning curve and know-how effects in semiconductors are such that early entry into the market for a new chip will give the first mover significant advantages over competitors. Investment is then made to capture that position, and the investment is captured by the quasi-rents available from the first-mover advantage. In some cases, innovation is necessary in order to be able to produce at the state of the art. Firms participate in "Learning Networks" to gain the benefits of being at the state of the art, and sharing their respective improvements. However, they can only participate if they innovate. If they do not innovate, they lack the in-house capacity to understand the state of the art and play at it. Their investments are then recouped not from asserting their exclusive rights, but from the fact that they sell into one of a set of markets, access into which is protected by the relatively small number of firms with such absorption capacity, or the ability to function at the edge of the state of the art. Firms of this sort might barter their information for access, or simply be part of a small group of organizations with enough knowledge to exploit the information generated and informally shared by all participants in these learning networks. They obtain rents from the concentrated market structure, not from assertion of property rights.[9]

An excellent example of a business strategy based on nonexclusivity is IBM's. The firm has obtained the largest number of patents every year from 1993 to 2004, amassing in total more than 29,000 patents. IBM has also, however, been one of the firms most aggressively engaged in adapting its business model to the emergence of free software. Figure 2.1 shows what happened to the relative weight of patent royalties, licenses, and sales in IBM's revenues and revenues that the firm described as coming from "Linux-related services." Within a span of four years, the Linux-related services category moved from accounting for practically no revenues, to providing double the revenues from all patent-related sources, of the firm that has been the most patent-productive in the United States. IBM has described itself as investing more than a billion dollars in free software developers, hired programmers to help develop the Linux kernel and other free software; and donated patents to the Free Software Foundation. What this does for the firm is provide it with a better operating system for its server business— making the servers better, faster, more reliable, and therefore more valuable to consumers. Participating in free software development has also allowed IBM to develop service relationships with its customers, building on free software to offer customer-specific solutions. In other words, IBM has combined both supply-side and demand-side strategies to adopt a nonproprietary business model that has generated more than $2 billion yearly of business

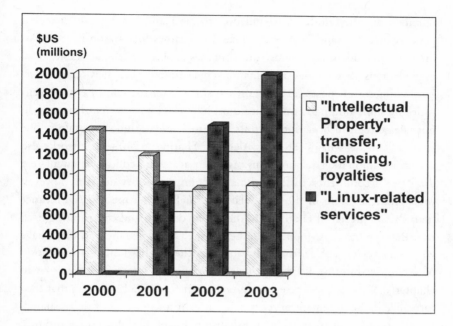

Figure 2.1: Selected IBM Revenues, 2000–2003

for the firm. Its strategy is, if not symbiotic, certainly complementary to free software.

I began this chapter with a puzzle—advanced economies rely on non-market organizations for information production much more than they do in other sectors. The puzzle reflects the fact that alongside the diversity of market-oriented business models for information production there is a wide diversity of nonmarket models as well. At a broad level of abstraction, I designate this diversity of motivations and organizational forms as "Joe Einstein"—to underscore the breadth of the range of social practices and practitioners of nonmarket production. These include universities and other research institutes; government research labs that publicize their work, or government information agencies like the Census Bureau. They also include individuals, like academics; authors and artists who play to "immortality" rather than seek to maximize the revenue from their creation. Eric von Hippel has for many years documented user innovation in areas ranging from surfboard design to new mechanisms for pushing electric wiring through insulation tiles.[10] The Oratorio Society of New York, whose chorus members are all volunteers, has filled Carnegie Hall every December with a performance of Handel's *Messiah* since the theatre's first season in 1891. Political parties, advocacy groups, and churches are but few of the stable social organizations that fill our information environment with news and views. For symmetry purposes in table 2.1, we also see reliance on internal inventories by some nonmarket organizations, like secret government labs that do not release their information outputs, but use it to continue to obtain public funding. This is what I call "Los Alamos." Sharing in limited networks also occurs in nonmarket relationships, as when academic colleagues circulate a draft to get comments. In the nonmarket, nonproprietary domain, however, these strategies were in the past relatively smaller in scope and significance than the simple act of taking from the public domain and contributing back to it that typifies most Joe Einstein behaviors. Only since the mid-1980s have we begun to see a shift from releasing into the public domain to adoption of commons-binding licensing, like the "copyleft" strategies I describe in chapter 3. What makes these strategies distinct from Joe Einstein is that they formalize the requirement of reciprocity, at least for some set of rights shared.

My point is not to provide an exhaustive list of all the ways we produce information. It is simply to offer some texture to the statement that information, knowledge, and culture are produced in diverse ways in contemporary society. Doing so allows us to understand the comparatively limited role that production based purely on exclusive rights—like patents, copyrights, and similar regulatory constraints on the use and exchange of information—has played in our information production system to this day. It is not new or mysterious to suggest that nonmarket production is important to information production. It is not new or mysterious to suggest that efficiency increases whenever it is possible to produce information in a way that allows the producer—whether market actor or not—to appropriate the benefits of production without actually charging a price for use of the information itself. Such strategies are legion among both market and nonmarket actors. Recognizing this raises two distinct questions: First, how does the cluster of mechanisms that make up intellectual property law affect this mix? Second, how do we account for the mix of strategies at any given time? Why, for example, did proprietary, market-based production become so salient in music and movies in the twentieth century, and what is it about the digitally networked environment that could change this mix?

THE EFFECTS OF EXCLUSIVE RIGHTS

Once we recognize that there are diverse strategies of appropriation for information production, we come to see a new source of inefficiency caused by strong "intellectual property"-type rights. Recall that in the mainstream analysis, exclusive rights always cause static inefficiency—that is, they allow producers to charge positive prices for products (information) that have a zero marginal cost. Exclusive rights have a more ambiguous effect dynamically. They raise the expected returns from information production, and thereby are thought to induce investment in information production and innovation. However, they also increase the costs of information inputs. If existing innovations are more likely covered by patent, then current producers will more likely have to pay for innovations or uses that in the past would have been available freely from the public domain. Whether, overall, any given regulatory change that increases the scope of exclusive rights improves or undermines new innovation therefore depends on whether, given the level of appropriability that preceded it, it increased input costs more or less than it increased the prospect of being paid for one's outputs.

The diversity of appropriation strategies adds one more kink to this story. Consider the following very simple hypothetical. Imagine an industry that produces "infowidgets." There are ten firms in the business. Two of them are infowidget publishers on the Romantic Maximizer model. They produce infowidgets as finished goods, and sell them based on patent. Six firms produce infowidgets on supply-side (Know-How) or demand-side (Scholarly Lawyer) effects: they make their Realwidgets or Servicewidgets more efficient or desirable to consumers, respectively. Two firms are nonprofit infowidget producers that exist on a fixed, philanthropically endowed income. Each firm produces five infowidgets, for a total market supply of fifty. Now imagine a change in law that increases exclusivity. Assume that this is a change in law that, absent diversity of appropriation, would be considered efficient. Say it increases input costs by 10 percent and appropriability by 20 percent, for a net expected gain of 10 percent. The two infowidget publishers would each see a 10 percent net gain, and let us assume that this would cause each to increase its efforts by 10 percent and produce 10 percent more infowidgets. Looking at these two firms alone, the change in law caused an increase from ten infowidgets to eleven—a gain for the policy change. Looking at the market as a whole, however, eight firms see an increase of 10 percent in costs, and no gain in appropriability. This is because none of these firms actually relies on exclusive rights to appropriate its product's value. If, commensurate with our assumption for the publishers, we assume that this results in a decline in effort and productivity of 10 percent for the eight firms, we would see these firms decline from forty infowidgets to thirty-six, and total market production would decline from fifty infowidgets to forty-seven.

Another kind of effect for the change in law may be to persuade some of the firms to shift strategies or to consolidate. Imagine, for example, that most of the inputs required by the two publishers were owned by the other infowidget publisher. If the two firms merged into one Mickey, each could use the outputs of the other at its marginal cost—zero—instead of at its exclusive-rights market price. The increase in exclusive rights would then not affect the merged firm's costs, only the costs of outside firms that would have to buy the merged firm's outputs from the market. Given this dynamic, strong exclusive rights drive concentration of inventory owners. We see this very clearly in the increasing sizes of inventory-based firms like Disney. Moreover, the increased appropriability in the exclusive-rights market will likely shift some firms at the margin of the nonproprietary business models to adopt proprietary business models. This, in turn, will increase the amount of information available only from proprietary sources. The feedback effect will further accelerate the rise in information input costs, increasing the gains from shifting to a proprietary strategy and to consolidating larger inventories with new production.

Given diverse strategies, the primary unambiguous effect of increasing the scope and force of exclusive rights is to shape the population of business strategies. Strong exclusive rights increase the attractiveness of exclusive-rights-based strategies at the expense of nonproprietary strategies, whether market-based or nonmarket based. They also increase the value and attraction of consolidation of large inventories of existing information with new production.

WHEN INFORMATION PRODUCTION MEETS
THE COMPUTER NETWORK

Music in the nineteenth century was largely a relational good. It was something people did in the physical presence of each other: in the folk way through hearing, repeating, and improvising; in the middle-class way of buying sheet music and playing for guests or attending public performances; or in the upper-class way of hiring musicians. Capital was widely distributed among musicians in the form of instruments, or geographically dispersed in the hands of performance hall (and drawing room) owners. Market-based production depended on performance through presence. It provided opportunities for artists to live and perform locally, or to reach stardom in cultural centers, but without displacing the local performers. With the introduction of the phonograph, a new, more passive relationship to played music was made possible in reliance on the high-capital requirements of recording, copying, and distributing specific instantiations of recorded music—records. What developed was a concentrated, commercial industry, based on massive financial investments in advertising, or preference formation, aimed at getting ever-larger crowds to want those recordings that the recording executives had chosen. In other words, the music industry took on a more industrial model of production, and many of the local venues—from the living room to the local dance hall—came to be occupied by mechanical recordings rather than amateur and professional local performances. This model crowded out some, but not all, of the live-performance-based markets (for example, jazz clubs, piano bars, or weddings), and created new live-performance markets—the megastar concert tour. The music industry shifted from a reliance on Scholarly Lawyer and Joe Einstein models to reliance on Romantic Maximizer and Mickey models. As computers became more music-capable and digital networks became a ubiquitously available distribution medium, we saw the emergence of the present conflict over the regulation of cultural production—the law of copyright—between the twentieth-century, industrial model recording industry and the emerging amateur distribution systems coupled, at least according to its supporters, to a reemergence of decentralized, relation-based markets for professional performance artists.

This stylized story of the music industry typifies the mass media more generally. Since the introduction of the mechanical press and the telegraph, followed by the phonograph, film, the high-powered radio transmitter, and through to the cable plant or satellite, the capital costs of fixing information and cultural goods in a transmission medium—a high-circulation newspaper, a record or movie, a radio or television program—have been high and increasing. The high physical and financial capital costs involved in making a widely accessible information good and distributing it to the increasingly larger communities (brought together by better transportation systems and more interlinked economic and political systems) muted the relative role of nonmarket production, and emphasized the role of those firms that could muster the financial and physical capital necessary to communicate on a mass scale. Just as these large, industrial-age machine requirements increased the capital costs involved in information and cultural production, thereby triggering commercialization and concentration of much of this sector, so too ubiquitously available cheap processors have dramatically reduced the capital input costs required to fix information and cultural expressions and communicate them globally. By doing so, they have rendered feasible a radical reorganization of our information and cultural production system, away from heavy reliance on commercial, concentrated business models and toward greater reliance on nonproprietary appropriation strategies, in particular nonmarket strategies whose efficacy was dampened throughout the industrial period by the high capital costs of effective communication.

Information and cultural production have three primary categories of inputs. The first is existing information and culture. We already know that existing information is a nonrival good—that is, its real marginal cost at any given moment is zero. The second major cost is that of the mechanical means of sensing our environment, processing it, and communicating new information goods. This is the high cost that typified the industrial model, and which has drastically declined in computer networks. The third factor is human communicative capacity—the creativity, experience, and cultural awareness necessary to take from the universe of existing information and cultural resources and turn them into new insights, symbols, or representations meaningful to others with whom we converse. Given the zero cost of existing information and the declining cost of communication and processing, human capacity becomes the primary scarce resource in the networked information economy.

Human communicative capacity, however, is an input with radically different characteristics than those of, say, printing presses or satellites. It is held by each individual, and cannot be "transferred" from one person to another or aggregated like so many machines. It is something each of us innately has, though in divergent quanta and qualities. Individual human capacities, rather than the capacity to aggregate financial capital, become the economic core of our information and cultural production. Some of that human capacity is currently, and will continue to be, traded through markets in creative labor. However, its liberation from the constraints of physical capital leaves creative human beings much freer to engage in a wide range of information and cultural production practices than those they could afford to participate in when, in addition to creativity, experience, cultural awareness and time, one needed a few million dollars to engage in information production. From our friendships to our communities we live life and exchange ideas, insights, and expressions in many more diverse relations than those mediated by the market. In the physical economy, these relationships were largely relegated to spaces outside of our economic production system. The promise of the networked information economy is to bring this rich diversity of social life smack into the middle of our economy and our productive lives.

Let's do a little experiment. Imagine that you were performing a Web search with me. Imagine that we were using Google as our search engine, and that what we wanted to do was answer the questions of an inquisitive six-year-old about Viking ships. What would we get, sitting in front of our computers and plugging in a search request for "Viking Ships"? The first site is Canadian, and includes a collection of resources, essays, and worksheets. An enterprising elementary school teacher at the Gander Academy in Newfoundland seems to have put these together. He has essays on different questions, and links to sites hosted by a wide range of individuals and organizations, such as a Swedish museum, individual sites hosted on geocities, and even to a specific picture of a replica Viking ship, hosted on a commercial site dedicated to selling nautical replicas. In other words, it is a Joe Einstein site that points to other sites, which in turn use either Joe Einstein or Scholarly Lawyer strategies. This multiplicity of sources of information that show up on the very first site is then replicated as one continues to explore the remaining links. The second link is to a Norwegian site called "the Viking Network," a Web ring dedicated to preparing and hosting short essays on Vikings. It includes brief essays, maps, and external links, such as one to an article in *Scientific American*. "To become a member you must produce an Information Sheet on the Vikings in your local area and send it in electronic format to Viking Network. Your info-sheet will then be included in the Viking Network web." The third site is maintained by a Danish commercial photographer, and hosted in Copenhagen, in a portion dedicated to photographs of archeological finds and replicas of Danish Viking ships. A retired professor from the University of Pittsburgh runs the fourth. The fifth is somewhere between a hobby and a showcase for the services of an individual, independent Web publisher offering publishing-related services. The sixth and seventh are museums, in Norway and Virginia, respectively. The eighth is the Web site of a hobbyists' group dedicated to building Viking Ship replicas. The ninth includes classroom materials and teaching guides made freely available on the Internet by PBS, the American Public Broadcasting Service. Certainly, if you perform this search now, as you read this book, the rankings will change from those I saw when I ran it; but I venture that the mix, the range and diversity of producers, and the relative salience of nonmarket producers will not change significantly.

The difference that the digitally networked environment makes is its capacity to increase the efficacy, and therefore the importance, of many more, and more diverse, nonmarket producers falling within the general category of Joe Einstein. It makes nonmarket strategies—from individual hobbyists to formal, well-funded nonprofits—vastly more effective than they could be in the mass-media environment. The economics of this phenomenon are neither mysterious nor complex. Imagine the grade-school teacher who wishes to put together ten to twenty pages of materials on Viking ships for schoolchildren. Pre-Internet, he would need to go to one or more libraries and museums, find books with pictures, maps, and text, or take his own photographs (assuming he was permitted by the museums) and write his own texts, combining this research. He would then need to select portions, clear the copyrights to reprint them, find a printing house that would set his text and pictures in a press, pay to print a number of copies, and then distribute them to all children who wanted them. Clearly, research today is simpler and cheaper. Cutting and pasting pictures and texts that are digital is cheaper. Depending on where the teacher is located, it is possible that these initial steps would have been insurmountable, particularly for a teacher in a poorly endowed community without easy access to books on the subject, where research would have required substantial travel. Even once these barriers were surmounted, in the precomputer, pre-Internet days, turning out materials that looked and felt like a high quality product, with high-resolution pictures and maps, and legible print required access to capital-intensive facilities. The cost of creating even one copy of such a product would likely dissuade the teacher from producing the booklet. At most, he might have produced a mimeographed bibliography, and perhaps some text reproduced on a photocopier. Now, place the teacher with a computer and a high-speed Internet connection, at home or in the school library. The cost of production and distribution of the products of his effort are trivial. A Web site can be maintained for a few dollars a month. The computer itself is widely accessible throughout the developed world. It becomes trivial for a teacher to produce the "booklet"—with more information, available to anyone in the world, anywhere, at any time, as long as he is willing to spend some of his free time putting together the booklet rather than watching television or reading a book.

When you multiply these very simple stylized facts by the roughly billion people who live in societies sufficiently wealthy to allow cheap ubiquitous Internet access, the breadth and depth of the transformation we are undergoing begins to become clear. A billion people in advanced economies may have between two billion and six billion spare hours among them, every day. In order to harness these billions of hours, it would take the whole workforce of almost 340,000 workers employed by the entire motion picture and recording industries in the United States put together, assuming each worker worked forty-hour weeks without taking a single vacation, for between three and eight and a half years! Beyond the sheer potential quantitative capacity, however one wishes to discount it to account for different levels of talent, knowledge, and motivation, a billion volunteers have qualities that make them more likely to produce what others want to read, see, listen to, or experience. They have diverse interests—as diverse as human culture itself. Some care about Viking ships, others about the integrity of voting machines. Some care about obscure music bands, others share a passion for baking. As Eben Moglen put it, "if you wrap the Internet around every person on the planet and spin the planet, software flows in the network. It's an emergent property of connected human minds that they create things for one another's pleasure and to conquer their uneasy sense of being too alone."[11] It is this combination of a will to create and to communicate with others, and a shared cultural experience that makes it likely that each of us wants to talk about something that we believe others will also want to talk about, that makes the billion potential participants in today's online conversation, and the six billion in tomorrow's conversation, affirmatively better than the commercial industrial model. When the economics of industrial production require high up-front costs and low marginal costs, the producers must focus on creating a few superstars and making sure that everyone tunes in to listen or watch them. This requires that they focus on averaging out what consumers are most likely to buy. This works reasonably well as long as there is no better substitute. As long as it is expensive to produce music or the evening news, there are indeed few competitors for top billing, and the star system can function. Once every person on the planet, or even only every person living in a wealthy economy and 10–20 percent of those living in poorer countries, can easily talk to their friends and compatriots, the competition becomes tougher. It does not mean that there is no continued role for the mass-produced and mass-marketed cultural products—be they Britney Spears or the broadcast news. It does, however, mean that many more "niche markets"—if markets, rather than conversations, are what they should be called—begin to play an ever-increasing role in the total mix of our cultural production system. The economics of production in a digital environment should lead us to expect an increase in the relative salience of nonmarket production models in the overall mix of our information production system, and it is efficient for this to happen—more information will be produced, and much of it will be available for its users at its marginal cost.

The known quirky characteristics of information and knowledge as production goods have always given nonmarket production a much greater role in this production system than was common in capitalist economies for tangible goods. The dramatic decline in the cost of the material means of producing and exchanging information, knowledge, and culture has substantially decreased the costs of information expression and exchange, and thereby increased the relative efficacy of nonmarket production. When these facts are layered over the fact that information, knowledge, and culture have become the central high-value-added economic activities of the most advanced economies, we find ourselves in a new and unfamiliar social and economic condition. Social behavior that traditionally was relegated to the peripheries of the economy has become central to the most advanced economies. Nonmarket behavior is becoming central to producing our information and cultural environment. Sources of knowledge and cultural edification, through which we come to know and comprehend the world, to form our opinions about it, and to express ourselves in communication with others about what we see and believe have shifted from heavy reliance on commercial, concentrated media, to being produced on a much more widely distributed model, by many actors who are not driven by the imperatives of advertising or the sale of entertainment goods.

STRONG EXCLUSIVE RIGHTS IN THE DIGITAL ENVIRONMENT

We now have the basic elements of a clash between incumbent institutions and emerging social practice. Technologies of information and cultural production initially led to the increasing salience of commercial, industrial-model production in these areas. Over the course of the twentieth century, in some of the most culturally visible industries like movies and music, copyright law coevolved with the industrial model. By the end of the twentieth century, copyright was longer, broader, and vastly more encompassing than it had been at the beginning of that century. Other exclusive rights in information, culture, and the fruits of innovation expanded following a similar logic. Strong, broad, exclusive rights like these have predictable effects. They preferentially improve the returns to business models that rely on exclusive rights, like copyrights and patents, at the expense of information and cultural production outside the market or in market relationships that do not depend on exclusive appropriation. They make it more lucrative to consolidate inventories of existing materials. The businesses that developed around the material capital required for production fed back into the political system, which responded by serially optimizing the institutional ecology to fit the needs of the industrial information economy firms at the expense of other information producers.

The networked information economy has upset the apple cart on the technical, material cost side of information production and exchange. The institutional ecology, the political framework (the lobbyists, the habits of legislatures), and the legal culture (the beliefs of judges, the practices of lawyers) have not changed. They are as they developed over the course of the twentieth century—centered on optimizing the conditions of those commercial firms that thrive in the presence of strong exclusive rights in information and culture. The outcome of the conflict between the industrial information economy and its emerging networked alternative will determine whether we evolve into a permission culture, as Lessig warns and projects, or into a society marked by social practice of nonmarket production and cooperative sharing of information, knowledge, and culture of the type I describe throughout this book, and which I argue will improve freedom and justice in liberal societies. Chapter 11 chronicles many of the arenas in which this basic conflict is played out. However, for the remainder of this part and part II, the basic economic understanding I offer here is all that is necessary.

There are diverse motivations and strategies for organizing information production. Their relative attractiveness is to some extent dependent on technology, to some extent on institutional arrangements. The rise that we see today in the efficacy and scope of nonmarket production, and of the peer production that I describe and analyze in the following two chapters, are well within the predictable, given our understanding of the economics of information production. The social practices of information production that form the basis of much of the normative analysis I offer in part II are internally sustainable given the material conditions of information production and exchange in the digitally networked environment. These patterns are unfamiliar to us. They grate on our intuitions about how production happens. They grate on the institutional arrangements we developed over the course of the twentieth century to regulate information and cultural production. But that is because they arise from a quite basically different set of material conditions. We must understand these new modes of production. We must learn to evaluate them and compare their advantages and disadvantages to those of the industrial information producers. And then we must adjust our institutional environment to make way for the new social practices made possible by the networked environment.

Chapter 3 Peer Production and Sharing

At the heart of the economic engine, of the world's most advanced economies, we are beginning to notice a persistent and quite amazing phenomenon. A new model of production has taken root; one that should not be there, at least according to our most widely held beliefs about economic behavior. It should not, the intuitions of the late-twentieth-century American would say, be the case that thousands of volunteers will come together to collaborate on a complex economic project. It certainly should not be that these volunteers will beat the largest and best-financed business enterprises in the world at their own game. And yet, this is precisely what is happening in the software world.

Industrial organization literature provides a prominent place for the transaction costs view of markets and firms, based on insights of Ronald Coase and Oliver Williamson. On this view, people use markets when the gains from doing so, net of transaction costs, exceed the gains from doing the same thing in a managed firm, net of the costs of organizing and managing a firm. Firms emerge when the opposite is true, and transaction costs can best be reduced by bringing an activity into a managed context that requires no individual transactions to allocate this resource or that effort. The emergence of free and open-source software, and the phenomenal success of its flagships, the GNU/ Linux operating system, the Apache Web server, Perl, and many others, should cause us to take a second look at this dominant paradigm.[1] Free software projects do not rely on markets or on managerial hierarchies to organize production. Programmers do not generally participate in a project because someone who is their boss told them to, though some do. They do not generally participate in a project because someone offers them a price to do so, though some participants do focus on long-term appropriation through money-oriented activities, like consulting or service contracts. However, the critical mass of participation in projects cannot be explained by the direct presence of a price or even a future monetary return. This is particularly true of the all-important, microlevel decisions: who will work, with what software, on what project. In other words, programmers participate in free software projects without following the signals generated by market-based, firm-based, or hybrid models. In chapter 2 I focused on how the networked information economy departs from the industrial information economy by improving the efficacy of nonmarket production generally. Free software offers a glimpse at a more basic and radical challenge. It suggests that the networked environment makes possible a new modality of organizing production: radically decentralized, collaborative, and nonproprietary; based on sharing resources and outputs among widely distributed, loosely connected individuals who cooperate with each other without relying on either market signals or managerial commands. This is what I call "commons-based peer production."

"Commons" refers to a particular institutional form of structuring the rights to access, use, and control resources. It is the opposite of "property" in the following sense: With property, law determines one particular person who has the authority to decide how the resource will be used. That person may sell it, or give it away, more or less as he or she pleases. "More or less" because property doesn't mean anything goes. We cannot, for example, decide that we will give our property away to one branch of our family, as long as that branch has boys, and then if that branch has no boys, decree that the property will revert to some other branch of the family. That type of provision, once common in English property law, is now legally void for public policy reasons. There are many other things we cannot do with our property—like build on wetlands. However, the core characteristic of property as the institutional foundation of markets is that the allocation of power to decide how a resource will be used is systematically and drastically asymmetric. That asymmetry permits the existence of "an owner" who can decide what to do, and with whom. We know that transactions must be made— rent, purchase, and so forth—if we want the resource to be put to some other use. The salient characteristic of commons, as opposed to property, is that no single person has exclusive control over the use and disposition of any particular resource in the commons. Instead, resources governed by commons may be used or disposed of by anyone among some (more or less well-defined) number of persons, under rules that may range from "anything goes" to quite crisply articulated formal rules that are effectively enforced.

Commons can be divided into four types based on two parameters. The first parameter is whether they are open to anyone or only to a defined group. The oceans, the air, and highway systems are clear examples of open commons. Various traditional pasture arrangements in Swiss villages or irrigation regions in Spain are now classic examples, described by Eleanor Ostrom, of limited-access common resources—where access is limited only to members of the village or association that collectively "owns" some defined pasturelands or irrigation system.[2] As Carol Rose noted, these are better thought of as limited common property regimes, rather than commons, because they behave as property vis-à-vis the entire world except members of the group who together hold them in common. The second parameter is whether a commons system is regulated or unregulated. Practically all well-studied, limited common property regimes are regulated by more or less elaborate rules—some formal, some social-conventional—governing the use of the resources. Open commons, on the other hand, vary widely. Some commons, called open access, are governed by no rule. Anyone can use resources within these types of commons at will and without payment. Air is such a resource, with respect to air intake (breathing, feeding a turbine). However, air is a regulated commons with regard to outtake. For individual human beings, breathing out is mildly regulated by social convention—you do not breath too heavily on another human being's face unless forced to. Air is a more extensively regulated commons for industrial exhalation—in the shape of pollution controls. The most successful and obvious regulated commons in contemporary landscapes are the sidewalks, streets, roads, and highways that cover our land and regulate the material foundation of our ability to move from one place to the other. In all these cases, however, the characteristic of commons is that the constraints, if any, are symmetric among all users, and cannot be unilaterally controlled by any single individual. The term "commons-based" is intended to underscore that what is characteristic of the cooperative enterprises I describe in this chapter is that they are not built around the asymmetric exclusion typical of property. Rather, the inputs and outputs of the process are shared, freely or conditionally, in an institutional form that leaves them equally available for all to use as they choose at their individual discretion. This latter characteristic— that commons leave individuals free to make their own choices with regard to resources managed as a commons—is at the foundation of the freedom they make possible. This is a freedom I return to in the discussion of autonomy. Not all commons-based production efforts qualify as peer production. Any production strategy that manages its inputs and outputs as commons locates that production modality outside the proprietary system, in a framework of social relations. It is the freedom to interact with resources and projects without seeking anyone's permission that marks commons-based production generally, and it is also that freedom that underlies the particular efficiencies of peer production, which I explore in chapter 4.

The term "peer production" characterizes a subset of commons-based production practices. It refers to production systems that depend on individual action that is self-selected and decentralized, rather than hierarchically assigned. "Centralization" is a particular response to the problem of how to make the behavior of many individual agents cohere into an effective pattern or achieve an effective result. Its primary attribute is the separation of the locus of opportunities for action from the authority to choose the action that the agent will undertake. Government authorities, firm managers, teachers in a classroom, all occupy a context in which potentially many individual wills could lead to action, and reduce the number of people whose will is permitted to affect the actual behavior patterns that the agents will adopt. "Decentralization" describes conditions under which the actions of many agents cohere and are effective despite the fact that they do not rely on reducing the number of people whose will counts to direct effective action. A substantial literature in the past twenty years, typified, for example, by Charles Sabel's work, has focused on the ways in which firms have tried to overcome the rigidities of managerial pyramids by decentralizing learning, planning, and execution of the firm's functions in the hands of employees or teams. The most pervasive mode of "decentralization," however, is the ideal market. Each individual agent acts according to his or her will. Coherence and efficacy emerge because individuals signal their wishes, and plan their behavior not in cooperation with others, but by coordinating, understanding the will of others and expressing their own through the price system.

What we are seeing now is the emergence of more effective collective action practices that are decentralized but do not rely on either the price system or a managerial structure for coordination. In this, they complement the increasing salience of uncoordinated nonmarket behavior that we saw in chapter 2. The networked environment not only provides a more effective platform for action to nonprofit organizations that organize action like firms or to hobbyists who merely coexist coordinately. It also provides a platform for new mechanisms for widely dispersed agents to adopt radically decentralized cooperation strategies other than by using proprietary and contractual claims to elicit prices or impose managerial commands. This kind of information production by agents operating on a decentralized, nonproprietary model is not completely new. Science is built by many people contributing incrementally—not operating on market signals, not being handed their research marching orders by a boss—independently deciding what to research, bringing their collaboration together, and creating science. What we see in the networked information economy is a dramatic increase in the importance and the centrality of information produced in this way.

FREE/OPEN-SOURCE SOFTWARE

The quintessential instance of commons-based peer production has been free software. Free software, or open source, is an approach to software development that is based on shared effort on a nonproprietary model. It depends on many individuals contributing to a common project, with a variety of motivations, and sharing their respective contributions without any single person or entity asserting rights to exclude either from the contributed components or from the resulting whole. In order to avoid having the joint product appropriated by any single party, participants usually retain copyrights in their contribution, but license them to anyone—participant or stranger—on a model that combines a universal license to use the materials with licensing constraints that make it difficult, if not impossible, for any single contributor or third party to appropriate the project. This model of licensing is the most important institutional innovation of the free software movement. Its central instance is the GNU General Public License, or GPL.

This requires anyone who modifies software and distributes the modified version to license it under the same free terms as the original software. While there have been many arguments about how widely the provisions that prevent downstream appropriation should be used, the practical adoption patterns have been dominated by forms of licensing that prevent anyone from exclusively appropriating the contributions or the joint product. More than 85 percent of active free software projects include some version of the GPL or similarly structured license.[3]

Free software has played a critical role in the recognition of peer production, because software is a functional good with measurable qualities. It can be more or less authoritatively tested against its market-based competitors. And, in many instances, free software has prevailed. About 70 percent of Web server software, in particular for critical e-commerce sites, runs on the Apache Web server—free software.[4] More than half of all back-office e-mail functions are run by one free software program or another. Google, Amazon, and CNN.com, for example, run their Web servers on the GNU/Linux operating system. They do this, presumably, because they believe this peer-produced operating system is more reliable than the alternatives, not because the system is "free." It would be absurd to risk a higher rate of failure in their core business activities in order to save a few hundred thousand dollars on licensing fees. Companies like IBM and Hewlett Packard, consumer electronics manufacturers, as well as military and other mission-critical government agencies around the world have begun to adopt business and service strategies that rely and extend free software. They do this because it allows them to build better equipment, sell better services, or better fulfill their public role, even though they do not control the software development process and cannot claim proprietary rights of exclusion in the products of their contributions.

The story of free software begins in 1984, when Richard Stallman started working on a project of building a nonproprietary operating system he called GNU (GNU's Not Unix). Stallman, then at the Massachusetts Institute of Technology (MIT), operated from political conviction. He wanted a world in which software enabled people to use information freely, where no one would have to ask permission to change the software they use to fit their needs or to share it with a friend for whom it would be helpful. These freedoms to share and to make your own software were fundamentally incompatible with a model of production that relies on property rights and markets, he thought, because in order for there to be a market in uses of software, owners must be able to make the software unavailable to people who need it. These people would then pay the provider in exchange for access to the software or modification they need. If anyone can make software or share software they possess with friends, it becomes very difficult to write software on a business model that relies on excluding people from software they need unless they pay. As a practical matter, Stallman started writing software himself, and wrote a good bit of it. More fundamentally, he adopted a legal technique that started a snowball rolling. He could not write a whole operating system by himself. Instead, he released pieces of his code under a license that allowed anyone to copy, distribute, and modify the software in whatever way they pleased. He required only that, if the person who modified the software then distributed it to others, he or she do so under the exact same conditions that he had distributed his software. In this way, he invited all other programmers to collaborate with him on this development program, if they wanted to, on the condition that they be as generous with making their contributions available to others as he had been with his. Because he retained the copyright to the software he distributed, he could write this condition into the license that he attached to the software. This meant that anyone using or distributing the software as is, without modifying it, would not violate Stallman's license. They could also modify the software for their own use, and this would not violate the license. However, if they chose to distribute the modified software, they would violate Stallman's copyright unless they included a license identical to his with the software they distributed. This license became the GNU General Public License, or GPL. The legal jujitsu Stallman used—asserting his own copyright claims, but only to force all downstream users who wanted to rely on his contributions to make their own contributions available to everyone else—came to be known as "copyleft," an ironic twist on copyright. This legal artifice allowed anyone to contribute to the GNU project without worrying that one day they would wake up and find that someone had locked them out of the system they had helped to build.

The next major step came when a person with a more practical, rather than prophetic, approach to his work began developing one central component of the operating system—the kernel. Linus Torvalds began to share the early implementations of his kernel, called Linux, with others, under the GPL. These others then modified, added, contributed, and shared among themselves these pieces of the operating system. Building on top of Stallman's foundation, Torvalds crystallized a model of production that was fundamentally different from those that preceded it. His model was based on voluntary contributions and ubiquitous, recursive sharing; on small incremental improvements to a project by widely dispersed people, some of whom contributed a lot, others a little. Based on our usual assumptions about volunteer projects and decentralized production processes that have no managers, this was a model that could not succeed. But it did.

It took almost a decade for the mainstream technology industry to recognize the value of free or open-source software development and its collaborative production methodology. As the process expanded and came to encompass more participants, and produce more of the basic tools of Internet connectivity—Web server, e-mail server, scripting—more of those who participated sought to "normalize" it, or, more specifically, to render it apolitical. Free software is about freedom ("free as in free speech, not free beer" is Stallman's epitaph for it). "Open-source software" was chosen as a term that would not carry the political connotations. It was simply a mode of organizing software production that may be more effective than market-based production. This move to depoliticize peer production of software led to something of a schism between the free software movement and the communities of open source software developers. It is important to understand, however, that from the perspective of society at large and the historical trajectory of information production generally the abandonment of political motivation and the importation of free software into the mainstream have not made it less politically interesting, but more so. Open source and its wide adoption in the business and bureaucratic mainstream allowed free software to emerge from the fringes of the software world and move to the center of the public debate about practical alternatives to the current way of doing things.

So what is open-source software development? The best source for a phenomenology of open-source development continues to be Eric Raymond's *Cathedral and Bazaar*, written in 1998. Imagine that one person, or a small group of friends, wants a utility. It could be a text editor, photo-retouching software, or an operating system. The person or small group starts by developing a part of this project, up to a point where the whole utility—if it is simple enough—or some important part of it, is functional, though it might have much room for improvement. At this point, the person makes the program freely available to others, with its source code—instructions in a human-readable language that explain how the software does whatever it does when compiled into a machine-readable language. When others begin to use it, they may find bugs, or related utilities that they want to add (e.g., the photo-retouching software only increases size and sharpness, and one of its users wants it to allow changing colors as well). The person who has found the bug or is interested in how to add functions to the software may or may not be the best person in the world to actually write the software fix. Nevertheless, he reports the bug or the new need in an Internet forum of users of the software. That person, or someone else, then thinks that they have a way of tweaking the software to fix the bug or add the new utility. They then do so, just as the first person did, and release a new version of the software with the fix or the added utility. The result is a collaboration between three people—the first author, who wrote the initial software; the second person, who identified a problem or shortcoming; and the third person, who fixed it. This collaboration is not managed by anyone who organizes the three, but is instead the outcome of them all reading the same Internet-based forum and using the same software, which is released under an open, rather than proprietary, license. This enables some of its users to identify problems and others to fix these problems without asking anyone's permission and without engaging in any transactions.

The most surprising thing that the open source movement has shown, in real life, is that this simple model can operate on very different scales, from the small, three-person model I described for simple projects, up to the many thousands of people involved in writing the Linux kernel and the GNU/Linux operating system—an immensely difficult production task. Source-Forge, the most popular hosting-meeting place of such projects, has close to 100,000 registered projects, and nearly a million registered users. The economics of this phenomenon are complex. In the larger-scale models, actual organization form is more diverse than the simple, three-person model. In particular, in some of the larger projects, most prominently the Linux kernel development process, a certain kind of meritocratic hierarchy is clearly present. However, it is a hierarchy that is very different in style, practical implementation, and organizational role than that of the manager in the firm. I explain this in chapter 4, as part of the analysis of the organizational forms of peer production. For now, all we need is a broad outline of how peer-production projects look, as we turn to observe case studies of kindred production models in areas outside of software.

PEER PRODUCTION OF INFORMATION,
KNOWLEDGE, AND CULTURE GENERALLY

Free software is, without a doubt, the most visible instance of peer production at the turn of the twenty-first century. It is by no means, however, the only instance. Ubiquitous computer communications networks are bringing about a dramatic change in the scope, scale, and efficacy of peer production throughout the information and cultural production system. As computers become cheaper and as network connections become faster, cheaper, and ubiquitous, we are seeing the phenomenon of peer production of information scale to much larger sizes, performing more complex tasks than were possible in the past for nonprofessional production. To make this phenomenon more tangible, I describe a number of such enterprises, organized to demonstrate the feasibility of this approach throughout the information production and exchange chain. While it is possible to break an act of communication into finer-grained subcomponents, largely we see three distinct functions involved in the process. First, there is an initial utterance of a humanly meaningful statement. Writing an article or drawing a picture, whether done by a professional or an amateur, whether high quality or low, is such an action. Second, there is a separate function of mapping the initial utterances on a knowledge map. In particular, an utterance must be understood as "relevant" in some sense, and "credible." Relevance is a subjective question of mapping an utterance on the conceptual map of a given user seeking information for a particular purpose defined by that individual. Credibility is a question of quality by some objective measure that the individual adopts as appropriate for purposes of evaluating a given utterance. The distinction between the two is somewhat artificial, however, because very often the utility of a piece of information will depend on a combined valuation of its credibility and relevance. I therefore refer to "relevance/accreditation" as a single function for purposes of this discussion, keeping in mind that the two are complementary and not entirely separable functions that an individual requires as part of being able to use utterances that others have uttered in putting together the user's understanding of the world. Finally, there is the function of distribution, or how one takes an utterance produced by one person and distributes it to other people who find it credible and relevant. In the mass-media world, these functions were often, though by no means always, integrated. NBC news produced the utterances, gave them credibility by clearing them on the evening news, and distributed them simultaneously. What the Internet is permitting is much greater dis-aggregation of these functions.

Uttering Content

NASA Clickworkers was "an experiment to see if public volunteers, each working for a few minutes here and there can do some routine science analysis that would normally be done by a scientist or graduate student working for months on end." Users could mark craters on maps of Mars, classify craters that have already been marked, or search the Mars landscape for "honeycomb" terrain. The project was "a pilot study with limited fund-ing, run part-time by one software engineer, with occasional input from two scientists." In its first six months of operation, more than 85,000 users visited the site, with many contributing to the effort, making more than 1.9 million entries (including redundant entries of the same craters, used to average out errors). An analysis of the quality of markings showed "that the automatically-computed consensus of a large number of clickworkers is virtually indistin-guishable from the inputs of a geologist with years of experience in identi-fying Mars craters."[5] The tasks performed by clickworkers (like marking craters) were discrete, each easily performed in a matter of minutes. As a result, users could choose to work for a few minutes doing a single iteration or for hours by doing many. An early study of the project suggested that some clickworkers indeed worked on the project for weeks, but that 37 percent of the work was done by one-time contributors.[6]

The clickworkers project was a particularly clear example of how a com-plex professional task that requires a number of highly trained individuals on full-time salaries can be reorganized so as to be performed by tens of thousands of volunteers in increments so minute that the tasks could be performed on a much lower budget. The low budget would be devoted to coordinating the volunteer effort. However, the raw human capital needed would be contributed for the fun of it. The professionalism of the original scientists was replaced by a combination of high modularization of the task. The organizers broke a large, complex task into small, independent modules. They built in redundancy and automated averaging out of both errors and purposeful erroneous markings—like those of an errant art student who thought it amusing to mark concentric circles on the map. What the NASA scientists running this experiment had tapped into was a vast pool of five-minute increments of human judgment, applied with motivation to partic-ipate in a task unrelated to "making a living."

While clickworkers was a distinct, self-conscious experiment, it suggests characteristics of distributed production that are, in fact, quite widely observable. We have already seen in chapter 2, in our little search for Viking ships, how the Internet can produce encyclopedic or almanac-type information. The power of the Web to answer such an encyclopedic question comes not from the fact that one particular site has all the great answers. It is not an *Encyclopedia Britannica*. The power comes from the fact that it allows a user looking for specific information at a given time to collect answers from a sufficiently large number of contributions. The task of sifting and accrediting falls to the user, motivated by the need to find an answer to the question posed. As long as there are tools to lower the cost of that task to a level acceptable to the user, the Web shall have "produced" the information content the user was looking for. These are not trivial considerations, but they are also not intractable. As we shall see, some of the solutions can themselves be peer produced, and some solutions are emerging as a function of the speed of computation and communication, which enables more efficient technological solutions.

Encyclopedic and almanac-type information emerges on the Web out of the coordinate but entirely independent action of millions of users. This type of information also provides the focus on one of the most successful collaborative enterprises that has developed in the first five years of the twenty-first century, *Wikipedia*. *Wikipedia* was founded by an Internet entrepreneur, Jimmy Wales. Wales had earlier tried to organize an encyclopedia named Nupedia, which was built on a traditional production model, but whose outputs were to be released freely: its contributors were to be PhDs, using a formal, peer-reviewed process. That project appears to have failed to generate a sufficient number of high-quality contributions, but its outputs were used in *Wikipedia* as the seeds for a radically new form of encyclopedia writing. Founded in January 2001, *Wikipedia* combines three core characteristics: First, it uses a collaborative authorship tool, Wiki. This platform enables anyone, including anonymous passersby, to edit almost any page in the entire project. It stores all versions, makes changes easily visible, and enables anyone to revert a document to any prior version as well as to add changes, small and large. All contributions and changes are rendered transparent by the software and database. Second, it is a self-conscious effort at creating an encyclopedia—governed first and foremost by a collective informal undertaking to strive for a neutral point of view, within the limits of substantial self-awareness as to the difficulties of such an enterprise. An effort to represent sympathetically all views on a subject, rather than to achieve objectivity, is the core operative characteristic of this effort. Third, all the content generated by this collaboration is released under the GNU Free Documentation License, an adaptation of the GNU GPL to texts.

The shift in strategy toward an open, peer-produced model proved enormously successful. The site saw tremendous growth both in the number of contributors, including the number of active and very active contributors, and in the number of articles included in the encyclopedia (table 3.1). Most of the early growth was in English, but more recently there has been an increase in the number of articles in many other languages: most notably in German (more than 200,000 articles), Japanese (more than 120,000 articles), and French (about 100,000), but also in another five languages that have between 40,000 and 70,000 articles each, another eleven languages with 10,000 to 40,000 articles each, and thirty-five languages with between 1,000 and 10,000 articles each.

The first systematic study of the quality of *Wikipedia* articles was published as this book was going to press. The journal *Nature* compared 42 science articles from *Wikipedia* to the gold standard of the *Encyclopedia Britannica*, and concluded that "the difference in accuracy was not particularly great."[7] On November 15, 2004, Robert McHenry, a former editor in chief of the *Encyclopedia Britannica*, published an article criticizing *Wikipedia* as "The Faith-Based Encyclopedia."[8] As an example, McHenry mocked the *Wikipedia* article on Alexander Hamilton. He noted that Hamilton biographers have a problem fixing his birth year—whether it is 1755 or 1757. *Wikipedia* glossed over this error, fixing the date at 1755. McHenry then went on to criticize the way the dates were treated throughout the article, using it as an anchor to his general claim: *Wikipedia* is unreliable because it is not professionally produced. What McHenry did not note was that the other major online encyclopedias—like *Columbia* or *Encarta*—similarly failed to deal with the ambiguity surrounding Hamilton's birth date. Only the *Britannica* did. However, McHenry's critique triggered the *Wikipedia* distributed correction mechanism. Within hours of the publication of McHenry's Web article, the reference was corrected. The following few days saw intensive cleanup efforts to conform all references in the biography to the newly corrected version. Within a week or so, *Wikipedia* had a correct, reasonably clean version. It now stood alone with the *Encyclopedia Britannica* as a source of accurate basic encyclopedic information. In coming to curse it, McHenry found himself blessing *Wikipedia*. He had demonstrated

Table 3.1: Contributors to *Wikipedia*, January 2001–June 2005

	Jan. 2001	Jan. 2002	Jan. 2003	Jan. 2004	July 2004	June 2005
Contributors*	10	472	2,188	9,653	25,011	48,721
Active contributors**	9	212	846	3,228	8,442	16,945
Very active contributors***	0	31	190	692	1,637	3,016
No. of English language articles	25	16,000	101,000	190,000	320,000	630,000
No. of articles, all languages	25	19,000	138,000	409,000	862,000	1,600,000

* Contributed at least ten times; ** at least 5 times in last month; *** more than 100 times in last month.

precisely the correction mechanism that makes *Wikipedia*, in the long term, a robust model of reasonably reliable information.

Perhaps the most interesting characteristic about *Wikipedia* is the self-conscious social-norms-based dedication to objective writing. Unlike some of the other projects that I describe in this chapter, *Wikipedia* does not include elaborate software-controlled access and editing capabilities. It is generally open for anyone to edit the materials, delete another's change, debate the desirable contents, survey archives for prior changes, and so forth. It depends on self-conscious use of open discourse, usually aimed at consensus. While there is the possibility that a user will call for a vote of the participants on any given definition, such calls can, and usually are, ignored by the community unless a sufficiently large number of users have decided that debate has been exhausted. While the system operators and server host—Wales—have the practical power to block users who are systematically disruptive, this power seems to be used rarely. The project relies instead on social norms to secure the dedication of project participants to objective writing. So, while not entirely anarchic, the project is nonetheless substantially more social, human, and intensively discourse- and trust-based than the other major projects described here. The following fragments from an early version of the self-described essential characteristics and basic policies of *Wikipedia* are illustrative:

> First and foremost, the Wikipedia project is self-consciously an encyclopedia—rather than a dictionary, discussion forum, web portal, etc. Wikipedia's partici-

pants commonly follow, and enforce, a few basic policies that seem essential to keeping the project running smoothly and productively. First, because we have a huge variety of participants of all ideologies, and from around the world, Wikipedia is committed to making its articles as unbiased as possible. The aim is not to write articles from a single *objective* point of view—this is a common misunderstanding of the policy—but rather, to fairly and sympathetically present all views on an issue. See "neutral point of view" page for further explanation.[9]

The point to see from this quotation is that the participants of *Wikipedia* are plainly people who like to write. Some of them participate in other collaborative authorship projects. However, when they enter the common project of *Wikipedia*, they undertake to participate in a particular way—a way that the group has adopted to make its product be an encyclopedia. On their interpretation, that means conveying in brief terms the state of the art on the item, including divergent opinions about it, but not the author's opinion. Whether that is an attainable goal is a subject of interpretive theory, and is a question as applicable to a professional encyclopedia as it is to *Wikipedia*. As the project has grown, it has developed more elaborate spaces for discussing governance and for conflict resolution. It has developed structures for mediation, and if that fails, arbitration, of disputes about particular articles.

The important point is that *Wikipedia* requires not only mechanical cooperation among people, but a commitment to a particular style of writing and describing concepts that is far from intuitive or natural to people. It requires self-discipline. It enforces the behavior it requires primarily through appeal to the common enterprise that the participants are engaged in, coupled with a thoroughly transparent platform that faithfully records and renders all individual interventions in the common project and facilitates discourse among participants about how their contributions do, or do not, contribute to this common enterprise. This combination of an explicit statement of common purpose, transparency, and the ability of participants to identify each other's actions and counteract them—that is, edit out "bad" or "faithless" definitions—seems to have succeeded in keeping this community from devolving into inefficacy or worse. A case study by IBM showed, for example, that while there were many instances of vandalism on *Wikipedia*, including deletion of entire versions of articles on controversial topics like "abortion," the ability of users to see what was done and to fix it with a single click by reverting to a past version meant that acts of vandalism were corrected within minutes. Indeed, corrections were so rapid that vandalism acts and their corrections did not even appear on a mechanically generated image of the abortion definition as it changed over time.[10] What is perhaps surprising is that this success occurs not in a tightly knit community with many social relations to reinforce the sense of common purpose and the social norms embodying it, but in a large and geographically dispersed group of otherwise unrelated participants. It suggests that even in a group of this size, social norms coupled with a facility to allow any participant to edit out purposeful or mistaken deviations in contravention of the social norms, and a robust platform for largely unmediated conversation, keep the group on track.

A very different cultural form of distributed content production is presented by the rise of massive multiplayer online games (MMOGs) as immersive entertainment. These fall in the same cultural "time slot" as television shows and movies of the twentieth century. The interesting thing about these types of games is that they organize the production of "scripts" very differently from movies or television shows. In a game like Ultima Online or EverQuest, the role of the commercial provider is not to tell a finished, highly polished story to be consumed start to finish by passive consumers. Rather, the role of the game provider is to build tools with which users collaborate to tell a story. There have been observations about this approach for years, regarding MUDs (Multi-User Dungeons) and MOOs (Multi-User Object Oriented games). The point to understand about MMOGs is that they produce a discrete element of "content" that was in the past dominated by centralized professional production. The screenwriter of an immersive entertainment product like a movie is like the scientist marking Mars craters—a professional producer of a finished good. In MMOGs, this function is produced by using the appropriate software platform to allow the story to be written by the many users as they experience it. The individual contributions of the users/coauthors of the story line are literally done for fun— they are playing a game. However, they are spending real economic goods— their attention and substantial subscription fees—on a form of entertainment that uses a platform for active coproduction of a story line to displace what was once passive reception of a finished, commercially and professionally manufactured good.

By 2003, a company called Linden Lab took this concept a major step forward by building an online game environment called Second Life. Second Life began almost entirely devoid of content. It was tools all the way down.

Within a matter of months, it had thousands of subscribers, inhabiting a "world" that had thousands of characters, hundreds of thousands of objects, multiple areas, villages, and "story lines." The individual users themselves had created more than 99 percent of all objects in the game environment, and all story lines and substantive frameworks for interaction—such as a particular village or group of theme-based participants. The interactions in the game environment involved a good deal of gift giving and a good deal of trade, but also some very surprising structured behaviors. Some users set up a university, where lessons were given in both in-game skills and in programming. Others designed spaceships and engaged in alien abductions (undergoing one seemed to become a status symbol within the game). At one point, aiming (successfully) to prevent the company from changing its pricing policy, users staged a demonstration by making signs and picketing the entry point to the game; and a "tax revolt" by placing large numbers of "tea crates" around an in-game reproduction of the Washington Monument. Within months, Second Life had become an immersive experience, like a movie or book, but one where the commercial provider offered a platform and tools, while the users wrote the story lines, rendered the "set," and performed the entire play.

Relevance/Accreditation

How are we to know that the content produced by widely dispersed individuals is not sheer gobbledygook? Can relevance and accreditation itself be produced on a peer-production model? One type of answer is provided by looking at commercial businesses that successfully break off precisely the "accreditation and relevance" piece of their product, and rely on peer production to perform that function. Amazon and Google are probably the two most prominent examples of this strategy.

Amazon uses a mix of mechanisms to get in front of their buyers of books and other products that the users are likely to purchase. A number of these mechanisms produce relevance and accreditation by harnessing the users themselves. At the simplest level, the recommendation "customers who bought items you recently viewed also bought these items" is a mechanical means of extracting judgments of relevance and accreditation from the actions of many individuals, who produce the datum of relevance as byproduct of making their own purchasing decisions. Amazon also allows users to create topical lists and track other users as their "friends and favorites." Amazon, like many consumer sites today, also provides users with the ability to rate books they buy, generating a peer-produced rating by averaging the ratings. More fundamentally, the core innovation of Google, widely recognized as the most efficient general search engine during the first half of the 2000s, was to introduce peer-based judgments of relevance. Like other search engines at the time, Google used a text-based algorithm to retrieve a given universe of Web pages initially. Its major innovation was its PageRank algorithm, which harnesses peer production of ranking in the following way. The engine treats links from other Web sites pointing to a given Web site as votes of confidence. Whenever someone who authors a Web site links to someone else's page, that person has stated quite explicitly that the linked page is worth a visit. Google's search engine counts these links as distributed votes of confidence in the quality of the page pointed to. Pages that are heavily linked-to count as more important votes of confidence. If a highly linked-to site links to a given page, that vote counts for more than the vote of a site that no one else thinks is worth visiting. The point to take home from looking at Google and Amazon is that corporations that have done immensely well at acquiring and retaining users have harnessed peer production to enable users to find things they want quickly and efficiently.

The most prominent example of a distributed project self-consciously devoted to peer production of relevance is the Open Directory Project. The site relies on more than sixty thousand volunteer editors to determine which links should be included in the directory. Acceptance as a volunteer requires application. Quality relies on a peer-review process based substantially on seniority as a volunteer and level of engagement with the site. The site is hosted and administered by Netscape, which pays for server space and a small number of employees to administer the site and set up the initial guidelines. Licensing is free and presumably adds value partly to America Online's (AOL's) and Netscape's commercial search engine/portal and partly through goodwill. Volunteers are not affiliated with Netscape and receive no compensation. They spend time selecting sites for inclusion in the directory (in small increments of perhaps fifteen minutes per site reviewed), producing the most comprehensive, highest-quality human-edited directory of the Web—at this point outshining the directory produced by the company that pioneered human edited directories of the Web: Yahoo!.

Perhaps the most elaborate platform for peer production of relevance and accreditation, at multiple layers, is used by Slashdot. Billed as "News for Nerds," Slashdot has become a leading technology newsletter on the Web, coproduced by hundreds of thousands of users. Slashdot primarily consists of users commenting on initial submissions that cover a variety of technology-related topics. The submissions are typically a link to an off-site story, coupled with commentary from the person who submits the piece. Users follow up the initial submission with comments that often number in the hundreds. The initial submissions themselves, and more importantly, the approach to sifting through the comments of users for relevance and accreditation, provide a rich example of how this function can be performed on a distributed, peer-production model.

First, it is important to understand that the function of posting a story from another site onto Slashdot, the first "utterance" in a chain of comments on Slashdot, is itself an act of relevance production. The person submitting the story is telling the community of Slashdot users, "here is a story that 'News for Nerds' readers should be interested in." This initial submission of a link is itself very coarsely filtered by editors who are paid employees of Open Source Technology Group (OSTG), which runs a number of similar platforms—like SourceForge, the most important platform for free software developers. OSTG is a subsidiary of VA Software, a software services company. The FAQ (Frequently Asked Question) response to, "how do you verify the accuracy of Slashdot stories?" is revealing: "We don't. You do. If something seems outrageous, we might look for some corroboration, but as a rule, we regard this as the responsibility of the submitter and the audience. This is why it's important to read comments. You might find something that refutes, or supports, the story in the main." In other words, Slashdot very self-consciously is organized as a means of facilitating peer production of accreditation; it is at the comments stage that the story undergoes its most important form of accreditation—peer review ex-post.

Filtering and accreditation of comments on Slashdot offer the most interesting case study of peer production of these functions. Users submit comments that are displayed together with the initial submission of a story. Think of the "content" produced in these comments as a cross between academic peer review of journal submissions and a peer-produced substitute for television's "talking heads." It is in the means of accrediting and evaluating these comments that Slashdot's system provides a comprehensive example of peer production of relevance and accreditation. Slashdot implements an automated system to select moderators from the pool of users. Moderators are chosen according to several criteria; they must be logged in (not anonymous), they must be regular users (who use the site averagely, not one-time page loaders or compulsive users), they must have been using the site for a while (this defeats people who try to sign up just to moderate), they must be willing, and they must have positive "karma." Karma is a number assigned to a user that primarily reflects whether he or she has posted good or bad comments (according to ratings from other moderators). If a user meets these criteria, the program assigns the user moderator status and the user gets five "influence points" to review comments. The moderator rates a comment of his choice using a drop-down list with words such as "flamebait" and "informative." A positive word increases the rating of a comment one point and a negative word decreases the rating a point. Each time a moderator rates a comment, it costs one influence point, so he or she can only rate five comments for each moderating period. The period lasts for three days and if the user does not use the influence points, they expire. The moderation setup is designed to give many users a small amount of power. This decreases the effect of users with an ax to grind or with poor judgment. The site also implements some automated "troll filters," which prevent users from sabotaging the system. Troll filters stop users from posting more than once every sixty seconds, prevent identical posts, and will ban a user for twenty-four hours if he or she has been moderated down several times within a short time frame. Slashdot then provides users with a "threshold" filter that allows each user to block lower-quality comments. The scheme uses the numerical rating of the comment (ranging from -1 to 5). Comments start out at 0 for anonymous posters, 1 for registered users, and 2 for registered users with good "karma." As a result, if a user sets his or her filter at 1, the user will not see any comments from anonymous posters unless the comments' ratings were increased by a moderator. A user can set his or her filter anywhere from -1 (viewing all of the comments) to 5 (where only the posts that have been upgraded by several moderators will show up).

Relevance, as distinct from accreditation, is also tied into the Slashdot scheme because off-topic posts should receive an "off topic" rating by the moderators and sink below the threshold level (assuming the user has the threshold set above the minimum). However, the moderation system is limited to choices that sometimes are not mutually exclusive. For instance, a moderator may have to choose between "funny" ($+1$) and "off topic" (-1) when a post is both funny and off topic. As a result, an irrelevant post can increase in ranking and rise above the threshold level because it is funny or informative. It is unclear, however, whether this is a limitation on relevance, or indeed mimics our own normal behavior, say in reading a newspaper or browsing a library, where we might let our eyes linger longer on a funny or informative tidbit, even after we have ascertained that it is not exactly relevant to what we were looking for.

The primary function of moderation is to provide accreditation. If a user sets a high threshold level, they will only see posts that are considered of high quality by the moderators. Users also receive accreditation through their karma. If their posts consistently receive high ratings, their karma will increase. At a certain karma level, their comments will start off with a rating of 2, thereby giving them a louder voice in the sense that users with a threshold of 2 will now see their posts immediately, and fewer upward moderations are needed to push their comments even higher. Conversely, a user with bad karma from consistently poorly rated comments can lose accreditation by having his or her posts initially start off at 0 or −1. In addition to the mechanized means of selecting moderators and minimizing their power to skew the accreditation system, Slashdot implements a system of peer-review accreditation for the moderators themselves. Slashdot accomplishes this "metamoderation" by making any user that has an account from the first 90 percent of accounts created on the system eligible to evaluate the moderators. Each eligible user who opts to perform metamoderation review is provided with ten random moderator ratings of comments. The user/metamoderator then rates the moderator's rating as either unfair, fair, or neither. The metamoderation process affects the karma of the original moderator, which, when lowered sufficiently by cumulative judgments of unfair ratings, will remove the moderator from the moderation system.

Together, these mechanisms allow for distributed production of both relevance and accreditation. Because there are many moderators who can moderate any given comment, and thanks to the mechanisms that explicitly limit the power of any one moderator to overinfluence the aggregate judgment, the system evens out differences in evaluation by aggregating judgments. It then allows individual users to determine what level of accreditation pronounced by this aggregate system fits their particular time and needs by setting their filter to be more or less inclusive. By introducing "karma," the system also allows users to build reputation over time, and to gain greater control over the accreditation of their own work relative to the power of the critics. Users, moderators, and metamoderators are all volunteers.

The primary point to take from the Slashdot example is that the same dynamic that we saw used for peer production of initial utterances, or content, can be implemented to produce relevance and accreditation. Rather than using the full-time effort of professional accreditation experts, the system is designed to permit the aggregation of many small judgments, each of which entails a trivial effort for the contributor, regarding both relevance and accreditation of the materials. The software that mediates the communication among the collaborating peers embeds both the means to facilitate the participation and a variety of mechanisms designed to defend the common effort from poor judgment or defection.

Value-Added Distribution

Finally, when we speak of information or cultural goods that exist (content has been produced) and are made usable through some relevance and accreditation mechanisms, there remains the question of distribution. To some extent, this is a nonissue on the Internet. Distribution is cheap. All one needs is a server and large pipes connecting one's server to the world. Nonetheless, this segment of the publication process has also provided us with important examples of peer production, including one of its earliest examples—Project Gutenberg.

Project Gutenberg entails hundreds of volunteers who scan in and correct books so that they are freely available in digital form. It has amassed more than 13,000 books, and makes the collection available to everyone for free. The vast majority of the "e-texts" offered are public domain materials. The site itself presents the e-texts in ASCII format, the lowest technical common denominator, but does not discourage volunteers from offering the e-texts in markup languages. It contains a search engine that allows a reader to search for typical fields such as subject, author, and title. Project Gutenberg volunteers can select any book that is in the public domain to transform into an e-text. The volunteer submits a copy of the title page of the book to Michael Hart—who founded the project—for copyright research. The volunteer is notified to proceed if the book passes the copyright clearance. The decision on which book to convert to e-text is left up to the volunteer, subject to copyright limitations. Typically, a volunteer converts a book to ASCII format using OCR (optical character recognition) and proofreads it one time in order to screen it for major errors. He or she then passes the ASCII file to a volunteer proofreader. This exchange is orchestrated with very little supervision. The volunteers use a Listserv mailing list and a bulletin board to initiate and supervise the exchange. In addition, books are labeled with a version number indicating how many times they have been proofed. The site encourages volunteers to select a book that has a low number and proof it. The Project Gutenberg proofing process is simple.

Proofreaders (aside from the first pass) are not expected to have access to the book, but merely review the e-text for self-evident errors.

Distributed Proofreading, a site originally unaffiliated with Project Gutenberg, is devoted to proofing Project Gutenberg e-texts more efficiently, by distributing the volunteer proofreading function in smaller and more information-rich modules. Charles Franks, a computer programmer from Las Vegas, decided that he had a more efficient way to proofread these e-texts. He built an interface that allowed volunteers to compare scanned images of original texts with the e-texts available on Project Gutenberg. In the Distributed Proofreading process, scanned pages are stored on the site, and volunteers are shown a scanned page and a page of the e-text simultaneously so that they can compare the e-text to the original page. Because of the fine-grained modularity, proofreaders can come on the site and proof one or a few pages and submit them. By contrast, on the Project Gutenberg site, the entire book is typically exchanged, or at minimum, a chapter. In this fashion, Distributed Proofreading clears the proofing of tens of thousands of pages every month. After a couple of years of working independently, Franks joined forces with Hart. By late 2004, the site had proofread more than five thousand volumes using this method.

Sharing of Processing, Storage, and Communications Platforms

All the examples of peer production that we have seen up to this point have been examples where individuals pool their time, experience, wisdom, and creativity to form new information, knowledge, and cultural goods. As we look around the Internet, however, we find that users also cooperate in similar loosely affiliated groups, without market signals or managerial commands, to build supercomputers and massive data storage and retrieval systems. In their radical decentralization and reliance on social relations and motivations, these sharing practices are similar to peer production of information, knowledge, and culture. They differ in one important aspect: Users are not sharing their innate and acquired human capabilities, and, unlike information, their inputs and outputs are not public goods. The participants are, instead, sharing material goods that they privately own, mostly personal computers and their components. They produce economic, not public, goods—computation, storage, and communications capacity.

As of the middle of 2004, the fastest supercomputer in the world was SETI@home. It ran about 75 percent faster than the supercomputer that was then formally known as "the fastest supercomputer in the world": the IBM Blue Gene/L. And yet, there was and is no single SETI@home computer. Instead, the SETI@home project has developed software and a collaboration platform that have enabled millions of participants to pool their computation resources into a single powerful computer. Every user who participates in the project must download a small screen saver. When a user's personal computer is idle, the screen saver starts up, downloads problems for calculation—in SETI@home, these are radio astronomy signals to be analyzed for regularities—and calculates the problem it has downloaded. Once the program calculates a solution, it automatically sends its results to the main site. The cycle continues for as long as, and repeats every time that, the computer is idle from its user's perspective. As of the middle of 2004, the project had harnessed the computers of 4.5 million users, allowing it to run computations at speeds greater than those achieved by the fastest supercomputers in the world that private firms, using full-time engineers, developed for the largest and best-funded government laboratories in the world. SETI@home is the most prominent, but is only one among dozens of similarly structured Internet-based distributed computing platforms. Another, whose structure has been the subject of the most extensive formal analysis by its creators, is Folding@home. As of mid-2004, Folding@home had amassed contributions of about 840,000 processors contributed by more than 365,000 users.

SETI@home and Folding@home provide a good basis for describing the fairly common characteristics of Internet-based distributed computation projects. First, these are noncommercial projects, engaged in pursuits understood as scientific, for the general good, seeking to harness contributions of individuals who wish to contribute to such larger-than-themselves goals. SETI@home helps in the search for extraterrestrial intelligence. Folding@home helps in protein folding research. Fightaids@home is dedicated to running models that screen compounds for the likelihood that they will provide good drug candidates to fight HIV/AIDS. Genome@home is dedicated to modeling artificial genes that would be created to generate useful proteins. Other sites, like those dedicated to cryptography or mathematics, have a narrower appeal, and combine "altruistic" with hobby as their basic motivational appeal. The absence of money is, in any event, typical of the large majority of active distributed computing projects. Less than one-fifth of these projects mention money at all. Most of those that do mention money refer to the contributors' eligibility for a share of a generally available prize for solving a scientific or mathematical challenge, and mix an appeal to hobby and altruism with the promise of money. Only two of about sixty projects active in 2004 were built on a pay-per-contribution basis, and these were quite small-scale by comparison to many of the others.

Most of the distributed computing projects provide a series of utilities and statistics intended to allow contributors to attach meaning to their contributions in a variety of ways. The projects appear to be eclectic in their implicit social and psychological theories of the motivations for participation in the projects. Sites describe the scientific purpose of the models and the specific scientific output, including posting articles that have used the calculations. In these components, the project organizers seem to assume some degree of taste for generalized altruism and the pursuit of meaning in contributing to a common goal. They also implement a variety of mechanisms to reinforce the sense of purpose, such as providing aggregate statistics about the total computations performed by the project as a whole. However, the sites also seem to assume a healthy dose of what is known in the anthropology of gift literature as agonistic giving—that is, giving intended to show that the person giving is greater than or more important than others, who gave less. For example, most of the sites allow individuals to track their own contributions, and provide "user of the month"-type rankings. An interesting characteristic of quite a few of these is the ability to create "teams" of users, who in turn compete on who has provided more cycles or work units. SETI@home in particular taps into ready-made nationalisms, by offering country-level statistics. Some of the team names on Folding@home also suggest other, out-of-project bonding measures, such as national or ethnic bonds (for example, Overclockers Australia or Alliance Francophone), technical minority status (for example, Linux or MacAddict4Life), and organizational affiliation (University of Tennessee or University of Alabama), as well as shared cultural reference points (Knights who say Ni!). In addition, the sites offer platforms for simple connectedness and mutual companionship, by offering user fora to discuss the science and the social participation involved. It is possible that these sites are shooting in the dark, as far as motivating sharing is concerned. It also possible, however, that they have tapped into a valuable insight, which is that people behave sociably and generously for all sorts of different reasons, and that at least in this domain, adding reasons to participate—some agonistic, some altruistic, some reciprocity-seeking—does not have a crowding-out effect.

Like distributed computing projects, peer-to-peer file-sharing networks are an excellent example of a highly efficient system for storing and accessing data in a computer network. These networks of sharing are much less "mysterious," in terms of understanding the human motivation behind participation. Nevertheless, they provide important lessons about the extent to which large-scale collaboration among strangers or loosely affiliated users can provide effective communications platforms. For fairly obvious reasons, we usually think of peer-to-peer networks, beginning with Napster, as a "problem." This is because they were initially overwhelmingly used to perform an act that, by the analysis of almost any legal scholar, was copyright infringement. To a significant extent, they are still used in this form. There were, and continue to be, many arguments about whether the acts of the firms that provided peer-to-peer software were responsible for the violations. However, there has been little argument that anyone who allows thousands of other users to make copies of his or her music files is violating copyright—hence the public interpretation of the creation of peer-to-peer networks as primarily a problem. From the narrow perspective of the law of copyright or of the business model of the recording industry and Hollywood, this may be an appropriate focus. From the perspective of diagnosing what is happening to our social and economic structure, the fact that the files traded on these networks were mostly music in the first few years of this technology's implementation is little more than a distraction. Let me explain why.

Imagine for a moment that someone—be it a legislator defining a policy goal or a businessperson defining a desired service—had stood up in mid-1999 and set the following requirements: "We would like to develop a new music and movie distribution system. We would like it to store all the music and movies ever digitized. We would like it to be available from anywhere in the world. We would like it to be able to serve tens of millions of users at any given moment." Any person at the time would have predicted that building such a system would cost tens if not hundreds of millions of dollars; that running it would require large standing engineering staffs; that managing it so that users could find what they wanted and not drown in the sea of content would require some substantial number of "curators"—DJs and movie buffs—and that it would take at least five to ten years to build. Instead, the system was built cheaply by a wide range of actors, starting with Shawn Fanning's idea and implementation of Napster. Once the idea was out, others perfected the idea further, eliminating the need for even the one centralized feature that Napster included—a list of who had what files on which computer that provided the matchmaking function in the Napster network. Since then, under the pressure of suits from the recording industry and a steady and persistent demand for peer-to-peer music software, rapid successive generations of Gnutella, and then the FastTrack clients KaZaa and Morpheus, Overnet and eDonkey, the improvements of BitTorrent, and many others have enhanced the reliability, coverage, and speed of the peer-to-peer music distribution system—all under constant threat of litigation, fines, police searches and even, in some countries, imprisonment of the developers or users of these networks.

What is truly unique about peer-to-peer networks as a signal of what is to come is the fact that with ridiculously low financial investment, a few teenagers and twenty-something-year-olds were able to write software and protocols that allowed tens of millions of computer users around the world to cooperate in producing the most efficient and robust file storage and retrieval system in the world. No major investment was necessary in creating a server farm to store and make available the vast quantities of data represented by the media files. The users' computers are themselves the "server farm." No massive investment in dedicated distribution channels made of high-quality fiber optics was necessary. The standard Internet connections of users, with some very intelligent file transfer protocols, sufficed. Architecture oriented toward enabling users to cooperate with each other in storage, search, retrieval, and delivery of files was all that was necessary to build a content distribution network that dwarfed anything that existed before.

Again, there is nothing mysterious about why users participate in peer-to-peer networks. They want music; they can get it from these networks for free; so they participate. The broader point to take from looking at peer-to-peer file-sharing networks, however, is the sheer effectiveness of large-scale collaboration among individuals once they possess, under their individual control, the physical capital necessary to make their cooperation effective. These systems are not "subsidized," in the sense that they do not pay the full marginal cost of their service. Remember, music, like all information, is a nonrival public good whose marginal cost, once produced, is zero. Moreover, digital files are not "taken" from one place in order to be played in the other. They are replicated wherever they are wanted, and thereby made more ubiquitous, not scarce. The only actual social cost involved at the time of the transmission is the storage capacity, communications capacity, and processing capacity necessary to store, catalog, search, retrieve, and transfer the information necessary to replicate the files from where copies reside to where more copies are desired. As with any nonrival good, if Jane is willing to spend the actual social costs involved in replicating the music file that already exists and that Jack possesses, then it is efficient that she do so without paying the creator a dime. It may throw a monkey wrench into the particular way in which our society has chosen to pay musicians and recording executives. This, as we saw in chapter 2, trades off efficiency for longer-term incentive effects for the recording industry. However, it is efficient within the normal meaning of the term in economics in a way that it would not have been had Jane and Jack used subsidized computers or network connections.

As with distributed computing, peer-to-peer file-sharing systems build on the fact that individual users own vast quantities of excess capacity embedded in their personal computers. As with distributed computing, peer-to-peer networks developed architectures that allowed users to share this excess capacity with each other. By cooperating in these sharing practices, users construct together systems with capabilities far exceeding those that they could have developed by themselves, as well as the capabilities that even the best-financed corporations could provide using techniques that rely on components they fully owned. The network components owned by any single music delivery service cannot match the collective storage and retrieval capabilities of the universe of users' hard drives and network connections. Similarly, the processors arrayed in the supercomputers find it difficult to compete with the vast computation resource available on the millions of personal computers connected to the Internet, and the proprietary software development firms find themselves competing, and in some areas losing to, the vast pool of programming talent connected to the Internet in the form of participants in free and open source software development projects.

In addition to computation and storage, the last major element of computer communications networks is connectivity. Here, too, perhaps more dramatically than in either of the two other functionalities, we have seen the development of sharing-based techniques. The most direct transfer of the design characteristics of peer-to-peer networks to communications has been the successful development of Skype—an Internet telephony utility that allows the owners of computers to have voice conversations with each other over the Internet for free, and to dial into the public telephone network for a fee. As of this writing, Skype is already used by more than two million users at any given moment in time. They use a FastTrack-like architecture to share their computing and communications resources to create a global telephone system running on top of the Internet. It was created, and is run by, the developers of KaZaa.

Most dramatically, however, we have seen these techniques emerging in wireless communications. Throughout almost the entire twentieth century, radio communications used a single engineering approach to allow multiple messages to be sent wirelessly in a single geographic area. This approach was to transmit each of the different simultaneous messages by generating separate electromagnetic waves for each, which differed from each other by the frequency of oscillation, or wavelength. The receiver could then separate out the messages by ignoring all electromagnetic energy received at its antenna unless it oscillated at the frequency of the desired message. This engineering technique, adopted by Marconi in 1900, formed the basis of our notion of "spectrum": the range of frequencies at which we know how to generate electromagnetic waves with sufficient control and predictability that we can encode and decode information with them, as well as the notion that there are "channels" of spectrum that are "used" by a communication. For more than half a century, radio communications regulation was thought necessary because spectrum was scarce, and unless regulated, everyone would transmit at all frequencies causing chaos and an inability to send messages. From 1959, when Ronald Coase first published his critique of this regulatory approach, until the early 1990s, when spectrum auctions began, the terms of the debate over "spectrum policy," or wireless communications regulation, revolved around whether the exclusive right to transmit radio signals in a given geographic area should be granted as a regulatory license or a tradable property right. In the 1990s, with the introduction of auctions, we began to see the adoption of a primitive version of a property-based system through "spectrum auctions." By the early 2000s, this system allowed the new "owners" of these exclusive rights to begin to shift what were initially purely mobile telephony systems to mobile data communications as well.

By this time, however, the century-old engineering assumptions that underlay the regulation-versus-property conceptualization of the possibilities open for the institutional framework of wireless communications had been rendered obsolete by new computation and network technologies.[11] The dramatic decline in computation cost and improvements in digital signal processing, network architecture, and antenna systems had fundamentally changed the design space of wireless communications systems. Instead of having one primary parameter with which to separate out messages—the frequency of oscillation of the carrier wave—engineers could now use many different mechanisms to allow much smarter receivers to separate out the message they wanted to receive from all other sources of electromagnetic radiation in the geographic area they occupied. Radio transmitters could now transmit at the same frequency, simultaneously, without "interfering" with each other—that is, without confusing the receivers as to which radiation carried the required message and which did not. Just like automobiles that can share a commons-based medium—the road—and unlike railroad cars, which must use dedicated, owned, and managed railroad tracks—these new radios could share "the spectrum" as a commons. It was no longer necessary, or even efficient, to pass laws—be they in the form of regulations or of exclusive property-like rights—that carved up the usable spectrum into exclusively controlled slices. Instead, large numbers of transceivers, owned and operated by end users, could be deployed and use equipment-embedded protocols to coordinate their communications.

The reasons that owners would share the excess capacity of their new radios are relatively straightforward in this case. Users want to have wireless connectivity all the time, to be reachable and immediately available everywhere. However, they do not actually want to communicate every few microseconds. They will therefore be willing to purchase and keep turned on equipment that provides them with such connectivity. Manufacturers, in turn, will develop and adhere to standards that will improve capacity and connectivity. As a matter of engineering, what has been called "cooperation gain"—the improved quality of the system gained when the nodes cooperate—is the most promising source of capacity scaling for distributed wireless systems.[12] Cooperation gain is easy to understand from day-to-day interactions. When we sit in a lecture and miss a word or two, we might turn to a neighbor and ask, "Did you hear what she said?" In radio systems, this kind of cooperation among the antennae (just like the ears) of neighbors is called antenna diversity, and is the basis for the design of a number of systems to improve reception. We might stand in a loud crowd without being able to shout or walk over to the other end of the room, but ask a friend: "If you see so and so, tell him *x*"; that friend then bumps into a friend of so and so and tells that person: "If you see so and so, tell him *x*"; and so forth. When we do this, we are using what in radio engineering is called repeater networks. These kinds of cooperative systems can carry much higher loads without interference, sharing wide swaths of spectrum, in ways that are more efficient than systems that rely on explicit market transactions based on property in the right to emit power in discrete frequencies. The design of such "ad hoc mesh networks"—that is, networks of radios that can configure themselves into cooperative networks as need arises, and help each other forward messages and decipher incoming messages over the din of radio emissions—are the most dynamic area in radio engineering today.

This technological shift gave rise to the fastest-growing sector in the wireless communications arena in the first few years of the twenty-first century—WiFi and similar unlicensed wireless devices. The economic success of the equipment market that utilizes the few primitive "spectrum commons" available in the United States—originally intended for low-power devices like garage openers and the spurious emissions of microwave ovens—led toward at first slow, and more recently quite dramatic, change in U.S. wireless policy. In the past two years alone, what have been called "commons-based" approaches to wireless communications policy have come to be seen as a legitimate, indeed a central, component of the Federal Communication Commission's (FCC's) wireless policy.[13] We are beginning to see in this space the most prominent example of a system that was entirely oriented toward regulation aimed at improving the institutional conditions of market-based production of wireless transport capacity sold as a finished good (connectivity minutes), shifting toward enabling the emergence of a market in shareable goods (smart radios) designed to provision transport on a sharing model.

I hope these detailed examples provide a common set of mental pictures of what peer production looks like. In the next chapter I explain the economics of peer production of information and the sharing of material resources for computation, communications, and storage in particular, and of nonmarket, social production more generally: why it is efficient, how we can explain the motivations that lead people to participate in these great enterprises of nonmarket cooperation, and why we see so much more of it online than we do off-line. The moral and political discussion throughout the remainder of the book does not, however, depend on your accepting the particular analysis I offer in chapter 4 to "domesticate" these phenomena within more or less standard economics. At this point, it is important that the stories have provided a texture for, and established the plausibility of, the claim that nonmarket production in general and peer production in particular are phenomena of much wider application than free software, and exist in important ways throughout the networked information economy. For purposes of understanding the political implications that occupy most of this book, that is all that is necessary.

Chapter 4 The Economics of Social Production

The increasing salience of nonmarket production in general, and peer production in particular, raises three puzzles from an economics perspective. First, why do people participate? What is their motivation when they work for or contribute resources to a project for which they are not paid or directly rewarded? Second, why now, why here? What, if anything, is special about the digitally networked environment that would lead us to believe that peer production is here to stay as an important economic phenomenon, as opposed to a fad that will pass as the medium matures and patterns of behavior settle toward those more familiar to us from the economy of steel, coal, and temp agencies. Third, is it efficient to have all these people sharing their computers and donating their time and creative effort? Moving through the answers to these questions, it becomes clear that the diverse and complex patterns of behavior observed on the Internet, from Viking ship hobbyists to the developers of the GNU/Linux operating system, are perfectly consistent with much of our contemporary understanding of human economic behavior. We need to assume no fundamental change in the nature of humanity;

we need not declare the end of economics as we know it. We merely need to see that the material conditions of production in the networked information economy have changed in ways that increase the relative salience of social sharing and exchange as a modality of economic production. That is, behaviors and motivation patterns familiar to us from social relations generally continue to cohere in their own patterns. What has changed is that now these patterns of behavior have become effective beyond the domains of building social relations of mutual interest and fulfilling our emotional and psychological needs of companionship and mutual recognition. They have come to play a substantial role as modes of motivating, informing, and organizing productive behavior at the very core of the information economy. And it is this increasing role as a modality of information production that ripples through the rest this book. It is the feasibility of producing information, knowledge, and culture through social, rather than market and proprietary relations—through cooperative peer production and coordinate individual action—that creates the opportunities for greater autonomous action, a more critical culture, a more discursively engaged and better informed republic, and perhaps a more equitable global community.

MOTIVATION

Much of economics achieves analytic tractability by adopting a very simple model of human motivation. The basic assumption is that all human motivations can be more or less reduced to something like positive and negative utilities—things people want, and things people want to avoid. These are capable of being summed, and are usually translatable into a universal medium of exchange, like money. Adding more of something people want, like money, to any given interaction will, all things considered, make that interaction more desirable to rational people. While simplistic, this highly tractable model of human motivation has enabled policy prescriptions that have proven far more productive than prescriptions that depended on other models of human motivation—such as assuming that benign administrators will be motivated to serve their people, or that individuals will undertake self-sacrifice for the good of the nation or the commune.

Of course, this simple model underlying much of contemporary economics is wrong. At least it is wrong as a universal description of human motivation. If you leave a fifty-dollar check on the table at the end of a dinner party at a friend's house, you do not increase the probability that you will be invited again. We live our lives in diverse social frames, and money has a complex relationship with these—sometimes it adds to the motivation to participate, sometimes it detracts from it. While this is probably a trivial observation outside of the field of economics, it is quite radical within that analytic framework. The present generation's efforts to formalize and engage it began with the Titmuss-Arrow debate of the early 1970s. In a major work, Richard Titmuss compared the U.S. and British blood supply systems. The former was largely commercial at the time, organized by a mix of private for-profit and nonprofit actors; the latter entirely voluntary and organized by the National Health Service. Titmuss found that the British system had higher-quality blood (as measured by the likelihood of recipients contracting hepatitis from transfusions), less blood waste, and fewer blood shortages at hospitals. Titmuss also attacked the U.S. system as inequitable, arguing that the rich exploited the poor and desperate by buying their blood. He concluded that an altruistic blood procurement system is both more ethical and more efficient than a market system, and recommended that the market be kept out of blood donation to protect the "right to give."[1] Titmuss's argument came under immediate attack from economists. Most relevant for our purposes here, Kenneth Arrow agreed that the differences in blood quality indicated that the U.S. blood system was flawed, but rejected Titmuss's central theoretical claim that markets reduce donative activity. Arrow reported the alternative hypothesis held by "economists typically," that if some people respond to exhortation/moral incentives (donors), while others respond to prices and market incentives (sellers), these two groups likely behave independently—neither responds to the other's incentives. Thus, the decision to allow or ban markets should have no effect on donative behavior. Removing a market could, however, remove incentives of the "bad blood" suppliers to sell blood, thereby improving the overall quality of the blood supply. Titmuss had not established his hypothesis analytically, Arrow argued, and its proof or refutation would lie in empirical study.[2] Theoretical differences aside, the U.S. blood supply system did in fact transition to an all-volunteer system of social donation since the 1970s. In surveys since, blood donors have reported that they "enjoy helping" others, experienced a sense of moral obligation or responsibility, or exhibited characteristics of reciprocators after they or their relatives received blood.

A number of scholars, primarily in psychology and economics, have attempted to resolve this question both empirically and theoretically. The most systematic work within economics is that of Swiss economist Bruno Frey and various collaborators, building on the work of psychologist Edward Deci.[3] A simple statement of this model is that individuals have intrinsic and extrinsic motivations. Extrinsic motivations are imposed on individuals from the outside. They take the form of either offers of money for, or prices imposed on, behavior, or threats of punishment or reward from a manager or a judge for complying with, or failing to comply with, specifically pre-scribed behavior. Intrinsic motivations are reasons for action that come from within the person, such as pleasure or personal satisfaction. Extrinsic moti-vations are said to "crowd out" intrinsic motivations because they (a) impair self-determination—that is, people feel pressured by an external force, and therefore feel overjustified in maintaining their intrinsic motivation rather than complying with the will of the source of the extrinsic reward; or (b) impair self-esteem—they cause individuals to feel that their internal moti-vation is rejected, not valued, and as a result, their self-esteem is diminished, causing them to reduce effort. Intuitively, this model relies on there being a culturally contingent notion of what one "ought" to do if one is a well-adjusted human being and member of a decent society. Being offered money to do something you know you "ought" to do, and that self-respecting members of society usually in fact do, implies that the person offering the money believes that you are not a well-adjusted human being or an equally respectable member of society. This causes the person offered the money either to believe the offerer, and thereby lose self-esteem and reduce effort, or to resent him and resist the offer. A similar causal explanation is formal-ized by Roland Benabou and Jean Tirole, who claim that the person receiv-ing the monetary incentives infers that the person offering the compensation does not trust the offeree to do the right thing, or to do it well of their own accord. The offeree's self-confidence and intrinsic motivation to succeed are reduced to the extent that the offeree believes that the offerer—a manager or parent, for example—is better situated to judge the offeree's abilities.[4]

More powerful than the theoretical literature is the substantial empirical literature—including field and laboratory experiments, econometrics, and surveys—that has developed since the mid-1990s to test the hypotheses of this model of human motivation. Across many different settings, researchers have found substantial evidence that, under some circumstances, adding money for an activity previously undertaken without price compensation reduces, rather than increases, the level of activity. The work has covered contexts as diverse as the willingness of employees to work more or to share their experience and knowledge with team members, of communities to accept locally undesirable land uses, or of parents to pick up children from day-care centers punctually.[5] The results of this empirical literature strongly suggest that across various domains some displacement or crowding out can be identified between monetary rewards and nonmonetary motivations. This does not mean that offering monetary incentives does not increase extrinsic rewards—it does. Where extrinsic rewards dominate, this will increase the activity rewarded as usually predicted in economics. However, the effect on intrinsic motivation, at least sometimes, operates in the opposite direction. Where intrinsic motivation is an important factor because pricing and contracting are difficult to achieve, or because the payment that can be offered is relatively low, the aggregate effect may be negative. Persuading experienced employees to communicate their tacit knowledge to the teams they work with is a good example of the type of behavior that is very hard to specify for efficient pricing, and therefore occurs more effectively through social motivations for teamwork than through payments. Negative effects of small payments on participation in work that was otherwise volunteer-based are an example of low payments recruiting relatively few people, but making others shift their efforts elsewhere and thereby reducing, rather than increasing, the total level of volunteering for the job.

The psychology-based alternative to the "more money for an activity will mean more of the activity" assumption implicit in most of these new economic models is complemented by a sociology-based alternative. This comes from one branch of the social capital literature—the branch that relates back to Mark Granovetter's 1974 book, *Getting a Job,* and was initiated as a crossover from sociology to economics by James Coleman.[6] This line of literature rests on the claim that, as Nan Lin puts it, "there are two ultimate (or primitive) rewards for human beings in a social structure: economic standing and social standing."[7] These rewards are understood as instrumental and, in this regard, are highly amenable to economics. Both economic and social aspects represent "standing"—that is, a relational measure expressed in terms of one's capacity to mobilize resources. Some resources can be mobilized by money. Social relations can mobilize others. For a wide range of reasons— institutional, cultural, and possibly technological—some resources are more readily capable of being mobilized by social relations than by money. If you want to get your nephew a job at a law firm in the United States today, a friendly relationship with the firm's hiring partner is more likely to help than passing on an envelope full of cash. If this theory of social capital is correct, then sometimes you should be willing to trade off financial rewards for social capital. Critically, the two are not fungible or cumulative. A hiring partner paid in an economy where monetary bribes for job interviews are standard does not acquire a social obligation. That same hiring partner in that same culture, who is also a friend and therefore forgoes payment, however, probably does acquire a social obligation, tenable for a similar social situation in the future. The magnitude of the social debt, however, may now be smaller. It is likely measured by the amount of money saved from not having to pay the price, not by the value of getting the nephew a job, as it would likely be in an economy where jobs cannot be had for bribes. There are things and behaviors, then, that simply cannot be commodified for market exchange, like friendship. Any effort to mix the two, to pay for one's friendship, would render it something completely different—perhaps a psychoanalysis session in our culture. There are things that, even if commodified, can still be used for social exchange, but the meaning of the social exchange would be diminished. One thinks of borrowing eggs from a neighbor, or lending a hand to friends who are moving their furniture to a new apartment. And there are things that, even when commodified, continue to be available for social exchange with its full force. Consider gamete donations as an example in contemporary American culture. It is important to see, though, that there is nothing intrinsic about any given "thing" or behavior that makes it fall into one or another of these categories. The categories are culturally contingent and cross-culturally diverse. What matters for our purposes here, though, is only the realization that for any given culture, there will be some acts that a person would prefer to perform not for money, but for social standing, recognition, and probably, ultimately, instrumental value obtainable only if that person has performed the action through a social, rather than a market, transaction.

It is not necessary to pin down precisely the correct or most complete theory of motivation, or the full extent and dimensions of crowding out nonmarket rewards by the introduction or use of market rewards. All that is required to outline the framework for analysis is recognition that there is some form of social and psychological motivation that is neither fungible with money nor simply cumulative with it. Transacting within the price system may either increase or decrease the social-psychological rewards (be they intrinsic or extrinsic, functional or symbolic). The intuition is simple. As I have already said, leaving a fifty-dollar check on the table after one has finished a pleasant dinner at a friend's house would not increase the host's social and psychological gains from the evening. Most likely, it would diminish them sufficiently that one would never again be invited. A bottle of wine or a bouquet of flowers would, to the contrary, improve the social gains. And if dinner is not intuitively obvious, think of sex. The point is simple. Money-oriented motivations are different from socially oriented motivations. Sometimes they align. Sometimes they collide. Which of the two will be the case is historically and culturally contingent. The presence of money in sports or entertainment reduced the social psychological gains from performance in late-nineteenth-century Victorian England, at least for members of the middle and upper classes. This is reflected in the long-standing insistence on the "amateur" status of the Olympics, or the status of "actors" in the Victorian society. This has changed dramatically more than a century later, where athletes' and popular entertainers' social standing is practically measured in the millions of dollars their performances can command.

The relative relationships of money and social-psychological rewards are, then, dependent on culture and context. Similar actions may have different meanings in different social or cultural contexts. Consider three lawyers contemplating whether to write a paper presenting their opinion—one is a practicing attorney, the second is a judge, and the third is an academic. For the first, money and honor are often, though not always, positively correlated. Being able to command a very high hourly fee for writing the requested paper is a mode of expressing one's standing in the profession, as well as a means of putting caviar on the table. Yet, there are modes of acquiring esteem—like writing the paper as a report for a bar committee—that are not improved by the presence of money, and are in fact undermined by it. This latter effect is sharpest for the judge. If a judge is approached with an offer of money for writing an opinion, not only is this not a mark of honor, it is a subversion of the social role and would render corrupt the writing of the opinion. For the judge, the intrinsic "rewards" for writing the opinion when matched by a payment for the product would be guilt and shame, and the offer therefore an expression of disrespect. Finally, if the same paper is requested of the academic, the presence of money is located somewhere in between the judge and the practitioner. To a high degree, like the judge, the academic who writes for money is rendered suspect in her community of scholarship. A paper clearly funded by a party, whose results support the party's regulatory or litigation position, is practically worthless as an academic work. In a mirror image of the practitioner, however, there are some forms of money that add to and reinforce an academic's social psychological rewards—peer-reviewed grants and prizes most prominent among them.

Moreover, individuals are not monolithic agents. While it is possible to posit idealized avaricious money-grubbers, altruistic saints, or social climbers, the reality of most people is a composite of these all, and one that is not like any of them. Clearly, some people are more focused on making money, and others are more generous; some more driven by social standing and esteem, others by a psychological sense of well-being. The for-profit and nonprofit systems probably draw people with different tastes for these desiderata. Academic science and commercial science also probably draw scientists with similar training but different tastes for types of rewards. However, well-adjusted, healthy individuals are rarely monolithic in their requirements. We would normally think of someone who chose to ignore and betray friends and family to obtain either more money or greater social recognition as a fetishist of some form or another. We spend some of our time making money, some of our time enjoying it hedonically; some of our time being with and helping family, friends, and neighbors; some of our time creatively expressing ourselves, exploring who we are and what we would like to become. Some of us, because of economic conditions we occupy, or because of our tastes, spend very large amounts of time trying to make money— whether to become rich or, more commonly, just to make ends meet. Others spend more time volunteering, chatting, or writing.

For all of us, there comes a time on any given day, week, and month, every year and in different degrees over our lifetimes, when we choose to act in some way that is oriented toward fulfilling our social and psychological needs, not our market-exchangeable needs. It is that part of our lives and our motivational structure that social production taps, and on which it thrives. There is nothing mysterious about this. It is evident to any of us who rush home to our family or to a restaurant or bar with friends at the end of a workday, rather than staying on for another hour of overtime or to increase our billable hours; or at least regret it when we cannot. It is evident to any of us who has ever brought a cup of tea to a sick friend or relative, or received one; to anyone who has lent a hand moving a friend's belongings; played a game; told a joke, or enjoyed one told by a friend. What needs to be understood now, however, is under what conditions these many and diverse social actions can turn into an important modality of economic production. When can all these acts, distinct from our desire for money and motivated by social and psychological needs, be mobilized, directed, and made effective in ways that we recognize as economically valuable?

SOCIAL PRODUCTION: FEASIBILITY
CONDITIONS AND ORGANIZATIONAL FORM

The core technologically contingent fact that enables social relations to become a salient modality of production in the networked information economy is that all the inputs necessary to effective productive activity are under the control of individual users. Human creativity, wisdom, and life experience are all possessed uniquely by individuals. The computer processors, data storage devices, and communications capacity necessary to make new meaningful conversational moves from the existing universe of information and stimuli, and to render and communicate them to others near and far are also under the control of these same individual users—at least in the advanced economies and in some portions of the population of developing economies. This does not mean that all the physical capital necessary to process, store, and communicate information is under individual user control. That is not necessary. It is, rather, that the majority of individuals in these societies have the threshold level of material capacity required to explore the information environment they occupy, to take from it, and to make their own contributions to it.

There is nothing about computation or communication that naturally or necessarily enables this fact. It is a felicitous happenstance of the fabrication technology of computing machines in the last quarter of the twentieth century, and, it seems, in the reasonably foreseeable future. It is cheaper to build freestanding computers that enable their owners to use a wide and dynamically changing range of information applications, and that are cheap enough that each machine is owned by an individual user or household, than it is to build massive supercomputers with incredibly high-speed communications to yet cheaper simple terminals, and to sell information services to individuals on an on-demand or standardized package model. Natural or contingent, it is nevertheless a fact of the industrial base of the networked information economy that individual users—susceptible as they are to acting on diverse motivations, in diverse relationships, some market-based, some social—possess and control the physical capital necessary to make effective the human capacities they uniquely and individually possess.

Now, having the core inputs of information production ubiquitously distributed in society is a core enabling fact, but it alone cannot assure that social production will become economically significant. Children and teenagers, retirees, and very rich individuals can spend most of their lives socializing or volunteering; most other people cannot. While creative capacity and judgment are universally distributed in a population, available time and attention are not, and human creative capacity cannot be fully dedicated to nonmarket, nonproprietary production all the time. Someone needs to work for money, at least some of the time, to pay the rent and put food on the table. Personal computers too are only used for earnings-generating activities some of the time. In both these resources, there remain large quantities of excess capacity—time and interest in human beings; processing, storage, and communications capacity in computers—available to be used for activities whose rewards are not monetary or monetizable, directly or indirectly.

For this excess capacity to be harnessed and become effective, the information production process must effectively integrate widely dispersed contributions, from many individual human beings and machines. These contributions are diverse in their quality, quantity, and focus, in their timing and geographic location. The great success of the Internet generally, and peer-production processes in particular, has been the adoption of technical and organizational architectures that have allowed them to pool such diverse efforts effectively. The core characteristics underlying the success of these enterprises are their modularity and their capacity to integrate many fine-grained contributions.

"Modularity" is a property of a project that describes the extent to which it can be broken down into smaller components, or modules, that can be independently produced before they are assembled into a whole. If modules are independent, individual contributors can choose what and when to contribute independently of each other. This maximizes their autonomy and flexibility to define the nature, extent, and timing of their participation in the project. Breaking up the maps of Mars involved in the clickworkers project (described in chapter 3) and rendering them in small segments with a simple marking tool is a way of modularizing the task of mapping craters. In the SETI@home project (see chapter 3), the task of scanning radio astronomy signals is broken down into millions of little computations as a way of modularizing the calculations involved.

"Granularity" refers to the size of the modules, in terms of the time and effort that an individual must invest in producing them. The five minutes required for moderating a comment on Slashdot, or for metamoderating a moderator, is more fine-grained than the hours necessary to participate in writing a bug fix in an open-source project. More people can participate in the former than in the latter, independent of the differences in the knowledge required for participation. The number of people who can, in principle, participate in a project is therefore inversely related to the size of the smallest-scale contribution necessary to produce a usable module. The granularity of the modules therefore sets the smallest possible individual investment necessary to participate in a project. If this investment is sufficiently low, then "incentives" for producing that component of a modular project can be of trivial magnitude. Most importantly for our purposes of understanding the rising role of nonmarket production, the time can be drawn from the excess time we normally dedicate to having fun and participating in social interactions. If the finest-grained contributions are relatively large and would require a large investment of time and effort, the universe of potential contributors decreases. A successful large-scale peer-production project must therefore have a predominate portion of its modules be relatively fine-grained.

Perhaps the clearest example of how large-grained modules can make projects falter is the condition, as of the middle of 2005, of efforts to peer produce open textbooks. The largest such effort is Wikibooks, a site associated with *Wikipedia*, which has not taken off as did its famous parent project. Very few texts there have reached maturity to the extent that they could be usable as a partial textbook, and those few that have were largely written by one individual with minor contributions by others. Similarly, an ambitious initiative launched in California in 2004 still had not gone far beyond an impassioned plea for help by mid-2005. The project that seems most successful as of 2005 was a South African project, Free High School Science Texts (FHSST), founded by a physics graduate student, Mark Horner. As of this writing, that three-year-old project had more or less completed a physics text, and was about halfway through chemistry and mathematics textbooks. The whole FHSST project involves a substantially more managed approach than is common in peer-production efforts, with a core group of dedicated graduate student administrators recruiting contributors, assigning tasks, and integrating the contributions. Horner suggests that the basic limiting factor is that in order to write a high school textbook, the output must comply with state-imposed guidelines for content and form. To achieve these requirements, the various modules must cohere to a degree much larger than necessary in a project like *Wikipedia*, which can endure high diversity in style and development without losing its utility. As a result, the individual contributions have been kept at a high level of abstraction— an idea or principle explained at a time. The minimal time commitment required of each contributor is therefore large, and has led many of those who volunteered initially to not complete their contributions. In this case, the guideline requirements constrained the project's granularity, and thereby impeded its ability to grow and capture the necessary thousands of small-grained contributions. With orders of magnitude fewer contributors, each must be much more highly motivated and available than is necessary in *Wikipedia*, Slashdot, and similar successful projects.

It is not necessary, however, that each and every chunk or module be fine grained. Free software projects in particular have shown us that successful peer-production projects may also be structured, technically and culturally, in ways that make it possible for different individuals to contribute vastly different levels of effort commensurate with their ability, motivation, and availability. The large free software projects might integrate thousands of people who are acting primarily for social psychological reasons—because it is fun or cool; a few hundred young programmers aiming to make a name for themselves so as to become employable; and dozens of programmers who are paid to write free software by firms that follow one of the nonproprietary strategies described in chapter 2. IBM and Red Hat are the quintessential examples of firms that contribute paid employee time to peer-production projects in this form. This form of link between a commercial firm and a peer production community is by no means necessary for a peer-production process to succeed; it does, however, provide one constructive interface between market- and nonmarket-motivated behavior, through which actions on the two types of motivation can reinforce, rather than undermine, each other.

The characteristics of planned modularization of a problem are highly visible and explicit in some peer-production projects—the distributed computing projects like SETI@home are particularly good examples of this. However, if we were to step back and look at the entire phenomenon of Web-based publication from a bird's-eye view, we would see that the architecture of the World Wide Web, in particular the persistence of personal Web pages and blogs and their self-contained, technical independence of each other, give the Web as a whole the characteristics of modularity and variable but fine-grained granularity. Imagine that you were trying to evaluate how, if at all, the Web is performing the task of media watchdog. Consider one example, which I return to in chapter 7: The Memory Hole, a Web site created and maintained by Russ Kick, a freelance author and editor. Kick spent some number of hours preparing and filing a Freedom of Information Act request with the Defense Department, seeking photographs of coffins of U.S. military personnel killed in Iraq. He was able to do so over some period, not having to rely on "getting the scoop" to earn his dinner. At the same time, tens of thousands of other individual Web publishers and bloggers were similarly spending their time hunting down stories that moved them, or that they happened to stumble across in their own daily lives. When Kick eventually got the photographs, he could upload them onto his Web site, where they were immediately available for anyone to see. Because each contribution like Kick's can be independently created and stored, because no single permission point or failure point is present in the architecture of the Web—it is merely a way of conveniently labeling documents stored independently by many people who are connected to the Internet and use HTML (hypertext markup language) and HTTP (hypertext transfer protocol)—as an "information service," it is highly modular and diversely granular. Each independent contribution comprises as large or small an investment as its owner-operator chooses to make. Together, they form a vast almanac, trivia trove, and news and commentary facility, to name but a few, produced by millions of people at their leisure—whenever they can or want to, about whatever they want.

The independence of Web sites is what marks their major difference from more organized peer-production processes, where contributions are marked not by their independence but by their interdependence. The Web as a whole requires no formal structure of cooperation. As an "information good" or medium, it emerges as a pattern out of coordinate coexistence of millions of entirely independent acts. All it requires is a pattern recognition utility superimposed over the outputs of these acts—a search engine or directory. Peer-production processes, to the contrary, do generally require some substantive cooperation among users. A single rating of an individual comment on Slashdot does not by itself moderate the comment up or down, neither does an individual marking of a crater. Spotting a bug in free software, proposing a fix, reviewing the proposed fix, and integrating it into the software are interdependent acts that require a level of cooperation. This necessity for cooperation requires peer-production processes to adopt more engaged strategies for assuring that everyone who participates is doing so in good faith, competently, and in ways that do not undermine the whole, and weeding out those would-be participants who are not.

Cooperation in peer-production processes is usually maintained by some combination of technical architecture, social norms, legal rules, and a technically backed hierarchy that is validated by social norms. *Wikipedia* is the strongest example of a discourse-centric model of cooperation based on social norms. However, even *Wikipedia* includes, ultimately, a small number of people with system administrator privileges who can eliminate accounts or block users in the event that someone is being genuinely obstructionist. This technical fallback, however, appears only after substantial play has been given to self-policing by participants, and to informal and quasi-formal community-based dispute resolution mechanisms. Slashdot, by contrast, provides a strong model of a sophisticated technical system intended to assure that no one can "defect" from the cooperative enterprise of commenting and moderating comments. It limits behavior enabled by the system to avoid destructive behavior before it happens, rather than policing it after the fact. The Slash code does this by technically limiting the power any given person has to moderate anyone else up or down, and by making every moderator the subject of a peer review system whose judgments are enforced technically— that is, when any given user is described by a sufficiently large number of other users as unfair, that user automatically loses the technical ability to moderate the comments of others. The system itself is a free software project, licensed under the GPL (General Public License)—which is itself the quintessential example of how law is used to prevent some types of defection from the common enterprise of peer production of software. The particular type of defection that the GPL protects against is appropriation of the joint product by any single individual or firm, the risk of which would make it less attractive for anyone to contribute to the project to begin with. The GPL assures that, as a legal matter, no one who contributes to a free software project need worry that some other contributor will take the project and make it exclusively their own. The ultimate quality judgments regarding what is incorporated into the "formal" releases of free software projects provide the clearest example of the extent to which a meritocratic hierarchy can be used to integrate diverse contributions into a finished single product. In the case of the Linux kernel development project (see chapter 3), it was always within the power of Linus Torvalds, who initiated the project, to decide which contributions should be included in a new release, and which should not. But it is a funny sort of hierarchy, whose quirkiness Steve Weber well explicates.[8] Torvalds's authority is persuasive, not legal or technical, and certainly not determinative. He can do nothing except persuade others to prevent them from developing anything they want and add it to their kernel, or to distribute that alternative version of the kernel. There is nothing he can do to prevent the entire community of users, or some subsection of it, from rejecting his judgment about what ought to be included in the kernel. Anyone is legally free to do as they please. So these projects are based on a hierarchy of meritocratic respect, on social norms, and, to a great extent, on the mutual recognition by most players in this game that it is to everybody's advantage to have someone overlay a peer review system with some leadership.

In combination then, three characteristics make possible the emergence of information production that is not based on exclusive proprietary claims, not aimed toward sales in a market for either motivation or information, and not organized around property and contract claims to form firms or market exchanges. First, the physical machinery necessary to participate in information and cultural production is almost universally distributed in the population of the advanced economies. Certainly, personal computers as capital goods are under the control of numbers of individuals that are orders of magnitude larger than the number of parties controlling the use of mass-production-capable printing presses, broadcast transmitters, satellites, or cable systems, record manufacturing and distribution chains, and film studios and distribution systems. This means that the physical machinery can be put in service and deployed in response to any one of the diverse motivations individual human beings experience. They need not be deployed in order to maximize returns on the financial capital, because financial capital need not be mobilized to acquire and put in service any of the large capital goods typical of the industrial information economy. Second, the primary raw materials in the information economy, unlike the industrial economy, are public goods—existing information, knowledge, and culture. Their actual marginal social cost is zero. Unless regulatory policy makes them purposefully expensive in order to sustain the proprietary business models, acquiring raw materials also requires no financial capital outlay. Again, this means that these raw materials can be deployed for any human motivation. They need not maximize financial returns. Third, the technical architectures, organizational models, and social dynamics of information production and exchange on the Internet have developed so that they allow us to structure the solution to problems—in particular to information production problems—in ways that are highly modular. This allows many diversely motivated people to act for a wide range of reasons that, in combination, cohere into new useful information, knowledge, and cultural goods. These architectures and organizational models allow both independent creation that coexists and coheres into usable patterns, and interdependent cooperative enterprises in the form of peer-production processes.

Together, these three characteristics suggest that the patterns of social production of information that we are observing in the digitally networked environment are not a fad. They are, rather, a sustainable pattern of human production given the characteristics of the networked information economy. The diversity of human motivation is nothing new. We now have a substantial literature documenting its importance in free and open-source software development projects, from Josh Lerner and Jean Tirole, Rishab Ghosh, Eric Von Hippel and Karim Lakhani, and others. Neither is the public goods nature of information new. What is new are the technological conditions that allow these facts to provide the ingredients of a much larger role in the networked information economy for nonmarket, nonproprietary production to emerge. As long as capitalization and ownership of the physical capital base of this economy remain widely distributed and as long as regulatory policy does not make information inputs artificially expensive, individuals will be able to deploy their own creativity, wisdom, conversational capacities, and connected computers, both independently and in loose interdependent cooperation with others, to create a substantial portion of the information environment we occupy. Moreover, we will be able to do so for whatever reason we choose—through markets or firms to feed and clothe ourselves, or through social relations and open communication with others, to give our lives meaning and context.

TRANSACTION COSTS AND EFFICIENCY

For purposes of analyzing the political values that are the concern of most of this book, all that is necessary is that we accept that peer production in particular, and nonmarket information production and exchange in general, are sustainable in the networked information economy. Most of the remainder of the book seeks to evaluate why, and to what extent, the presence of a substantial nonmarket, commons-based sector in the information production system is desirable from the perspective of various aspects of freedom and justice. Whether this sector is "efficient" within the meaning of the word in welfare economics is beside the point to most of these considerations. Even a strong commitment to a pragmatic political theory, one that accepts and incorporates into its consideration the limits imposed by material and economic reality, need not aim for "efficient" policy in the welfare sense. It is sufficient that the policy is economically and socially sustainable on its own bottom—in other words, that it does not require constant subsidization at the expense of some other area excluded from the analysis. It is nonetheless worthwhile spending a few pages explaining why, and under what conditions, commons-based peer production, and social production more generally, are not only sustainable but actually efficient ways of organizing information production.

The efficient allocation of two scarce resources and one public good are at stake in the choice between social production—whether it is peer production or independent nonmarket production—and market-based production. Because most of the outputs of these processes are nonrival goods—information, knowledge, and culture—the fact that the social production system releases them freely, without extracting a price for using them, means that it would, all other things being equal, be more efficient for information to be produced on a nonproprietary social model, rather than on a proprietary market model. Indeed, all other things need not even be equal for this to hold. It is enough that the net value of the information produced by commons-based social production processes and released freely for anyone to use as they please is no less than the total value of information produced through property-based systems minus the deadweight loss caused by the above-marginal-cost pricing practices that are the intended result of the intellectual property system.

The two scarce resources are: first, human creativity, time, and attention; and second, the computation and communications resources used in information production and exchange. In both cases, the primary reason to choose among proprietary and nonproprietary strategies, between market-based systems—be they direct market exchange or firm-based hierarchical production—and social systems, are the comparative transaction costs of each, and the extent to which these transaction costs either outweigh the benefits of working through each system, or cause the system to distort the information it generates so as to systematically misallocate resources.

The first thing to recognize is that markets, firms, and social relations are three distinct transactional frameworks. Imagine that I am sitting in a room and need paper for my printer. I could (a) order paper from a store; (b) call the storeroom, if I am in a firm or organization that has one, and ask the clerk to deliver the paper I need; or (c) walk over to a neighbor and borrow some paper. Choice (a) describes the market transactional framework. The store knows I need paper immediately because I am willing to pay for it now. Alternative (b) is an example of the firm as a transactional framework. The paper is in the storeroom because someone in the organization planned that someone else would need paper today, with some probability, and ordered enough to fill that expected need. The clerk in the storeroom gives it to me because that is his job; again, defined by someone who planned to have someone available to deliver paper when someone else in the proper channels of authority says that she needs it. Comparing and improving the efficiency of (a) and (b), respectively, has been a central project in transaction-costs organization theory. We might compare, for example, the costs of taking my call, verifying the credit card information, and sending a delivery truck for my one batch of paper, to the costs of someone planning for the average needs of a group of people like me, who occasionally run out of paper, and stocking a storeroom with enough paper and a clerk to fill our needs in a timely manner. However, notice that (c) is also an alternative transactional framework. I could, rather than incurring the costs of transacting through the market with the local store or of building a firm with sufficient lines of authority to stock and manage the storeroom, pop over to my neighbor and ask for some paper. This would make sense even within an existing firm when, for example, I need two or three pages immediately and do not want to wait for the storeroom clerk to do his rounds, or more generally, if I am working at home and the costs of creating "a firm," stocking a storeroom, and paying a clerk are too high for my neighbors and me. Instead, we develop a set of neighborly social relations, rather than a firm-based organization, to deal with shortfalls during periods when it would be too costly to assure a steady flow of paper from the market—for example, late in the evening, on a weekend, or in a sparsely populated area.

The point is not, of course, to reduce all social relations and human decency to a transaction-costs theory. Too many such straight planks have already been cut from the crooked timber of humanity to make that exercise useful or enlightening. The point is that most of economics internally has been ignoring the social transactional framework as an alternative whose relative efficiency can be accounted for and considered in much the same way as the relative cost advantages of simple markets when compared to the hierarchical organizations that typify much of our economic activity—firms.

A market transaction, in order to be efficient, must be clearly demarcated as to what it includes, so that it can be priced efficiently. That price must then be paid in equally crisply delineated currency. Even if a transaction initially may be declared to involve sale of "an amount reasonably required to produce the required output," for a "customary" price, at some point what was provided and what is owed must be crystallized and fixed for a formal exchange. The crispness is a functional requirement of the price system. It derives from the precision and formality of the medium of exchange—currency—and the ambition to provide refined representations of the comparative value of marginal decisions through denomination in an exchange medium that represents these incremental value differences. Similarly, managerial hierarchies require a crisp definition of who should be doing what, when, and how, in order to permit the planning and coordination process to be effective.

Social exchange, on the other hand, does not require the same degree of crispness at the margin. As Maurice Godelier put it in *The Enigma of the Gift*, "the mark of the gift between close friends and relatives . . . is not the absence of obligations, it is the absence of 'calculation.' "[9] There are, obviously, elaborate and formally ritualistic systems of social exchange, in both ancient societies and modern. There are common-property regimes that monitor and record calls on the common pool very crisply. However, in many of the common-property regimes, one finds mechanisms of bounding or fairly allocating access to the common pool that more coarsely delineate the entitlements, behaviors, and consequences than is necessary for a proprietary system. In modern market society, where we have money as a formal medium of precise exchange, and where social relations are more fluid than in traditional societies, social exchange certainly occurs as a fuzzier medium. Across many cultures, generosity is understood as imposing a debt of obligation; but none of the precise amount of value given, the precise nature of the debt to be repaid, or the date of repayment need necessarily be specified. Actions enter into a cloud of goodwill or membership, out of which each agent can understand him- or herself as being entitled to a certain flow of dependencies or benefits in exchange for continued cooperative behavior. This may be an ongoing relationship between two people, a small group like a family or group of friends, and up to a general level of generosity among strangers that makes for a decent society. The point is that social exchange does not require defining, for example, "I will lend you my car and help you move these five boxes on Monday, and in exchange you will feed my fish next July," in the same way that the following would: "I will move five boxes on Tuesday for $100, six boxes for $120." This does not mean that social systems are cost free—far from it. They require tremendous investment, acculturation, and maintenance. This is true in this case every bit as much as it is true for markets or states. Once functional, however, social exchanges require less information crispness at the margin.

Both social and market exchange systems require large fixed costs—the setting up of legal institutions and enforcement systems for markets, and creating social networks, norms, and institutions for the social exchange. Once these initial costs have been invested, however, market transactions systematically require a greater degree of precise information about the content of actions, goods, and obligations, and more precision of monitoring and enforcement on a per-transaction basis than do social exchange systems.

This difference between markets and hierarchical organizations, on the one hand, and peer-production processes based on social relations, on the other, is particularly acute in the context of human creative labor—one of the central scarce resources that these systems must allocate in the networked information economy. The levels and focus of individual effort are notoriously hard to specify for pricing or managerial commands, considering all aspects of individual effort and ability—talent, motivation, workload, and focus—as they change in small increments over the span of an individual's full day, let alone months. What we see instead is codification of effort types—a garbage collector, a law professor—that are priced more or less finely. However, we only need to look at the relative homogeneity of law firm starting salaries as compared to the high variability of individual ability and motivation levels of graduating law students to realize that pricing of individual effort can be quite crude. Similarly, these attributes are also difficult to monitor and verify over time, though perhaps not quite as difficult as predicting them *ex ante*. Pricing therefore continues to be a function of relatively crude information about the actual variability among people. More importantly, as aspects of performance that are harder to fully specify in advance or monitor—like creativity over time given the occurrence of new opportunities to be creative, or implicit know-how—become a more significant aspect of what is valuable about an individual's contribution, market mechanisms become more and more costly to maintain efficiently, and, as a practical matter, simply lose a lot of information.

People have different innate capabilities; personal, social, and educational histories; emotional frameworks; and ongoing lived experiences, which make for immensely diverse associations with, idiosyncratic insights into, and divergent utilization of existing information and cultural inputs at different times and in different contexts. Human creativity is therefore very difficult to standardize and specify in the contracts necessary for either market-cleared or hierarchically organized production. As the weight of human intellectual effort increases in the overall mix of inputs into a given production process, an organization model that does not require contractual specification of the individual effort required to participate in a collective enterprise, and which allows individuals to self-identify for tasks, will be better at gathering and utilizing information about who should be doing what than a system that does require such specification. Some firms try to solve this problem by utilizing market- and social-relations-oriented hybrids, like incentive compensation schemes and employee-of-the-month–type social motivational frameworks. These may be able to improve on firm-only or market-only approaches. It is unclear, though, how well they can overcome the core difficulty: that is, that both markets and firm hierarchies require significant specification of the object of organization and pricing—in this case, human intellectual input. The point here is qualitative. It is not only, or even primarily, that more people can participate in production in a commons-based effort. It is that the widely distributed model of information production will better identify the best person to produce a specific component of a project, considering all abilities and availability to work on the specific module within a specific time frame. With enough uncertainty as to the value of various productive activities, and enough variability in the quality of both information inputs and human creative talent vis-à-vis any set of production opportunities, freedom of action for individuals coupled with continuous communications among the pool of potential producers and consumers can generate better information about the most valuable productive actions, and the best human inputs available to engage in these actions at a given time. Markets and firm incentive schemes are aimed at producing precisely this form of self-identification. However, the rigidities associated with collecting and comprehending bids from individuals through these systems (that is, transaction costs) limit the efficacy of self-identification by comparison to a system in which, once an individual self-identifies for a task, he or she can then undertake it without permission, contract, or instruction from another. The emergence of networked organizations (described and analyzed in the work of Charles Sabel and others) suggests that firms are in fact trying to overcome these limitations by developing parallels to the freedom to learn, innovate, and act on these innovations that is intrinsic to peer-production processes by loosening the managerial bonds, locating more of the conception and execution of problem solving away from the managerial core of the firm, and implementing these through social, as well as monetary, motivations. However, the need to assure that the value created is captured within the organization limits the extent to which these strategies can be implemented within a single enterprise, as opposed to their implementation in an open process of social production. This effect, in turn, is in some sectors attenuated through the use of what Walter Powell and others have described as learning networks. Engineers and scientists often create frameworks that allow them to step out of their organizational affiliations, through conferences or workshops. By reproducing the social production characteristics of academic exchange, they overcome some of the information loss caused by the boundary of the firm. While these organizational strategies attenuate the problem, they also underscore the degree to which it is widespread and understood by organizations as such. The fact that the direction of the solutions business organizations choose tends to shift elements of the production process away from market- or firm-based models and toward networked social production models is revealing. Now, the self-identification that is central to the relative information efficiency of peer production is not always perfect. Some mechanisms used by firms and markets to codify effort levels and abilities—like formal credentials—are the result of experience with substantial errors or misstatements by individuals of their capacities. To succeed, therefore, peer-production systems must also incorporate mechanisms for smoothing out incorrect self-assessments—as peer review does in traditional academic research or in the major sites like *Wikipedia* or Slashdot, or as redundancy and statistical averaging do in the case of NASA clickworkers. The prevalence of misperceptions that individual contributors have about their own ability and the cost of eliminating such errors will be part of the transaction costs associated with this form of organization. They parallel quality control problems faced by firms and markets.

The lack of crisp specification of who is giving what to whom, and in exchange for what, also bears on the comparative transaction costs associated with the allocation of the second major type of scarce resource in the networked information economy: the physical resources that make up the networked information environment—communications, computation, and storage capacity. It is important to note, however, that these are very different from creativity and information as inputs: they are private goods, not a public good like information, and they are standardized goods with well-specified capacities, not heterogeneous and highly uncertain attributes like human creativity at a given moment and context. Their outputs, unlike information, are not public goods. The reasons that they are nonetheless subject to efficient sharing in the networked environment therefore require a different economic explanation. However, the sharing of these material resources, like the sharing of human creativity, insight, and attention, nonetheless relies on both the comparative transaction costs of markets and social relations and the diversity of human motivation.

Personal computers, wireless transceivers, and Internet connections are "shareable goods." The basic intuition behind the concept of shareable goods is simple. There are goods that are "lumpy": given a state of technology, they can only be produced in certain discrete bundles that offer discontinuous amounts of functionality or capacity. In order to have any ability to run a computation, for example, a consumer must buy a computer processor. These, in turn, only come in discrete units with a certain speed or capacity. One could easily imagine a world where computers are very large and their owners sell computation capacity to consumers "on demand," whenever they needed to run an application. That is basically the way the mainframe world of the 1960s and 1970s worked. However, the economics of microchip fabrication and of network connections over the past thirty years, followed by storage technology, have changed that. For most functions that users need, the price-performance trade-off favors stand-alone, general-purpose personal computers, owned by individuals and capable of running locally most applications users want, over remote facilities capable of selling on-demand computation and storage. So computation and storage today come in discrete, lumpy units. You can decide to buy a faster or slower chip, or a larger or smaller hard drive, but once you buy them, you have the capacity of these machines at your disposal, whether you need it or not.

Lumpy goods can, in turn, be fine-, medium-, or large-grained. A large-grained good is one that is so expensive it can only be used by aggregating demand for it. Industrial capital equipment, like a steam engine, is of this type. Fine-grained goods are of a granularity that allows consumers to buy precisely as much of the goods needed for the amount of capacity they require. Medium-grained goods are small enough for an individual to justify buying for her own use, given their price and her willingness and ability to pay for the functionality she plans to use. A personal computer is a medium-grained lumpy good in the advanced economies and among the more well-to-do in poorer countries, but is a large-grained capital good for most people in poor countries. If, given the price of such a good and the wealth of a society, a large number of individuals buy and use such medium-grained lumpy goods, that society will have a large amount of excess capacity "out there," in the hands of individuals. Because these machines are put into service to serve the needs of individuals, their excess capacity is available for these individuals to use as they wish—for their own uses, to sell to others, or to share with others. It is the combination of the fact that these machines are available at prices (relative to wealth) that allow users to put them in service based purely on their value for personal use, and the fact that they have enough capacity to facilitate additionally the action and fulfill the needs of others, that makes them "shareable." If they were so expensive that they could only be bought by pooling the value of a number of users, they would be placed in service either using some market mechanism to aggregate that demand, or through formal arrangements of common ownership by all those whose demand was combined to invest in purchasing the resource. If they were so finely grained in their capacity that there would be nothing left to share, again, sharing would be harder to sustain. The fact that they are both relatively inexpensive and have excess capacity makes them the basis for a stable model of individual ownership of resources combined with social sharing of that excess capacity.

Because social sharing requires less precise specification of the transactional details with each transaction, it has a distinct advantage over market-based mechanisms for reallocating the excess capacity of shareable goods, particularly when they have small quanta of excess capacity relative to the amount necessary to achieve the desired outcome. For example, imagine that there are one thousand people in a population of computer owners. Imagine that each computer is capable of performing one hundred computations per second, and that each computer owner needs to perform about eighty operations per second. Every owner, in other words, has twenty operations of excess capacity every second. Now imagine that the marginal transaction costs of arranging a sale of these twenty operations—exchanging PayPal (a widely used low-cost Internet-based payment system) account information, insurance against nonpayment, specific statement of how much time the computer can be used, and so forth—cost ten cents more than the marginal transaction costs of sharing the excess capacity socially. John wants to render a photograph in one second, which takes two hundred operations per second. Robert wants to model the folding of proteins, which takes ten thousand operations per second. For John, a sharing system would save fifty cents—assuming he can use his own computer for half of the two hundred operations he needs. He needs to transact with five other users to "rent" their excess capacity of twenty operations each. Robert, on the other hand, needs to transact with five hundred individual owners in order to use their excess capacity, and for him, using a sharing system is fifty dollars cheaper. The point of the illustration is simple. The cost advantage of sharing as a transactional framework relative to the price system increases linearly with the number of transactions necessary to acquire the level of resources necessary for an operation. If excess capacity in a society is very widely distributed in small dollops, and for any given use of the excess capacity it is necessary to pool the excess capacity of thousands or even millions of individual users, the transaction-cost advantages of the sharing system become significant.

The transaction-cost effect is reinforced by the motivation crowding out theory. When many discrete chunks of excess capacity need to be pooled, each distinct contributor cannot be paid a very large amount. Motivation crowding out theory would predict that when the monetary rewards to an activity are low, the negative effect of crowding out the social-psychological motivation will weigh more heavily than any increased incentive that is created by the promise of a small payment to transfer one's excess capacity. The upshot is that when the technological state results in excess capacity of physical capital being widely distributed in small dollops, social sharing can outperform secondary markets as a mechanism for harnessing that excess capacity. This is so because of both transaction costs and motivation. Fewer owners will be willing to sell their excess capacity cheaply than to give it away for free in the right social context and the transaction costs of selling will be higher than those of sharing.

From an efficiency perspective, then, there are clear reasons to think that social production systems—both peer production of information, knowledge, and culture and sharing of material resources—can be more efficient than market-based systems to motivate and allocate both human creative effort and the excess computation, storage, and communications capacity that typify the networked information economy. That does not mean that all of us will move out of market-based productive relationships all of the time. It does mean that alongside our market-based behaviors we generate substantial amounts of human creativity and mechanical capacity. The transaction costs of clearing those resources through the price system or through firms are substantial, and considerably larger for the marginal transaction than clearing them through social-sharing mechanisms as a transactional framework. With the right institutional framework and peer-review or quality-control mechanisms, and with well-modularized organization of work, social sharing is likely to identify the best person available for a job and make it feasible for that person to work on that job using freely available information inputs. Similarly, social transactional frameworks are likely to be substantially less expensive than market transactions for pooling large numbers of discrete, small increments of the excess capacity of the personal computer processors, hard drives, and network connections that make up the physical capital base of the networked information economy. In both cases, given that much of what is shared is excess capacity from the perspective of the contributors, available to them after they have fulfilled some threshold level of their market-based consumption requirements, social-sharing systems are likely to tap in to social psychological motivations that money cannot tap, and, indeed, that the presence of money in a transactional framework could nullify. Because of these effects, social sharing and collaboration can provide not only a sustainable alternative to market-based and firm-based models of provisioning information, knowledge, culture, and communications, but also an alternative that more efficiently utilizes the human and physical capital base of the networked information economy. A society whose institutional ecology permitted social production to thrive would be more productive under these conditions than a society that optimized its institutional environment solely for market- and firm-based production, ignoring its detrimental effects to social production.

THE EMERGENCE OF SOCIAL PRODUCTION IN
THE DIGITALLY NETWORKED ENVIRONMENT

There is a curious congruence between the anthropologists of the gift and mainstream economists today. Both treat the gift literature as being about the periphery, about societies starkly different from modern capitalist societies. As Godelier puts it, "What a contrast between these types of society, these social and mental universes, and today's capitalist society where the majority of social relations are impersonal (involving the individual as citizen and the state, for instance), and where the exchange of things and services is conducted for the most part in an anonymous marketplace, leaving little room for an economy and moral code based on gift-giving."[10] And yet, sharing is everywhere around us in the advanced economies. Since the 1980s, we have seen an increasing focus, in a number of literatures, on production practices that rely heavily on social rather than price-based or governmental policies. These include, initially, the literature on social norms and social capital, or trust.[11] Both these lines of literature, however, are statements of the institutional role of social mechanisms for enabling market exchange and production. More direct observations of social production and exchange systems are provided by the literature on social provisioning of public goods— like social norm enforcement as a dimension of policing criminality, and the literature on common property regimes.[12] The former are limited by their focus on public goods provisioning. The latter are usually limited by their focus on discretely identifiable types of resources—common pool resources— that must be managed as among a group of claimants while retaining a proprietary outer boundary toward nonmembers. The focus of those who study these phenomena is usually on relatively small and tightly knit communities, with clear boundaries between members and nonmembers.[13]

These lines of literature point to an emerging understanding of social production and exchange as an alternative to markets and firms. Social production is not limited to public goods, to exotic, out-of-the-way places like surviving medieval Spanish irrigation regions or the shores of Maine's lobster fishing grounds, or even to the ubiquitous phenomenon of the household. As SETI@home and Slashdot suggest, it is not necessarily limited to stable communities of individuals who interact often and know each other, or who expect to continue to interact personally. Social production of goods and services, both public and private, is ubiquitous, though unnoticed. It sometimes substitutes for, and sometimes complements, market and state production everywhere. It is, to be fanciful, the dark matter of our economic production universe.

Consider the way in which the following sentences are intuitively familiar, yet as a practical matter, describe the provisioning of goods or services that have well-defined NAICS categories (the categories used by the Economic Census to categorize economic sectors) whose provisioning through the markets is accounted for in the Economic Census, but that are commonly provisioned in a form consistent with the definition of sharing—on a radically distributed model, without price or command.

NAICS 624410624410 [Babysitting services, child day care]
"John, could you pick up Bobby today when you take Lauren to soccer? I have a conference call I have to make."

"Are you doing homework with Zoe today, or shall I?"

NAICS 484210 [Trucking used household, office, or institutional furniture and equipment]

"Jane, could you lend a hand moving this table to the dining room?"

"Here, let me hold the elevator door for you, this looks heavy."

NAICS 484122 [Trucking, general freight, long-distance, less-than-truckload]

"Jack, do you mind if I load my box of books in your trunk so you can drop it off at my brother's on your way to Boston?"

NAICS 514110 [Traffic reporting services]

"Oh, don't take I-95, it's got horrible construction traffic to exit 39."

NAICS 711510 [Newspaper columnists, independent (freelance)]

"I don't know about Kerry, he doesn't move me, I think he should be more aggressive in criticizing Bush on Iraq."

NAICS 621610 [Home health-care services]

"Can you please get me my medicine? I'm too wiped to get up."

"Would you like a cup of tea?"

NAICS 561591 [Tourist information bureaus]

"Excuse me, how do I get to Carnegie Hall?"

NAICS 561321 [Temporary help services]

"I've got a real crunch on the farm, can you come over on Saturday and lend a hand?"

"This is crazy, I've got to get this document out tonight, could you lend me a hand with proofing and pulling it all together tonight?"

NAICS 71 [Arts, entertainment, and recreation]

"Did you hear the one about the Buddhist monk, the Rabbi, and the Catholic priest . . . ?"

"Roger, bring out your guitar. . . ."

"Anybody up for a game of . . . ?"

The litany of examples generalizes through a combination of four dimensions that require an expansion from the current focus of the literatures related to social production. First, they relate to production of goods and services, not only of norms or rules. Social relations provide the very motivations for, and information relating to, production and exchange, not only the institutional framework for organizing action, which itself is motivated, informed, and organized by markets or managerial commands. Second, they relate to all kinds of goods, not only public goods. In particular, the paradigm cases of free software development and distributed computing involve labor and shareable goods—each plainly utilizing private goods as inputs, and, in the case of distributed computing, producing private goods as outputs. Third, at least some of them relate not only to relations of production within well-defined communities of individuals who have repeated interactions, but extend to cover baseline standards of human decency. These enable strangers to ask one another for the time or for directions, enable drivers to cede the road to each other, and enable strangers to collaborate on software projects, on coauthoring an online encyclopedia, or on running simulations of how proteins fold. Fourth, they may either complement or substitute for market and state production systems, depending on the social construction of mixed provisioning. It is hard to measure the weight that social and sharing-based production has in the economy. Our intuitions about capillary systems would suggest that the total volume of boxes or books moved or lifted, instructions given, news relayed, and meals prepared by family, friends, neighbors, and minimally decent strangers would be very high relative to the amount of substitutable activity carried on through market exchanges or state provisioning.

Why do we, despite the ubiquity of social production, generally ignore it as an economic phenomenon, and why might we now reconsider its importance? A threshold requirement for social sharing to be a modality of economic production, as opposed to one purely of social reproduction, is that sharing-based action be effective. Efficacy of individual action depends on the physical capital requirements for action to become materially effective, which, in turn, depend on technology. Effective action may have very low physical capital requirements, so that every individual has, by natural capacity, "the physical capital" necessary for action. Social production or sharing can then be ubiquitous (though in practice, it may not). Vocal cords to participate in a sing-along or muscles to lift a box are obvious examples. When the capital requirements are nontrivial, but the capital good is widely distributed and available, sharing can similarly be ubiquitous and effective. This is true both when the shared resource or good is the capacity of the capital good itself—as in the case of shareable goods—and when some widely distributed human capacity is made effective through the use of the widely distributed capital goods—as in the case of human creativity, judgment, experience, and labor shared in online peer-production processes—in which participants contribute using the widespread availability of connected computers. When use of larger-scale physical capital goods is a threshold requirement of effective action, we should not expect to see widespread reliance on decentralized sharing as a standard modality of production. Industrial mass-manufacture of automobiles, steel, or plastic toys, for example, is not the sort of thing that is likely to be produced on a social-sharing basis, because of the capital constraints. This is not to say that even for large-scale capital projects, like irrigation systems and dams, social production systems cannot step into the breach. We have those core examples in the common-property regime literature, and we have worker-owned firms as examples of mixed systems. However, those systems tend to replicate the characteristics of firm, state, or market production—using various combinations of quotas, scrip systems, formal policing by "professional" officers, or management within worker-owned firms. By comparison, the "common property" arrangements described among lobster gangs of Maine or fishing groups in Japan, where capital requirements are much lower, tend to be more social-relations-based systems, with less formalized or crisp measurement of contributions to, and calls on, the production system.

To say that sharing is technology dependent is not to deny that it is a ubiquitous human phenomenon. Sharing is so deeply engrained in so many of our cultures that it would be difficult to argue that with the "right" (or perhaps "wrong") technological contingencies, it would simply disappear. My claim, however, is narrower. It is that the relative economic role of sharing changes with technology. There are technological conditions that require more or less capital, in larger or smaller packets, for effective provisioning of goods, services, and resources the people value. As these conditions change, the relative scope for social-sharing practices to play a role in production changes. When goods, services, and resources are widely dispersed, their owners can choose to engage with each other through social sharing instead of through markets or a formal, state-based relationship, because individuals have available to them the resources necessary to engage in such behavior without recourse to capital markets or the taxation power of the state. If technological changes make the resources necessary for effective action rare or expensive, individuals may wish to interact in social relations, but they can now only do so ineffectively, or in different fields of endeavor that do not similarly require high capitalization. Large-packet, expensive physical capital draws the behavior into one or the other of the modalities of production that can collect the necessary financial capital—through markets or taxation. Nothing, however, prevents change from happening in the opposite direction. Goods, services, and resources that, in the industrial stage of the information economy required large-scale, concentrated capital investment to provision, are now subject to a changing technological environment that can make sharing a better way of achieving the same results than can states, markets, or their hybrid, regulated industries.

Because of changes in the technology of the industrial base of the most advanced economies, social sharing and exchange is becoming a common modality of production at their very core—in the information, culture, education, computation, and communications sectors. Free software, distributed computing, ad hoc mesh wireless networks, and other forms of peer production offer clear examples of large-scale, measurably effective sharing practices. The highly distributed capital structure of contemporary communications and computation systems is largely responsible for this increased salience of social sharing as a modality of economic production in that environment. By lowering the capital costs required for effective individual action, these technologies have allowed various provisioning problems to be structured in forms amenable to decentralized production based on social relations, rather than through markets or hierarchies.

My claim is not, of course, that we live in a unique moment of humanistic sharing. It is, rather, that our own moment in history suggests a more general observation. The technological state of a society, in particular the extent to which individual agents can engage in efficacious production activities with material resources under their individual control, affects the opportunities for, and hence the comparative prevalence and salience of, social, market—both price-based and managerial—and state production modalities. The capital cost of effective economic action in the industrial economy shunted sharing to its economic peripheries—to households in the advanced economies, and to the global economic peripheries that have been the subject of the anthropology of gift or the common-property regime literatures. The emerging restructuring of capital investment in digital networks—in particular, the phenomenon of user-capitalized computation and communications capabilities—are at least partly reversing that effect. Technology does not determine the level of sharing. It does, however, set threshold constraints on the effective domain of sharing as a modality of economic production. Within the domain of the practically feasible, the actual level of sharing practices will be culturally driven and cross-culturally diverse.

Most practices of production—social or market-based—are already embedded in a given technological context. They present no visible "problem" to solve or policy choice to make. We do not need to be focused consciously on improving the conditions under which friends lend a hand to each other to move boxes, make dinner, or take kids to school. We feel no need to reconsider the appropriateness of market-based firms as the primary modality for the production of automobiles. However, in moments where a field of action is undergoing a technological transition that changes the opportunities for sharing as a modality of production, understanding that sharing *is* a modality of production becomes more important, as does understanding how it functions as such. This is so, as we are seeing today, when prior technologies have already set up market- or state-based production systems that have the law and policy-making systems already designed to fit their requirements. While the prior arrangement may have been the most efficient, or even may have been absolutely necessary for the incumbent production system, its extension under new technological conditions may undermine, rather than improve, the capacity of a society to produce and provision the goods, resources, or capacities that are the object of policy analysis. This is, as I discuss in part III, true of wireless communications regulation, or "spectrum management," as it is usually called; of the regulation of information, knowledge, and cultural production, or "intellectual property," as it is usually now called; and it may be true of policies for computation and wired communications networks, as distributed computing and the emerging peer-to-peer architectures suggest.

THE INTERFACE OF SOCIAL PRODUCTION AND MARKET-BASED BUSINESSES

The rise of social production does not entail a decline in market-based production. Social production first and foremost harnesses impulses, time, and resources that, in the industrial information economy, would have been wasted or used purely for consumption. Its immediate effect is therefore likely to increase overall productivity in the sectors where it is effective. But that does not mean that its effect on market-based enterprises is neutral. A newly effective form of social behavior, coupled with a cultural shift in tastes as well as the development of new technological and social solution spaces to problems that were once solved through market-based firms, exercises a significant force on the shape and conditions of market action. Understanding the threats that these developments pose to some incumbents explains much of the political economy of law in this area, which will occupy chapter 11. At the simplest level, social production in general and peer production in particular present new sources of competition to incumbents that produce information goods for which there are now socially produced substitutes.

Open source software development, for example, first received mainstream media attention in 1998 due to publication of a leaked internal memorandum from Microsoft, which came to be known as The Halloween Memo. In it, a Microsoft strategist identified the open source methodology as the one major potential threat to the company's dominance over the desktop. As we have seen since, definitively in the Web server market and gradually in segments of the operating system market, this prediction proved prescient. Similarly, *Wikipedia* now presents a source of competition to online encyclopedias like *Columbia*, *Grolier*, or *Encarta*, and may well come to be seen as an adequate substitute for *Britannica* as well. Most publicly visible, peer-to-peer file sharing networks have come to compete with the recording industry as an alternative music distribution system, to the point where the long-term existence of that industry is in question. Some scholars like William Fisher, and artists like Jenny Toomey and participants in the Future of Music Coalition, are already looking for alternative ways of securing for artists a living from the music they make.

The competitive threat from social production, however, is merely a surface phenomenon. Businesses often face competition or its potential, and this is a new source, with new economics, which may or may not put some of the incumbents out of business. But there is nothing new about entrants with new business models putting slow incumbents out of business. More basic is the change in opportunity spaces, the relationships of firms to users, and, indeed, the very nature of the boundary of the firm that those businesses that are already adapting to the presence and predicted persistence of social production are exhibiting. Understanding the opportunities social production presents for businesses begins to outline how a stable social production system can coexist and develop a mutually reinforcing relationship with market-based organizations that adapt to and adopt, instead of fight, them.

Consider the example I presented in chapter 2 of IBM's relationship to the free and open source software development community. IBM, as I explained there, has shown more than $2 billion a year in "Linux-related revenues." Prior to IBM's commitment to adapting to what the firm sees as the inevitability of free and open source software, the company either developed in house or bought from external vendors the software it needed as part of its hardware business, on the one hand, and its software services—customization, enterprise solutions, and so forth—on the other hand. In each case, the software development follows a well-recognized supply chain model. Through either an employment contract or a supply contract the company secures a legal right to require either an employee or a vendor to deliver a given output at a given time. In reliance on that notion of a supply chain that is fixed or determined by a contract, the company turns around and promises to its clients that it will deliver the integrated product or service that includes the contracted-for component. With free or open source software, that relationship changes. IBM is effectively relying for its inputs on a loosely defined cloud of people who are engaged in productive social relations. It is making the judgment that the probability that a sufficiently good product will emerge out of this cloud is high enough that it can undertake a contractual obligation to its clients, even though no one in the cloud is specifically contractually committed to it to produce the specific inputs the firm needs in the timeframe it needs it. This apparent shift from a contractually deterministic supply chain to a probabilistic supply chain is less dramatic, however, than it seems. Even when contracts are signed with employees or suppliers, they merely provide a probability that the employee or the supplier will in fact supply in time and at appropriate quality, given the difficulties of coordination and implementation. A broad literature in organization theory has developed around the effort to map the various strategies of collaboration and control intended to improve the likelihood that the different components of the production process will deliver what they are supposed to: from early efforts at vertical integration, to relational contracting, pragmatic collaboration, or Toyota's fabled flexible specialization. The presence of a formalized enforceable contract, for outputs in which the supplier can claim and transfer a property right, may change the probability of the desired outcome, but not the fact that in entering its own contract with its clients, the company is making a prediction about the required availability of necessary inputs in time. When the company turns instead to the cloud of social production for its inputs, it is making a similar prediction. And, as with more engaged forms of relational contracting, pragmatic collaborations, or other models of iterated relations with coproducers, the company may engage with the social process in order to improve the probability that the required inputs will in fact be produced in time. In the case of companies like IBM or Red Hat, this means, at least partly, paying employees to participate in the open source development projects. But managing this relationship is tricky. The firms must do so without seeking to, or even seeming to seek to, take over the project; for to take over the project in order to steer it more "predictably" toward the firm's needs is to kill the goose that lays the golden eggs. For IBM and more recently Nokia, supporting the social processes on which they rely has also meant contributing hundreds of patents to the Free Software Foundation, or openly licensing them to the software development community, so as to extend the protective umbrella created by these patents against suits by competitors. As the companies that adopt this strategic reorientation become more integrated into the peer-production process itself, the boundary of the firm becomes more porous. Participation in the discussions and governance of open source development projects creates new ambiguity as to where, in relation to what is "inside" and "outside" of the firm boundary, the social process is. In some cases, a firm may begin to provide utilities or platforms for the users whose outputs it then uses in its own products. The Open Source Development Group (OSDG), for example, provides platforms for Slashdot and Source-Forge. In these cases, the notion that there are discrete "suppliers" and "consumers," and that each of these is clearly demarcated from the other and outside of the set of stable relations that form the inside of the firm becomes somewhat attenuated.

As firms have begun to experience these newly ambiguous relationships with individuals and social groups, they have come to wrestle with questions of leadership and coexistence. Businesses like IBM, or eBay, which uses peer production as a critical component of its business ecology—the peer reviewed system of creating trustworthiness, without which person-to-person transactions among individual strangers at a distance would be impossible—have to structure their relationship to the peer-production processes that they co-exist with in a helpful and non-threatening way. Sometimes, as we saw in the case of IBM's contributions to the social process, this may mean support without attempting to assume "leadership" of the project. Sometimes, as when peer production is integrated more directly into what is otherwise a commercially created and owned platform—as in the case of eBay—the relationship is more like that of a peer-production leader than of a commercial actor. Here, the critical and difficult point for business managers to accept is that bringing the peer-production community into the newly semi-porous boundary of the firm—taking those who used to be customers and turning them into participants in a process of coproduction—changes the relationship of the firm's managers and its users. Linden Labs, which runs Second Life, learned this in the context of the tax revolt described in chapter 3. Users cannot be ordered around like employees. Nor can they be simply advertised-to and manipulated, or even passively surveyed, like customers. To do that would be to lose the creative and generative social character that makes integration of peer production into a commercial business model so valuable for those businesses that adopt it. Instead, managers must be able to identify patterns that emerge in the community and inspire trust that they are correctly judging the patterns that are valuable from the perspective of the users, not only the enterprise, so that the users in fact coalesce around and extend these patterns.

The other quite basic change wrought by the emergence of social production, from the perspective of businesses, is a change in taste. Active users require and value new and different things than passive consumers did. The industrial information economy specialized in producing finished goods, like movies or music, to be consumed passively, and well-behaved appliances, like televisions, whose use was fully specified at the factory door. The emerging businesses of the networked information economy are focusing on serving the demand of active users for platforms and tools that are much more loosely designed, late-binding—that is, optimized only at the moment of use and not in advance—variable in their uses, and oriented toward providing users with new, flexible platforms for relationships. Personal computers, camera phones, audio and video editing software, and similar utilities are examples of tools whose value increases for users as they are enabled to explore new ways to be creative and productively engaged with others. In the network, we are beginning to see business models emerge to allow people to come together, like MeetUp, and to share annotations of Web pages they read, like del.icio.us, or photographs they took, like Flickr. Services like Blogger and Technorati similarly provide platforms for the new social and cultural practices of personal journals, or the new modes of expression described in chapters 7 and 8.

The overarching point is that social production is reshaping the market conditions under which businesses operate. To some of the incumbents of the industrial information economy, the pressure from social production is experienced as pure threat. It is the clash between these incumbents and the new practices that was most widely reported in the media in the first five years of the twenty-first century, and that has driven much of policy making, legislation, and litigation in this area. But the much more fundamental effect on the business environment is that social production is changing the relationship of firms to individuals outside of them, and through this changing the strategies that firms internally are exploring. It is creating new sources of inputs, and new tastes and opportunities for outputs. Consumers are changing into users—more active and productive than the consumers of the industrial information economy. The change is reshaping the relationships necessary for business success, requiring closer integration of users into the process of production, both in inputs and outputs. It requires different leadership talents and foci. By the time of this writing, in 2005, these new opportunities and adaptations have begun to be seized upon as strategic advantages by some of the most successful companies working around the Internet and information technology, and increasingly now around information and cultural production more generally. Eric von Hippel's work has shown how the model of user innovation has been integrated into the business model of innovative firms even in sectors far removed from either the network or from information production—like designing kite-surfing equipment or mountain bikes. As businesses begin to do this, the platforms and tools for collaboration improve, the opportunities and salience of social production increases, and the political economy begins to shift. And as these firms and social processes coevolve, the dynamic accommodation they are developing provides us with an image of what the future stable interface between market-based businesses and the newly salient social production is likely to look like.

Part Two The Political Economy of Property and Commons

How a society produces its information environment goes to the very core of freedom. Who gets to say what, to whom? What is the state of the world? What counts as credible information? How will different forms of action affect the way the world can become? These questions go to the foundations of effective human action. They determine what individuals understand to be the range of options open to them, and the range of consequences to their actions. They determine what is understood to be open for debate in a society, and what is considered impossible as a collective goal or a collective path for action. They determine whose views count toward collective action, and whose views are lost and never introduced into the debate of what we should do as political entities or social communities. Freedom depends on the information environment that those individuals and societies occupy. Information underlies the very possibility of individual self-direction. Information and communication constitute the practices that enable a community to form a common range of understandings of what is at stake and what paths are open for the taking. They are constitutive components of both formal and informal mechanisms for deciding on collective action. Societies that embed the emerging networked information economy in an institutional ecology that accommodates nonmarket production, both individual and cooperative, will improve the freedom of their constituents along all these dimensions.

The networked information economy makes individuals better able to do things for and by themselves, and makes them less susceptible to manipulation by others than they were in the mass-media culture. In this sense, the emergence of this new set of technical, economic, social, and institutional relations can increase the relative role that each individual is able to play in authoring his or her own life. The networked information economy also promises to provide a much more robust platform for public debate. It enables citizens to participate in public conversation continuously and pervasively, not as passive recipients of "received wisdom" from professional talking heads, but as active participants in conversations carried out at many levels of political and social structure. Individuals can find out more about what goes on in the world, and share it more effectively with others. They can check the claims of others and produce their own, and they can be heard by others, both those who are like-minded and opponents. At a more foundational level of collective understanding, the shift from an industrial to a networked information economy increases the extent to which individuals can become active participants in producing their own cultural environment. It opens the possibility of a more critical and reflective culture.

Unlike the relationship of information production to freedom, the relationship between the organization of information production and distributive justice is not intrinsic. However, the importance of knowledge in contemporary economic production makes a change in the modality of information production important to justice as well. The networked information economy can provide opportunities for global development and for improvements in the justice of distribution of opportunities and capacities everywhere. Economic opportunity and welfare today—of an individual, a social group, or a nation—depend on the state of knowledge and access to opportunities to learn and apply practical knowledge. Transportation networks, global financial markets, and institutional trade arrangements have made material resources and outputs capable of flowing more efficiently from any one corner of the globe to another than they were at any previous period. Economic welfare and growth now depend more on knowledge and social organization than on natural sources. Knowledge transfer and social reform, probably more than any other set of changes, can affect the economic opportunities and material development of different parts of the global economic system, within economies both advanced and less developed. The emergence of a substantial nonmarket sector in the networked information economy offers opportunities for providing better access to knowledge and information as input from, and better access for information outputs of, developing and less-developed economies and poorer geographic and social sectors in the advanced economies. Better access to knowledge and the emergence of less capital-dependent forms of productive social organization offer the possibility that the emergence of the networked information economy will open up opportunities for improvement in economic justice, on scales both global and local.

The basic intuition and popular belief that the Internet will bring greater freedom and global equity has been around since the early 1990s. It has been the technophile's basic belief, just as the horrors of cyberporn, cybercrime, or cyberterrorism have been the standard gut-wrenching fears of the technophobe. The technophilic response is reminiscent of claims made in the past for electricity, for radio, or for telegraph, expressing what James Carey described as "the mythos of the electrical sublime." The question this part of the book explores is whether this claim, given the experience of the past decade, can be sustained on careful analysis, or whether it is yet another instance of a long line of technological utopianism. The fact that earlier utopias were overly optimistic does not mean that these previous technologies did not in fact alter the conditions of life—material, social, and intellectual. They did, but they did so differently in different societies, and in ways that diverged from the social utopias attached to them. Different nations absorbed and used these technologies differently, diverging in social and cultural habits, but also in institutional strategies for adoption—some more state-centric, others more market based; some more controlled, others less so. Utopian or at least best-case conceptions of the emerging condition are valuable if they help diagnose the socially and politically significant attributes of the emerging networked information economy correctly and allow us to form a normative conception of their significance. At a minimum, with these in hand, we can begin to design our institutional response to the present technological perturbation in order to improve the conditions of freedom and justice over the next few decades.

The chapters in this part focus on major liberal commitments or concerns. Chapter 5 addresses the question of individual autonomy. Chapters 6, 7, and 8 address democratic participation: first in the political public sphere and then, more broadly, in the construction of culture. Chapter 9 deals with justice and human development. Chapter 10 considers the effects of the networked information economy on community.

Chapter 5 Individual Freedom:

Autonomy, Information, and Law

The emergence of the networked information economy has the potential to increase individual autonomy. First, it increases the range and diversity of things that individuals can do for and by themselves. It does this by lifting, for one important domain of life, some of the central material constraints on what individuals can do that typified the industrial information economy. The majority of materials, tools, and platforms necessary for effective action in the information environment are in the hands of most individuals in advanced economies. Second, the networked information economy provides nonproprietary alternative sources of communications capacity and information, alongside the proprietary platforms of mediated communications. This decreases the extent to which individuals are subject to being acted upon by the owners of the facilities on which they depend for communications. The construction of consumers as passive objects of manipulation that typified television culture has not disappeared overnight, but it is losing its dominance in the information environment. Third, the networked information environment qualitatively increases the range and diversity of information available to individuals. It does so by enabling sources commercial and noncommercial, mainstream and fringe, domestic or foreign, to produce information and communicate with anyone. This diversity radically changes the universe of options that individuals can consider as open for them to pursue. It provides them a richer basis to form critical judgments about how they could live their lives, and, through this opportunity for critical reflection, why they should value the life they choose.

FREEDOM TO DO MORE FOR ONESELF, BY ONESELF, AND WITH OTHERS

Rory Cejas was a twenty-six-year-old firefighter/paramedic with the Miami Fire Department in 2003, when he enlisted the help of his brother, wife, and a friend to make a *Star Wars*–like fan film. Using a simple camcorder and tripod, and widely available film and image generation and editing software on his computer, he made a twenty-minute film he called *The Jedi Saga*. The film is not a parody. It is not social criticism. It is a straightforward effort to make a movie in the genre of *Star Wars*, using the same type of characters and story lines. In the predigital world, it would have been impossible, as a practical matter, for Cejas to do this. It would have been an implausible part of his life plan to cast his wife as a dark femme fatale, or his brother as a Jedi Knight, so they could battle shoulder-to-shoulder, light sabers drawn, against a platoon of Imperial clone soldiers. And it would have been impossible for him to distribute the film he had made to friends and strangers. The material conditions of cultural production have changed, so that it has now become part of his feasible set of options. He needs no help from government to do so. He needs no media access rules that give him access to fancy film studios. He needs no cable access rules to allow him to distribute his fantasy to anyone who wants to watch it. The new set of feasible options open to him includes not only the option passively to sit in the theatre or in front of the television and watch the images created by George Lucas, but also the option of trying his hand at making this type of film by himself.

Jedi Saga will not be a blockbuster. It is not likely to be watched by many people. Those who do watch it are not likely to enjoy it in the same way that they enjoyed any of Lucas's films, but that is not its point. When someone like Cejas makes such a film, he is not displacing what Lucas does. He is changing what he himself does—from sitting in front of a screen that is painted by another to painting his own screen. Those who watch it will enjoy it in the same way that friends and family enjoy speaking to each other or singing together, rather than watching talking heads or listening to Talking Heads. Television culture, the epitome of the industrial information economy, structured the role of consumers as highly passive. While media scholars like John Fiske noted the continuing role of viewers in construing and interpreting the messages they receive, the role of the consumer in this model is well defined. The media product is a finished good that they consume, not one that they make. Nowhere is this clearer than in the movie theatre, where the absence of light, the enveloping sound, and the size of the screen are all designed to remove the viewer as agent, leaving only a set of receptors—eyes, ears—through which to receive the finished good that is the movie. There is nothing wrong with the movies as one mode of entertainment. The problem emerges, however, when the movie theatre becomes an apt metaphor for the relationship the majority of people have with most of the information environment they occupy. That increasing passivity of television culture came to be a hallmark of life for most people in the late stages of the industrial information economy. The couch potato, the eyeball bought and sold by Madison Avenue, has no part in making the information environment he or she occupies.

Perhaps no single entertainment product better symbolizes the shift that the networked information economy makes possible from television culture than the massive multiplayer online game. These games are typified by two central characteristics. First, they offer a persistent game environment. That is, any action taken or "object" created anywhere in the game world persists over time, unless and until it is destroyed by some agent in the game; and it exists to the same extent for all players. Second, the games are effectively massive collaboration platforms for thousands, tens of thousands—or in the case of Lineage, the most popular game in South Korea, more than four million—users. These platforms therefore provide individual players with various contexts in which to match their wits and skills with other human players. The computer gaming environment provides a persistent relational database of the actions and social interactions of players. The first games that became mass phenomena, like Ultima Online or Everquest, started with an already richly instantiated context. Designers of these games continue to play a large role in defining the range of actions and relations feasible for players. The basic medieval themes, the role of magic and weapons, and the types and ranges of actions that are possible create much of the context, and therefore the types of relationships pursued. Still, these games leave qualitatively greater room for individual effort and personal taste in producing the experience, the relationships, and hence the story line, relative to a television or movie experience. Second Life, a newer game by Linden Labs, offers us a glimpse into the next step in this genre of immersive entertainment. Like other massively multiplayer online games, Second Life is a persistent collaboration platform for its users. Unlike other games, however, Second Life offers only tools, with no story line, stock objects, or any cultural or meaning-oriented context whatsoever. Its users have created 99 percent of the objects in the game environment. The medieval village was nothing but blank space when they started. So was the flying vehicle design shop, the futuristic outpost, or the university, where some of the users are offering courses in basic programming skills and in-game design. Linden Labs charges a flat monthly subscription fee. Its employees focus on building tools that enable users to do everything from basic story concept down to the finest details of their own appearance and of objects they use in the game world. The in-game human relationships are those made by the users as they interact with each other in this immersive entertainment experience. The game's relationship to its users is fundamentally different from that of the movie or television studio. Movies and television seek to control the entire experience—rendering the viewer inert, but satisfied. Second Life sees the users as active makers of the entertainment environment that they occupy, and seeks to provide them with the tools they need to be so. The two models assume fundamentally different conceptions of play. Whereas in front of the television, the consumer is a passive receptacle, limited to selecting which finished good he or she will consume from a relatively narrow range of options, in the world of Second Life, the individual is treated as a fundamentally active, creative human being, capable of building his or her own fantasies, alone and in affiliation with others.

Second Life and *Jedi Saga* are merely examples, perhaps trivial ones, within the entertainment domain. They represent a shift in possibilities open both to human beings in the networked information economy and to the firms that sell them the tools for becoming active creators and users of their information environment. They are stark examples because of the centrality of the couch potato as the image of human action in television culture. Their characteristics are representative of the shift in the individual's role that is typical of the networked information economy in general and of peer production in particular. Linus Torvalds, the original creator of the Linux kernel development community, was, to use Eric Raymond's characterization, a designer with an itch to scratch. Peer-production projects often are composed of people who want to do something in the world and turn to the network to find a community of peers willing to work together to make that wish a reality. Michael Hart had been working in various contexts for more than thirty years when he—at first gradually, and more recently with increasing speed—harnessed the contributions of hundreds of volunteers to Project Gutenberg in pursuit of his goal to create a globally accessible library of public domain e-texts. Charles Franks was a computer programmer from Las Vegas when he decided he had a more efficient way to proofread those e-texts, and built an interface that allowed volunteers to compare scanned images of original texts with the e-texts available on Project Gutenberg. After working independently for a couple of years, he joined forces with Hart. Franks's facility now clears the volunteer work of more than one thousand proofreaders, who proof between two hundred and three hundred books a month. Each of the thousands of volunteers who participate in free software development projects, in *Wikipedia*, in the Open Directory Project, or in any of the many other peer-production projects, is living some version, as a major or minor part of their lives, of the possibilities captured by the stories of a Linus Torvalds, a Michael Hart, or *The Jedi Saga*. Each has decided to take advantage of some combination of technical, organizational, and social conditions within which we have come to live, and to become an active creator in his or her world, rather than merely to accept what was already there. The belief that it is possible to make something valuable happen in the world, and the practice of actually acting on that belief, represent a qualitative improvement in the condition of individual freedom. They mark the emergence of new practices of self-directed agency as a lived experience, going beyond mere formal permissibility and theoretical possibility.

Our conception of autonomy has not only been forged in the context of the rise of the democratic, civil rights–respecting state over its major competitors as a political system. In parallel, we have occupied the context of the increasing dominance of market-based industrial economy over its competitors. The culture we have developed over the past century is suffused with images that speak of the loss of agency imposed by that industrial economy. No cultural image better captures the way that mass industrial production reduced workers to cogs and consumers to receptacles than the one-dimensional curves typical of welfare economics—those that render human beings as mere production and demand functions. Their cultural, if not intellectual, roots are in Fredrick Taylor's *Theory of Scientific Management*: the idea of abstracting and defining all motions and actions of employees in the production process so that all the knowledge was in the system, while the employees were barely more than its replaceable parts. Taylorism, ironically, was a vast improvement over the depredations of the first industrial age, with its sweatshops and child labor. It nonetheless resolved into the kind of mechanical existence depicted in Charlie Chaplin's tragic-comic portrait, *Modern Times*. While the grind of industrial Taylorism seems far from the core of the advanced economies, shunted as it is now to poorer economies, the basic sense of alienation and lack of effective agency persists. Scott Adams's *Dilbert* comic strip, devoted to the life of a white-collar employee in a nameless U.S. corporation, thoroughly alienated from the enterprise, crimped by corporate hierarchy, resisting in all sorts of ways—but trapped in a cubicle—powerfully captures this sense for the industrial information economy in much the same way that Chaplin's *Modern Times* did for the industrial economy itself.

In the industrial economy and its information adjunct, most people live most of their lives within hierarchical relations of production, and within relatively tightly scripted possibilities after work, as consumers. It did not necessarily have to be this way. Michael Piore and Charles Sabel's *Second Industrial Divide* and Roberto Mangabeira Unger's *False Necessity* were central to the emergence of a "third way" literature that developed in the 1980s and 1990s to explore the possible alternative paths to production processes that did not depend so completely on the displacement of individual agency by hierarchical production systems. The emergence of radically decentralized, nonmarket production provides a new outlet for the attenuation of the constrained and constraining roles of employees and consumers. It is not limited to Northern Italian artisan industries or imagined for emerging economies, but is at the very heart of the most advanced market economies. Peer production and otherwise decentralized nonmarket production can alter the producer/consumer relationship with regard to culture, entertainment, and information. We are seeing the emergence of the user as a new category of relationship to information production and exchange. Users are individuals who are sometimes consumers and sometimes producers. They are substantially more engaged participants, both in defining the terms of their productive activity and in defining what they consume and how they consume it. In these two great domains of life—production and consumption, work and play—the networked information economy promises to enrich individual autonomy substantively by creating an environment built less around control and more around facilitating action.

The emergence of radically decentralized nonmarket production in general and of peer production in particular as feasible forms of action opens new classes of behaviors to individuals. Individuals can now justifiably believe that they can in fact do things that they want to do, and build things that they want to build in the digitally networked environment, and that this pursuit of their will need not, perhaps even cannot, be frustrated by insurmountable cost or an alien bureaucracy. Whether their actions are in the domain of political organization (like the organizers of MoveOn.org), or of education and professional attainment (as with the case of Jim Cornish, who decided to create a worldwide center of information on the Vikings from his fifth-grade schoolroom in Gander, Newfoundland), the networked information environment opens new domains for productive life that simply were not there before. In doing so, it has provided us with new ways to imagine our lives as productive human beings. Writing a free operating system or publishing a free encyclopedia may have seemed quixotic a mere few years ago, but these are now far from delusional. Human beings who live in a material and social context that lets them aspire to such things as possible for them to do, in their own lives, by themselves and in loose affiliation with others, are human beings who have a greater realm for their agency. We can live a life more authored by our own will and imagination than by the material and social conditions in which we find ourselves. At least we can do so more effectively than we could until the last decade of the twentieth century.

This new practical individual freedom, made feasible by the digital environment, is at the root of the improvements I describe here for political participation, for justice and human development, for the creation of a more critical culture, and for the emergence of the networked individual as a more fluid member of community. In each of these domains, the improvements in the degree to which these liberal commitments are honored and practiced emerge from new behaviors made possible and effective by the networked information economy. These behaviors emerge now precisely because individuals have a greater degree of freedom to act effectively, unconstrained by a need to ask permission from anyone. It is this freedom that increases the salience of nonmonetizable motivations as drivers of production. It is this freedom to seek out whatever information we wish, to write about it, and to join and leave various projects and associations with others that underlies the new efficiencies we see in the networked information economy. These behaviors underlie the cooperative news and commentary production that form the basis of the networked public sphere, and in turn enable us to look at the world as potential participants in discourse, rather than as potential viewers only. They are at the root of making a more transparent and reflective culture. They make possible the strategies I suggest as feasible avenues to assure equitable access to opportunities for economic participation and to improve human development globally.

Treating these new practical opportunities for action as improvements in autonomy is not a theoretically unproblematic proposition. For all its intuitive appeal and centrality, autonomy is a notoriously nebulous concept. In particular, there are deep divisions within the literature as to whether it is appropriate to conceive of autonomy in substantive terms—as Gerald Dworkin, Joseph Raz, and Joel Feinberg most prominently have, and as I have here—or in formal terms. Formal conceptions of autonomy are committed to assuming that all people have the capacity for autonomous choice, and do not go further in attempting to measure the degree of freedom people actually exercise in the world in which they are in fact constrained by circumstances, both natural and human. This commitment is not rooted in some stubborn unwillingness to recognize the slings and arrows of outrageous fortune that actually constrain our choices. Rather, it comes from the sense that only by treating people as having these capacities and abilities can we accord them adequate respect as free, rational beings, and avoid sliding into overbearing paternalism. As Robert Post put it, while autonomy may well be something that needs to be "achieved" as a descriptive matter, the "structures of social authority" will be designed differently depending on whether or not individuals are treated as autonomous. "From the point of view of the designer of the structure, therefore, the presence or absence of autonomy functions as an axiomatic and foundational principle."[1] Autonomy theory that too closely aims to understand the degree of autonomy people actually exercise under different institutional arrangements threatens to form the basis of an overbearing benevolence that would undermine the very possibility of autonomous action.

While the fear of an overbearing bureaucracy benevolently guiding us through life toward becoming more autonomous is justifiable, the formal conception of autonomy pays a high price in its bluntness as a tool to diagnose the autonomy implications of policy. Given how we are: situated, context-bound, messy individuals, it would be a high price to pay to lose the ability to understand how law and policy actually affect whatever capacity we do have to be the authors of our own life choices in some meaningful sense. We are individuals who have the capacity to form beliefs and to change them, to form opinions and plans and defend them—but also to listen to arguments and revise our beliefs. We experience some decisions as being more free than others; we mock or lament ourselves when we find ourselves trapped by the machine or the cubicle, and we do so in terms of a sense of helplessness, a negation of freedom, not only, or even primarily, in terms of lack of welfare; and we cherish whatever conditions those are that we experience as "free" precisely for that freedom, not for other reasons. Certainly, the concerns with an overbearing state, whether professing benevolence or not, are real and immediate. No one who lives with the near past of the totalitarianism of the twentieth century or with contemporary authoritarianism and fundamentalism can belittle these. But the great evils that the state can impose through formal law should not cause us to adopt methodological commitments that would limit our ability to see the many ways in which ordinary life in democratic societies can nonetheless be more or less free, more or less conducive to individual self-authorship.

If we take our question to be one concerned with diagnosing the condition of freedom of individuals, we must observe the conditions of life from a first-person, practical perspective—that is, from the perspective of the person whose autonomy we are considering. If we accept that all individuals are always constrained by personal circumstances both physical and social, then the way to think about autonomy of human agents is to inquire into the relative capacity of individuals to be the authors of their lives within the constraints of context. From this perspective, whether the sources of constraint are private actors or public law is irrelevant. What matters is the extent to which a particular configuration of material, social, and institutional conditions allows an individual to be the author of his or her life, and to what extent these conditions allow others to act upon the individual as an object of manipulation. As a means of diagnosing the conditions of individual freedom in a given society and context, we must seek to observe the extent to which people are, in fact, able to plan and pursue a life that can reasonably be described as a product of their own choices. It allows us to compare different conditions, and determine that a certain condition allows individuals to do more for themselves, without asking permission from anyone. In this sense, we can say that the conditions that enabled Cejas to make *Jedi Saga* are conditions that made him more autonomous than he would have been without the tools that made that movie possible. It is in this sense that the increased range of actions we can imagine for ourselves in loose affiliation with others—like creating a Project Gutenberg—increases our ability to imagine and pursue life plans that would have been impossible in the recent past.

From the perspective of the implications of autonomy for how people act in the digital environment, and therefore how they are changing the conditions of freedom and justice along the various dimensions explored in these chapters, this kind of freedom to act is central. It is a practical freedom sufficient to sustain the behaviors that underlie the improvements in these other domains. From an internal perspective of the theory of autonomy, however, this basic observation that people can do more by themselves, alone or in loose affiliation with others, is only part of the contribution of the networked information economy to autonomy, and a part that will only be considered an improvement by those who conceive of autonomy as a substantive concept. The implications of the networked information economy for autonomy are, however, broader, in ways that make them attractive across many conceptions of autonomy. To make that point, however, we must focus more specifically on law as the source of constraint, a concern common to both substantive and formal conceptions of autonomy. As a means of analyzing the implications of law to autonomy, the perspective offered here requires that we broaden our analysis beyond laws that directly limit autonomy. We must also look to laws that structure the conditions of action for individuals living within the ambit of their effect. In particular, where we have an opportunity to structure a set of core resources necessary for individuals to perceive the state of the world and the range of possible actions, and to communicate their intentions to others, we must consider whether the way we regulate these resources will create systematic limitations on the capacity of individuals to control their own lives, and in their susceptibility to manipulation and control by others. Once we recognize that there cannot be a person who is ideally "free," in the sense of being unconstrained or uncaused by the decisions of others, we are left to measure the effects of all sorts of constraints that predictably flow from a particular legal arrangement, in terms of the effect they have on the relative role that individuals play in authoring their own lives.

AUTONOMY, PROPERTY, AND COMMONS

The first legal framework whose role is altered by the emergence of the networked information economy is the property-like regulatory structure of patents, copyrights, and similar exclusion mechanisms applicable to information, knowledge, and culture. Property is usually thought in liberal theory to enhance, rather than constrain, individual freedom, in two quite distinct ways. First, it provides security of material context—that is, it allows one to know with some certainty that some set of resources, those that belong to her, will be available for her to use to execute her plans over time. This is the core of Kant's theory of property, which relies on a notion of positive liberty, the freedom to do things successfully based on life plans we can lay for ourselves. Second, property and markets provide greater freedom of action for the individual owner as compared both, as Marx diagnosed, to the feudal arrangements that preceded them, and, as he decidedly did not but Hayek did, to the models of state ownership and regulation that competed with them throughout most of the twentieth century.

Markets are indeed institutional spaces that enable a substantial degree of free choice. "Free," however, does not mean "anything goes." If John possesses a car and Jane possesses a gun, a market will develop only if John is prohibited from running Jane over and taking her gun, and also if Jane is prohibited from shooting at John or threatening to shoot him if he does not give her his car. A market that is more or less efficient will develop only if many other things are prohibited to, or required of, one or both sides—like monopolization or disclosure. Markets are, in other words, structured relationships intended to elicit a particular datum—the comparative willingness and ability of agents to pay for goods or resources. The most basic set of constraints that structure behavior in order to enable markets are those we usually call property. Property is a cluster of background rules that determine what resources each of us has when we come into relations with others, and, no less important, what "having" or "lacking" a resource entails in our relations with these others. These rules impose constraints on who can do what in the domain of actions that require access to resources that are the subjects of property law. They are aimed to crystallize asymmetries of power over resources, which then form the basis for exchanges—I will allow you to do X, which I am asymmetrically empowered to do (for example, watch television using this cable system), and you, in turn, will allow me to do Y, which you are asymmetrically empowered to do (for example, receive payment from your bank account). While a necessary precondition for markets, property also means that choice in markets is itself not free of constraints, but is instead constrained in a particular pattern. It makes some people more powerful with regard to some things, and must constrain the freedom of action of others in order to achieve this asymmetry.[2]

Commons are an alternative form of institutional space, where human agents can act free of the particular constraints required for markets, and where they have some degree of confidence that the resources they need for their plans will be available to them. Both freedom of action and security of resource availability are achieved in very different patterns than they are in property-based markets. As with markets, commons do not mean that anything goes. Managing resources as commons does, however, mean that individuals and groups can use those resources under different types of constraints than those imposed by property law. These constraints may be social, physical, or regulatory. They may make individuals more free or less so, in the sense of permitting a greater or lesser freedom of action to choose among a range of actions that require access to resources governed by them than would property rules in the same resources. Whether having a particular type of resource subject to a commons, rather than a property-based market, enhances freedom of action and security, or harms them, is a context-specific question. It depends on how the commons is structured, and how property rights in the resource would have been structured in the absence of a commons. The public spaces in New York City, like Central Park, Union Square, or any sidewalk, afford more people greater freedom than does a private backyard—certainly to all but its owner. Given the diversity of options that these public spaces make possible as compared to the social norms that neighbors enforce against each other, they probably offer more freedom of action than a backyard offers even to its owner in many loosely urban and suburban communities. Swiss pastures or irrigation districts of the type that Elinor Ostrom described as classic cases of long-standing sustainable commons offer their participants security of holdings at least as stable as any property system, but place substantial traditional constraints on who can use the resources, how they can use them, and how, if at all, they can transfer their rights and do something completely different. These types of commons likely afford their participants less, rather than more, freedom of action than would have been afforded had they owned the same resource in a market-alienable property arrangement, although they retain security in much the same way. Commons, like the air, the sidewalk, the road and highway, the ocean, or the public beach, achieve security on a very different model. I can rely on the resources so managed in a probabilistic, rather than deterministic sense. I can plan to meet my friends for a picnic in the park, not because I own the park and can direct that it be used for my picnic, but because I know there will be a park, that it is free for me to use, and that there will be enough space for us to find a corner to sit in. This is also the sort of security that allows me to plan to leave my house at some hour, and plan to be at work at some other hour, relying not on owning the transportation path, but on the availability to me of the roads and highways on symmetric terms to its availability to everyone else. If we look more closely, we will see that property and markets also offer only a probabilistic security of context, whose parameters are different—for example, the degree of certainty we have as to whether the resource we rely on as our property will be stolen or damaged, whether it will be sufficient for what we need, or if we need more, whether it will be available for sale and whether we will be able to afford it.

Like property and markets, then, commons provide both freedom of action and security of context. They do so, however, through the imposition of different constraints than do property and market rules. In particular, what typifies all these commons in contradistinction to property is that no actor is empowered by law to act upon another as an object of his or her will. I can impose conditions on your behavior when you are walking on my garden path, but I have no authority to impose on you when you walk down the sidewalk. Whether one or the other of the two systems, used exclusively, will provide "greater freedom" in some aggregate sense is not a priori determinable. It will depend on the technical characteristics of the resource, the precise contours of the rules of, respectively, the proprietary market and the commons, and the distribution of wealth in society. Given the diversity of resources and contexts, and the impossibility of a purely "anything goes" absence of rules for either system, some mix of the two different institutional frameworks is likely to provide the greatest diversity of freedom to act in a material context. This diversity, in turn, enables the greatest freedom to plan action within material contexts, allowing individuals to trade off the availabilities of, and constraints on, different resources to forge a context sufficiently provisioned to enable them to execute their plans, while being sufficiently unregulated to permit them to do so. Freedom inheres in diversity of constraint, not in the optimality of the balance of freedom and constraint represented by any single institutional arrangement. It is the diversity of constraint that allows individuals to plan to live out different portions and aspects of their lives in different institutional contexts, taking advantage of the different degrees of freedom and security they make possible.

In the context of information, knowledge, and culture, because of the nonrivalry of information and its characteristic as input as well as output of the production process, the commons provides substantially greater security of context than it does when material resources, like parks or roadways, are at stake. Moreover, peer production and the networked information economy provide an increasingly robust source of new information inputs. This reduces the risk of lacking resources necessary to create new expressions or find out new things, and renders more robust the freedom to act without being susceptible to constraint from someone who holds asymmetrically greater power over the information resources one needs. As to information, then, we can say with a high degree of confidence that a more expansive commons improves individual autonomy, while enclosure of the public domain undermines it. This is less determinate with communications systems. Because computers and network connections are rival goods, there is less certainty that a commons will deliver the required resources. Under present conditions, a mixture of commons-based and proprietary communications systems is likely to improve autonomy. If, however, technological and social conditions change so that, for example, sharing on the model of peer-to-peer networks, distributed computation, or wireless mesh networks will be able to offer as dependable a set of communications and computation resources as the Web offers information and knowledge resources, the relative attractiveness of commons-oriented communications policies will increase from the perspective of autonomy.

AUTONOMY AND THE INFORMATION ENVIRONMENT

The structure of our information environment is constitutive of our autonomy, not only functionally significant to it. While the capacity to act free of constraints is most immediately and clearly changed by the networked information economy, information plays an even more foundational role in our very capacity to make and pursue life plans that can properly be called our own. A fundamental requirement of self-direction is the capacity to perceive the state of the world, to conceive of available options for action, to connect actions to consequences, to evaluate alternative outcomes, and to decide upon and pursue an action accordingly. Without these, no action, even if mechanically self-directed in the sense that my brain consciously directs my body to act, can be understood as autonomous in any normatively interesting sense. All of the components of decision making prior to action, and those actions that are themselves communicative moves or require communication as a precondition to efficacy, are constituted by the information and communications environment we, as agents, occupy. Conditions that cause failures at any of these junctures, which place bottlenecks, failures of communication, or provide opportunities for manipulation by a gatekeeper in the information environment, create threats to the autonomy of individuals in that environment. The shape of the information environment, and the distribution of power within it to control information flows to and from individuals, are, as we have seen, the contingent product of a combination of technology, economic behavior, social patterns, and institutional structure or law.

In 1999, Cisco Systems issued a technical white paper, which described a new router that the company planned to sell to cable broadband providers. In describing advantages that these new "policy routers" offer cable providers, the paper explained that if the provider's users want to subscribe to a service that "pushes" information to their computer: "You could restrict the incoming push broadcasts as well as subscribers' outgoing access to the push site to discourage its use. At the same time, you could promote your own or a partner's services with full speed features to encourage adoption of your services."[3]

In plain English, the broadband provider could inspect the packets flowing to and from a customer, and decide which packets would go through faster and more reliably, and which would slow down or be lost. Its engineering purpose was to improve quality of service. However, it could readily be used to make it harder for individual users to receive information that they want to subscribe to, and easier for them to receive information from sites preferred by the provider—for example, the provider's own site, or sites of those who pay the cable operator for using this function to help "encourage" users to adopt their services. There are no reports of broadband providers using these capabilities systematically. But occasional events, such as when Canada's second largest telecommunications company blocked access for all its subscribers and those of smaller Internet service providers that relied on its network to the website of the Telecommunications Workers Union in 2005, suggest that the concern is far from imaginary.

It is fairly clear that the new router increases the capacity of cable operators to treat their subscribers as objects, and to manipulate their actions in order to make them act as the provider wills, rather than as they would have had they had perfect information. It is less obvious whether this is a violation of, or a decrease in, the autonomy of the users. At one extreme, imagine the home as a black box with no communications capabilities save one—the cable broadband connection. Whatever comes through that cable is, for all practical purposes, "the state of the world," as far as the inhabitants of that home know. In this extreme situation, the difference between a completely neutral pipe that carries large amounts of information indiscriminately, and a pipe finely controlled by the cable operator is a large one, in terms of the autonomy of the home's inhabitants. If the pipe is indiscriminate, then the choices of the users determine what they know; decisions based on that knowledge can be said to be autonomous, at least to the extent that whether they are or are not autonomous is a function of the state of the agent's knowledge when forming a decision. If the pipe is finely controlled and purposefully manipulated by the cable operator, by contrast, then decisions that individuals make based on the knowledge they acquire through that pipe are substantially a function of the choices of the controller of the pipe, not of the users. At the other extreme, if each agent has dozens of alternative channels of communication to the home, and knows how the information flow of each one is managed, then the introduction of policy routers into one or some of those channels has no real implications for the agent's autonomy. While it may render one or more channels manipulable by their provider, the presence of alternative, indiscriminate channels, on the one hand, and of competition and choice among various manipulated channels, on the other hand, attenuates the extent to which the choices of the provider structure the universe of information within which the individual agent operates. The provider no longer can be said to shape the individual's choices, even if it tries to shape the information environment observable through its channel with the specific intent of manipulating the actions of users who view the world through its pipe. With sufficient choice among pipes, and sufficient knowledge about the differences between pipes, the very choice to use the manipulated pipe can be seen as an autonomous act. The resulting state of knowledge is self-selected by the user. Even if that state of knowledge then is partial and future actions constrained by it, the limited range of options is itself an expression of the user's autonomy, not a hindrance on it. For example, consider the following: Odysseus and his men mix different forms of freedom and constraint in the face of the Sirens. Odysseus maintains his capacity to acquire new information by leaving his ears unplugged, but binds himself to stay on the ship by having his men tie him to the mast. His men choose the same course at the same time, but bind themselves to the ship by having Odysseus stop their ears with wax, so that they do not get the new information—the siren songs—that might change their minds and cause them not to stay the course. Both are autonomous when they pass by the Sirens, though both are free only because of their current incapacity. Odysseus's incapacity to jump into the water and swim to the Sirens and his men's incapacity to hear the siren songs are a result of their autonomously chosen past actions.

The world we live in is neither black box nor cornucopia of well-specified communications channels. However, characterizing the range of possible configurations of the communications environment we occupy as lying on a spectrum from one to the other provides us with a framework for describing the degree to which actual conditions of a communications environment are conducive to individual autonomy. More important perhaps, it allows us to characterize policy and law that affects the communications environment as improving or undermining individual autonomy. Law can affect the range of channels of communications available to individuals, as well as the rules under which they are used. How many communications channels and sources of information can an individual receive? How many are available for him or her to communicate with others? Who controls these communications channels? What does control over the communications channels to an agent entail? What can the controller do, and what can it not? All of these questions are the subject of various forms of policy and law. Their implications affect the degree of autonomy possessed by individuals operating with the institutional-technical-economic framework thus created.

There are two primary types of effects that information law can have on personal autonomy. The first type is concerned with the relative capacity of some people systematically to constrain the perceptions or shape the preferences of others. A law that systematically gives some people the power to control the options perceived by, or the preferences of, others, is a law that harms autonomy. Government regulation of the press and its propaganda that attempts to shape its subjects' lives is a special case of this more general concern. This concern is in some measure quantitative, in the sense that a greater degree of control to which one is subject is a greater offense to autonomy. More fundamentally, a law that systematically makes one adult susceptible to the control of another offends the autonomy of the former. Law has created the conditions for one person to act upon another as an object. This is the nonpragmatic offense to autonomy committed by abortion regulations upheld in *Planned Parenthood v. Casey*—such as requirements that women who seek abortions listen to lectures designed to dissuade them. These were justified by the plurality there, not by the claim that they did not impinge on a woman's autonomy, but that the state's interest in the potential life of a child trumps the autonomy of the pregnant woman.

The second type of effect that law can have on autonomy is to reduce significantly the range and variety of options open to people in society generally, or to certain classes of people. This is different from the concern with government intervention generally. It is not focused on whether the state prohibits these options, but only on whether the effect of the law is to remove options. It is less important whether this effect is through prohibition or through a set of predictable or observable behavioral adaptations among individuals and organizations that, as a practical matter, remove these options. I do not mean to argue for the imposition of restraints, in the name of autonomy, on any lawmaking that results in a removal of any single option, irrespective of the quantity and variety of options still open. Much of law does that. Rather, the autonomy concern is implicated by laws that systematically and significantly reduce the number, and more important, impoverish the variety, of options open to people in the society for which the law is passed.

"Number and variety" is intended to suggest two dimensions of effect on the options open to an individual. The first is quantitative. For an individual to author her own life, she must have a significant set of options from which to choose; otherwise, it is the choice set—or whoever, if anyone, made it so—and not the individual, that is governing her life. This quantitative dimension, however, does not mean that more choices are always better, from the individual's perspective. It is sufficient that the individual have some adequate threshold level of options in order for him or her to exercise substantive self-authorship, rather than being authored by circumstances. Beyond that threshold level, additional options may affect one's welfare and success as an autonomous agent, but they do not so constrain an individual's choices as to make one not autonomous. Beyond quantitative adequacy, the options available to an individual must represent meaningfully different paths, not merely slight variations on a theme. Qualitatively, autonomy requires the availability of options in whose adoption or rejection the individual can practice critical reflection and life choices. In order to sustain the autonomy of a person born and raised in a culture with a set of socially embedded conventions about what a good life is, one would want a choice set that included at least some unconventional, non-mainstream, if you will, critical options. If all the options one has—even if, in a purely quantitative sense, they are "adequate"—are conventional or mainstream, then one loses an important dimension of self-creation. The point is not that to be truly autonomous one necessarily must be unconventional. Rather, if self-governance for an individual consists in critical reflection and re-creation by making choices over the course of his life, then some of the options open must be different from what he would choose simply by drifting through life, adopting a life plan for no reason other than that it is accepted by most others. A person who chooses a conventional life in the presence of the option to live otherwise makes that conventional life his or her own in a way that a person who lives a conventional life without knowing about alternatives does not.

As long as our autonomy analysis of information law is sensitive to these two effects on information flow to, from, and among individuals and organizations in the regulated society, it need not conflict with the concerns of those who adopt the formal conception of autonomy. It calls for no therapeutic agenda to educate adults in a wide range of options. It calls for no one to sit in front of educational programs. It merely focuses on two core effects that law can have through the way it structures the relationships among people with regard to the information environment they occupy. If a law—passed for any reason that may or may not be related to autonomy concerns—creates systematic shifts of power among groups in society, so that some have a greater ability to shape the perceptions of others with regard to available options, consequences of action, or the value of preferences, then that law is suspect from an autonomy perspective. It makes the choices of some people less their own and more subject to manipulation by those to whom the law gives the power to control perceptions. Furthermore, a law that systematically and severely limits the range of options known to individuals is one that imposes a normative price, in terms of autonomy, for whatever value it is intended to deliver. As long as the focus of autonomy as an institutional design desideratum is on securing the best possible information flow to the individual, the designer of the legal structure need not assume that individuals are not autonomous, or have failures of autonomy, in order to serve autonomy. All the designer need assume is that individuals will not act in order to optimize the autonomy of their neighbors. Law then responds by avoiding institutional designs that facilitate the capacity of some groups of individuals to act on others in ways that are systematically at the expense of the ability of those others to control their own lives, and by implementing policies that predictably diversify the set of options that all individuals are able to see as open to them.

Throughout most of the 1990s and currently, communications and information policy around the globe was guided by a wish to "let the private sector lead," interpreted in large measure to mean that various property and property-like regulatory frameworks should be strengthened, while various regulatory constraints on property-like rights should be eased. The drive toward proprietary, market-based provisioning of communications and information came from disillusionment with regulatory systems and state-owned communications networks. It saw the privatization of national postal, telephone, and telegraph authorities (PTTs) around the world. Even a country with a long tradition of state-centric communications policy, like France, privatized much of its telecommunications systems. In the United States, this model translated into efforts to shift telecommunications from the regulated monopoly model it followed throughout most of the twentieth century to a competitive market, and to shift Internet development from being primarily a government-funded exercise, as it had been from the late 1960s to the mid 1990s, to being purely private property, market based. This model was declared in the Clinton administration's 1993 *National Information Infrastructure: Agenda for Action*, which pushed for privatization of Internet deployment and development. It was the basis of that administration's 1995 *White Paper on Intellectual Property*, which mapped the most aggressive agenda ever put forward by any American administration in favor of perfect enclosure of the public domain; and it was in those years when the Federal Communications Commission (FCC) first implemented spectrum auctions aimed at more thorough privatization of wireless communications in the United States. The general push for stronger intellectual property rights and more marketcentric telecommunications systems also became a central tenet of international trade regimes, pushing similar policies in smaller and developing economies.

The result of the push toward private provisioning and deregulation has led to the emergence of a near-monopolistic market structure for wired physical broadband services. By the end of 2003, more than 96 percent of homes and small offices in the United States that had any kind of "high-speed"

Internet services received their service from either their incumbent cable operator or their incumbent local telephone company. If one focuses on the subset of these homes and offices that get service that provides more substantial room for autonomous communicative action—that is, those that have upstream service at high-speed, enabling them to publish and participate in online production efforts and not simply to receive information at high speeds—the picture is even more dismal. Less than 2 percent of homes and small offices receive their broadband connectivity from someone other than their cable carrier or incumbent telephone carrier. More than 83 percent of these users get their access from their cable operator. Moreover, the growth rate in adoption of cable broadband and local telephone digital subscriber line (DSL) has been high and positive, whereas the growth rate of the few competing platforms, like satellite broadband, has been stagnant or shrinking. The proprietary wired environment is gravitating toward a high-speed connectivity platform that will be either a lopsided duopoly, or eventually resolve into a monopoly platform.[4] These owners are capable, both technically and legally, of installing the kind of policy routers with which I opened the discussion of autonomy and information law—routers that would allow them to speed up some packets and slow down or reject others in ways intended to shape the universe of information available to users of their networks.

The alternative of building some portions of our telecommunications and information production and exchange systems as commons was not understood in the mid-1990s, when the policy that resulted in this market structure for communications was developed. As we saw in chapter 3, however, wireless communications technology has progressed to the point where it is now possible for users to own equipment that cooperates in mesh networks to form a "last-mile" infrastructure that no one other than the users own. Radio networks can now be designed so that their capital structure more closely approximates the Internet and personal computer markets, bringing with it a greater scope for commons-based peer production of telecommunications infrastructure. Throughout most of the twentieth century, wireless communications combined high-cost capital goods (radio transmitters and antennae towers) with cheaper consumer goods (radio receivers), using regulated proprietary infrastructure, to deliver a finished good of wireless communications on an industrial model. Now WiFi is marking the possibility of an inversion of the capital structure of wireless communication. We see end-user equipment manufacturers like Intel, Cisco, and others producing and selling radio "transceivers" that are shareable goods. By using ad hoc mesh networking techniques, some early versions of which are already being deployed, these transceivers allow their individual owners to cooperate and coprovision their own wireless communications network, without depending on any cable carrier or other wired provider as a carrier of last resort. Almost the entire debate around spectrum policy and the relative merits of markets and commons in wireless policy is conducted today in terms of efficiency and innovation. A common question these days is which of the two approaches will lead to greater growth of wireless communications capacity and will more efficiently allocate the capacity we already have. I have contributed my fair share of this form of analysis, but the question that concerns us here is different. We must ask what, if any, are the implications of the emergence of a feasible, sustainable model of a commons-based physical infrastructure for the first and last mile of the communications environment, in terms of individual autonomy?

The choice between proprietary and commons-based wireless data networks takes on new significance in light of the market structure of the wired network, and the power it gives owners of broadband networks to control the information flow into the vast majority of homes. Commons-based wireless systems become the primary legal form of communications capacity that does not systematically subject its users to manipulation by an infrastructure owner.

Imagine a world with four agents—A, B, C, and D—connected to each other by a communications network. Each component, or route, of the network could be owned or unowned. If all components are unowned, that is, are organized as a commons, each agent has an equal privilege to use any component of the network to communicate with any other agent. If all components are owned, the owner of any network component can deny to any other agent use of that network component to communicate with anyone else. This translates in the real world into whether or not there is a "spectrum owner" who "owns" the link between any two users, or whether the link is simply a consequence of the fact that two users are communicating with each other in a way that no one has a right to prevent them from doing.

In this simple model, if the network is unowned, then for any communication all that is required is a willing sender and a willing recipient. No third agent gets a say as to whether any other pair will communicate with each other. Each agent determines independently of the others whether to participate in a communicative exchange, and communication occurs whenever all its participants, and only they, agree to communicate with each other. For example, A can exchange information with B, as long as B consents. The only person who has a right to prevent A from receiving information from, or sending information to, B, is B, in the exercise of B's own autonomous choice whether to change her information environment. Under these conditions, neither A nor B is subject to control of her information environment by others, except where such control results from denying her the capacity to control the information environment of another. If all network components are owned, on the other hand, then for any communication there must be a willing sender, a willing recipient, and a willing infrastructure owner. In a pure property regime, infrastructure owners have a say over whether, and the conditions under which, others in their society will communicate with each other. It is precisely the power to prevent others from communicating that makes infrastructure ownership a valuable enterprise: One can charge for granting one's permission to communicate. For example, imagine that D owns all lines connecting A to B directly or through D, and C owns all lines connecting A or B to C. As in the previous scenario, A wishes to exchange information with B. Now, in addition to B, A must obtain either C's or D's consent. A now functions under two distinct types of constraint. The first, as before, is a constraint imposed by B's autonomy: A cannot change B's information environment (by exchanging information with her) without B's consent. The second constraint is that A must persuade an owner of whatever carriage medium connects A to B to permit A and B to communicate. The communication is not sent to or from C or D. It does not change C's or D's information environment, and that is not A's intention. C and D's ability to consent or withhold consent is not based on the autonomy principle. It is based, instead, on an instrumental calculus: namely, that creating such property rights in infrastructure will lead to the right incentives for the deployment of infrastructure necessary for A and B to communicate in the first place.

Now imagine that D owns the entire infrastructure. If A wants to get information from B or to communicate to C in order to persuade C to act in a way that is beneficial to A, A needs D's permission. D may grant or withhold permission, and may do so either for a fee or upon the imposition of conditions on the communication. Most significantly, D can choose to prevent anyone from communicating with anyone else, or to expose each participant to the communications of only some, but not all, members of society. This characteristic of her ownership gives D the power to shape A's information environment by selectively exposing A to information in the form of communications from others. Most commonly, we might see this where D decides that B will pay more if all infrastructure is devoted to permitting B to communicate her information to A and C, rather than any of it used to convey A's statements to C. D might then refuse to carry A's message to C and permit only B to communicate to A and C. The point is that from A's perspective, A is dependent upon D's decisions as to what information can be carried on the infrastructure, among whom, and in what directions. To the extent of that dependence, A's autonomy is compromised. We might call the requirement that D can place on A as a precondition to using the infrastructure an "influence exaction."

The magnitude of the negative effect on autonomy, or of the influence exaction, depends primarily on (a) the degree to which it is hard or easy to get around D's facility, and (b) the degree of transparency of the exaction. Compare, for example, Cisco's policy router for cable broadband, which allows the cable operator to speed up and slow down packets based on its preferences, to Amazon's brief experiment in 1998–1999 with accepting undisclosed payments from publishers in exchange for recommending their books. If a cable operator programs its routers to slow down packets of competitors, or of information providers that do not pay, this practice places a significant exaction on users. First, the exaction is entirely nontransparent. There are many reasons that different sites load at different speeds, or even fail to load altogether. Users, the vast majority of whom are unaware that the provider could, if it chose, regulate the flow of information to them, will assume that it is the target site that is failing, not that their own service provider is manipulating what they can see. Second, there is no genuine work-around. Cable broadband covers roughly two-thirds of the home market, in many places without alternative; and where there is an alternative, there is only one—the incumbent telephone company. Without one of these noncompetitive infrastructure owners, the home user has no broadband access to the Internet. In Amazon's case, the consumer outrage when the practice was revealed focused on the lack of transparency. Users had little objection to clearly demarcated advertisement. The resistance was to the nontransparent manipulation of the recommendation system aimed at causing the consumers to act in ways consistent with Amazon's goals, rather than their own. In that case, however, there were alternatives. There are many different places from which to find book reviews and recommendations, and at the time, barnesandnoble.com was already available as an online book-seller—and had not significantly adopted similar practices. The exaction was therefore less significant. Moreover, once the practice was revealed, Amazon publicly renounced it and began to place advertisements in a clearly recognizable separate category. The lesson was not lost on others. When Google began at roughly the same time as a search engine, it broke with the then-common practice of selling search-result location. When the company later introduced advertised links, it designed its interface to separate out clearly the advertisements from the algorithm-based results, and to give the latter more prominent placement than the former. This does not necessarily mean that any search engine that accepts payments for linking is necessarily bad. A search engine like Overture, which explicitly and publicly returns results ranked according to which, among the sites retrieved, paid Overture the most, has its own value for consumers looking for commercial sites. A transparent, nonmonopolistic option of this sort increases, rather than decreases, the freedom of users to find the information they want and act on it. The problem would be with search engines that mix the two strategies and hide the mix, or with a monopolistic search engine.

Because of the importance of the possibility to work around the owned infrastructure, the degree of competitiveness of any market in such infrastructure is important. Before considering the limits of even competitive markets by comparison to commons, however, it is important to recognize that a concern with autonomy provides a distinct justification for the policy concern with media concentration. To understand the effects of concentration, we can think of freedom from constraint as a dimension of welfare. Just as we have no reason to think that in a concentrated market, total welfare, let alone consumer welfare, will be optimal, we also have no reason to think that a component of welfare—freedom from constraint as a condition to access one's communicative environment—will be optimal. Moreover, when we use a "welfare" calculus as a metaphor for the degree of autonomy users have in the system, we must optimize not total welfare, as we do in economic analysis, but only what in the metaphorical calculus would count as "consumer surplus." In the domain of influence and autonomy, only "consumer surplus" counts as autonomy enhancing. "Producer surplus," the degree of successful imposition of influence on others as a condition of service, translates in an autonomy calculus into control exerted by some people (providers) over others (consumers). It reflects the successful negation of autonomy. The monopoly case therefore presents a new normative dimension of the well-known critiques of media concentration. Why, however, is this not solely an analysis of media concentration? Why does a competitive market in infrastructure not solve the autonomy deficit of property?

If we make standard assumptions of perfectly competitive markets and apply them to our A-B-D example, one would think that the analysis must change. D no longer has monopoly power. We would presume that the owners of infrastructure would be driven by competition to allocate infrastructure to uses that users value most highly. If one owner "charges" a high price in terms of conditions imposed on users, say to forgo receiving certain kinds of speech uncongenial to the owner, then the users will go to a competitor who does not impose that condition. This standard market response is far from morally irrelevant if one is concerned with autonomy. If, in fact, every individual can choose precisely the package of influence exactions and the cash-to-influence trade-off under which he or she is willing to communicate, then the autonomy deficit that I suggest is created by property rights in communications infrastructure is minimal. If all possible degrees of freedom from the influence of others are available to autonomous individuals, then respecting their choices, including their decisions to subject themselves to the influence of others in exchange for releasing some funds so they are available for other pursuits, respects their autonomy.

Actual competition, however, will not eliminate the autonomy deficit of privately owned communications infrastructure, for familiar reasons. The most familiar constraint on the "market will solve it" hunch is imposed by transaction costs—in particular, information-gathering and negotiation costs. Influence exactions are less easily homogenized than prices expressed in currency. They will therefore be more expensive to eliminate through transactions. Some people value certain kinds of information lobbed at them positively; others negatively. Some people are more immune to suggestion, others less. The content and context of an exaction will have a large effect on its efficacy as a device for affecting the choices of the person subject to its influence, and these could change from communication to communication for the same person, let alone for different individuals. Both users and providers have imperfect information about the users' susceptibility to manipulated information flows; they have imperfect information about the value that each user would place on being free of particular exactions. Obtaining the information necessary to provide a good fit for each consumer's preferences regarding the right influence-to-cash ratio for a given service would be prohibitively expensive. Even if the information were obtained, negotiating the precise cash-to-influence trade-off would be costly. Negotiation also may fail because of strategic behavior. The consumer's ideal outcome is to labor under an exaction that is ineffective. If the consumer can reduce the price by submitting to constraints on communication that would affect an average consumer, but will not change her agenda or subvert her capacity to author her life, she has increased her welfare without compromising her autonomy. The vendor's ideal outcome, however, is that the influence exaction be effective—that it succeed in changing the recipient's preferences or her agenda to fit those of the vendor. The parties, therefore, will hide their true beliefs about whether a particular condition to using proprietary infrastructure is of a type that is likely to be effective at influencing the particular recipient. Under anything less than a hypothetical and practically unattainable perfect market in communications infrastructure services, users of a proprietary infrastructure will face a less-than-perfect menu of influence exactions that they must accept before they can communicate using owned infrastructure.

Adopting a regulatory framework under which all physical means of communication are based on private property rights in the infrastructure will therefore create a cost for users, in terms of autonomy. This cost is the autonomy deficit of exclusive reliance on proprietary models. If ownership of infrastructure is concentrated, or if owners can benefit from exerting political, personal, cultural, or social influence over others who seek access to their infrastructure, they will impose conditions on use of the infrastructure that will satisfy their will to exert influence. If agents other than owners (advertisers, tobacco companies, the U.S. drug czar) value the ability to influence users of the infrastructure, then the influence-exaction component of the price of using the infrastructure will be sold to serve the interests of these third parties. To the extent that these influence exactions are effective, a pure private-property regime for infrastructure allows owners to constrain the autonomy of users. The owners can do this by controlling and manipulating the users' information environment to shape how they perceive their life choices in ways that make them more likely to act in a manner that the owners prefer.

The traditional progressive or social-democratic response to failures of property-based markets has been administrative regulation. In the area of communications, these responses have taken the form of access regulations—ranging from common carriage to more limited right-of-reply, fairness doctrine-type regulations. Perfect access regulation—in particular, common-carrier obligations—like a perfectly competitive market, could in principle alleviate the autonomy deficit of property. Like markets, however, actual regulation that limits the powers that go with property in infrastructure suffers from a number of limitations. First, the institutional details of the common-carriage regime can skew incentives for what types of communications will be available, and with what degree of freedom. If we learned one thing from the history of American communications policy in the twentieth century, it is that regulated entities are adept at shaping their services, pricing, and business models to take advantage of every weakness in the common-carriage regulatory system. They are even more adept at influencing the regulatory process to introduce lucrative weaknesses into the regulatory system. At present, cable broadband has succeeded in achieving a status almost entirely exempt from access requirements that might mitigate its power to control how the platform is used, and broadband over legacy telephone systems is increasingly winning a parallel status of unregulated semi-monopoly. Second, the organization that owns the infrastructure retains the same internal incentives to control content as it would in the absence of common carriage and will do so to the extent that it can sneak by any imperfections in either the carriage regulations or their enforcement. Third, as long as the network is built to run through a central organizational clearinghouse, that center remains a potential point at which regulators can reassert control or delegate to owners the power to prevent unwanted speech by purposefully limiting the scope of the common-carriage requirements.

As a practical matter, then, if all wireless systems are based on property, just like the wired systems are, then wireless will offer some benefits through the introduction of some, albeit imperfect, competition. However, it will not offer the autonomy-enhancing effects that a genuine diversity of constraint can offer. If, on the other hand, policies currently being experimented with in the United States do result in the emergence of a robust, sustainable wireless communications infrastructure, owned and shared by its users and freely available to all under symmetric technical constraints, it will offer a genuinely alternative communications platform. It may be as technically good as the wired platforms for all users and uses, or it may not. Nevertheless, because of its radically distributed capitalization, and its reliance on commons rendered sustainable by equipment-embedded technical protocols, rather than on markets that depend on institutionally created asymmetric power over communications, a commons-based wireless system will offer an infrastructure that operates under genuinely different institutional constraints. Such a system can become an infrastructure of first and last resort for uses that would not fit the constraints of the proprietary market, or for users who find the price-to-influence exaction bundles offered in the market too threatening to their autonomy.

The emerging viability of commons-based strategies for the provisioning of communications, storage, and computation capacity enables us to take a practical, real world look at the autonomy deficit of a purely property-based communications system. As we compare property to commons, we see that property, by design, introduces a series of legal powers that asymmetrically enable owners of infrastructure to exert influence over users of their systems. This asymmetry is necessary for the functioning of markets. Predictably and systematically, however, it allows one group of actors—owners—to act upon another group of actors—consumers—as objects of manipulation. No single idiom in contemporary culture captures this characteristic better than the term "the market in eyeballs," used to describe the market in advertising slots. Commons, on the other hand, do not rely on asymmetric constraints. They eliminate points of asymmetric control over the resources necessary for effective communication, thereby eliminating the legal bases of the objectification of others. These are not spaces of perfect freedom from all constraints. However, the constraints they impose are substantively different from those generated by either the property system or by an administrative regulatory system. Their introduction alongside proprietary networks therefore diversifies the constraints under which individuals operate. By offering alternative transactional frameworks for alternative information flows, these networks substantially and qualitatively increase the freedom of individuals to perceive the world through their own eyes, and to form their own perceptions of what options are open to them and how they might evaluate alternative courses of action.

AUTONOMY, MASS MEDIA, AND NONMARKET INFORMATION PRODUCERS

The autonomy deficit of private communications and information systems is a result of the formal structure of property as an institutional device and the role of communications and information systems as basic requirements in the ability of individuals to formulate purposes and plan actions to fit their lives. The gains flow directly from the institutional characteristics of commons. The emergence of the networked information economy makes one other important contribution to autonomy. It qualitatively diversifies the information available to individuals. Information, knowledge, and culture are now produced by sources that respond to a myriad of motivations, rather than primarily the motivation to sell into mass markets. Production is organized in any one of a myriad of productive organizational forms, rather than solely the for-profit business firm. The supplementation of the profit motive and the business organization by other motivations and organizational forms—ranging from individual play to large-scale peer-production projects—provides not only a discontinuously dramatic increase in the number of available information sources but, more significantly, an increase in available information sources that are qualitatively different from others.

Imagine three storytelling societies: the Reds, the Blues, and the Greens. Each society follows a set of customs as to how they live and how they tell stories. Among the Reds and the Blues, everyone is busy all day, and no one tells stories except in the evening. In the evening, in both of these societies, everyone gathers in a big tent, and there is one designated storyteller who sits in front of the audience and tells stories. It is not that no one is allowed to tell stories elsewhere. However, in these societies, given the time constraints people face, if anyone were to sit down in the shade in the middle of the day and start to tell a story, no one else would stop to listen. Among the Reds, the storyteller is a hereditary position, and he or she alone decides which stories to tell. Among the Blues, the storyteller is elected every night by simple majority vote. Every member of the community is eligible to offer him- or herself as that night's storyteller, and every member is eligible to vote. Among the Greens, people tell stories all day, and everywhere. Everyone tells stories. People stop and listen if they wish, sometimes in small groups of two or three, sometimes in very large groups. Stories in each of these societies play a very important role in understanding and evaluating the world. They are the way people describe the world as they know it. They serve as testing grounds to imagine how the world might be, and as a way to work out what is good and desirable and what is bad and undesirable. The societies are isolated from each other and from any other source of information.

Now consider Ron, Bob, and Gertrude, individual members of the Reds, Blues, and Greens, respectively. Ron's perception of the options open to him and his evaluation of these options are largely controlled by the hereditary storyteller. He can try to contact the storyteller to persuade him to tell different stories, but the storyteller is the figure who determines what stories are told. To the extent that these stories describe the universe of options Ron knows about, the storyteller defines the options Ron has. The storyteller's perception of the range of options largely will determine the size and diversity of the range of options open to Ron. This not only limits the range of known options significantly, but it also prevents Ron from choosing to become a storyteller himself. Ron is subjected to the storyteller's control to the extent that, by selecting which stories to tell and how to tell them, the storyteller can shape Ron's aspirations and actions. In other words, both the freedom to be an active producer and the freedom from the control of another are constrained. Bob's autonomy is constrained not by the storyteller, but by the majority of voters among the Blues. These voters select the storyteller, and the way they choose will affect Bob's access to stories profoundly. If the majority selects only a small group of entertaining, popular, pleasing, or powerful (in some other dimension, like wealth or political power) storytellers, then Bob's perception of the range of options will be only slightly wider than Ron's, if at all. The locus of power to control Bob's sense of what he can and cannot do has shifted. It is not the hereditary storyteller, but rather the majority. Bob can participate in deciding which stories can be told. He can offer himself as a storyteller every night. He cannot, however, decide to become a storyteller independently of the choices of a majority of Blues, nor can he decide for himself what stories he will hear. He is significantly constrained by the preferences of a simple majority. Gertrude is in a very different position. First, she can decide to tell a story whenever she wants to, subject only to whether there is any other Green who wants to listen. She is free to become an active producer except as constrained by the autonomy of other individual Greens. Second, she can select from the stories that any other Green wishes to tell, because she and all those surrounding her can sit in the shade and tell a story. No one person, and no majority, determines for her whether she can or cannot tell a story. No one can unilaterally control whose stories Gertrude can listen to. And no one can determine for her the range and diversity of stories that will be available to her from any other member of the Greens who wishes to tell a story.

The difference between the Reds, on the one hand, and the Blues or Greens, on the other hand, is formal. Among the Reds, only the storyteller may tell the story as a matter of formal right, and listeners only have a choice of whether to listen to this story or to no story at all. Among the

Blues and the Greens anyone may tell a story as a matter of formal right, and listeners, as a matter of formal right, may choose from whom they will hear. The difference between the Reds and the Blues, on the one hand, and the Greens, on the other hand, is economic. In the former, opportunities for storytelling are scarce. The social cost is higher, in terms of stories unavailable for hearing, or of choosing one storyteller over another. The difference between the Blues and the Greens, then, is not formal, but practical. The high cost of communication created by the Blues' custom of listening to stories only in the evening, in a big tent, together with everyone else, makes it practically necessary to select "a storyteller" who occupies an evening. Since the stories play a substantive role in individuals' perceptions of how they might live their lives, that practical difference alters the capacity of individual Blues and Greens to perceive a wide and diverse set of options, as well as to exercise control over their perceptions and evaluations of options open for living their lives and to exercise the freedom themselves to be storytellers. The range of stories Bob is likely to listen to, and the degree to which he can choose unilaterally whether he will tell or listen, and to which story, are closer, as a practical matter, to those of Ron than to those of Gertrude. Gertrude has many more stories and storytelling settings to choose from, and many more instances where she can offer her own stories to others in her society. She, and everyone else in her society, can be exposed to a wider variety of conceptions of how life can and ought to be lived. This wider diversity of perceptions gives her greater choice and increases her ability to compose her own life story out of the more varied materials at her disposal. She can be more self-authored than either Ron or Bob. This diversity replicates, in large measure, the range of perceptions of how one might live a life that can be found among all Greens, precisely because the storytelling customs make every Green a potential storyteller, a potential source of information and inspiration about how one might live one's life.

All this could sound like a morality tale about how wonderfully the market maximizes autonomy. The Greens easily could sound like Greenbacks, rather than like environmentalists staking out public parks as information commons. However, this is not the case in the industrial information economy, where media markets have high entry barriers and large economies of scale. It is costly to start up a television station, not to speak of a network, a newspaper, a cable company, or a movie distribution system. It is costly to produce the kind of content delivered over these systems. Once production costs or the costs of laying a network are incurred, the additional marginal cost of making information available to many users, or of adding users to the network, is much smaller than the initial cost. This is what gives information and cultural products and communications facilities supply-side economies of scale and underlies the industrial model of producing them. The result is that the industrial information economy is better stylized by the Reds and Blues rather than by the Greens. While there is no formal limitation on anyone producing and disseminating information products, the economic realities limit the opportunities for storytelling in the mass-mediated environment and make storytelling opportunities a scarce good. It is very costly to tell stories in the mass-mediated environment. Therefore, most storytellers are commercial entities that seek to sell their stories to the audience. Given the discussion earlier in this chapter, it is fairly straightforward to see how the Greens represent greater freedom to choose to become an active producer of one's own information environment. It is similarly clear that they make it exceedingly difficult for any single actor to control the information flow to any other actor. We can now focus on how the story provides a way of understanding the justification and contours of the third focus of autonomy-respecting policy: the requirement that government not limit the quantity and diversity of information available.

The fact that our mass-mediated environment is mostly commercial makes it more like the Blues than the Reds. These outlets serve the tastes of the majority—expressed in some combination of cash payment and attention to advertising. I do not offer here a full analysis—covered so well by Baker in *Media, Markets, and Democracy*—as to why mass-media markets do not reflect the preferences of their audiences very well. Presented here is a tweak of an older set of analyses of whether monopoly or competition is better in mass-media markets to illustrate the relationship between markets, channels, and diversity of content. In chapter 6, I describe in greater detail the Steiner-Beebe model of diversity and number of channels. For our purposes here, it is enough to note that this model shows how advertiser-supported media tend to program lowest-common-denominator programs, intended to "capture the eyeballs" of the largest possible number of viewers. These media do not seek to identify what viewers intensely want to watch, but tend to clear programs that are tolerable enough to viewers so that they do not switch off their television. The presence or absence of smaller-segment oriented television depends on the shape of demand in an audience, the number of channels available to serve that audience, and the ownership structure. The relationship between diversity of content and diversity of structure or ownership is not smooth. It occurs in leaps. Small increases in the number of outlets continue to serve large clusters of low-intensity preferences—that is, what people find acceptable. A new channel that is added will more often try to take a bite out of a large pie represented by some lowest-common-denominator audience segment than to try to serve a new niche market. Only after a relatively high threshold number of outlets are reached do advertiser-supported media have sufficient reason to try to capture much smaller and higher-intensity preference clusters—what people are really interested in. The upshot is that if all storytellers in society are profit maximizing and operate in a market, the number of storytellers and venues matters tremendously for the diversity of stories told in a society. It is quite possible to have very active market competition in how well the same narrow set of stories are told, as opposed to what stories are told, even though there are many people who would rather hear different stories altogether, but who are in clusters too small, too poor, or too uncoordinated to persuade the storytellers to change their stories rather than their props.

The networked information economy is departing from the industrial information economy along two dimensions that suggest a radical increase in the number of storytellers and the qualitative diversity of stories told. At the simplest level, the cost of a channel is so low that some publication capacity is becoming available to practically every person in society. Ranging from an e-mail account, to a few megabytes of hosting capacity to host a subscriber's Web site, to space on a peer-to-peer distribution network available for any kind of file (like FreeNet or eDonkey), individuals are now increasingly in possession of the basic means necessary to have an outlet for their stories. The number of channels is therefore in the process of jumping from some infinitesimally small fraction of the population—whether this fraction is three networks or five hundred channels almost does not matter by comparison—to a number of channels roughly equal to the number of users. This dramatic increase in the number of channels is matched by the fact that the low costs of communications and production enable anyone who wishes to tell a story to do so, whether or not the story they tell will predictably capture enough of a paying (or advertising-susceptible) audience to recoup production costs. Self-expression, religious fervor, hobby, community seeking, political mobilization, any one of the many and diverse reasons that might drive us to want to speak to others is now a sufficient reason to enable us to do so in mediated form to people both distant and close. The basic filter of marketability has been removed, allowing anything that emerges out of the great diversity of human experience, interest, taste, and expressive motivation to flow to and from everyone connected to everyone else. Given that all diversity within the industrial information economy needed to flow through the marketability filter, the removal of that filter marks a qualitative increase in the range and diversity of life options, opinions, tastes, and possible life plans available to users of the networked information economy.

The image of everyone being equally able to tell stories brings, perhaps more crisply than any other image, two critical objections to the attractiveness of the networked information economy: quality and cacophony. The problem of quality is easily grasped, but is less directly connected to autonomy. Having many high school plays and pickup basketball games is not the same as having Hollywood movies or the National Basketball Association (NBA). The problem of quality understood in these terms, to the extent that the shift from industrial to networked information production in fact causes it, does not represent a threat to autonomy as much as a welfare cost of making the autonomy-enhancing change. More troubling from the perspective of autonomy is the problem of information overload, which is related to, but distinct from, production quality. The cornucopia of stories out of which each of us can author our own will only enhance autonomy if it does not resolve into a cacophony of meaningless noise. How, one might worry, can a system of information production enhance the ability of an individual to author his or her life, if it is impossible to tell whether this or that particular story or piece of information is credible, or whether it is relevant to the individual's particular experience? Will individuals spend all their time sifting through mounds of inane stories and fairy tales, instead of evaluating which life is best for them based on a small and manageable set of credible and relevant stories? None of the philosophical accounts of substantive autonomy suggests that there is a linearly increasing relationship between the number of options open to an individual—or in this case, perceivable by an individual—and that person's autonomy. Information overload and decision costs can get in the way of actually living one's autonomously selected life.

The quality problem is often raised in public discussions of the Internet, and takes the form of a question: Where will high-quality information products, like movies, come from? This form of the objection, while common, is underspecified normatively and overstated descriptively. First, it is not at all clear what might be meant by "quality," insofar as it is a characteristic of information, knowledge, and cultural production that is negatively affected by the shift from an industrial to a networked information economy. Chapter 2 explains that information has always been produced in various modalities, not only in market-oriented organizations and certainly not in proprietary strategies. Political theory is not "better" along any interesting dimension when written by someone aiming to maximize her own or her publisher's commercial profits. Most of the commercial, proprietary online encyclopedias are not better than *Wikipedia* along any clearly observable dimension. Moreover, many information and cultural goods are produced on a relational model, rather than a packaged-goods model. The emergence of the digitally networked environment does not much change their economics or sustainability. Professional theatre that depends on live performances is an example, as are musical performances. To the extent, therefore, that the emergence of substantial scope for nonmarket, distributed production in a networked information economy places pressure on "quality," it is quality of a certain kind. The threatened desiderata are those that are uniquely attractive about industrially produced mass-market products. The high-production-cost Hollywood movie or television series are the threatened species. Even that species is not entirely endangered, and the threat varies for different industries, as explained in some detail in chapter 11. Some movies, particularly those currently made for video release only, may well, in fact, recede. However, truly high-production-value movies will continue to have a business model through release windows other than home video distribution. Independently, the pressure on advertising-supported television from multichannel video— cable and satellite—on the other hand, is pushing for more low-cost productions like reality TV. That internal development in mass media, rather than the networked information economy, is already pushing industrial producers toward low-cost, low-quality productions. Moreover, as a large section of chapter 7 illustrates, peer production and nonmarket production are producing desirable public information—news and commentary—that offer qualities central to democratic discourse. Chapter 8 discusses how these two forms of production provide a more transparent and plastic cultural environment—both central to the individual's capacity for defining his or her goals and options. What emerges in the networked information environment, therefore, will not be a system for low-quality amateur mimicry of existing commercial products. What will emerge is space for much more expression, from diverse sources and of diverse qualities. Freedom—the freedom to speak, but also to be free from manipulation and to be cognizant of many and diverse options—inheres in this radically greater diversity of information, knowledge, and culture through which to understand the world and imagine how one could be.

Rejecting the notion that there will be an appreciable loss of quality in some absolute sense does not solve the deeper problem of information overload, or having too much information to be able to focus or act upon it. Having too much information with no real way of separating the wheat from the chaff forms what we might call the Babel objection. Individuals must have access to some mechanism that sifts through the universe of information, knowledge, and cultural moves in order to whittle them down to a manageable and usable scope. The question then becomes whether the networked information economy, given the human need for filtration, actually improves the information environment of individuals relative to the industrial information economy. There are three elements to the answer: First, as a baseline, it is important to recognize the power that inheres in the editorial function. The extent to which information overload inhibits autonomy relative to the autonomy of an individual exposed to a well-edited information flow depends on how much the editor who whittles down the information flow thereby gains power over the life of the user of the editorial function, and how he or she uses that power. Second, there is the question of whether users can select and change their editor freely, or whether the editorial function is bundled with other communicative functions and sold by service providers among which users have little choice. Finally, there is the understanding that filtration and accreditation are themselves information goods, like any other, and that they too can be produced on a commons-based, nonmarket model, and therefore without incurring the autonomy deficit that a reintroduction of property to solve the Babel objection would impose.

Relevance filtration and accreditation are integral parts of all communications. A communication must be relevant for a given sender to send to a given recipient and relevant for the recipient to receive. Accreditation further filters relevant information for credibility. Decisions of filtration for purposes of relevance and accreditation are made with reference to the values of the person filtering the information, not the values of the person receiving the information. For instance, the editor of a cable network newsmagazine decides whether a given story is relevant to send out. The owner of the cable system decides whether it is, in the aggregate, relevant to its viewers to see that newsmagazine on its system. Only if both so decide, does each viewer get the residual choice of whether to view the story. Of the three decisions that must coincide to mark the newsmagazine as relevant to the viewer, only one is under the control of the individual recipient. And, while the editor's choice might be perceived in some sense as inherent to the production of the information, the cable operator's choice is purely a function of its role as proprietor of the infrastructure. The point to focus on is that the recipient's judgment is dependent on the cable operator's decision as to whether to release the program. The primary benefit of proprietary systems as mechanisms of avoiding the problem of information overload or the Babel objection is precisely the fact that the individual cannot exercise his own judgment as to all the programs that the cable operator—or other commercial intermediary between someone who makes a statement and someone who might receive it—has decided not to release.

As with any flow, control over a necessary passageway or bottleneck in the course of a communication gives the person controlling that point the power to direct the entire flow downstream from it. This power enables the provision of a valuable filtration service, which promises the recipient that he or she will not spend hours gazing at irrelevant materials. However, filtration only enhances the autonomy of users if the editor's notions of relevance and quality resemble those of the sender and the recipient. Imagine a recipient who really wants to be educated about African politics, but also likes sports. Under perfect conditions, he would seek out information on African politics most of the time, with occasional searches for information on sports. The editor, however, makes her money by selling advertising. For her, the relevant information is whatever will keep the viewer's attention most closely on the screen while maintaining a pleasantly acquisitive mood. Given a choice between transmitting information about famine in Sudan, which she worries will make viewers feel charitable rather than acquisitive, and transmitting a football game that has no similar adverse effects, she will prefer the latter. The general point should be obvious. For purposes of enhancing the autonomy of the user, the filtering and accreditation function suffers from an agency problem. To the extent that the values of the editor diverge from those of the user, an editor who selects relevant information based on her values and plans for the users does not facilitate user autonomy, but rather imposes her own preferences regarding what should be relevant to users given her decisions about their life choices. A parallel effect occurs with accreditation. An editor might choose to treat as credible a person whose views or manner of presentation draw audiences, rather than necessarily the wisest or best-informed of commentators. The wide range in quality of talking heads on television should suffice as an example. The Babel objection may give us good reason to pause before we celebrate the networked information economy, but it does not provide us with reasons to celebrate the autonomy effects of the industrial information economy.

The second component of the response to the Babel objection has to do with the organization of filtration and accreditation in the industrial information economy. The cable operator owns its cable system by virtue of capital investment and (perhaps) expertise in laying cables, hooking up homes, and selling video services. However, it is control over the pipeline into the home that gives it the editorial role in the materials that reach the home. Given the concentrated economics of cable systems, this editorial power is not easy to replace and is not subject to open competition. The same phenomenon occurs with other media that are concentrated and where the information production and distribution functions are integrated with relevance filtration and accreditation: from one-newspaper towns to broadcasters or cable broadband service providers. An edited environment that frees the individual to think about and choose from a small selection of information inputs becomes less attractive when the editor takes on that role as a result of the ownership of carriage media, a large printing press, or copyrights in existing content, rather than as a result of selection by the user as a preferred editor or filter. The existence of an editor means that there is less information for an individual to process. It does not mean that the values according to which the information was pared down are those that the user would have chosen absent the tied relationship between editing and either proprietary content production or carriage.

Finally, and most important, just like any other form of information, knowledge, and culture, relevance and accreditation can be, and are, produced in a distributed fashion. Instead of relying on the judgment of a record label and a DJ of a commercial radio station for what music is worth listening to, users can compare notes as to what they like, and give music to friends whom they think will like it. This is the virtue of music file-sharing systems as distribution systems. Moreover, some of the most interesting experiments in peer production described in chapter 3 are focused on filtration. From the discussions of *Wikipedia* to the moderation and metamoderation scheme of Slashdot, and from the sixty thousand volunteers that make up the Open Directory Project to the PageRank system used by Google, the means of filtering data are being produced within the networked information economy using peer production and the coordinate patterns of nonproprietary production more generally. The presence of these filters provides the most important answer to the Babel objection. The presence of filters that do not depend on proprietary control, and that do not bundle proprietary content production and carriage services with filtering, offers a genuinely distinct approach toward presenting autonomous individuals with a choice among different filters that reflect genuinely diverse motivations and organizational forms of the providers.

Beyond the specific efforts at commons-based accreditation and relevance filtration, we are beginning to observe empirically that patterns of use of the Internet and the World Wide Web exhibit a significant degree of order. In chapter 7, I describe in detail and apply the literature that has explored network topology to the Babel objection in the context of democracy and the emerging networked public sphere, but its basic lesson applies here as well. In brief, the structure of linking on the Internet suggests that, even without quasi-formal collaborative filtering, the coordinate behavior of many autonomous individuals settles on an order that permits us to make sense of the tremendous flow of information that results from universal practical ability to speak and create. We observe the Web developing an order—with high-visibility nodes, and clusters of thickly connected "regions" where groups of Web sites accredit each other by mutual referencing. The high-visibility Web sites provide points of condensation for informing individual choices, every bit as much as they form points of condensation for public discourse. The enormous diversity of topical and context-dependent clustering, whose content is nonetheless available for anyone to reach from anywhere, provides both a way of slicing through the information and rendering it comprehensible, and a way of searching for new sources of information beyond those that one interacts with as a matter of course. The Babel objection is partly solved, then, by the fact that people tend to congregate around common choices. We do this not as a result of purposeful manipulation, but rather because in choosing whether or not to read something, we probably give some weight to whether or not other people have chosen to read it. Unless one assumes that individual human beings are entirely dissimilar from each other, then the fact that many others have chosen to read something is a reasonable signal that it may be worthwhile for me to read. This phenomenon is both universal—as we see with the fact that Google successfully provides useful ranking by aggregating all judgments around the Web as to the relevance of any given Web site—and recursively present within interest-based and context-based clusters or groups. The clustering and actual degree distribution in the Web suggests, however, that people do not simply follow the herd—they will not read whatever a majority reads. Rather, they will make additional rough judgments about which other people's preferences are most likely to predict their own, or which topics to look in. From these very simple rules—other people share something with me in their tastes, and some sets of other people share more with me than others—we see the Babel objection solved on a distributed model, without anyone exerting formal legal control or practical economic power.

Why, however, is this not a simple reintroduction of heteronomy, of dependence on the judgment of others that subjects individuals to their control? The answer is that, unlike with proprietary filters imposed at bottlenecks or gateways, attention-distribution patterns emerge from many small-scale, independent choices where free choice exists. They are not easily manipulable by anyone. Significantly, the millions of Web sites that do not have high traffic do not "go out of business." As Clay Shirky puts it, while my thoughts about the weekend are unlikely to be interesting to three random users, they may well be interesting, and a basis for conversation, for three of my close friends. The fact that power law distributions of attention to Web sites result from random distributions of interests, not from formal or practical bottlenecks that cannot be worked around, means that whenever an individual chooses to search based on some mechanism other than the simplest, thinnest belief that individuals are all equally similar and dissimilar, a different type of site will emerge as highly visible. Topical sites cluster, unsurprisingly, around topical preference groups; one site does not account for all readers irrespective of their interests. We, as individuals, also go through an iterative process of assigning a likely relevance to the judgments of others. Through this process, we limit the information overload that would threaten to swamp our capacity to know; we diversify the sources of information to which we expose ourselves; and we avoid a stifling dependence on an editor whose judgments we cannot circumvent. We might spend some of our time using the most general, "human interest has some overlap" algorithm represented by Google for some things, but use political common interest, geographic or local interest, hobbyist, subject matter, or the like, to slice the universe of potential others with whose judgments we will choose to affiliate for any given search. By a combination of random searching and purposeful deployment of social mapping—who is likely to be interested in what is relevant to me now—we can solve the Babel objection while subjecting ourselves neither to the legal and market power of proprietors of communications infrastructure or media products nor to the simple judgments of the undifferentiated herd. These observations have the virtue of being not only based on rigorous mathematical and empirical studies, as we see in chapter 7, but also being more consistent with intuitive experience of anyone who has used the Internet for any decent length of time. We do not degenerate into mindless meandering through a cacophonous din. We find things we want quite well. We stumble across things others suggest to us. When we do go on an unplanned walk, within a very short number of steps we either find something interesting or go back to looking in ways that are more self-conscious and ordered.

The core response to the Babel objection is, then, to accept that filtration is crucial to an autonomous individual. Nonetheless, that acknowledgement does not suggest that the filtration and accreditation systems that the industrial information economy has in fact produced, tied to proprietary control over content production and exchange, are the best means to protect autonomous individuals from the threat of paralysis due to information overload. Property in infrastructure and content affords control that can be used to provide filtration. To that extent, property provides the power for some people to shape the will-formation processes of others. The adoption of distributed information-production systems—both structured as cooperative peer-production enterprises and unstructured coordinate results of individual behavior, like the clustering of preferences around Web sites—does not mean that filtration and accreditation lose their importance. It only means that autonomy is better served when these communicative functions, like others, are available from a nonproprietary, open model of production alongside the proprietary mechanisms of filtration. Being autonomous in this context does not mean that we have to make all the information, read it all, and sift through it all by ourselves. It means that the combination of institutional and practical constraints on who can produce information, who can access it, and who can determine what is worth reading leaves each individual with a substantial role in determining what he shall read, and whose judgment he shall adhere to in sifting through the information environment, for what purposes, and under what circumstances. As always in the case of autonomy for context-bound individuals, the question is the relative role that individuals play, not some absolute, context-independent role that could be defined as being the condition of freedom.

The increasing feasibility of nonmarket, nonproprietary production of in-

formation, knowledge, and culture, and of communications and computation capacity holds the promise of increasing the degree of autonomy for
individuals in the networked information economy. By removing basic capital and organizational constraints on individual action and effective cooperation, the networked information economy allows individuals to do more
for and by themselves, and to form associations with others whose help they
require in pursuing their plans. We are beginning to see a shift from the
highly constrained roles of employee and consumer in the industrial economy, to more flexible, self-authored roles of user and peer participant in
cooperative ventures, at least for some part of life. By providing as commons
a set of core resources necessary for perceiving the state of the world, constructing one's own perceptions of it and one's own contributions to the
information environment we all occupy, the networked information economy diversifies the set of constraints under which individuals can view the
world and attenuates the extent to which users are subject to manipulation
and control by the owners of core communications and information systems
they rely on. By making it possible for many more diversely motivated and
organized individuals and groups to communicate with each other, the
emerging model of information production provides individuals with radically different sources and types of stories, out of which we can work to
author our own lives. Information, knowledge, and culture can now be
produced not only by many more people than could do so in the industrial
information economy, but also by individuals and in subjects and styles that
could not pass the filter of marketability in the mass-media environment.
The result is a proliferation of strands of stories and of means of scanning
the universe of potential stories about how the world is and how it might
become, leaving individuals with much greater leeway to choose, and
therefore a much greater role in weaving their own life tapestry.

Chapter 6 Political Freedom Part 1:
The Trouble with Mass Media

Modern democracies and mass media have coevolved throughout the twentieth century. The first modern national republics—the early American Republic, the French Republic from the Revolution to the Terror, the Dutch Republic, and the early British parliamentary monarchy—preexisted mass media. They provide us with some model of the shape of the public sphere in a republic without mass media, what Jurgen Habermas called the bourgeois public sphere. However, the expansion of democracies in complex modern societies has largely been a phenomenon of the late nineteenth and twentieth centuries—in particular, the post–World War II years. During this period, the platform of the public sphere was dominated by mass media—print, radio, and television. In authoritarian regimes, these means of mass communication were controlled by the state. In democracies, they operated either under state ownership, with varying degrees of independence from the sitting government, or under private ownership financially dependent on advertising markets. We do not, therefore, have examples of complex modern democracies whose public sphere is built on a platform that is widely

distributed and independent of both government control and market demands. The Internet as a technology, and the networked information economy as an organizational and social model of information and cultural production, promise the emergence of a substantial alternative platform for the
public sphere. The networked public sphere, as it is currently developing,
suggests that it will have no obvious points of control or exertion of influence—either by fiat or by purchase. It seems to invert the mass-media model
in that it is driven heavily by what dense clusters of users find intensely
interesting and engaging, rather than by what large swathes of them find
mildly interesting on average. And it promises to offer a platform for engaged
citizens to cooperate and provide observations and opinions, and to serve as
a watchdog over society on a peer-production model.

The claim that the Internet democratizes is hardly new. "Everyone a pamphleteer" has been an iconic claim about the Net since the early 1990s. It is
a claim that has been subjected to significant critique. What I offer, therefore,
in this chapter and the next is not a restatement of the basic case, but a
detailed analysis of how the Internet and the emerging networked information economy provide us with distinct improvements in the structure of
the public sphere over the mass media. I will also explain and discuss the
solutions that have emerged within the networked environment itself to
some of the persistent concerns raised about democracy and the Internet:
the problems of information overload, fragmentation of discourse, and the
erosion of the watchdog function of the media.

For purposes of considering political freedom, I adopt a very limited definition of "public sphere." The term is used in reference to the set of practices that members of a society use to communicate about matters they
understand to be of public concern and that potentially require collective
action or recognition. Moreover, not even all communications about matters
of potential public concern can be said to be part of the public sphere.
Communications within self-contained relationships whose boundaries are
defined independently of the political processes for collective action are "private," if those communications remain purely internal. Dinner-table conversations, grumblings at a bridge club, or private letters have that characteristic, if they occur in a context where they are not later transmitted across
the associational boundaries to others who are not part of the family or the
bridge club. Whether these conversations are, or are not, part of the public
sphere depends on the actual communications practices in a given society.
The same practices can become an initial step in generating public opinion

in the public sphere if they are nodes in a network of communications that do cross associational boundaries. A society with a repressive regime that controls the society-wide communications facilities nonetheless may have an active public sphere if social networks and individual mobility are sufficient to allow opinions expressed within discrete associational settings to spread throughout a substantial portion of the society and to take on political meaning for those who discuss them. The public sphere is, then, a sociologically descriptive category. It is a term for signifying how, if at all, people in a given society speak to each other in their relationship as constituents about what their condition is and what they ought or ought not to do as a political unit. This is a purposefully narrow conception of the public sphere. It is intended to focus on the effects of the networked environment on what has traditionally been understood to be political participation in a republic. I postpone consideration of a broader conception of the public sphere, and of the political nature of who gets to decide meaning and how cultural interpretations of the conditions of life and the alternatives open to a society are created and negotiated in a society until chapter 8.

The practices that define the public sphere are structured by an interaction of culture, organization, institutions, economics, and technical communications infrastructure. The technical platforms of ink and rag paper, handpresses, and the idea of a postal service were equally present in the early American Republic, Britain, and France of the late eighteenth and early nineteenth centuries. However, the degree of literacy, the social practices of newspaper reading, the relative social egalitarianism as opposed to elitism, the practices of political suppression or subsidy, and the extent of the postal system led to a more egalitarian, open public sphere, shaped as a network of smaller-scale local clusters in the United States, as opposed to the more tightly regulated and elitist national and metropolis-centered public spheres of France and Britain. The technical platforms of mass-circulation print and radio were equally available in the Soviet Union and Nazi Germany, in Britain, and in the United States in the 1930s. Again, however, the vastly different political and legal structures of the former created an authoritarian public sphere, while the latter two, both liberal public spheres, differed significantly in the business organization and economic model of production, the legal framework and the cultural practices of reading and listening— leading to the then still elitist overlay on the public sphere in Britain relative to a more populist public sphere in the United States.

Mass media structured the public sphere of the twentieth century in all advanced modern societies. They combined a particular technical architecture, a particular economic cost structure, a limited range of organizational forms, two or three primary institutional models, and a set of cultural practices typified by consumption of finished media goods. The structure of the mass media resulted in a relatively controlled public sphere—although the degree of control was vastly different depending on whether the institutional model was liberal or authoritarian—with influence over the debate in the public sphere heavily tilted toward those who controlled the means of mass communications. The technical architecture was a one-way, hub-and-spoke structure, with unidirectional links to its ends, running from the center to the periphery. A very small number of production facilities produced large amounts of identical copies of statements or communications, which could then be efficiently sent in identical form to very large numbers of recipients. There was no return loop to send observations or opinions back from the edges to the core of the architecture in the same channel and with similar salience to the communications process, and no means within the mass-media architecture for communication among the end points about the content of the exchanges. Communications among the individuals at the ends were shunted to other media—personal communications or telephones—which allowed communications among the ends. However, these edge media were either local or one-to-one. Their social reach, and hence potential political efficacy, was many orders of magnitude smaller than that of the mass media.

The economic structure was typified by high-cost hubs and cheap, ubiquitous, reception-only systems at the ends. This led to a limited range of organizational models available for production: those that could collect sufficient funds to set up a hub. These included: state-owned hubs in most countries; advertising-supported commercial hubs in some of the liberal states, most distinctly in the United States; and, particularly for radio and television, the British Broadcasting Corporation (BBC) model or hybrid models like the Canadian Broadcasting Corporation (CBC) in Canada. The role of hybrid and purely commercial, advertising-supported media increased substantially around the globe outside the United States in the last two to three decades of the twentieth century. Over the course of the century, there also emerged civil-society or philanthropy-supported hubs, like the party presses in Europe, nonprofit publications like *Consumer Reports* (later, in the United States), and, more important, public radio and television. The one-way technical architecture and the mass-audience organizational model underwrote the development of a relatively passive cultural model of media consumption. Consumers (or subjects, in authoritarian systems) at the ends of these systems would treat the communications that filled the public sphere as finished goods. These were to be treated not as moves in a conversation, but as completed statements whose addressees were understood to be passive: readers, listeners, and viewers.

The Internet's effect on the public sphere is different in different societies, depending on what salient structuring components of the existing public sphere its introduction perturbs. In authoritarian countries, it is the absence of a single or manageably small set of points of control that is placing the greatest pressure on the capacity of the regimes to control their public sphere, and thereby to simplify the problem of controlling the actions of the population. In liberal countries, the effect of the Internet operates through its implications for economic cost and organizational form. In both cases, however, the most fundamental and potentially long-standing effect that Internet communications are having is on the cultural practice of public communication. The Internet allows individuals to abandon the idea of the public sphere as primarily constructed of finished statements uttered by a small set of actors socially understood to be "the media" (whether state owned or commercial) and separated from society, and to move toward a set of social practices that see individuals as participating in a debate. Statements in the public sphere can now be seen as invitations for a conversation, not as finished goods. Individuals can work their way through their lives, collecting observations and forming opinions that they understand to be practically capable of becoming moves in a broader public conversation, rather than merely the grist for private musings.

DESIGN CHARACTERISTICS OF A
COMMUNICATIONS PLATFORM FOR A
LIBERAL PUBLIC PLATFORM OR A LIBERAL
PUBLIC SPHERE

How is private opinion about matters of collective, formal, public action formed? How is private opinion communicated to others in a form and in channels that allow it to be converted into a public, political opinion, and a position worthy of political concern by the formal structures of governance of a society? How, ultimately, is such a political and public opinion converted into formal state action? These questions are central to understanding how individuals in complex contemporary societies, located at great distances from each other and possessing completely different endowments of material, intellectual, social, and formal ties and capabilities, can be citizens of the same democratic polity rather than merely subjects of a more or less responsive authority. In the idealized Athenian agora or New England town hall, the answers are simple and local. All citizens meet in the agora, they speak in a way that all relevant citizens can hear, they argue with each other, and ultimately they also constitute the body that votes and converts the opinion that emerges into a legitimate action of political authority. Of course, even in those small, locally bounded polities, things were never quite so simple. Nevertheless, the idealized version does at least give us a set of functional characteristics that we might seek in a public sphere: a place where people can come to express and listen to proposals for agenda items—things that ought to concern us as members of a polity and that have the potential to become objects of collective action; a place where we can make and gather statements of fact about the state of our world and about alternative courses of action; where we can listen to opinions about the relative quality and merits of those facts and alternative courses of action; and a place where we can bring our own concerns to the fore and have them evaluated by others.

Understood in this way, the public sphere describes a social communication process. Habermas defines the public sphere as "a network for communicating information and points of view (i.e., opinions expressing affirmative or negative attitudes)"; which, in the process of communicating this information and these points of view, filters and synthesizes them "in such a way that they coalesce into bundles of topically specified public opinions."[1] Taken in this descriptive sense, the public sphere does not relate to a particular form of public discourse that is normatively attractive from some perspective or another. It defines a particular set of social practices that are necessary for the functioning of any complex social system that includes elements of governing human beings. There are authoritarian public spheres, where communications are regimented and controlled by the government in order to achieve acquiescence and to mobilize support, rather than relying solely on force to suppress dissent and opposition. There are various forms of liberal public spheres, constituted by differences in the political and communications systems scattered around liberal democracies throughout the world. The BBC or the state-owned televisions throughout postwar Western European democracies, for example, constituted the public spheres in different ways than did the commercial mass media that dominated the American public sphere. As advertiser-supported mass media have come to occupy a larger role even in places where they were not dominant before the last quarter of the twentieth century, the long American experience with this form provides useful insight globally.

In order to consider the relative advantages and failures of various platforms for a public sphere, we need to define a minimal set of desiderata that such a platform must possess. My point is not to define an ideal set of constraints and affordances of the public sphere that would secure legitimacy or would be most attractive under one conception of democracy or another. Rather, my intention is to define a design question: What characteristics of a communications system and practices are sufficiently basic to be desired by a wide range of conceptions of democracy? With these in hand, we will be able to compare the commercial mass media and the emerging alternatives in the digitally networked environment.

Universal Intake.   Any system of government committed to the idea that, in principle, the concerns of all those governed by that system are equally respected as potential proper subjects for political action and that all those governed have a say in what government should do requires a public sphere that can capture the observations of all constituents. These include at least their observations about the state of the world as they perceive and understand it, and their opinions of the relative desirability of alternative courses of action with regard to their perceptions or those of others. It is important not to confuse "universal intake" with more comprehensive ideas, such as that every voice must be heard in actual political debates, or that all concerns deserve debate and answer. Universal intake does not imply these broader requirements. It is, indeed, the role of filtering and accreditation to whittle down what the universal intake function drags in and make it into a manageable set of political discussion topics and interventions. However, the basic requirement of a public sphere is that it must in principle be susceptible to perceiving and considering the issues of anyone who believes that their condition is a matter appropriate for political consideration and collective action. The extent to which that personal judgment about what the political discourse should be concerned with actually coincides with what the group as a whole will consider in the public sphere is a function of the filtering and accreditation functions.

Filtering for Potential Political Relevance.   Not everything that someone considers to be a proper concern for collective action is perceived as such by most other participants in the political debate. A public sphere that has some successful implementation of universal intake must also have a filter to separate out those matters that are plausibly within the domain of organized political action and those that are not. What constitutes the range of plausible political topics is locally contingent, changes over time, and is itself a contested political question, as was shown most obviously by the "personal is political" feminist intellectual campaign. While it left "my dad won't buy me the candy I want" out of the realm of the political, it insisted on treating "my husband is beating me" as critically relevant in political debate. An overly restrictive filtering system is likely to impoverish a public sphere and rob it of its capacity to develop legitimate public opinion. It tends to exclude views and concerns that are in fact held by a sufficiently large number of people, or to affect people in sufficiently salient ways that they turn out, in historical context, to place pressure on the political system that fails to consider them or provide a legitimate answer, if not a solution. A system that is too loose tends to fail because it does not allow a sufficient narrowing of focus to provide the kind of sustained attention and concentration necessary to consider a matter and develop a range of public opinions on it.

Filtering for Accreditation.   Accreditation is different from relevance, requires different kinds of judgments, and may be performed in different ways than basic relevance filtering. A statement like "the president has sold out space policy to Martians" is different from "my dad won't buy me the candy I want." It is potentially as relevant as "the president has sold out energy policy to oil companies." What makes the former a subject for entertainment, not political debate, is its lack of credibility. Much of the function of journalistic professional norms is to create and preserve the credibility of the professional press as a source of accreditation for the public at large. Parties provide a major vehicle for passing the filters of both relevance and accreditation. Academia gives its members a source of credibility, whose force (ideally) varies with the degree to which their statements come out of, and pertain to, their core roles as creators of knowledge through their disciplinary constraints. Civil servants in reasonably professional systems can provide a source of accreditation. Large corporations have come to play such a role, though with greater ambiguity. The emerging role of nongovernment organizations

(NGOs), very often is intended precisely to preorganize opinion that does not easily pass the relevant public sphere's filters of relevance and accreditation and provide it with a voice that will. Note that accreditation of a move in political discourse is very different from accreditation of a move in, for example, academic discourse, because the objective of each system is different. In academic discourse, the fact that a large number of people hold a particular opinion ("the universe was created in seven days") does not render that opinion credible enough to warrant serious academic discussion. In political discourse, say, about public school curricula, the fact that a large number of people hold the same view and are inclined to have it taught in public schools makes that claim highly relevant and "credible." In other words, it is credible that this could become a political opinion that forms a part of public discourse with the potential to lead to public action.

Filters, both for relevance and accreditation, provide a critical point of control over the debate, and hence are extremely important design elements.

Synthesis of "Public Opinion." The communications system that offers the platform for the public sphere must also enable the synthesis of clusters of individual opinion that are sufficiently close and articulated to form something more than private opinions held by some number of individuals. How this is done is tricky, and what counts as "public opinion" may vary among different theories of democracy. In deliberative conceptions, this might make requirements of the form of discourse. Civic republicans would focus on open deliberation among people who see their role as deliberating about the common good. Habermas would focus on deliberating under conditions that assure the absence of coercion, while Bruce Ackerman would admit to deliberation only arguments formulated so as to be neutral as among conceptions of the good. In pluralist conceptions, like John Rawls's in *Political Liberalism*, which do not seek ultimately to arrive at a common understanding but instead seek to peaceably clear competing positions as to how we ought to act as a polity, this might mean the synthesis of a position that has sufficient overlap among those who hold it that they are willing to sign on to a particular form of statement in order to get the bargaining benefits of scale as an interest group with a coherent position. That position then comes to the polls and the bargaining table as one that must be considered, overpowered, or bargained with. In any event, the platform has to provide some capacity to synthesize the finely disparate and varied versions of beliefs and positions held by actual individuals into articulated positions amenable for consideration and adoption in the formal political sphere and by a system of government, and to render them in ways that make them sufficiently salient in the overall mix of potential opinions to form a condensation point for collective action.

Independence from Government Control. The core role of the political public sphere is to provide a platform for converting privately developed observations, intuitions, and opinions into public opinions that can be brought to bear in the political system toward determining collective action. One core output of these communications is instructions to the administration sitting in government. To the extent that the platform is dependent on that same sitting government, there is a basic tension between the role of debate in the public sphere as issuing instructions to the executive and the interests of the sitting executive to retain its position and its agenda and have it ratified by the public. This does not mean that the communications system must exclude government from communicating its positions, explaining them, and advocating them. However, when it steps into the public sphere, the locus of the formation and crystallization of public opinion, the sitting administration must act as a participant in explicit conversation, and not as a platform controller that can tilt the platform in its direction.

THE EMERGENCE OF THE COMMERCIAL MASS-MEDIA PLATFORM FOR THE PUBLIC SPHERE

Throughout the twentieth century, the mass media have played a fundamental constitutive role in the construction of the public sphere in liberal democracies. Over this period, first in the United States and later throughout the world, the commercial, advertising-supported form of mass media has become dominant in both print and electronic media. Sometimes, these media have played a role that has drawn admiration as "the fourth estate." Here, the media are seen as a critical watchdog over government processes, and as a major platform for translating the mobilization of social movements into salient, and ultimately actionable, political statements. These same media, however, have also drawn mountains of derision for the power they wield, as well as fail to wield, and for the shallowness of public communication they promote in the normal course of the business of selling eyeballs to advertisers. Nowhere was this clearer than in the criticism of the large role that television came to play in American public culture and its public sphere. Contemporary debates bear the imprint of the three major networks, which in the early 1980s still accounted for 92 percent of television viewers and were turned on and watched for hours a day in typical American homes. These inspired works like Neil Postman's *Amusing Ourselves to Death* or Robert Putnam's claim, in *Bowling Alone*, that television seemed to be the primary identifiable discrete cause of the decline of American civic life. Nevertheless, whether positive or negative, variants of the mass-media model of communications have been dominant throughout the twentieth century, in both print and electronic media. The mass-media model has been the dominant model of communications in both democracies and their authoritarian rivals throughout the period when democracy established itself, first against monarchies, and later against communism and fascism. To say that mass media were dominant is not to say that only technical systems of remote communications form the platform of the public sphere. As Theda Skocpol and Putnam have each traced in the context of the American and Italian polities, organizations and associations of personal civic involvement form an important platform for public participation. And yet, as both have recorded, these platforms have been on the decline. So "dominant" does not mean sole, but instead means overridingly important in the structuring of the public sphere. It is this dominance, not the very existence, of mass media that is being challenged by the emergence of the networked public sphere.

The roots of the contemporary industrial structure of mass media presage both the attractive and unattractive aspects of the media we see today. Pioneered by the Dutch printers of the seventeenth century, a commercial press that did not need to rely on government grants and printing contracts, or on the church, became a source of a constant flow of heterodox literature and political debate.[2] However, a commercial press has always also been sensitive to the conditions of the marketplace—costs, audience, and competition. In seventeenth-century England, the Stationers' Monopoly provided its insiders enough market protection from competitors that its members were more than happy to oblige the Crown with a compliant press in exchange for monopoly. It was only after the demise of that monopoly that a genuinely political press appeared in earnest, only to be met by a combination of libel prosecutions, high stamp taxes, and outright bribery and acquisition by government.[3] These, like the more direct censorship and sponsorship relationships that typified the prerevolutionary French press, kept newspapers and gazettes relatively compliant, and their distribution largely limited to elite audiences. Political dissent did not form part of a stable and independent market-based business model. As Paul Starr has shown, the evolution of the British colonies in America was different. While the first century or so of settlement saw few papers, and those mostly "authorized" gazettes, competition began to increase over the course of the eighteenth century. The levels of literacy, particularly in New England, were exceptionally high, the population was relatively prosperous, and the regulatory constraints that applied in England, including the Stamp Tax of 1712, did not apply in the colonies. As second and third newspapers emerged in cities like Boston, Philadelphia, and New York, and were no longer supported by the colonial governments through postal franchises, the public sphere became more contentious. This was now a public sphere whose voices were self-supporting, like Benjamin Franklin's *Pennsylvania Gazette*. The mobilization of much of this press during the revolutionary era, and the broad perception that it played an important role in constituting the American public, allowed the commercial press to continue to play an independent and critical role after the revolution as well, a fate not shared by the brief flowering of the press immediately after the French Revolution. A combination of high literacy and high government tolerance, but also of postal subsidies, led the new United States to have a number and diversity of newspapers unequalled anywhere else, with a higher weekly circulation by 1840 in the 17-million-strong United States than in all of Europe with its population then of 233 million. By 1830, when Tocqueville visited America, he was confronted with a widespread practice of newspaper reading—not only in towns, but in far-flung farms as well, newspapers that were a primary organizing mechanism for political association.[4]

This widespread development of small-circulation, mostly local, competitive commercial press that carried highly political and associational news and opinion came under pressure not from government, but from the economies of scale of the mechanical press, the telegraph, and the ever-expanding political and economic communities brought together by rail and industrialization. Harold Innis argued more than half a century ago that the increasing costs of mechanical presses, coupled with the much-larger circulation they enabled and the availability of a flow of facts from around the world through telegraph, reoriented newspapers toward a mass-circulation, relatively low-denominator advertising medium. These internal economies, as Alfred Chandler and, later, James Beniger showed in their work, intersected with the vast increase in industrial output, which in turn required new mechanisms of demand management—in other words, more sophisticated advertising to generate and channel demand. In the 1830s, the *Sun* and *Herald* were published in New York on large-circulation scales, reducing prices to a penny a copy and shifting content from mostly politics and business news to new forms of reporting: petty crimes from the police courts, human-interest stories, and outright entertainment-value hoaxes.[5] The start-up cost of founding such mass-circulation papers rapidly increased over the second quarter of the nineteenth century, as figure 6.1 illustrates. James Gordon Bennett founded the *Herald* in 1835, with an investment of five hundred dollars, equal to a little more than $10,400 in 2005 dollars. By 1840, the necessary investment was ten to twenty times greater, between five and ten thousand dollars, or $106,000–$212,000 in 2005 terms. By 1850, that amount had again grown tenfold, to $100,000, about $2.38 million in 2005.[6] In the span of fifteen years, the costs of starting a newspaper rose from a number that many could conceive of spending for a wide range of motivations using a mix of organizational forms, to something that required a more or less industrial business model to recoup a very substantial financial investment. The new costs reflected mutually reinforcing increases in organizational cost (because of the professionalization of the newspaper publishing model) and the introduction of high-capacity, higher-cost equipment: electric presses (1839); the Hoe double-cylinder rotary press (1846), which raised output from the five hundred to one thousand sheets per hour of the early steam presses (up from 250 sheets for the handpress) to twelve thousand sheets per hour; and eventually William Bullock's roll-fed rotary press that produced twelve thousand complete newspapers per hour by 1865. The introduction of telegraph and the emergence of news agencies—particularly the Associated Press (AP) in the United States and Reuters in England—completed the basic structure of the commercial printed press. These characteristics—relatively high cost, professional, advertising supported, dependent on access to a comparatively small number of news agencies (which, in the case of the AP, were often used to anticompetitive advantage by their members until the mid-twentieth-century antitrust case)—continued to typify print media. With the introduction of competition from radio and television, these effects tended to lead to greater concentration, with a majority of papers facing no local competition, and an ever-increasing number of papers coming under the joint ownership of a very small number of news publishing houses.

The introduction of radio was the next and only serious potential inflection point, prior to the emergence of the Internet, at which some portion of the public sphere could have developed away from the advertiser-

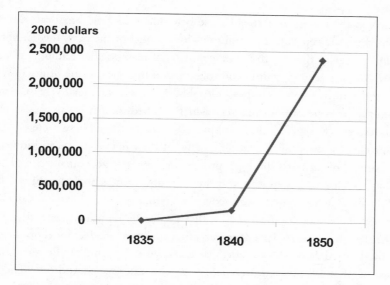

Figure 6.1: Start-up Costs of a Daily Newspaper, 1835–1850 (in 2005 dollars)

supported mass-media model. In most of Europe, radio followed the path of state-controlled media, with variable degrees of freedom from the executive at different times and places. Britain developed the BBC, a public organization funded by government-imposed levies, but granted sufficient operational freedom to offer a genuine platform for a public sphere, as opposed to a reflection of the government's voice and agenda. While this model successfully developed what is perhaps the gold standard of broadcast journalism, it also grew as a largely elite institution throughout much of the twentieth century. The BBC model of state-based funding and monopoly with genuine editorial autonomy became the basis of the broadcast model in a number of former colonies: Canada and Australia adopted a hybrid model in the 1930s. This included a well-funded public broadcaster, but did not impose a monopoly in its favor, allowing commercial broadcasters to grow alongside it. Newly independent former colonies in the postwar era that became democracies, like India and Israel, adopted the model with monopoly, levy-based funding, and a degree of editorial independence. The most currently visible adoption of a hybrid model based on some state funding but with editorial freedom is Al Jazeera, the Arab satellite station partly funded by the Emir of Qatar, but apparently free to pursue its own editorial policy, whose coverage stands in sharp contrast to that of the state-run broadcasters in the region. In none of these BBC-like places did broadcast diverge from the basic centralized communications model of the mass media, but it followed a path distinct from the commercial mass media. Radio, and later television, was a more tightly controlled medium than was the printed press; its intake, filtering, and synthesis of public discourse were relatively insulated from the pressure of both markets, which typified the American model, and politics, which typified the state-owned broadcasters. These were instead controlled by the professional judgments of their management and journalists, and showed both the high professionalism that accompanied freedom along both those dimensions and the class and professional elite filters that typify those who control the media under that organizational model. The United States took a different path that eventually replicated, extended, and enhanced the commercial, advertiser-supported mass-media model originated in the printed press. This model was to become the template for the development of similar broadcasters alongside the state-owned and independent BBC-model channels adopted throughout much of the rest of the world, and of programming production for newer distribution technologies, like cable and satellite stations. The birth of radio as a platform for the public sphere in the United States was on election night in 1920.[7] Two stations broadcast the election returns as their launchpad for an entirely new medium—wireless broadcast to a wide audience. One was the Detroit News amateur station, 8MK, a broadcast that was framed and understood as an internal communication of a technical fraternity—the many amateurs who had been trained in radio communications for World War I and who then came to form a substantial and engaged technical community. The other was KDKA Pittsburgh, launched by Westinghouse as a bid to create demand for radio receivers of a kind that it had geared up to make during the war. Over the following four or five years, it was unclear which of these two models of communication would dominate the new medium. By 1926, however, the industrial structure that would lead radio to follow the path of commercial, advertiser-supported, concentrated mass media, dependent on government licensing and specializing in influencing its own regulatory oversight process was already in place.

Although this development had its roots in the industrial structure of radio production as it emerged from the first two decades of innovation and businesses in the twentieth century, it was shaped significantly by political-regulatory choices during the 1920s. At the turn of the twentieth century, radio was seen exclusively as a means of wireless telegraphy, emphasizing ship-to-shore and ship-to-ship communications. Although some amateurs experimented with voice programs, broadcast was a mode of point-to-point communications; entertainment was not seen as its function until the 1920s. The first decade and a half of radio in the United States saw rapid innovation and competition, followed by a series of patent suits aimed to consolidate control over the technology. By 1916, the ideal transmitter based on technology available at the time required licenses of patents held by Marconi, AT&T, General Electric (GE), and a few individuals. No licenses were in fact granted. The industry had reached stalemate. When the United States joined the war, however, the navy moved quickly to break the stalemate, effectively creating a compulsory cross-licensing scheme for war production, and brought in Westinghouse, the other major potential manufacturer of vacuum tubes alongside GE, as a participant in the industry. The two years following the war saw intervention by the U.S. government to assure that American radio industry would not be controlled by British Marconi because of concerns in the navy that British control over radio would render the United States vulnerable to the same tactic Britain used against Germany at the start of the war—cutting off all transoceanic telegraph communications. The navy brokered a deal in 1919 whereby a new company was created— the Radio Corporation of America (RCA)—which bought Marconi's American business. By early 1920, RCA, GE, and AT&T entered into a patent cross-licensing model that would allow each to produce for a market segment: RCA would control transoceanic wireless telegraphy, while GE and AT&T's Western Electric subsidiary would make radio transmitters and sell them under the RCA brand. This left Westinghouse with production facilities developed for the war, but shut out of the existing equipment markets by the patent pool. Launching KDKA Pittsburgh was part of its response: Westinghouse would create demand for small receivers that it could manufacture without access to the patents held by the pool. The other part of its strategy consisted of acquiring patents that, within a few months, enabled Westinghouse to force its inclusion in the patent pool, redrawing the market division map to give Westinghouse 40 percent of the receiving equipment market. The first part of Westinghouse's strategy, adoption of broadcasting to generate demand for receivers, proved highly successful and in the long run more important. Within two years, there were receivers in 10 percent of American homes. Throughout the 1920s, equipment sales were big business.

Radio stations, however, were not dominated by the equipment manufacturers, or by anyone else for that matter, in the first few years. While the equipment manufacturers did build powerful stations like KDKA Pittsburgh, WJZ Newark, KYW Chicago (Westinghouse), and WGY Schenectady (GE), they did not sell advertising, but rather made their money from equipment sales. These stations did not, in any meaningful sense of the word, dominate the radio sphere in the first few years of radio, as the networks would indeed come to do within a decade. In November 1921, the first five licenses were issued by the Department of Commerce under the new category of "broad-casting" of "news, lectures, entertainment, etc." Within eight months, the department had issued another 453 licenses. Many of these went to univer-sities, churches, and unions, as well as local shops hoping to attract business with their broadcasts. Universities, seeing radio as a vehicle for broadening their role, began broadcasting lectures and educational programming. Seventy-four institutes of higher learning operated stations by the end of 1922. The University of Nebraska offered two-credit courses whose lectures were transmitted over the air. Churches, newspapers, and department stores each forayed into this new space, much as we saw the emergence of Web sites for every organization over the course of the mid-1990s. Thousands of amateurs were experimenting with technical and format innovations. While receivers were substantially cheaper than transmitters, it was still possible to assemble and sell relatively cheap transmitters, for local communications, at prices sufficiently low that thousands of individual amateurs could take to the air. At this point in time, then, it was not yet foreordained that radio would follow the mass-media model, with a small number of well-funded speakers and hordes of passive listeners. Within a short period, however, a combination of technology, business practices, and regulatory decisions did in fact settle on the model, comprised of a small number of advertiser-supported national networks, that came to typify the American broadcast system throughout most of the rest of the century and that became the template for television as well.

Herbert Hoover, then secretary of commerce, played a pivotal role in this development. Throughout the first few years after the war, Hoover had po-sitioned himself as the champion of making control over radio a private market affair, allying himself both with commercial radio interests and with the amateurs against the navy and the postal service, each of which sought some form of nationalization of radio similar to what would happen more or less everywhere else in the world. In 1922, Hoover assembled the first of four annual radio conferences, representing radio manufacturers, broadcast-ers, and some engineers and amateurs. This forum became Hoover's primary stage. Over the next four years, he used its annual meeting to derive policy recommendations, legitimacy, and cooperation for his regulatory action, all without a hint of authority under the Radio Act of 1912. Hoover relied heavily on the rhetoric of public interest and on the support of amateurs to justify his system of private broadcasting coordinated by the Department of Commerce. From 1922 on, however, he followed a pattern that would systematically benefit large commercial broadcasters over small ones; commercial broadcasters over educational and religious broadcasters; and the one-to-many broadcasts over the point-to-point, small-scale wireless telephony and telegraphy that the amateurs were developing. After January 1922, the department inserted a limitation on amateur licenses, excluding from their coverage the broadcast of "weather reports, market reports, music, concerts, speeches, news or similar information or entertainment." This, together with a Department of Commerce order to all amateurs to stop broadcasting at 360 meters (the wave assigned broadcasting), effectively limited amateurs to shortwave radiotelephony and telegraphy in a set of frequencies then thought to be commercially insignificant. In the summer, the department assigned broadcasters, in addition to 360 meters, another band, at 400 meters. Licenses in this Class B category were reserved for transmitters operating at power levels of 500–1,000 watts, who did not use phonograph records. These limitations on Class B licenses made the newly created channel a feasible home only to broadcasters who could afford the much-more-expensive, high-powered transmitters and could arrange for live broadcasts, rather than simply play phonograph records. The success of this new frequency was not immediate, because many receivers could not tune out stations broadcasting at the two frequencies in order to listen to the other. Hoover, failing to move Congress to amend the radio law to provide him with the power necessary to regulate broadcasting, relied on the recommendations of the Second Radio Conference in 1923 as public support for adopting a new regime, and continued to act without legislative authority. He announced that the broadcast band would be divided in three: high-powered (500–1,000 watts) stations serving large areas would have no interference in those large areas, and would not share frequencies. They would transmit on frequencies between 300 and 545 meters. Medium-powered stations served smaller areas without interference, and would operate at assigned channels between 222 and 300 meters. The remaining low-powered stations would not be eliminated, as the bigger actors wanted, but would remain at 360 meters, with limited hours of operation and geographic reach. Many of these lower-powered broadcasters were educational and religious institutions that perceived Hoover's allocation as a preference for the RCA-GE-AT&T-Westinghouse alliance. Despite his protestations against commercial broadcasting ("If a speech by the President is to be used as the meat in a sandwich of two patent medicine advertisements, there will be no radio left"), Hoover consistently reserved clear channels and issued high-power licenses to commercial broadcasters. The final policy action based on the radio conferences came in 1925, when the Department of Commerce stopped issuing licenses. The result was a secondary market in licenses, in which some religious and educational stations were bought out by commercial concerns. These purchases further gravitated radio toward commercial ownership. The licensing preference for stations that could afford high-powered transmitters, long hours of operation, and compliance with high technical constraints continued after the Radio Act of 1927. As a practical matter, it led to assignment of twenty-one out of the twenty-four clear channel licenses created by the Federal Radio Commission to the newly created network-affiliated stations.

Over the course of this period, tensions also began to emerge within the patent alliance. The phenomenal success of receiver sales tempted Western Electric into that market. In the meantime, AT&T, almost by mistake, began to challenge GE, Westinghouse, and RCA in broadcasting as an outgrowth of its attempt to create a broadcast common-carriage facility. Despite the successes of broadcast and receiver sales, it was not clear in 1922–1923 how the cost of setting up and maintaining stations would be paid for. In England, a tax was levied on radio sets, and its revenue used to fund the BBC. No such proposal was considered in the United States, but the editor of *Radio Broadcast* proposed a national endowed fund, like those that support public libraries and museums, and in 1924, a committee of New York businessmen solicited public donations to fund broadcasters (the response was so pitiful that the funds were returned to their donors). AT&T was the only company to offer a solution. Building on its telephone service experience, it offered radio telephony to the public for a fee. Genuine wireless telephony, even mobile telephony, had been the subject of experimentation since the second decade of radio, but that was not what AT&T offered. In February 1922, AT&T established WEAF in New York, a broadcast station over which AT&T was to provide no programming of its own, but instead would enable the public or program providers to pay on a per-time basis. AT&T treated this service as a form of wireless telephony so that it would fall, under the patent alliance agreements of 1920, under the exclusive control of AT&T.

RCA, Westinghouse, and GE could not compete in this area. "Toll broad-casting" was not a success by its own terms. There was insufficient demand for communicating with the public to sustain a full schedule that would justify listeners tuning into the station. As a result, AT&T produced its own programming. In order to increase the potential audience for its transmissions while using its advantage in wired facilities, AT&T experimented with remote transmissions, such as live reports from sports events, and with simultaneous transmissions of its broadcasts by other stations, connected to its New York feed by cable. In its effort to launch toll broadcasting, AT&T found itself by mid-1923 with the first functioning precursor to an advertiser-supported broadcast network.

The alliance members now threatened each other: AT&T threatened to enter into receiver manufacturing and broadcast, and the RCA alliance, with its powerful stations, threatened to adopt "toll broadcasting," or advertiser-supported radio. The patent allies submitted their dispute to an arbitrator, who was to interpret the 1920 agreements, reached at a time of wireless telegraphy, to divide the spoils of the broadcast world of 1924. In late 1924, the arbitrator found for RCA-GE-Westinghouse on almost all issues. Capitalizing on RCA's difficulties with the antitrust authorities and congressional hearings over aggressive monopolization practices in the receiving set market, however, AT&T countered that if the 1920 agreements meant what the arbitrator said they meant, they were a combination in restraint of trade to which AT&T would not adhere. Bargaining in the shadow of the mutual threats of contract and antitrust actions, the former allies reached a solution that formed the basis of future radio broadcasting. AT&T would leave broadcasting. A new company, owned by RCA, GE, and Westinghouse would be formed, and would purchase AT&T's stations. The new company would enter into a long-term contract with AT&T to provide the long-distance communications necessary to set up the broadcast network that David Sarnoff envisioned as the future of broadcast. This new entity would, in 1926, become the National Broadcasting Company (NBC). AT&T's WEAF station would become the center of one of NBC's two networks, and the division arrived at would thereafter form the basis of the broadcast system in the United States.

By the middle of 1926, then, the institutional and organizational elements that became the American broadcast system were, to a great extent, in place. The idea of government monopoly over broadcasting, which became dominant in Great Britain, Europe, and their former colonies, was forever abandoned. The idea of a private-property regime in spectrum, which had been advocated by commercial broadcasters to spur investment in broadcast, was rejected on the backdrop of other battles over conservation of federal resources. The Radio Act of 1927, passed by Congress in record speed a few months after a court invalidated Hoover's entire regulatory edifice as lacking legal foundation, enacted this framework as the basic structure of American broadcast. A relatively small group of commercial broadcasters and equipment manufacturers took the lead in broadcast development. A governmental regulatory agency, using a standard of "the public good," allocated frequency, time, and power assignments to minimize interference and to resolve conflicts. The public good, by and large, correlated to the needs of commercial broadcasters and their listeners. Later, the broadcast networks supplanted the patent alliance as the primary force to which the Federal Radio Commission paid heed. The early 1930s still saw battles over the degree of freedom that these networks had to pursue their own commercial interests, free of regulation (studied in Robert McChesney's work).[8] By that point, however, the power of the broadcasters was already too great to be seriously challenged. Interests like those of the amateurs, whose romantic pioneering mantle still held strong purchase on the process, educational institutions, and religious organizations continued to exercise some force on the allocation and management of the spectrum. However, they were addressed on the periphery of the broadcast platform, leaving the public sphere to be largely mediated by a tiny number of commercial entities running a controlled, advertiser-supported platform of mass media. Following the settlement around radio, there were no more genuine inflection points in the structure of mass media. Television followed radio, and was even more concentrated. Cable networks and satellite networks varied to some extent, but retained the basic advertiser-supported model, oriented toward luring the widest possible audience to view the advertising that paid for the programming.

BASIC CRITIQUES OF MASS MEDIA

The cluster of practices that form the mass-media model was highly conducive to social control in authoritarian countries. The hub-and-spoke technical architecture and unidirectional endpoint-reception model of these systems made it very simple to control, by controlling the core—the state-owned television, radio, and newspapers. The high cost of providing high-circulation statements meant that subversive publications were difficult to make and communicate across large distances and to large populations of potential supporters. Samizdat of various forms and channels have existed in most if not all authoritarian societies, but at great disadvantage relative to public communication. The passivity of readers, listeners, and viewers coincided nicely with the role of the authoritarian public sphere—to manage opinion in order to cause the widest possible willing, or at least quiescent, compliance, and thereby to limit the need for using actual repressive force.

In liberal democracies, the same technical and economic cost characteristics resulted in a very different pattern of communications practices. However, these practices relied on, and took advantage of, some of the very same basic architectural and cost characteristics. The practices of commercial mass media in liberal democracies have been the subject of a vast literature, criticizing their failures and extolling their virtues as a core platform for the liberal public sphere. There have been three primary critiques of these media: First, their intake has been seen as too limited. Too few information collection points leave too many views entirely unexplored and unrepresented because they are far from the concerns of the cadre of professional journalists, or cannot afford to buy their way to public attention. The debates about localism and diversity of ownership of radio and television stations have been the clearest policy locus of this critique in the United States. They are based on the assumption that local and socially diverse ownership of radio stations will lead to better representation of concerns as they are distributed in society. Second, concentrated mass media has been criticized as giving the owners too much power—which they either employ themselves or sell to the highest bidder—over what is said and how it is evaluated. Third, the advertising-supported media needs to attract large audiences, leading programming away from the genuinely politically important, challenging, and engaging, and toward the titillating or the soothing. This critique has emphasized the tension between business interests and journalistic ethics, and the claims that market imperatives and the bottom line lead to shoddy or cowering reporting; quiescence in majority tastes and positions in order to maximize audience; spectacle rather than substantive conversation of issues even when political matters are covered; and an emphasis on entertainment over news and analysis.

Three primary defenses or advantages have also been seen in these media: first is their independence from government, party, or upper-class largesse, particularly against the background of the state-owned media in authoritarian regimes, and given the high cost of production and communication, commercial mass media have been seen as necessary to create a public sphere grounded outside government. Second is the professionalism and large newsrooms that commercial mass media can afford to support to perform the watchdog function in complex societies. Because of their market-based revenues, they can replace universal intake with well-researched observations that citizens would not otherwise have made, and that are critical to a well-functioning democracy. Third, their near-universal visibility and independence enable them to identify important issues percolating in society. They can provide a platform to put them on the public agenda. They can express, filter, and accredit statements about these issues, so that they become well-specified subjects and feasible objects for public debate among informed citizens. That is to say, the limited number of points to which all are tuned and the limited number of "slots" available for speaking on these media form the basis for providing the synthesis required for public opinion and raising the salience of matters of public concern to the point of potential collective action. In the remainder of this chapter, I will explain the criticisms of the commercial mass media in more detail. I then take up in chapter 7 the question of how the Internet in general, and the rise of nonmarket and cooperative individual production in the networked information economy in particular, can solve or alleviate those problems while fulfilling some of the important roles of mass media in democracies today.

Mass Media as a Platform for the Public Sphere

The structure of mass media as a mode of communications imposes a certain set of basic characteristics on the kind of public conversation it makes possible. First, it is always communication from a small number of people, organized into an even smaller number of distinct outlets, to an audience several orders of magnitude larger, unlimited in principle in its membership except by the production capacity of the media itself—which, in the case of print, may mean the number of copies, and in radio, television, cable, and the like, means whatever physical-reach constraints, if any, are imposed by the technology and business organizational arrangements used by these outlets. In large, complex, modern societies, no one knows everything. The initial function of a platform for the public sphere is one of intake—taking into the system the observations and opinions of as many members of society as possible as potential objects of public concern and consideration. The radical difference between the number of intake points the mass media have and the range and diversity of human existence in large complex societies assures a large degree of information loss at the intake stage. Second, the vast difference between the number of speakers and the number of listeners, and the finished-goods style of mass-media products, imposes significant constraints on the extent to which these media can be open to feedback— that is, to responsive communications that are tied together as a conversation with multiple reciprocal moves from both sides of the conversation. Third, the immense and very loosely defined audience of mass media affects the filtering and synthesis functions of the mass media as a platform for the public sphere. One of the observations regarding the content of newspapers in the late eighteenth to mid-nineteenth centuries was the shift they took as their circulation increased—from party-oriented, based in relatively thick communities of interest and practice, to fact- and sensation-oriented, with content that made thinner requirements on their users in order to achieve broader and more weakly defined readership. Fourth, and finally, because of the high costs of organizing these media, the functions of intake, sorting for relevance, accrediting, and synthesis are all combined in the hands of the same media operators, selected initially for their capacity to pool the capital necessary to communicate the information to wide audiences. While all these functions are necessary for a usable public sphere, the correlation of capacity to pool capital resources with capacity to offer the best possible filtering and synthesis is not obvious. In addition to basic structural constraints that come from the characteristic of a communications modality that can properly be called "mass media," there are also critiques that arise more specifically from the business models that have characterized the commercial mass media over the course of most of the twentieth century. Media markets are relatively concentrated, and the most common business model involves selling the attention of large audiences to commercial advertisers.

Media Concentration: The Power of Ownership and Money

The Sinclair Broadcast Group is one of the largest owners of television broadcast stations in the United States. The group's 2003 Annual Report proudly states in its title, "Our Company. Your Message. 26 Million Households"; that is, roughly one quarter of U.S. households. Sinclair owns and operates or provides programming and sales to sixty-two stations in the United States, including multiple local affiliates of NBC, ABC, CBS, and

Fox. In April 2004, ABC News's program *Nightline* dedicated a special program to reading the names of American service personnel who had been killed in the Iraq War. The management of Sinclair decided that its seven ABC affiliates would not air the program, defending its decision because the program "appears to be motivated by a political agenda designed to undermine the efforts of the United States in Iraq."[9] At the time, the rising number of American casualties in Iraq was already a major factor in the 2004 presidential election campaign, and both ABC's decision to air the program, and Sinclair's decision to refuse to carry it could be seen as interventions by the media in setting the political agenda and contributing to the public debate. It is difficult to gauge the politics of a commercial organization, but one rough proxy is political donations. In the case of Sinclair, 95 percent of the donations made by individuals associated with the company during the 2004 election cycle went to Republicans, while only 5 percent went to Democrats.[10] Contributions of Disney, on the other hand, the owner of the ABC network, split about seventy-thirty in favor of contribution to Democrats. It is difficult to parse the extent to which political leanings of this sort are personal to the executives and professional employees who make decisions about programming, and to what extent these are more organizationally self-interested, depending on the respective positions of the political parties on the conditions of the industry's business. In some cases, it is quite obvious that the motives are political. When one looks, for example, at contributions by Disney's film division, they are distributed 100 percent in favor of Democrats. This mostly seems to reflect the large contributions of the Weinstein brothers, who run the semi-independent studio Miramax, which also distributed Michael Moore's politically explosive criticism of the Bush administration, *Fahrenheit 9/11,* in 2004. Sinclair's contributions were aligned with, though more skewed than, those of the National Association of Broadcasters political action committee, which were distributed 61 percent to 39 percent in favor of Republicans. Here the possible motivation is that Republicans have espoused a regulatory agenda at the Federal Communications Commission that allows broadcasters greater freedom to consolidate and to operate more as businesses and less as public trustees.

The basic point is not, of course, to trace the particular politics of one programming decision or another. It is the relative power of those who manage the mass media when it so dominates public discourse as to shape public perceptions and public debate. This power can be brought to bear throughout the components of the platform, from the intake function (what facts about the world are observed) to the filtration and synthesis (the selection of materials, their presentation, and the selection of who will debate them and in what format). These are all central to forming the agenda that the public perceives, choreographing the discussion, the range of opinions perceived and admitted into the conversation, and through these, ultimately, choreographing the perceived consensus and the range of permissible debate. One might think of this as "the Berlusconi effect." Thinking in terms of a particular individual, known for a personal managerial style, who translated the power of control over media into his election as prime minister of his country symbolizes well the concern, but of course does not exhaust the problem, which is both broader and more subtle than the concern with the possibility that mass media will be owned by individuals who would exert total control over these media and translate their control into immediate political power, manufacturing and shaping the appearance of a public sphere, rather than providing a platform for one.

The power of the commercial mass media depends on the degree of concentration in mass-media markets. A million equally watched channels do not exercise power. Concentration is a common word used to describe the power media exercise when there are only few outlets, but a tricky one because it implies two very distinct phenomena. The first is a lack of competition in a market, to a degree sufficient to allow a firm to exercise power over its pricing. This is the antitrust sense. The second, very different concern might be called "mindshare." That is, media is "concentrated" when a small number of media firms play a large role as the channel from and to a substantial majority of readers, viewers, and listeners in a given politically relevant social unit.

If one thinks that commercial firms operating in a market will always "give the audience what it wants" and that what the audience wants is a fully representative cross-section of all observations and opinions relevant to public discourse, then the antitrust sense would be the only one that mattered. A competitive market would force any market actor simply to reflect the range of available opinions actually held in the public. Even by this measure, however, there continue to be debates about how one should define the relevant market and what one is measuring. The more one includes all potential nationally available sources of information, newspapers, magazines, television, radio, satellite, cable, and the like, the less concentrated the market seems. However, as Eli Noam's recent work on local media concentration has argued, treating a tiny television station on Long Island as equivalent to

WCBS in New York severely underrepresents the power of mass media over their audience. Noam offered the most comprehensive analysis currently available of the patterns of concentration where media are actually accessed—locally, where people live—from 1984 to 2001–2002. Most media are consumed locally—because of the cost of national distribution of paper newspapers, and because of the technical and regulatory constraints on nationwide distribution of radio and television. Noam computed two measures of market concentration for each of thirty local markets: the Herfindahl-Hirschman Index (HHI), a standard method used by the Department of Justice to measure market concentration for antitrust purposes; and what he calls a C4 index—that is, the market share of the top four firms in a market, and C1, the share of the top single firm in the market. He found that, based on the HHI index, all the local media markets are highly concentrated. In the standard measure, a market with an index of less than 1,000 is not concentrated, a market with an index of 1,000–1,800 is moderately concentrated, and a market with an index of above 1,800 on the HHI is highly concentrated. Noam found that local radio, which had an index below 1,000 between 1984 and 1992, rose over the course of the following years substantially. Regulatory restrictions were loosened over the course of the 1990s, resulting by the end of the decade in an HHI index measure of 2,400 for big cities, and higher for medium-sized and small markets. And yet, radio is less concentrated than local multichannel television (cable and satellite) with an HHI of 6,300, local magazines with an HHI of 6,859, and local newspapers with an HHI of 7,621. The only form of media whose concentration has declined to less than highly concentrated (HHI 1,714) is local television, as the rise of new networks and local stations' viability on cable has moved us away from the three-network world of 1984. It is still the case, however, that the top four television stations capture 73 percent of the viewers in most markets, and 62 percent in large markets. The most concentrated media in local markets are newspapers, which, except for the few largest markets, operate on a one-newspaper town model. C1 concentration has grown in this area to 83 percent of readership for the leading papers, and an HHI of 7,621.

The degree of concentration in media markets supports the proposition that owners of media can either exercise power over the programming they provide or what they write, or sell their power over programming to those who would like to shape opinions. Even if one were therefore to hold the Pollyannaish view that market-based media in a competitive market would be constrained by competition to give citizens what they need, as Ed Baker put it, there is no reason to think the same in these kinds of highly concentrated markets. As it turns out, a long tradition of scholarship has also developed the claim that even without such high levels of concentration in the antitrust sense, advertiser-supported media markets are hardly good mechanisms for assuring that the contents of the media provide a good reflection of the information citizens need to know as members of a polity, the range of opinions and views about what ought to occupy the public, and what solutions are available to those problems that are perceived and discussed.[11] First, we have long known that advertiser-supported media suffer from more or less well-defined failures, purely as market mechanisms, at representing the actual distribution of first-best preferences of audiences. As I describe in more detail in the next section, whether providers in any market structure, from monopoly to full competition, will even try to serve first-best preferences of their audience turns out to be a function of the distribution of actual first-best and second-best preferences, and the number of "channels." Second, there is a systematic analytic problem with defining consumer demand for information. Perfect information is a precondition to an efficient market, not its output. In order for consumers to value information or an opinion fully, they must know it and assimilate it to their own worldview and understanding. However, the basic problem to be solved by media markets is precisely to select which information people will value if they in fact come to know it, so it is impossible to gauge the value of a unit of information before it has been produced, and hence to base production decisions on actual existing user preferences. The result is that, even if media markets were perfectly competitive, a substantial degree of discretion and influence would remain in the hands of commercial media owners.

The actual cultural practice of mass-media production and consumption is more complex than either the view of "efficient media markets" across the board or the general case against media concentration and commercialism. Many of the relevant companies are public companies, answerable to at least large institutional shareholders, and made up of managements that need not be monolithic in their political alignment or judgment as to the desirability of making political gains as opposed to market share. Unless there is economic or charismatic leadership of the type of a William Randolph Hearst or a Rupert Murdoch, organizations usually have complex structures, with varying degrees of freedom for local editors, reporters, and midlevel managers to tug and pull at the fabric of programming. Different media companies also have different business models, and aim at different market segments. The *New York Times*, *Wall Street Journal*, and *Washington Post* do not aim at the same audience as most daily local newspapers in the United States. They are aimed at elites, who want to buy newspapers that can credibly claim to embody highly professional journalism. This requires separation of editorial from business decisions—at least for some segments of the newspapers that are critical in attracting those readers. The degree to which the Berlusconi effect in its full-blown form of individual or self-consciously directed political power through shaping of the public sphere will apply is not one that can necessarily be answered as a matter of a priori theoretical framework for all mass media. Instead, it is a concern, a tendency, whose actual salience in any given public sphere or set of firms is the product of historical contingency, different from one country to another and one period to another. It will depend on the strategies of particular companies and their relative mindshare in a society. However, it is clear and structurally characteristic of mass media that a society that depends for its public sphere on a relatively small number of actors, usually firms, to provide most of the platform of its public sphere, is setting itself up for, at least, a form of discourse elitism. In other words, those who are on the inside of the media will be able to exert substantially greater influence over the agenda, the shape of the conversation, and through these the outcomes of public discourse, than other individuals or groups in society. Moreover, for commercial organizations, this power could be sold—and as a business model, one should expect it to be. The most direct way to sell influence is explicit political advertising, but just as we see "product placement" in movies as a form of advertising, we see advertiser influence on the content of the editorial materials. Part of this influence is directly substantive and political. Another is the source of the second critique of commercial mass media.

Commercialism, Journalism, and
Political Inertness

The second cluster of concerns about the commercial mass media is the degree to which their commercialism undermines their will and capacity to provide a platform for public, politically oriented discourse. The concern is, in this sense, the opposite of the concern with excessive power. Rather than the fear that the concentrated mass media will exercise its power to pull opinion in its owners' interest, the fear is that the commercial interests of these media will cause them to pull content away from matters of genuine political concern altogether. It is typified in a quote offered by Ben Bagdikian, attributed to W. R. Nelson, publisher of the *Kansas City Star* in 1915: "Newspapers are read at the breakfast table and dinner tables. God's great gift to man is appetite. Put nothing in the paper that will destroy it."[12] Examples abound, but the basic analytic structure of the claim is fairly simple and consists of three distinct components. First, advertiser-supported media need to achieve the largest audience possible, not the most engaged or satisfied audience possible. This leads such media to focus on lowest-common-denominator programming and materials that have broad second-best appeal, rather than trying to tailor their programming to the true first-best preferences of well-defined segments of the audience. Second, issues of genuine public concern and potential political contention are toned down and structured as a performance between iconic representations of large bodies of opinion, in order to avoid alienating too much of the audience. This is the reemergence of spectacle that Habermas identified in *The Transformation of the Public Sphere*. The tendency toward lowest-common-denominator programming translates in the political sphere into a focus on fairly well-defined, iconic views, and to avoidance of genuinely controversial material, because it is easier to lose an audience by offending its members than by being only mildly interesting. The steady structuring of the media as professional, commercial, and one way over 150 years has led to a pattern whereby, when political debate is communicated, it is mostly communicated as performance. Someone represents a party or widely known opinion, and is juxtaposed with others who similarly represent alternative widely known views. These avatars of public opinion then enact a clash of opinion, orchestrated in order to leave the media neutral and free of blame, in the eyes of their viewers, for espousing an offensively partisan view. Third, and finally, this business logic often stands in contradiction to journalistic ethic. While there are niche markets for high-end journalism and strong opinion, outlets that serve those markets are specialized. Those that cater to broader markets need to subject journalistic ethic to business necessity, emphasizing celebrities or local crime over distant famines or a careful analysis of economic policy.

The basic drive behind programming choices in advertising-supported mass media was explored in the context of the problem of "program diversity" and competition. It relies on a type of analysis introduced by Peter Steiner in 1952. The basic model argued that advertiser-supported media are sensitive only to the number of viewers, not the intensity of their satisfaction. This created an odd situation, where competitors would tend to divide among them the largest market segments, and leave smaller slices of the audience unserved, whereas a monopolist would serve each market segment, in order of size, until it ran out of channels. Because it has no incentive to divide all the viewers who want, for example, sitcoms, among two or more stations, a monopolist would program a sitcom on one channel, and the next-most-desired program on the next channel. Two competitors, on the other hand, would both potentially program sitcoms, if dividing those who prefer sitcoms in half still yields a larger total audience size than airing the next-most-desired program. To illustrate this effect with a rather extreme hypothetical example, imagine that we are in a television market of 10 million viewers. Suppose that the distribution of preferences in the audience is as follows: 1,000,000 want to watch sitcoms; 750,000 want sports; 500,000 want local news; 250,000 want action movies; 9,990 are interested in foreign films; and 9,980 want programs on gardening. The stark drop-off between action movies and foreign films and gardening is intended to reflect the fact that the 7.5 million potential viewers who do not fall into one of the first four clusters are distributed in hundreds of small clusters, none commanding more than 10,000 viewers. Before we examine why this extreme assumption is likely correct, let us first see what happens if it were. Table 6.1 presents the programming choices that would typify those of competing channels, based on the number of channels competing and the distribution of preferences in the audience. It reflects the assumptions that each programmer wants to maximize the number of viewers of its channel and that the viewers are equally likely to watch one channel as another if both offer the same type of programming. The numbers in parentheses next to the programming choice represent the number of viewers the programmer can hope to attract given these assumptions, not including the probability that some of the 7.5 million viewers outside the main clusters will also tune in. In this extreme example, one would need a system with more than 250 channels in order to start seeing something other than sitcoms, sports, local news, and action movies. Why, however, is such a distribution likely, or even plausible? The assumption is not intended to represent an actual distribution of what people most prefer to watch. Rather, it reflects the notion that many people have best preferences, fallback preferences, and tolerable options. Their first-best preferences reflect what they really want to watch, and people are highly diverse in this dimension. Their fallback and tolerable preferences reflect the kinds of things they would be willing to watch if nothing else is available, rather than getting up off the sofa and going to a local café or reading a

Table 6.1: Distribution of Channels Hypothetical

No. of channels	Programming Available (in thousands of viewers)
1	sitcom (1000)
2	sitcom (1000), sports (750)
3	sitcom (1000 or 500), sports (750), indifferent between sitcoms and local news (500)
4	sitcom (500), sports (750), sitcom (500), local news (500)
5	sitcom (500), sports (375), sitcom (500), local news (500), sports (375)
6	sitcom (333), sports (375), sitcom (333), local news (500), sports (375), sitcom (333)
7	sitcom (333), sports (375), sitcom (333), local news (500), sports (375), sitcom (333), action movies (250)
8	sitcom (333), sports (375), sitcom (333), local news (250), sports (375), sitcom (333), action movies (250), local news (250)
9	sitcom (250), sports (375), sitcom (250), local news (250), sports (375), sitcom (250), action movies (250), local news (250), sitcom (250)
* * *	* * *
250	100 channels of sitcom (10); 75 channels of sports (10); 50 channels of local news (10); 25 channels of action movies (10)
251	100 channels of sitcom (10); 75 channels of sports (10); 50 channels of local news (10); 25 channels of action movies (10); 1 foreign film channel (9.99)
252	100 channels of sitcom (10); 75 channels of sports (10); 50 channels of local news (10); 25 channels of action movies (10); 1 foreign film channel (9.99); 1 gardening channel (9.98)

book. Here represented by sitcoms, sports, and the like, fallback options are more widely shared, even among people whose first-best preferences differ widely, because they represent what people will tolerate before switching, a much less strict requirement than what they really want. This assumption follows Jack Beebe's refinement of Steiner's model. Beebe established that media monopolists would show nothing but common-denominator programs and that competition among broadcasters would begin to serve the smaller preference clusters only if a large enough number of channels were available. Such a model would explain the broad cultural sense of Bruce Springsteen's song, "57 Channels (And Nothin' On)," and why we saw the emergence of channels like Black Entertainment Television, Univision (Spanish channel in the United States), or The History Channel only when cable systems significantly expanded channel capacity, as well as why direct-broadcast satellite and, more recently, digital cable offerings were the first venue for twenty-four-hour-a-day cooking channels and smaller minority-language channels.[13]

   While this work was developed in the context of analyzing media diversity of offerings, it provides a foundation for understanding the programming choices of all advertiser-supported mass media, including the press, in domains relevant to the role they play as a platform for the public sphere. It provides a framework for understanding, but also limiting, the applicability of the idea that mass media will put nothing in the newspaper that will destroy the reader's appetite. Controversial views and genuinely disturbing images, descriptions, or arguments have a higher likelihood of turning readers, listeners, and viewers away than entertainment, mildly interesting and amusing human-interest stories, and a steady flow of basic crime and courtroom dramas, and similar fare typical of local television newscasts and newspapers. On the other hand, depending on the number of channels, there are clearly market segments for people who are "political junkies," or engaged elites, who can support some small number of outlets aimed at that crowd. The *New York Times* or the *Wall Street Journal* are examples in print, programs like *Meet the Press* or *Nightline* and perhaps channels like CNN and Fox News are examples of the possibility and limitations of this exception to the general entertainment-oriented, noncontroversial, and politically inert style of commercial mass media. The dynamic of programming to the lowest common denominator can, however, iteratively replicate itself even within relatively news- and elite-oriented media outlets. Even among news junkies, larger news outlets must cater relatively to the mainstream of its intended audience. Too strident a position or too probing an inquiry may slice the market segment to which they sell too thin. This is likely what leads to the common criticism, from both the Right and Left, that the same media are too "liberal" and too "conservative," respectively. By contrast, magazines, whose business model can support much lower circulation levels, exhibit a substantially greater will for political engagement and analysis than even the relatively political-readership-oriented, larger-circulation mass media. By definition, however, the media that cater to these niche markets serve only a small segment of the political community. Fox News in the United States appears to be a powerful counterexample to this trend. It is difficult to pinpoint why. The channel likely represents a composite of the Berlusconi effect, the high market segmentation made possible by high-capacity cable systems, the very large market segment of Republicans, and the relatively polarized tone of American political culture since the early 1990s.

The mass-media model as a whole, with the same caveat for niche markets, does not lend itself well to in-depth discussion and dialog. High professionalism can, to some extent, compensate for the basic structural problem of a medium built on the model of a small number of producers transmitting to an audience that is many orders of magnitude larger. The basic problem occurs at the intake and synthesis stages of communication. However diligent they may be, a small number of professional reporters, embedded as they are within social segments that are part of social, economic, and political elites, are a relatively stunted mechanism for intake. If one seeks to collect the wide range of individual observations, experiences, and opinions that make up the actual universe of concerns and opinions of a large public as a basic input into the public sphere, before filtering, the centralized model of mass media provides a limited means of capturing those insights. On the back end of the communication of public discourse, concentrated media of necessity must structure most "participants" in the debate as passive recipients of finished messages and images. That is the core characteristic of mass media: Content is produced prior to transmission in a relatively small number of centers, and when finished is then transmitted to a mass audience, which consumes it. This is the basis of the claim of the role of professional journalism to begin with, separating it from nonprofessional observations of those who consume its products. The result of this basic structure of the media product is that discussion and analysis of issues of common concern is an iconic representation of discussion, a choreographed enactment of public debate. The participants are selected for the fact that they represent well-understood, well-defined positions among those actually prevalent in a population, the images and stories are chosen to represent issues, and the public debate that is actually facilitated (and is supposedly where synthesis of the opinions in public debate actually happens) is in fact an already presynthesized portrayal of an argument among avatars of relatively large segments of opinion as perceived by the journalists and stagers of the debate. In the United States, this translates into fairly standard formats of "on the left X, on the right Y," or "the Republicans' position" versus "the Democrats' position." It translates into "photo-op" moments of publicly enacting an idea, a policy position, or a state of affairs—whether it is a president landing on an aircraft carrier to represent security and the successful completion of a controversial war, or a candidate hunting with his buddies to represent a position on gun control. It is important to recognize that by describing these characteristics, I am not identifying failures of imagination, thoughtfulness, or professionalism on the part of media organizations. These are simply characteristics of a mass-mediated public sphere; modes of communication that offer the path of least resistance given the characteristics of the production and distribution process of mass media, particularly commercial mass media. There are partial exceptions, as there are to the diversity of content or the emphasis on entertainment value, but these do not reflect what most citizens read, see, or hear. The phenomenon of talk radio and call-in shows represents a very different, but certainly not more reflective form. They represent the pornography and violence of political discourse—a combination of exhibitionism and voyeurism intended to entertain us with opportunities to act out suppressed desires and to glimpse what we might be like if we allowed ourselves more leeway from what it means to be a well-socialized adult.

The two basic critiques of commercial mass media coalesce on the conflict between journalistic ethics and the necessities of commercialism. If professional journalists seek to perform a robust watchdog function, to inform their readers and viewers, and to provoke and explore in depth, then the dynamics of both power and lowest-common-denominator appeal push back. Different organizations, with different degrees of managerial control, editorial independence, internal organizational culture, and freedom from competitive pressures, with different intended market segments, will resolve these tensions differently. A quick reading of the conclusions of some media scholarship, and more commonly, arguments made in public debates over the media, would tend to lump "the media" as a single entity, with a single set of failures. In fact, unsurprisingly, the literature suggests substantial heterogeneity among organizations and media. Television seems to be the worst culprit on the dimension of political inertness. Print media, both magazines and some newspapers, include significant variation in the degree to which they fit these general models of failure.

As we turn now to consider the advantages of the introduction of Internet communications, we shall see how this new model can complement the mass media and alleviate its worst weaknesses. In particular, the discussion focuses on the emergence of the networked information economy and the relatively larger role it makes feasible for nonmarket actors and for radically distributed production of information and culture. One need not adopt the position that the commercial mass media are somehow abusive, evil, corporate-controlled giants, and that the Internet is the ideal Jeffersonian republic in order to track a series of genuine improvements represented by what the new emerging modalities of public communication can do as platforms for the public sphere. Greater access to means of direct individual communications, to collaborative speech platforms, and to nonmarket producers more generally can complement the commercial mass media and contribute to a significantly improved public sphere.

Chapter 7 Political Freedom Part 2:
Emergence of the Networked
Public Sphere

The fundamental elements of the difference between the networked information economy and the mass media are network architecture and the cost of becoming a speaker. The first element is the shift from a hub-and-spoke architecture with unidirectional links to the end points in the mass media, to distributed architecture with multidirectional connections among all nodes in the networked information environment. The second is the practical elimination of communications costs as a barrier to speaking across associational boundaries. Together, these characteristics have fundamentally altered the capacity of individuals, acting alone or with others, to be active participants in the public sphere as opposed to its passive readers, listeners, or viewers. For authoritarian countries, this means that it is harder and more costly, though not perhaps entirely impossible, to both be networked and maintain control over their public spheres. China seems to be doing too good a job of this in the middle of the first decade of this century for us to say much more than that it is harder to maintain control, and therefore that at least in some authoritarian regimes, control will be looser. In liberal democracies, ubiquitous individual ability to produce information creates the potential for near-universal intake. It therefore portends significant, though not inevitable, changes in the structure of the public sphere from the commercial mass-media environment. These changes raise challenges for filtering. They underlie some of the critiques of the claims about the democratizing effect of the Internet that I explore later in this chapter. Fundamentally, however, they are the roots of possible change. Beginning with the cost of sending an e-mail to some number of friends or to a mailing list of people interested in a particular subject, to the cost of setting up a Web site or a blog, and through to the possibility of maintaining interactive conversations with large numbers of people through sites like Slashdot, the cost of being a speaker in a regional, national, or even international political conversation is several orders of magnitude lower than the cost of speaking in the mass-mediated environment. This, in turn, leads to several orders of magnitude more speakers and participants in conversation and, ultimately, in the public sphere.

The change is as much qualitative as it is quantitative. The qualitative change is represented in the experience of being a potential speaker, as opposed to simply a listener and voter. It relates to the self-perception of individuals in society and the culture of participation they can adopt. The easy possibility of communicating effectively into the public sphere allows individuals to reorient themselves from passive readers and listeners to potential speakers and participants in a conversation. The way we listen to what we hear changes because of this; as does, perhaps most fundamentally, the way we observe and process daily events in our lives. We no longer need to take these as merely private observations, but as potential subjects for public communication. This change affects the relative power of the media. It affects the structure of intake of observations and views. It affects the presentation of issues and observations for discourse. It affects the way issues are filtered, for whom and by whom. Finally, it affects the ways in which positions are crystallized and synthesized, sometimes still by being amplified to the point that the mass media take them as inputs and convert them into political positions, but occasionally by direct organization of opinion and action to the point of reaching a salience that drives the political process directly.

The basic case for the democratizing effect of the Internet, as seen from the perspective of the mid-1990s, was articulated in an opinion of the U.S. Supreme Court in *Reno v. ACLU*:

The Web is thus comparable, from the readers' viewpoint, to both a vast library including millions of readily available and indexed publications and a sprawling mall offering goods and services. From the publishers' point of view, it constitutes a vast platform from which to address and hear from a world-wide audience of millions of readers, viewers, researchers, and buyers. Any person or organization with a computer connected to the Internet can "publish" information. Publishers include government agencies, educational institutions, commercial entities, advocacy groups, and individuals. . . .

Through the use of chat rooms, any person with a phone line can become a town crier with a voice that resonates farther than it could from any soapbox. Through the use of Web pages, mail exploders, and newsgroups, the same individual can become a pamphleteer. As the District Court found, "the content on the Internet is as diverse as human thought."[1]

The observations of what is different and unique about this new medium relative to those that dominated the twentieth century are already present in the quotes from the Court. There are two distinct types of effects. The first, as the Court notes from "the readers' perspective," is the abundance and diversity of human expression available to anyone, anywhere, in a way that was not feasible in the mass-mediated environment. The second, and more fundamental, is that anyone can be a publisher, including individuals, educational institutions, and nongovernmental organizations (NGOs), alongside the traditional speakers of the mass-media environment—government and commercial entities.

Since the end of the 1990s there has been significant criticism of this early conception of the democratizing effects of the Internet. One line of critique includes variants of the Babel objection: the concern that information overload will lead to fragmentation of discourse, polarization, and the loss of political community. A different and descriptively contradictory line of critique suggests that the Internet is, in fact, exhibiting concentration: Both infrastructure and, more fundamentally, patterns of attention are much less distributed than we thought. As a consequence, the Internet diverges from the mass media much less than we thought in the 1990s and significantly less than we might hope.

I begin the chapter by offering a menu of the core technologies and usage patterns that can be said, as of the middle of the first decade of the twenty-first century, to represent the core Internet-based technologies of democratic discourse. I then use two case studies to describe the social and economic practices through which these tools are implemented to construct the public sphere, and how these practices differ quite radically from the mass-media model. On the background of these stories, we are then able to consider the critiques that have been leveled against the claim that the Internet democratizes. Close examination of the application of networked information economy to the production of the public sphere suggests that the emerging networked public sphere offers significant improvements over one dominated by commercial mass media. Throughout the discussion, it is important to keep in mind that the relevant comparison is always between the public sphere that we in fact had throughout the twentieth century, the one dominated by mass media, that is the baseline for comparison, not the utopian image of the "everyone a pamphleteer" that animated the hopes of the 1990s for Internet democracy. Departures from the naïve utopia are not signs that the Internet does not democratize, after all. They are merely signs that the medium and its analysis are maturing.

BASIC TOOLS OF NETWORKED COMMUNICATION

Analyzing the effect of the networked information environment on public discourse by cataloging the currently popular tools for communication is, to some extent, self-defeating. These will undoubtedly be supplanted by new ones. Analyzing this effect without having a sense of what these tools are or how they are being used is, on the other hand, impossible. This leaves us with the need to catalog what is, while trying to abstract from what is being used to what relationships of information and communication are emerging, and from these to transpose to a theory of the networked information economy as a new platform for the public sphere.

E-mail is the most popular application on the Net. It is cheap and trivially easy to use. Basic e-mail, as currently used, is not ideal for public communications. While it provides a cheap and efficient means of communicating with large numbers of individuals who are not part of one's basic set of social associations, the presence of large amounts of commercial spam and the amount of mail flowing in and out of mailboxes make indiscriminate e-mail distributions a relatively poor mechanism for being heard. E-mails to smaller groups, preselected by the sender for having some interest in a subject or relationship to the sender, do, however, provide a rudimentary mechanism for communicating observations, ideas, and opinions to a significant circle, on an ad hoc basis. Mailing lists are more stable and self-selecting, and therefore more significant as a basic tool for the networked public sphere. Some mailing lists are moderated or edited, and run by one or a small number of editors. Others are not edited in any significant way. What separates mailing lists from most Web-based uses is the fact that they push the information on them into the mailbox of subscribers. Because of their attention limits, individuals restrict their subscriptions, so posting on a mailing list tends to be done by and for people who have self-selected as having a heightened degree of common interest, substantive or contextual. It therefore enhances the degree to which one is heard by those already interested in a topic. It is not a communications model of one-to-many, or few-to-many as broadcast is to an open, undefined class of audience members. Instead, it allows one, or a few, or even a limited large group to communicate to a large but limited group, where the limit is self-selection as being interested or even immersed in a subject.

The World Wide Web is the other major platform for tools that individuals use to communicate in the networked public sphere. It enables a wide range of applications, from basic static Web pages, to, more recently, blogs and various social-software–mediated platforms for large-scale conversations of the type described in chapter 3—like Slashdot. Static Web pages are the individual's basic "broadcast" medium. They allow any individual or organization to present basic texts, sounds, and images pertaining to their position. They allow small NGOs to have a worldwide presence and visibility. They allow individuals to offer thoughts and commentaries. They allow the creation of a vast, searchable database of information, observations, and opinions, available at low cost for anyone, both to read and write into. This does not yet mean that all these statements are heard by the relevant others to whom they are addressed. Substantial analysis is devoted to that problem, but first let us complete the catalog of tools and information flow structures.

One Web-based tool and an emerging cultural practice around it that extends the basic characteristics of Web sites as media for the political public sphere are Web logs, or blogs. Blogs are a tool and an approach to using the Web that extends the use of Web pages in two significant ways. Technically, blogs are part of a broader category of innovations that make the web "writable." That is, they make Web pages easily capable of modification through a simple interface. They can be modified from anywhere with a networked computer, and the results of writing onto the Web page are immediately available to anyone who accesses the blog to read. This technical change resulted in two divergences from the cultural practice of Web sites in the 1990s. First, they allowed the evolution of a journal-style Web page, where individual short posts are added to the Web site in short or large intervals. As practice has developed over the past few years, these posts are usually archived chronologically. For many users, this means that blogs have become a form of personal journal, updated daily or so, for their own use and perhaps for the use of a very small group of friends. What is significant about this characteristic from the perspective of the construction of the public sphere is that blogs enable individuals to write to their Web pages in journalism time—that is, hourly, daily, weekly—whereas Web page culture that preceded it tended to be slower moving: less an equivalent of reportage than of the essay. Today, one certainly finds individuals using blog software to maintain what are essentially static Web pages, to which they add essays or content occasionally, and Web sites that do not use blogging technology but are updated daily. The public sphere function is based on the content and cadence—that is, the use practice—not the technical platform.

The second critical innovation of the writable Web in general and of blogs in particular was the fact that in addition to the owner, readers/users could write to the blog. Blogging software allows the person who runs a blog to permit some, all, or none of the readers to post comments to the blog, with or without retaining power to edit or moderate the posts that go on, and those that do not. The result is therefore not only that many more people write finished statements and disseminate them widely, but also that the end product is a weighted conversation, rather than a finished good. It is a conversation because of the common practice of allowing and posting comments, as well as comments to these comments. Blog writers—bloggers— often post their own responses in the comment section or address comments in the primary section. Blog-based conversation is weighted, because the culture and technical affordances of blogging give the owner of the blog greater weight in deciding who gets to post or comment and who gets to decide these questions. Different blogs use these capabilities differently; some opt for broader intake and discussion on the board, others for a more tightly edited blog. In all these cases, however, the communications model or information-flow structure that blogs facilitate is a weighted conversation that takes the form of one or a group of primary contributors/authors, to-gether with some larger number, often many, secondary contributors, com-municating to an unlimited number of many readers.

The writable Web also encompasses another set of practices that are dis-tinct, but that are often pooled in the literature together with blogs. These are the various larger-scale, collaborative-content production systems available on the Web, of the type described in chapter 3. Two basic characteristics make sites like Slashdot or Wikipedia different from blogs. First, they are intended for, and used by, very large groups, rather than intended to facilitate a conversation weighted toward one or a small number of primary speakers. Unlike blogs, they are not media for individual or small group expression with a conversation feature. They are intrinsically group communication media. They therefore incorporate social software solutions to avoid deterioration into chaos—peer review, structured posting privileges, reputation systems, and so on. Second, in the case of Wikis, the conversation platform is anchored by a common text. From the perspective of facilitating the synthesis of positions and opinions, the presence of collaborative authorship of texts offers an additional degree of viscosity to the conversation, so that views "stick" to each other, must jostle for space, and accommodate each other. In the process, the output is more easily recognizable as a collective output and a salient opinion or observation than where the form of the conversation is more free-flowing exchange of competing views.

Common to all these Web-based tools—both static and dynamic, individual and cooperative—are linking, quotation, and presentation. It is at the very core of the hypertext markup language (HTML) to make referencing easy. And it is at the very core of a radically distributed network to allow materials to be archived by whoever wants to archive them, and then to be accessible to whoever has the reference. Around these easy capabilities, the cultural practice has emerged to reference through links for easy transition from your own page or post to the one you are referring to—whether as inspiration or in disagreement. This culture is fundamentally different from the mass-media culture, where sending a five-hundred-page report to millions of users is hard and expensive. In the mass media, therefore, instead of allowing readers to read the report alongside its review, all that is offered is the professional review in the context of a culture that trusts the reviewer. On the Web, linking to original materials and references is considered a core characteristic of communication. The culture is oriented toward "see for yourself." Confidence in an observation comes from a combination of the reputation of the speaker as it has emerged over time, reading underlying sources you believe you have some competence to evaluate for yourself, and knowing that for any given referenced claim or source, there is some group of people out there, unaffiliated with the reviewer or speaker, who will have access to the source and the means for making their disagreement with the speaker's views known. Linking and "see for yourself" represent a radically different and more participatory model of accreditation than typified the mass media.

Another dimension that is less well developed in the United States than it is in Europe and East Asia is mobility, or the spatial and temporal ubiquity of basic tools for observing and commenting on the world we inhabit. Dan Gillmor is clearly right to include these basic characteristics in his book *We the Media*, adding to the core tools of what he describes as a transformation in journalism, short message service (SMS), and mobile connected cameras to mailing lists, Web logs, Wikis, and other tools. The United States has remained mostly a PC-based networked system, whereas in Europe and Asia, there has been more substantial growth in handheld devices, primarily mobile phones. In these domains, SMS—the "e-mail" of mobile phones—and camera phones have become critical sources of information, in real time. In some poor countries, where cell phone minutes remain very (even prohibitively) expensive for many users and where landlines may not exist, text messaging is becoming a central and ubiquitous communication tool. What these suggest to us is a transition, as the capabilities of both systems converge, to widespread availability of the ability to register and communicate observations in text, audio, and video, wherever we are and whenever we wish. Drazen Pantic tells of how listeners of Internet-based Radio B-92 in Belgrade reported events in their neighborhoods after the broadcast station had been shut down by the Milosevic regime. Howard Rheingold describes in *Smart Mobs* how citizens of the Philippines used SMS to organize real-time movements and action to overthrow their government. In a complex modern society, where things that matter can happen anywhere and at any time, the capacities of people armed with the means of recording, rendering, and communicating their observations change their relationship to the events that surround them. Whatever one sees and hears can be treated as input into public debate in ways that were impossible when capturing, rendering, and communicating were facilities reserved to a handful of organizations and a few thousands of their employees.

NETWORKED INFORMATION ECONOMY MEETS
THE PUBLIC SPHERE

The networked public sphere is not made of tools, but of social production practices that these tools enable. The primary effect of the Internet on the

public sphere in liberal societies relies on the information and cultural production activity of emerging nonmarket actors: individuals working alone
and cooperatively with others, more formal associations like NGOs, and
their feedback effect on the mainstream media itself. These enable the networked public sphere to moderate the two major concerns with commercial
mass media as a platform for the public sphere: (1) the excessive power it
gives its owners, and (2) its tendency, when owners do not dedicate their
media to exert power, to foster an inert polity. More fundamentally, the
social practices of information and discourse allow a very large number of
actors to see themselves as potential contributors to public discourse and as
potential actors in political arenas, rather than mostly passive recipients of
mediated information who occasionally can vote their preferences. In this
section, I offer two detailed stories that highlight different aspects of the
effects of the networked information economy on the construction of the
public sphere. The first story focuses on how the networked public sphere
allows individuals to monitor and disrupt the use of mass-media power, as
well as organize for political action. The second emphasizes in particular
how the networked public sphere allows individuals and groups of intense
political engagement to report, comment, and generally play the role traditionally assigned to the press in observing, analyzing, and creating political
salience for matters of public interest. The case studies provide a context
both for seeing how the networked public sphere responds to the core failings
of the commercial, mass-media-dominated public sphere and for considering
the critiques of the Internet as a platform for a liberal public sphere.

Our first story concerns Sinclair Broadcasting and the 2004 U.S. presidential election. It highlights the opportunities that mass-media owners have
to exert power over the public sphere, the variability within the media itself
in how this power is used, and, most significant for our purposes here, the
potential corrective effect of the networked information environment. At its
core, it suggests that the existence of radically decentralized outlets for individuals and groups can provide a check on the excessive power that media
owners were able to exercise in the industrial information economy.

Sinclair, which owns major television stations in a number of what were
considered the most competitive and important states in the 2004 election—
including Ohio, Florida, Wisconsin, and Iowa—informed its staff and stations that it planned to preempt the normal schedule of its sixty-two stations
to air a documentary called *Stolen Honor: The Wounds That Never Heal*, as
a news program, a week and a half before the elections.[2] The documentary

was reported to be a strident attack on Democratic candidate John Kerry's Vietnam War service. One reporter in Sinclair's Washington bureau, who objected to the program and described it as "blatant political propaganda," was promptly fired.[3] The fact that Sinclair owns stations reaching one quarter of U.S. households, that it used its ownership to preempt local broadcast schedules, and that it fired a reporter who objected to its decision, make this a classic "Berlusconi effect" story, coupled with a poster-child case against media concentration and the ownership of more than a small number of outlets by any single owner. The story of Sinclair's plans broke on Saturday, October 9, 2004, in the *Los Angeles Times*. Over the weekend, "official" responses were beginning to emerge in the Democratic Party. The Kerry campaign raised questions about whether the program violated election laws as an undeclared "in-kind" contribution to the Bush campaign. By Tuesday, October 12, the Democratic National Committee announced that it was filing a complaint with the Federal Elections Commission (FEC), while seventeen Democratic senators wrote a letter to the chairman of the Federal Communications Commission (FCC), demanding that the commission investigate whether Sinclair was abusing the public trust in the airwaves. Neither the FEC nor the FCC, however, acted or intervened throughout the episode.

Alongside these standard avenues of response in the traditional public sphere of commercial mass media, their regulators, and established parties, a very different kind of response was brewing on the Net, in the blogosphere. On the morning of October 9, 2004, the *Los Angeles Times* story was blogged on a number of political blogs—Josh Marshall on talkingpointsmemo.com, Chris Bower on MyDD.com, and Markos Moulitsas on dailyKos.com. By midday that Saturday, October 9, two efforts aimed at organizing opposition to Sinclair were posted in the dailyKos and MyDD. A "boycott-Sinclair" site was set up by one individual, and was pointed to by these blogs. Chris Bowers on MyDD provided a complete list of Sinclair stations and urged people to call the stations and threaten to picket and boycott. By Sunday, October 10, the dailyKos posted a list of national advertisers with Sinclair, urging readers to call them. On Monday, October 11, MyDD linked to that list, while another blog, theleftcoaster.com, posted a variety of action agenda items, from picketing affiliates of Sinclair to suggesting that readers oppose Sinclair license renewals, providing a link to the FCC site explaining the basic renewal process and listing public-interest organizations to work with. That same day, another individual, Nick Davis, started a Web site,

BoycottSBG.com, on which he posted the basic idea that a concerted boycott of local advertisers was the way to go, while another site, stopsinclair.org, began pushing for a petition. In the meantime, TalkingPoints published a letter from Reed Hundt, former chairman of the FCC, to Sinclair, and continued finding tidbits about the film and its maker. Later on Monday, TalkingPoints posted a letter from a reader who suggested that stockholders of Sinclair could bring a derivative action. By 5:00 A.M. on the dawn of Tuesday, October 12, however, TalkingPoints began pointing toward Davis's database on BoycottSBG.com. By 10:00 that morning, Marshall posted on TalkingPoints a letter from an anonymous reader, which began by saying: "I've worked in the media business for 30 years and I guarantee you that sales is what these local TV stations are all about. They don't care about license renewal or overwhelming public outrage. They care about sales only, so only local advertisers can affect their decisions." This reader then outlined a plan for how to watch and list all local advertisers, and then write to the sales managers—not general managers—of the local stations and tell them which advertisers you are going to call, and then call those. By 1:00 P.M. Marshall posted a story of his own experience with this strategy. He used Davis's database to identify an Ohio affiliate's local advertisers. He tried to call the sales manager of the station, but could not get through. He then called the advertisers. The post is a "how to" instruction manual, including admonitions to remember that the advertisers know nothing of this, the story must be explained, and accusatory tones avoided, and so on. Marshall then began to post letters from readers who explained with whom they had talked—a particular sales manager, for example—and who were then referred to national headquarters. He continued to emphasize that advertisers were the right addressees. By 5:00 P.M. that same Tuesday, Marshall was reporting more readers writing in about experiences, and continued to steer his readers to sites that helped them to identify their local affiliate's sales manager and their advertisers.[4]

By the morning of Wednesday, October 13, the boycott database already included eight hundred advertisers, and was providing sample letters for users to send to advertisers. Later that day, BoycottSBG reported that some participants in the boycott had received reply e-mails telling them that their unsolicited e-mail constituted illegal spam. Davis explained that the CAN-SPAM Act, the relevant federal statute, applied only to commercial spam, and pointed users to a law firm site that provided an overview of CAN-SPAM. By October 14, the boycott effort was clearly bearing fruit. Davis reported that Sinclair affiliates were threatening advertisers who cancelled advertisements with legal action, and called for volunteer lawyers to help respond. Within a brief period, he collected more than a dozen volunteers to help the advertisers. Later that day, another blogger at grassroots nation.com had set up a utility that allowed users to send an e-mail to all advertisers in the BoycottSBG database. By the morning of Friday, October 15, Davis was reporting more than fifty advertisers pulling ads, and three or four mainstream media reports had picked up the boycott story and reported on it. That day, an analyst at Lehman Brothers issued a research report that downgraded the expected twelve-month outlook for the price of Sinclair stock, citing concerns about loss of advertiser revenue and risk of tighter regulation. Mainstream news reports over the weekend and the following week systematically placed that report in context of local advertisers pulling their ads from Sinclair. On Monday, October 18, the company's stock price dropped by 8 percent (while the S&P 500 rose by about half a percent). The following morning, the stock dropped a further 6 percent, before beginning to climb back, as Sinclair announced that it would not show *Stolen Honor*, but would provide a balanced program with only portions of the documentary and one that would include arguments on the other side. On that day, the company's stock price had reached its lowest point in three years. The day after the announced change in programming decision, the share price bounced back to where it had been on October 15. There were obviously multiple reasons for the stock price losses, and Sinclair stock had been losing ground for many months prior to these events. Nonetheless, as figure 7.1 demonstrates, the market responded quite sluggishly to the announcements of regulatory and political action by the Democratic establishment earlier in the week of October 12, by comparison to the precipitous decline and dramatic bounce-back surrounding the market projections that referred to advertising loss. While this does not prove that the Web-organized, blog-driven and -facilitated boycott was the determining factor, as compared to fears of formal regulatory action, the timing strongly suggests that the efficacy of the boycott played a very significant role.

The first lesson of the Sinclair *Stolen Honor* story is about commercial mass media themselves. The potential for the exercise of inordinate power by media owners is not an imaginary concern. Here was a publicly traded firm whose managers supported a political party and who planned to use their corporate control over stations reaching one quarter of U.S. households, many in swing states, to put a distinctly political message in front of this

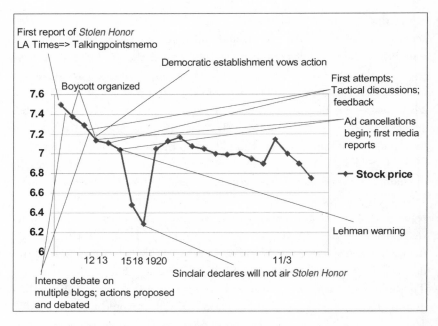

Figure 7.1: Sinclair Stock, October 8–November 5, 2004

large audience. We also learn, however, that in the absence of monopoly, such decisions do not determine what everyone sees or hears, and that other mass-media outlets will criticize each other under these conditions. This criticism alone, however, cannot stop a determined media owner from trying to exert its influence in the public sphere, and if placed as Sinclair was, in locations with significant political weight, such intervention could have substantial influence. Second, we learn that the new, network-based media can exert a significant counterforce. They offer a completely new and much more widely open intake basin for insight and commentary. The speed with which individuals were able to set up sites to stake out a position, to collect and make available information relevant to a specific matter of public concern, and to provide a platform for others to exchange views about the appropriate political strategy and tactics was completely different from anything that the economics and organizational structure of mass media make feasible. The third lesson is about the internal dynamics of the networked public sphere. Filtering and synthesis occurred through discussion, trial, and error. Multiple proposals for action surfaced, and the practice of linking allowed most anyone interested who connected to one of the nodes in the network to follow quotations and references to get a sense of the broad range of proposals. Different people could coalesce on different modes of action—150,000 signed the petition on stopsinclair.org, while others began to work on the boycott. Setting up the mechanism was trivial, both technically and as a matter of cost—something a single committed individual could choose to do. Pointing and adoption provided the filtering, and feedback about the efficacy, again distributed through a system of cross-references, allowed for testing and accreditation of this course of action. High-visibility sites, like Talkingpointsmemo or the dailyKos, offered transmissions hubs that disseminated information about the various efforts and provided a platform for interest-group-wide tactical discussions. It remains ambiguous to what extent these dispersed loci of public debate still needed mass-media exposure to achieve broad political salience. BoycottSBG.com received more than three hundred thousand unique visitors during its first week of operations, and more than one million page views. It successfully coordinated a campaign that resulted in real effects on advertisers in a large number of geographically dispersed media markets. In this case, at least, mainstream media reports on these efforts were few, and the most immediate "transmission mechanism" of their effect was the analyst's report from Lehman, not the media. It is harder to judge the extent to which those few mainstream media reports that did appear featured in the decision of the analyst to credit the success of the boycott efforts. The fact that mainstream media outlets may have played a role in increasing the salience of the boycott does not, however, take away from the basic role played by these new mechanisms of bringing information and experience to bear on a broad public conversation combined with a mechanism to organize political action across many different locations and social contexts.

Our second story focuses not on the new reactive capacity of the networked public sphere, but on its generative capacity. In this capacity, it begins to outline the qualitative change in the role of individuals as potential investigators and commentators, as active participants in defining the agenda and debating action in the public sphere. This story is about Diebold Election Systems (one of the leading manufacturers of electronic voting machines and a subsidiary of one of the foremost ATM manufacturers in the world, with more than $2 billion a year in revenue), and the way that public criticism of its voting machines developed. It provides a series of observations about how the networked information economy operates, and how it allows large numbers of people to participate in a peer-production enterprise of news gathering, analysis, and distribution, applied to a quite unsettling set of claims. While the context of the story is a debate over electronic voting, that is not what makes it pertinent to democracy. The debate could have centered on any corporate and government practice that had highly unsettling implications, was difficult to investigate and parse, and was largely ignored by mainstream media. The point is that the networked public sphere did engage, and did successfully turn something that was not a matter of serious public discussion to a public discussion that led to public action.

Electronic voting machines were first used to a substantial degree in the United States in the November 2002 elections. Prior to, and immediately following that election, there was sparse mass-media coverage of electronic voting machines. The emphasis was mostly on the newness, occasional slips, and the availability of technical support staff to help at polls. An *Atlanta Journal-Constitution* story, entitled "Georgia Puts Trust in Electronic Voting, Critics Fret about Absence of Paper Trails,"[5] is not atypical of coverage at the time, which generally reported criticism by computer engineers, but conveyed an overall soothing message about the efficacy of the machines and about efforts by officials and companies to make sure that all would be well. The *New York Times* report of the Georgia effort did not even mention the critics.[6] The *Washington Post* reported on the fears of failure with the newness of the machines, but emphasized the extensive efforts that the manufacturer, Diebold, was making to train election officials and to have hundreds of technicians available to respond to failure.[7] After the election, the *Atlanta Journal-Constitution* reported that the touch-screen machines were a hit, burying in the text any references to machines that highlighted the wrong candidates or the long lines at the booths, while the *Washington Post* highlighted long lines in one Maryland county, but smooth operation elsewhere. Later, the *Post* reported a University of Maryland study that surveyed users and stated that quite a few needed help from election officials, compromising voter privacy.[8] Given the centrality of voting mechanisms for democracy, the deep concerns that voting irregularities determined the 2000 presidential elections, and the sense that voting machines would be a solution to the "hanging chads" problem (the imperfectly punctured paper ballots that came to symbolize the Florida fiasco during that election), mass-media reports were remarkably devoid of any serious inquiry into how secure and accurate voting machines were, and included a high quotient of soothing comments from election officials who bought the machines and executives of the manufacturers who sold them. No mass-media outlet sought to go behind the claims of the manufacturers about their machines, to inquire into their security or the integrity of their tallying and transmission mechanisms against vote tampering. No doubt doing so would have been difficult. These systems were protected as trade secrets. State governments charged with certifying the systems were bound to treat what access they had to the inner workings as confidential. Analyzing these systems requires high degrees of expertise in computer security. Getting around these barriers is difficult. However, it turned out to be feasible for a collection of volunteers in various settings and contexts on the Net.

In late January 2003, Bev Harris, an activist focused on electronic voting machines, was doing research on Diebold, which has provided more than 75,000 voting machines in the United States and produced many of the machines used in Brazil's purely electronic voting system. Harris had set up a whistle-blower site as part of a Web site she ran at the time, blackboxvoting.com. Apparently working from a tip, Harris found out about an openly available site where Diebold stored more than forty thousand files about how its system works. These included specifications for, and the actual code of, Diebold's machines and vote-tallying system. In early February 2003, Harris published two initial journalistic accounts on an online journal in New Zealand, Scoop.com—whose business model includes providing an unedited platform for commentators who wish to use it as a platform to publish their materials. She also set up a space on her Web site for technically literate users to comment on the files she had retrieved. In early July of that year, she published an analysis of the results of the discussions on her site, which pointed out how access to the Diebold open site could have been used to affect the 2002 election results in Georgia (where there had been a tightly contested Senate race). In an editorial attached to the publication, entitled "Bigger than Watergate," the editors of Scoop claimed that what Harris had found was nothing short of a mechanism for capturing the U.S. elections process. They then inserted a number of lines that go to the very heart of how the networked information economy can use peer production to play the role of watchdog:

> We can now reveal for the first time the location of a complete online copy of the original data set. As we anticipate attempts to prevent the distribution of this information we encourage supporters of democracy to make copies of these files and to make them available on websites and file sharing networks: http://users.actrix.co.nz/dolly/. As many of the files are zip password protected you may need some assistance in opening them, we have found that the utility available at

the following URL works well: http://www.lostpassword.com. Finally some of the zip files are partially damaged, but these too can be read by using the utility at: http://www.zip-repair.com/. At this stage in this inquiry we do not believe that we have come even remotely close to investigating all aspects of this data; i.e., there is no reason to believe that the security flaws discovered so far are the only ones. Therefore we expect many more discoveries to be made. We want the assistance of the online computing community in this enterprise and we encourage you to file your findings at the forum HERE [providing link to forum].

A number of characteristics of this call to arms would have been simply infeasible in the mass-media environment. They represent a genuinely different mind-set about how news and analysis are produced and how censorship and power are circumvented. First, the ubiquity of storage and communications capacity means that public discourse can rely on "see for yourself" rather than on "trust me." The first move, then, is to make the raw materials available for all to see. Second, the editors anticipated that the company would try to suppress the information. Their response was not to use a counterweight of the economic and public muscle of a big media corporation to protect use of the materials. Instead, it was widespread distribution of information—about where the files could be found, and about where tools to crack the passwords and repair bad files could be found— matched with a call for action: get these files, copy them, and store them in many places so they cannot be squelched. Third, the editors did not rely on large sums of money flowing from being a big media organization to hire experts and interns to scour the files. Instead, they posed a challenge to whoever was interested—there are more scoops to be found, this is important for democracy, good hunting!! Finally, they offered a platform for integration of the insights on their own forum. This short paragraph outlines a mechanism for radically distributed storage, distribution, analysis, and reporting on the Diebold files.

As the story unfolded over the next few months, this basic model of peer production of investigation, reportage, analysis, and communication indeed worked. It resulted in the decertification of some of Diebold's systems in California, and contributed to a shift in the requirements of a number of states, which now require voting machines to produce a paper trail for recount purposes. The first analysis of the Diebold system based on the files Harris originally found was performed by a group of computer scientists at the Information Security Institute at Johns Hopkins University and released as a working paper in late July 2003. The Hopkins Report, or Rubin Report as it was also named after one of its authors, Aviel Rubin, presented deep criticism of the Diebold system and its vulnerabilities on many dimensions. The academic credibility of its authors required a focused response from Diebold. The company published a line-by-line response. Other computer scientists joined in the debate. They showed the limitations and advantages of the Hopkins Report, but also where the Diebold response was adequate and where it provided implicit admission of the presence of a number of the vulnerabilities identified in the report. The report and comments to it sparked two other major reports, commissioned by Maryland in the fall of 2003 and later in January 2004, as part of that state's efforts to decide whether to adopt electronic voting machines. Both studies found a wide range of flaws in the systems they examined and required modifications (see figure 7.2).

Meanwhile, trouble was brewing elsewhere for Diebold. In early August 2003, someone provided *Wired* magazine with a very large cache containing thousands of internal e-mails of Diebold. *Wired* reported that the e-mails were obtained by a hacker, emphasizing this as another example of the laxity of Diebold's security. However, the magazine provided neither an analysis of the e-mails nor access to them. Bev Harris, the activist who had originally found the Diebold materials, on the other hand, received the same cache, and posted the e-mails and memos on her site. Diebold's response was to threaten litigation. Claiming copyright in the e-mails, the company demanded from Harris, her Internet service provider, and a number of other sites where the materials had been posted, that the e-mails be removed. The e-mails were removed from these sites, but the strategy of widely distributed replication of data and its storage in many different topological and organizationally diverse settings made Diebold's efforts ultimately futile. The protagonists from this point on were college students. First, two students at Swarthmore College in Pennsylvania, and quickly students in a number of other universities in the United States, began storing the e-mails and scouring them for evidence of impropriety. In October 2003, Diebold proceeded to write to the universities whose students were hosting the materials. The company invoked provisions of the Digital Millennium Copyright Act that require Web-hosting companies to remove infringing materials when copyright owners notify them of the presence of these materials on their sites. The universities obliged, and required the students to remove the materials from their sites. The students, however, did not disappear quietly into the

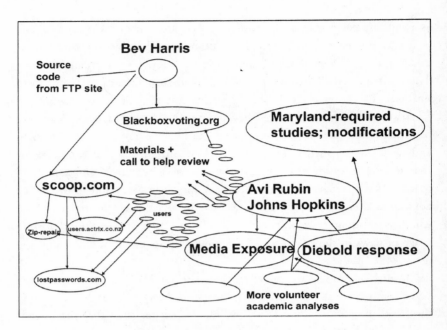

Figure 7.2: Analysis of the Diebold Source Code Materials

night. On October 21, 2003, they launched a multipronged campaign of what they described as "electronic civil disobedience." First, they kept moving the files from one student to another's machine, encouraging students around the country to resist the efforts to eliminate the material. Second, they injected the materials into FreeNet, the anticensorship peer-to-peer publication network, and into other peer-to-peer file-sharing systems, like eDonkey and BitTorrent. Third, supported by the Electronic Frontier Foundation, one of the primary civil-rights organizations concerned with Internet freedom, the students brought suit against Diebold, seeking a judicial declaration that their posting of the materials was privileged. They won both the insurgent campaign and the formal one. As a practical matter, the materials remained publicly available throughout this period. As a matter of law, the litigation went badly enough for Diebold that the company issued a letter promising not to sue the students. The court nonetheless awarded the students damages and attorneys' fees because it found that Diebold had "knowingly and materially misrepresented" that the publication of the e-mail archive was a copyright violation in its letters to the Internet service providers.[9]

Central from the perspective of understanding the dynamics of the net-worked public sphere is not, however, the court case—it was resolved almost a year later, after most of the important events had already unfolded—but the efficacy of the students' continued persistent publication in the teeth of the cease-and-desist letters and the willingness of the universities to comply. The strategy of replicating the files everywhere made it impracticable to keep the documents from the public eye. And the public eye, in turn, scrutinized. Among the things that began to surface as users read the files were internal e-mails recognizing problems with the voting system, with the security of the FTP site from which Harris had originally obtained the specifications of the voting systems, and e-mail that indicated that the machines implemented in California had been "patched" or updated after their certification. That is, the machines actually being deployed in California were at least somewhat different from the machines that had been tested and certified by the state. This turned out to have been a critical find.

California had a Voting Systems Panel within the office of the secretary of state that reviewed and certified voting machines. On November 3, 2003, two weeks after the students launched their electronic disobedience cam-paign, the agenda of the panel's meeting was to include a discussion of proposed modifications to one of Diebold's voting systems. Instead of dis-cussing the agenda item, however, one of the panel members made a motion to table the item until the secretary of state had an opportunity to investigate, because "It has come to our attention that some very disconcerting infor-mation regarding this item [sic] and we are informed that this company, Diebold, may have installed uncertified software in at least one county before it was certified."[10] The source of the information is left unclear in the minutes. A later report in *Wired* cited an unnamed source in the secretary of state's office as saying that somebody within the company had provided this information. The timing and context, however, suggest that it was the revelation and discussion of the e-mail memoranda online that played that role. Two of the members of the public who spoke on the record mention information from within the company. One specifically mentions the infor-mation gleaned from company e-mails. In the next committee meeting, on December 16, 2003, one member of the public who was in attendance spe-cifically referred to the e-mails on the Internet, referencing in particular a January e-mail about upgrades and changes to the certified systems. By that December meeting, the independent investigation by the secretary of state had found systematic discrepancies between the systems actually installed and those tested and certified by the state. The following few months saw more studies, answers, debates, and the eventual decertification of many of the Diebold machines installed in California (see figures 7.3a and 7.3b).

The structure of public inquiry, debate, and collective action exemplified by this story is fundamentally different from the structure of public inquiry and debate in the mass-media-dominated public sphere of the twentieth century. The initial investigation and analysis was done by a committed activist, operating on a low budget and with no financing from a media company. The output of this initial inquiry was not a respectable analysis by a major player in the public debate. It was access to raw materials and initial observations about them, available to start a conversation. Analysis then emerged from a widely distributed process undertaken by Internet users of many different types and abilities. In this case, it included academics studying electronic voting systems, activists, computer systems practitioners, and mobilized students. When the pressure from a well-financed corporation mounted, it was not the prestige and money of a *Washington Post* or a *New York Times* that protected the integrity of the information and its availability for public scrutiny. It was the radically distributed cooperative efforts of students and peer-to-peer network users around the Internet. These efforts were, in turn, nested in other communities of cooperative production—like the free software community that developed some of the applications used to disseminate the e-mails after Swarthmore removed them from the students' own site. There was no single orchestrating power—neither party nor professional commercial media outlet. There was instead a series of uncoordinated but mutually reinforcing actions by individuals in different settings and contexts, operating under diverse organizational restrictions and affordances, to expose, analyze, and distribute criticism and evidence for it. The networked public sphere here does not rely on advertising or capturing large audiences to focus its efforts. What became salient for the public agenda and shaped public discussion was what intensely engaged active participants, rather than what kept the moderate attention of large groups of passive viewers. Instead of the lowest-common-denominator focus typical of commercial mass media, each individual and group can—and, indeed, most likely will—focus precisely on what is most intensely interesting to its participants. Instead of iconic representation built on the scarcity of time slots and space on the air or on the page, we see the emergence of a "see for yourself" culture. Access to underlying documents and statements, and to

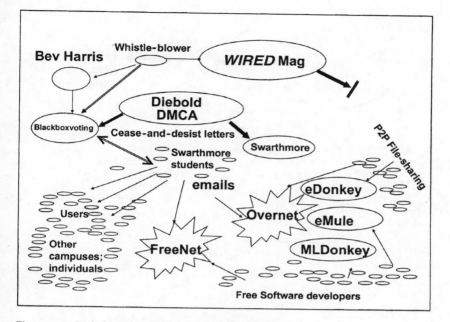

Figure 7.3a: Diebold Internal E-mails Discovery and Distribution

the direct expression of the opinions of others, becomes a central part of the medium.

CRITIQUES OF THE CLAIMS THAT THE INTERNET HAS DEMOCRATIZING EFFECTS

It is common today to think of the 1990s, out of which came the Supreme Court's opinion in *Reno v. ACLU*, as a time of naïve optimism about the Internet, expressing in political optimism the same enthusiasm that drove the stock market bubble, with the same degree of justifiability. An ideal liberal public sphere did not, in fact, burst into being from the Internet, fully grown like Athena from the forehead of Zeus. The detailed criticisms of the early claims about the democratizing effects of the Internet can be characterized as variants of five basic claims:

1. *Information overload.* A basic problem created when everyone can speak is that there will be too many statements, or too much information. Too

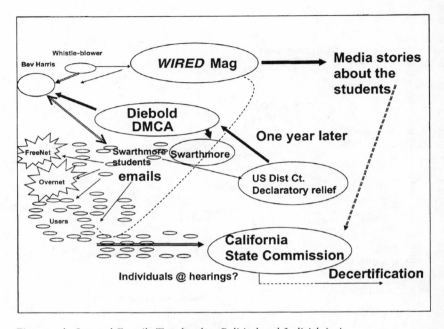

Figure 7.3b: Internal E-mails Translated to Political and Judicial Action

many observations and too many points of view make the problem of sifting through them extremely difficult, leading to an unmanageable din. This overall concern, a variant of the Babel objection, underlies three more specific arguments: that money will end up dominating anyway, that there will be fragmentation of discourse, and that fragmentation of discourse will lead to its polarization.

Money will end up dominating anyway. A point originally raised by Eli Noam is that in this explosively large universe, getting attention will be as difficult as getting your initial message out in the mass-media context, if not more so. The same means that dominated the capacity to speak in the mass-media environment—money—will dominate the capacity to be heard on the Internet, even if it no longer controls the capacity to speak.

Fragmentation of attention and discourse. A point raised most explicitly by Cass Sunstein in *Republic.com* is that the ubiquity of information and the absence of the mass media as condensation points will impoverish public discourse by fragmenting it. There will be no public sphere.

Individuals will view the world through millions of personally customized windows that will offer no common ground for political discourse or action, except among groups of highly similar individuals who customize their windows to see similar things.

Polarization. A descriptively related but analytically distinct critique of Sunstein's was that the fragmentation would lead to polarization. When information and opinions are shared only within groups of like-minded participants, he argued, they tend to reinforce each other's views and beliefs without engaging with alternative views or seeing the concerns and critiques of others. This makes each view more extreme in its own direction and increases the distance between positions taken by opposing camps.

2. *Centralization of the Internet.* A second-generation criticism of the democratizing effects of the Internet is that it turns out, in fact, not to be as egalitarian or distributed as the 1990s conception had suggested. First, there is concentration in the pipelines and basic tools of communications. Second, and more intractable to policy, even in an open network, a high degree of attention is concentrated on a few top sites—a tiny number of sites are read by the vast majority of readers, while many sites are never visited by anyone. In this context, the Internet is replicating the mass-media model, perhaps adding a few channels, but not genuinely changing anything structural.

Note that the concern with information overload is in direct tension with the second-generation concerns. To the extent that the concerns about Internet concentration are correct, they suggest that the information overload is not a deep problem. Sadly, from the perspective of democracy, it turns out that according to the concentration concern, there are few speakers to which most people listen, just as in the mass-media environment. While this means that the supposed benefits of the networked public sphere are illusory, it also means that the information overload concerns about what happens when there is no central set of speakers to whom most people listen are solved in much the same way that the mass-media model deals with the factual diversity of information, opinion, and observations in large societies—by consigning them to public oblivion. The response to both sets of concerns will therefore require combined consideration of a series of questions: To what extent are the claims of concentration correct? How do they solve the information overload problem? To what extent does the observed concentration replicate the mass-media model?

3. *Centrality of commercial mass media to the Fourth Estate function.* The importance of the press to the political process is nothing new. It earned the press the nickname "the Fourth Estate" (a reference to the three estates that made up the prerevolutionary French Estates-General, the clergy, nobility, and townsmen), which has been in use for at least a hundred and fifty years. In American free speech theory, the press is often described as fulfilling "the watchdog function," deriving from the notion that the public representatives must be watched over to assure they do the public's business faithfully. In the context of the Internet, the concern, most clearly articulated by Neil Netanel, has been that in the modern complex societies in which we live, commercial mass media are critical for preserving the watchdog function of the media. Big, sophisticated, well-funded government and corporate market actors have enormous resources at their disposal to act as they please and to avoid scrutiny and democratic control. Only similarly big, powerful, independently funded media organizations, whose basic market roles are to observe and criticize other large organizations, can match these established elite organizational actors. Individuals and collections of volunteers talking to each other may be nice, but they cannot seriously replace well-funded, economically and politically powerful media.

4. *Authoritarian countries can use filtering and monitoring to squelch Internet use.* A distinct set of claims and their critiques have to do with the effects of the Internet on authoritarian countries. The critique is leveled at a basic belief supposedly, and perhaps actually, held by some cyber-libertarians, that with enough access to Internet tools freedom will burst out everywhere. The argument is that China, more than any other country, shows that it is possible to allow a population access to the Internet—it is now home to the second-largest national population of Internet users—and still control that use quite substantially.

5. *Digital divide.* While the Internet may increase the circle of participants in the public sphere, access to its tools is skewed in favor of those who already are well-off in society—in terms of wealth, race, and skills. I do not respond to this critique in this chapter. First, in the United States, this is less stark today than it was in the late 1990s. Computers and Internet connections are becoming cheaper and more widely available in public libraries and schools. As they become more central to life, they

seem to be reaching higher penetration rates, and growth rates among underrepresented groups are higher than the growth rate among the highly represented groups. The digital divide with regard to basic access within advanced economies is important as long as it persists, but seems to be a transitional problem. Moreover, it is important to recall that the democratizing effects of the Internet must be compared to democracy in the context of mass media, not in the context of an idealized utopia. Computer literacy and skills, while far from universal, are much more widely distributed than the skills and instruments of mass-media production. Second, I devote chapter 9 to the question of how and why the emergence specifically of nonmarket production provides new avenues for substantial improvements in equality of access to various desiderata that the market distributes unevenly, both within advanced economies and globally, where the maldistribution is much more acute. While the digital divide critique can therefore temper our enthusiasm for how radical the change represented by the networked information economy may be in terms of democracy, the networked information economy is itself an avenue for alleviating maldistribution.

The remainder of this chapter is devoted to responding to these critiques, providing a defense of the claim that the Internet can contribute to a more attractive liberal public sphere. As we work through these objections, we can develop a better understanding of how the networked information economy responds to or overcomes the particular systematic failures of mass media as platforms for the public sphere. Throughout this analysis, it is comparison of the attractiveness of the networked public sphere to that baseline—the mass-media-dominated public sphere—not comparison to a nonexistent ideal public sphere or to the utopia of "everyone a pamphleteer," that should matter most to our assessment of its democratic promise.

IS THE INTERNET TOO CHAOTIC, TOO CONCENTRATED, OR NEITHER?

The first-generation critique of the claims that the Internet democratizes focused heavily on three variants of the information overload or Babel objection. The basic descriptive proposition that animated the Supreme Court in *Reno v. ACLU* was taken as more or less descriptively accurate: Everyone would be equally able to speak on the Internet. However, this basic observation was then followed by a descriptive or normative explanation of why this development was a threat to democracy, or at least not much of a boon. The basic problem that is diagnosed by this line of critique is the problem of attention. When everyone can speak, the central point of failure becomes the capacity to be heard—who listens to whom, and how that question is decided. Speaking in a medium that no one will actually hear with any reasonable likelihood may be psychologically satisfying, but it is not a move in a political conversation. Noam's prediction was, therefore, that there would be a reconcentration of attention: money would reemerge in this environment as a major determinant of the capacity to be heard, certainly no less, and perhaps even more so, than it was in the mass-media environment.[11] Sunstein's theory was different. He accepted Nicholas Negroponte's prediction that people would be reading "The Daily Me," that is, that each of us would create highly customized windows on the information environment that would be narrowly tailored to our unique combination of interests. From this assumption about how people would be informed, he spun out two distinct but related critiques. The first was that discourse would be fragmented. With no six o'clock news to tell us what is on the public agenda, there would be no public agenda, just a fragmented multiplicity of private agendas that never coalesce into a platform for political discussion. The second was that, in a fragmented discourse, individuals would cluster into groups of self-reinforcing, self-referential discussion groups. These types of groups, he argued from social scientific evidence, tend to render their participants' views more extreme and less amenable to the conversation across political divides necessary to achieve reasoned democratic decisions.

Extensive empirical and theoretical studies of actual use patterns of the Internet over the past five to eight years has given rise to a second-generation critique of the claim that the Internet democratizes. According to this critique, attention is much more concentrated on the Internet than we thought a few years ago: a tiny number of sites are highly linked, the vast majority of "speakers" are not heard, and the democratic potential of the Internet is lost. If correct, these claims suggest that Internet use patterns solve the problem of discourse fragmentation that Sunstein was worried about. Rather than each user reading a customized and completely different "newspaper," the vast majority of users turn out to see the same sites. In a network with a small number of highly visible sites that practically everyone reads, the discourse fragmentation problem is resolved. Because they are seen by most people, the polarization problem too is solved—the highly visible sites are not small-group interactions with homogeneous viewpoints. While resolving Sunstein's concerns, this pattern is certainly consistent with Noam's prediction that money would have to be paid to reach visibility, effectively replicating the mass-media model. While centralization would resolve the Babel objection, it would do so only at the expense of losing much of the democratic promise of the Net.

Therefore, we now turn to the question: Is the Internet in fact too chaotic or too concentrated to yield a more attractive democratic discourse than the mass media did? I suggest that neither is the case. At the risk of appearing a chimera of Goldilocks and Pangloss, I argue instead that the observed use of the network exhibits an order that is not too concentrated and not too chaotic, but rather, if not "just right," at least structures a networked public sphere more attractive than the mass-media-dominated public sphere.

There are two very distinct types of claims about Internet centralization. The first, and earlier, has the familiar ring of media concentration. It is the simpler of the two, and is tractable to policy. The second, concerned with the emergent patterns of attention and linking on an otherwise open network, is more difficult to explain and intractable to policy. I suggest, however, that it actually stabilizes and structures democratic discourse, providing a better answer to the fears of information overload than either the mass media or any efforts to regulate attention to matters of public concern.

The media-concentration type argument has been central to arguments about the necessity of open access to broadband platforms, made most forcefully over the past few years by Lawrence Lessig. The argument is that the basic instrumentalities of Internet communications are subject to concentrated markets. This market concentration in basic access becomes a potential point of concentration of the power to influence the discourse made possible by access. Eli Noam's recent work provides the most comprehensive study currently available of the degree of market concentration in media industries. It offers a bleak picture.[12] Noam looked at markets in basic infrastructure components of the Internet: Internet backbones, Internet service providers (ISPs), broadband providers, portals, search engines, browser software, media player software, and Internet telephony. Aggregating across all these sectors, he found that the Internet sector defined in terms of these components was, throughout most of the period from 1984 to 2002, concentrated according to traditional antitrust measures. Between 1992 and 1998, however, this sector was "highly concentrated" by the Justice Department's measure of market concentration for antitrust purposes. Moreover, the power of the top ten firms in each of these markets, and in aggregate for firms that had large market segments in a number of these markets, shows that an ever-smaller number of firms were capturing about 25 percent of the revenues in the Internet sector. A cruder, but consistent finding is the FCC's, showing that 96 percent of homes and small offices get their broadband access either from their incumbent cable operator or their incumbent local telephone carrier.[13] It is important to recognize that these findings are suggesting potential points of failure for the networked information economy. They are not a critique of the democratic potential of the networked public sphere, but rather show us how we could fail to develop it by following the wrong policies.

The risk of concentration in broadband access services is that a small number of firms, sufficiently small to have economic power in the antitrust sense, will control the markets for the basic instrumentalities of Internet communications. Recall, however, that the low cost of computers and the open-ended architecture of the Internet protocol itself are the core enabling facts that have allowed us to transition from the mass-media model to the networked information model. As long as these basic instrumentalities are open and neutral as among uses, and are relatively cheap, the basic economics of nonmarket production described in part I should not change. Under competitive conditions, as technology makes computation and communications cheaper, a well-functioning market should ensure that outcome. Under oligopolistic conditions, however, there is a threat that the network will become too expensive to be neutral as among market and nonmarket production. If basic upstream network connections, server space, and up-to-date reading and writing utilities become so expensive that one needs to adopt a commercial model to sustain them, then the basic economic characteristic that typifies the networked information economy—the relatively large role of nonproprietary, nonmarket production—will have been reversed. However, the risk is not focused solely or even primarily on explicit pricing. One of the primary remaining scarce resources in the networked environment is user time and attention. As chapter 5 explained, owners of communications facilities can extract value from their users in ways that are more subtle than increasing price. In particular, they can make some sites and statements easier to reach and see—more prominently displayed on the screen, faster to load—and sell that relative ease to those who are willing to pay.[14] In that environment, nonmarket sites are systematically disadvantaged irrespective of the quality of their content.

The critique of concentration in this form therefore does not undermine the claim that the networked information economy, if permitted to flourish, will improve the democratic public sphere. It underscores the threat of excessive monopoly in infrastructure to the sustainability of the networked public sphere. The combination of observations regarding market concentration and an understanding of the importance of a networked public sphere to democratic societies suggests that a policy intervention is possible and desirable. Chapter 11 explains why the relevant intervention is to permit substantial segments of the core common infrastructure—the basic physical transport layer of wireless or fiber and the software and standards that run communications—to be produced and provisioned by users and managed as a commons.

ON POWER LAW DISTRIBUTIONS, NETWORK TOPOLOGY, AND BEING HEARD

A much more intractable challenge to the claim that the networked information economy will democratize the public sphere emerges from observations of a set or phenomena that characterize the Internet, the Web, the blogosphere, and, indeed, most growing networks. In order to extract information out of the universe of statements and communications made possible by the Internet, users are freely adopting practices that lead to the emergence of a new hierarchy. Rather than succumb to the "information overload" problem, users are solving it by congregating in a small number of sites. This conclusion is based on a new but growing literature on the likelihood that a Web page will be linked to by others. The distribution of that probability turns out to be highly skew. That is, there is a tiny probability that any given Web site will be linked to by a huge number of people, and a very large probability that for a given Web site only one other site, or even no site, will link to it. This fact is true of large numbers of very different networks described in physics, biology, and social science, as well as in communications networks. If true in this pure form about Web usage, this phenomenon presents a serious theoretical and empirical challenge to the claim that Internet communications of the sorts we have seen here meaningfully decentralize democratic discourse. It is not a problem that is tractable to policy. We cannot as a practical matter force people to read different things than what they choose to read; nor should we wish to. If users avoid information overload by focusing on a small subset of sites in an otherwise open network that allows them to read more or less whatever they want and whatever anyone has written, policy interventions aimed to force a different pattern would be hard to justify from the perspective of liberal democratic theory.

The sustained study of the distribution of links on the Internet and the Web is relatively new—only a few years old. There is significant theoretical work in a field of mathematics called graph theory, or network topology, on power law distributions in networks, on skew distributions that are not pure power law, and on the mathematically related small-worlds phenomenon in networks. The basic intuition is that, if indeed a tiny minority of sites gets a large number of links, and the vast majority gets few or no links, it will be very difficult to be seen unless you are on the highly visible site. Attention patterns make the open network replicate mass media. While explaining this literature over the next few pages, I show that what is in fact emerging is very different from, and more attractive than, the mass-media-dominated public sphere.

While the Internet, the Web, and the blogosphere are indeed exhibiting much greater order than the freewheeling, "everyone a pamphleteer" image would suggest, this structure does not replicate a mass-media model. We are seeing a newly shaped information environment, where indeed few are read by many, but clusters of moderately read sites provide platforms for vastly greater numbers of speakers than were heard in the mass-media environment. Filtering, accreditation, synthesis, and salience are created through a system of peer review by information affinity groups, topical or interest based. These groups filter the observations and opinions of an enormous range of people, and transmit those that pass local peer review to broader groups and ultimately to the polity more broadly, without recourse to market-based points of control over the information flow. Intense interest and engagement by small groups that share common concerns, rather than lowest-common-denominator interest in wide groups that are largely alienated from each other, is what draws attention to statements and makes them more visible. This makes the emerging networked public sphere more responsive to intensely held concerns of a much wider swath of the population than the mass media were capable of seeing, and creates a communications process that is more resistant to corruption by money.

In what way, first, is attention concentrated on the Net? We are used to seeing probability distributions that describe social phenomena following a Gaussian distribution: where the mean and the median are the same and the probabilities fall off symmetrically as we describe events that are farther from the median. This is the famous Bell Curve. Some phenomena, however, observed initially in Pareto's work on income distribution and Zipf's on the probability of the use of English words in text and in city populations, exhibit completely different probability distributions. These distributions have very long "tails"—that is, they are characterized by a very small number of very high-yield events (like the number of words that have an enormously high probability of appearing in a randomly chosen sentence, like "the" or "to") and a very large number of events that have a very low probability of appearing (like the probability that the word "probability" or "blogosphere" will appear in a randomly chosen sentence). To grasp intuitively how un-intuitive such distributions are to us, we could think of radio humorist Garrison Keillor's description of the fictitious Lake Wobegon, where "all the children are above average." That statement is amusing because we assume intelligence follows a normal distribution. If intelligence were distributed according to a power law, most children there would actually be below average—the median is well below the mean in such distributions (see figure 7.4). Later work by Herbert Simon in the 1950s, and by Derek de Solla Price in the 1960s, on cumulative advantage in scientific citations[15] presaged an emergence at the end of the 1990s of intense interest in power law characterizations of degree distributions, or the number of connections any point in a network has to other points, in many kinds of networks—from networks of neurons and axons, to social networks and communications and information networks.

The Internet and the World Wide Web offered a testable setting, where large-scale investigation could be done automatically by studying link structure (who is linked-in to and by whom, who links out and to whom, how these are related, and so on), and where the practical applications of better understanding were easily articulated—such as the design of better search engines. In 1999, Albert-László Barabási and Reka Albert published a paper in *Science* showing that a variety of networked phenomena have a predictable topology: The distribution of links into and out of nodes on the network follows a power law. There is a very low probability that any vertex, or node, in the network will be very highly connected to many others, and a very large probability that a very large number of nodes will be connected only very loosely, or perhaps not at all. Intuitively, a lot of Web sites link to information that is located on Yahoo!, while very few link to any randomly selected individual's Web site. Barabási and Albert hypothesized a mechanism

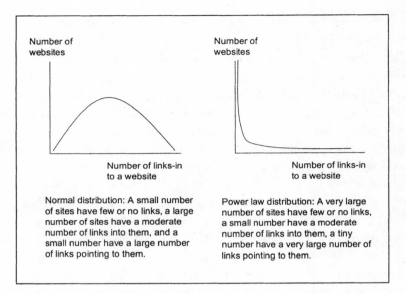

Figure 7.4: Illustration of How Normal Distribution and Power Law Distribution Would Differ in Describing How Many Web Sites Have Few or Many Links Pointing at Them

for this distribution to evolve, which they called "preferential attachment." That is, new nodes prefer to attach to already well-attached nodes. Any network that grows through the addition of new nodes, and in which nodes preferentially attach to nodes that are already well attached, will eventually exhibit this distribution.[16] In other words, the rich get richer. At the same time, two computer scientists, Lada Adamic and Bernardo Huberman, published a study in *Nature* that identified the presence of power law distributions in the number of Web pages in a given site. They hypothesized not that new nodes preferentially attach to old ones, but that each site has an intrinsically different growth rate, and that new sites are formed at an exponential rate.[17] The intrinsically different growth rates could be interpreted as quality, interest, or perhaps investment of money in site development and marketing. They showed that on these assumptions, a power law distribution would emerge. Since the publication of these articles we have seen an explosion of theoretical and empirical literature on graph theory, or the structure and growth of networks, and particularly on link structure in the World Wide Web. It has consistently shown that the number of links into and out of Web sites follows power laws and that the exponent (the exponential factor that determines that the drop-off between the most linked-to site and the second most linked-to site, and the third, and so on, will be so dramatically rapid, and how rapid it is) for inlinks is roughly 2.1 and for outlinks 2.7.

If one assumes that most people read things by either following links, or by using a search engine, like Google, that heavily relies on counting inlinks to rank its results, then it is likely that the number of visitors to a Web page, and more recently, the number of readers of blogs, will follow a similarly highly skew distribution. The implication for democracy that comes most immediately to mind is dismal. While, as the Supreme Court noted with enthusiasm, on the Internet everyone can be a pamphleteer or have their own soapbox, the Internet does not, in fact, allow individuals to be heard in ways that are substantially more effective than standing on a soapbox in a city square. Many Web pages and blogs will simply go unread, and will not contribute to a more engaged polity. This argument was most clearly made in Barabási's popularization of his field, *Linked*: "The most intriguing result of our Web-mapping project was the *complete* absence of democracy, fairness, and egalitarian values on the Web. We learned that the topology of the Web prevents us from seeing anything but a mere handful of the billion documents out there."[18]

The stories offered in this chapter and throughout this book present a puzzle for this interpretation of the power law distribution of links in the network as re-creating a concentrated medium. The success of Nick Davis's site, BoycottSBG, would be a genuine fluke. The probability that such a site could be established on a Monday, and by Friday of the same week would have had three hundred thousand unique visitors and would have orchestrated a successful campaign, is so small as to be negligible. The probability that a completely different site, StopSinclair.org, of equally network-obscure origins, would be established on the very same day and also successfully catch the attention of enough readers to collect 150,000 signatures on a petition to protest Sinclair's broadcast, rather than wallowing undetected in the mass of self-published angry commentary, is practically insignificant. And yet, intuitively, it seems unsurprising that a large population of individuals who are politically mobilized on the same side of the political map and share a political goal in the public sphere—using a network that makes it trivially simple to set up new points of information and coordination, tell each other about them, and reach and use them from anywhere—would, in fact, inform each other and gather to participate in a political demonstration. We saw that the boycott technique that Davis had designed his Web site to facilitate was discussed on TalkingPoints—a site near the top of the power law distribution of political blogs—but that it was a proposal by an anonymous individual who claimed to know what makes local affiliates tick, not of TalkingPoints author Josh Marshall. By midweek, after initially stoking the fires of support for Davis's boycott, Marshall had stepped back, and Davis's site became the clearing point for reports, tactical conversations, and mobilization. Davis not only was visible, but rather than being drowned out by the high-powered transmitter, TalkingPoints, his relationship with the high-visibility site was part of his success. This story alone cannot, of course, "refute" the power law distribution of network links, nor is it offered as a refutation. It does, however, provide a context for looking more closely at the emerging understanding of the topology of the Web, and how it relates to the fears of concentration of the Internet, and the problems of information overload, discourse fragmentation, and the degree to which money will come to dominate such an unstructured and wide-open environment. It suggests a more complex story than simply "the rich get richer" and "you might speak, but no one will hear you." In this case, the topology of the network allowed rapid emergence of a position, its filtering and synthesis, and its rise to salience. Network topology helped facilitate all these components of the public sphere, rather than undermined them. We can go back to the mathematical and computer science literature to begin to see why.

Within two months of the publication of Barabási and Albert's article, Adamic and Huberman had published a letter arguing that, if Barabási and Albert were right about preferential attachment, then older sites should systematically be among those that are at the high end of the distribution, while new ones will wallow in obscurity. The older sites are already attached, so newer sites would preferentially attach to the older sites. This, in turn, would make them even more attractive when a new crop of Web sites emerged and had to decide which sites to link to. In fact, however, Adamic and Huberman showed that there is no such empirical correlation among Web sites. They argued that their mechanism—that nodes have intrinsic growth rates that are different—better describes the data. In their response, Barabási and Albert showed that on their data set, the older nodes are actually more connected in a way that follows a power law, but only on average—that is to say, the average number of connections of a class of older nodes related to the average number of links to a younger class of nodes follows a power law. This argued that their basic model was sound, but required that they modify their equations to include something similar to what Huberman and Adamic had proposed—an intrinsic growth factor for each node, as well as the preferential connection of new nodes to established nodes.[19] This modification is important because it means that not every new node is doomed to be unread relative to the old ones, only that on average they are much less likely to be read. It makes room for rapidly growing new nodes, but does not theorize what might determine the rate of growth. It is possible, for example, that money could determine growth rates: In order to be seen, new sites or statements would have to spend money to gain visibility and salience. As the BoycottSBG and Diebold stories suggest, however, as does the Lott story described later in this chapter, there are other ways of achieving immediate salience. In the case of BoycottSBG, it was providing a solution that resonated with the political beliefs of many people and was useful to them for their expression and mobilization. Moreover, the continued presence of preferential attachment suggests that noncommercial Web sites that are already highly connected because of the time they were introduced (like the Electronic Frontier Foundation), because of their internal attractiveness to large communities (like Slashdot), or because of their salience to the immediate interests of users (like BoycottSBG), will have persistent visibility even in the face of large infusions of money by commercial sites.

Developments in network topology theory and its relationship to the structure of the empirically mapped real Internet offer a map of the networked information environment that is indeed quite different from the naïve model of "everyone a pamphleteer." To the limited extent that these findings have been interpreted for political meaning, they have been seen as a disappointment—the real world, as it turns out, does not measure up to anything like that utopia. However, that is the wrong baseline. There never has been a complex, large modern democracy in which everyone could speak and be heard by everyone else. The correct baseline is the one-way structure of the commercial mass media. The normatively relevant descriptive questions are whether the networked public sphere provides broader intake, participatory filtering, and relatively incorruptible platforms for creating public salience. I suggest that it does. Four characteristics of network topology structure the Web and the blogosphere in an ordered, but nonetheless meaningfully participatory form. First, at a microlevel, sites cluster—in particular, topically and interest-related sites link much more heavily to each other than to other sites. Second, at a macrolevel, the Web and the blogosphere have giant, strongly connected cores—"areas" where 20–30 percent of all sites are highly and redundantly interlinked; that is, tens or hundreds of millions of sites, rather than ten, fifty, or even five hundred television stations. That pattern repeats itself in smaller subclusters as well. Third, as the clusters get small enough, the obscurity of sites participating in the cluster diminishes, while the visibility of the superstars remains high, forming a filtering and transmission backbone for universal intake and local filtering. Fourth and finally, the Web exhibits "small-world" phenomena, making most Web sites reachable through shallow paths from most other Web sites. I will explain each of these below, as well as how they interact to form a reasonably attractive image of the networked public sphere.

First, links are not smoothly distributed throughout the network. Sites cluster into densely linked "regions" or communities of interest. Computer scientists have looked at clustering from the perspective of what topical or other correlated characteristics describe these relatively high-density interconnected regions of nodes. What they found was perhaps entirely predictable from an intuitive perspective of the network users, but important as we try to understand the structure of information flow on the Web. Web sites cluster into topical and social/organizational clusters. Early work done in the IBM Almaden Research Center on how link structure could be used as a search technique showed that by mapping densely interlinked sites without looking at content, one could find communities of interest that identify very fine-grained topical connections, such as Australian fire brigades or Turkish students in the United States.[20] A later study out of the NEC Research Institute more formally defined the interlinking that would identify a "community" as one in which the nodes were more densely connected to each other than they were to nodes outside the cluster by some amount. The study also showed that topically connected sites meet this definition. For instance, sites related to molecular biology clustered with each other—in the sense of being more interlinked with each other than with off-topic sites—as did sites about physics and black holes.[21] Lada Adamic and Natalie Glance recently showed that liberal political blogs and conservative political blogs densely interlink with each other, mostly pointing within each political leaning but with about 15 percent of links posted by the most visible sites also linking across the political divide.[22] Physicists analyze clustering as the property of transitivity in networks: the increased probability that if node A is connected to node B, and node B is connected to node C, that node A also will be connected to node C, forming a triangle. Newman has shown that the clustering coefficient of a network that exhibits power law distribution of connections or degrees—that is, its tendency to cluster—is related to the exponent of the distribution. At low exponents, below 2.333, the clustering coefficient becomes high. This explains analytically the empirically observed high level of clustering on the Web, whose exponent for inlinks has been empirically shown to be 2.1.[23]

Second, at a macrolevel and in smaller subclusters, the power law distribution does not resolve into everyone being connected in a mass-media model relationship to a small number of major "backbone" sites. As early as 1999, Broder and others showed that a very large number of sites occupy what has been called a giant, strongly connected core.[24] That is, nodes within this core are heavily linked and interlinked, with multiple redundant paths among them. Empirically, as of 2001, this structure was comprised of about 28 percent of nodes. At the same time, about 22 percent of nodes had links into the core, but were not linked to from it—these may have been new sites, or relatively lower-interest sites. The same proportion of sites was linked-to from the core, but did not link back to it—these might have been ultimate depositories of documents, or internal organizational sites. Finally, roughly the same proportion of sites occupied "tendrils" or "tubes" that cannot reach, or be reached from, the core. Tendrils can be reached from the group of sites that link into the strongly connected core or can reach into the group that can be connected to from the core. Tubes connect the inlinking sites to the outlinked sites without going through the core. About 10 percent of sites are entirely isolated. This structure has been called a "bow tie"—with a large core and equally sized in- and outflows to and from that core (see figure 7.5).

One way of interpreting this structure as counterdemocratic is to say: This means that half of all Web sites are not reachable from the other half—the "IN," "tendrils," and disconnected portions cannot be reached from any of the sites in SCC and OUT. This is indeed disappointing from the "everyone a pamphleteer" perspective. On the other hand, one could say that half of all Web pages, the SCC and OUT components, *are* reachable from IN and SCC. That is, hundreds of millions of pages are reachable from hundreds of millions of potential entry points. This represents a very different intake function and freedom to speak in a way that is potentially accessible to others than a five-hundred-channel, mass-media model. More significant yet, Dill and others showed that the bow tie structure appears not only at the level of the Web as a whole, but repeats itself within clusters. That is, the Web

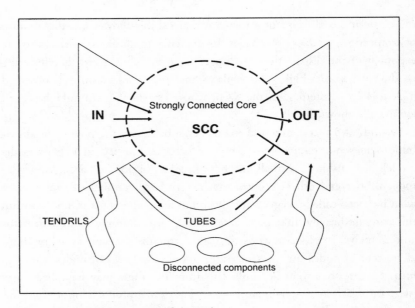

Figure 7.5: Bow Tie Structure of the Web

appears to show characteristics of self-similarity, up to a point—links within clusters also follow a power law distribution and cluster, and have a bow tie structure of similar proportions to that of the overall Web. Tying the two points about clustering and the presence of a strongly connected core, Dill and his coauthors showed that what they called "thematically unified clusters," such as geographically or content-related groupings of Web sites, themselves exhibit these strongly connected cores that provided a thematically defined navigational backbone to the Web. It is not that one or two major sites were connected to by all thematically related sites; rather, as at the network level, on the order of 25–30 percent were highly interlinked, and another 25 percent were reachable from within the strongly connected core.[25] Moreover, when the data was pared down to treat only the home page, rather than each Web page within a single site as a distinct "node" (that is, everything that came under www.foo.com was treated as one node, as opposed to the usual method where www.foo.com, www.foo.com/nonsuch, and www.foo.com/somethingelse are each treated as a separate node), fully 82 percent of the nodes were in the strongly connected core, and an additional 13 percent were reachable from the SCC as the OUT group.

Third, another finding of Web topology and critical adjustment to the basic Barabási and Albert model is that when the topically or organizationally related clusters become small enough—on the order of hundreds or even low thousands of Web pages—they no longer follow a pure power law distribution. Instead, they follow a distribution that still has a very long tail— these smaller clusters still have a few genuine "superstars"—but the body of the distribution is substantially more moderate: beyond the few superstars, the shape of the link distribution looks a little more like a normal distribution. Instead of continuing to drop off exponentially, many sites exhibit a moderate degree of connectivity. Figure 7.6 illustrates how a hypothetical distribution of this sort would differ both from the normal and power law distributions illustrated in figure 7.4. David Pennock and others, in their paper describing these empirical findings, hypothesized a uniform component added to the purely exponential original Barabási and Albert model. This uniform component could be random (as they modeled it), but might also stand for quality of materials, or level of interest in the site by participants in the smaller cluster. At large numbers of nodes, the exponent dominates the uniform component, accounting for the pure power law distribution when looking at the Web as a whole, or even at broadly defined topics. In smaller clusters of sites, however, the uniform component begins to exert a stronger pull on the distribution. The exponent keeps the long tail intact, but the uniform component accounts for a much more moderate body. Many sites will have dozens, or even hundreds of links. The Pennock paper looked at sites whose number was reduced by looking only at sites of certain organizations—universities or public companies. Chakrabarti and others later confirmed this finding for topical clusters as well. That is, when they looked at small clusters of topically related sites, the distribution of links still has a long tail for a small number of highly connected sites in every topic, but the body of the distribution diverges from a power law distribution, and represents a substantial proportion of sites that are moderately linked.[26] Even more specifically, Daniel Drezner and Henry Farrell reported that the Pennock modification better describes distribution of links specifically to and among political blogs.[27]

These findings are critical to the interpretation of the distribution of links as it relates to human attention and communication. There is a big difference between a situation where no one is looking at any of the sites on the low end of the distribution, because everyone is looking only at the superstars, and a situation where dozens or hundreds of sites at the low end are looking at each other, as well as at the superstars. The former leaves all but the very

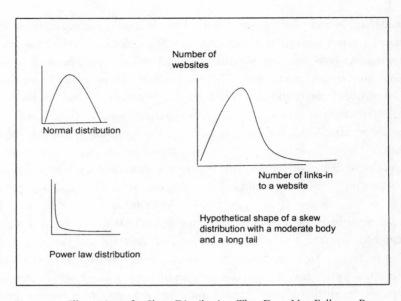

Figure 7.6: Illustration of a Skew Distribution That Does Not Follow a Power Law

few languishing in obscurity, with no one to look at them. The latter, as explained in more detail below, offers a mechanism for topically related and interest-based clusters to form a peer-reviewed system of filtering, accreditation, and salience generation. It gives the long tail on the low end of the distribution heft (and quite a bit of wag).

The fourth and last piece of mapping the network as a platform for the public sphere is called the "small-worlds effect." Based on Stanley Milgram's sociological experiment and on mathematical models later proposed by Duncan Watts and Steven Strogatz, both theoretical and empirical work has shown that the number of links that must be traversed from any point in the network to any other point is relatively small.[28] Fairly shallow "walks"— that is, clicking through three or four layers of links—allow a user to cover a large portion of the Web.

What is true of the Web as a whole turns out to be true of the blogosphere as well, and even of the specifically political blogosphere. Early 2003 saw increasing conversations in the blogosphere about the emergence of an "A-list," a number of highly visible blogs that were beginning to seem more like mass media than like blogs. In two blog-based studies, Clay Shirky and then Jason Kottke published widely read explanations of how the blogosphere was simply exhibiting the power law characteristics common on the Web.[29] The emergence in 2003 of discussions of this sort in the blogosphere is, it turns out, hardly surprising. In a time-sensitive study also published in 2003, Kumar and others provided an analysis of the network topology of the blogosphere. They found that it was very similar to that of the Web as a whole—both at the macro- and microlevels. Interestingly, they found that the strongly connected core only developed after a certain threshold, in terms of total number of nodes, had been reached, and that it began to develop extensively only in 2001, reached about 20 percent of all blogs in 2002, and continued to grow rapidly. They also showed that what they called the "community" structure—the degree of clustering or mutual pointing within groups—was high, an order of magnitude more than a random graph with a similar power law exponent would have generated. Moreover, the degree to which a cluster is active or inactive, highly connected or not, changes over time. In addition to time-insensitive superstars, there are also flare-ups of connectivity for sites depending on the activity and relevance of their community of interest. This latter observation is consistent with what we saw happen for BoycottSBG.com. Kumar and his collaborators explained these phenomena by the not-too-surprising claim that bloggers link to each other based on topicality—that is, their judgment of the quality and relevance of the materials—not only on the basis of how well connected they are already.[30]

This body of literature on network topology suggests a model for how order has emerged on the Internet, the World Wide Web, and the blogosphere. The networked public sphere allows hundreds of millions of people to publish whatever and whenever they please without disintegrating into an unusable cacophony, as the first-generation critics argued, and it filters and focuses attention without re-creating the highly concentrated model of the mass media that concerned the second-generation critique. We now know that the network at all its various layers follows a degree of order, where some sites are vastly more visible than most. This order is loose enough, however, and exhibits a sufficient number of redundant paths from an enormous number of sites to another enormous number, that the effect is fundamentally different from the small number of commercial professional editors of the mass media.

Individuals and individual organizations cluster around topical, organizational, or other common features. At a sufficiently fine-grained degree of clustering, a substantial proportion of the clustered sites are moderately connected, and each can therefore be a point of intake that will effectively transmit observations or opinions within and among the users of that topical or interest-based cluster. Because even in small clusters the distribution of links still has a long tail, these smaller clusters still include high-visibility nodes. These relatively high-visibility nodes can serve as points of transfer to larger clusters, acting as an attention backbone that transmits information among clusters. Subclusters within a general category—such as liberal and conservative blogs clustering within the broader cluster of political blogs—are also interlinked, though less densely than within-cluster connectivity. The higher level or larger clusters again exhibit a similar feature, where higher visibility nodes can serve as clearinghouses and connectivity points among clusters and across the Web. These are all highly connected with redundant links within a giant, strongly connected core—comprising more than a quarter of the nodes in any given level of cluster. The small-worlds phenomenon means that individual users who travel a small number of different links from similar starting points within a cluster cover large portions of the Web and can find diverse sites. By then linking to them on their own Web sites, or giving them to others by e-mail or blog post, sites provide multiple redundant paths open to many users to and from most statements on the Web. High-visibility nodes amplify and focus on given statements, and in this regard, have greater power in the information environment they occupy. However, there is sufficient redundancy of paths through high-visibility nodes that no single node or small collection of nodes can control the flow of information in the core and around the Web. This is true both at the level of the cluster and at the level of the Web as a whole.

The result is an ordered system of intake, filtering, and synthesis that can in theory emerge in networks generally, and empirically has been shown to have emerged on the Web. It does not depend on single points of control. It avoids the generation of a din through which no voice can be heard, as the fears of fragmentation predicted. And, while money may be useful in achieving visibility, the structure of the Web means that money is neither necessary nor sufficient to grab attention—because the networked information economy, unlike its industrial predecessor, does not offer simple points of dissemination and control for purchasing assured attention. What the network topology literature allows us to do, then, is to offer a richer, more detailed, and empirically supported picture of how the network can be a platform for the public sphere that is structured in a fundamentally different way than the mass-media model. The problem is approached through a self-organizing principle, beginning with communities of interest on smallish scales, practices of mutual pointing, and the fact that, with freedom to choose what to see and who to link to, with some codependence among the choices of individuals as to whom to link, highly connected points emerge even at small scales, and continue to be replicated with ever-larger visibility as the clusters grow. Without forming or requiring a formal hierarchy, and without creating single points of control, each cluster generates a set of sites that offer points of initial filtering, in ways that are still congruent with the judgments of participants in the highly connected small cluster. The process is replicated at larger and more general clusters, to the point where positions that have been synthesized "locally" and "regionally" can reach Web-wide visibility and salience. It turns out that we are not intellectual lemmings. We do not use the freedom that the network has made possible to plunge into the abyss of incoherent babble. Instead, through iterative processes of cooperative filtering and "transmission" through the high visibility nodes, the low-end thin tail turns out to be a peer-produced filter and transmission medium for a vastly larger number of speakers than was imaginable in the mass-media model.

The effects of the topology of the network are reinforced by the cultural forms of linking, e-mail lists, and the writable Web. The network topology literature treats every page or site as a node. The emergence of the writable Web, however, allows each node to itself become a cluster of users and posters who, collectively, gain salience as a node. Slashdot is "a node" in the network as a whole, one that is highly linked and visible. Slashdot itself, however, is a highly distributed system for peer production of observations and opinions about matters that people who care about information technology and communications ought to care about. Some of the most visible blogs, like the dailyKos, are cooperative blogs with a number of authors. More important, the major blogs receive input—through posts or e-mails—from their users. Recall, for example, that the original discussion of a Sinclair boycott that would focus on local advertisers arrived on TalkingPoints through an e-mail comment from a reader. Talkingpoints regularly solicits and incorporates input from and research by its users. The cultural practice of writing to highly visible blogs with far greater ease than writing a letter to the editor and with looser constraints on what gets posted makes these nodes themselves platforms for the expression, filtering, and synthesis of observations and opinions. Moreover, as Drezner and Farrell have shown, blogs have developed cultural practices of mutual citation—when one blogger finds a source by reading another, the practice is to link to the original blog, not only directly to the underlying source. Jack Balkin has argued that the culture of linking more generally and the "see for yourself" culture also significantly militate against fragmentation of discourse, because users link to materials they are commenting on, even in disagreement.

Our understanding of the emerging structure of the networked information environment, then, provides the basis for a response to the family of criticisms of the first generation claims that the Internet democratizes. Recall that these criticisms, rooted in the problem of information overload, or the Babel objection, revolved around three claims. The first claim was that the Internet would result in a fragmentation of public discourse. The clustering of topically related sites, such as politically oriented sites, and of communities of interest, the emergence of high-visibility sites that the majority of sites link to, and the practices of mutual linking show quantitatively and qualitatively what Internet users likely experience intuitively. While there is enormous diversity on the Internet, there are also mechanisms and practices that generate a common set of themes, concerns, and public knowledge around which a public sphere can emerge. Any given site is likely to be within a very small number of clicks away from a site that is visible from a very large number of other sites, and these form a backbone of common materials, observations, and concerns. All the findings of power law distribution of linking, clustering, and the presence of a strongly connected core, as well as the linking culture and "see for yourself," oppose the fragmentation prediction. Users self-organize to filter the universe of information that is generated in the network. This self-organization includes a number of highly salient sites that provide a core of common social and cultural experiences and knowledge that can provide the basis for a common public sphere, rather than a fragmented one.

The second claim was that fragmentation would cause polarization. Because like-minded people would talk only to each other, they would tend to amplify their differences and adopt more extreme versions of their positions. Given that the evidence demonstrates there is no fragmentation, in the sense of a lack of a common discourse, it would be surprising to find higher polarization because of the Internet. Moreover, as Balkin argued, the fact that the Internet allows widely dispersed people with extreme views to find each other and talk is not a failure for the liberal public sphere, though it may present new challenges for the liberal state in constraining extreme action. Only polarization of discourse in society as a whole can properly be considered a challenge to the attractiveness of the networked public sphere. However, the practices of linking, "see for yourself," or quotation of the position one is criticizing, and the widespread practice of examining and criticizing the assumptions and assertions of one's interlocutors actually point the other way, militating against polarization. A potential counterargument, however, was created by the most extensive recent study of the political blogosphere. In that study, Adamic and Glance showed that only about 10 percent of the links on any randomly selected political blog linked to a site across the ideological divide. The number increased for the "A-list" political blogs, which linked across the political divide about 15 percent of the time. The picture that emerges is one of distinct "liberal" and "conservative" spheres of conversation, with very dense links within, and more sparse links between them. On one interpretation, then, although there are salient sites that provide a common subject matter for discourse, actual conversations occur in distinct and separate spheres—exactly the kind of setting that Sunstein argued would lead to polarization. Two of the study's findings, however, suggest a different interpretation. The first was that there was still a substantial amount of cross-divide linking. One out of every six or seven links in the top sites on each side of the divide linked to the other side in roughly equal proportions (although conservatives tended to link slightly more overall—both internally and across the divide). The second was, that in an effort to see whether the more closely interlinked conservative sites therefore showed greater convergence "on message," Adamic and Glance found that greater interlinking did not correlate with less diversity in external (outside of the blogosphere) reference points.[31] Together, these findings suggest a different interpretation. Each cluster of more or less like-minded blogs tended to read each other and quote each other much more than they did the other side. This operated not so much as an echo chamber as a forum for working out of observations and interpretations internally, among like-minded people. Many of these initial statements or inquiries die because the community finds them uninteresting or fruitless. Some reach greater salience, and are distributed through the high-visibility sites throughout the community of interest. Issues that in this form reached political salience became topics of conversation and commentary across the divide. This is certainly consistent with both the BoycottSBG and Diebold stories, where we saw a significant early working out of strategies and observations before the criticism reached genuine political salience. There would have been no point for opponents to link to and criticize early ideas kicked around within the community, like opposing Sinclair station renewal applications. Only after a few days, when the boycott was crystallizing, would opponents have reason to point out the boycott effort and discuss it. This interpretation also well characterizes the way in which the Trent Lott story described later in this chapter began percolating on the liberal side of the blogosphere, but then migrated over to the center-right.

The third claim was that money would reemerge as the primary source of power brokerage because of the difficulty of getting attention on the Net. Descriptively, it shares a prediction with the second-generation claims: Namely, that the Internet will centralize discourse. It differs in the mechanism of concentration: it will not be the result of an emergent property of large-scale networks, but rather of an old, tried-and-true way of capturing the political arena—money. But the peer-production model of filtering and discussion suggests that the networked public sphere will be substantially less corruptible by money. In the interpretation that I propose, filtering for the network as a whole is done as a form of nested peer-review decisions, beginning with the speaker's closest information affinity group. Consistent with what we have been seeing in more structured peer-production projects like *Wikipedia*, Slashdot, or free software, communities of interest use clustering and mutual pointing to peer produce the basic filtering mechanism necessary for the public sphere to be effective and avoid being drowned in the din of the crowd. The nested structure of the Web, whereby subclusters form relatively dense higher-level clusters, which then again combine into even higher-level clusters, and in each case, have a number of high-end salient sites, allows for the statements that pass these filters to become globally salient in the relevant public sphere. This structure, which describes the analytic and empirical work on the Web as a whole, fits remarkably well as a description of the dynamics we saw in looking more closely at the success of the boycott on Sinclair, as well as the successful campaign to investigate and challenge Diebold's voting machines.

The peer-produced structure of the attention backbone suggests that money is neither necessary nor sufficient to attract attention in the networked public sphere (although nothing suggests that money has become irrelevant to political attention given the continued importance of mass media). It renders less surprising Howard Dean's strong campaign for the Democratic presidential primaries in 2003 and the much more stable success of MoveOn.org since the late 1990s. These suggest that attention on the network has more to do with mobilizing the judgments, links, and cooperation of large bodies of small-scale contributors than with applying large sums of money. There is no obvious broadcast station that one can buy in order to assure salience. There are, of course, the highly visible sites, and they do offer a mechanism of getting your message to large numbers of people. However, the degree of engaged readership, interlinking, and clustering suggests that, in fact, being exposed to a certain message in one or a small number of highly visible places accounts for only a small part of the range of "reading" that gets done. More significantly, it suggests that reading, as opposed to having a conversation, is only part of what people do in the networked environment. In the networked public sphere, receiving information or getting out a finished message are only parts, and not necessarily the most important parts, of democratic discourse. The central desideratum of a political campaign that is rooted in the Internet is the capacity to engage users to the point that they become effective participants in a conversation and an effort; one that they have a genuine stake in and that is linked to a larger, society-wide debate. This engagement is not easily purchased, nor is it captured by the concept of a well-educated public that receives all the information it needs to be an informed citizenry. Instead, it is precisely the varied modes of participation in small-, medium-, and large-scale conversations, with varied but sustained degrees of efficacy, that make the public sphere of the networked environment different, and more attractive, than was the mass-media-based public sphere.

The networked public sphere is not only more resistant to control by money, but it is also less susceptible to the lowest-common-denominator orientation that the pursuit of money often leads mass media to adopt. Because communication in peer-produced media starts from an intrinsic motivation—writing or commenting about what one cares about—it begins with the opposite of lowest common denominator. It begins with what irks you, the contributing peer, individually, the most. This is, in the political world, analogous to Eric Raymond's claim that every free or open-source software project begins with programmers with an itch to scratch—something directly relevant to their lives and needs that they want to fix. The networked information economy, which makes it possible for individuals alone and in cooperation with others to scour the universe of politically relevant events, to point to them, and to comment and argue about them, follows a similar logic. This is why one freelance writer with lefty leanings, Russ Kick, is able to maintain a Web site, The Memory Hole, with documents that he gets by filing Freedom of Information Act requests. In April

2004, Kick was the first to obtain the U.S. military's photographs of the coffins of personnel killed in Iraq being flown home. No mainstream news organization had done so, but many published the photographs almost immediately after Kick had obtained them. Like free software, like Davis and the bloggers who participated in the debates over the Sinclair boycott, or the students who published the Diebold e-mails, the decision of what to publish does not start from a manager's or editor's judgment of what would be relevant and interesting to many people without being overly upsetting to too many others. It starts with the question: What do I care about most now?

To conclude, we need to consider the attractiveness of the networked public sphere not from the perspective of the mid-1990s utopianism, but from the perspective of how it compares to the actual media that have dominated the public sphere in all modern democracies. The networked public sphere provides an effective nonmarket alternative for intake, filtering, and synthesis outside the market-based mass media. This nonmarket alternative can attenuate the influence over the public sphere that can be achieved through control over, or purchase of control over, the mass media. It offers a substantially broader capture basin for intake of observations and opinions generated by anyone with a stake in the polity, anywhere. It appears to have developed a structure that allows for this enormous capture basin to be filtered, synthesized, and made part of a polity-wide discourse. This nested structure of clusters of communities of interest, typified by steadily increasing visibility of superstar nodes, allows for both the filtering and salience to climb up the hierarchy of clusters, but offers sufficient redundant paths and interlinking to avoid the creation of a small set of points of control where power can be either directly exercised or bought.

There is, in this story, an enormous degree of contingency and factual specificity. That is, my claims on behalf of the networked information economy as a platform for the public sphere are not based on general claims about human nature, the meaning of liberal discourse, context-independent efficiency, or the benevolent nature of the technology we happen to have stumbled across at the end of the twentieth century. They are instead based on, and depend on the continued accuracy of, a description of the economics of fabrication of computers and network connections, and a description of the dynamics of linking in a network of connected nodes. As such, my claim is not that the Internet inherently liberates. I do not claim that commons-based production of information, knowledge, and culture will win out by some irresistible progressive force. That is what makes the study of the political economy of information, knowledge, and culture in the networked environment directly relevant to policy. The literature on network topology suggests that, as long as there are widely distributed capabilities to publish, link, and advise others about what to read and link to, networks enable intrinsic processes that allow substantial ordering of the information. The pattern of information flow in such a network is more resistant to the application of control or influence than was the mass-media model. But things can change. Google could become so powerful on the desktop, in the e-mail utility, and on the Web, that it will effectively become a supernode that will indeed raise the prospect of a reemergence of a mass-media model. Then the politics of search engines, as Lucas Introna and Helen Nissenbaum called it, become central. The zeal to curb peer-to-peer file sharing of movies and music could lead to a substantial redesign of computing equipment and networks, to a degree that would make it harder for end users to exchange information of their own making. Understanding what we will lose if such changes indeed warp the topology of the network, and through it the basic structure of the networked public sphere, is precisely the object of this book as a whole. For now, though, let us say that the networked information economy as it has developed to this date has a capacity to take in, filter, and synthesize observations and opinions from a population that is orders of magnitude larger than the population that was capable of being captured by the mass media. It has done so without re-creating identifiable and reliable points of control and manipulation that would replicate the core limitation of the mass-media model of the public sphere—its susceptibility to the exertion of control by its regulators, owners, or those who pay them.

WHO WILL PLAY THE WATCHDOG FUNCTION?

A distinct critique leveled at the networked public sphere as a platform for democratic politics is the concern for who will fill the role of watchdog. Neil Netanel made this argument most clearly. His concern was that, perhaps freedom of expression for all is a good thing, and perhaps we could even overcome information overflow problems, but we live in a complex world with powerful actors. Government and corporate power is large, and individuals, no matter how good their tools, cannot be a serious alternative to a well-funded, independent press that can pay investigative reporters, defend lawsuits, and generally act like the *New York Times* and the *Washington Post* when they published the Pentagon Papers in the teeth of the Nixon administration's resistance, providing some of the most damning evidence against the planning and continued prosecution of the war in Vietnam. Netanel is cognizant of the tensions between the need to capture large audiences and sell advertising, on the one hand, and the role of watchdog, on the other. He nonetheless emphasizes that the networked public sphere cannot investigate as deeply or create the public salience that the mass media can. These limitations make commercial mass media, for all their limitations, necessary for a liberal public sphere.

This diagnosis of the potential of the networked public sphere underrepresents its productive capacity. The Diebold story provides in narrative form a detailed response to each of the concerns. The problem of voting machines has all the characteristics of an important, hard subject. It stirs deep fears that democracy is being stolen, and is therefore highly unsettling. It involves a difficult set of technical judgments about the functioning of voting machines. It required exposure and analysis of corporate-owned materials in the teeth of litigation threats and efforts to suppress and discredit the criticism. At each juncture in the process, the participants in the critique turned iteratively to peer production and radically distributed methods of investigation, analysis, distribution, and resistance to suppression: the initial observations of the whistle-blower or the hacker; the materials made available on a "see for yourself" and "come analyze this and share your insights" model; the distribution by students; and the fallback option when their server was shut down of replication around the network. At each stage, a peer-production solution was interposed in place of where a well-funded, high-end mass-media outlet would have traditionally applied funding in expectation of sales of copy. And it was only after the networked public sphere developed the analysis and debate that the mass media caught on, and then only gingerly.

The Diebold case was not an aberration, but merely a particularly rich case study of a much broader phenomenon, most extensively described in Dan Gilmore's *We the Media*. The basic production modalities that typify the networked information economy are now being applied to the problem of producing politically relevant information. In 2005, the most visible example of application of the networked information economy—both in its peer-production dimension and more generally by combining a wide range of nonproprietary production models—to the watchdog function of the media is the political blogosphere. The founding myth of the blogosphere's journalistic potency was built on the back of then Senate majority leader Trent Lott. In 2002, Lott had the indiscretion of saying, at the one-hundredth-birthday party of Republican Senator Strom Thurmond, that if Thurmond had won his Dixiecrat presidential campaign, "we wouldn't have had all these problems over all these years." Thurmond had run on a seg-regationist campaign, splitting from the Democratic Party in opposition to Harry Truman's early civil rights efforts, as the post–World War II winds began blowing toward the eventual demise of formal, legal racial segregation in the United States. Few positions are taken to be more self-evident in the national public morality of early twenty-first-century America than that for-mal, state-imposed, racial discrimination is an abomination. And yet, the first few days after the birthday party at which Lott made his statement saw almost no reporting on the statement. ABC News and the *Washington Post* made small mention of it, but most media outlets reported merely on a congenial salute and farewell celebration of the Senate's oldest and longest-serving member. Things were different in the blogosphere. At first liberal blogs, and within three days conservative bloggers as well, began to excavate past racist statements by Lott, and to beat the drums calling for his censure or removal as Senate leader. Within about a week, the story surfaced in the mainstream media, became a major embarrassment, and led to Lott's resig-nation as Senate majority leader about a week later. A careful case study of this event leaves it unclear why the mainstream media initially ignored the story.[32] It may have been that the largely social event drew the wrong sort of reporters. It may have been that reporters and editors who depend on major Washington, D.C., players were reluctant to challenge Lott. Perhaps they thought it rude to emphasize this indiscretion, or too upsetting to us all to think of just how close to the surface thoughts that we deem abom-inable can lurk. There is little disagreement that the day after the party, the story was picked up and discussed by Marshall on TalkingPoints, as well as by another liberal blogger, Atrios, who apparently got it from a post on Slate's "Chatterbox," which picked it up from ABC News's own *The Note*, a news summary made available on the television network's Web site. While the mass media largely ignored the story, and the two or three mainstream reporters who tried to write about it were getting little traction, bloggers were collecting more stories about prior instances where Lott's actions tended to suggest support for racist causes. Marshall, for example, found that Lott had filed a 1981 amicus curiae brief in support of Bob Jones University's effort to retain its tax-exempt status. The U.S. government had rescinded that status because the university practiced racial discrimination—such as prohibiting interracial dating. By Monday of the following week, four days after the remarks, conservative bloggers like Glenn Reynolds on Instapundit, Andrew Sullivan, and others were calling for Lott's resignation. It is possible that, absent the blogosphere, the story would still have flared up. There were two or so mainstream reporters still looking into the story. Jesse Jackson had come out within four days of the comment and said Lott should resign as majority leader. Eventually, when the mass media did enter the fray, its coverage clearly dominated the public agenda and its reporters uncovered materials that helped speed Lott's exit. However, given the short news cycle, the lack of initial interest by the media, and the large time lag between the event itself and when the media actually took the subject up, it seems likely that without the intervention of the blogosphere, the story would have died. What happened instead is that the cluster of political blogs—starting on the Left but then moving across the Left-Right divide—took up the subject, investigated, wrote opinions, collected links and public interest, and eventually captured enough attention to make the comments a matter of public importance. Free from the need to appear neutral and not to offend readers, and free from the need to keep close working relationships with news subjects, bloggers were able to identify something that grated on their sensibilities, talk about it, dig deeper, and eventually generate a substantial intervention into the public sphere. That intervention still had to pass through the mass media, for we still live in a communications environment heavily based on those media. However, the new source of insight, debate, and eventual condensation of effective public opinion came from within the networked information environment.

The point is not to respond to the argument with a litany of anecdotes. The point is that the argument about the commercial media's role as watchdog turns out to be a familiar argument—it is the same argument that was made about software and supercomputers, encyclopedias and immersive entertainment scripts. The answer, too, is by now familiar. Just as the World Wide Web can offer a platform for the emergence of an enormous and effective almanac, just as free software can produce excellent software and peer production can produce a good encyclopedia, so too can peer production produce the public watchdog function. In doing so, clearly the unorganized collection of Internet users lacks some of the basic tools of the mass media: dedicated full-time reporters; contacts with politicians who need media to survive, and therefore cannot always afford to stonewall questions; or public visibility and credibility to back their assertions. However, network-based peer production also avoids the inherent conflicts between investigative reporting and the bottom line—its cost, its risk of litigation, its risk of withdrawal of advertising from alienated corporate subjects, and its risk of alienating readers. Building on the wide variation and diversity of knowledge, time, availability, insight, and experience, as well as the vast communications and information resources on hand for almost anyone in advanced economies, we are seeing that the watchdog function too is being peer produced in the networked information economy.

Note that while my focus in this chapter has been mostly the organization of public discourse, both the Sinclair and the Diebold case studies also identify characteristics of distributed political action. We see collective action emerging from the convergence of independent individual actions, with no hierarchical control like that of a political party or an organized campaign. There may be some coordination and condensation points—like BoycottSBG.com or blackboxvoting.org. Like other integration platforms in peer-production systems, these condensation points provide a critical function. They do not, however, control the process. One manifestation of distributed coordination for political action is something Howard Rheingold has called "smart mobs"—large collections of individuals who are able to coordinate real-world action through widely distributed information and communications technology. He tells of the "People Power II" revolution in Manila in 2001, where demonstrations to oust then president Estrada were coordinated spontaneously through extensive text messaging.[33] Few images in the early twenty-first century can convey this phenomenon more vividly than the demonstrations around the world on February 15, 2003. Between six and ten million protesters were reported to have gone to the streets of major cities in about sixty countries in opposition to the American-led invasion of Iraq. There had been no major media campaign leading up to the demonstrations—though there was much media attention to them later. There had been no organizing committee. Instead, there was a network of roughly concordant actions, none controlling the other, all loosely discussing what ought to be done and when. MoveOn.org in the United States provides an example of a coordination platform for a network of politically mobilized activities. It builds on e-mail and Web-based media to communicate opportunities for political action to those likely to be willing and able to take it. Radically distributed, network-based solutions to the problems of political mobilization rely on the same characteristics as networked information production

more generally: extensive communications leading to concordant and cooperative patterns of behavior without the introduction of hierarchy or the
interposition of payment.

USING NETWORKED COMMUNICATION TO
WORK AROUND AUTHORITARIAN CONTROL

The Internet and the networked public sphere offer a different set of potential benefits, and suffer a different set of threats, as a platform for liberation
in authoritarian countries. State-controlled mass-media models are highly
conducive to authoritarian control. Because they usually rely on a small
number of technical and organizational points of control, mass media offer
a relatively easy target for capture and control by governments. Successful
control of such universally visible media then becomes an important tool of
information manipulation, which, in turn, eases the problem of controlling
the population. Not surprisingly, capture of the national television and radio
stations is invariably an early target of coups and revolutions. The highly
distributed networked architecture of the Internet makes it harder to control
communications in this way.

The case of Radio B92 in Yugoslavia offers an example. B92 was founded
in 1989, as an independent radio station. Over the course of the 1990s, it
developed a significant independent newsroom broadcast over the station
itself, and syndicated through thirty affiliated independent stations. B92 was
banned twice after the NATO bombing of Belgrade, in an effort by the
Milosevic regime to control information about the war. In each case, however, the station continued to produce programming, and distributed it over
the Internet from a server based in Amsterdam. The point is a simple one.
Shutting down a broadcast station is simple. There is one transmitter with
one antenna, and police can find and hold it. It is much harder to shut
down all connections from all reporters to a server and from the server back
into the country wherever a computer exists.

This is not to say that the Internet will of necessity in the long term lead
all authoritarian regimes to collapse. One option open to such regimes is
simply to resist Internet use. In 2003, Burma, or Myanmar, had 28,000
Internet users out of a population of more than 42 million, or one in fifteen
hundred, as compared, for example, to 6 million out of 65 million in neighboring Thailand, or roughly one in eleven. Most countries are not, however,
willing to forgo the benefits of connectivity to maintain their control. Iran's

population of 69 million includes 4.3 million Internet users, while China
has about 80 million users, second only to the United States in absolute
terms, out of a population of 1.3 billion. That is, both China and Iran have
a density of Internet users of about one in sixteen.[34] Burma's negligible level
of Internet availability is a compound effect of low gross domestic product
(GDP) per capita and government policies. Some countries with similar
GDP levels still have levels of Internet users in the population that are two
orders of magnitude higher: Cameroon (1 Internet user for every 27 residents), Moldova (1 in 30), and Mongolia (1 in 55). Even very large poor
countries have several times more users per population than Myanmar: like
Pakistan (1 in 100), Mauritania (1 in 300), and Bangladesh (1 in 580).
Lawrence Solum and Minn Chung outline how Myanmar achieves its high
degree of control and low degree of use.[35] Myanmar has only one Internet
service provider (ISP), owned by the government. The government must
authorize anyone who wants to use the Internet or create a Web page within
the country. Some of the licensees, like foreign businesses, are apparently
permitted and enabled only to send e-mail, while using the Web is limited
to security officials who monitor it. With this level of draconian regulation,
Myanmar can avoid the liberating effects of the Internet altogether, at the
cost of losing all its economic benefits. Few regimes are willing to pay that
price.

Introducing Internet communications into a society does not, however,
immediately and automatically mean that an open, liberal public sphere
emerges. The Internet is technically harder to control than mass media. It
increases the cost and decreases the efficacy of information control. However,
a regime willing and able to spend enough money and engineering power,
and to limit its population's access to the Internet sufficiently, can have
substantial success in controlling the flow of information into and out of its
country. Solum and Chung describe in detail one of the most extensive and
successful of these efforts, the one that has been conducted by China—
home to the second-largest population of Internet users in the world, whose
policies controlled use of the Internet by two out of every fifteen Internet
users in the world in 2003. In China, the government holds a monopoly
over all Internet connections going into and out of the country. It either
provides or licenses the four national backbones that carry traffic throughout
China and connect it to the global network. ISPs that hang off these backbones are licensed, and must provide information about the location and
workings of their facilities, as well as comply with a code of conduct. In-

dividual users must register and provide information about their machines, and the many Internet cafes are required to install filtering software that will filter out subversive sites. There have been crackdowns on Internet cafes to enforce these requirements. This set of regulations has replicated one aspect of the mass-medium model for the Internet—it has created a potential point of concentration or centralization of information flow that would make it easier to control Internet use. The highly distributed production capabilities of the networked information economy, however, as opposed merely to the distributed carriage capability of the Internet, mean that more must be done at this bottleneck to squelch the flow of information and opinion than would have to be done with mass media. That "more" in China has consisted of an effort to employ automatic filters—some at the level of the cybercafe or the local ISP, some at the level of the national backbone networks. The variability of these loci and their effects is reflected in partial efficacy and variable performance for these mechanisms. The most extensive study of the efficacy of these strategies for controlling information flows over the Internet to China was conducted by Jonathan Zittrain and Ben Edelman. From servers within China, they sampled about two hundred thousand Web sites and found that about fifty thousand were unavailable at least once, and close to nineteen thousand were unavailable on two distinct occasions. The blocking patterns seemed to follow mass-media logic—BBC News was consistently unavailable, as CNN and other major news sites often were; the U.S. court system official site was unavailable. However, Web sites that provided similar information—like those that offered access to all court cases but were outside the official system—were available. The core Web sites of human rights organizations or of Taiwan and Tibet-related organizations were blocked, and about sixty of the top one hundred results for "Tibet" on Google were blocked. What is also apparent from their study, however, and confirmed by Amnesty International's reports on Internet censorship in China, is that while censorship is significant, it is only partially effective.[36] The Amnesty report noted that Chinese users were able to use a variety of techniques to avoid the filtering, such as the use of proxy servers, but even Zittrain and Edelman, apparently testing for filtering as experienced by unsophisticated or compliant Internet users in China, could access many sites that would, on their face, seem potentially destabilizing.

This level of censorship may indeed be effective enough for a government negotiating economic and trade expansion with political stability and control. It suggests, however, limits of the ability of even a highly dedicated government to control the capacity of Internet communications to route around censorship and to make it much easier for determined users to find information they care about, and to disseminate their own information to others. Iran's experience, with a similar level of Internet penetration, emphasizes the difficulty of maintaining control of Internet publication.[37] Iran's network emerged from 1993 onward from the university system, quite rapidly complemented by commercial ISPs. Because deployment and use of the Internet preceded its regulation by the government, its architecture is less amenable to centralized filtering and control than China's. Internet access through university accounts and cybercafes appears to be substantial, and until the past three or four years, had operated free of the crackdowns and prison terms suffered by opposition print publications and reporters. The conservative branches of the regime seem to have taken a greater interest in suppressing Internet communications since the publication of imprisoned Ayatollah Montazeri's critique of the foundations of the Islamic state on the Web in December 2000. While the original Web site, montazeri.com, seems to have been eliminated, the site persists as montazeri.ws, using a Western Samoan domain name, as do a number of other Iranian publications. There are now dozens of chat rooms, blogs, and Web sites, and e-mail also seems to be playing an increasing role in the education and organization of an opposition. While the conservative branches of the Iranian state have been clamping down on these forms, and some bloggers and Web site operators have found themselves subject to the same mistreatment as journalists, the efficacy of these efforts to shut down opposition seems to be limited and uneven.

Media other than static Web sites present substantially deeper problems for regimes like those of China and Iran. Scanning the text of e-mail messages of millions of users who can encrypt their communications with widely available tools creates a much more complex problem. Ephemeral media like chat rooms and writable Web tools allow the content of an Internet communication or Web site to be changed easily and dynamically, so that blocking sites becomes harder, while coordinating moves to new sites to route around blocking becomes easier. At one degree of complexity deeper, the widely distributed architecture of the Net also allows users to build censorship-resistant networks by pooling their own resources. The pioneering example of this approach is Freenet, initially developed in 1999–2000 by Ian Clarke, an Irish programmer fresh out of a degree in computer science and artificial intelligence at Edinburgh University. Now a broader free-software project, Freenet is a peer-to-peer application specifically designed to be censorship resistant. Unlike the more famous peer-to-peer network developed at the time—Napster—Freenet was not intended to store music files on the hard drives of users. Instead, it stores bits and pieces of publications, and then uses sophisticated algorithms to deliver the documents to whoever seeks them, in encrypted form. This design trades off easy availability for a series of security measures that prevent even the owners of the hard drives on which the data resides—or government agents that search their computers—from knowing what is on their hard drive or from controlling it. As a practical matter, if someone in a country that prohibits certain content but enables Internet connections wants to publish content—say, a Web site or blog—safely, they can inject it into the Freenet system. The content will be encrypted and divided into little bits and pieces that are stored in many different hard drives of participants in the network. No single computer will have all the information, and shutting down any given computer will not make the information unavailable. It will continue to be accessible to anyone running the Freenet client. Freenet indeed appears to be used in China, although the precise scope is hard to determine, as the network is intended to mask the identity and location of both readers and publishers in this system. The point to focus on is not the specifics of Freenet, but the feasibility of constructing user-based censorship-resistant storage and retrieval systems that would be practically impossible for a national censorship system to identify and block subversive content.

To conclude, in authoritarian countries, the introduction of Internet communications makes it harder and more costly for governments to control the public sphere. If these governments are willing to forgo the benefits of Internet connectivity, they can avoid this problem. If they are not, they find themselves with less control over the public sphere. There are, obviously, other means of more direct repression. However, control over the mass media was, throughout most of the twentieth century, a core tool of repressive governments. It allowed them to manipulate what the masses of their populations knew and believed, and thus limited the portion of the population that the government needed to physically repress to a small and often geographically localized group. The efficacy of these techniques of repression is blunted by adoption of the Internet and the emergence of a networked information economy. Low-cost communications, distributed technical and organizational structure, and ubiquitous presence of dynamic authorship tools make control over the public sphere difficult, and practically never perfect.

TOWARD A NETWORKED PUBLIC SPHERE

The first generation of statements that the Internet democratizes was correct but imprecise. The Internet does restructure public discourse in ways that give individuals a greater say in their governance than the mass media made possible. The Internet does provide avenues of discourse around the bottle-necks of older media, whether these are held by authoritarian governments or by media owners. But the mechanisms for this change are more complex than those articulated in the past. And these more complex mechanisms respond to the basic critiques that have been raised against the notion that the Internet enhances democracy.

Part of what has changed with the Internet is technical infrastructure. Network communications do not offer themselves up as easily for single points of control as did the mass media. While it is possible for authoritarian regimes to try to retain bottlenecks in the Internet, the cost is higher and the efficacy lower than in mass-media-dominated systems. While this does not mean that introduction of the Internet will automatically result in global democratization, it does make the work of authoritarian regimes harder. In liberal democracies, the primary effect of the Internet runs through the emer-gence of the networked information economy. We are seeing the emergence to much greater significance of nonmarket, individual, and cooperative peer-production efforts to produce universal intake of observations and opinions about the state of the world and what might and ought to be done about it. We are seeing the emergence of filtering, accreditation, and synthesis mecha-nisms as part of network behavior. These rely on clustering of communities of interest and association and highlighting of certain sites, but offer tre-mendous redundancy of paths for expression and accreditation. These prac-tices leave no single point of failure for discourse: no single point where observations can be squelched or attention commanded—by fiat or with the application of money. Because of these emerging systems, the networked information economy is solving the information overload and discourse frag-mentation concerns without reintroducing the distortions of the mass-media model. Peer production, both long-term and organized, as in the case of Slashdot, and ad hoc and dynamically formed, as in the case of blogging or

the Sinclair or Diebold cases, is providing some of the most important functionalities of the media. These efforts provide a watchdog, a source of salient
observations regarding matters of public concern, and a platform for discussing the alternatives open to a polity.

In the networked information environment, everyone is free to observe,
report, question, and debate, not only in principle, but in actual capability.
They can do this, if not through their own widely read blog, then through
a cycle of mailing lists, collective Web-based media like Slashdot, comments
on blogs, or even merely through e-mails to friends who, in turn, have
meaningful visibility in a smallish-scale cluster of sites or lists. We are wit-
nessing a fundamental change in how individuals can interact with their
democracy and experience their role as citizens. Ideal citizens need not be
seen purely as trying to inform themselves about what others have found,
so that they can vote intelligently. They need not be limited to reading the
opinions of opinion makers and judging them in private conversations. They
are no longer constrained to occupy the role of mere readers, viewers, and
listeners. They can be, instead, participants in a conversation. Practices that
begin to take advantage of these new capabilities shift the locus of content
creation from the few professional journalists trolling society for issues and
observations, to the people who make up that society. They begin to free
the public agenda setting from dependence on the judgments of managers,
whose job it is to assure that the maximum number of readers, viewers, and
listeners are sold in the market for eyeballs. The agenda thus can be rooted
in the life and experience of individual participants in society—in their
observations, experiences, and obsessions. The network allows all citizens to
change their relationship to the public sphere. They no longer need be
consumers and passive spectators. They can become creators and primary
subjects. It is in this sense that the Internet democratizes.

Chapter 8 Cultural Freedom: A
Culture Both Plastic and Critical

Gone with the Wind

There was a land of Cavaliers
and Cotton Fields called the
Old South. Here in this
pretty world, Gallantry took
its last bow. Here was the
last ever to be seen of
Knights and their Ladies
Fair, of Master and of Slave.
Look for it only in books,
for it is no more than a
dream remembered, a Civili-
zation gone with the wind.

> —MGM (1939) film
> adaptation of Margaret
> Mitchell's novel (1936)

Strange Fruit

Southern trees bear strange fruit,
Blood on the leaves and blood at the root,
Black bodies swinging in the southern
  breeze,
Strange fruit hanging from the poplar trees.

Pastoral scene of the gallant south,
The bulging eyes and the twisted mouth,
Scent of magnolias, sweet and fresh,
Then the sudden smell of burning flesh.

Here is the fruit for the crows to pluck,
For the rain to gather, for the wind to
  suck,
For the sun to rot, for the trees to drop,
Here is a strange and bitter crop.

> —Billie Holiday (1939) from lyrics by
> Abel Meeropol (1937)

In 1939, *Gone with the Wind* reaped seven Oscars, while Billie Holiday's song reached number 16 on the charts, even though Columbia Records refused to release it: Holiday had to record it with a small company that was run out of a storefront in midtown Manhattan. On the eve of the second reconstruction era, which was to overhaul the legal framework of race relations over the two decades beginning with the desegregation of the armed forces in the late 1940s and culminating with the civil rights acts passed between 1964–1968, the two sides of the debate over desegregation and the legacy of slavery were minting new icons through which to express their most basic beliefs about the South and its peculiar institutions. As the following three decades unfolded and the South was gradually forced to change its ways, the cultural domain continued to work out the meaning of race relations in the United States and the history of slavery. The actual slogging of regulation of discrimination, implementation of desegregation and later affirmative action, and the more local politics of hiring and firing were punctuated throughout this period by salient iconic retellings of the stories of race relations in the United States, from *Guess Who's Coming to Dinner?* to *Roots*. The point of this chapter, however, is not to discuss race relations, but to understand culture and cultural production in terms of political theory. *Gone with the Wind* and *Strange Fruit* or *Guess Who's Coming to Dinner?* offer us intuitively accessible instances of a much broader and more basic characteristic of human understanding and social relations. Culture, shared meaning, and symbols are how we construct our views of life across a wide range of domains—personal, political, and social. How culture is produced is therefore an essential ingredient in structuring how freedom and justice are perceived, conceived, and pursued. In the twentieth century, Hollywood and the recording industry came to play a very large role in this domain. The networked information economy now seems poised to attenuate that role in favor of a more participatory and transparent cultural production system.

Cultural freedom occupies a position that relates to both political freedom and individual autonomy, but is synonymous with neither. The root of its importance is that none of us exist outside of culture. As individuals and as political actors, we understand the world we occupy, evaluate it, and act in it from within a set of understandings and frames of meaning and reference that we share with others. What institutions and decisions are considered "legitimate" and worthy of compliance or participation; what courses of action are attractive; what forms of interaction with others are considered appropriate—these are all understandings negotiated from within a set of shared frames of meaning. How those frames of meaning are shaped and by whom become central components of the structure of freedom for those individuals and societies that inhabit it and are inhabited by it. They define the public sphere in a much broader sense than we considered in the prior chapters.

The networked information economy makes it possible to reshape both the "who" and the "how" of cultural production relative to cultural production in the twentieth century. It adds to the centralized, market-oriented production system a new framework of radically decentralized individual and cooperative nonmarket production. It thereby affects the ability of individuals and groups to participate in the production of the cultural tools and frameworks of human understanding and discourse. It affects the way we, as individuals and members of social and political clusters, interact with culture, and through it with each other. It makes culture more transparent to its inhabitants. It makes the process of cultural production more participatory, in the sense that more of those who live within a culture can actively participate in its creation. We are seeing the possibility of an emergence of a new popular culture, produced on the folk-culture model and inhabited actively, rather than passively consumed by the masses. Through these twin characteristics—transparency and participation—the networked information economy also creates greater space for critical evaluation of cultural materials and tools. The practice of producing culture makes us all more sophisticated readers, viewers, and listeners, as well as more engaged makers.

Throughout the twentieth century, the making of widely shared images and symbols was a concentrated practice that went through the filters of Hollywood and the recording industry. The radically declining costs of manipulating video and still images, audio, and text have, however, made culturally embedded criticism and broad participation in the making of meaning much more feasible than in the past. Anyone with a personal computer can cut and mix files, make their own files, and publish them to a global audience. This is not to say that cultural bricolage, playfulness, and criticism did not exist before. One can go to the avant-garde movement, but equally well to African-Brazilian culture or to Our Lady of Guadalupe to find them. Even with regard to television, that most passive of electronic media, John Fiske argued under the rubric of "semiotic democracy" that viewers engage in creative play and meaning making around the TV shows they watch. However, the technical characteristics of digital information technology, the economics of networked information production, and the social practices of networked discourse qualitatively change the role individuals can play in cultural production.

The practical capacity individuals and noncommercial actors have to use and manipulate cultural artifacts today, playfully or critically, far outstrips anything possible in television, film, or recorded music, as these were organized throughout the twentieth century. The diversity of cultural moves and statements that results from these new opportunities for creativity vastly increases the range of cultural elements accessible to any individual. Our ability, therefore, to navigate the cultural environment and make it our own, both through creation and through active selection and attention, has increased to the point of making a qualitative difference. In the academic law literature, Niva Elkin Koren wrote early about the potential democratization of "meaning making processes," William Fisher about "semiotic democracy," and Jack Balkin about a "democratic culture." Lessig has explored the generative capacity of the freedom to create culture, its contribution to creativity itself. These efforts revolve around the idea that there is something normatively attractive, from the perspective of "democracy" as a liberal value, about the fact that anyone, using widely available equipment, can take from the existing cultural universe more or less whatever they want, cut it, paste it, mix it, and make it their own—equally well expressing their adoration as their disgust, their embrace of certain images as their rejection of them.

Building on this work, this chapter seeks to do three things: First, I claim that the modalities of cultural production and exchange are a proper subject for normative evaluation within a broad range of liberal political theory. Culture is a social-psychological-cognitive fact of human existence. Ignoring it, as rights-based and utilitarian versions of liberalism tend to do, disables political theory from commenting on central characteristics of a society and its institutional frameworks. Analyzing the attractiveness of any given political institutional system without considering how it affects cultural production, and through it the production of the basic frames of meaning through which individual and collective self-determination functions, leaves a large hole in our analysis. Liberal political theory needs a theory of culture and agency that is viscous enough to matter normatively, but loose enough to give its core foci—the individual and the political system—room to be effective independently, not as a mere expression or extension of culture. Second, I argue that cultural production in the form of the networked information economy offers individuals a greater participatory role in making the culture they occupy, and makes this culture more transparent to its inhabitants. This descriptive part occupies much of the chapter. Third, I suggest the relatively straightforward conclusion of the prior two observations. From the perspective of liberal political theory, the kind of open, participatory, transparent folk culture that is emerging in the networked environment is normatively more attractive than was the industrial cultural production system typified by Hollywood and the recording industry.

A nine-year-old girl searching Google for Barbie will quite quickly find links to AdiosBarbie.com, to the Barbie Liberation Organization (BLO), and to other, similarly critical sites interspersed among those dedicated to selling and playing with the doll. The contested nature of the doll becomes publicly and everywhere apparent, liberated from the confines of feminist-criticism symposia and undergraduate courses. This simple Web search represents both of the core contributions of the networked information economy. First, from the perspective of the searching girl, it represents a new transparency of cultural symbols. Second, from the perspective of the participants in AdiosBarbie or the BLO, the girl's use of their site completes their own quest to participate in making the cultural meaning of Barbie. The networked information environment provides an outlet for contrary expression and a medium for shaking what we accept as cultural baseline assumptions. Its radically decentralized production modes provide greater freedom to participate effectively in defining the cultural symbols of our day. These characteristics make the networked environment attractive from the perspectives of both personal freedom of expression and an engaged and self-aware political discourse.

We cannot, however, take for granted that the technological capacity to participate in the cultural conversation, to mix and make our own, will translate into the freedom to do so. The practices of cultural and countercultural creation are at the very core of the battle over the institutional ecology of the digital environment. The tension is perhaps not new or unique to the Internet, but its salience is now greater. The makers of the 1970s comic strip *Air Pirates* already found their comics confiscated when they portrayed Mickey and Minnie and Donald and Daisy in various compromising countercultural postures. Now, the ever-increasing scope and expanse of copyright law and associated regulatory mechanisms, on the one hand, and of individual and collective nonmarket creativity, on the other hand, have heightened the conflict between cultural freedom and the regulatory framework on which the industrial cultural production system depends. As Lessig, Jessica Litman, and Siva Vaidhyanathan have each portrayed elegantly and in detail, the copyright industries have on many dimensions persuaded both Congress and courts that individual, nonmarket creativity using the cultural outputs of the industrial information economy is to be prohibited. As we stand today, freedom to play with the cultural environment is nonetheless preserved in the teeth of the legal constraints, because of the high costs of enforcement, on the one hand, and the ubiquity and low cost of the means to engage in creative cultural bricolage, on the other hand. These social, institutional, and technical facts still leave us with quite a bit of unauthorized creative expression. These facts, however, are contingent and fragile. Chapter 11 outlines in some detail the long trend toward the creation of ever-stronger legal regulation of cultural production, and in particular, the enclosure movement that began in the 1970s and gained steam in the mid-1990s. A series of seemingly discrete regulatory moves threatens the emerging networked folk culture. Ranging from judicial interpretations of copyright law to efforts to regulate the hardware and software of the networked environment, we are seeing a series of efforts to restrict nonmarket use of twentieth-century cultural materials in order to preserve the business models of Hollywood and the recording industry. These regulatory efforts threaten the freedom to participate in twenty-first-century cultural production, because current creation requires taking and mixing the twentieth-century cultural materials that make up who we are as culturally embedded beings. Here, however, I focus on explaining how cultural participation maps onto the project of liberal political theory, and why the emerging cultural practices should be seen as attractive within that normative framework. I leave development of the policy implications to part III.

CULTURAL FREEDOM IN LIBERAL
POLITICAL THEORY

Utilitarian and rights-based liberal political theories have an awkward relationship to culture. Both major strains of liberal theory make a certain set of assumptions about the autonomous individuals with which they are concerned. Individuals are assumed to be rational and knowledgeable, at least about what is good for them. They are conceived of as possessing a capacity for reason and a set of preferences prior to engagement with others. Political theory then proceeds to concern itself with political structures that respect the autonomy of individuals with such characteristics. In the political domain, this conception of the individual is easiest to see in pluralist theories, which require institutions for collective decision making that clear what are treated as already-formed preferences of individuals or voluntary groupings.

Culture represents a mysterious category for these types of liberal political theories. It is difficult to specify how it functions in terms readily amenable to a conception of individuals whose rationality and preferences for their own good are treated as though they preexist and are independent of society. A concept of culture requires some commonly held meaning among these individuals. Even the simplest intuitive conception of what culture might mean would treat this common frame of meaning as the result of social processes that preexist any individual, and partially structure what it is that individuals bring to the table as they negotiate their lives together, in society or in a polity. Inhabiting a culture is a precondition to any interpretation of what is at stake in any communicative exchange among individuals. A partly subconscious, lifelong dynamic social process of becoming and changing as a cultural being is difficult to fold into a collective decision-making model that focuses on designing a discursive platform for individuated discrete participants who are the bearers of political will. It is easier to model respect for an individual's will when one adopts a view of that will as independent, stable, and purely internally generated. It is harder to do so when one conceives of that individual will as already in some unspecified degree rooted in exchange with others about what an individual is to value and prefer.

Culture has, of course, been incorporated into political theory as a central part of the critique of liberalism. The politics of culture have been a staple of critical theory since Marx first wrote that "Religion . . . is the opium of the people" and that "to call on them to give up their illusions about their condition is to call on them to give up a condition that requires illusions."[1] The twentieth century saw a wide array of critique, from cultural Marxism to poststructuralism and postmodernism. However, much of mainstream liberal political theory has chosen to ignore, rather than respond and adapt to, these critiques. In *Political Liberalism*, for example, Rawls acknowledges "the fact" of reasonable pluralism—of groups that persistently and reasonably hold competing comprehensive doctrines—and aims for political pluralism as a mode of managing the irreconcilable differences. This leaves the formation of the comprehensive doctrine and the systems of belief within which it is rendered "reasonable" a black box to liberal theory. This may be an adequate strategy for analyzing the structure of formal political institutions at the broadest level of abstraction. However, it disables liberal political theory from dealing with more fine-grained questions of policy that act within the black box.

As a practical matter, treating culture as a black box disables a political theory as a mechanism for diagnosing the actual conditions of life in a society in terms of its own political values. It does so in precisely the same way that a formal conception of autonomy disables those who hold it from diagnosing the conditions of autonomy in practical life. Imagine for a moment that we had received a revelation that a crude version of Antonio Gramsci's hegemony theory was perfectly correct as a matter of descriptive sociology. Ruling classes do, in fact, consciously and successfully manipulate the culture in order to make the oppressed classes compliant. It would be difficult, then, to continue to justify holding a position about political institutions, or autonomy, that treated the question of how culture, generally, or even the narrow subset of reasonably held comprehensive doctrines like religion, are made, as a black box. It would be difficult to defend respect for autonomous choices as respect for an individual's will, if an objective observer could point to a social process, external to the individual and acting upon him or her, as the cause of the individual holding that will. It would be difficult to focus one's political design imperatives on public processes that allow people to express their beliefs and preferences, argue about them, and ultimately vote on them, if it is descriptively correct that those beliefs and preferences are themselves the product of manipulation of some groups by others.

The point is not, of course, that Gramsci was descriptively right or that any of the broad range of critical theories of culture is correct as a descriptive matter. It is that liberal theories that ignore culture are rendered incapable of answering some questions that arise in the real world and have real implications for individuals and polities. There is a range of sociological, psychological, or linguistic descriptions that could characterize the culture of a society as more or less in accord with the concern of liberalism with individual and collective self-determination. Some such descriptive theory of culture can provide us with enough purchase on the role of culture to diagnose the attractiveness of a cultural production system from a political-theory perspective. It does not require that liberal theory abandon individuals as the bearers of the claims of political morality. It does not require that liberal political theory refocus on culture as opposed to formal political institutions. It does require, however, that liberal theory at least be able to diagnose different conditions in the practical cultural life of a society as more or less attractive from the perspective of liberal political theory.

The efforts of deliberative liberal theories to account for culture offer the most obvious source of such an insight. These political theories have worked to develop a conception of culture and its relationship to liberalism precisely because at a minimum, they require mutual intelligibility across individuals, which cannot adequately be explained without some conception of culture. In Jurgen Habermas's work, culture plays the role of a basis for mutual intelligibility. As the basis for "interpersonal intelligibility," we see culture playing such a role in the work of Bruce Ackerman, who speaks of acculturation as the necessary condition to liberal dialogue. "Cultural coherence" is something he sees children requiring as a precondition to becoming liberal citizens: it allows them to "Talk" and defend their claims in terms without which there can be no liberal conversation.[2] Michael Walzer argues that, "in matters of morality, argument is simply the appeal to common meanings."[3] Will Kymlicka claims that for individual autonomy, "freedom involves making choices amongst various options, and our societal culture not only provides these options, but makes them meaningful to us." A societal culture, in turn, is a "shared vocabulary of tradition and convention" that is "embodied in social life[,] institutionally embodied—in schools, media, economy, government, etc."[4] Common meanings in all these frameworks must mean more than simple comprehension of the words of another. It provides a common baseline, which is not itself at that moment the subject of conversation or inquiry, but forms the background on which conversation and inquiry take place. Habermas's definition of lifeworld as "background knowledge," for example, is a crisp rendering of culture in this role:

> the lifeworld embraces us as an unmediated certainty, out of whose immediate proximity we live and speak. This all-penetrating, yet latent and unnoticed presence of the background of communicative action can be described as a more intense, yet deficient, form of knowledge and ability. To begin with, we make use of this knowledge involuntarily, without reflectively knowing *that* we possess it at all. What enables background knowledge to acquire absolute certainty in this way, and even augments its epistemic quality from a subjective standpoint, is precisely the property that robs it of a constitutive feature of knowledge: we make use of

such knowledge without the awareness that it *could* be false. Insofar as all knowledge is fallible and is known to be such, background knowledge does not represent knowledge at all, in a strict sense. As background knowledge, it lacks the possibility of being challenged, that is, of being raised to the level of criticizable validity claims. One can do this only by converting it from a resource into a topic of discussion, at which point—just when it is thematized—it no longer functions as a lifeworld background but rather *disintegrates* in its background modality.[5]

In other words, our understanding of meaning—how we are, how others are, what ought to be—are in some significant portion unexamined assumptions that we share with others, and to which we appeal as we engage in communication with them. This does not mean that culture is a version of false consciousness. It does not mean that background knowledge cannot be examined rationally or otherwise undermines the very possibility or coherence of a liberal individual or polity. It does mean, however, that at any given time, in any given context, there will be some set of historically contingent beliefs, attitudes, and social and psychological conditions that will in the normal course remain unexamined, and form the unexamined foundation of conversation. Culture is revisable through critical examination, at which point it ceases to be "common knowledge" and becomes a contested assumption. Nevertheless, some body of unexamined common knowledge is necessary for us to have an intelligible conversation that does not constantly go around in circles, challenging the assumptions on whichever conversational move is made.

Culture, in this framework, is not destiny. It does not predetermine who we are, or what we can become or do, nor is it a fixed artifact. It is the product of a dynamic process of engagement among those who make up a culture. It is a frame of meaning from within which we must inevitably function and speak to each other, and whose terms, constraints, and affordances we always negotiate. There is no point outside of culture from which to do otherwise. An old Yiddish folktale tells of a naïve rabbi who, for safekeeping, put a ten-ruble note inside his copy of the Torah, at the page of the commandment, "thou shalt not steal." That same night, a thief stole into the rabbi's home, took the ten-ruble note, and left a five-ruble note in its place, at the page of the commandment, "thou shalt love thy neighbor as thyself." The rabbi and the thief share a common cultural framework (as do we, across the cultural divide), through which their various actions can be understood; indeed, without which their actions would be unintelligible.

The story offers a theory of culture, power, and freedom that is more congenial to liberal political theory than critical theories, and yet provides a conception of the role of culture in human relations that provides enough friction, or viscosity, to allow meaning making in culture to play a role in the core concerns of liberal political theory. Their actions are part strategic and part communicative—that is to say, to some extent they seek to force an outcome, and to some extent they seek to engage the other in a conversation in order to achieve a commonly accepted outcome. The rabbi places the ten-ruble note in the Bible in order to impress upon the putative thief that he should leave the money where it is. He cannot exert force on the thief by locking the money up in a safe because he does not own one. Instead, he calls upon a shared understanding and a claim of authority within the governed society to persuade the thief. The thief, to the contrary, could have physically taken the ten-ruble note without replacing it, but he does not. He engages the rabbi in the same conversation. In part, he justifies his claim to five rubles. In part, he resists the authority of the rabbi—not by rejecting the culture that renders the rabbi a privileged expert, but by playing the game of Talmudic disputation. There is a price, though, for participating in the conversation. The thief must leave the five-ruble note; he cannot take the whole amount.

In this story, culture is open to interpretation and manipulation, but not infinitely so. Some moves may be valid within a cultural framework and alter it; others simply will not. The practical force of culture, on the other hand, is not brute force. It cannot force an outcome, but it can exert a real pull on the range of behaviors that people will seriously consider undertaking, both as individuals and as polities. The storyteller relies on the listener's cultural understanding about the limits of argument, or communicative action. The story exploits the open texture of culture, and the listener's shared cultural belief that stealing is an act of force, not a claim of justice; that those who engage in it do not conceive of themselves as engaged in legitimate defensible acts. The rabbi was naïve to begin with, but the thief's disputation is inconsistent with our sense of the nature of the act of stealing in exactly the same way that the rabbi's was, but inversely. The thief, the rabbi, and the storyteller participate in making, and altering, the meaning of the commandments.

Culture changes through the actions of individuals in the cultural context. Beliefs, claims, communicative moves that have one meaning before an intervention may begin to shift in their meaning as a result of other moves, made by other participants in the same cultural milieu. One need not adopt any given fully fledged meme theory of culture—like Richard Dawkins's, or Balkin's political adaptation of it as a theory of ideology—to accept that culture is created through communication among human beings, that it exerts some force on what they can say to each other and how it will be received, and that the parameters of a culture as a platform for making meaning in interaction among human beings change over time with use. How cultural moves are made, by whom, and with what degree of perfect replication or subtle (and not so subtle) change, become important elements in determining the rate and direction of cultural change. These changes, over time, alter the platform individuals must use to make sense of the world they occupy, and for participants in conversation to be able to make intelligible communications to each other about the world they share and where it can and ought to go. Culture so understood is a social fact about particular sets of human beings in historical context. As a social fact, it constrains and facilitates the development, expression, and questioning of beliefs and positions. Whether and how Darwinism should be taught in public schools, for example, is a live political question in vast regions of the United States, and is played out as a debate over whether evolution is "merely a theory." Whether racial segregation should be practiced in these schools is no longer a viable or even conceivable political agenda. The difference between Darwinism and the undesirability of racial segregation is not that one is scientifically true and the other is not. The difference is that the former is not part of the "common knowledge" of a large section of society, whereas the latter is, in a way that no longer requires proof by detailed sociological and psychological studies of the type cited by the Supreme Court in support of its holding, in *Brown v. Board of Education*, that segregation in education was inherently unequal.

If culture is indeed part of how we form a shared sense of unexamined common knowledge, it plays a significant role in framing the meaning of the state of the world, the availability and desirability of choices, and the organization of discourse. The question of how culture is framed (and through it, meaning and the baseline conversational moves) then becomes germane to a liberal political theory. Between the Scylla of a fixed culture (with hierarchical, concentrated power to control its development and interpretation) and the Charybdis of a perfectly open culture (where nothing is fixed and everything is up for grabs, offering no anchor for meaning and mutual intelligibility), there is a wide range of practical social and economic arrangements around the production and use of culture. In evaluating the attractiveness of various arrangements from the perspective of liberal theory, we come to an already familiar trade-off, and an already familiar answer. As in the case of autonomy and political discourse, a greater ability of individuals to participate in the creation of the cultural meaning of the world they occupy is attractive from the perspective of the liberal commitments to individual freedom and democratic participation. As in both areas that we have already considered, a Babel objection appears: Too much freedom to challenge and remake our own cultural environment will lead to a lack of shared meaning. As in those two cases, however, the fears of too active a community of meaning making are likely exaggerated. Loosening the dominant power of Hollywood and television over contemporary culture is likely to represent an incremental improvement, from the perspective of liberal political commitments. It will lead to a greater transparency of culture, and therefore a greater capacity for critical reflection, and it will provide more opportunities for participating in the creation of culture, for interpolating individual glosses on it, and for creating shared variations on common themes.

THE TRANSPARENCY OF INTERNET CULTURE

If you run a search for "Barbie" on three separate search engines—Google, Overture, and Yahoo!—you will get quite different results. Table 8.1 lists these results in the order in which they appear on each search engine. Overture is a search engine that sells placement to the parties who are being searched. Hits on this search engine are therefore ranked based on whoever paid Overture the most in order to be placed highly in response to a query. On this list, none of the top ten results represent anything other than sales-related Barbie sites. Critical sites begin to appear only around the twenty-fifth result, presumably after all paying clients have been served. Google, as we already know, uses a radically decentralized mechanism for assigning relevance. It counts how many sites on the Web have linked to a particular site that has the search term in it, and ranks the search results by placing a site with a high number of incoming links above a site with a low number of incoming links. In effect, each Web site publisher "votes" for a site's

Table 8.1: Results for "Barbie"—Google versus Overture and Yahoo!

Google	Overture	Yahoo!
Barbie.com (Mattel's site)	Barbie at Amazon.com	Barbie.com
Barbie Collector: Official Mattel Web site for hobbyists and collectors	Toys and Leisure at QVC—Barbie	*Barbie Bazaar* Magazine
AdiosBarbie.com: A Body Image for Every Body (site created by women critical of Barbie's projected body image)	Barbie on Sale at KBToys	Barbie Collector
Barbie Bazaar Magazine (Barbie collectible news and Information)	Target.com: Barbies	My Scene.com
If You Were a Barbie, Which Messed Up Version Would You Be?	Barbie: Best prices and selection (bizrate.com)	EverythingGirl.com
Visible Barbie Project (macabre images of Barbie sliced as though in a science project)	Barbies, New and Pre-owned at NetDoll	Barbie History (fan-type history, mostly when various dolls were released)
Barbie: The Image of Us All (1995 undergraduate paper about Barbie's cultural history)	Barbies—compare prices (nextag.com)	Mattel, Inc.
Andigraph.free.fr (Barbie and Ken sex animation)	Barbie Toys (complete line of Barbie electronics online)	Spatula Jackson's Barbies (pictures of Barbie as various countercultural images).
Suicide bomber Barbie (Barbie with explosives strapped to waist)	Barbie Party supplies	Barbie! (fan site)
Barbies (Barbie dressed and painted as countercultural images)	Barbie and her accessories online	The Distorted Barbie

relevance by linking to it, and Google aggregates these votes and renders them on their results page as higher ranking. The little girl who searches for Barbie on Google will encounter a culturally contested figure. The same girl, searching on Overture, will encounter a commodity toy. In each case, the underlying efforts of Mattel, the producer of Barbie, have not changed. What is different is that in an environment where relevance is measured in non-market action—placing a link to a Web site because you deem it relevant to whatever you are doing with your Web site—as opposed to in dollars, Barbie has become a more transparent cultural object. It is easier for the little girl to see that the doll is not only a toy, not only a symbol of beauty and glamour, but also a symbol of how norms of female beauty in our society can be oppressive to women and girls. The transparency does not force the girl to choose one meaning of Barbie or another. It does, however, render transparent that Barbie can have multiple meanings and that choosing meanings is a matter of political concern for some set of people who coinhabit this culture. Yahoo! occupies something of a middle ground—its algorithm does link to two of the critical sites among the top ten, and within the top twenty, identifies most of the sites that appear on Google's top ten that are not related to sales or promotion.

A similar phenomenon repeats itself in the context of explicit efforts to define Barbie—encyclopedias. There are, as of this writing, six general-interest online encyclopedias that are reasonably accessible on the Internet—that is to say, can be found with reasonable ease by looking at major search engines, sites that focus on education and parenting, and similar techniques. Five are commercial, and one is a quintessential commons-based peer-production project—*Wikipedia*. Of the five commercial encyclopedias, only one is available at no charge, the *Columbia Encyclopedia*, which is packaged in two primary forms—as encyclopedia.com and as part of Bartleby.com.[6] The other four—*Britannica*, Microsoft's *Encarta*, the *World Book*, and *Grolier's Online Encyclopedia*—charge various subscription rates that range around fifty to sixty dollars a year. The *Columbia Encyclopedia* includes no reference to Barbie, the doll. The *World Book* has no "Barbie" entry, but does include a reference to Barbie as part of a fairly substantial article on "Dolls." The only information that is given is that the doll was introduced in 1959, that she has a large wardrobe, and in a different place, that dark-skinned Barbies were introduced in the 1980s. The article concludes with a guide of about three hundred words to good doll-collecting practices. Microsoft's *Encarta* also includes Barbie in the article on "Doll," but provides a brief separate definition as well, which replicates the *World Book* information in slightly different form: 1959, large wardrobe, and introduction of dark-skinned Barbies. The online photograph available with the definition is of a brown-skinned, black-haired Barbie. *Grolier's Online's* major general-purpose encyclopedia, *Americana*, also has no entry for Barbie, but makes reference to the doll as part of the article on dolls. Barbie is described as a revolutionary new doll, made to resemble a teenage fashion model as part of a trend to realism in dolls. *Grolier's Online* does, however, include a more specialized *American Studies* encyclopedia that has an article on Barbie. That article heavily emphasizes the number of dolls sold and their value, provides some description of the chronological history of the doll, and makes opaque references to Barbie's physique and her emphasis on consumption. While the encyclopedia includes bibliographic references to critical works about Barbie, the textual references to cultural critique or problems she raises are very slight and quite oblique.

Only two encyclopedias focus explicitly on Barbie's cultural meaning: *Britannica* and *Wikipedia*. The *Britannica* entry was written by M. G. Lord, a professional journalist who authored a book entitled *Forever Barbie: The Unauthorized Biography of a Real Doll*. It is a tightly written piece that underscores the critique of Barbie, both on body dimensions and its relationship to the body image of girls, and excessive consumerism. It also, however, makes clear the fact that Barbie was the first doll to give girls a play image that was not focused on nurturing and family roles, but was an independent, professional adult: playing roles such as airline pilot, astronaut, or presidential candidate. The article also provides brief references to the role of Barbie in a global market economy—its manufacture outside the United States, despite its marketing as an American cultural icon, and its manufacturer's early adoption of direct-to-children marketing. *Wikipedia* provides more or less all the information provided in the *Britannica* definition, including a reference to Lord's own book, and adds substantially more material from within Barbie lore itself and a detailed time line of the doll's history. It has a strong emphasis on the body image controversy, and emphasizes both the critique that Barbie encourages girls to focus on shallow consumption of fashion accessories, and that she represents an unattainable lifestyle for most girls who play with her. The very first version of the definition, posted January 3, 2003, included only a brief reference to a change in Barbie's waistline as a result of efforts by parents and anorexia groups concerned with the doll's impact on girls' nutrition. This remained the only reference to the critique of Barbie until December 15, 2003, when a user who was not logged in introduced a fairly roughly written section that emphasized both the body image concerns and the consumerism concerns with Barbie. During the same day, a number of regular contributors (that is, users with log-in names and their own talk pages) edited the new section and improved its language and flow, but kept the basic concepts intact. Three weeks later, on January 5, 2004, another regular user rewrote the section, reorganized the paragraphs so that the critique of Barbie's emphasis on high consumption was separated from the emphasis on Barbie's body dimensions, and also separated and clarified the qualifying claims that Barbie's independence and professional outfits may have had positive effects on girls' perception of possible life plans. This contributor also introduced a reference to the fact that the term "Barbie" is often used to denote a shallow or silly girl or woman. After that, with a change three weeks later from describing Barbie as available for most of her life only as "white Anglo-Saxon (and probably protestant)" to "white woman of apparently European descent" this part of the definition stabilized. As this description aims to make clear, *Wikipedia* makes the history of the evolution of the article entirely transparent. The software platform allows any reader to look at prior versions of the definition, to compare specific versions, and to read the "talk" pages— the pages where the participants discuss their definition and their thoughts about it.

The relative emphasis of Google and *Wikipedia*, on the one hand, and Overture, Yahoo!, and the commercial encyclopedias other than *Britannica*, on the other hand, is emblematic of a basic difference between markets and social conversations with regard to culture. If we focus on the role of culture as "common knowledge" or background knowledge, its relationship to the market—at least for theoretical economists—is exogenous. It can be taken as given and treated as "taste." In more practical business environments, culture is indeed a source of taste and demand, but it is not taken as exogenous. Culture, symbolism, and meaning, as they are tied with market-based goods, become a major focus of advertising and of demand management. No one who has been exposed to the advertising campaigns of Coca-Cola, Nike, or Apple Computers, as well as practically to any one of a broad range of advertising campaigns over the past few decades, can fail to see that these are not primarily a communication about the material characteristics or qualities of the products or services sold by the advertisers.

They are about meaning. These campaigns try to invest the act of buying their products or services with a cultural meaning that they cultivate, manipulate, and try to generalize in the practices of the society in which they are advertising, precisely in order to shape taste. They offer an opportunity to generate rents, because the consumer has to have this company's shoe rather than that one, because that particular shoe makes the customer this kind of person rather than that kind—cool rather than stuffy, sophisticated rather than common. Neither the theoretical economists nor the marketing executives have any interest in rendering culture transparent or writable. Whether one treats culture as exogenous or as a domain for limiting the elasticity of demand for one's particular product, there is no impetus to make it easier for consumers to see through the cultural symbols, debate their significance, or make them their own. If there is business reason to do anything about culture, it is to try to shape the cultural meaning of an object or practice, in order to shape the demand for it, while keeping the role of culture hidden and assuring control over the careful cultural choreography of the symbols attached to the company. Indeed, in 1995, the U.S. Congress enacted a new kind of trademark law, the Federal Antidilution Act, which for the first time disconnects trademark protection from protecting consumers from confusion by knockoffs. The Antidilution Act of 1995 gives the owner of any famous mark—and only famous marks—protection from any use that dilutes the meaning that the brand owner has attached to its own mark. It can be entirely clear to consumers that a particular use does not come from the owner of the brand, and still, the owner has a right to prevent this use. While there is some constitutional free-speech protection for criticism, there is also a basic change in the understanding of trademark law—from a consumer protection law intended to assure that consumers can rely on the consistency of goods marked in a certain way, to a property right in controlling the meaning of symbols a company has successfully cultivated so that they are, in fact, famous. This legal change marks a major shift in the understanding of the role of law in assigning control for cultural meaning generated by market actors.

Unlike market production of culture, meaning making as a social, non-market practice has no similar systematic reason to accept meaning as it comes. Certainly, some social relations do. When girls play with dolls, collect them, or exhibit them, they are rarely engaged in reflection on the meaning of the dolls, just as fans of Scarlett O'Hara, of which a brief Internet search suggests there are many, are not usually engaged in critique of *Gone with the*

Wind as much as in replication and adoption of its romantic themes. Plainly, however, some conversations we have with each other are about who we are, how we came to be who we are, and whether we view the answers we find to these questions as attractive or not. In other words, some social interactions do have room for examining culture as well as inhabiting it, for considering background knowledge for what it is, rather than taking it as a given input into the shape of demand or using it as a medium for managing meaning and demand. People often engage in conversations with each other precisely to understand themselves in the world, their relationship to others, and what makes them like and unlike those others. One major domain in which this formation of self- and group identity occurs is the adoption or rejection of, and inquiry into, cultural symbols and sources of meaning that will make a group cohere or splinter; that will make people like or unlike each other.

The distinction I draw here between market-based and nonmarket-based activities is purposefully overstated to clarify the basic structural differences between these two modes of organizing communications and the degree of transparency of culture they foster. As even the very simple story of how Barbie is defined in Internet communications demonstrates, practices are not usually as cleanly divided. Like the role of the elite newspapers in providing political coverage, discussed in chapter 6, some market-based efforts do provide transparency; indeed, their very market rationale pushes them to engage in a systematic effort to provide transparency. Google's strategy from the start has been to assume that what individuals are interested in is a reflection of what other individuals—who are interested in roughly the same area, but spend more time on it, that is, Web page authors—think is worthwhile. The company built its business model around rendering transparent what people and organizations that make their information available freely consider relevant. Occasionally, Google has had to deal with "search engine optimizers," who have advised companies on how to game its search engine to achieve a high ranking. Google has fought these optimizers; sometimes by outright blocking access to traffic that originates with them. In these cases, we see a technical competition between firms—the optimizers—whose interest is in capturing attention based on the interests of those who pay them, and a firm, Google, whose strategic choice is to render the distributed judgments of relevance on the Web more or less faithfully. There, the market incentive actually drives Google's investment affirmatively toward transparency. However, the market decision must be strategic, not tactical, for this to be the case. Fear of litigation has, for example, caused Google to bury links that threatened it with liability. The most prominent of these cases occurred when the Church of Scientology threatened to sue Google over presenting links to www.xenu.net, a site dedicated to criticizing scientology. Google initially removed the link. However, its strategic interest was brought to the fore by widespread criticism of its decision on the Internet, and the firm relented. A search for "Scientology" as of this writing reveals a wide range of sites, many critical of scientology, and xenu.net is the second link. A search for "scientology Google" will reveal many stories, not quite flattering either to Google or to the Church of Scientology, as the top links. We see similar diversity among the encyclopedias. *Britannica* offered as clear a presentation of the controversy over Barbie as *Wikipedia*. *Britannica* has built its reputation and business model on delivery of the knowledge and opinions of those in positions to claim authority in the name of high culture professional competence, and delivering that perspective to those who buy the encyclopedia precisely to gain access to that kind of knowledge base, judgment, and formal credibility. In both cases, the long-term business model of the companies calls for reflecting the views and insights of agents who are not themselves thoroughly within the market—whether they are academics who write articles for *Britannica*, or the many and diverse Web page owners on the Internet. In both cases, these business models lead to a much more transparent cultural representation than what Hollywood or Madison Avenue produce. Just as not all market-based organizations render culture opaque, not all nonmarket or social-relations-based conversations aim to explore and expose cultural assumptions. Social conversations can indeed be among the most highly deferential to cultural assumptions, and can repress critique more effectively and completely than market-based conversations. Whether in communities of unquestioning religious devotion or those that enforce strict egalitarian political correctness, we commonly see, in societies both traditional and contemporary, significant social pressures against challenging background cultural assumptions within social conversations. We have, for example, always had more cultural experimentation and fermentation in cities, where social ties are looser and communities can exercise less social control over questioning minds and conversation. Ubiquitous Internet communications expand something of the freedom of city parks and streets, but also the freedom of cafés and bars—commercial platforms for social interaction—so that it is available everywhere.

The claim I make here, as elsewhere throughout this book, is not that nonmarket production will, in fact, generally displace market production, or that such displacement is necessary to achieve the improvement in the degree of participation in cultural production and legibility. My claim is that the emergence of a substantial nonmarket alternative path for cultural conversation increases the degrees of freedom available to individuals and groups to engage in cultural production and exchange, and that doing so increases the transparency of culture to its inhabitants. It is a claim tied to the particular technological moment and its particular locus of occurrence—our networked communications environment. It is based on the fact that it is displacing the particular industrial form of information and cultural production of the twentieth century, with its heavy emphasis on consumption in mass markets. In this context, the emergence of a substantial sector of nonmarket production, and of peer production, or the emergence of individuals acting cooperatively as a major new source of defining widely transmissible statements and conversations about the meaning of the culture we share, makes culture substantially more transparent and available for reflection, and therefore for revision.

Two other dimensions are made very clear by the *Wikipedia* example. The first is the degree of self-consciousness that is feasible with open, conversation-based definition of culture that is itself rendered more transparent. The second is the degree to which the culture is writable, the degree to which individuals can participate in mixing and matching and making their own emphases, for themselves and for others, on the existing set of symbols. Fisher, for example, has used the term "semiotic democracy" to describe the potential embodied in the emerging openness of Internet culture to participation by users. The term originates from Fiske's *Television Culture* as a counterpoint to the claim that television was actually a purely one-way medium that only enacted culture on viewers. Instead, Fiske claimed that viewers resist these meanings, put them in their own contexts, use them in various ways, and subvert them to make their own meaning. However, much of this resistance is unstated, some of it unself-conscious. There are the acts of reception and interpretation, or of using images and sentences in different contexts of life than those depicted in the television program; but these acts are local, enacted within small-scale local cultures, and are not the result of a self-conscious conversation among users of the culture about its limits, its meanings, and its subversions. One of the phenomena we are beginning to observe on the Internet is an emerging culture of conversation about culture, which is both self-conscious and informed by linking or quoting from specific reference points. The *Wikipedia* development of the definition of Barbie, its history, and the availability of a talk page alongside it for discussion about the definition, are an extreme version of self-conscious discussion about culture. The basic tools enabled by the Internet—cutting, pasting, rendering, annotating, and commenting—make active utilization and conscious discussion of cultural symbols and artifacts easier to create, sustain, and read more generally.

The flexibility with which cultural artifacts—meaning-carrying objects—can be rendered, preserved, and surrounded by different context and discussion makes it easy for anyone, anywhere, to make a self-conscious statement about culture. They enable what Balkin has called "glomming on"—taking that which is common cultural representation and reworking it into your own move in a cultural conversation.[7] The low cost of storage, and the ubiquitous possibility of connecting from any connection location to any storage space make any such statement persistent and available to others. The ease of commenting, linking, and writing to other locations of statements, in turn, increases the possibility of response and counterresponse. These conversations can then be found by others, and at least read if not contributed to. In other words, as with other, purposeful peer-produced projects like *Wikipedia*, the basic characteristics of the Internet in general and the World Wide Web in particular have made it possible for anyone, anywhere, for any reason to begin to contribute to an accretion of conversation about well-defined cultural objects or about cultural trends and characteristics generally. These conversations can persist across time and exist across distance, and are available for both active participation and passive reading by many people in many places. The result is, as we are already seeing it, the emergence of widely accessible, self-conscious conversation about the meaning of contemporary culture by those who inhabit it. This "writability" is also the second characteristic that the *Wikipedia* definition process makes very clear, and the second major change brought about by the networked information economy in the digital environment.

THE PLASTICITY OF INTERNET CULTURE:
THE FUTURE OF HIGH-PRODUCTION-VALUE
FOLK CULTURE

I have already described the phenomena of blogs, of individually created movies like *The Jedi Saga*, and of Second Life, the game platform where users have made all the story lines and all the objects, while the commercial provider created the tools and hosts the platform for their collective storytelling. We are seeing the broad emergence of business models that are aimed precisely at providing users with the tools to write, compose, film, and mix existing materials, and to publish, play, render, and distribute what we have made to others, everywhere. Blogger, for example, provides simple tools for online publication of written materials. Apple Computer offers a product called GarageBand, that lets users compose and play their own music. It includes a large library of prerecorded building blocks—different instruments, riffs, loops—and an interface that allows the user to mix, match, record and add their own, and produce their own musical composition and play it. Video-editing utilities, coupled with the easy malleability of digital video, enable people to make films—whether about their own lives or, as in the case of *The Jedi Saga*, of fantasies. The emerging phenomenon of Machinima—short movies that are made using game platforms—underscores how digital platforms can also become tools for creation in unintended ways. Creators use the 3-D rendering capabilities of an existing game, but use the game to stage a movie scene or video presentation, which they record as it is played out. This recording is then distributed on the Internet as a stand-alone short film. While many of these are still crude, the basic possibilities they present as modes of making movies is significant. Needless to say, not everyone is Mozart. Not everyone is even a reasonably talented musician, author, or filmmaker. Much of what can be and is done is not wildly creative, and much of it takes the form of Balkin's "glomming on": That is, users take existing popular culture, or otherwise professionally created culture, and perform it, sometimes with an effort toward fidelity to the professionals, but often with their own twists, making it their own in an immediate and unmediated way. However, just as learning how to read music and play an instrument can make one a better-informed listener, so too a ubiquitous practice of making cultural artifacts of all forms enables individuals in society to be better readers, listeners, and viewers of professionally produced culture, as well as contributors of our own statements into this mix of collective culture.

People have always created their own culture. Popular music did not begin with Elvis. There has always been a folk culture—of music, storytelling, and theater. What happened over the course of the twentieth century in advanced economies, and to a lesser extent but still substantially around the globe, is the displacement of folk culture by commercially produced mass popular

culture. The role of the individuals and communities vis-à-vis cultural artifacts changed, from coproducers and replicators to passive consumers. The
time frame where elders might tell stories, children might put on a show for
the adults, or those gathered might sing songs came to be occupied by
background music, from the radio or phonograph, or by television. We came
to assume a certain level of "production values"—quality of sound and image, quality of rendering and staging—that are unattainable with our crude
means and our relatively untrained voices or use of instruments. Not only
time for local popular creation was displaced, therefore, but also a sense of
what counted as engaging, delightful articulation of culture. In a now-classic
article from 1937, "The Work of Art in the Age of Mechanical Reproduction," Walter Benjamin authored one of the only instances of critical theory
that took an optimistic view of the emergence of popular culture in the
twentieth century as a potentially liberating turn. Benjamin's core claim was
that with mechanical replication of art, the "aura" that used to attach to
single works of art is dissipated. Benjamin saw this aura of unique works of
art as reinforcing a distance between the masses and the representations of
culture, reinforcing the perception of their weakness and distance from truly
great things. He saw in mechanical reproducibility the possibility of bringing
copies down to earth, to the hands of the masses, and reversing the sense
of distance and relative weakness of the mass culture. What Benjamin did
not yet see were the ways in which mechanical reproduction would insert a
different kind of barrier between many dispersed individuals and the capacity
to make culture. The barrier of production costs, production values, and the
star system that came along with them, replaced the iconic role of the unique
work of art with new, but equally high barriers to participation in making
culture. It is precisely those barriers that the capabilities provided by digital
media begin to erode. It is becoming feasible for users to cut and paste,
"glom on," to existing cultural materials; to implement their intuitions,
tastes, and expressions through media that render them with newly acceptable degrees of technical quality, and to distribute them among others, both
near and far. As Hollywood begins to use more computer-generated special
effects, but more important, whole films—2004 alone saw major releases
like *Shrek 2*, *The Incredibles*, and *Polar Express*—and as the quality of widely
available image-generation software and hardware improves, the production
value gap between individual users or collections of users and the
commercial-professional studios will decrease. As this book is completed in
early 2005, nothing makes clearer the value of retelling basic stories through

the prism of contemporary witty criticism of prevailing culture than do *Shrek 2* and *The Incredibles*, and, equally, nothing exposes the limits of purely technical, movie-star-centered quality than the lifelessness of *Polar Express*. As online games like Second Life provide users with new tools and platforms to tell and retell their own stories, or their own versions of well-trodden paths, as digital multimedia tools do the same for individuals outside of the collaborative storytelling platforms, we can begin to see a reemergence of folk stories and songs as widespread cultural practices. And as network connections become ubiquitous, and search engines and filters improve, we can begin to see this folk culture emerging to play a substantially greater role in the production of our cultural environment.

A PARTICIPATORY CULTURE: TOWARD POLICY

Culture is too broad a concept to suggest an all-encompassing theory centered around technology in general or the Internet in particular. My focus is therefore much narrower, along two dimensions. First, I am concerned with thinking about the role of culture to human interactions that can be understood in terms of basic liberal political commitments—that is to say, a concern for the degree of freedom individuals have to form and pursue a life plan, and the degree of participation they can exercise in debating and determining collective action. Second, my claim is focused on the relative attractiveness of the twentieth-century industrial model of cultural production and what appears to be emerging as the networked model in the early twenty-first century, rather than on the relationship of the latter to some theoretically defined ideal culture.

A liberal political theory cannot wish away the role of culture in structuring human events. We engage in wide ranges of social practices of making and exchanging symbols that are concerned with how our life is and how it might be, with which paths are valuable for us as individuals to pursue and which are not, and with what objectives we as collective communities—from the local to the global—ought to pursue. This unstructured, ubiquitous conversation is centrally concerned with things that a liberal political system speaks to, but it is not amenable to anything like an institutionalized process that could render its results "legitimate." Culture operates as a set of background assumptions and common knowledge that structure our understanding of the state of the world and the range of possible actions and outcomes open to us individually and collectively. It constrains the range of conversational moves open to us to consider what we are doing and how we might act differently. In these regards, it is a source of power in the critical-theory sense—a source that exerts real limits on what we can do and how we can be. As a source of power, it is not a natural force that stands apart from human endeavor and is therefore a fact that is not itself amenable to political evaluation. As we see well in the efforts of parents and teachers, advertising agencies and propaganda departments, culture is manipulable, manageable, and a direct locus of intentional action aimed precisely at harnessing its force as a way of controlling the lives of those who inhabit it. At the same time, however, culture is not the barrel of a gun or the chains of a dungeon. There are limits on the degree to which culture can actually control those who inhabit it. Those degrees depend to a great extent on the relative difficulty or ease of seeing through culture, of talking about it with others, and of seeing other alternatives or other ways of symbolizing the possible and the desirable.

Understanding that culture is a matter of political concern even within a liberal framework does not, however, translate into an agenda of intervention in the cultural sphere as an extension of legitimate political decision making. Cultural discourse is systematically not amenable to formal regulation, management, or direction from the political system. First, participation in cultural discourse is intimately tied to individual self-expression, and its regulation would therefore require levels of intrusion in individual autonomy that would render any benefits in terms of a participatory political system Pyrrhic indeed. Second, culture is much more intricately woven into the fabric of everyday life than political processes and debates. It is language— the basic framework within which we can comprehend anything, and through which we do so everywhere. To regulate culture is to regulate our very comprehension of the world we occupy. Third, therefore, culture infuses our thoughts at a wide range of levels of consciousness. Regulating culture, or intervening in its creation and direction, would entail self-conscious action to affect citizens at a subconscious or weakly conscious level. Fourth, and finally, there is no Archimedean point outside of culture on which to stand and decide—let us pour a little bit more of this kind of image or that, so that we achieve a better consciousness, one that better fits even our most just and legitimately arrived-at political determinations.

A systematic commitment to avoid direct intervention in cultural exchange does not leave us with nothing to do or say about culture, and about law or policy as it relates to it. What we have is the capacity and need to observe a cultural production and exchange system and to assure that it is as unconstraining and free from manipulation as possible. We must diagnose what makes a culture more or less opaque to its inhabitants; what makes it more or less liable to be strictly constraining of the conversations that rely on it; and what makes the possibility of many and diverse sources and forms of cultural intervention more or less likely. On the background of this project, I suggest that the emergence of Internet culture is an attractive development from the perspective of liberal political theory. This is so both because of the technical characteristics of digital objects and computer network communications, and because of the emerging industrial structure of the networked information economy—typified by the increased salience of nonmarket production in general and of individual production, alone or in concert with others, in particular. The openness of digital networks allows for a much wider range of perspectives on any particular symbol or range of symbols to be visible for anyone, everywhere. The cross section of views that makes it easy to see that Barbie is a contested symbol makes it possible more generally to observe very different cultural forms and perspectives for any individual. This transparency of background unstated assumptions and common knowledge is the beginning of self-reflection and the capacity to break out of given molds. Greater transparency is also a necessary element in, and a consequence of, collaborative action, as various participants either explicitly, or through negotiating the divergence of their nonexplicit different perspectives, come to a clearer statement of their assumptions, so that these move from the background to the fore, and become more amenable to examination and revision. The plasticity of digital objects, in turn, improves the degree to which individuals can begin to produce a new folk culture, one that already builds on the twentieth-century culture that was highly unavailable for folk retelling and re-creation. This plasticity, and the practices of writing your own culture, then feed back into the transparency, both because the practice of making one's own music, movie, or essay makes one a more self-conscious user of the cultural artifacts of others, and because in retelling anew known stories, we again come to see what the originals were about and how they do, or do not, fit our own sense of how things are and how they ought to be. There is emerging a broad practice of learning by doing that makes the entire society more effective readers and writers of their own culture.

By comparison to the highly choreographed cultural production system of the industrial information economy, the emergence of a new folk culture and of a wider practice of active personal engagement in the telling and retelling of basic cultural themes and emerging concerns and attachments offers new avenues for freedom. It makes culture more participatory, and renders it more legible to all its inhabitants. The basic structuring force of culture is not eliminated, of course. The notion of floating monads disconnected from a culture is illusory. Indeed, it is undesirable. However, the framework that culture offers us, the language that makes it possible for us to make statements and incorporate the statements of others in the daily social conversation that pervades life, is one that is more amenable to our own remaking. We become more sophisticated users of this framework, more self-conscious about it, and have a greater capacity to recognize, challenge, and change that which we find oppressive, and to articulate, exchange, and adopt that which we find enabling. As chapter 11 makes clear, however, the tension between the industrial model of cultural production and the networked information economy is nowhere more pronounced than in the question of the degree to which the new folk culture of the twenty-first century will be permitted to build upon the outputs of the twentieth-century industrial model. In this battle, the stakes are high. One cannot make new culture ex nihilo. We are as we are today, as cultural beings, occupying a set of common symbols and stories that are heavily based on the outputs of that industrial period. If we are to make this culture our own, render it legible, and make it into a new platform for our needs and conversations today, we must find a way to cut, paste, and remix present culture. And it is precisely this freedom that most directly challenges the laws written for the twentieth-century technology, economy, and cultural practice.

Chapter 9 Justice and Development

How will the emergence of a substantial sector of nonmarket, commons-based production in the information economy affect questions of distribution and human well-being? The pessimistic answer is, very little. Hunger, disease, and deeply rooted racial, ethnic, or class stratification will not be solved by a more decentralized, nonproprietary information production system. Without clean water, basic literacy, moderately well-functioning governments, and universal practical adoption of the commitment to treat all human beings as fundamentally deserving of equal regard, the fancy Internet-based society will have little effect on the billions living in poverty or deprivation, either in the rich world, or, more urgently and deeply, in poor and middle-income economies. There is enough truth in this pessimistic answer to require us to tread lightly in embracing the belief that the shift to a networked information economy can indeed have meaningful effects in the domain of justice and human development.

Despite the caution required in overstating the role that the networked information economy can play in solving issues of justice, it is important to recognize that information, knowledge, and culture are core inputs into human welfare. Agricultural knowledge and biological innovation are central to food security. Medical innovation and access to its fruits are central to living a long and healthy life. Literacy and education are central to individual growth, to democratic self-governance, and to economic capabilities. Economic growth itself is critically dependent on innovation and information. For all these reasons, information policy has become a critical element of development policy and the question of how societies attain and distribute human welfare and well-being. Access to knowledge has become central to human development. The emergence of the networked information economy offers definable opportunities for improvement in the normative domain of justice, as it does for freedom, by comparison to what was achievable in the industrial information economy.

We can analyze the implications of the emergence of the networked information economy for justice or equality within two quite different frames. The first is liberal, and concerned primarily with some form of equality of opportunity. The second is social-democratic, or development oriented, and focused on universal provision of a substantial set of elements of human well-being. The availability of information from nonmarket sources and the range of opportunities to act within a nonproprietary production environment improve distribution in both these frameworks, but in different ways. Despite the differences, within both frameworks the effect crystallizes into one of access—access to opportunities for one's own action, and access to the outputs and inputs of the information economy. The industrial economy creates cost barriers and transactional-institutional barriers to both these domains. The networked information economy reduces both types of barriers, or creates alternative paths around them. It thereby equalizes, to some extent, both the opportunities to participate as an economic actor and the practical capacity to partake of the fruits of the increasingly information-based global economy.

The opportunities that the network information economy offers, however, often run counter to the central policy drive of both the United States and the European Union in the international trade and intellectual property systems. These two major powers have systematically pushed for ever-stronger proprietary protection and increasing reliance on strong patents, copyrights, and similar exclusive rights as the core information policy for growth and development. Chapter 2 explains why such a policy is suspect from a purely economic perspective concerned with optimizing innovation.

A system that relies too heavily on proprietary approaches to information production is not, however, merely inefficient. It is unjust. Proprietary rights are designed to elicit signals of people's willingness and ability to pay. In the presence of extreme distribution differences like those that characterize the global economy, the market is a poor measure of comparative welfare. A system that signals what innovations are most desirable and rations access to these innovations based on ability, as well as willingness, to pay, over-represents welfare gains of the wealthy and underrepresents welfare gains of the poor. Twenty thousand American teenagers can simply afford, and will be willing to pay, much more for acne medication than the more than a million Africans who die of malaria every year can afford to pay for a vaccine. A system that relies too heavily on proprietary models for managing information production and exchange is unjust because it is geared toward serving small welfare increases for people who can pay a lot for incremental improvements in welfare, and against providing large welfare increases for people who cannot pay for what they need.

LIBERAL THEORIES OF JUSTICE AND THE
NETWORKED INFORMATION ECONOMY

Liberal theories of justice can be categorized according to how they characterize the sources of inequality in terms of luck, responsibility, and structure. By luck, I mean reasons for the poverty of an individual that are beyond his or her control, and that are part of that individual's lot in life unaffected by his or her choices or actions. By responsibility, I mean causes for the poverty of an individual that can be traced back to his or her actions or choices. By structure, I mean causes for the inequality of an individual that are beyond his or her control, but are traceable to institutions, economic organizations, or social relations that form a society's transactional framework and constrain the behavior of the individual or undermine the efficacy of his or her efforts at self-help.

We can think of John Rawls's *Theory of Justice* as based on a notion that the poorest people are the poorest because of dumb luck. His proposal for a systematic way of defending and limiting redistribution is the "difference principle." A society should organize its redistribution efforts in order to make those who are least well-off as well-off as they can be. The theory of desert is that, because any of us could in principle be the victim of this dumb luck, we would all have agreed, if none of us had known where we would be on the distribution of bad luck, to minimize our exposure to really horrendous conditions. The practical implication is that while we might be bound to sacrifice some productivity to achieve redistribution, we cannot sacrifice too much. If we did that, we would most likely be hurting, rather than helping, the weakest and poorest. Libertarian theories of justice, most prominently represented by Robert Nozick's entitlement theory, on the other hand, tend to ignore bad luck or impoverishing structure. They focus solely on whether the particular holdings of a particular person at any given moment are unjustly obtained. If they are not, they may not justly be taken from the person who holds them. Explicitly, these theories ignore the poor. As a practical matter and by implication, they treat responsibility as the source of the success of the wealthy, and by negation, the plight of the poorest—leading them to be highly resistant to claims of redistribution.

The basic observation that an individual's economic condition is a function of his or her own actions does not necessarily resolve into a blanket rejection of redistribution, as we see in the work of other liberals. Ronald Dworkin's work on inequality offers a critique of Rawls's, in that it tries to include a component of responsibility alongside recognition of the role of luck. In his framework, if (1) resources were justly distributed and (2) bad luck in initial endowment were compensated through some insurance scheme, then poverty that resulted from bad choices, not bad luck, would not deserve help through redistribution. While Rawls's theory ignores personal responsibility, and in this regard, is less attractive from the perspective of a liberal theory that respects individual autonomy, it has the advantage of offering a much clearer metric for a just system. One can measure the welfare of the poorest under different redistribution rules in market economies. One can then see how much redistribution is too much, in the sense that welfare is reduced to the point that the poorest are actually worse off than they would be under a less-egalitarian system. You could compare the Soviet Union, West Germany, and the United States of the late 1960s–early 1970s, and draw conclusions. Dworkin's insurance scheme would require too fine an ability to measure the expected incapacitating effect of various low endowments—from wealth to intelligence to health—in a market economy, and to calibrate wealth endowments to equalize them, to offer a measuring rod for policy. It does, however, have the merit of distinguishing—for purposes of judging desert to benefit from society's redistribution efforts—between a child of privilege who fell into poverty through bad investments coupled with sloth and a person born into a poor family with severe mental defects. Bruce Ackerman's *Social Justice and the Liberal State* also provides a mechanism of differentiating the deserving from the undeserving, but adds policy tractability by including the dimension of structure to luck and responsibility. In addition to the dumb luck of how wealthy your parents are when you are born and what genetic endowment you are born with, there are also questions of the education system you grow up with and the transactional framework through which you live your life—which opportunities it affords, and which it cuts off or burdens. His proposals therefore seek to provide basic remedies for those failures, to the extent that they can, in fact, be remedied. One such proposal is Anne Alstott and Ackerman's idea of a government-funded personal endowment at birth, coupled with the freedom to squander it and suffer the consequential reduction in welfare.[1] He also emphasizes a more open and egalitarian transactional framework that would allow anyone access to opportunities to transact with others, rather than depending on, for example, unequal access to social links as a precondition to productive behavior.

The networked information economy improves justice from the perspective of every single one of these theories of justice. Imagine a good that improves the welfare of its users—it could be software, or an encyclopedia, or a product review. Now imagine a policy choice that could make production of that good on a nonmarket, peer-production basis too expensive to perform, or make it easy for an owner of an input to exclude competitors—both market-based and social-production based. For example, a government might decide to: recognize patents on software interfaces, so that it would be very expensive to buy the right to make your software work with someone else's; impose threshold formal education requirements on the authors of any encyclopedia available for school-age children to read, or impose very strict copyright requirements on using information contained in other sources (as opposed to only prohibiting copying their language) and impose high penalties for small omissions; or give the putative subjects of reviews very strong rights to charge for the privilege of reviewing a product—such as by expanding trademark rights to refer to the product, or prohibiting a reviewer to take apart a product without permission. The details do not matter. I offer them only to provide a sense of the commonplace kinds of choices that governments could make that would, as a practical matter, differentially burden nonmarket producers, whether nonprofit organizations or informal peer-production collaborations. Let us call a rule set that is looser from the perspective of access to existing information resources Rule Set A, and a rule set that imposes higher costs on access to information inputs Rule Set B. As explained in chapter 2, it is quite likely that adopting B would depress information production and innovation, even if it were intended to increase the production of information by, for example, strengthening copyright or patent. This is because the added incentives for some producers who produce with the aim of capturing the rents created by copyright or patents must be weighed against their costs. These include (a) the higher costs even for those producers and (b) the higher costs for all producers who do not rely on exclusive rights at all, but instead use either a nonproprietary market model—like service—or a nonmarket model, like nonprofits and individual authors, and that do not benefit in any way from the increased appropriation. However, let us make here a much weaker assumption—that an increase in the rules of exclusion will not affect overall production. Let us assume that there will be exactly enough increased production by producers who rely on a proprietary model to offset the losses of production in the nonproprietary sectors.

It is easy to see why a policy shift from A to B would be regressive from the perspective of theories like Rawls's or Ackerman's. Under Rule A, let us say that in this state of affairs, State A, there are five online encyclopedias. One of them is peer produced and freely available for anyone to use. Rule B is passed. In the new State B, there are still five encyclopedias. It has become too expensive to maintain the free encyclopedia, however, and more profitable to run commercial online encyclopedias. A new commercial encyclopedia has entered the market in competition with the four commercial encyclopedias that existed in State A, and the free encyclopedia folded. From the perspective of the difference principle, we can assume that the change has resulted in a stable overall welfare in the Kaldor-Hicks sense. (That is, overall welfare has increased enough so that, even though some people may be worse off, those who have been made better off are sufficiently better off that they could, in principle, compensate everyone who is worse off enough to make everyone either better off or no worse off than they were before.) There are still five encyclopedias. However, now they all charge a subscription fee. The poorest members of society are worse off, even if we posit that total social welfare has remained unchanged. In State A, they had access for free to an encyclopedia. They could use the information (or the software utility, if the example were software) without having to give up any other sources of welfare. In State B, they must choose between the same amount of encyclopedia usage as they had before, and less of some other source of welfare, or the same welfare from other sources, and no encyclopedia. If we assume, contrary to theory and empirical evidence from the innovation economics literature, that the move to State B systematically and predictably improves the incentives and investments of the commercial producers, that would still by itself not justify the policy shift from the perspective of the difference principle. One would have to sustain a much stricter claim: that the marginal improvement in the quality of the encyclopedias, and a decline in price from the added market competition that was not felt by the commercial producers when they were competing with the free, peer-produced version, would still make the poorest better off, even though they now must pay for any level of encyclopedia access, than they were when they had four commercial competitors with their prior levels of investment operating in a competitive landscape of four commercial and one free encyclopedia.

From the perspective of Ackerman's theory of justice, the advantages of the networked information economy are clearer yet. Ackerman characterizes some of the basic prerequisites for participating in a market economy as access to a transactional framework, to basic information, and to an adequate educational endowment. To the extent that any of the basic utilities required to participate in an information economy at all are available without sensitivity to price—that is, free to anyone—they are made available in a form that is substantially insulated from the happenstance of initial wealth endowments. In this sense at least, the development of a networked information economy overcomes some of the structural components of continued poverty—lack of access to information about market opportunities for production and cheaper consumption, about the quality of goods, or lack of communications capacity to people or places where one can act productively. While Dworkin's theory does not provide a similarly clear locus for mapping the effect of the networked information economy on justice, there is some advantage, and no loss, from this perspective, in having more of the information economy function on a nonmarket basis. As long as one recognizes bad luck as a partial reason for poverty, then having information resources available for free use is one mechanism of moderating the effects of bad luck in endowment, and lowers the need to compensate for those effects insofar as they translate to lack of access to information resources. This added access results from voluntary communication by the producers and a respect for their willingness to communicate what they produced freely.

While the benefits flow to individuals irrespective of whether their present state is due to luck or irresponsibility, it does not involve a forced redistribution from responsible individuals to irresponsible individuals.

From the perspective of liberal theories of justice, then, the emergence of the networked information economy is an unqualified improvement. Except under restrictive assumptions inconsistent with what we know as a matter of both theory and empirics about the economics of innovation and information production, the emergence of a substantial sector of information production and exchange that is based on social transactional frameworks, rather than on a proprietary exclusion business model, improves distribution in society. Its outputs are available freely to anyone, as basic inputs into their own actions—whether market-based or nonmarket-based. The facilities it produces improve the prospects of all who are connected to the Internet— whether they are seeking to use it as consumers or as producers. It softens some of the effects of resource inequality. It offers platforms for greater equality of opportunity to participate in market- and nonmarket-based enterprises. This characteristic is explored in much greater detail in the next segment of this chapter, but it is important to emphasize here that equality of opportunity to act in the face of unequal endowment is central to all liberal theories of justice. As a practical matter, these characteristics of the networked information economy make the widespread availability of Internet access a more salient objective of redistribution policy. They make policy debates, which are mostly discussed in today's political sphere in terms of innovation and growth, and sometimes in terms of freedom, also a matter of liberal justice.

COMMONS-BASED STRATEGIES FOR HUMAN WELFARE AND DEVELOPMENT

There is a long social-democratic tradition of focusing not on theoretical conditions of equality in a liberal society, but on the actual well-being of human beings in a society. This conception of justice shares with liberal theories the acceptance of market economy as a fundamental component of free societies. However, its emphasis is not equality of opportunity or even some level of social insurance that still allows the slothful to fall, but on assuring a basic degree of well-being to everyone in society. Particularly in the European social democracies, the ambition has been to make that basic level quite high, but the basic framework of even American Social Security—

unless it is fundamentally changed in the coming years—has this character-istic. The literature on global poverty and its alleviation was initially inde-pendent of this concern, but as global communications and awareness in-creased, and as the conditions of life in most advanced market economies for most people improved, the lines between the concerns with domestic conditions and global poverty blurred. We have seen an increasing merging of the concerns into a concern for basic human well-being everywhere. It is represented in no individual's work more clearly than in that of Amartya Sen, who has focused on the centrality of development everywhere to the definition not only of justice, but of freedom as well.

The emerging salience of global development as the core concern of dis-tributive justice is largely based on the sheer magnitude of the problems faced by much of the world's population.[2] In the world's largest democracy, 80 percent of the population—slightly more people than the entire popu-lation of the United States and the expanded European Union combined—lives on less than two dollars a day, 39 percent of adults are illiterate, and 47 percent of children under the age of five are underweight for their age. In Africa's wealthiest democracy, a child at birth has a 45 percent probability of dying before he or she reaches the age of forty. India and South Africa are far from being the worst-off countries. The scope of destitution around the globe exerts a moral pull on any acceptable discussion of justice. Intui-tively, these problems seem too fundamental to be seriously affected by the networked information economy—what has *Wikipedia* got to do with the 49 percent of the population of Congo that lacks sustainable access to im-proved water sources? It is, indeed, important not to be overexuberant about the importance of information and communications policy in the context of global human development. But it is also important not to ignore the centrality of information to most of our more-advanced strategies for pro-ducing core components of welfare and development. To see this, we can begin by looking at the components of the Human Development Index (HDI).

The Human Development Report was initiated in 1990 as an effort to measure a broad set of components of what makes a life livable, and, ulti-mately, attractive. It was developed in contradistinction to indicators cen-tered on economic output, like gross domestic product (GDP) or economic growth alone, in order to provide a more refined sense of what aspects of a nation's economy and society make it more or less livable. It allows a more nuanced approach toward improving the conditions of life everywhere. As

Sen pointed out, the people of China, Kerala in India, and Sri Lanka lead much longer and healthier lives than other countries, like Brazil or South Africa, which have a higher per capita income.[3] The Human Development Report measures a wide range of outcomes and characteristics of life. The major composite index it tracks is the Human Development Index. The HDI tries to capture the capacity of people to live long and healthy lives, to be knowledgeable, and to have material resources sufficient to provide a decent standard of living. It does so by combining three major components: life expectancy at birth, adult literacy and school enrollment, and GDP per capita. As Figure 9.1 illustrates, in the global information economy, each and every one of these measures is significantly, though not solely, a function of access to information, knowledge, and information-embedded goods and services. Life expectancy is affected by adequate nutrition and access to life-saving medicines. Biotechnological innovation for agriculture, along with agronomic innovation in cultivation techniques and other, lower-tech modes of innovation, account for a high portion of improvements in the capacity of societies to feed themselves and in the availability of nutritious foods. Medicines depend on pharmaceutical research and access to its products, and health care depends on research and publication for the development and dissemination of information about best-care practices. Education is also heavily dependent, not surprisingly, on access to materials and facilities for teaching. This includes access to basic textbooks, libraries, computation and communications systems, and the presence of local academic centers. Finally, economic growth has been understood for more than half a century to be centrally driven by innovation. This is particularly true of latecomers, who can improve their own condition most rapidly by adopting best practices and advanced technology developed elsewhere, and then adapting to local conditions and adding their own from the new technological platform achieved in this way. All three of these components are, then, substantially affected by access to, and use of, information and knowledge. The basic premise of the claim that the emergence of the networked information economy can provide significant benefits to human development is that the manner in which we produce new information—and equally important, the institutional framework we use to manage the stock of existing information and knowledge around the world—can have significant impact on human development.

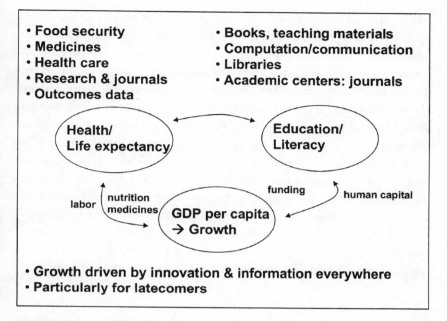

- **Food security**
- **Medicines**
- **Health care**
- **Research & journals**
- **Outcomes data**

- **Books, teaching materials**
- **Computation/communication**
- **Libraries**
- **Academic centers: journals**

Health/
Life expectancy

Education/
Literacy

labor nutrition medicines funding human capital

GDP per capita
→ Growth

- **Growth driven by innovation & information everywhere**
- **Particularly for latecomers**

Figure 9.1: HDI and Information

INFORMATION-EMBEDDED GOODS AND
TOOLS, INFORMATION, AND KNOWLEDGE

One can usefully idealize three types of information-based advantages that developed economies have, and that would need to be available to developing and less-developed economies if one's goal were the improvement in conditions in those economies and the opportunities for innovation in them. These include information-embedded material resources—consumption goods and production tools—information, and knowledge.

Information-Embedded Goods. These are goods that are not themselves information, but that are better, more plentiful, or cheaper because of some technological advance embedded in them or associated with their production. Pharmaceuticals and agricultural goods are the most obvious examples in the areas of health and food security, respectively. While there are other constraints on access to innovative products in these areas—regulatory and political in nature—a perennial barrier is cost. And a perennial barrier to competition that could reduce the cost is the presence of exclusive rights, mostly in the form of patents, but also in the form of internationally recognized breeders' rights and regulatory data exclusivity. In the areas of computation and communication, hardware and software are the primary domains of concern. With hardware, there have been some efforts toward developing cheaper equipment—like the simputer and the Jhai computer efforts to develop inexpensive computers. Because of the relatively commoditized state of most components of these systems, however, marginal cost, rather than exclusive rights, has been the primary barrier to access. The solution, if one has emerged, has been aggregation of demand—a networked computer for a village, rather than an individual. For software, the initial solution was piracy. More recently, we have seen an increased use of free software instead. The former cannot genuinely be described as a "solution," and is being eliminated gradually by trade policy efforts. The latter—adoption of free software to obtain state-of-the-art software—forms the primary template for the class of commons-based solutions to development that I explore in this chapter.

Information-Embedded Tools.   One level deeper than the actual useful material things one would need to enhance welfare are tools necessary for innovation itself. In the areas of agricultural biotechnology and medicines, these include enabling technologies for advanced research, as well as access to materials and existing compounds for experimentation. Access to these is perhaps the most widely understood to present problems in the patent system of the developed world, as much as it is for the developing world—an awareness that has mostly crystallized under Michael Heller's felicitous phrase "anti-commons," or Carl Shapiro's "patent thicket." The intuition, whose analytic basis is explained in chapter 2, is that innovation is encumbered more than it is encouraged when basic tools for innovation are proprietary, where the property system gives owners of these tools proprietary rights to control innovation that relies on their tools, and where any given new innovation requires the consent of, and payment to, many such owners. This problem is not unique to the developing world. Nonetheless, because of the relatively small dollar value of the market for medicines that treat diseases that affect only poorer countries or of crop varieties optimized for those countries, the cost hurdle weighs more heavily on the public or nonprofit efforts to achieve food security and health in poor and middle-income countries. These nonmarket-based research efforts into diseases and crops of concern purely to these areas are not constructed to appropriate gains from exclusive rights to research tools, but only bear their costs on downstream innovation.

Information.   The distinction between information and knowledge is a tricky one. I use "information" here colloquially, to refer to raw data, scientific reports of the output of scientific discovery, news, and factual reports. I use "knowledge" to refer to the set of cultural practices and capacities necessary for processing the information into either new statements in the information exchange, or more important in our context, for practical use of the information in appropriate ways to produce more desirable actions or outcomes from action. Three types of information that are clearly important for purposes of development are scientific publications, scientific and economic data, and news and factual reports. Scientific publication has seen a tremendous cost escalation, widely perceived to have reached crisis proportions even by the terms of the best-endowed university libraries in the wealthiest countries. Over the course of the 1990s, some estimates saw a 260 percent increase in the prices of scientific publications, and libraries were reported choosing between journal subscription and monograph purchases.[4] In response to this crisis, and in reliance on what were perceived to be the publication cost-reduction opportunities for Internet publication, some scientists—led by Nobel laureate and then head of the National Institutes of Health Harold Varmus—began to agitate for a scientist-based publication system.[5] The debates were, and continue to be, heated in this area. However, currently we are beginning to see the emergence of scientist-run and -driven publication systems that distribute their papers for free online, either within a traditional peer-review system like the Public Library of Science (PLoS), or within tightly knit disciplines like theoretical physics, with only post-publication peer review and revision, as in the case of the Los Alamos Archive, or ArXiv.org. Together with free software and peer production on the Internet, the PLoS and ArXiv.org models offer insights into the basic shape of the class of commons-based, nonproprietary production solutions to problems of information production and exchange unhampered by intellectual property.

Scientific and economic data present a parallel conceptual problem, but in a different legal setting. In the case of both types of data, much of it is produced by government agencies. In the United States, however, raw data is in the public domain, and while initial access may require payment of the cost of distribution, reworking of the data as a tool in information production and innovation—and its redistribution by those who acquired access initially—is considered to be in the public domain. In Europe, this has not been the case since the 1996 Database Directive, which created a property-like right in raw data in an effort to improve the standing of European database producers. Efforts to pass similar legislation in the United States have been mounted and stalled in practically every Congress since the mid-1990s. These laws continue to be introduced, driven by the lobby of the largest owners of nongovernment databases, and irrespective of the fact that for almost a decade, Europe's database industry has grown only slowly in the presence of a right, while the U.S. database industry has flourished without an exclusive rights regime.

News, market reports, and other factual reporting seem to have escaped the problems of barriers to access. Here it is most likely that the value-appropriation model simply does not depend on exclusive rights. Market data is generated as a by-product of the market function itself. Tiny time delays are sufficient to generate a paying subscriber base, while leaving the price trends necessary for, say, farmers to decide at what prices to sell their grain in the local market, freely available.[6] As I suggested in chapter 2, the advertising-supported press has never been copyright dependent, but has instead depended on timely updating of news to capture attention, and then attach that attention to advertising. This has not changed, but the speed of the update cycle has increased and, more important, distribution has become global, so that obtaining most information is now trivial to anyone with access to an Internet connection. While this continues to raise issues with deployment of communications hardware and the knowledge of how to use it, these issues can be, and are being, approached through aggregation of demand in either public or private forms. These types of information do not themselves appear to exhibit significant barriers to access once network connectivity is provided.

Knowledge.   In this context, I refer mostly to two types of concern. The first is the possibility of the transfer of implicit knowledge, which resists codification into what would here be treated as "information"—for example, training manuals. The primary mechanism for transfer of knowledge of this type is learning by doing, and knowledge transfer of this form cannot happen except through opportunities for local practice of the knowledge. The second type of knowledge transfer of concern here is formal instruction in an education context (as compared with dissemination of codified outputs for self-teaching). Here, there is a genuine limit on the capacity of the networked information economy to improve access to knowledge. Individual, face-to-face instruction does not scale across participants, time, and distance. However, some components of education, at all levels, are nonetheless susceptible to improvement with the increase in nonmarket and radically decentralized production processes. The MIT Open Courseware initiative is instructive as to how the universities of advanced economies can attempt to make at least their teaching materials and manuals freely available to teachers throughout the world, thereby leaving the pedagogy in local hands but providing more of the basic inputs into the teaching process on a global scale. More important perhaps is the possibility that teachers and educators can collaborate, both locally and globally, on an open platform model like *Wikipedia*, to coauthor learning objects, teaching modules, and, more ambitiously, textbooks that could then be widely accessed by local teachers

INDUSTRIAL ORGANIZATION OF HDI-RELATED
INFORMATION INDUSTRIES

The production of information and knowledge is very different from the production of steel or automobiles. Chapter 2 explains in some detail that information production has always included substantial reliance on nonmarket actors and on nonmarket, nonproprietary settings as core modalities of production. In software, for example, we saw that Mickey and romantic maximizer-type producers, who rely on exclusive rights directly, have accounted for a stable 36–37 percent of market-based revenues for software developers, while the remainder was focused on both supply-side and demand-side improvements in the capacity to offer software services. This number actually overstates the importance of software publishing, because it does not at all count free software development except when it is monetized by an IBM or a Red Hat, leaving tremendous value unaccounted for. A very large portion of the investments and research in any of the information production fields important to human development occur within the category that I have broadly described as "Joe Einstein." These include both those places formally designated for the pursuit of information and knowledge in themselves, like universities, and those that operate in the social sphere, but produce information and knowledge as a more or less central part of their existence—like churches or political parties. Moreover, individuals acting as social beings have played a central role in our information production and exchange system. In order to provide a more sector-specific analysis of how commons-based, as opposed to proprietary, strategies can contribute to development, I offer here a more detailed breakdown specifically of software, scientific publication, agriculture, and biomedical innovation than is provided in chapter 2. Table 9.1 presents a higher-resolution statement of the major actors in these fields, within both the market and the nonmarket sectors, from which we can then begin to analyze the path toward, and the sustainability of, more significant commons-based production of the necessities of human development.

Table 9.1 identifies the relative role of each of the types of main actors in information and knowledge production across the major sectors relevant to contemporary policy debates. It is most important to extract from this table the diversity of business models and roles not only in each industry, but also among industries. This diversity means that different types of actors can have different relative roles: nonprofits as opposed to individuals, universities as opposed to government, or nonproprietary market actors—that is, market actors whose business model is service based or otherwise does not depend on exclusive appropriation of information—as compared to nonmarket actors. The following segments look at each of these sectors more specifically, and describe the ways in which commons-based strategies are already, or could be, used to improve the access to information, knowledge, and the information-embedded goods and tools for human development. However, even a cursory look at the table shows that the current production landscape of software is particularly well suited to having a greater role for commons-based production. For example, exclusive proprietary producers account for only one-third of software-related revenues, even within the market. The remainder is covered by various services and relationships that are compatible with nonproprietary treatment of the software itself. Individuals and nonprofit associations also have played a very large role, and continue to do so, not only in free software development, but in the development of standards as well. As we look at each sector, we see that they differ in their incumbent industrial landscape, and these differences mean that each sector may be more or less amenable to commons-based strategies, and, even if in principle amenable, may present harder or easier transition problems.

Table 9.1: Map of Players and Roles in Major Relevant Sectors

Actor Sector	Government	Universities, Libraries, etc.	IP-Based Industry	Non-IP-Based Industry	NGOs/ Nonprofits	Individuals
Software	Research funding, defense, procurement	Basic research and design; components "incubate" much else	Software publishing (1/3 annual revenue)	Software services, customization (~2/3 annual revenue)	FSF; Apache; W3C; IETF	Free/open-source software
Scientific publication	Research funding	University presses; salaries; promotion and tenure	Elsevier Science; professional associations	Biomed Central	PLoS; ArXiv	Working papers; Web-based self-publishing
Agricultural Biotech	Grants and government labs; NARS	Basic research; tech transfer (24% of patenting activity)	Monsanto, DuPont, Syngenta (~74% of patents)	No obvious equivalent	CAMBIA BIOS CGIAR	Farmers
Biomed/ Health	Grants and government labs	Basic research; tech transfer (~50%?)	Big Pharma; Biotech (~50%?)	Generics	OneWorld Health	None

TOWARD ADOPTING COMMONS-BASED STRATEGIES FOR DEVELOPMENT

The mainstream understanding of intellectual property by its dominant policy-making institutions—the Patent Office and U.S. trade representative in the United States, the Commission in the European Union, and the World Intellectual Property Organization (WIPO) and Trade-Related Aspects of Intellectual Property (TRIPS) systems internationally—is that strong protection is good, and stronger protection is better. In development and trade policy, this translates into a belief that the primary mechanism for knowledge transfer and development in a global information economy is for all nations, developing as well as developed, to ratchet up their intellectual property law standards to fit the most protective regimes adopted in the United States and Europe. As a practical political matter, the congruence between the United States and the European Union in this area means that this basic understanding is expressed in the international trade system, in the World Trade Organization (WTO) and its TRIPS agreement, and in international intellectual property treaties, through the WIPO. The next few segments present an alternative view. Intellectual property as an institution is substantially more ambiguous in its effects on information production than the steady drive toward expansive rights would suggest. The full argument is in chapter 2.

Intellectual property is particularly harmful to net information importers. In our present world trade system, these are the poor and middle-income nations. Like all users of information protected by exclusive rights, these nations are required by strong intellectual property rights to pay more than the marginal cost of the information at the time that they buy it. In the standard argument, this is intended to give producers incentives to create information that users want. Given the relative poverty of these countries, however, practically none of the intellectual-property-dependent producers develop products specifically with returns from poor or even middle-income markets in mind. The pharmaceutical industry receives about 5 percent of its global revenues from low- and middle-income countries. That is why we have so little investment in drugs for diseases that affect only those parts of the world. It is why most agricultural research that has focused on agriculture in poorer areas of the world has been public sector and nonprofit. Under these conditions, the above-marginal-cost prices paid in these poorer countries are purely regressive redistribution. The information, knowledge, and information-embedded goods paid for would have been developed in expectation of rich world rents alone. The prospects of rents from poorer countries do not affect their development. They do not affect either the rate or the direction of research and development. They simply place some of the rents that pay for technology development in the rich countries on consumers in poor and middle-income countries. The morality of this redistribution from the world's poor to the world's rich has never been confronted or defended in the European or American public spheres. It simply goes unnoticed. When crises in access to information-embedded goods do appear—such as in the AIDS/HIV access to medicines crisis—these are seldom tied to our basic institutional choice. In our trade policies, Americans and Europeans push for ever-stronger protection. We thereby systematically benefit those who own much of the stock of usable human knowledge. We do so at the direct expense of those who need access to knowledge in order to feed themselves and heal their sick.

The practical politics of the international intellectual property and trade regime make it very difficult to reverse the trend toward ever-increasing exclusive property protections. The economic returns to exclusive proprietary rights in information are highly concentrated in the hands of those who own such rights. The costs are widely diffuse in the populations of both the developing and developed world. The basic inefficiency of excessive property protection is difficult to understand by comparison to the intuitive, but mistaken, Economics 101 belief that property is good, more property is better, and intellectual property must be the same. The result is that pressures on the governments that represent exporters of intellectual property rights per-missions—in particular, the United States and the European Union—come in this area mostly from the owners, and they continuously push for ever-stronger rights. Monopoly is a good thing to have if you can get it. Its value for rent extraction is no less valuable for a database or patent-based company than it is for the dictator's nephew in a banana republic. However, its value to these supplicants does not make it any more efficient or desirable.

The political landscape is, however, gradually beginning to change. Since the turn of the twenty-first century, and particularly in the wake of the urgency with which the HIV/AIDS crisis in Africa has infused the debate over access to medicines, there has been a growing public interest advocacy movement focused on the intellectual property trade regime. This movement is, however, confronted with a highly playable system. A victory for devel-oping world access in one round in the TRIPS context always leaves other places to construct mechanisms for exclusivity. Bilateral trade negotiations are one domain that is beginning to play an important role. In these, the United States or the European Union can force a rice- or cotton-exporting country to concede a commitment to strong intellectual property protection in exchange for favorable treatment for their core export. The intellectual property exporting nations can then go to WIPO, and push for new treaties based on the emerging international practice of bilateral agreements. This, in turn, would cycle back and be generalized and enforced through the trade regimes. Another approach is for the exporting nations to change their own laws, and then drive higher standards elsewhere in the name of "harmonization." Because the international trade and intellectual property system is highly "playable" and manipulable in these ways, systematic resistance to the expansion of intellectual property laws is difficult.

The promise of the commons-based strategies explored in the remainder of this chapter is that they can be implemented without changes in law—either national or international. They are paths that the emerging networked information economy has opened to individuals, nonprofits, and public-sector organizations that want to help in improving human development in the poorer regions of the world to take action on their own. As with decentralized speech for democratic discourse, and collaborative production by individuals of the information environment they occupy as autonomous agents, here too we begin to see that self-help and cooperative action outside the proprietary system offer an opportunity for those who wish to pursue it. In this case, it is an opportunity to achieve a more just distribution of the world's resources and a set of meaningful improvements in human development. Some of these solutions are "commons-based," in the sense that they rely on free access to existing information that is in the commons, and they facilitate further use and development of that information and those information-embedded goods and tools by releasing their information outputs openly, and managing them as a commons, rather than as property. Some of the solutions are specifically peer-production solutions. We see this most clearly in software, and to some extent in the more radical proposals for scientific publication. I will also explore here the viability of peer-production efforts in agricultural and biomedical innovation, although in those fields, commons-based approaches grafted onto traditional public-sector and nonprofit organizations at present hold the more clearly articulated alternatives.

Software

The software industry offers a baseline case because of the proven large scope for peer production in free software. As in other information-intensive industries, government funding and research have played an enormously important role, and university research provides much of the basic science. However, the relative role of individuals, nonprofits, and nonproprietary market producers is larger in software than in the other sectors. First, two-thirds of revenues derived from software in the United States are from services and do not depend on proprietary exclusion. Like IBM's "Linux-related services" category, for which the company claimed more than two billion dollars of revenue for 2003, these services do not depend on exclusion from the software, but on charging for service relationships.[7] Second, some of the most basic elements of the software environment—like standards and protocols—are developed in nonprofit associations, like the Internet Engineering Taskforce or the World Wide Web Consortium. Third, the role of individuals engaged in peer production—the free and open-source software development communities—is very large. Together, these make for an organizational ecology highly conducive to nonproprietary production, whose outputs can be freely usable around the globe. The other sectors have some degree of similar components, and commons-based strategies for development can focus on filling in the missing components and on leveraging nonproprietary components already in place.

In the context of development, free software has the potential to play two distinct and significant roles. The first is offering low-cost access to high-performing software for developing nations. The second is creating the potential for participation in software markets based on human ability, even without access to a stock of exclusive rights in existing software. At present, there is a movement in both developing and the most advanced economies to increase reliance on free software. In the United States, the Presidential Technology Advisory Commission advised the president in 2000 to increase use of free software in mission-critical applications, arguing the high quality and dependability of such systems. To the extent that quality, reliability, and ease of self-customization are consistently better with certain free software products, they are attractive to developing-country governments for the same reasons that they are to the governments of developed countries. In the context of developing nations, the primary additional arguments that have been made include cost, transparency, freedom from reliance on a single foreign source (read, Microsoft), and the potential of local software programmers to learn the program, acquire skills, and therefore easily enter the global market with services and applications for free software.[8] The question of cost, despite the confusion that often arises from the word "free," is not obvious. It depends to some extent on the last hope—that local software developers will become skilled in the free software platforms. The cost of software to any enterprise includes the extent, cost, and efficacy with which the software can be maintained, upgraded, and fixed when errors occur. Free software may or may not involve an up-front charge. Even if it does not, that does not make it cost-free. However, free software enables an open market in free software servicing, which in turn improves and lowers the cost of servicing the software over time. More important, because the software is open for all to see and because developer communities are often multinational, local developers can come, learn the software, and become relatively low-cost software service providers for their own government. This, in turn, helps realize the low-cost promise over and above the licensing fees avoided. Other arguments in favor of government procurement of free software focus on the value of transparency of software used for public purposes. The basic thrust of these arguments is that free software makes it possible for constituents to monitor the behavior of machines used in governments, to make sure that they are designed to do what they are publicly reported to do. The most significant manifestation of this sentiment in the United States is the hitherto-unsuccessful, but fairly persistent effort to require states to utilize voting machines that use free software, or at a minimum, to use software whose source code is open for public inspection. This is a consideration that, if valid, is equally suitable for developing nations. The concern with independence from a single foreign provider, in the case of operating systems, is again not purely a developing-nation concern. Just as the United States required American Marconi to transfer its assets to an American company, RCA, so that it would not be dependent for a critical infrastructure on a foreign provider, other countries may have similar concerns about Microsoft. Again, to the extent that this is a valid concern, it is so for rich nations as much as it is for poor, with the exceptions of the European Union and Japan, which likely do have bargaining power with Microsoft to a degree that smaller markets do not.

The last and quite distinct potential gain is the possibility of creating a context and an anchor for a free software development sector based on service. This was cited as the primary reason behind Brazil's significant push to use free software in government departments and in telecenters that the federal government is setting up to provide Internet service access to some of its poorer and more remote areas. Software services represent a very large industry. In the United States, software services are an industry roughly twice the size of the movie and video industry. Software developers from low- and middle-income countries can participate in the growing free software segment of this market by using their skills alone. Unlike with service for the proprietary domain, they need not buy licenses to learn and practice the services. Moreover, if Brazil, China, India, Indonesia, and other major developing countries were to rely heavily on free software, then the "internal market," within the developing world, for free software–related services would become very substantial. Building public-sector demand for these services would be one place to start. Moreover, because free software development is a global phenomenon, free software developers who learn their skills within the developing world would be able to export those skills elsewhere. Just as India's call centers leverage the country's colonial past with its resulting broad availability of English speakers, so too countries like Brazil can leverage their active free software development community to provide software services for free software platforms anywhere in the developed and developing worlds. With free software, the developing-world providers can compete as equals. They do not need access to permissions to operate. Their relationships need not replicate the "outsourcing" model so common in proprietary industries, where permission to work on a project is the point of control over the ability to do so. There will still be branding issues that undoubtedly will affect access to developed markets. However, there will be no baseline constraints of minimal capital necessary to enter the market and try to develop a reputation for reliability. As a development strategy, then, utilization of free software achieves transfer of information-embedded goods for free or at low cost. It also transfers information about the nature of the product and its operation—the source code. Finally, it enables transfer, at least potentially, of opportunities for learning by doing and of opportunities for participating in the global market. These would depend on knowledge of a free software platform that anyone is free to learn, rather than on access to financial capital or intellectual property inventories as preconditions to effective participation.

Scientific Publication

Scientific publication is a second sector where a nonproprietary strategy can be implemented readily and is already developing to supplant the proprietary model. Here, the existing market structure is quite odd in a way that likely makes it unstable. Authoring and peer review, the two core value-creating activities, are done by scientists who perform neither task in expectation of royalties or payment. The model of most publications, however, is highly proprietary. A small number of business organizations, like Elsevier Science, control most of the publications. Alongside them, professional associations of scientists also publish their major journals using a proprietary model.

Universities, whose scientists need access to the papers, incur substantial cost burdens to pay for the publications as a basic input into their own new work. While the effects of this odd system are heavily felt in universities in rich countries, the burden of subscription rates that go into the thousands of dollars per title make access to up-to-date scientific research prohibitive for universities and scientists working in poorer economies. Nonproprietary solutions are already beginning to emerge in this space. They fall into two large clusters.

The first cluster is closer to the traditional peer-review publication model. It uses Internet communications to streamline the editorial and peer-review system, but still depends on a small, salaried editorial staff. Instead of relying on subscription payments, it relies on other forms of payments that do not require charging a price for the outputs. In the case of the purely nonprofit Public Library of Science (PLoS), the sources of revenue combine author's payments for publication, philanthropic support, and university memberships. In the case of the for-profit BioMed Central, based in the United Kingdom, it is a combination of author payments, university memberships, and a variety of customized derivative products like subscription-based literature reviews and customized electronic update services. Author payments—fees authors must pay to have their work published—are built into the cost of scientific research and included in grant applications. In other words, they are intended to be publicly funded. Indeed, in 2005, the National Institutes of Health (NIH), the major funding agency for biomedical science in the United States, announced a requirement that all NIH-funded research be made freely available on the Web within twelve months of publication. Both PLoS and BioMed Central have waiver processes for scientists who cannot pay the publication fees. The articles on both systems are available immediately for free on the Internet. The model exists. It works internally and is sustainable as such. What is left in determining the overall weight that these open-access journals will have in the landscape of scientific publication is the relatively conservative nature of universities themselves. The established journals, like *Science* or *Nature*, still carry substantially more prestige than the new journals. As long as this is the case, and as long as hiring and promotion decisions continue to be based on the prestige of the journal in which a scientist's work is published, the ability of the new journals to replace the traditional ones will be curtailed. Some of the established journals, however, are operated by professional associations of scientists. There is an internal tension between the interests of the associations in securing their revenue and the growing interest of scientists in open-access publication. Combined with the apparent economic sustainability of the open-access journals, it seems that some of these established journals will likely shift over to the open-access model. At a minimum, policy interventions like those proposed by the NIH will force traditional publications to adapt their business model by making access free after a few months. The point here, however, is not to predict the overall likely success of open-access journals. It is to combine them with what we have seen happening in software as another example of a reorganization of the components of the industrial structure of an information production system. Individual scientists, government funding agencies, nonprofits and foundations, and nonproprietary commercial business models can create the same good—scientific publication—but without the cost barrier that the old model imposed on access to its fruits. Such a reorientation would significantly improve the access of universities and physicians in developing nations to the most advanced scientific publication.

The second approach to scientific publication parallels more closely free software development and peer production. This is typified by ArXiv and the emerging practices of self-archiving or self-publishing. ArXiv.org is an online repository of working papers in physics, mathematics, and computer science. It started out focusing on physics, and that is where it has become the sine qua non of publication in some subdisciplines. The archive does not perform review except for technical format compliance. Quality control is maintained by postpublication review and commentary, as well as by hosting updated versions of the papers with explanations (provided by authors) of the changes. It is likely that the reason ArXiv.org has become so successful in physics is the very small and highly specialized nature of the discipline. The universe of potential readers is small, and their capacity to distinguish good arguments from bad is high. Reputation effects of poor publications are likely immediate.

While ArXiv offers a single repository, a much broader approach has been the developing practice of self-archiving. Academics post their completed work on their own Web sites and make it available freely. The primary limitation of this mechanism is the absence of an easy, single location where one can search for papers on a topic of concern. And yet we are already seeing the emergence of tagging standards and protocols that allow anyone to search the universe of self-archived materials. Once completed, such a development process would in principle render archiving by single points of reference unnecessary. The University of Michigan Digital Library Production Service, for example, has developed a protocol called OAIster (pronounced like oyster, with the tagline "find the pearls"), which combines the acronym of Open Archives Initiative with the "ster" ending made popular in reference to peer-to-peer distribution technologies since Napster (AIMster, Grokster, Friendster, and the like). The basic impulse of the Open Archives Initiative is to develop a sufficiently refined set of meta-data tags that would allow anyone who archives their materials with OAI-compliant tagging to be searched easily, quickly, and accurately on the Web. In that case, a general Web search becomes a targeted academic search in a "database" of scientific publications. However, the database is actually a network of self-created, small personal databases that comply with a common tagging and search standard. Again, my point here is not to explore the details of one or another of these approaches. If scientists and other academics adopt this approach of self-archiving coupled with standardized interfaces for global, well-delimited searches, the problem of lack of access to academic publication because of their high-cost publication will be eliminated.

Other types of documents, for example, primary- and secondary-education textbooks, are in a much more rudimentary stage of the development of peer-production models. First, it should be recognized that responses to illiteracy and low educational completion in the poorer areas of the world are largely a result of lack of schoolteachers, physical infrastructure for classrooms, demand for children's schooling among parents who are themselves illiterate, and lack of effectively enforced compulsory education policy. The cost of textbooks contributes only a portion of the problem of cost. The opportunity cost of children's labor is probably the largest factor. Nonetheless, outdated materials and poor quality of teaching materials are often cited as one limit on the educational achievement of those who do attend school. The costs of books, school fees, uniforms, and stationery can amount to 20–30 percent of a family's income.[9] The component of the problem contributed by the teaching materials may be alleviated by innovative approaches to textbook and education materials authoring. Chapter 4 already discussed some textbook initiatives. The most successful commons-based textbook authoring project, which is also the most relevant from the perspective of development, is the South African project, Free High School Science Texts (FHSST). The FHSST initiative is more narrowly focused than the broader efforts of Wikibooks or the California initiative, more managed, and more successful. Nonetheless, in three years of substantial effort by a group of dedicated volunteers who administer the project, its product is one physics high school text, and advanced drafts of two other science texts. The main constraint on the efficacy of collaborative textbook authoring is that compliance requirements imposed by education ministries tend to require a great degree of coherence, which constrains the degree of modularity that these text-authoring projects adopt. The relatively large-grained contributions required limit the number of contributors, slowing the process. The future of these efforts is therefore likely to be determined by the extent to which their designers are able to find ways to make finer-grained modules without losing the coherence required for primary- and secondary-education texts. Texts at the post-secondary level likely present less of a problem, because of the greater freedom instructors have to select texts. This allows an initiative like MIT's Open Courseware Initiative to succeed. That initiative provides syllabi, lecture notes, problem sets, etc. from over 1,100 courses. The basic creators of the materials are paid academics who produce these materials for one of their core professional roles: teaching college- and graduate-level courses. The content is, by and large, a "side-effect" of teaching. What is left to be done is to integrate, create easy interfaces and search capabilities, and so forth. The university funds these functions through its own resources and dedicated grant funding. In the context of MIT, then, these functions are performed on a traditional model—a large, well-funded nonprofit provides an important public good through the application of full-time staff aimed at non-wealth-maximizing goals. The critical point here was the radical departure of MIT from the emerging culture of the 1980s and 1990s in American academia. When other universities were thinking of "distance education" in terms of selling access to taped lectures and materials so as to raise new revenue, MIT thought of what its basic mandate to advance knowledge and educate students in a networked environment entailed. The answer was to give anyone, anywhere, access to the teaching materials of some of the best minds in the world. As an intervention in the ecology of free knowledge and information and an act of leadership among universities, the MIT initiative was therefore a major event. As a model for organizational innovation in the domain of information production generally and the creation of educational resources in particular, it was less significant.

Software and academic publication, then, offer the two most advanced examples of commons-based strategies employed in a sector whose outputs are important to development, in ways that improve access to basic information, knowledge, and information-embedded tools. Building on these basic cases, we can begin to see how similar strategies can be employed to create a substantial set of commons-based solutions that could improve the distribution of information germane to human development.

COMMONS-BASED RESEARCH FOR
FOOD AND MEDICINES

While computation and access to existing scientific research are important in the development of any nation, they still operate at a remove from the most basic needs of the world poor. On its face, it is far from obvious how the emergence of the networked information economy can grow rice to feed millions of malnourished children or deliver drugs to millions of HIV/AIDS patients. On closer observation, however, a tremendous proportion of the way modern societies grow food and develop medicines is based on scientific research and technical innovation. We have seen how the functions of mass media can be fulfilled by nonproprietary models of news and commentary. We have seen the potential of free and open source software and open-access publications to replace and redress some of the failures of proprietary software and scientific publication, respectively. These cases suggest that the basic choice between a system that depends on exclusive rights and business models that use exclusion to appropriate research outputs and a system that weaves together various actors—public and private, organized and individual—in a nonproprietary social network of innovation, has important implications for the direction of innovation and for access to its products. Public attention has focused mostly on the HIV/AIDS crisis in Africa and the lack of access to existing drugs because of their high costs. However, that crisis is merely the tip of the iceberg. It is the most visible to many because of the presence of the disease in rich countries and its cultural and political salience in the United States and Europe. The exclusive rights system is a poor institutional mechanism for serving the needs of those who are worst off around the globe. Its weaknesses pervade the problems of food security and agricultural research aimed at increasing the supply of nourishing food throughout the developing world, and of access to medicines in general, and to medicines for developing-world diseases in particular. Each of these areas has seen a similar shift in national and international policy toward greater reliance on exclusive rights, most important of which are patents. Each area has also begun to see the emergence of commons-based models to alleviate the problems of patents. However, they differ from each other still. Agriculture offers more immediate opportunities for improvement because of the relatively larger role of public research—national, international, and academic—and of the long practices of farmer innovation in seed associations and local and regional frameworks. I explore it first in some detail, as it offers a template for what could be a path for development in medical research as well.

Food Security: Commons-Based Agricultural Innovation

Agricultural innovation over the past century has led to a vast increase in crop yields. Since the 1960s, innovation aimed at increasing yields and improving quality has been the centerpiece of efforts to secure the supply of food to the world's poor, to avoid famine and eliminate chronic malnutrition. These efforts have produced substantial increases in the production of food and decreases in its cost, but their benefits have varied widely in different regions of the world. Now, increases in productivity are not alone a sufficient condition to prevent famine. Sen's observations that democracies have no famines—that is, that good government and accountability will force public efforts to prevent famine—are widely accepted today. The contributions of the networked information economy to democratic participation and transparency are discussed in chapters 6–8, and to the extent that those chapters correctly characterize the changes in political discourse, should help alleviate human poverty through their effects on democracy. However, the cost and quality of food available to accountable governments of poor countries, or to international aid organizations or nongovernment organizations (NGOs) that step in to try to alleviate the misery caused by ineffective or malicious governments, affect how much can be done to avoid not only catastrophic famine, but also chronic malnutrition. Improvements in agriculture make it possible for anyone addressing food security to perform better than they could have if food production had lower yields, of less nutritious food, at higher prices. Despite its potential benefits, however, agricultural innovation has been subject to an unusual degree of sustained skepticism aimed at the very project of organized scientific and scientifically based innovation. Criticism combines biological-ecological concerns with social and economic concerns. Nowhere is this criticism more strident, or more successful at moving policy, than in current European resistance to genetically modified (GM) foods. The emergence of commons-based production strategies can go some way toward allaying the biological-ecological fears by locating much of the innovation at the local level. Its primary benefit, however, is likely to be in offering a path for agricultural and biological innovation that is sustainable and low cost, and that need not result in appropriation of the food production chain by a small number of multinational businesses, as many critics fear.

Scientific plant improvement in the United States dates back to the establishment of the U.S. Department of Agriculture, the land-grant universities, and later the state agricultural experiment stations during the Civil War and in the decades that followed. Public-sector investment dominated agricultural research at the time, and with the rediscovery of Mendel's work in 1900, took a turn toward systematic selective breeding. Through crop improvement associations, seed certification programs, and open-release policies allowing anyone to breed and sell the certified new seeds, farmers were provided access to the fruits of public research in a reasonably efficient and open market. The development of hybrid corn through this system was the first major modern success that vastly increased agricultural yields. It reshaped our understanding not only of agriculture, but also more generally of the value of innovation, by comparison to efficiency, to growth. Yields in the United States doubled between the mid-1930s and the mid-1950s, and by the mid-1980s, cornfields had a yield six times greater than they had fifty years before. Beginning in the early 1960s, with funding from the Rockefeller and Ford foundations, and continuing over the following forty years, agricultural research designed to increase the supply of agricultural production and lower its cost became a central component of international and national policies aimed at securing the supply of food to the world's poor populations, avoiding famines and, ultimately, eliminating chronic malnutrition. The International Rice Research Institute (IRRI) in the Philippines was the first such institute, founded in the 1960s, followed by the International Center for Wheat and Maize Improvement (CIM-MYT) in Mexico (1966), and the two institutes for tropical agriculture in Colombia and Nigeria (1967). Together, these became the foundation for the Consultative Group for International Agricultural Research (CGIAR), which now includes sixteen centers. Over the same period, National Agricultural Research Systems (NARS) also were created around the world, focusing on research specific to local agroecological conditions. Research in these centers preceded the biotechnology revolution, and used various experimental breeding techniques to obtain high-yielding plants: for example, plants with shorter growing seasons, or more adapted to intensive fertilizer use. These efforts later introduced varieties that were resistant to local pests, diseases, and to various harsh environmental conditions.

The "Green Revolution," as the introduction of these new, scientific-research-based varieties has been called, indeed resulted in substantial increases in yields, initially in rice and wheat, in Asia and Latin America. The term "Green Revolution" is often limited to describing these changes in those regions in the 1960s and 1970s. A recent study shows, however, that the growth in yields has continued throughout the last forty years, and has, with varying degrees, occurred around the world.[10] More than eight thousand modern varieties of rice, wheat, maize, other major cereals, and root and protein crops have been released over the course of this period by more than four hundred public breeding programs. One of the most interesting finds of this study was that fewer than 1 percent of these modern varieties had any crosses with public or private breeding programs in the developed world, and that private-sector contributions in general were limited to hybrid maize, sorghum, and millet. The effort, in other words, was almost entirely public sector, and almost entirely based in the developing world, with complementary efforts of the international and national programs. Yields in Asia increased sevenfold from 1961 to 2000, and fivefold in Latin America, the Middle East/North Africa, and Sub-Saharan Africa. More than 60 percent of the growth in Asia and Latin America occurred in the 1960s–1980s, while the primary growth in Sub-Saharan Africa began in the 1980s. In Latin America, most of the early-stage increases in yields came from increasing cultivated areas (~40 percent), and from other changes in cultivation— increased use of fertilizer, mechanization, and irrigation. About 15 percent of the growth in the early period was attributable to the use of modern varieties. In the latter twenty years, however, more than 40 percent of the total increase in yields was attributable to the use of new varieties. In Asia in the early period, about 19 percent of the increase came from modern varieties, but almost the entire rest of the increase came from increased use of fertilizer, mechanization, and irrigation, not from increased cultivated areas. It is trivial to see why changes of this sort would elicit both environmental and a social-economic critique of the industrialization of farm work. Again, though, in the latter twenty years, 46 percent of the increase in yields is attributable to the use of modern varieties. Modern varieties played a significantly less prominent role in the Green Revolution of the Middle East and Africa, contributing 5–6 percent of the growth in yields. In Sub-Saharan Africa, for example, early efforts to introduce varieties from Asia and Latin America failed, and local developments only began to be adopted in the 1980s. In the latter twenty-year period, however, the Middle East and North Africa did see a substantial role for modern varieties—accounting for close to 40 percent of a more than doubling of yields. In Sub-Saharan Africa, the overwhelming majority of the tripling of yields came from increasing area of cultivation, and about 16 percent came from modern varieties. Over the past forty years, then, research-based improvements in plants have come to play a larger role in increasing agricultural yields in the developing world. Their success was, however, more limited in the complex and very difficult environments of Sub-Saharan Africa. Much of the benefit has to do with local independence, as opposed to heavier dependence on food imports. Evenson and Gollin, for example, conservatively estimate that higher prices and a greater reliance on imports in the developing world in the absence of the Green Revolution would have resulted in 13–14 percent lower caloric intake in the developing world, and in a 6–8 percent higher proportion of malnourished children. While these numbers may not seem eye-popping, for populations already living on marginal nutrition, they represent significant differences in quality of life and in physical and mental development for millions of children and adults.

The agricultural research that went into much of the Green Revolution did not involve biotechnology—that is, manipulation of plant varieties at the genetic level through recombinant DNA techniques. Rather, it occurred at the level of experimental breeding. In the developed world, however, much of the research over the past twenty-five years has been focused on the use of biotechnology to achieve more targeted results than breeding can, has been more heavily based on private-sector investment, and has resulted in more private-sector ownership over the innovations. The promise of biotechnology, and particularly of genetically engineered or modified foods, has been that they could provide significant improvements in yields as well as in health effects, quality of the foods grown, and environmental effects. Plants engineered to be pest resistant could decrease the need to use pesticides, resulting in environmental benefits and health benefits to farmers. Plants engineered for ever-higher yields without increasing tilled acreage could limit the pressure for deforestation. Plants could be engineered to carry specific nutritional supplements, like golden rice with beta-carotene, so as to introduce necessarily nutritional requirements into subsistence diets. Beyond the hypothetically optimistic possibilities, there is little question that genetic engineering has already produced crops that lower the cost of production for farmers by increasing herbicide and pest tolerance. As of 2002, more than 50 percent of the world's soybean acreage was covered with genetically modified (GM) soybeans, and 20 percent with cotton. Twenty-seven percent of acreage covered with GM crops is in the developing world. This number will grow significantly now that Brazil has decided to permit the introduction of GM crops, given its growing agricultural role, and now that India, as the world's largest cotton producer, has approved the use of Bt cotton—a GM form of cotton that improves its resistance to a common pest. There are, then, substantial advantages to farmers, at least, and widespread adoption of GM crops both in the developed world outside of Europe and in the developing world.

This largely benign story of increasing yields, resistance, and quality has not been without critics, to put it mildly. The criticism predates biotechnology and the development of transgenic varieties. Its roots are in criticism of experimental breeding programs of the American agricultural sectors and the Green Revolution. However, the greatest public visibility and political success of these criticisms has been in the context of GM foods. The critique brings together odd intellectual and political bedfellows, because it includes five distinct components: social and economic critique of the industrialization of agriculture, environmental and health effects, consumer preference for "natural" or artisan production of foodstuffs, and, perhaps to a more limited extent, protectionism of domestic farm sectors.

Perhaps the oldest component of the critique is the social-economic critique. One arm of the critique focuses on how mechanization, increased use of chemicals, and ultimately the use of nonreproducing proprietary seed led to incorporation of the agricultural sector into the capitalist form of production. In the United States, even with its large "family farm" sector, purchased inputs now greatly exceed nonpurchased inputs, production is highly capital intensive, and large-scale production accounts for the majority of land tilled and the majority of revenue captured from farming.[11] In 2003, 56 percent of farms had sales of less than $10,000 a year. Roughly 85 percent of farms had less than $100,000 in sales.[12] These farms account for only 42 percent of the farmland. By comparison, 3.4 percent of farms have sales of more than $500,000 a year, and account for more than 21 percent of land. In the aggregate, the 7.5 percent of farms with sales over $250,000 account for 37 percent of land cultivated. Of all principal owners of farms in the United States in 2002, 42.5 percent reported something other than farming as their principal occupation, and many reported spending two hundred or more days off-farm, or even no work days at all on the farm. The growth of large-scale "agribusiness," that is, mechanized, rationalized industrial-scale production of agricultural products, and more important, of agricultural inputs, is seen as replacing the family farm and the small-scale, self-sufficient farm, and bringing farm labor into the capitalist mode of production. As scientific development of seeds and chemical applications increases, the seed as input becomes separated from the grain as output, making farmers dependent on the purchase of industrially produced seed. This further removes farmwork from traditional modes of self-sufficiency and craftlike production to an industrial mode. This basic dynamic is repeated in the critique of the Green Revolution, with the added overlay that the industrial producers of seed are seen to be multinational corporations, and the industrialization of agriculture is seen as creating dependencies in the periphery on the industrial-scientific core of the global economy.

The social-economic critique has been enmeshed, as a political matter, with environmental, health, and consumer-oriented critiques as well. The environmental critiques focus on describing the products of science as monocultures, which, lacking the genetic diversity of locally used varieties, are more susceptible to catastrophic failure. Critics also fear contamination of existing varieties, unpredictable interactions with pests, and negative effects on indigenous species. The health effects concern focused initially on how breeding for yield may have decreased nutritional content, and in the more recent GM food debates, the concern that genetically altered foods will have some unanticipated negative health reactions that would only become apparent many years from now. The consumer concerns have to do with quality and an aesthetic attraction to artisan-mode agricultural products and aversion to eating industrial outputs. These social-economic and environmental-health-consumer concerns tend also to be aligned with protectionist lobbies, not only for economic purposes, but also reflecting a strong cultural attachment to the farming landscape and human ecology, particularly in Europe.

This combination of social-economic and postcolonial critique, environmentalism, public-health concerns, consumer advocacy, and farm-sector protectionism against the relatively industrialized American agricultural sector reached a height of success in the 1999 five-year ban imposed by the European Union on all GM food sales. A recent study of a governmental Science Review Board in the United Kingdom, however, found that there was no evidence for any of the environmental or health critiques of GM foods.[13] Indeed, as Peter Pringle masterfully chronicled in *Food, Inc.*, both sides of the political debate could be described as having buffed their cases significantly. The successes and potential benefits have undoubtedly been overstated by enamored scientists and avaricious vendors. There is little doubt, too, that the near-hysterical pitch at which the failures and risks of GM foods have been trumpeted has little science to back it, and the debate has degenerated to a state that makes reasoned, evidence-based consideration difficult. In Europe in general, however, there is wide acceptance of what is called a "precautionary principle." One way of putting it is that absence of evidence of harm is not evidence of absence of harm, and caution counsels against adoption of the new and at least theoretically dangerous. It was this precautionary principle rather than evidence of harm that was at the base of the European ban. This ban has recently been lifted, in the wake of a WTO trade dispute with the United States and other major producers who challenged the ban as a trade barrier. However, the European Union retained strict labeling requirements. This battle among wealthy countries, between the conservative "Fortress Europe" mentality and the growing reliance of American agriculture on biotechnological innovation, would have little moral valence if it did not affect funding for, and availability of, biotechnological research for the populations of the developing world. Partly as a consequence of the strong European resistance to GM foods, the international agricultural research centers that led the way in the development of the Green Revolution varieties, and that released their developments freely for anyone to sell and use without proprietary constraint, were slow to develop capacity in genetic engineering and biotechnological research more generally. Rather than the public national and international efforts leading the way, a study of GM use in developing nations concluded that practically all GM acreage is sown with seed obtained in the finished form from a developed-world supplier, for a price premium or technology licensing fee.[14] The seed, and its improvements, is proprietary to the vendor in this model. It is not supplied in a form or with the rights to further improve locally and independently. Because of the critique of innovation in agriculture as part of the process of globalization and industrialization, of environmental degradation, and of consumer exploitation, the political forces that would have been most likely to support public-sector investment in agricultural innovation are in opposition to such investments. The result has not been retardation of biotechnological innovation in agriculture, but its increasing privatization: primarily in the United States and now increasingly in Latin America, whose role in global agricultural production is growing.

Private-sector investment, in turn, operates within a system of patents and other breeders' exclusive rights, whose general theoretical limitations are discussed in chapter 2. In agriculture, this has two distinct but mutually reinforcing implications. The first is that, while private-sector innovation has indeed accounted for most genetically engineered crops in the developing world, research aimed at improving agricultural production in the neediest places has not been significantly pursued by the major private-sector firms. A sector based on expectation of sales of products embedding its patents will not focus its research where human welfare will be most enhanced. It will focus where human welfare can best be expressed in monetary terms. The poor are systematically underserved by such a system. It is intended to elicit investments in research in directions that investors believe will result in outputs that serve the needs of those with the highest willingness and ability to pay for their outputs. The second is that even where the products of innovation can, as a matter of biological characteristics, be taken as inputs into local research and development—by farmers or by national agricultural research systems—the international system of patents and plant breeders' rights enforcement makes it illegal to do so without a license. This again retards the ability of poor countries and their farmers and research institutes to conduct research into local adaptations of improved crops.

The central question raised by the increasing privatization of agricultural biotechnology over the past twenty years is: What can be done to employ commons-based strategies to provide a foundation for research that will be focused on the food security of developing world populations? Is there a way of managing innovation in this sector so that it will not be heavily weighted in favor of populations with a higher ability to pay, and so that its outputs allow farmers and national research efforts to improve and adapt to highly variable local agroecological environments? The continued presence of the public-sector research infrastructure—including the international and national research centers, universities, and NGOs dedicated to the problem of food security—and the potential of harnessing individual farmers and scientists to cooperative development of open biological innovation for agriculture suggest that commons-based paths for development in the area of food security and agricultural innovation are indeed feasible.

First, some of the largest and most rapidly developing nations that still have large poor populations—most prominently, China, India, and Brazil—can achieve significant advances through their own national agricultural research systems. Their research can, in turn, provide a platform for further innovation and adaptation by projects in poorer national systems, as well as in nongovernmental public and peer-production efforts. In this regard, China seems to be leading the way. The first rice genome to be sequenced was japonica, apparently sequenced in 2000 by scientists at Monsanto, but not published. The second, an independent and published sequence of japonica, was sequenced by scientists at Syngenta, and published as the first published rice genome sequence in *Science* in April 2002. To protect its proprietary interests, Syngenta entered a special agreement with *Science*, which permitted the authors not to deposit the genomic information into the public Genbank maintained by the National Institutes of Health in the United States.[15] Depositing the information in GenBank makes it immediately available for other scientists to work with freely. All the major scientific publications require that such information be deposited and made publicly available as a standard condition of publication, but *Science* waved this requirement for the Syngenta japonica sequence. The same issue of *Science*, however, carried a similar publication, the sequence of Oryza sativa L.ssp. indica, the most widely cultivated subspecies in China. This was sequenced by a public Chinese effort, and its outputs were immediately deposited in GenBank. The simultaneous publication of the rice genome by a major private firm and a Chinese public effort was the first public exposure to the enormous advances that China's public sector has made in agricultural biotechnology, and its focus first and foremost on improving Chinese agriculture. While its investments are still an order of magnitude smaller than those of public and private sectors in the developed countries, China has been reported as the source of more than half of all expenditures in the developing world.[16] China's longest experience with GM agriculture is with Bt cotton, which was introduced in 1997. By 2000, 20 percent of China's cotton acreage was sown to Bt cotton. One study showed that the average acreage of a farm was less than 0.5 hectare of cotton, and the trait that was most valuable to them was Bt cotton's reduced pesticide needs. Those who adopted Bt cotton used less pesticide, reducing labor for pest control and the pesticide cost per kilogram of cotton produced. This allowed an average cost savings of 28 percent. Another effect suggested by survey data—which, if confirmed over time, would be very important as a matter of public health, but also to the political economy of the agricultural biotechnology debate—is that farmers who do not use Bt cotton are four times as likely to report symptoms of a degree of toxic exposure following application of pesticides than farmers who did adopt Bt cotton.[17] The point is not, of course, to sing the praises of GM cotton or the Chinese research system. China's efforts offer an example of how the larger national research systems can provide an anchor for agricultural research, providing solutions both for their own populations, and, by making the products of their research publicly and freely available, offer a foundation for the work of others.

Alongside the national efforts in developing nations, there are two major paths for commons-based research and development in agriculture that could serve the developing world more generally. The first is based on existing research institutes and programs cooperating to build a commons-based system, cleared of the barriers of patents and breeders' rights, outside and alongside the proprietary system. The second is based on the kind of loose affiliation of university scientists, nongovernmental organizations, and individuals that we saw play such a significant role in the development of free and open-source software. The most promising current efforts in the former vein are the PIPRA (Public Intellectual Property for Agriculture) coalition of public-sector universities in the United States, and, if it delivers on its theoretical promises, the Generation Challenge Program led by CGIAR (the Consultative Group on International Agricultural Research). The most promising model of the latter, and probably the most ambitious commons-based project for biological innovation currently contemplated, is BIOS (Biological Innovation for an Open Society).

PIPRA is a collaboration effort among public-sector universities and agricultural research institutes in the United States, aimed at managing their rights portfolio in a way that will give their own and other researchers freedom to operate in an institutional ecology increasingly populated by patents and other rights that make work difficult. The basic thesis and underlying problem that led to PIPRA's founding were expressed in an article in *Science* coauthored by fourteen university presidents.[18] They underscored the centrality of public-sector, land-grant university-based research to American agriculture, and the shift over the last twenty-five years toward increased use of intellectual property rules to cover basic discoveries and tools necessary for agricultural innovation. These strategies have been adopted by both commercial firms and, increasingly, by public-sector universities as the primary mechanism for technology transfer from the scientific institute to the commercializing firms. The problem they saw was that in agricultural research, innovation was incremental. It relies on access to existing germplasm and crop varieties that, with each generation of innovation, brought with them an ever-increasing set of intellectual property claims that had to be licensed in order to obtain permission to innovate further. The universities decided to use the power that ownership over roughly 24 percent of the patents in agricultural biotechnology innovations provides them as a lever with which to unravel the patent thickets and to reduce the barriers to research that they increasingly found themselves dealing with. The main story, one might say the "founding myth" of PIPRA, was the story of golden rice. Golden rice is a variety of rice that was engineered to provide dietary vitamin A. It was developed with the hope that it could introduce vitamin A supplement to populations in which vitamin A deficiency causes roughly 500,000 cases of blindness a year and contributes to more than 2 million deaths a year. However, when it came to translating the research into deliverable plants, the developers encountered more than seventy patents in a number of countries and six materials transfer agreements that restricted the work and delayed it substantially. PIPRA was launched as an effort of public-sector universities to cooperate in achieving two core goals that would respond to this type of barrier—preserving the right to pursue applications to subsistence crops and other developing-world-related crops, and preserving their own freedom to operate vis-à-vis each other's patent portfolios.

The basic insight of PIPRA, which can serve as a model for university alliances in the context of the development of medicines as well as agriculture, is that universities are not profit-seeking enterprises, and university scientists are not primarily driven by a profit motive. In a system that offers opportunities for academic and business tracks for people with similar basic skills, academia tends to attract those who are more driven by nonmonetary motivations. While universities have invested a good deal of time and money since the Bayh-Dole Act of 1980 permitted and indeed encouraged them to patent innovations developed with public funding, patent and other exclusive-rights-based revenues have not generally emerged as an important part of the revenue scheme of universities. As table 9.2 shows, except for one or two outliers, patent revenues have been all but negligible in university budgets.[19] This fact makes it fiscally feasible for universities to use their patent portfolios to maximize the global social benefit of their research, rather than trying to maximize patent revenue. In particular, universities can aim to include provisions in their technology licensing agreements that are aimed at the dual goals of (a) delivering products embedding their innova-

Table 9.2: Selected University Gross Revenues and Patent Licensing Revenues

	Total Revenues (millions $)	Licensing and Royalties (millions $)	% of total	Government Grants & Contracts (millions $)	% of total
All universities	$227,000	$ 1270	0.56%	$31,430	13.85%
Columbia University	$ 2,074	$178.4	8.6%	$532	25.65%
		$100–120[a]	4.9–5.9%		
University of California	$ 14,166	$ 81.3	0.57%	$2372	16.74%
		$ 55 (net)[b]	0.39%		
Stanford University	$ 3,475	$ 43.3	1.25%	$860	24.75%
		$ 36.8[c]	1.06%		
Florida State	$ 2,646	$ 35.6	1.35%	$238	8.99%
University of Wisconsin-Madison	$ 1,696	$ 32	1.89%	$417.4	24.61%
University of Minnesota	$ 1,237	$ 38.7	3.12%	$323.5	26.15%
Harvard	$ 2,473	$ 47.9	1.94%	$416	16.82%
				$548.7[d]	22.19%
Cal Tech	$ 531	$ 26.7[e]	5.02%	$268	50.47%
		$ 15.7[f]	2.95%		

Sources: Aggregate revenues: U.S. Dept. of Education, National Center for Education Statistics, *Enrollment in Postsecondary Institutions, Fall 2001, and Financial Statistics, Fiscal Year 2001* (2003), Table F; Association of University Technology Management, *Annual Survey Summary FY 2002* (AUTM 2003), Table S-12. Individual institutions: publicly available annual reports of each university and/or its technology transfer office for FY 2003.

Notes:

a. Large ambiguity results because technology transfer office reports increased revenues for year-end 2003 as $178M without reporting expenses; University Annual Report reports licensing revenue with all "revenue from other educational and research activities," and reports a 10 percent decline in this category, "reflecting an anticipated decline in royalty and license income" from the $133M for the previous year-end, 2002. The table reflects an assumed net contribution to university revenues between $100-120M (the entire decline in the category due to royalty/royalties decreased proportionately with the category).

b. University of California Annual Report of the Office of Technology Transfer is more transparent than most in providing expenses—both net legal expenses and tech transfer direct operating expenses, which allows a clear separation of net revenues from technology transfer activities.

c. Minus direct expenses, not including expenses for unlicensed inventions.

d. Federal- and nonfederal-sponsored research.

e. Almost half of this amount is in income from a single Initial Public Offering, and therefore does not represent a recurring source of licensing revenue.

f. Technology transfer gross revenue minus the one-time event of an initial public offering of LiquidMetal Technologies.

tions to developing nations at reasonable prices and (b) providing researchers and plant breeders the freedom to operate that would allow them to research, develop, and ultimately produce crops that would improve food security in the developing world.

While PIPRA shows an avenue for collaboration among universities in the public interest, it is an avenue that does not specifically rely on, or benefit in great measure from, the information networks or the networked information economy. It continues to rely on the traditional model of publicly funded research. More explicit in its effort to leverage the cost savings made possible by networked information systems is the Generation Challenge Program (GCP). The GCP is an effort to bring the CGIAR into the biotechnology sphere, carefully, given the political resistance to genetically modified foods, and quickly, given the already relatively late start that the international research centers have had in this area. Its stated emphasis is on building an architecture of innovation, or network of research relationships, that will provide low-cost techniques for the basic contemporary technologies of agricultural research. The program has five primary foci, but the basic thrust is to generate improvements both in basic genomics science and in breeding and farmer education, in both cases for developing world agriculture. One early focus would be on building a communications system that allows participating institutions and scientists to move information efficiently and utilize computational resources to pursue research. There are hundreds of thousands of samples of germplasm, from "landrace" (that is, locally agriculturally developed) and wild varieties to modern varieties, located in databases around the world in international, national, and academic institutions. There are tremendous high-capacity computation resources in some of the most advanced research institutes, but not in many of the national and international programs. One of the major goals articulated for the GCP is to develop Web-based interfaces to share these data and computational resources. Another is to provide a platform for sharing new questions and directions of research among participants. The work in this network will, in turn, rely on materials that have proprietary interests attached to them, and will produce outputs that could have proprietary interests attached to them as well. Just like the universities, the GCP institutes (national, international, and nonprofit) are looking for an approach aimed to secure open access to research materials and tools and to provide humanitarian access to its products, particularly for subsistence crop development and use. As of this writing, however, the GCP is still in a formative stage, more an aspiration than a working model. Whether it will succeed in overcoming the political constraints placed on the CGIAR as well as the relative latecomer status of the international public efforts to this area of work remains to be seen. But the elements of the GCP certainly exhibit an understanding of the possibilities presented by commons-based networked collaboration, and an ambition to both build upon them and contribute to their development.

The most ambitious effort to create a commons-based framework for biological innovation in this field is BIOS. BIOS is an initiative of CAMBIA (Center for the Application of Molecular Biology to International Agriculture), a nonprofit agricultural research institute based in Australia, which was founded and is directed by Richard Jefferson, a pioneer in plant biotechnology. BIOS is based on the observation that much of contemporary agricultural research depends on access to tools and enabling technologies—such as mechanisms to identify genes or for transferring them into target plants. When these tools are appropriated by a small number of firms and available only as part of capital-intensive production techniques, they cannot serve as the basis for innovation at the local level or for research organized on nonproprietary models. One of the core insights driving the BIOS initiative is the recognition that when a subset of necessary tools is available in the public domain, but other critical tools are not, the owners of those tools appropriate the full benefits of public domain innovation without at the same time changing the basic structural barriers to use of the proprietary technology. To overcome these problems, the BIOS initiative includes both a strong informatics component and a fairly ambitious "copyleft"-like model (similar to the GPL described in chapter 3) of licensing CAMBIA's basic tools and those of other members of the BIOS initiative. The informatics component builds on a patent database that has been developed by CAMBIA for a number of years, and whose ambition is to provide as complete as possible a dataset of who owns what tools, what the contours of ownership are, and by implication, who needs to be negotiated with and where research paths might emerge that are not yet appropriated and therefore may be open to unrestricted innovation.

The licensing or pooling component is more proactive, and is likely the most significant of the project. BIOS is setting up a licensing and pooling arrangement, "primed" by CAMBIA's own significant innovations in tools, which are licensed to all of the initiative's participants on a free model, with grant-back provisions that perform an openness-binding function similar to copyleft.[20] In coarse terms, this means that anyone who builds upon the contributions of others must contribute improvements back to the other participants. One aspect of this model is that it does not assume that all research comes from academic institutions or from traditional government-funded, nongovernmental, or intergovernmental research institutes. It tries to create a framework that, like the open-source development community, engages commercial and noncommercial, public and private, organized and individual participants into a cooperative research network. The platform for this collaboration is "BioForge," styled after Sourceforge, one of the major free and open-source software development platforms. The commitment to engage many different innovators is most clearly seen in the efforts of BIOS to include major international commercial providers and local potential commercial breeders alongside the more likely targets of a commons-based initiative. Central to this move is the belief that in agricultural science, the basic tools can, although this may be hard, be separated from specific applications or products. All actors, including the commercial ones, therefore have an interest in the open and efficient development of tools, leaving competition and profit making for the market in applications. At the other end of the spectrum, BIOS's focus on making tools freely available is built on the proposition that innovation for food security involves more than biotechnology alone. It involves environmental management, locale-specific adaptations, and social and economic adoption in forms that are locally and internally sustainable, as opposed to dependent on a constant inflow of commoditized seed and other inputs. The range of participants is, then, much wider than envisioned by PIPRA or the GCP. It ranges from multinational corporations through academic scientists, to farmers and local associations, pooling their efforts in a communications platform and institutional model that is very similar to the way in which the GNU/Linux operating system has been developed. As of this writing, the BIOS project is still in its early infancy, and cannot be evaluated by its outputs. However, its structure offers the crispest example of the extent to which the peer-production model in particular, and commons-based production more generally, can be transposed into other areas of innovation at the very heart of what makes for human development—the ability to feed oneself adequately.

PIPRA and the BIOS initiative are the most salient examples of, and the most significant first steps in the development of commons-based strategies to achieve food security. Their vitality and necessity challenge the conventional wisdom that ever-increasing intellectual property rights are necessary to secure greater investment in research, or that the adoption of proprietary rights is benign. Increasing appropriation of basic tools and enabling tech-nologies creates barriers to entry for innovators—public-sector, nonprofit organizations, and the local farmers themselves—concerned with feeding those who cannot signal with their dollars that they are in need. The emer-gence of commons-based techniques—particularly, of an open innovation platform that can incorporate farmers and local agronomists from around the world into the development and feedback process through networked collaboration platforms—promises the most likely avenue to achieve research oriented toward increased food security in the developing world. It promises a mechanism of development that will not increase the relative weight and control of a small number of commercial firms that specialize in agricultural production. It will instead release the products of innovation into a self-binding commons—one that is institutionally designed to defend itself against appropriation. It promises an iterative collaboration platform that would be able to collect environmental and local feedback in the way that a free software development project collects bug reports—through a contin-uous process of networked conversation among the user-innovators them-selves. In combination with public investments from national governments in the developing world, from the developed world, and from more tradi-tional international research centers, agricultural research for food security may be on a path of development toward constructing a sustainable commons-based innovation ecology alongside the proprietary system. Whether it follows this path will be partly a function of the engagement of the actors themselves, but partly a function of the extent to which the international intellectual property/trade system will refrain from raising obstacles to the emergence of these commons-based efforts.

Access to Medicines: Commons-Based
Strategies for Biomedical Research

Nothing has played a more important role in exposing the systematic prob-lems that the international trade and patent system presents for human de-velopment than access to medicines for HIV/AIDS. This is so for a number of reasons. First, HIV/AIDS has reached pandemic proportions. One quarter of all deaths from infectious and parasitic diseases in 2002 were caused by AIDS, accounting for almost 5 percent of all deaths in the world that year.[21] Second, it is a new condition, unknown to medicine a mere twenty-five years ago, is communicable, and in principle is of a type—infectious dis-eases—that we have come to see modern medicine as capable of solving.

This makes it different from much bigger killers—like the many cancers and forms of heart disease—which account for about nine times as many deaths globally. Third, it has a significant presence in the advanced economies. Because it was perceived there as a disease primarily affecting the gay community, it had a strong and well-defined political lobby and high cultural salience. Fourth, and finally, there have indeed been enormous advances in the development of medicines for HIV/AIDS. Mortality for patients who are treated is therefore much lower than for those who are not. These treatments are new, under patent, and enormously expensive. As a result, death—as opposed to chronic illness—has become overwhelmingly a consequence of poverty. More than 75 percent of deaths caused by AIDS in 2002 were in Africa. HIV/AIDS drugs offer a vivid example of an instance where drugs exist for a disease but cannot be afforded in the poorest countries. They represent, however, only a part, and perhaps the smaller part, of the limitations that a patent-based drug development system presents for providing medicines to the poor. No less important is the absence of a market pull for drugs aimed at diseases that are solely or primarily developing-world diseases—like drugs for tropical diseases, or the still-elusive malaria vaccine.

To the extent that the United States and Europe are creating a global innovation system that relies on patents and market incentives as its primary driver of research and innovation, these wealthy democracies are, of necessity, choosing to neglect diseases that disproportionately affect the poor. There is nothing evil about a pharmaceutical company that is responsible to its shareholders deciding to invest where it expects to reap profit. It is not immoral for a firm to invest its research funds in finding a drug to treat acne, which might affect 20 million teenagers in the United States, rather than a drug that will cure African sleeping sickness, which affects 66 million Africans and kills about fifty thousand every year. If there is immorality to be found, it is in the legal and policy system that relies heavily on the patent system to induce drug discovery and development, and does not adequately fund and organize biomedical research to solve the problems that cannot be solved by relying solely on market pull. However, the politics of public response to patents for drugs are similar in structure to those that have to do with agricultural biotechnology exclusive rights. There is a very strong patent-based industry—much stronger than in any other patent-sensitive area. The rents from strong patents are enormous, and a rational monopolist will pay up to the value of its rents to maintain and improve its monopoly. The primary potential political push-back in the pharmaceutical area, which does not exist in the agricultural innovation area, is that the exorbitant costs of drugs developed under this system is hurting even the well-endowed purses of developed-world populations. The policy battles in the United States and throughout the developed world around drug cost containment may yet result in a sufficient loosening of the patent constraints to deliver positive side effects for the developing world. However, they may also work in the opposite direction. The unwillingness of the wealthy populations in the developed world to pay high rents for drugs retards the most immediate path to lower-cost drugs in the developing world—simple subsidy of below-cost sales in poor countries cross-subsidized by above-cost rents in wealthy countries.

The industrial structure of biomedical research and pharmaceutical development is different from that of agricultural science in ways that still leave a substantial potential role for commons-based strategies. However, these would be differently organized and aligned than in agriculture. First, while governments play an enormous role in funding basic biomedical science, there are no real equivalents of the national and international agricultural research institutes. In other words, there are few public-sector laboratories that actually produce finished drugs for delivery in the developing world, on the model of the International Rice Research Institute or one of the national agricultural research systems. On the other hand, there is a thriving generics industry, based in both advanced and developing economies, that stands ready to produce drugs once these are researched. The primary constraint on harnessing its capacity for low-cost drug production and delivery for poorer nations is the international intellectual property system. The other major difference is that, unlike with software, scientific publication, or farmers in agriculture, there is no existing framework for individuals to participate in research and development on drugs and treatments. The primary potential source of nongovernmental investment of effort and thought into biomedical research and development are universities as institutions and scientists, if they choose to organize themselves into effective peer-production communities.

Universities and scientists have two complementary paths open to them to pursue commons-based strategies to provide improved research on the relatively neglected diseases of the poor and improved access to existing drugs that are available in the developed world but unaffordable in the developing. The first involves leveraging existing university patent portfolios—much as the universities allied in PIPRA are exploring and as CAMBIA is doing more aggressively. The second involves work in an entirely new model—constructing collaboration platforms to allow scientists to engage in peer production, cross-cutting the traditional grant-funded lab, and aiming toward research into diseases that do not exercise a market pull on the biomedical research system in the advanced economies.

Leveraging University Patents.   In February 2001, the humanitarian organization Doctors Without Borders (also known as Médecins Sans Frontières, or MSF) asked Yale University, which held the key South African patent on stavudine—one of the drugs then most commonly used in combination therapies—for permission to use generic versions in a pilot AIDS treatment program. At the time, the licensed version of the drug, sold by Bristol-Myers-Squibb (BMS), cost $1,600 per patient per year. A generic version, manufactured in India, was available for $47 per patient per year. At that point in history, thirty-nine drug manufacturers were suing the South African government to strike down a law permitting importation of generics in a health crisis, and no drug company had yet made concessions on pricing in developing nations. Within weeks of receiving MSF's request, Yale negotiated with BMS to secure the sale of stavudine for fifty-five dollars a year in South Africa. Yale, the University of California at Berkeley, and other universities have, in the years since, entered into similar ad hoc agreements with regard to developing-world applications or distribution of drugs that depend on their patented technologies. These successes provide a template for a much broader realignment of how universities use their patent portfolios to alleviate the problems of access to medicines in developing nations.

We have already seen in table 9.2 that while universities own a substantial and increasing number of patents, they do not fiscally depend in any significant way on patent revenue. These play a very small part in the overall scheme of revenues. This makes it practical for universities to reconsider how they use their patents and to reorient toward using them to maximize their beneficial effects on equitable access to pharmaceuticals developed in the advanced economies. Two distinct moves are necessary to harness publicly funded university research toward building an information commons that is easily accessible for global redistribution. The first is internal to the university process itself. The second has to do with the interface between the university and patent-dependent and similar exclusive-rights-dependent market actors.

Universities are internally conflicted about their public and market goals.

Dating back to the passage of the Bayh-Dole Act, universities have increased their patenting practices for the products of publicly funded research. Technology transfer offices that have been set up to facilitate this practice are, in many cases, measured by the number of patent applications, grants, and dollars they bring in to the university. These metrics for measuring the success of these offices tend to make them function, and understand their role, in a way that is parallel to exclusive-rights-dependent market actors, instead of as public-sector, publicly funded, and publicly minded institutions. A technology transfer officer who has successfully provided a royalty-free license to a nonprofit concerned with developing nations has no obvious metric in which to record and report the magnitude of her success (saving X millions of lives or displacing Y misery), unlike her colleague who can readily report X millions of dollars from a market-oriented license, or even merely Y dozens of patents filed. Universities must consider more explicitly their special role in the global information and knowledge production system. If they recommit to a role focused on serving the improvement of the lot of humanity, rather than maximization of their revenue stream, they should adapt their patenting and licensing practices appropriately. In particular, it will be important following such a rededication to redefine the role of technology transfer offices in terms of lives saved, quality-of-life measures improved, or similar substantive measures that reflect the mission of university research, rather than the present metrics borrowed from the very different world of patent-dependent market production. While the internal process is culturally and politically difficult, it is not, in fact, analytically or technically complex. Universities have, for a very long time, seen themselves primarily as dedicated to the advancement of knowledge and human welfare through basic research, reasoned inquiry, and education. The long-standing social traditions of science have always stood apart from market incentives and orientations. The problem is therefore one of reawakening slightly dormant cultural norms and understandings, rather than creating new ones in the teeth of long-standing contrary traditions. The problem should be substantially simpler than, say, persuading companies that traditionally thought of their innovation in terms of patents granted or royalties claimed, as some technology industry participants have, to adopt free software strategies.

If universities do make the change, then the more complex problem will remain: designing an institutional interface between universities and the pharmaceutical industry that will provide sustainable significant benefits for developing-world distribution of drugs and for research opportunities into developing-world diseases. As we already saw in the context of agriculture, patents create two discrete kinds of barriers: The first is on distribution, because of the monopoly pricing power they purposefully confer on their owners. The second is on research that requires access to tools, enabling technologies, data, and materials generated by the developed-world research process, and that could be useful to research on developing-world diseases. Universities working alone will not provide access to drugs. While universities perform more than half of the basic scientific research in the United States, this effort means that more than 93 percent of university research expenditures go to basic and applied science, leaving less than 7 percent for development—the final research necessary to convert a scientific project into a usable product.[22] Universities therefore cannot simply release their own patents and expect treatments based on their technologies to become accessible. Instead, a change is necessary in licensing practices that takes an approach similar to a synthesis of the general public license (GPL), of BIOS's licensing approach, and PIPRA.

Universities working together can cooperate to include in their licenses provisions that would secure freedom to operate for anyone conducting research into developing-world diseases or production for distribution in poorer nations. The institutional details of such a licensing regime are relatively complex and arcane, but efforts are, in fact, under way to develop such licenses and to have them adopted by universities.[23] What is important here, for understanding the potential, is the basic idea and framework. In exchange for access to the university's patents, the pharmaceutical licensees will agree not to assert any of their own rights in drugs that require a university license against generics manufacturers who make generic versions of those drugs purely for distribution in low- and middle-income countries. An Indian or American generics manufacturer could produce patented drugs that relied on university patents and were licensed under this kind of an equitable-access license, as long as it distributed its products solely in poor countries. A government or nonprofit research institute operating in South Africa could work with patented research tools without concern that doing so would violate the patents. However, neither could then import the products of their production or research into the developed world without violating the patents of both the university and the drug company. The licenses would create a mechanism for redistribution of drug products and research tools from the developed economies to the developing. It would do so without requiring the kind of regulatory changes advocated by others, such as

Jean Lanjouw, who have advocated policy changes aimed similarly to achieve differential pricing in the developing and developed worlds.[24] Because this redistribution could be achieved by universities acting through licensing, instead of through changes in law, it offers a more feasible political path for achieving the desired result. Such action by universities would, of course, not solve all the problems of access to medicines. First, not all health-related products are based on university research. Second, patents do not account for all, or perhaps even most, of the reason that patients in poor nations are not treated. A lack of delivery infrastructure, public-health monitoring and care, and stable conditions to implement disease-control policy likely weigh more heavily. Nonetheless, there are successful and stable government and nonprofit programs that could treat hundreds of thousands or millions of patients more than they do now, if the cost of drugs were lower. Achieving improved access for those patients seems a goal worthy of pursuit, even if it is no magic bullet to solve all the illnesses of poverty.

Nonprofit Research.   Even a successful campaign to change the licensing practices of universities in order to achieve inexpensive access to the products of pharmaceutical research would leave the problem of research into diseases that affect primarily the poor. This is because, unless universities themselves undertake the development process, the patent-based pharmaceuticals have no reason to. The "simple" answer to this problem is more funding from the public sector or foundations for both basic research and development. This avenue has made some progress, and some foundations—particularly, in recent years, the Gates Foundation—have invested enormous amounts of money in searching for cures and improving basic public-health conditions of disease in Africa and elsewhere in the developing world. It has received a particularly interesting boost since 2000, with the founding of the Institute for One World Health, a nonprofit pharmaceutical dedicated to research and development specifically into developing-world diseases. The basic model of One World Health begins by taking contributions of drug leads that are deemed unprofitable by the pharmaceutical industry—from both universities and pharmaceutical companies. The firms have no reason not to contribute their patents on leads purely for purposes they do not intend to pursue. The group then relies on foundation and public-sector funding to perform synthesis, preclinical and clinical trials, in collaboration with research centers in the United States, India, Bangladesh, and Thailand, and when the time comes around for manufacturing, the institute collaborates with manufacturers in developing nations to produce low-cost instances of the drugs, and with government and NGO public-health providers to organize distribution. This model is new, and has not yet had enough time to mature and provide measurable success. However, it is promising.

Peer Production of Drug Research and Development. Scientists, scientists-in-training, and to some extent, nonscientists can complement university licensing practices and formally organized nonprofit efforts as a third component of the ecology of commons-based producers. The initial response to the notion that peer production can be used for drug development is that the process is too complex, expensive, and time consuming to succumb to commons-based strategies. This may, at the end of the day, prove true. However, this was also thought of complex software projects or of supercomputing, until free software and distributed computing projects like SETI@Home and Folding@Home came along and proved them wrong. The basic point is to see how distributed nonmarket efforts are organized, and to see how the scientific production process can be broken up to fit a peer-production model.

First, anything that can be done through computer modeling or data analysis can, in principle, be done on a peer-production basis. Increasing portions of biomedical research are done today through modeling, computer simulation, and data analysis of the large and growing databases, including a wide range of genetic, chemical, and biological information. As more of the process of drug discovery of potential leads can be done by modeling and computational analysis, more can be organized for peer production. The relevant model here is open bioinformatics. Bioinformatics generally is the practice of pursuing solutions to biological questions using mathematics and information technology. Open bioinformatics is a movement within bioinformatics aimed at developing the tools in an open-source model, and in providing access to the tools and the outputs on a free and open basis. Projects like these include the Ensmbl Genome Browser, operated by the European Bioinformatics Institute and the Sanger Centre, or the National Center for Biotechnology Information (NCBI), both of which use computer databases to provide access to data and to run various searches on combinations, patterns, and so forth, in the data. In both cases, access to the data and the value-adding functionalities are free. The software too is developed on a free software model. These, in turn, are complemented by database policies like those of the International HapMap Project, an effort to map common variations in the human genome, whose participants have committed to releasing all the data they collect freely into the public domain. The economics of this portion of research into drugs are very similar to the economics of software and computation. The models are just software. Some models will be able to run on the ever-more-powerful basic machines that the scientists themselves use. However, anything that requires serious computation could be modeled for distributed computing. This would allow projects to harness volunteer computation resources, like Folding@Home, Genome@Home, or FightAIDS@Home—sites that already harness the computing power of hundreds of thousands of users to attack biomedical science questions. This stage of the process is the one that most directly can be translated into a peer-production model, and, in fact, there have been proposals, such as the Tropical Disease Initiative proposed by Maurer, Sali, and Rai.[25]

Second, and more complex, is the problem of building wet-lab science on a peer-production basis. Some efforts would have to focus on the basic science. Some might be at the phase of optimization and chemical synthesis. Some, even more ambitiously, would be at the stage of preclinical animal trials and even clinical trials. The wet lab seems to present an insurmountable obstacle for a serious role for peer production in biomedical science. Nevertheless, it is not clear that it is actually any more so than it might have seemed for the development of an operating system, or a supercomputer, before these were achieved. Laboratories have two immensely valuable resources that may be capable of being harnessed to peer production. Most important by far are postdoctoral fellows. These are the same characters who populate so many free software projects, only geeks of a different feather. They are at a similar life stage. They have the same hectic, overworked lives, and yet the same capacity to work one more hour on something else, something interesting, exciting, or career enhancing, like a special grant announced by the government. The other resources that have overcapacity might be thought of as petri dishes, or if that sounds too quaint and old-fashioned, polymerase chain reaction (PCR) machines or electrophoresis equipment. The point is simple. Laboratory funding currently is silo-based. Each lab is usually funded to have all the equipment it needs for run-of-the-mill work, except for very large machines operated on time-share principles. Those machines that are redundantly provisioned in laboratories have downtime. That downtime coupled with a postdoctoral fellow in the lab is an experiment waiting to happen. If a group that is seeking to start a project defines discrete modules of a common experiment, and provides a communications platform to allow people to download project modules, perform them, and upload results, it would be possible to harness the overcapacity that exists in laboratories. In principle, although this is a harder empirical question, the same could be done for other widely available laboratory materials and even animals for preclinical trials on the model of, "brother, can you spare a mouse?" One fascinating proposal and early experiment at the University of Indiana-Purdue University Indianapolis was suggested by William Scott, a chemistry professor. Scott proposed developing simple, low-cost kits for training undergraduate students in chemical synthesis, but which would use targets and molecules identified by computational biology as potential treatments for developing-world diseases as their output. With enough redundancy across different classrooms and institutions around the world, the results could be verified while screening and synthesizing a significant number of potential drugs. The undergraduate educational experience could actually contribute to new experiments, as opposed simply to synthesizing outputs that are not really needed by anyone. Clinical trials provide yet another level of complexity, because the problem of delivering consistent drug formulations for testing to physicians and patients stretches the imagination. One option would be that research centers in countries affected by the diseases in question could pick up the work at this point, and create and conduct clinical trials. These too could be coordinated across regions and countries among the clinicians administering the tests, so that accruing patients and obtaining sufficient information could be achieved more rapidly and at lower cost. As in the case of One World Health, production and regulatory approval, from this stage on, could be taken up by the generics manufacturers. In order to prevent the outputs from being appropriated at this stage, every stage in the process would require a public-domain-binding license that would prevent a manufacturer from taking the outputs and, by making small changes, patenting the ultimate drug.

This proposal about medicine is, at this stage, the most imaginary among the commons-based strategies for development suggested here. However, it is analytically consistent with them, and, in principle, should be attainable. In combination with the more traditional commons-based approaches, university research, and the nonprofit world, peer production could contribute to an innovation ecology that could overcome the systematic inability of a purely patent-based system to register and respond to the health needs of the world's poor.

COMMONS-BASED STRATEGIES FOR
DEVELOPMENT: CONCLUSION

Welfare, development, and growth outside of the core economies heavily depend on the transfer of information-embedded goods and tools, information, and knowledge from the technologically advanced economies to the developing and less-developed economies and societies around the globe. These are important partly as finished usable components of welfare. Perhaps more important, however, they are necessary as tools and platforms on which innovation, research, and development can be pursued by local actors in the developing world itself—from the free software developers of Brazil to the agricultural scientists and farmers of Southeast Asia. The primary obstacles to diffusion of these desiderata in the required direction are the institutional framework of intellectual property and trade and the political power of the patent-dependent business models in the information-exporting economies. This is not because the proprietors of information goods and tools are evil. It is because their fiduciary duty is to maximize shareholder value, and the less-developed and developing economies have little money. As rational maximizers with a legal monopoly, the patent holders restrict output and sell at higher rates. This is not a bug in the institutional system we call "intellectual property." It is a known feature that has known undesirable side effects of inefficiently restricting access to the products of innovation. In the context of vast disparities in wealth across the globe, however, this known feature does not merely lead to less than theoretically optimal use of the information. It leads to predictable increase of morbidity and mortality and to higher barriers to development.

The rise of the networked information economy provides a new framework for thinking about how to work around the barriers that the international intellectual property regime places on development. Public-sector and other nonprofit institutions that have traditionally played an important role in development can do so with a greater degree of efficacy. Moreover, the emergence of peer production provides a model for new solutions to some of the problems of access to information and knowledge. In software and communications, these are directly available. In scientific information and some educational materials, we are beginning to see adaptations of these models to support core elements of development and learning. In food security and health, the translation process may be more difficult. In agriculture, we are seeing more immediate progress in the development of a woven fabric of public-sector, academic, nonprofit, and individual innovation and learning to pursue biological innovation outside of the markets based on patents and breeders' rights. In medicine, we are still at a very early stage of organizational experiments and institutional proposals. The barriers to implementation are significant. However, there is growing awareness of the human cost of relying solely on the patent-based production system, and of the potential of commons-based strategies to alleviate these failures.

Ideally, perhaps, the most direct way to arrive at a better system for harnessing innovation to development would pass through a new international politics of development, which would result in a better-designed international system of trade and innovation policy. There is in fact a global movement of NGOs and developing nations pursuing this goal. It is possible, however, that the politics of international trade are sufficiently bent to the purposes of incumbent industrial information economy proprietors and the governments that support them as a matter of industrial policy that the political path of formal institutional reform will fail. Certainly, the history of the TRIPS agreement and, more recently, efforts to pass new expansive treaties through the WIPO suggest this. However, one of the lessons we learn as we look at the networked information economy is that the work of governments through international treaties is not the final word on innovation and its diffusion across boundaries of wealth. The emergence of social sharing as a substantial mode of production in the networked environment offers an alternative route for individuals and nonprofit entities to take a much more substantial role in delivering actual desired outcomes independent of the formal system. Commons-based and peer production efforts may not be a cure-all. However, as we have seen in the software world, these strategies can make a big contribution to quite fundamental aspects of human welfare and development. And this is where freedom and justice coincide.

The practical freedom of individuals to act and associate freely—free from the constraints of proprietary endowment, free from the constraints of formal relations of contract or stable organizations—allows individual action in ad hoc, informal association to emerge as a new global mover. It frees the ability of people to act in response to all their motivations. In doing so, it offers a new path, alongside those of the market and formal governmental investment in public welfare, for achieving definable and significant improvements in human development throughout the world.

Chapter 10 Social Ties: Networking Together

Increased practical individual autonomy has been central to my claims throughout this book. It underlies the efficiency and sustainability of nonproprietary production in the networked information economy. It underlies the improvements I describe in both freedom and justice. Many have raised concerns that this new freedom will fray social ties and fragment social relations. On this view, the new freedom is one of detached monads, a freedom to live arid, lonely lives free of the many constraining attachments that make us grounded, well-adjusted human beings. Bolstered by early sociological studies, this perspective was one of two diametrically opposed views that typified the way the Internet's effect on community, or close social relations, was portrayed in the 1990s. The other view, popular among the digerati, was that "virtual communities" would come to represent a new form of human communal existence, providing new scope for building a shared experience of human interaction. Within a few short years, however, empirical research suggests that while neither view had it completely right, it was the dystopian view that got it especially wrong. The effects of the Internet on social relations are obviously complex. It is likely too soon to tell which social practices this new mode of communication will ultimately settle on. The most recent research, however, suggests that the Internet has some fairly well-defined effects on human community and intimate social relations. These effects mark neither breakdown nor transcendence, but they do represent an improvement over the world of television and telephone along most dimensions of normative concern with social relations.

We are seeing two effects: first, and most robustly, we see a thickening of preexisting relations with friends, family, and neighbors, particularly with those who were not easily reachable in the pre-Internet-mediated environment. Parents, for example, use instant messages to communicate with their children who are in college. Friends who have moved away from each other are keeping in touch more than they did before they had e-mail, because e-mail does not require them to coordinate a time to talk or to pay long-distance rates. However, this thickening of contacts seems to occur alongside a loosening of the hierarchical aspects of these relationships, as individuals weave their own web of supporting peer relations into the fabric of what might otherwise be stifling familial relationships. Second, we are beginning to see the emergence of greater scope for limited-purpose, loose relationships. These may not fit the ideal model of "virtual communities." They certainly do not fit a deep conception of "community" as a person's primary source of emotional context and support. They are nonetheless effective and meaningful to their participants. It appears that, as the digitally networked environment begins to displace mass media and telephones, its salient communications characteristics provide new dimensions to thicken existing social relations, while also providing new capabilities for looser and more fluid, but still meaningful social networks. A central aspect of this positive improvement in loose ties has been the technical-organizational shift from an information environment dominated by commercial mass media on a one-to-many model, which does not foster group interaction among viewers, to an information environment that both technically and as a matter of social practice enables user-centric, group-based active cooperation platforms of the kind that typify the networked information economy. This is not to say that the Internet necessarily effects all people, all social groups, and networks identically. The effects on different people in different settings and networks will likely vary, certainly in their magnitude. My purpose here, however, is to respond to the concern that enhanced individual capabilities entail social fragmentation and alienation. The available data do not support that claim as a description of a broad social effect.

FROM "VIRTUAL COMMUNITIES" TO
FEAR OF DISINTEGRATION

Angst about the fragmentation of organic deep social ties, the gemeinschaft community, the family, is hardly a creature of the Internet. In some form or another, the fear that cities, industrialization, rapid transportation, mass communications, and other accoutrements of modern industrial society are leading to alienation, breakdown of the family, and the disruption of community has been a fixed element of sociology since at least the mid-nineteenth century. Its mirror image—the search for real or imagined, more or less idealized community, "grounded" in preindustrial pastoral memory or postindustrial utopia—was often not far behind. Unsurprisingly, this patterned opposition of fear and yearning was replayed in the context of the Internet, as the transformative effect of this new medium made it a new focal point for both strands of thought.

In the case of the Internet, the optimists preceded the pessimists. In his now-classic *The Virtual Community*, Howard Rheingold put it most succinctly in 1993:

> My direct observations of online behavior around the world over the past ten years have led me to conclude that whenever CMC [computer mediated communications] technology becomes available to people anywhere, they inevitably build virtual communities with it, just as microorganisms inevitably create colonies. I suspect that one of the explanations for this phenomenon is the hunger for community that grows in the breasts of people around the world as more and more informal public spaces disappear from our real lives. I also suspect that these new media attract colonies of enthusiasts because CMC enables people to do things with each other in new ways, and to do altogether new kinds of things— just as telegraphs, telephones, and televisions did.

The Virtual Community was grounded on Rheingold's own experience in the WELL (Whole Earth 'Lectronic Link). The WELL was one the earliest well-developed instances of large-scale social interaction among people who started out as strangers but came to see themselves as a community. Its members eventually began to organize meetings in real space to strengthen the bonds, while mostly continuing their interaction through computer-mediated communications. Note the structure of Rheingold's claim in this early passage. There is a hunger for community, no longer satisfied by the declining availability of physical spaces for human connection. There is a newly available medium that allows people to connect despite their physical distance. This new opportunity inevitably and automatically brings people to use its affordances—the behaviors it makes possible—to fulfill their need for human connection. Over and above this, the new medium offers new ways of communicating and new ways of doing things together, thereby enhancing what was previously possible. Others followed Rheingold over the course of the 1990s in many and various ways. The basic structure of the claim about the potential of cyberspace to forge a new domain for human connection, one that overcomes the limitations that industrial mass-mediated society places on community, was oft repeated. The basic observation that the Internet permits the emergence of new relationships that play a significant role in their participants' lives and are anchored in online communications continues to be made. As discussed below, however, much of the research suggests that the new online relationships develop in addition to, rather than instead of, physical face-to-face human interaction in community and family—which turns out to be alive and well.

It was not long before a very different set of claims emerged about the Internet. Rather than a solution to the problems that industrial society creates for family and society, the Internet was seen as increasing alienation by absorbing its users. It made them unavailable to spend time with their families. It immersed them in diversions from the real world with its real relationships. In a social-relations version of the Babel objection, it was seen as narrowing the set of shared cultural experiences to such an extent that people, for lack of a common sitcom or news show to talk about, become increasingly alienated from each other. One strand of this type of criticism questioned the value of online relationships themselves as plausible replacements for real-world human connection. Sherry Turkle, the most important early explorer of virtual identity, characterized this concern as: "is it really sensible to suggest that the way to revitalize community is to sit alone in our rooms, typing at our networked computers and filling our lives with virtual friends?"[1] Instead of investing themselves with real relationships, risking real exposure and connection, people engage in limited-purpose, low-intensity relationships. If it doesn't work out, they can always sign off, and no harm done.

Another strand of criticism focused less on the thinness, not to say vacuity, of online relations, and more on sheer time. According to this argument, the time and effort spent on the Net came at the expense of time spent with family and friends. Prominent and oft cited in this vein were two early studies. The first, entitled *Internet Paradox*, was led by Robert Kraut.[2] It was the first longitudinal study of a substantial number of users—169 users in the first year or two of their Internet use. Kraut and his collaborators found a slight, but statistically significant, correlation between increases in Internet use and (a) decreases in family communication, (b) decreases in the size of social circle, both near and far, and (c) an increase in depression and loneliness. The researchers hypothesized that use of the Internet replaces strong ties with weak ties. They ideal-typed these communications as exchanging knitting tips with participants in a knitting Listserv, or jokes with someone you would meet on a tourist information site. These trivialities, they thought, came to fill time that, in the absence of the Internet, would be spent with people with whom one has stronger ties. From a communications theory perspective, this causal explanation was more sophisticated than the more widely claimed assimilation of the Internet and television—that a computer monitor is simply one more screen to take away from the time one has to talk to real human beings.[3] It recognized that using the Internet is fundamentally different from watching TV. It allows users to communicate with each other, rather than, like television, encouraging passive reception in a kind of "parallel play." Using a distinction between strong ties and weak ties, introduced by Mark Granovetter in what later became the social capital literature, these researchers suggested that the kind of human contact that was built around online interactions was thinner and less meaningful, so that the time spent on these relationships, on balance, weakened one's stock of social relations.

A second, more sensationalist release of a study followed two years later. In 2000, the Stanford Institute for the Quantitative Study of Society's "preliminary report" on Internet and society, more of a press release than a report, emphasized the finding that "the more hours people use the Internet, the less time they spend with real human beings."[4] The actual results were somewhat less stark than the widely reported press release. As among all Internet users, only slightly more than 8 percent reported spending less time with family; 6 percent reported spending more time with family, and 86 percent spent about the same amount of time. Similarly, 9 percent reported spending less time with friends, 4 percent spent more time, and 87 percent spent the same amount of time.[5] The press release probably should not have read, "social isolation increases," but instead, "Internet seems to have indeterminate, but in any event small, effects on our interaction with family and friends"—hardly the stuff of front-page news coverage.[6] The strongest result supporting the "isolation" thesis in that study was that 27 percent of respondents who were heavy Internet users reported spending less time on the phone with friends and family. The study did not ask whether they used e-mail instead of the phone to keep in touch with these family and friends, and whether they thought they had more or less of a connection with these friends and family as a result. Instead, as the author reported in his press release, "E-mail is a way to stay in touch, but you can't share coffee or beer with somebody on e-mail, or give them a hug" (as opposed, one supposes, to the common practice of phone hugs).[7] As Amitai Etzioni noted in his biting critique of that study, the truly significant findings were that Internet users spent less time watching television and shopping. Forty-seven percent of those surveyed said that they watched less television than they used to, and that number reached 65 percent for heavy users and 27 percent for light users. Only 3 percent of those surveyed said they watched more TV. Nineteen percent of all respondents and 25 percent of those who used the Internet more than five hours a week said they shopped less in stores, while only 3 percent said they shopped more in stores. The study did not explore how people were using the time they freed by watching less television and shopping less in physical stores. It did not ask whether they used any of this newfound time to increase and strengthen their social and kin ties.[8]

A MORE POSITIVE PICTURE EMERGES
OVER TIME

The concerns represented by these early studies of the effects of Internet use on community and family seem to fall into two basic bins. The first is that sustained, more or less intimate human relations are critical to well-functioning human beings as a matter of psychological need. The claims that Internet use is associated with greater loneliness and depression map well onto the fears that human connection ground into a thin gruel of electronic bits simply will not give people the kind of human connectedness they need as social beings. The second bin of concerns falls largely within the "social capital" literature, and, like that literature itself, can be divided largely into two main subcategories. The first, following James Coleman and Mark Granovetter, focuses on the economic function of social ties and the ways in which people who have social capital can be materially better off than people who lack it. The second, exemplified by Robert Putnam's work, focuses on the political aspects of engaged societies, and on the ways in which communities with high social capital—defined as social relations with people in local, stable, face-to-face interactions—will lead to better results in terms of political participation and the provisioning of local public goods, like education and community policing. For this literature, the shape of social ties, their relative strength, and who is connected to whom become more prominent features.

There are, roughly speaking, two types of responses to these concerns. The first is empirical. In order for these concerns to be valid as applied to increasing use of Internet communications, it must be the case that Internet communications, with all of their inadequacies, come to supplant real-world human interactions, rather than simply to supplement them. Unless Internet connections actually displace direct, unmediated, human contact, there is no basis to think that using the Internet will lead to a decline in those nourishing connections we need psychologically, or in the useful connections we make socially, that are based on direct human contact with friends, family, and neighbors. The second response is theoretical. It challenges the notion that the socially embedded individual is a fixed entity with unchanging needs that are, or are not, fulfilled by changing social conditions and relations. Instead, it suggests that the "nature" of individuals changes over time, based on actual social practices and expectations. In this case, we are seeing a shift from individuals who depend on social relations that are dominated by locally embedded, thick, unmediated, given, and stable relations, into networked individuals—who are more dependent on their own combination of strong and weak ties, who switch networks, cross boundaries, and weave their own web of more or less instrumental, relatively fluid relationships. Manuel Castells calls this the "networked society,"[9] Barry Wellman, "networked individualism."[10] To simplify vastly, it is not that people cease to depend on others and their context for both psychological and social well-being and efficacy. It is that the kinds of connections that we come to rely on for these basic human needs change over time. Comparisons of current practices to the old ways of achieving the desiderata of community, and fears regarding the loss of community, are more a form of nostalgia than a diagnosis of present social malaise.

Users Increase Their Connections with
Preexisting Relations

The most basic response to the concerns over the decline of community and its implications for both the psychological and the social capital strands is the empirical one. Relations with one's local geographic community and with one's intimate friends and family do not seem to be substantially affected by Internet use. To the extent that these relationships are affected, the effect is positive. Kraut and his collaborators continued their study, for example, and followed up with their study subjects for an additional three years. They found that the negative effects they had reported in the first year or two dissipated over the total period of observation.[11] Their basic hypothesis that the Internet probably strengthened weak ties, however, is consistent with other research and theoretical work. One of the earliest systematic studies of high-speed Internet access and its effects on communities in this vein was by Keith Hampton and Barry Wellman.[12] They studied the aptly named Toronto suburb Netville, where homes had high-speed wiring years before broadband access began to be adopted widely in North America. One of their most powerful findings was that people who were connected recognized three times as many of their neighbors by name and regularly talked with twice as many as those who were not wired. On the other hand, however, stronger ties—indicated by actually visiting neighbors, as opposed to just knowing their name or stopping to say good morning—were associated with how long a person had lived in the neighborhood, not with whether or not they were wired. In other words, weak ties of the sort of knowing another's name or stopping to chat with them were significantly strengthened by Internet connection, even within a geographic neighborhood. Stronger ties were not. Using applications like a local e-mail list and personal e-mails, wired residents communicated with others in their neighborhood much more often than did nonwired residents. Moreover, wired residents recognized the names of people in a wider radius from their homes, while nonwired residents tended to know only people within their block, or even a few homes on each side. However, again, stronger social ties, like visiting and talking face-to-face, tended to be concentrated among physically proximate neighbors. Other studies also observed this increase of weak ties in a neighborhood with individuals who are more geographically distant than one's own immediate street or block.[13] Perhaps the most visible aspect of the social capital implications of a well-wired geographic community was the finding that wired neighbors began to sit on their front porches, instead of in their backyard, thereby providing live social reinforcement of community through daily brief greetings, as well as creating a socially enforced community policing mechanism.

We now have quite a bit of social science research on the side of a number of factual propositions.[14] Human beings, whether connected to the Internet or not, continue to communicate preferentially with people who are geographically proximate than with those who are distant.[15] Nevertheless, people who are connected to the Internet communicate more with people who are geographically distant without decreasing the number of local connections. While the total number of connections continues to be greatest with proximate family members, friends, coworkers, and neighbors, the Internet's greatest effect is in improving the ability of individuals to add to these proximate relationships new and better-connected relationships with people who are geographically distant. This includes keeping more in touch with friends and relatives who live far away, and creating new weak-tie relationships around communities of interest and practice. To the extent that survey data are reliable, the most comprehensive and updated surveys support these observations. It now seems clear that Internet users "buy" their time to use the Internet by watching less television, and that the more Internet experience they have, the less they watch TV. People who use the Internet claim to have increased the number of people they stay in touch with, while mostly reporting no effect on time they spend with their family.[16]

Connections with family and friends seemed to be thickened by the new channels of communication, rather than supplanted by them. Emblematic of this were recent results of a survey conducted by the Pew project on "Internet and American Life" on *Holidays Online*. Almost half of respondents surveyed reported using e-mail to organize holiday activities with family (48 percent) and friends (46 percent), 27 percent reported sending or receiving holiday greetings, and while a third described themselves as shopping online in order to save money, 51 percent said they went online to find an unusual or hard-to-find gift. In other words, half of those who used the Internet for holiday shopping did so in order to personalize their gift further, rather than simply to take advantage of the most obvious use of e-commerce—price comparison and time savings. Further support for this position is offered in another Pew study, entitled "Internet and Daily Life." In that survey, the two most common uses—both of which respondents claimed they did more of because of the Net than they otherwise would have—were connecting with family and friends and looking up information.[17] Further evidence that the Internet is used to strengthen and service preexisting relations, rather than create new ones, is the fact that 79 percent of those who use the Internet at all do so to communicate with friends and family, while only 26 percent use the Internet to meet new people or to arrange dates. Another point of evidence is the use of instant messaging (IM). IM is a synchronous communications medium that requires its users to set time aside to respond and provides information to those who wish to communicate with an individual about whether that person is or is not available at any given moment. Because it is so demanding, IM is preferentially useful for communicating with individuals with whom one already has a preexisting relationship. This preferential use for strengthening preexisting relations is also indicated by the fact that two-thirds of IM users report using IM with no more than five others, while only one in ten users reports instant messaging with more than ten people. A recent Pew study of instant messaging shows that 53 million adults—42 percent of Internet users in the United States—trade IM messages. Forty percent use IM to contact coworkers, one-third family, and 21 percent use it to communicate equally with both. Men and women IM in equal proportions, but women IM more than men do, averaging 433 minutes per month as compared to 366 minutes, respectively, and households with children IM more than households without children.

These studies are surveys and local case studies. They cannot offer a knockdown argument about how "we"—everyone, everywhere—are using the Internet. The same technology likely has different effects when it is introduced into cultures that differ from each other in their pre-Internet baseline.[18] Despite these cautions, these studies do offer the best evidence we have about Internet use patterns. As best we can tell from contemporary social science, Internet use increases the contact that people have with others who traditionally have been seen as forming a person's "community": family, friends, and neighbors. Moreover, the Internet is also used as a platform for forging new relationships, in addition to those that are preexisting. These relationships are more limited in nature than ties to friends and family. They are detached from spatial constraints, and even time synchronicity; they are usually interest or practice based, and therefore play a more limited role in people's lives than the more demanding and encompassing relationships with family or intimate friends. Each discrete connection or cluster of connections that forms a social network, or a network of social relations, plays some role, but not a definitive one, in each participant's life. There is little disagreement among researchers that these kinds of weak ties or limited-liability social relationships are easier to create on the Internet, and that we see some increase in their prevalence among Internet users. The primary disagreement is interpretive—in other words, is it, on balance, a good thing that we have multiple, overlapping, limited emotional liability relationships, or does it, in fact, undermine our socially embedded being?

Networked Individuals

The interpretive argument about the normative value of the increase in weak ties is colored by the empirical finding that the time spent on the Internet in these limited relationships does not come at the expense of the number of communications with preexisting, real-world relationships. Given our current state of sociological knowledge, the normative question cannot be whether online relations are a reasonable replacement for real-world friendship. Instead, it must be how we understand the effect of the interaction between an increasingly thickened network of communications with preexisting relations and the casting of a broader net that captures many more, and more varied, relations. What is emerging in the work of sociologists is a framework that sees the networked society or the networked individual as entailing an abundance of social connections and more effectively deployed attention. The concern with the decline of community conceives of a scarcity of forms of stable, nurturing, embedding relations, which are mostly fixed over the life of an individual and depend on long-standing and interdependent relations in stable groups, often with hierarchical relations. What we now see emerging is a diversity of forms of attachment and an abundance of connections that enable individuals to attain discrete components of the package of desiderata that "community" has come to stand for in sociology. As Wellman puts it: "Communities and societies have been changing towards networked societies where boundaries are more permeable, interactions are with diverse others, linkages switch between multiple networks, and hierarchies are flatter and more recursive. . . . Their work and community networks are diffuse, sparsely knit, with vague, overlapping, social and spatial boundaries."[19] In this context, the range and diversity of network connections beyond the traditional family, friends, stable coworkers, or village becomes a source of dynamic stability, rather than tension and disconnect.

The emergence of networked individuals is not, however, a mere overlay, "floating" on top of thickened preexisting social relations without touching them except to add more relations. The interpolation of new networked connections, and the individual's role in weaving those for him- or herself, allows individuals to reorganize their social relations in ways that fit them better. They can use their network connections to loosen social bonds that are too hierarchical and stifling, while filling in the gaps where their real-world relations seem lacking. Nowhere is this interpolation clearer than in Mizuko Ito's work on the use of mobile phones, primarily for text messaging and e-mail, among Japanese teenagers.[20] Japanese urban teenagers generally live in tighter physical quarters than their American or European counterparts, and within quite strict social structures of hierarchy and respect. Ito and others have documented how these teenagers use mobile phones—primarily as platforms for text messages—that is, as a mobile cross between e-mail and instant messaging and more recently images, to loosen the constraints under which they live. They text at home and in the classroom, making connections to meet in the city and be together, and otherwise succeed in constructing a network of time- and space-bending emotional connections with their friends, without—and this is the critical observation—breaking the social molds they otherwise occupy. They continue to spend time in their home, with their family. They continue to show respect and play the role of child at home and at school. However, they interpolate that role and those relations with a sub-rosa network of connections that fulfill otherwise suppressed emotional needs and ties.

The phenomenon is not limited to youths, but is applicable more generally to the capacity of users to rely on their networked connections to escape or moderate some of the more constraining effects of their stable social connections. In the United States, a now iconic case—mostly described in terms of privacy—was that of U.S. Navy sailor Timothy McVeigh (not the Oklahoma bomber). McVeigh was discharged from the navy when his superiors found out that he was gay by accessing his AOL (America Online) account. The case was primarily considered in terms of McVeigh's e-mail account privacy. It settled for an undisclosed sum, and McVeigh retired from the navy with benefits. However, what is important for us here is not the "individual rights" category under which the case was fought, but the practice that it revealed. Here was an eighteen-year veteran of the navy who used the space-time breaking possibilities of networked communications to loosen one of the most constraining attributes imaginable of the hierarchical framework that he nonetheless chose to be part of—the U.S. Navy. It would be odd to think that the navy did not provide McVeigh with a sense of identity and camaraderie that closely knit communities provide their members. Yet at the same time, it also stifled his ability to live one of the most basic of all human ties—his sexual identity. He used the network and its potential for anonymous and pseudonymous existence to coexist between these two social structures.

At the other end of the spectrum of social ties, we see new platforms emerging to generate the kinds of bridging relations that were so central to the identification of "weak ties" in social capital literature. Weak ties are described in the social capital literature as allowing people to transmit information across social networks about available opportunities and resources, as well as provide at least a limited form of vouching for others—as one introduces a friend to a friend of a friend. What we are seeing on the Net is an increase in the platforms developed to allow people to create these kinds of weak ties based on an interest or practice. Perhaps clearest of these is Meetup.com. Meetup is a Web site that allows users to search for others who share an interest and who are locally available to meet face-to-face. The search results show users what meetings are occurring within their requested area and interest. The groups then meet periodically, and those who sign up for them also are able to provide a profile and photo of themselves, to facilitate and sustain the real-world group meetings. The power of this platform is that it is not intended as a replacement for real-space meetings. It is intended as a replacement for the happenstance of social networks as they transmit information about opportunities for interest- and practice-based social relations. The vouching function, on the other hand, seems to have more mixed efficacy, as Dana Boyd's ethnography of Friendster suggests.[21] Friendster was started as a dating Web site. It was built on the assumption that dating a friend of a friend of a friend is safer and more likely to be successful than dating someone based on a similar profile, located on a general dating site like match.com—in other words, that vouching as friends provides valuable information. As Boyd shows, however, the attempt of Friendster to articulate and render transparent the social networks of its users met with less than perfect success. The platform only permits users to designate friend/not friend, without the finer granularity enabled by a face-to-face conversation about someone, where one can answer or anticipate the question, "just how well do you know this person?" with a variety of means, from tone to express reservations. On Friendster, it seems that people cast broader networks, and for fear of offending or alienating others, include many more "friendsters" than they actually have "friends." The result is a weak platform for mapping general connections, rather than a genuine articulation of vouching through social networks. Nonetheless, it does provide a visible rendering of at least the thinnest of weak ties, and strengthens their effect in this regard. It enables very weak ties to perform some of the roles of real-world weak social ties.

THE INTERNET AS A PLATFORM FOR
HUMAN CONNECTION

Communication is constitutive of social relations. We cannot have relationships except by communicating with others. Different communications media differ from each other—in who gets to speak to whom and in what can be said. These differences structure the social relations that rely on these various modes of communication so that they differ from each other in significant ways. Technological determinism is not required to accept this. Some aspects of the difference are purely technical. Script allows text and more or less crude images to be transmitted at a distance, but not voice, touch, smell, or taste. To the extent that there are human emotions, modes of submission and exertion of authority, irony, love or affection, or information that is easily encoded and conveyed in face-to-face communications but not in script, script-based communications are a poor substitute for presence. A long and romantic tradition of love letters and poems notwithstanding, there is a certain thinness to that mode in the hands of all but the most gifted writers relative to the fleshiness of unmediated love. Some aspects of the difference among media of communication are not necessarily technical, but are rather culturally or organizationally embedded. Television can transmit text. However, text distribution is not television's relative advantage in a sociocultural environment that already has mass-circulation print media, and in a technical context where the resolution of television images is relatively low. As a matter of cultural and business practice, therefore, from its inception, television emphasized moving images and sound, not text transmission. Radio could have been deployed as short-range, point-to-point personal communications systems, giving us a nation of walkie-talkies. However, as chapter 6 described, doing so would have required a very different set of regulatory and business decisions between 1919 and 1927. Communications media take on certain social roles, structures of control, and emphases of style that combine their technical capacities and limits with the sociocultural business context into which they were introduced, and through which they developed. The result is a cluster of use characteristics that define how a given medium is used within a given society, in a given historical context. They make media differ from each other, providing platforms with very different capacities and emphases for their users.

As a technical and organizational matter, the Internet allows for a radically more diverse suite of communications models than any of the twentieth-century systems permitted. It allows for textual, aural, and visual communications. It permits spatial and temporal asynchronicity, as in the case of e-mail or Web pages, but also enables temporal synchronicity—as in the case of IM, online game environments, or Voice over Internet Protocol (VoIP). It can even be used for subchannel communications within a spatially synchronous context, such as in a meeting where people pass electronic notes to each other by e-mail or IM. Because it is still highly textual, it requires more direct attention than radio, but like print, it is highly multiplexable—both between uses of the Internet and other media, and among Internet uses themselves. Similar to print media, you can pick your head up from the paper, make a comment, and get back to reading. Much more richly, one can be on a voice over IP conversation and e-mail at the same time, or read news interlaced with receiving and responding to e-mail. It offers one-to-one, one-to-few, few-to-few, one-to-many, and many-to-many communications capabilities, more diverse in this regard than any medium for social communication that preceded it, including—on the dimensions of distance, asynchronicity, and many-to-many capabilities—even that richest of media: face-to-face communications.

Because of its technical flexibility and the "business model" of Internet service providers as primarily carriers, the Internet lends itself to being used for a wide range of social relations. Nothing in "the nature of the technology" requires that it be the basis of rich social relations, rather than becoming, as some predicted in the early 1990s, a "celestial jukebox" for the mass distribution of prepackaged content to passive end points. In contradistinction to the dominant remote communications technologies of the twentieth century, however, the Internet offers some new easy ways to communicate that foster both of the types of social communication that the social science literature seems to be observing. Namely, it makes it easy to increase the number of communications with preexisting friends and family, and increases communication with geographically distant or more loosely affiliated others. Print, radio, television, film, and sound recording all operated largely on a one-to-many model. They did not, given the economics of production and transmission, provide a usable means of remote communication for individuals at the edges of these communication media. Television, film, sound recording, and print industries were simply too expensive, and their business organization was too focused on selling broadcast-model communications, to support significant individual communication. When cassette tapes were introduced, we might have seen people recording a tape instead of writing a letter to friends or family. However, this was relatively cumbersome, low quality, and time consuming. Telephones were the primary means of communications used by individuals, and they indeed became the primary form of mediated personal social communications. However, telephone conversations require synchronicity, which means that they can only be used for socializing purposes when both parties have time. They were also only usable throughout this period for serial, one-to-one conversations. Moreover, for most of the twentieth century, a long-distance call was a very expensive proposition for most nonbusiness users, and outside of the United States, local calls too carried nontrivial time-sensitive prices in most places. Telephones were therefore a reasonable medium for social relations with preexisting friends and family. However, their utility dropped off radically with the cost of communication, which was at a minimum associated with geographic distance. In all these dimensions, the Internet makes it easier and cheaper to communicate with family and friends, at close proximity or over great distances, through the barriers of busy schedules and differing time zones. Moreover, because of the relatively low-impact nature of these communications, the Internet allows people to experiment with looser relations more readily. In other words, the Internet does not make us more social beings. It simply offers more degrees of freedom for each of us to design our own communications space than were available in the past. It could have been that we would have used that design flexibility to re-create the mass-media model. But to predict that it would be used in this fashion requires a cramped view of human desire and connectedness. It was much more likely that, given the freedom to design our own communications environment flexibly and to tailor it to our own individual needs dynamically over time, we would create a system that lets us strengthen the ties that are most important to us. It was perhaps less predictable, but unsurprising after the fact, that this freedom would also be used to explore a wider range of relations than simply consuming finished media goods.

There is an appropriate wariness in contemporary academic commentary about falling into the trap of "the mythos of the electrical sublime" by adopting a form of Internet utopianism.[22] It is important, however, not to let this caution blind us to the facts about Internet use, and the technical, business, and cultural capabilities that the Internet makes feasible. The cluster of technologies of computation and communications that characterize the Internet today are, in fact, used in functionally different ways, and make for several different media of communication than we had in the twentieth century. The single technical platform might best be understood to enable several different "media"—in the sense of clusters of technical-social-economic practices of communication—and the number of these enabled media is growing. Instant messaging came many years after e-mail, and a few years after Web pages. Blogging one's daily journal on LiveJournal so that a group of intimates can check in on one's life as it unfolds was not a medium that was available to users until even more recently. The Internet is still providing its users with new ways to communicate with each other, and these represent a genuinely wide range of new capabilities. It is therefore unsurprising that connected social beings, such as we are, will take advantage of these new capabilities to form connections that were practically infeasible in the past. This is not media determinism. This is not millenarian utopianism. It is a simple observation. People do what they can, not what they cannot. In the daily humdrum of their lives, individuals do more of what is easier to do than what requires great exertion. When a new medium makes it easy for people to do new things, they may well, in fact, do them. And when these new things are systematically more user-centric, dialogic, flexible in terms of the temporal and spatial synchronicity they require or enable, and multiplexable, people will communicate with each other in ways and amounts that they could not before.

THE EMERGENCE OF SOCIAL SOFTWARE

The design of the Internet itself is agnostic as among the social structures and relations it enables. At its technical core is a commitment to push all the detailed instantiations of human communications to the edges of the network—to the applications that run on the computers of users. This technical agnosticism leads to a social agnosticism. The possibility of large-scale sharing and cooperation practices, of medium-scale platforms for collaboration and discussion, and of small-scale, one-to-one communications has led to the development of a wide range of software designs and applications to facilitate different types of communications. The World Wide Web was used initially as a global broadcast medium available to anyone and everyone, everywhere. In e-mail, we see a medium available for one-to-one, few-to-few, one-to-many and, to a lesser extent, many-to-many use. One of the more interesting phenomena of the past few years is the emergence of what is beginning to be called "social software." As a new design space, it is concerned with groups that are, as defined by Clay Shirky, who first articulated the concept, "Larger than a dozen, smaller than a few hundred, where people can actually have these conversational forms that can't be supported when you're talking about tens of thousands or millions of users, at least in a single group." The definition of the term is somewhat amorphous, but the basic concept is software whose design characteristic is that it treats genuine social phenomena as different from one-to-one or one-to-many communications. It seeks to build one's expectations about the social interactions that the software will facilitate into the design of the platform. The design imperative was most clearly articulated by Shirky when he wrote that from the perspective of the software designer, the user of social software is the group, not the individual.[23]

A simple example will help to illustrate. Take any given site that uses a collaborative authorship tool, like the Wiki that is the basis of *Wikipedia* and many other cooperative authorship exercises. From the perspective of an individual user, the ease of posting a comment on the Wiki, and the ease of erasing one's own comments from it, would be important characteristics: The fewer registration and sign-in procedures, the better. Not so from the perspective of the group. The group requires some "stickiness" to make the group as a group, and the project as a project, avoid the rending forces of individualism and self-reference. So, for example, design components that require registration for posting, or give users different rights to post and erase comments over time, depending on whether they are logged in or not, or depending on a record of their past cooperative or uncooperative behavior, are a burden for the individual user. However, that is precisely their point. They are intended to give those users with a greater stake in the common enterprise a slight, or sometimes large, edge in maintaining the group's cohesion. Similarly, erasing past comments may be useful for the individual, for example, if they were silly or untempered. Keeping the comments there is, however, useful to the group—as a source of experience about the individual or part of the group's collective memory about mistakes made in the past that should not be repeated by someone else. Again, the needs of the group as a group often differ from those of the individual participant. Thinking of the platform as social software entails designing it with characteristics that have a certain social-science or psychological model of the interactions of a group, and building the platform's affordances in order to enhance the survivability and efficacy of the group, even if it sometimes comes at the expense of the individual user's ease of use or comfort.

This emergence of social software—like blogs with opportunities to comment, Wikis, as well as social-norm-mediated Listservs or uses of the "cc" line in e-mail—underscores the nondeterministic nature of the claim about the relationship between the Internet and social relations. The Internet makes possible all sorts of human communications that were not technically feasible before its widespread adoption. Within this wide range of newly feasible communications patterns, we are beginning to see the emergence of different types of relationships—some positive, some, like spam (unsolicited commercial e-mail), decidedly negative. In seeking to predict and diagnose the relationship between the increasing use of Internet communications and the shape of social relations, we see that the newly emerging constructive social possibilities are leading to new design challenges. These, in turn, are finding engineers and enthusiasts willing and able to design for them. The genuinely new capability—connecting among few and many at a distance in a dialogic, recursive form—is leading to the emergence of new design problems. These problems come from the fact that the new social settings come with their own social dynamics, but without long-standing structures of mediation and constructive ordering. Hence the early infamy of the tendency of Usenet and Listservs discussions to deteriorate into destructive flame wars. As social habits of using these kinds of media mature, so that users already know that letting loose on a list will likely result in a flame war and will kill the conversation, and as designers understand that social dynamics—including both those that allow people to form and sustain groups and those that rend them apart with equal if not greater force—we are seeing the coevolution of social norms and platform designs that are intended to give play to the former, and mediate or moderate the latter. These platforms are less likely to matter for sustaining the group in preexisting relations—as among friends or family. The structuring of those relationships is dominated by social norms. However, they do offer a new form and a stabilizing context for the newly emerging diverse set of social relations—at a distance, across interests and contexts—that typify both peer production and many forms of social interaction aimed purely at social reproduction.

The peer-production processes that are described in primarily economic terms in chapter 3—like free software development, *Wikipedia*, or the Open Directory Project—represent one cluster of important instances of this new form of social relations. They offer a type of relationship that is nonhierarchical and organized in a radically decentralized pattern. Their social valence is given by some combination of the shared experience of joint creativity they enable, as well as their efficacy—their ability to give their users a sense of common purpose and mutual support in achieving it. Individuals adopt projects and purposes they consider worth pursuing. Through these projects they find others, with whom they initially share only a general sense of human connectedness and common practical interest, but with whom they then interact in ways that allow the relationship to thicken over time. Nowhere is this process clearer than on the community pages of *Wikipedia*. Because of the limited degree to which that platform uses technical means to constrain destructive behavior, the common enterprise has developed practices of user-to-user communication, multiuser mediation, and user-appointed mediation to resolve disputes and disagreements. Through their involvement in these, users increase their participation, their familiarity with other participants—at least in this limited role as coauthors—and their practices of mutual engagement with these others. In this way, peer production offers a new platform for human connection, bringing together otherwise unconnected individuals and replacing common background or geographic proximity with a sense of well-defined purpose and the successful common pursuit of this purpose as the condensation point for human connection. Individuals who are connected to each other in a peer-production community may or may not be bowling alone when they are off-line, but they are certainly playing together online.

THE INTERNET AND HUMAN COMMUNITY

This chapter began with a basic question. While the networked information economy may enhance the autonomy of individuals, does it not also facilitate the breakdown of community? The answer offered here has been partly empirical and partly conceptual.

Empirically, it seems that the Internet is allowing us to eat our cake and have it too, apparently keeping our (social) figure by cutting down on the social equivalent of deep-fried dough—television. That is, we communicate more, rather than less, with the core constituents of our organic communities—our family and our friends—and we seem, in some places, also to be communicating more with our neighbors. We also communicate more with loosely affiliated others, who are geographically remote, and who may share only relatively small slivers of overlapping interests, or for only short periods of life. The proliferation of potential connections creates the social parallel to the Babel objection in the context of autonomy—with all these possible links, will any of them be meaningful? The answer is largely that we do, in fact, employ very strong filtering on our Internet-based social connections in one obvious dimension: We continue to use the newly feasible lines of communication primarily to thicken and strengthen connections with preexisting relationships—family and friends. The clearest indication of this is the parsimony with which most people use instant messaging. The other mechanism we seem to be using to avoid drowning in the noise of potential chitchat with ever-changing strangers is that we tend to find networks of connections that have some stickiness from our perspective. This stickiness could be the efficacy of a cluster of connections in pursuit of a goal one cares about, as in the case of the newly emerging peer-production enterprises. It could be the ways in which the internal social interaction has combined social norms with platform design to offer relatively stable relations with others who share common interests. Users do not amble around in a social equivalent of Brownian motion. They tend to cluster in new social relations, albeit looser and for more limited purposes than the traditional pillars of community.

The conceptual answer has been that the image of "community" that seeks a facsimile of a distant pastoral village is simply the wrong image of how we interact as social beings. We are a networked society now—networked individuals connected with each other in a mesh of loosely knit, overlapping, flat connections. This does not leave us in a state of anomie. We are well-adjusted, networked individuals; well-adjusted socially in ways that those who seek community would value, but in new and different ways. In a substantial departure from the range of feasible communications channels available in the twentieth century, the Internet has begun to offer us new ways of connecting to each other in groups small and large. As we have come to take advantage of these new capabilities, we see social norms and software coevolving to offer new, more stable, and richer contexts for forging new relationships beyond those that in the past have been the focus of our social lives. These do not displace the older relations. They do not mark a fundamental shift in human nature into selfless, community-conscious characters. We continue to be complex beings, radically individual and self-interested at the same time that we are entwined with others who form the context out of which we take meaning, and in which we live our lives. However, we now have new scope for interaction with others. We have new opportunities for building sustained limited-purpose relations, weak and intermediate-strength ties that have significant roles in providing us with context, with a source of defining part of our identity, with potential sources for support, and with human companionship. That does not mean that these new relationships will come to displace the centrality of our more immediate relationships. They will, however, offer increasingly attractive supplements as we seek new and diverse ways to embed ourselves in relation to others, to gain efficacy in weaker ties, and to interpolate different social networks in combinations that provide us both stability of context and a greater degree of freedom from the hierarchical and constraining aspects of some of our social relations.

Part Three Policies of Freedom at a
Moment of Transformation

Part I of this book offers a descriptive, progressive account of emerging patterns of nonmarket individual and cooperative social behavior, and an analysis of why these patterns are internally sustainable and increase information economy productivity. Part II combines descriptive and normative analysis to claim that these emerging practices offer defined improvements in autonomy, democratic discourse, cultural creation, and justice. I have noted periodically, however, that the descriptions of emerging social practices and the analysis of their potential by no means imply that these changes will necessarily become stable or provide the benefits I ascribe them. They are not a deterministic consequence of the adoption of networked computers as core tools of information production and exchange. There is no inevitable historical force that drives the technological-economic moment toward an open, diverse, liberal equilibrium. If the transformation I describe actually generalizes and stabilizes, it could lead to substantial redistribution of power and money. The twentieth-century industrial producers of information, culture, and communications—like Hollywood, the recording industry, and some of the telecommunications giants—stand to lose much. The winners would be a combination of the widely diffuse population of individuals around the globe and the firms or other toolmakers and platform providers who supply these newly capable individuals with the context for participating in the networked information economy. None of the industrial giants of yore are taking this threat lying down. Technology will not overcome their resistance through an insurmountable progressive impulse of history. The reorganization of production and the advances it can bring in freedom and justice will emerge only as a result of social practices and political actions that successfully resist efforts to regulate the emergence of the networked information economy in order to minimize its impact on the incumbents.

Since the middle of the 1990s, we have seen intensifying battles over the institutional ecology within which the industrial mode of information production and the newly emerging networked modes compete. Partly, this has been a battle over telecommunications infrastructure regulation. Most important, however, this has meant a battle over "intellectual property" protection, very broadly defined. Building upon and extending a twenty-five-year trend of expansion of copyrights, patents, and similar exclusive rights, the last half-decade of the twentieth century saw expansion of institutional mechanisms for exerting exclusive control in multiple dimensions. The term of copyright was lengthened. Patent rights were extended to cover software and business methods. Trademarks were extended by the Antidilution Act of 1995 to cover entirely new values, which became the basis for liability in the early domain-name trademark disputes. Most important, we saw a move to create new legal tools with which information vendors could hermetically seal access to their materials to an extent never before possible. The Digital Millennium Copyright Act (DMCA) prohibited the creation and use of technologies that would allow users to get at materials whose owners control through encryption. It prohibited even technologies that users can employ to use the materials in ways that the owners have no right to prevent. Today we are seeing efforts to further extend similar technological regulations—down to the level of regulating hardware to make sure that it complies with design specifications created by the copyright industries. At other layers of the communications environment, we see efforts to expand software patents, to control the architecture of personal computing devices, and to create ever-stronger property rights in physical infrastructure—be it the telephone lines, cable plant, or wireless frequencies. Together, these legislative and judicial

acts have formed what many have been calling a second enclosure movement: A concerted effort to shape the institutional ecology in order to help
proprietary models of information production at the expense of burdening
nonmarket, nonproprietary production.[1] The new enclosure movement is
not driven purely by avarice and rent seeking—though it has much of that
too. Some of its components are based in well-meaning judicial and regulatory choices that represent a particular conception of innovation and its
relationship to exclusive rights. That conception, focused on mass-media-
type content, movies, and music, and on pharmaceutical-style innovation
systems, is highly solicitous of the exclusive rights that are the bread and
butter of those culturally salient formats. It is also suspicious of, and detrimental to, the forms of nonmarket, commons-based production emerging
in the networked information economy.

This new enclosure movement has been the subject of sustained and diverse academic critique since the mid-1980s.[2] The core of this rich critique
has been that the cases and statutes of the past decade or so have upset the
traditional balance, in copyrights in particular, between seeking to create
incentives through the grant of exclusive rights and assuring access to information through the judicious limitation of these rights and the privileging
of various uses. I do not seek to replicate that work here, or to offer a
comprehensive listing of all the regulatory moves that have increased the
scope of proprietary rights in digital communications networks. Instead, I
offer a way of framing these various changes as moves in a large-scale battle
over the institutional ecology of the digital environment. By "institutional
ecology," I mean to say that institutions matter to behavior, but in ways that
are more complex than usually considered in economic models. They interact
with the technological state, the cultural conceptions of behaviors, and with
incumbent and emerging social practices that may be motivated not only by
self-maximizing behavior, but also by a range of other social and psychological motivations. In this complex ecology, institutions—most prominently,
law—affect these other parameters, and are, in turn, affected by them. Institutions coevolve with technology and with social and market behavior.
This coevolution leads to periods of relative stability, punctuated by periods
of disequilibrium, which may be caused by external shocks or internally
generated phase shifts. During these moments, the various parameters will
be out of step, and will pull and tug at the pattern of behavior, at the
technology, and at the institutional forms of the behavior. After the tugging
and pulling has shaped the various parameters in ways that are more con-

sistent with each other, we should expect to see periods of relative stability and coherence.

Chapter 11 is devoted to an overview of the range of discrete policy areas that are shaping the institutional ecology of digital networks, in which proprietary, market-based models of information production compete with those that are individual, social, and peer produced. In almost all contexts, when presented with a policy choice, advanced economies have chosen to regulate information production and exchange in ways that make it easier to pursue a proprietary, exclusion-based model of production of entertainment goods at the expense of commons- and service-based models of information production and exchange. This has been true irrespective of the political party in power in the United States, or the cultural differences in the salience of market orientation between Europe and the United States. However, the technological trajectory, the social practices, and the cultural understanding are often working at cross-purposes with the regulatory impulse. The equilibrium on which these conflicting forces settle will shape, to a large extent, the way in which information, knowledge, and culture are produced and used over the coming few decades. Chapter 12 concludes the book with an overview of what we have seen about the political economy of information and what we might therefore understand to be at stake in the policy choices that liberal democracies and advanced economies will be making in the coming years.

Chapter 11 The Battle Over the Institutional Ecology of the Digital Environment

The decade straddling the turn of the twenty-first century has seen high levels of legislative and policy activity in the domains of information and communications. Between 1995 and 1998, the United States completely overhauled its telecommunications law for the first time in sixty years, departed drastically from decades of practice on wireless regulation, revolutionized the scope and focus of trademark law, lengthened the term of copyright, criminalized individual user infringement, and created new paracopyright powers for rights holders that were so complex that the 1998 Digital Millennium Copyright Act (DMCA) that enacted them was longer than the entire Copyright Act. Europe covered similar ground on telecommunications, and added a new exclusive right in raw facts in databases. Both the United States and the European Union drove for internationalization of the norms they adopted, through the new World Intellectual Property Organization (WIPO) treaties and, more important, though the inclusion of intellectual property concerns in the international trade regime. In the seven years since then, legal battles have raged over the meaning of these changes, as well as over efforts to extend them in other directions. From telecommunications law to copyrights, from domain name assignment to trespass to server, we have seen a broad range of distinct regulatory moves surrounding the question of control over the basic resources needed to create, encode, transmit, and receive information, knowledge, and culture in the digital environment. As we telescope up from the details of sundry regulatory skirmishes, we begin to see a broad pattern of conflict over the way that access to these core resources will be controlled.

Much of the formal regulatory drive has been to increase the degree to which private, commercial parties can gain and assert exclusivity in core resources necessary for information production and exchange. At the physical layer, the shift to broadband Internet has been accompanied by less competitive pressure and greater legal freedom for providers to exclude competitors from, and shape the use of, their networks. That freedom from both legal and market constraints on exercising control has been complemented by increasing pressures from copyright industries to require that providers exercise greater control over the information flows in their networks in order to enforce copyrights. At the logical layer, anticircumvention provisions and the efforts to squelch peer-to-peer sharing have created institutional pressures on software and protocols to offer a more controlled and controllable environment. At the content layer, we have seen a steady series of institutional changes aimed at tightening exclusivity.

At each of these layers, however, we have also seen countervailing forces. At the physical layer, the Federal Communications Commission's (FCC's) move to permit the development of wireless devices capable of self-configuring as user-owned networks offers an important avenue for a commons-based last mile. The open standards used for personal computer design have provided an open platform. The concerted resistance against efforts to require computers to be designed so they can more reliably enforce copyrights against their users has, to this point, prevented extension of the DMCA approach to hardware design. At the logical layer, the continued centrality of open standard-setting processes and the emergence of free software as a primary modality of producing mission-critical software provide significant resistance to efforts to enclose the logical layer. At the content layer, where law has been perhaps most systematically one-sided in its efforts to enclose, the cultural movements and the technical affordances that form the foundation of the transformation described throughout this book stand as the most significant barrier to enclosure.

It is difficult to tell how much is really at stake, from the long-term perspective, in all these legal battles. From one point of view, law would have to achieve a great deal in order to replicate the twentieth-century model of industrial information economy in the new technical-social context. It would have to curtail some of the most fundamental technical characteristics of computer networks and extinguish some of our most fundamental human motivations and practices of sharing and cooperation. It would have to shift the market away from developing ever-cheaper general-purpose computers whose value to users is precisely their on-the-fly configurability over time, toward more controllable and predictable devices. It would have to squelch the emerging technologies in wireless, storage, and computation that are permitting users to share their excess resources ever more efficiently. It would have to dampen the influence of free software, and prevent people, young and old, from doing the age-old human thing: saying to each other, "here, why don't you take this, you'll like it," with things they can trivially part with and share socially. It is far from obvious that law can, in fact, achieve such basic changes. From another viewpoint, there may be no need to completely squelch all these things. Lessig called this the principle of bovinity: a small number of rules, consistently applied, suffice to control a herd of large animals. There is no need to assure that all people in all contexts continue to behave as couch potatoes for the true scope of the networked information economy to be constrained. It is enough that the core enabling technologies and the core cultural practices are confined to small groups—some teenagers, some countercultural activists. There have been places like the East Village or the Left Bank throughout the period of the industrial information economy. For the gains in autonomy, democracy, justice, and a critical culture that are described in part II to materialize, the practices of nonmarket information production, individually free creation, and cooperative peer production must become more than fringe practices. They must become a part of life for substantial portions of the networked population. The battle over the institutional ecology of the digitally networked environment is waged precisely over how many individual users will continue to participate in making the networked information environment, and how much of the population of consumers will continue to sit on the couch and passively receive the finished goods of industrial information producers.

INSTITUTIONAL ECOLOGY AND
PATH DEPENDENCE

The century-old pragmatist turn in American legal thought has led to the development of a large and rich literature about the relationship of law to society and economy. It has both Right and Left versions, and has disciplinary roots in history, economics, sociology, psychology, and critical theory. Explanations are many: some simple, some complex; some analytically tractable, many not. I do not make a substantive contribution to that debate here, but rather build on some of its strains to suggest that the process is complex, and particularly, that the relationship of law to social relations is one of punctuated equilibrium—there are periods of stability followed by periods of upheaval, and then adaptation and stabilization anew, until the next cycle. Hopefully, the preceding ten chapters have provided sufficient reason to think that we are going through a moment of social-economic transformation today, rooted in a technological shock to our basic modes of information, knowledge, and cultural production. Most of this chapter offers a sufficient description of the legislative and judicial battles of the past few years to make the case that we are in the midst of a significant perturbation of some sort. I suggest that the heightened activity is, in fact, a battle, in the domain of law and policy, over the shape of the social settlement that will emerge around the digital computation and communications revolution.

The basic claim is made up of fairly simple components. First, law affects human behavior on a micromotivational level and on a macro-social-organizational level. This is in contradistinction to, on the one hand, the classical Marxist claim that law is epiphenomenal, and, on the other hand, the increasingly rare simple economic models that ignore transaction costs and institutional barriers and simply assume that people will act in order to maximize their welfare, irrespective of institutional arrangements. Second, the causal relationship between law and human behavior is complex. Simple deterministic models of the form "if law X, then behavior Y" have been used as assumptions, but these are widely understood as, and criticized for being, oversimplifications for methodological purposes. Laws do affect human behavior by changing the payoffs to regulated actions directly. However, they also shape social norms with regard to behaviors, psychological attitudes toward various behaviors, the cultural understanding of actions, and the politics of claims about behaviors and practices. These effects are not all linearly additive. Some push back and nullify the law, some amplify its effects; it is not always predictable which of these any legal change will be. Decreasing the length of a "Walk" signal to assure that pedestrians are not hit by cars may trigger wider adoption of jaywalking as a norm, affecting ultimate behavior in exactly the opposite direction of what was intended. This change may, in turn, affect enforcement regarding jaywalking, or the length of the signals set for cars, because the risks involved in different signal lengths change as actual expected behavior changes, which again may feed back on driving and walking practices. Third, and as part of the complexity of the causal relation, the effects of law differ in different material, social, and cultural contexts. The same law introduced in different societies or at different times will have different effects. It may enable and disable a different set of practices, and trigger a different cascade of feedback and countereffects. This is because human beings are diverse in their motivational structure and their cultural frames of meaning for behavior, for law, or for outcomes. Fourth, the process of lawmaking is not exogenous to the effects of law on social relations and human behavior. One can look at positive political theory or at the history of social movements to see that the shape of law itself is contested in society because it makes (through its complex causal mechanisms) some behaviors less attractive, valuable, or permissible, and others more so. The "winners" and the "losers" battle each other to tweak the institutional playing field to fit their needs. As a consequence of these, there is relatively widespread acceptance that there is path dependence in institutions and social organization. That is, the actual organization of human affairs and legal systems is not converging through a process of either Marxist determinism or its neoclassical economics mirror image, "the most efficient institutions win out in the end." Different societies will differ in initial conditions and their historically contingent first moves in response to similar perturbations, and variances will emerge in their actual practices and institutional arrangements that persist over time—irrespective of their relative inefficiency or injustice.

The term "institutional ecology" refers to this context-dependent, causally complex, feedback-ridden, path-dependent process. An example of this interaction in the area of communications practices is the description in chapter 6 of how the introduction of radio was received and embedded in different legal and economic systems early in the twentieth century. A series of organizational and institutional choices converged in all nations on a broadcast model, but the American broadcast model, the BBC model, and the state-run monopoly radio models created very different journalistic styles, consumption expectations and styles, and funding mechanisms in these various systems. These differences, rooted in a series of choices made during a short period in the 1920s, persisted for decades in each of the respective systems. Paul Starr has argued in *The Creation of the Media* that basic institutional choices—from postage pricing to freedom of the press—interacted with cultural practices and political culture to underwrite substantial differences in the print media of the United States, Britain, and much of the European continent in the late eighteenth and throughout much of the nineteenth centuries.[1] Again, the basic institutional and cultural practices were put in place around the time of the American Revolution, and were later overlaid with the introduction of mass-circulation presses and the telegraph in the mid-1800s. Ithiel de Sola Pool's *Technologies of Freedom* describes the battle between newspapers and telegraph operators in the United States and Britain over control of telegraphed news flows. In Britain, this resulted in the nationalization of telegraph and the continued dominance of London and *The Times*. In the United States, it resolved into the pooling model of the Associated Press, based on private lines for news delivery and sharing— the prototype for newspaper chains and later network-television models of mass media.[2] The possibility of multiple stable equilibria alongside each other evoked by the stories of radio and print media is a common characteristic to both ecological models and analytically tractable models of path dependency. Both methodological approaches depend on feedback effects and therefore suggest that for any given path divergence, there is a point in time where early actions that trigger feedbacks can cause large and sustained differences over time.

Systems that exhibit path dependencies are characterized by periods of relative pliability followed by periods of relative stability. Institutions and social practices coevolve through a series of adaptations—feedback effects from the institutional system to social, cultural, and psychological frameworks; responses into the institutional system; and success and failure of various behavioral patterns and belief systems—until a society reaches a stage of relative stability. It can then be shaken out of that stability by external shocks—like Admiral Perry's arrival in Japan—or internal buildup of pressure to a point of phase transition, as in the case of slavery in the United States. Of course, not all shocks can so neatly be categorized as external or internal—as in the case of the Depression and the New Deal. To say that there are periods of stability is not to say that in such periods, everything is just dandy for everyone. It is only to say that the political, social, economic settlement is too widely comfortable for, accepted or acquiesced in, by too many agents who in that society have the power to change practices for institutional change to have substantial effects on the range of lived human practices.

The first two parts of this book explained why the introduction of digital computer-communications networks presents a perturbation of transformative potential for the basic model of information production and exchange in modern complex societies. They focused on the technological, economic, and social patterns that are emerging, and how they differ from the industrial information economy that preceded them. This chapter offers a fairly detailed map of how law and policy are being tugged and pulled in response to these changes. Digital computers and networked communications as a broad category will not be rolled back by these laws. Instead, we are seeing a battle—often but not always self-conscious—over the precise shape of these technologies. More important, we are observing a series of efforts to shape the social and economic practices as they develop to take advantage of these new technologies.

A FRAMEWORK FOR MAPPING THE INSTITUTIONAL ECOLOGY

Two specific examples will illustrate the various levels at which law can operate to shape the use of information and its production and exchange. The first example builds on the story from chapter 7 of how embarrassing internal e-mails from Diebold, the electronic voting machine maker, were exposed by investigative journalism conducted on a nonmarket and peer-production model. After students at Swarthmore College posted the files, Diebold made a demand under the DMCA that the college remove the materials or face suit for contributory copyright infringement. The students were therefore forced to remove the materials. However, in order keep the materials available, the students asked students at other institutions to mirror the files, and injected them into the eDonkey, BitTorrent, and FreeNet file-sharing and publication networks. Ultimately, a court held that the unauthorized publication of files that were not intended for sale and carried such high public value was a fair use. This meant that the underlying publication of the files was not itself a violation, and therefore the Internet service provider was not liable for providing a conduit. However, the case was decided on September 30, 2004—long after the information would have been relevant to the voting equipment certification process in California. What kept the information available for public review was not the ultimate vindication of the students' publication. It was the fact that the materials were kept in the public sphere even under threat of litigation. Recall also that at least some of the earlier set of Diebold files that were uncovered by the activist who had started the whole process in early 2003 were zipped, or perhaps encrypted in some form. Scoop, the Web site that published the revelation of the initial files, published—along with its challenge to the Internet community to scour the files and find holes in the system—links to locations in which utilities necessary for reading the files could be found.

There are four primary potential points of failure in this story that could have conspired to prevent the revelation of the Diebold files, or at least to suppress the peer-produced journalistic mode that made them available. First, if the service provider—the college, in this case—had been a sole provider with no alternative physical transmission systems, its decision to block the materials under threat of suit would have prevented publication of the materials throughout the relevant period. Second, the existence of peer-to-peer networks that overlay the physical networks and were used to distribute the materials made expunging them from the Internet practically impossible. There was no single point of storage that could be locked down. This made the prospect of threatening other universities futile. Third, those of the original files that were not in plain text were readable with software utilities that were freely available on the Internet, and to which Scoop pointed its readers. This made the files readable to many more critical eyes than they otherwise would have been. Fourth, and finally, the fact that access to the raw materials—the e-mails—was ultimately found to be privileged under the fair-use doctrine in copyright law allowed all the acts that had been performed in the preceding period under a shadow of legal liability to proceed in the light of legality.

The second example does not involve litigation, but highlights more of the levers open to legal manipulation. In the weeks preceding the American-led invasion of Iraq, a Swedish video artist produced an audio version of Diana Ross and Lionel Richie's love ballad, "Endless Love," lip-synched to news footage of U.S. president George Bush and British prime minister Tony Blair. By carefully synchronizing the lip movements from the various news clips, the video produced the effect of Bush "singing" Richie's part, and Blair "singing" Ross's, serenading each other with an eternal love ballad. No legal action with regard to the release of this short video has been reported. However, the story adds two components not available in the context of the Diebold files context. First, it highlights that quotation from video and music requires actual copying of the digital file. Unlike text, you cannot simply transcribe the images or the sound. This means that access to the unencrypted bits is more important than in the case of text. Second, it is not at all clear that using the entire song, unmodified, is a "fair use." While it is true that the Swedish video is unlikely to cut into the market for the original song, there is nothing in the video that is a parody either of the song itself or of the news footage. The video uses "found materials," that is, materials produced by others, to mix them in a way that is surprising, creative, and creates a genuinely new statement. However, its use of the song is much more complete than the minimalist uses of digital sampling in recorded music, where using a mere two-second, three-note riff from another's song has been found to be a violation unless done with a negotiated license.[3]

Combined, the two stories suggest that we can map the resources necessary for a creative communication, whether produced on a market model or a nonmarket model, as including a number of discrete elements. First, there is the universe of "content" itself: existing information, cultural artifacts and communications, and knowledge structures. These include the song and video footage, or the e-mail files, in the two stories. Second, there is the cluster of machinery that goes into capturing, manipulating, fixing and communicating the new cultural utterances or communications made of these inputs, mixed with the creativity, knowledge, information, or communications capacities of the creator of the new statement or communication. These include the physical devices—the computers used by the students and the video artist, as well as by their readers or viewers—and the physical transmission mechanisms used to send the information or communications from one place to another. In the Diebold case, the firm tried to use the Internet service provider liability regime of the DMCA to cut off the machine storage and mechanical communications capacity provided to the students by the university. However, the "machinery" also includes the logical components— the software necessary to capture, read or listen to, cut, paste, and remake the texts or music; the software and protocols necessary to store, retrieve, search, and communicate the information across the Internet.

As these stories suggest, freedom to create and communicate requires use of diverse things and relationships—mechanical devices and protocols, information, cultural materials, and so forth. Because of this diversity of components and relationships, the institutional ecology of information production and exchange is a complex one. It includes regulatory and policy elements that affect different industries, draw on various legal doctrines and traditions, and rely on diverse economic and political theories and practices. It includes social norms of sharing and consumption of things conceived of as quite different—bandwidth, computers, and entertainment materials. To make these cohere into a single problem, for several years I have been using a very simple, three-layered representation of the basic functions involved in mediated human communications. These are intended to map how different institutional components interact to affect the answer to the basic questions that define the normative characteristics of a communications system—who gets to say what, to whom, and who decides?[4]

These are the physical, logical, and content layers. The physical layer refers to the material things used to connect human beings to each other. These include the computers, phones, handhelds, wires, wireless links, and the like. The content layer is the set of humanly meaningful statements that human beings utter to and with one another. It includes both the actual utterances and the mechanisms, to the extent that they are based on human communication rather than mechanical processing, for filtering, accreditation, and interpretation. The logical layer represents the algorithms, standards, ways of translating human meaning into something that machines can transmit, store, or compute, and something that machines process into communications meaningful to human beings. These include standards, protocols, and software—both general enabling platforms like operating systems, and more specific applications. A mediated human communication must use all three layers, and each layer therefore represents a resource or a pathway that the communication must use or traverse in order to reach its intended destination. In each and every one of these layers, we have seen the emergence of technical and practical capabilities for using that layer on a nonproprietary model that would make access cheaper, less susceptible to control by any single party or class of parties, or both. In each and every layer, we have seen significant policy battles over whether these nonproprietary or open-platform practices will be facilitated or even permitted. Looking at the aggregate effect, we see that at all these layers, a series of battles is being fought over the degree to which some minimal set of basic resources and capabilities necessary to use and participate in constructing the information environment will be available for use on a nonproprietary, nonmarket basis.

In each layer, the policy debate is almost always carried out in local, specific terms. We ask questions like, Will this policy optimize "spectrum management" in these frequencies, or, Will this decrease the number of CDs sold? However, the basic, overarching question that we must learn to ask in all these debates is: Are we leaving enough institutional space for the social-economic practices of networked information production to emerge? The networked information economy requires access to a core set of capabilities—existing information and culture, mechanical means to process, store, and communicate new contributions and mixes, and the logical systems necessary to connect them to each other. What nonmarket forms of production need is a core common infrastructure that anyone can use, irrespective of whether their production model is market-based or not, proprietary or not. In almost all these dimensions, the current trajectory of technological-economic-social trends is indeed leading to the emergence of such a core common infrastructure, and the practices that make up the networked information economy are taking advantage of open resources. Wireless equipment manufacturers are producing devices that let users build their own networks, even if these are now at a primitive stage. The open-innovation ethos of the programmer and Internet engineering community produce both free software and proprietary software that rely on open standards for providing an open logical layer. The emerging practices of free sharing of information, knowledge, and culture that occupy most of the discussion in this book are producing an ever-growing stream of freely and openly accessible content resources. The core common infrastructure appears to be emerging without need for help from a guiding regulatory hand. This may or may not be a stable pattern. It is possible that by some happenstance one or two firms, using one or two critical technologies, will be able to capture and control a bottleneck. At that point, perhaps regulatory intervention will be required. However, from the beginning of legal responses to the Internet and up to this writing in the middle of 2005, the primary role of law has been reactive and reactionary. It has functioned as a point of resistance to the emergence of the networked information economy. It has been used by incumbents from the industrial information economies to contain the risks posed by the emerging capabilities of the networked information environment. What the emerging networked information economy therefore needs, in almost all cases, is not regulatory protection, but regulatory abstinence.

The remainder of this chapter provides a more or less detailed presentation of the decisions being made at each layer, and how they relate to the freedom to create, individually and with others, without having to go through proprietary, market-based transactional frameworks. Because so many components are involved, and so much has happened since the mid-1990s, the discussion is of necessity both long in the aggregate and truncated in each particular category. To overcome this expositional problem, I have collected the various institutional changes in table 11.1. For readers interested only in the overarching claim of this chapter—that is, that there is, in fact, a battle over the institutional environment, and that many present choices interact to increase or decrease the availability of basic resources for information production and exchange—table 11.1 may provide sufficient detail. For those interested in a case study of the complex relationship between law, technology, social behavior, and market structure, the discussion of peer-to-peer networks may be particularly interesting to pursue.

A quick look at table 11.1 reveals that there is a diverse set of sources of openness. A few of these are legal. Mostly, they are based on technological and social practices, including resistance to legal and regulatory drives toward enclosure. Examples of policy interventions that support an open core common infrastructure are the FCC's increased permission to deploy open wireless networks and the various municipal broadband initiatives. The former is a regulatory intervention, but its form is largely removal of past prohibitions on an entire engineering approach to building wireless systems. Municipal efforts to produce open broadband networks are being resisted at the state legislation level, with statutes that remove the power to provision broadband from the home rule powers of municipalities. For the most part, the drive for openness is based on individual and voluntary cooperative action, not law. The social practices of openness take on a quasi-normative face when practiced in standard-setting bodies like the Internet Engineering Task Force (IETF) or the World Wide Web Consortium (W3C). However, none of these have the force of law. Legal devices also support openness when used in voluntaristic models like free software licensing and Creative Commons–type licensing. However, most often when law has intervened in its regulatory force, as opposed to its contractual-enablement force, it has done so almost entirely on the side of proprietary enclosure.

Another characteristic of the social-economic-institutional struggle is an alliance between a large number of commercial actors and the social sharing culture. We see this in the way that wireless equipment manufacturers are selling into a market of users of WiFi and similar unlicensed wireless devices. We see this in the way that personal computer manufacturers are competing

Table 11.1: Overview of the Institutional Ecology

	Enclosure	Openness
Physical Transport	• Broadband treated by FCC as information service • DMCA ISP liability • Municipal broadband barred by states	• Open wireless networks • Municipal broadband initiatives
Physical Devices	• CBDPTA: regulatory requirements to implement "trusted systems"; private efforts toward the same goal • Operator-controlled mobile phones	• Standardization • Fiercely competitive market in commodity components
Logical Transmission protocols	Privatized DNS/ICANN	• TCP/IP • IETF • p2p networks
Logical Software	DMCA anticircumvention; Proprietary OS; Web browser Software patents	• Free software • W3C • P2p software widely used • social acceptability of widespread hacking of copy protection

Content	• Copyright expansion
	  • "Right to read"
	  • No de minimis digital sampling
	  • "Fair use" narrowed: effect on potential market "commercial" defined broadly
	  • Criminalization
	  • Term extension
	• Contractual enclosure: UCITA
	• Trademark dilution
	• Database protection
	• Linking and trespass to chattels
	• International "harmonization" and trade enforcement of maximal exclusive rights regimes
		• Increasing sharing practices and adoption of sharing licensing practices
		• Musicians distribute music freely
		• Creative Commons; other open publication models
		• Widespread social disdain for copyright
		• International jurisdictional arbitrage
		• Early signs of a global access to knowledge movement combining developing nations with free information ecology advocates, both market and nonmarket, raising a challenge to the enclosure movement

over decreasing margins by producing the most general-purpose machines that would be most flexible for their users, rather than machines that would most effectively implement the interests of Hollywood and the recording industry. We see this in the way that service and equipment-based firms, like IBM and Hewlett-Packard (HP), support open-source and free software. The alliance between the diffuse users and the companies that are adapting their business models to serve them as users, instead of as passive consumers, affects the political economy of this institutional battle in favor of openness. On the other hand, security consciousness in the United States has led to some efforts to tip the balance in favor of closed proprietary systems, apparently because these are currently perceived as more secure, or at least more amenable to government control. While orthogonal in its political origins to the battle between proprietary and commons-based strategies for information production, this drive does tilt the field in favor of enclosure, at least at the time of this writing in 2005.

Over the past few years, we have also seen that the global character of the Internet is a major limit on effective enclosure, when openness is a function of technical and social practices, and enclosure is a function of law.[5] When Napster was shut down in the United States, for example, KaZaa emerged in the Netherlands, from where it later moved to Australia. This force is meeting the countervailing force of international harmonization—a series of bilateral and multilateral efforts to "harmonize" exclusive rights regimes internationally and efforts to coordinate international enforcement. It is difficult at this stage to predict which of these forces will ultimately have the upper hand. It is not too early to map in which direction each is pushing. And it is therefore not too early to characterize the normative implications of the success or failure of these institutional efforts.

THE PHYSICAL LAYER

The physical layer encompasses both transmission channels and devices for producing and communicating information. In the broadcast and telephone era, devices were starkly differentiated. Consumers owned dumb terminals. Providers owned sophisticated networks and equipment: transmitters and switches. Consumers could therefore consume whatever providers could produce most efficiently that the providers believed consumers would pay for. Central to the emergence of the freedom of users in the networked environment is an erosion of the differentiation between consumer and provider equipment. Consumers came to use general-purpose computers that could do whatever their owners wanted, instead of special-purpose terminals that could only do what their vendors designed them to do. These devices were initially connected over a transmission network—the public phone system— that was regulated as a common carrier. Common carriage required the network owners to carry all communications without differentiating by type or content. The network was neutral as among communications. The transition to broadband networks, and to a lesser extent the emergence of Internet services on mobile phones, are threatening to undermine that neutrality and nudge the network away from its end-to-end, user-centric model to one designed more like a five-thousand-channel broadcast model. At the same time, Hollywood and the recording industry are pressuring the U.S. Congress to impose regulatory requirements on the design of personal computers so that they can be relied on not to copy music and movies without permission. In the process, the law seeks to nudge personal computers away from being purely general-purpose computation devices toward being devices with factory-defined behaviors vis-à-vis predicted-use patterns, like glorified televisions and CD players. The emergence of the networked information economy as described in this book depends on the continued existence of an open transport network connecting general-purpose computers. It therefore also depends on the failure of the efforts to restructure the network on the model of proprietary networks connecting terminals with sufficiently controlled capabilities to be predictable and well behaved from the perspective of incumbent production models.

Transport: Wires and Wireless

Recall the Cisco white paper quoted in chapter 5. In it, Cisco touted the value of its then new router, which would allow a broadband provider to differentiate streams of information going to and from the home at the packet level. If the packet came from a competitor, or someone the user wanted to see or hear but the owner preferred that the user did not, the packet could be slowed down or dropped. If it came from the owner or an affiliate, it could be speeded up. The purpose of the router was not to enable evil control over users. It was to provide better-functioning networks. America Online (AOL), for example, has been reported as blocking its users from reaching Web sites that have been advertised in spam e-mails. The theory is that if spammers know their Web site will be inaccessible to AOL customers, they will stop.[6] The ability of service providers to block sites or packets from certain senders and promote packets from others may indeed be used to improve the network. However, whether this ability will in fact be used to improve service depends on the extent to which the interests of all users, and particularly those concerned with productive uses of the network, are aligned with the interests of the service providers. Clearly, when in 2005 Telus, Canada's second largest telecommunications company, blocked access to the Web site of the Telecommunications Workers Union for all of its own clients and those of internet service providers that relied on its backbone network, it was not seeking to improve service for those customers' benefit, but to control a conversation in which it had an intense interest. When there is a misalignment, the question is what, if anything, disciplines the service providers' use of the technological capabilities they possess? One source of discipline would be a genuinely competitive market. The transition to broadband has, however, severely constrained the degree of competition in Internet access services. Another would be regulation: requiring owners to treat all packets equally. This solution, while simple to describe, remains highly controversial in the policy world. It has strong supporters and strong opposition from the incumbent broadband providers, and has, as a practical matter, been rejected for the time being by the FCC. The third type of solution would be both more radical and less "interventionist" from the perspective of regulation. It would involve eliminating contemporary regulatory barriers to the emergence of a user-owned wireless infrastructure. It would allow users to deploy their own equipment, share their wireless capacity, and create a "last mile" owned by all users in common, and controlled by none. This would, in effect, put equipment manufacturers in competition to construct the "last mile" of broadband networks, and thereby open up the market in "middle-mile" Internet connection services.

Since the early 1990s, when the Clinton administration announced its "Agenda for Action" for what was then called "the information superhighway," it was the policy of the United States to "let the private sector lead" in deployment of the Internet. To a greater or lesser degree, this commitment to private provisioning was adopted in most other advanced economies in the world. In the first few years, this meant that investment in the backbone of the Internet was private, and heavily funded by the stock bubble of the late 1990s. It also meant that the last distribution bottleneck—the "last mile"—was privately owned. Until the end of the 1990s, the last mile was made mostly of dial-up connections over the copper wires of the incumbent local exchange carriers. This meant that the physical layer was not only proprietary, but that it was, for all practical purposes, monopolistically owned. Why, then, did the early Internet nonetheless develop into a robust, end-to-end neutral network? As Lessig showed, this was because the telephone carriers were regulated as common carriers. They were required to carry all traffic without discrimination. Whether a bit stream came from Cable News Network (CNN) or from an individual blog, all streams— upstream from the user and downstream to the user—were treated neutrally.

BROADBAND REGULATION

The end of the 1990s saw the emergence of broadband networks. In the United States, cable systems, using hybrid fiber-coaxial systems, moved first, and became the primary providers. The incumbent local telephone carriers have been playing catch-up ever since, using digital subscriber line (DSL) techniques to squeeze sufficient speed out of their copper infrastructure to remain competitive, while slowly rolling out fiber infrastructure closer to the home. As of 2003, the incumbent cable carriers and the incumbent local telephone companies accounted for roughly 96 percent of all broadband access to homes and small offices.[7] In 1999–2000, as cable was beginning to move into a more prominent position, academic critique began to emerge, stating that the cable broadband architecture could be manipulated to deviate from the neutral, end-to-end architecture of the Internet. One such paper was written by Jerome Saltzer, one of the authors of the paper that originally defined the "end-to-end" design principle of the Internet in 1980, and Lessig and Mark Lemley wrote another. These papers began to emphasize that cable broadband providers technically could, and had commercial incentive to, stop treating all communications neutrally. They could begin to move from a network where almost all functions are performed by user-owned computers at the ends of the network to one where more is done by provider equipment at the core. The introduction of the Cisco policy router was seen as a stark marker of how things could change.

The following two years saw significant regulatory battles over whether the cable providers would be required to behave as commons carriers. In particular, the question was whether they would be required to offer competitors nondiscriminatory access to their networks, so that these competitors could compete in Internet services. The theory was that competition would discipline the incumbents from skewing their networks too far away from what users valued as an open Internet. The first round of battles occurred at the municipal level. Local franchising authorities tried to use their power over cable licenses to require cable operators to offer open access to their competitors if they chose to offer cable broadband. The cable providers challenged these regulations in courts. The most prominent decision came out of Portland, Oregon, where the Federal Court of Appeals for the Ninth Circuit held that broadband was part information service and part telecommunications service, but not a cable service. The FCC, not the cable franchising authority, had power to regulate it.[8] At the same time, as part of the approval of the AOL–Time Warner merger, the Federal Trade Commission (FTC) required the new company to give at least three competitors open access to its broadband facilities, should AOL be offered cable broadband facilities over Time Warner.

The AOL–Time Warner merger requirements, along with the Ninth Circuit's finding that cable broadband included a telecommunications component, seemed to indicate that cable broadband transport would come to be treated as a common carrier. This was not to be. In late 2001 and the middle of 2002, the FCC issued a series of reports that would reach the exact opposite result. Cable broadband, the commission held, was an information service, not a telecommunications service. This created an imbalance with the telecommunications status of broadband over telephone infrastructure, which at the time was treated as a telecommunications service. The commission dealt with this imbalance by holding that broadband over telephone infrastructure, like broadband over cable, was now to be treated as an information service. Adopting this definition was perhaps admissible as a matter of legal reasoning, but it certainly was not required by either sound legal reasoning or policy. The FCC's reasoning effectively took the business model that cable operators had successfully used to capture two-thirds of the market in broadband—bundling two discrete functionalities, transport (carrying bits) and higher-level services (like e-mail and Web hosting)—and treated it as though it described the intrinsic nature of "broadband cable" as a service. Because that service included more than just carriage of bits, it could be called an information service. Of course, it would have been as legally admissible, and more technically accurate, to do as the Ninth Circuit had done. That is, to say that cable broadband bundles two distinct services: carriage and information-use tools. The former is a telecommunications service. In June of 2005, the Supreme Court in the *Brand X* case upheld the FCC's authority to make this legally admissible policy error, upholding as a matter of deference to the expert agency the Commission's position that cable broadband services should be treated as information services.[9] As a matter of policy, the designation of broadband services as "information services" more or less locked the FCC into a "no regulation" approach. As information services, broadband providers obtained the legal power to "edit" their programming, just like any operator of an information service, like a Web site. Indeed, this new designation has placed a serious question mark over whether future efforts to regulate carriage decisions would be considered constitutional, or would instead be treated as violations of the carriers' "free speech" rights as a provider of information. Over the course of the 1990s, there were a number of instances where carriers—particularly cable, but also telephone companies—were required by law to carry some signals from competitors. In particular, cable providers were required to carry over-the-air broadcast television, telephone carriers, in FCC rules called "video dialtone," were required to offer video on a common carriage basis, and cable providers that chose to offer broadband were required to make their infrastructure available to competitors on a common carrier model. In each of these cases, the carriage requirements were subjected to First Amendment scrutiny by courts. In the case of cable carriage of broadcast television, the carriage requirements were only upheld after six years of litigation.[10] In cases involving video common carriage requirements applied to telephone companies and cable broadband, lower courts struck down the carriage requirements as violating the telephone and cable companies' free-speech rights.[11] To a large extent, then, the FCC's regulatory definition left the incumbent cable and telephone providers—who control 96 percent of broadband connections to home and small offices—unregulated, and potentially constitutionally immune to access regulation and carriage requirements.

Since 2003 the cable access debate—over whether competitors should get access to the transport networks of incumbent broadband carriers—has been replaced with an effort to seek behavioral regulation in the form of "network neutrality." This regulatory concept would require broadband providers to treat all packets equally, without forcing them to open their network up to competitors or impose any other of the commitments associated with common carriage. The concept has the backing of some very powerful actors, including Microsoft, and more recently MCI, which still owns much of the Internet backbone, though not the last mile. For this reason, if for no other, it remains as of this writing a viable path for institutional reform that would balance the basic structural shift of Internet infrastructure from a common-carriage to a privately controlled model. Even if successful, the drive to network neutrality would keep the physical infrastructure a technical bottleneck, owned by a small number of firms facing very limited competition, with wide legal latitude for using that control to affect the flow of information over their networks.

OPEN WIRELESS NETWORKS

A more basic and structural opportunity to create an open broadband infrastructure is, however, emerging in the wireless domain. To see how, we must first recognize that opportunities to control the broadband infrastructure in general are not evenly distributed throughout the networked infrastructure. The long-haul portions of the network have multiple redundant paths with no clear choke points. The primary choke point over the physical transport of bits across the Internet is in the last mile of all but the most highly connected districts. That is, the primary bottleneck is the wire or cable connecting the home and small office to the network. It is here that cable and local telephone incumbents control the market. It is here that the high costs of digging trenches, pulling fiber, and getting wires through and into walls pose a prohibitive barrier to competition. And it is here, in the last mile, that unlicensed wireless approaches now offer the greatest promise to deliver a common physical infrastructure of first and last resort, owned by its users, shared as a commons, and offering no entity a bottleneck from which to control who gets to say what to whom.

As discussed in chapter 6, from the end of World War I and through the mid-twenties, improvements in the capacity of expensive transmitters and a series of strategic moves by the owners of the core patents in radio transmission led to the emergence of the industrial model of radio communications that typified the twentieth century. Radio came to be dominated by a small number of professional, commercial networks, based on high-capital-cost transmitters. These were supported by a regulatory framework tailored to making the primary model of radio utilization for most Americans passive reception, with simple receivers, of commercial programming delivered with high-powered transmitters. This industrial model, which assumed large-scale capital investment in the core of the network and small-scale investments at the edges, optimized for receiving what is generated at the core, imprinted on wireless communications systems both at the level of design and at the level of regulation. When mobile telephony came along, it replicated the same model, using relatively cheap handsets oriented toward an infrastructure-centric deployment of towers. The regulatory model followed Hoover's initial pattern and perfected it. A government agency strictly controlled who may place a transmitter, where, with what antenna height, and using what power. The justification was avoidance of interference. The presence of strict licensing was used as the basic assumption in the engineering of wireless systems throughout this period. Since 1959, economic analysis of wireless regulation has criticized this approach, but only on the basis that it inefficiently regulated the legal right to construct a wireless system by using strictly regulated spectrum licenses, instead of creating a market in "spectrum use" rights.[12] This critique kept the basic engineering assumptions stable—for radio to be useful, a high-powered transmitter must be received by simple receivers. Given this engineering assumption, someone had to control the right to emit energy in any range of radio frequencies. The economists wanted the controller to be a property owner with a flexible, transferable right. The regulators wanted it to be a licensee subject to regulatory oversight and approval by the FCC.

As chapter 3 explained, by the time that legislatures in the United States and around the world had begun to accede to the wisdom of the economists' critique, it had been rendered obsolete by technology. In particular, it had been rendered obsolete by the fact that the declining cost of computation and the increasing sophistication of communications protocols among end-user devices in a network made possible new, sharing-based solutions to the problem of how to allow users to communicate without wires. Instead of having a regulation-determined exclusive right to transmit, which may or may not be subject to market reallocation, it is possible to have a market in smart radio equipment owned by individuals. These devices have the technical ability to share capacity and cooperate in the creation of wireless carriage capacity. These radios can, for example, cooperate by relaying each other's messages or temporarily "lending" their antennae to neighbors to help them decipher messages of senders, without anyone having exclusive use of the spectrum. Just as PCs can cooperate to create a supercomputer in SETI@Home by sharing their computation, and a global-scale, peer-to-peer data-storage and retrieval system by sharing their hard drives, computationally intensive radios can share their capacity to produce a local wireless broadband infrastructure. Open wireless networks allow users to install their own wireless device—much like the WiFi devices that have become popular. These devices then search automatically for neighbors with similar capabilities, and self-configure into a high-speed wireless data network. Reaching this goal does not, at this point, require significant technological innovation. The technology is there, though it does require substantial engineering effort to implement. The economic incentives to develop such devices are fairly straightforward. Users already require wireless local networks. They will gain added utility from extending their range for themselves, which would be coupled with the possibility of sharing with others to provide significant wide-area network capacity for whose availability they need not rely on any particular provider. Ultimately, it would be a way for users to circumvent the monopoly last mile and recapture some of the rents they currently pay. Equipment manufacturers obviously have an incentive to try to cut into the rents captured by the broadband monopoly/oligopoly by offering an equipment-embedded alternative.

My point here is not to consider the comparative efficiency of a market in wireless licenses and a market in end-user equipment designed for sharing channels that no one owns. It is to highlight the implications of the emergence of a last mile that is owned by no one in particular, and is the product of cooperation among neighbors in the form of, "I'll carry your bits if you carry mine." At the simplest level, neighbors could access locally relevant information directly, over a wide-area network. More significant, the fact that users in a locality coproduced their own last-mile infrastructure would allow commercial Internet providers to set up Internet points of presence anywhere within the "cloud" of the locale. The last mile would be provided not by these competing Internet service providers, but by the cooperative efforts of the residents of local neighborhoods. Competitors in providing the "middle mile"—the connection from the last mile to the Internet cloud— could emerge, in a way that they cannot if they must first lay their own last mile all the way to each home. The users, rather than the middle-mile providers, shall have paid the capital cost of producing the local transmission system—their own cooperative radios. The presence of a commons-based, coproduced last mile alongside the proprietary broadband network eliminates the last mile as a bottleneck for control over who speaks, with what degree of ease, and with what types of production values and interactivity.

The development of open wireless networks, owned by their users and focused on sophisticated general-purpose devices at their edges also offers a counterpoint to the emerging trend among mobile telephony providers to offer a relatively limited and controlled version of the Internet over the phones they sell. Some wireless providers are simply offering mobile Internet connections throughout their networks, for laptops. Others, however, are using their networks to allow customers to use their ever-more-sophisticated phones to surf portions of the Web. These latter services diverge in their styles. Some tend to be limited, offering only a set of affiliated Web sites rather than genuine connectivity to the Internet itself with a general-purpose device. Sprint's "News" offerings, for example, connects users to CNNtoGo, ABCNews.com, and the like, but will not enable a user to reach the blogosphere to upload a photo of protesters being manhandled, for example. So while mobility in principle increases the power of the Web, and text messaging puts e-mail-like capabilities everywhere, the effect of the implementations of the Web on phones is more ambiguous. It could be more like a Web-enabled reception device than a genuinely active node in a multidirectional network. Widespread adoption of open wireless networks would give mobile phone manufacturers a new option. They could build into the mobile telephones the ability to tap into open wireless networks, and use them as general-purpose access points to the Internet. The extent to which this will be a viable option for the mobile telephone manufacturers depends on how much the incumbent mobile telephone service providers, those who purchased their licenses at high-priced auctions, will resist this move. Most users buy their phones from their providers, not from general electronic equipment stores. Phones are often tied to specific providers in ways that users are not able to change for themselves. In these conditions, it is likely that mobile providers will resist the competition from free open wireless systems for "data minutes" by refusing to sell dual-purpose equipment. Worse, they may boycott manufacturers who make mobile phones that are also general-purpose Web-surfing devices over open wireless networks. How that conflict will go, and whether users would be willing to carry a separate small device to enable them to have open Internet access alongside their mobile phone, will determine the extent to which the benefits of open wireless networks will be transposed into the mobile domain. Normatively, that outcome has significant implications. From the perspective of the citizen watchdog function, ubiquitous availability of capture, rendering, and communication capabilities are important. From the perspective of personal autonomy as informed action in context, extending openness to mobile units would provide significant advantages to allow individuals to construct their own information environment on the go, as they are confronting decisions and points of action in their daily lives.

MUNICIPAL BROADBAND INITIATIVES

One alternative path for the emergence of basic physical information transport infrastructure on a nonmarket model is the drive to establish municipal systems. These proposed systems would not be commons-based in the sense that they would not be created by the cooperative actions of individuals without formal structure. They would be public, like highways, sidewalks, parks, and sewage systems. Whether they are, or are not, ultimately to perform as commons would depend on how they would be regulated. In the United States, given the First Amendment constraints on government preferring some speech to other speech in public fora, it is likely that municipal systems would be managed as commons. In this regard, they would have parallel beneficial characteristics to those of open wireless systems. The basic thesis underlying municipal broadband initiatives is similar to that which has led some municipalities to create municipal utilities or transportation hubs. Connectivity has strong positive externalities. It makes a city's residents more available for the information economy and the city itself a more attractive locale for businesses. Most of the efforts have indeed been phrased in these instrumental terms. The initial drive has been the creation of municipal fiber-to-the-home networks. The town of Bristol, Virginia, is an example. It has a population of slightly more than seventeen thousand. Median household income is 68 percent of the national median. These statistics made it an unattractive locus for early broadband rollout by incumbent providers. However, in 2003, Bristol residents had one of the most advanced residential fiber-to-the-home networks in the country, available for less than forty dollars a month. Unsurprisingly, therefore, the city had broadband penetration rivaling many of the top U.S. markets with denser and wealthier populations. The "miracle" of Bristol is that the residents of the town, fed up with waiting for the local telephone and cable companies, built their own, municipally owned network. Theirs has become among the most ambitious and successful of more than five hundred publicly owned utilities in the United States that offer high-speed Internet, cable, and telephone services to their residents. Some of the larger cities—Chicago and Philadelphia, most prominently—are moving as of this writing in a similar direction. The idea in Chicago is that basic "dark fiber"—that is, the physical fiber going to the home, but without the electronics that would determine what kinds of uses the connectivity could be put to—would be built by the city. Access to use this entirely neutral, high-capacity platform would then be open to anyone— commercial and noncommercial alike. The drive in Philadelphia emphasizes the other, more recently available avenue—wireless. The quality of WiFi and the widespread adoption of wireless techniques have moved other municipalities to adopt wireless or mixed-fiber wireless strategies. Municipalities are proposing to use publicly owned facilities to place wireless points of access around the town, covering the area in a cloud of connectivity and providing open Internet access from anywhere in the city. Philadelphia's initiative has received the widest public attention, although other, smaller cities are closer to having a wireless cloud over the city already.

The incumbent broadband providers have not taken kindly to the municipal assault on their monopoly (or oligopoly) profits. When the city of Abilene, Texas, tried to offer municipal broadband service in the late-1990s, Southwestern Bell (SBC) persuaded the Texas legislature to pass a law that prohibited local governments from providing high-speed Internet access. The town appealed to the FCC and the Federal Court of Appeals in Washington, D.C. Both bodies held that when Congress passed the 1996 Telecommunications Act, and said that, "no state . . . regulation . . . may prohibit . . . the ability of any entity to provide . . . telecommunications service," municipalities were not included in the term "any entity." As the D.C. Circuit put it, "any" might have some significance "depending on the speaker's tone of voice," but here it did not really mean "*any* entity," only some. And states could certainly regulate the actions of municipalities, which are treated in U.S. law as merely their subdivisions or organs.[13] Bristol, Virginia, had to fight off similar efforts to prohibit its plans through state law before it was able to roll out its network. In early 2004, the U.S. Supreme Court was presented with the practice of state preemption of municipal broadband efforts and chose to leave the municipalities to fend for themselves. A coalition of Missouri municipalities challenged a Missouri law that, like the Texas law, prohibited them from stepping in to offer their citizens broadband service. The Court of the Appeals for the Eighth Circuit agreed with the municipalities. The 1996 Act, after all, was intended precisely to allow anyone to compete with the incumbents. The section that prohibited states from regulating the ability of "any entity" to enter the telecommunications service market precisely anticipated that the local incumbents would use their clout in state legislatures to thwart the federal policy of introducing competition into the local loop. Here, the incumbents were doing just that, but the Supreme Court reversed the Eighth Circuit decision. Without dwelling too much on the wisdom of allowing citizens of municipalities to decide for themselves whether they want a municipal system, the court issued an opinion that was technically defensible in terms of statutory interpretation, but effectively invited the incumbent broadband providers to put their lobbying efforts into persuading state legislators to prohibit municipal efforts.[14] After

Philadelphia rolled out its wireless plan, it was not long before the Pennsylvania legislature passed a similar law prohibiting municipalities from offering broadband. While Philadelphia's plan itself was grandfathered, future expansion from a series of wireless "hot spots" in open area to a genuine municipal network will likely be challenged under the new state law. Other municipalities in Pennsylvania are entirely foreclosed from pursuing this option. In this domain, at least as of 2005, the incumbents seem to have had some substantial success in containing the emergence of municipal broadband networks as a significant approach to eliminating the bottleneck in local network infrastructure.

Devices

The second major component of the physical layer of the networked environment is comprised of the devices people use to compute and communicate. Personal computers, handhelds, game consoles, and to a lesser extent, but lurking in the background, televisions, are the primary relevant devices. In the United States, personal computers are the overwhelmingly dominant mode of connectivity. In Europe and Japan, mobile handheld devices occupy a much larger space. Game consoles are beginning to provide an alternative computationally intensive device, and Web-TV has been a background idea for a while. The increasing digitization of both over-the-air and cable broadcast makes digital TV a background presence, if not an immediate alternative avenue, to Internet communications. None of these devices are constructed by a commons—in the way that open wireless networks, free software, or peer-produced content can be. Personal computers, however, are built on open architecture, using highly standardized commodity components and open interfaces in an enormously competitive market. As a practical matter, therefore, PCs provide an open-platform device. Handhelds, game consoles, and digital televisions, on the other hand, use more or less proprietary architectures and interfaces and are produced in a less-competitive market— not because there is no competition among the manufacturers, but because the distribution chain, through the service providers, is relatively controlled. The result is that configurations and features can more readily be customized for personal computers. New uses can be developed and implemented in the hardware without permission from any owner of a manufacturing or distribution outlet. As handhelds grow in their capabilities, and personal computers collapse in size, the two modes of communicating are bumping into each other's turf. At the moment, there is no obvious regulatory push to nudge one or the other out. Observing the evolution of these markets therefore has less to do with policy. As we look at these markets, however, it is important to recognize that the outcome of this competition is not normatively neutral. The capabilities made possible by personal computers underlie much of the social and economic activity described throughout this book. Proprietary handhelds, and even more so, game consoles and televisions, are, presently at least, platforms that choreograph their use. They structure their users' capabilities according to design requirements set by their producers and distributors. A physical layer usable with general-purpose computers is one that is pliable and open for any number of uses by individuals, in a way that a physical layer used through more narrowly scripted devices is not.

The major regulatory threat to the openness of personal computers comes from efforts to regulate the use of copyrighted materials. This question is explored in greater depth in the context of discussing the logical layer. Here, I only note that peer-to-peer networks, and what Fisher has called "promiscuous copying" on the Internet, have created a perceived threat to the very existence of the major players in the industrial cultural production system—Hollywood and the recording industry. These industries are enormously adept at driving the regulation of their business environment—the laws of copyright, in particular. As the threat of copying and sharing of their content by users increased, these industries have maintained a steady pressure on Congress, the courts, and the executive to ratchet up the degree to which their rights are enforced. As we will see in looking at the logical and content layers, these efforts have been successful in changing the law and pushing for more aggressive enforcement. They have not, however, succeeded in suppressing widespread copying. Copying continues, if not entirely unabated, certainly at a rate that was impossible a mere six years ago.

One major dimension of the effort to stop copying has been a drive to regulate the design of personal computers. Pioneered by Senator Fritz Hollings in mid-2001, a number of bills were drafted and lobbied for: the first was the Security Systems Standards and Certification Act; the second, Consumer Broadband and Digital Television Promotion Act (CBDTPA), was actually introduced in the Senate in 2002.[15] The basic structure of these proposed statutes was that they required manufacturers to design their computers to be "trusted systems." The term "trusted," however, had a very odd meaning. The point is that the system, or computer, can be trusted to perform in certain predictable ways, irrespective of what its owner wishes.

The impulse is trivial to explain. If you believe that most users are using their personal computers to copy films and music illegally, then you can think of these users as untrustworthy. In order to be able to distribute films and music in the digital environment that is trustworthy, one must disable the users from behaving as they would choose to. The result is a range of efforts at producing what has derisively been called "the Fritz chip": legal mandates that systems be designed so that personal computers cannot run programs that are not certified properly to the chip. The most successful of these campaigns was Hollywood's achievement in persuading the FCC to require manufacturers of all devices capable of receiving digital television signals from the television set to comply with a particular "trusted system" standard. This "broadcast flag" regulation was odd in two distinct ways. First, the rule-making documents show quite clearly that this was a rule driven by Hollywood, not by the broadcasters. This is unusual because the industries that usually play a central role in these rule makings are those regulated by the FCC, such as broadcasters and cable systems. Second, the FCC was not, in fact, regulating the industries that it normally has jurisdiction to regulate. Instead, the rule applied to any device that could use digital television signals *after* they had already been received in the home. In other words, they were regulating practically every computer and digital-video-capable consumer electronics device imaginable. The Court of Appeals ultimately indeed struck down the regulation as wildly beyond the agency's jurisdiction, but the broadcast flag nonetheless is the closest that the industrial information economy incumbents have come to achieving regulatory control over the design of computers.

The efforts to regulate hardware to fit the distribution model of Hollywood and the recording industry pose a significant danger to the networked information environment. The core design principle of general-purpose computers is that they are open for varied uses over time, as their owners change their priorities and preferences. It is this general-purpose character that has allowed personal computers to take on such varied roles since their adoption in the 1980s. The purpose of the Fritz chip–style laws is to make computing devices less flexible. It is to define a range of socially, culturally, and economically acceptable uses of the machines that are predicted by the legislature and the industry actors, and to implement factory-defined capabilities that are not flexible, and do not give end users the freedom to change the intended use over time and to adapt to changing social and economic conditions and opportunities.

The political economy of this regulatory effort, and similar drives that have been more successful in the logical and content layers, is uncharacteristic of American politics. Personal computers, software, and telecommunications services are significantly larger industries than Hollywood and the recording industry. Verizon alone has roughly similar annual revenues to the entire U.S. movie industry. Each one of the industries that the content industries have tried to regulate has revenues several times greater than do the movie and music industries combined. The relative successes of Hollywood and the recording industry in regulating the logical and content layers, and the viability of their efforts to pass a Fritz chip law, attest to the remarkable cultural power of these industries and to their lobbying prowess. The reason is likely historical. The software and hardware industries in particular have developed mostly outside of the regulatory arena; only around 2002 did they begin to understand that what goes on in Washington could really hurt them. The telecommunications carriers, which are some of the oldest hands at the regulatory game, have had some success in preventing regulations that would force them to police their users and limit Internet use. However, the bulk of their lobbying efforts have been aimed elsewhere. The institutions of higher education, which have found themselves under attack for not policing their students' use of peer-to-peer networks, have been entirely ineffective at presenting their cultural and economic value and the importance of open Internet access to higher education, as compared to the hypothetical losses of Hollywood and the recording industry. Despite the past successes of these entertainment-industry incumbents, two elements suggest that physical device regulation of the CBDPTA form will not follow the same successful path of similar legislation at the logical layer, the DMCA of 1998. The first element is the fact that, unlike in 1998, the technology industries have now realized that Hollywood is seeking to severely constrain their design space. Industries with half a trillion dollars a year in revenues tend to have significant pull in American and international lawmaking bodies, even against industries, like movies and sound recording, that have high cultural visibility but no more than seventy-five billion dollars a year in revenues. The second is that in 1998, there were very few public advocacy organizations operating in the space of intellectual property and trying to play watchdog and to speak for the interests of users. By 2004, a number of organizations dedicated to users' rights in the digital environment emerged to make that conflict clear. The combination of well-defined business interests with increasing representation of user interests creates a political landscape in which it will be difficult to pass sweeping laws to limit the flexibility of personal computers. The most recent iteration of the Fritz chip agenda, the Inducing Infringement of Copyrights Act of 2004 was indeed defeated, for the time being, by a coalition of high-technology firms and people who would have formerly been seen as left-of-center media activists.

Regulation of device design remains at the frontier of the battles over the institutional ecology of the digital environment. It is precisely ubiquitous access to basic, general-purpose computers, as opposed to glorified televisions or telephone handsets, that lies at the very heart of the networked information economy. And it is therefore precisely ubiquitous access to such basic machines that is a precondition to the improvements in freedom and justice that we can see emerging in the digital environment.

THE LOGICAL LAYER

At the logical layer, most of the efforts aimed to secure a proprietary model and a more tightly controlled institutional ecology follow a similar pattern to the efforts to regulate device design. They come from the needs of the content-layer businesses—Hollywood and the recording industry, in particular. Unlike the physical transmission layer, which is historically rooted in a proprietary but regulated organizational form, most of the logical layer of the Internet has its roots in open, nonproprietary protocols and standards. The broad term "logical layer" combines a wide range of quite different functionalities. The most basic logical components—the basic protocols and standards for Internet connectivity—have from the beginning of the Internet been open, unowned, and used in common by all Internet users and applications. They were developed by computer scientists funded primarily with public money. The basic Internet Protocol (IP) and Transmission Control Protocol (TCP) are open for all to use. Most of the basic standards for communicating were developed in the IETF, a loosely defined standards-setting body that works almost entirely on a meritocratic basis—a body that Michael Froomkin once suggested is the closest earthly approximation of Habermas's ideal speech situation. Individual computer engineers contributed irrespective of formal status or organizational affiliation, and the organization ran on the principle that Dave Clark termed "rough consensus and running code." The World Wide Web protocols and authoring conventions HTTP and HTML were created, and over the course of their lives, shepherded by Tim Berners Lee, who has chosen to dedicate his efforts to making the Web a public good rather than cashing in on his innovation. The sheer technical necessity of these basic protocols and the cultural stature of their achievement within the engineering community have given these open processes and their commonslike institutional structure a strong gravitational pull on the design of other components of the logical layer, at least insofar as it relates to the communication side of the Internet.

This basic open model has been in constant tension with the proprietary models that have come to use and focus on the Internet in the past decade. By the mid-1990s, the development of graphical-user interfaces to the Web drove Internet use out of universities and into homes. Commercial actors began to look for ways to capture the commercial value of the human potential of the World Wide Web and the Internet, while Hollywood and the recording industry saw the threat of one giant worldwide copying machine looming large. At the same time, the Clinton administration's search of "third-way" liberal agenda manifested in these areas as a commitment to "let the private sector lead" in deployment of the Internet, and an "intellectual property" policy based on extreme protectionism for the exclusive-rights-dependent industries aimed, in the metaphors of that time, to get cars on the information superhighway or help the Internet become a celestial jukebox. The result was a series of moves designed to make the institutional ecology of the Internet more conducive to the proprietary model.

The Digital Millennium Copyright Act of 1998

No piece of legislation more clearly represents the battle over the institutional ecology of the digital environment than the pompously named Digital Millennium Copyright Act of 1998 (DMCA). The DMCA was the culmination of more than three years of lobbying and varied efforts, both domestically in the United States and internationally, over the passage of two WIPO treaties in 1996. The basic worldview behind it, expressed in a 1995 white paper issued by the Clinton administration, was that in order for the National Information Infrastructure (NII) to take off, it had to have "content," and that its great promise was that it could deliver the equivalent of thousands of channels of entertainment. This would only happen, however, if the NII was made safe for delivery of digital content without making it easily copied and distributed without authorization and without payment. The two core recommendations of that early road map were focused on regulating technology and organizational responsibility. First, law was to regulate the development of technologies that might defeat any encryption or other mechanisms that the owners of copyrighted materials would use to prevent use of their works. Second, Internet service providers were to be held accountable for infringements made by their users, so that they would have an incentive to police their systems. Early efforts to pass this agenda in legislation were resisted, primarily by the large telecommunications service providers. The Baby Bells—U.S. regional telephone companies that were created from the breakup of AT&T (Ma Bell) in 1984, when the telecommunications company was split up in order to introduce a more competitive structure to the telecom industry—also played a role in partly defeating implementation of this agenda in the negotiations toward new WIPO treaties in 1996, treaties that ultimately included a much-muted version of the white paper agenda. Nonetheless, the following year saw significant lobbying for "implementing legislation" to bring U.S. law in line with the requirements of the new WIPO treaties. This new posture placed the emphasis of congressional debates on national industrial policy and the importance of strong protection to the export activities of the U.S. content industries. It was enough to tip the balance in favor of passage of the DMCA. The Internet service provider liability portions bore the marks of a hard-fought battle. The core concerns of the telecommunications companies were addressed by creating an explicit exemption for pure carriage of traffic. Furthermore, providers of more sophisticated services, like Web hosting, were provided immunity from liability for simple failure to police their system actively. In exchange, however, service providers were required to respond to requests by copyright owners by immediately removing materials that the copyright owners deemed infringing. This was the provision under which Diebold forced Swarthmore to remove the embarrassing e-mail records from the students' Web sites. The other, more basic, element of the DMCA was the anticircumvention regime it put in place. Pamela Samuelson has described the anticircumvention provisions of the DMCA as the result of a battle between Hollywood and Silicon Valley. At the time, unlike the telecommunications giants who were born of and made within the regulatory environment, Silicon Valley did not quite understand that what happened in Washington, D.C., could affect its business. The Act was therefore an almost unqualified victory for Hollywood, moderated only by a long list of weak exemptions for various parties that bothered to show up and lobby against it.

The central feature of the DMCA, a long and convoluted piece of legislation, is its anticircumvention and antidevice provisions. These provisions made it illegal to use, develop, or sell technologies that had certain properties. Copyright owners believed that it would be possible to build strong encryption into media products distributed on the Internet. If they did so successfully, the copyright owners could charge for digital distribution and users would not be able to make unauthorized copies of the works. If this outcome was achieved, the content industries could simply keep their traditional business model—selling movies or music as discrete packages—at lower cost, and with a more refined ability to extract the value users got from using their materials. The DMCA was intended to make this possible by outlawing technologies that would allow users to get around, or circumvent, the protection measures that the owners of copyrighted materials put in place. At first blush, this proposition sounds entirely reasonable. If you think of the content of a music file as a home, and of the copy protection mechanism as its lock, then all the DMCA does is prohibit the making and distributing of burglary tools. This is indeed how the legislation was presented by its supporters. From this perspective, even the relatively draconian consequences spelled out in the DMCA's criminal penalties seem defensible.

There are two distinct problems with this way of presenting what the DMCA does. First, copyrights are far from coextensive with real property. There are many uses of existing works that are permissible to all. They are treated in copyright law like walking on the sidewalk or in a public park is treated in property law, not like walking across the land of a neighbor. This is true, most obviously, for older works whose copyright has expired. This is true for certain kinds of uses of a work, like quoting it for purposes of criticism or parody. Encryption and other copy-protection techniques are not limited by the definition of legal rights. They can be used to protect all kinds of digital files—whether their contents are still covered by copyright or not, and whether the uses that users wish to make of them are privileged or not. Circumvention techniques, similarly, can be used to circumvent copy-protection mechanisms for purposes both legitimate and illegitimate. A barbed wire cutter, to borrow Boyle's metaphor, could be a burglary tool if the barbed wire is placed at the property line. However, it could equally be a tool for exercising your privilege if the private barbed wire has been drawn around public lands or across a sidewalk or highway. The DMCA prohibited all wire cutters, even though there were many uses of these technologies that could be used for legal purposes. Imagine a ten-year-old girl doing her homework on the history of the Holocaust. She includes in her multimedia paper a clip from Steven Spielberg's film, *Schindler's List*, in which a little girl in red, the only color image on an otherwise black-and-white screen, walks through the pandemonium of a deportation. In her project, the child painstakingly superimposes her own face over that of the girl in the film for the entire sequence, frame by frame. She calls the paper, "My Grandmother." There is little question that most copyright lawyers (not retained by the owner of the movie) would say that this use would count as a "fair use," and would be privileged under the Copyright Act. There is also little question that if *Schindler's List* was only available in encrypted digital form, a company would have violated the DMCA if it distributed a product that enabled the girl to get around the encryption in order to use the snippet she needed, and which by traditional copyright law she was permitted to use. It is in the face of this concern about overreaching by those who employ technological protection measures that Julie Cohen argued for the "right to hack"—to circumvent code that impedes one's exercise of one's privileged uses.

The second problem with the DMCA is that its definitions are broad and malleable. Simple acts like writing an academic paper on how the encryption works, or publishing a report on the Web that tells users where they can find information about how to circumvent a copy-protection mechanism could be included in the definition of providing a circumvention device. Edward Felten is a computer scientist at Princeton. As he was preparing to publish an academic paper on encryption, he received a threatening letter from the Recording Industry Association of America (RIAA), telling him that publication of the paper constituted a violation of the DMCA. The music industry had spent substantial sums on developing encryption for digital music distribution. In order to test the system before it actually entrusted music with this wrapper, the industry issued a public challenge, inviting cryptographers to try to break the code. Felten succeeded in doing so, but did not continue to test his solutions because the industry required that, in order to continue testing, he sign a nondisclosure agreement. Felten is an academic, not a businessperson. He works to make knowledge public, not to keep it secret. He refused to sign the nondisclosure agreement, and prepared to publish his initial findings, which he had made without entering any nondisclosure agreement. As he did so, he received the RIAA's threatening letter. In response, he asked a federal district court to declare that publication of his findings was not a violation of the DMCA. The RIAA, realizing that trying to silence academic publication of a criticism of the weakness of its approach to encryption was not the best litigation stance, moved to dismiss the case by promising it would never bring suit.[16]

Another case did not end so well for the defendant. It involved a suit by the eight Hollywood studios against a hacker magazine, *2600*. The studios sought an injunction prohibiting *2600* from making available a program called DeCSS, which circumvents the copy-protection scheme used to control access to DVDs, named CSS. CSS prevents copying or any use of DVDs unauthorized by the vendor. DeCSS was written by a fifteen-year-old Norwegian named Jon Johanson, who claimed (though the district court discounted his claim) to have written it as part of an effort to create a DVD player for GNU/Linux-based machines. A copy of DeCSS, together with a story about it was posted on the *2600* site. The industry obtained an injunction against *2600*, prohibiting not only the posting of DeCSS, but also its linking to other sites that post the program—that is, telling users where they can get the program, rather than actually distributing a circumvention program. That decision may or may not have been correct on the merits. There are strong arguments in favor of the proposition that making DVDs compatible with GNU/Linux systems is a fair use. There are strong arguments that the DMCA goes much farther than it needs to in restricting speech of software programmers and Web authors, and so is invalid under the First Amendment. The court rejected these arguments.

The point here is not, however, to revisit the legal correctness of that decision, but to illustrate the effects of the DMCA as an element in the institutional ecology of the logical layer. The DMCA is intended as a strong legal barrier to certain technological paths of innovation at the logical layer of the digital environment. It is intended specifically to preserve the "thing-" or "goods"-like nature of entertainment products—music and movies, in particular. As such, it is intended to, and does to some extent, shape the technological development toward treating information and culture as finished goods, rather than as the outputs of social and communications processes that blur the production-consumption distinction. It makes it more difficult for individuals and nonmarket actors to gain access to digital materials that the technology, the market, and the social practices, left unregulated, would have made readily available. It makes practices of cutting and pasting, changing and annotating existing cultural materials harder to do than the technology would have made possible. I have argued elsewhere that when Congress self-consciously makes it harder for individuals to use whatever technology is available to them, to speak as they please and to whomever they please, in the interest of some public goal (in this case, preservation of Hollywood and the recording industry for the public good), it must justify its acts under the First Amendment. However, the important question is not one of U.S. constitutional law.

The more general claim, true for any country that decides to enforce a DMCA-like law, is that prohibiting technologies that allow individuals to make flexible and creative uses of digital cultural materials burdens the development of the networked information economy and society. It burdens individual autonomy, the emergence of the networked public sphere and critical culture, and some of the paths available for global human development that the networked information economy makes possible. All these losses will be incurred in expectation of improvements in creativity, even though it is not at all clear that doing so would actually improve, even on a simple utilitarian calculus, the creative production of any given country or region. Passing a DMCA-type law will not by itself squelch the development of nonmarket and peer production. Indeed, many of these technological and social-economic developments emerged and have flourished after the DMCA was already in place. It does, however, represent a choice to tilt the institutional ecology in favor of industrial production and distribution of cultural packaged goods, at the expense of commons-based relations of sharing information, knowledge, and culture. Twentieth-century cultural materials provide the most immediate and important source of references and images for contemporary cultural creation. Given the relatively recent provenance of movies, recorded music, and photography, much of contemporary culture was created in these media. These basic materials for the creation of contemporary multimedia culture are, in turn, encoded in formats that cannot simply be copied by hand, as texts might be even in the teeth of technical protection measures. The capacity to copy mechanically is a necessary precondition for the capacity to quote and combine existing materials of these kinds into new cultural statements and conversational moves. Preserving the capacity of industrial cultural producers to maintain a hermetic seal on the use of materials to which they own copyright can be bought only at the cost of disabling the newly emerging modes of cultural production from quoting and directly building upon much of the culture of the last century.

The Battle over Peer-to-Peer Networks

The second major institutional battle over the technical and social trajectory of Internet development has revolved around peer-to-peer (p2p) networks. I offer a detailed description of it here, but not because I think it will be the make-it-or-break-it of the networked information economy. If any laws have that determinative a power, they are the Fritz chip and DMCA. However, the peer-to-peer legal battle offers an excellent case study of just how difficult it is to evaluate the effects of institutional ecology on technology, economic organization, and social practice.

Peer-to-peer technologies as a global phenomenon emerged from Napster and its use by tens of millions of users around the globe for unauthorized sharing of music files. In the six years since their introduction, p2p networks have developed robust and impressive technical capabilities. They have been adopted by more than one hundred million users, and are increasingly applied to uses well beyond music sharing. These developments have occurred despite a systematic and aggressive campaign of litigation and criminal enforcement in a number of national systems against both developers and users. Technically, p2p networks are algorithms that run on top of the Internet and allow users to connect directly from one end user's machine to another. In theory, that is how the whole Internet works—or at least how it worked when there were a small number of computers attached to it. In practice, most users connect through an Internet service provider, and most content available for access on the Internet was available on a server owned and operated by someone distinct from its users. In the late 1990s, there were rudimentary utilities that allowed one user to access information stored on the computer of another, but no widely used utility allowed large numbers of individuals to search each other's hard drives and share data directly from one user to another. Around 1998–1999, early Internet music distribution models, like MP3.com, therefore provided a centralized distribution point for music. This made them highly vulnerable to legal attack. Shawn Fanning, then eighteen years old, was apparently looking for ways to do what teenagers always do—share their music with friends—in a way that would not involve a central point of storing and copying. He developed Napster—the first major, widely adopted p2p technology. Unlike MP3.com, users of Napster could connect their computers directly—one person could download a song stored on the computer of another without mediation. All that the Napster site itself did, in addition to providing the end-user software, was to provide a centralized directory of which songs resided on which machine. There is little disagreement in the literature that it is an infringement under U.S. copyright law for any given user to allow others to duplicate copyrighted music from his or her computer to theirs. The centralizing role of Napster in facilitating these exchanges, alongside a number of ill-considered statements by some of its principals, were enough to render the company liable for contributory copyright infringement.

The genie of p2p technology and the social practice of sharing music, however, were already out of the bottle. The story of the following few years, to the extent that one can tell a history of the present and the recent past, offers two core insights. First, it shows how institutional design can be a battleground over the conditions of cultural production in the digital environment. Second, it exposes the limits of the extent to which the institutional ecology can determine the ultimate structure of behavior at a moment of significant and rapid technological and social perturbation. Napster's judicial closure provided no real respite for the recording industry. As Napster was winding down, Gnutella, a free software alternative, had already begun to replace it. Gnutella did not depend on any centralized component, not even to facilitate search. This meant that there was no central provider. There was no firm against which to bring action. Even if there were, it would be impossible to "shut down" use of the program. Gnutella was a freestanding program that individual users could install. Once installed, its users could connect to anyone else who had installed the program, without passing through any choke point. There was no central server to shut down. Gnutella had some technical imperfections, but these were soon overcome by other implementations of p2p. The most successful improvement over Gnutella was the FastTrack architecture, now used by Kazaa, Grokster, and other applications, including some free software applications. It improves on the search capabilities of Gnutella by designating some users as "supernodes," which store information about what songs are available in their "neighborhood." This avoids Gnutella's primary weakness, the relatively high degree of network overhead traffic. The supernodes operate on an ad hoc basis. They change based on whose computer is available with enough storage and bandwidth. They too, therefore, provide no litigation target. Other technologies have developed to speed up or make more robust the distribution of files, including BitTorrent, eDonkey and its free-software relative eMule, and many others. Within less than two years of Napster's closure, more people were using these various platforms to share files than Napster had users at its height. Some of these new firms found themselves again under legal assault—both in the United States and abroad.

As the technologies grew and developed, and as the legal attacks increased, the basic problem presented by the litigation against technology manufacturers became evident. Peer-to-peer techniques can be used for a wide range of uses, only some of which are illegal. At the simplest level, they can be used to distribute music that is released by an increasing number of bands freely. These bands hope to get exposure that they can parley into concert performances. As recorded music from the 1950s begins to fall into the public domain in Europe and Australia, golden oldies become another legitimate reason to use p2p technologies. More important, p2p systems are being adapted to different kinds of uses. Chapter 7 discusses how FreeNet is being used to disseminate subversive documents, using the persistence and robustness of p2p networks to evade detection and suppression by authoritarian regimes. BitTorrent was initially developed to deal with the large file transfers required for free software distributions. BitTorrent and eDonkey were both used by the Swarthmore students when their college shut down their Internet connection in response to Diebold's letter threatening action under the service provider liability provisions of the DMCA. The founders of KaZaa have begun to offer an Internet telephony utility, Skype, which allows users to make phone calls from one computer to another for free, and from their computer to the telephone network for a small fee. Skype is a p2p technology.

In other words, p2p is developing as a general approach toward producing distributed data storage and retrieval systems, just as open wireless networks and distributed computing are emerging to take advantage of personal devices to produce distributed communications and computation systems, respectively. As the social and technological uses of p2p technologies grow and diversify, the legal assault on all p2p developers becomes less sustainable— both as a legal matter and as a social-technical matter. KaZaa was sued in the Netherlands, and moved to Australia. It was later subject to actions in Australia, but by that time, the Dutch courts found the company not to be liable to the music labels. Grokster, a firm based in the United States, was initially found to have offered a sufficiently diverse set of capabilities, beyond merely facilitating copyright infringements, that the Court of Appeals for the Ninth Circuit refused to find it liable simply for making and distributing its software. The Supreme Court reversed that holding, however, returning the case to the lower courts to find, factually, whether Grokster had actual intent to facilitate illegal copying.[17] Even if Grokster ultimately loses, the FastTrack network architecture will not disappear; clients (that is, end user software) will continue to exist, including free software clients. Perhaps it will be harder to raise money for businesses located within the United States to operate in this technological space, because the new rule announced by the Supreme Court in *Grokster* raises the risk of litigation for innovators in the p2p space. However, as with encryption regulation in the mid-1990s, it is not clear that the United States can unilaterally prevent the development of technology for which there is worldwide demand and with regard to whose development there is globally accessible talent.

How important more generally are these legal battles to the organization of cultural production in the networked environment? There are two components to the answer: The first component considers the likely effect of the legal battles on the development and adoption of the technology and the social practice of promiscuous copying. In this domain, law seems unlikely to prevent the continued development of p2p technologies. It has, however, had two opposite results. First, it has affected the path of the technological evolution in a way that is contrary to the industry interests but consistent with increasing distribution of the core functions of the logical layer. Second, it seems to have dampened somewhat the social practice of file sharing. The second component assumes that a range of p2p technologies will continue to be widely adopted, and that some significant amount of sharing will continue to be practiced. The question then becomes what effect this will have on the primary cultural industries that have fought this technology— movies and recorded music. Within this new context, music will likely change more radically than movies, and the primary effect will be on the accreditation function—how music is recognized and adopted by fans. Film, if it is substantially affected, will likely be affected largely by a shift in tastes.

MP3.com was the first major music distribution site shut down by litigation. From the industry's perspective, it should have represented an entirely unthreatening business model. Users paid a subscription fee, in exchange for which they were allowed to download music. There were various quirks and kinks in this model that made it unattractive to the music industry at the time: the industry did not control this major site, and therefore had to share the rents from the music, and more important, there was no effective control over the music files once downloaded. However, from the perspective of 2005, MP3.com was a vastly more manageable technology for the sound recording business model than a free software file-sharing client. MP3.com was a single site, with a corporate owner that could be (and was) held responsible. It controlled which user had access to what files—by requiring each user to insert a CD into the computer to prove that he or she had bought the CD—so that usage could in principle be monitored and, if desired, compensation could be tied to usage. It did not fundamentally change the social practice of choosing music. It provided something that was more like a music-on-demand jukebox than a point of music sharing. As a legal matter, MP3.com's infringement was centered on the fact that it stored and delivered the music from this central server instead of from the licensed individual copies. In response to the shutdown of MP3.com, Napster redesigned the role of the centralized mode, and left storage in the hands of users, keeping only the directory and search functions centralized. When Napster was shut down, Gnutella and later FastTrack further decentralized the system, offering a fully decentralized, ad hoc reconfigurable cataloging and search function. Because these algorithms represent architecture and a protocol-based network, not a particular program, they are usable in many different implementations. This includes free software programs like MLDonkey—which is a nascent file-sharing system that is aimed to run simultaneously across most of the popular file-sharing networks, including FastTrack, BitTorrent, and Overnet, the eDonkey network. These programs are now written by, and available from, many different jurisdictions. There is no central point of control over their distribution. There is no central point through which to measure and charge for their use. They are, from a technical perspective, much more resilient to litigation attack, and much less friendly to various possible models of charging for downloads or usage. From a technological perspective, then, the litigation backfired. It created a network that is less susceptible to integration into an industrial model of music distribution based on royalty payments per user or use.

It is harder to gauge, however, whether the litigation was a success or a failure from a social-practice point of view. There have been conflicting reports on the effects of file sharing and the litigation on CD sales. The recording industry claimed that CD sales were down because of file sharing, but more independent academic studies suggested that CD sales were not independently affected by file sharing, as opposed to the general economic downturn.[18] The Pew project on Internet and American Life user survey data suggests that the litigation strategy against individual users has dampened the use of file sharing, though file sharing is still substantially more common among users than paying for files from the newly emerging pay-per-download authorized services. In mid-2003, the Pew study found that 29 percent of Internet users surveyed said they had downloaded music files, identical to the percentage of users who had downloaded music in the first quarter of 2001, the heyday of Napster. Twenty-one percent responded that they allow others to download from their computer.[19] This meant that somewhere between twenty-six and thirty-five million adults in the United States alone were sharing music files in mid-2003, when the recording industry began to sue individual users. Of these, fully two-thirds expressly stated that they did not care whether the files they downloaded were or were not copyrighted. By the end of 2003, five months after the industry began to sue individuals, the number of respondents who admitted to downloading music dropped by half. During the next few months, these numbers increased slightly to twenty-three million adults, remaining below the mid-2003 numbers in absolute terms and more so in terms of percentage of Internet users. Of those who had at one point downloaded, but had stopped, roughly a third said that the threat of suit was the reason they had stopped file sharing.[20] During this same period, use of pay online music download services, like iTunes, rose to about 7 percent of Internet users. Sharing of all kinds of media files—music, movies, and games—was at 23 percent of adult Internet users. These numbers do indeed suggest that, in the aggregate, music downloading is reported somewhat less often than it was in the past. It is hard to tell how much of this reduction is due to actual behavioral change as compared to an unwillingness to self-report on behavior that could subject one to litigation. It is impossible to tell how much of an effect the litigation has had specifically on sharing by younger people—teenagers and college students—who make up a large portion of both CD buyers and file sharers. Nonetheless, the reduction in the total number of self-reported users and the relatively steady percentage of total Internet users who share files of various kinds suggest that the litigation does seem to have had a moderating effect on file sharing as a social practice. It has not, however, prevented file sharing from continuing to be a major behavioral pattern among one-fifth to one-quarter of Internet users, and likely a much higher proportion in the most relevant populations from the perspective of the music and movie industries—teenagers and young adults.

From the perspective of understanding the effects of institutional ecology, then, the still-raging battle over peer-to-peer networks presents an ambiguous picture. One can speculate with some degree of confidence that, had Napster not been stopped by litigation, file sharing would have been a much wider social practice than it is today. The application was extremely easy to use; it offered a single network for all file-sharing users, thereby offering an extremely diverse and universal content distribution network; and for a brief period, it was a cultural icon and a seemingly acceptable social practice. The period of regrouping that followed its closure; the imperfect interfaces of early Gnutella clients; the relative fragmentation of file sharing into a number of networks, each with a smaller coverage of content than was present; and the fear of personal litigation risk are likely to have limited adoption. On the other hand, in the longer run, the technological developments have created platforms that are less compatible with the industrial model, and which would be harder to integrate into a stable settlement for music distribution in the digital environment.

Prediction aside, it is not immediately obvious why peer-to-peer networks contribute to the kinds of nonmarket production and creativity that I have focused on as the core of the networked information economy. At first blush, they seem simply to be mechanisms for fans to get industrially produced recorded music without paying musicians. This has little to do with democratization of creativity. To see why p2p networks nonetheless are a part of the development of a more attractive cultural production system, and how they can therefore affect the industrial organization of cultural production, we can look first at music, and then, independently, at movies. The industrial structure of each is different, and the likely effects of p2p networks are different in each case.

Recorded music began with the phonograph—a packaged good intended primarily for home consumption. The industry that grew around the ability to stamp and distribute records divided the revenue structure such that artists have been paid primarily from live public performances and merchandizing. Very few musicians, including successful recording artists, make money from recording royalties. The recording industry takes almost all of the revenues from record and CD sales, and provides primarily promotion and distribution. It does not bear the capital cost of the initial musical creation; artists do. With the declining cost of computation, that cost has become relatively low, often simply a computer owned by artists themselves, much as they own their instruments. Because of this industrial structure, peer-to-peer networks are a genuine threat to displacing the entire recording industry, while leaving musicians, if not entirely unaffected, relatively insulated from the change and perhaps mildly better off. Just as the recording industry stamps CDs, promotes them on radio stations, and places them on distribution chain shelves, p2p networks produce the physical and informational aspects of a music distribution system. However, p2p networks do so collaboratively, by sharing the capacity of their computers, hard drives, and network connections. Filtering and accreditation, or "promotion," are produced on the model that Eben Moglen called "anarchist distribution." Jane's friends and friends of her friends are more likely to know exactly what music would make her happy than are recording executives trying to predict which song to place, on which station and which shelf, to expose her to exactly the music she is most likely to buy in a context where she would buy it. File-sharing systems produce distribution and "promotion" of music in a social-sharing modality. Alongside peer-produced music reviews, they could entirely supplant the role of the recording industry.

Musicians and songwriters seem to be relatively insulated from the effects of p2p networks, and on balance, are probably affected positively. The most comprehensive survey data available, from mid-2004, shows that 35 percent of musicians and songwriters said that free downloads have helped their careers. Only 5 percent said it has hurt them. Thirty percent said it increased attendance at concerts, 21 percent that it helped them sell CDs and other merchandise, and 19 percent that it helped them gain radio playing time. These results are consistent with what one would expect given the revenue structure of the industry, although the study did not separate answers out based on whether the respondent was able to live entirely or primarily on their music, which represented only 16 percent of the respondents to the survey. In all, it appears that much of the actual flow of revenue to artists—from performances and other sources—is stable. This is likely to remain true even if the CD market were entirely displaced by peer-to-peer distribution. Musicians will still be able to play for their dinner, at least not significantly less so than they can today. Perhaps there will be fewer millionaires. Perhaps fewer mediocre musicians with attractive physiques will be sold as "geniuses," and more talented musicians will be heard than otherwise would have, and will as a result be able to get paying gigs instead of waiting tables or "getting a job." But it would be silly to think that music, a cultural form without which no human society has existed, will cease to be in our world if we abandon the industrial form it took for the blink of a historical eye that was the twentieth century. Music was not born with the phonograph, nor will it die with the peer-to-peer network. The terms of the debate, then, are about cultural policy; perhaps about industrial policy. Will we get the kind of music we want in this system, whoever "we" are? Will American recording companies continue to get the export revenue streams they do? Will artists be able to live from making music? Some of these arguments are serious. Some are but a tempest in a monopoly-rent teapot. It is clear that a tech-nological change has rendered obsolete a particular mode of distributing information and culture. Distribution, once the sole domain of market-based firms, now can be produced by decentralized networks of users, sharing instantiations of music they deem attractive with others, using equipment they own and generic network connections. This distribution network, in turn, allows a much more diverse range of musicians to reach much more finely grained audiences than were optimal for industrial production and distribution of mechanical instantiations of music in vinyl or CD formats. The legal battles reflect an effort by an incumbent industry to preserve its very lucrative business model. The industry has, to this point, delayed the transition to peer-based distribution, but it is unclear for how long or to what extent it will be successful in preventing the gradual transition to user-based distribution.

The movie industry has a different industrial structure and likely a different trajectory in its relations to p2p networks. First and foremost, movies began as a relatively high capital cost experience good. Making a movie, as opposed to writing a song, was something that required a studio and a large workforce. It could not be done by a musician with a guitar or a piano. Furthermore, movies were, throughout most of their history, collective experience goods. They were a medium for public performance experienced outside of the home, in a social context. With the introduction of television, it was easy to adapt movie revenue structure by delaying release of films to television viewing until after demand for the movie at the theater declined, as well as to develop their capabilities into a new line of business—television production. However, theatrical release continued to be the major source of revenue. When video came along, the movie industry cried murder in the Sony Betamax case, but actually found it quite easy to work videocassettes into yet another release window, like television, and another medium, the made-for-video movie. Digital distribution affects the distribution of cultural artifacts as packaged goods for home consumption. It does not affect the social experience of going out to the movies. At most, it could affect the consumption of the twenty-year-old mode of movie distribution: videos and DVDs. As recently as the year 2000, when the Hollywood studios were litigating the DeCSS case, they represented to the court that home video sales were roughly 40 percent of revenue, a number consistent with other reports.[21] The remainder, composed of theatrical release revenues and various television releases, remains reasonably unthreatened as a set of modes of revenue capture to sustain the high-production value, high-cost movies that typify Hollywood. Forty percent is undoubtedly a large chunk, but unlike the recording industry, which began with individually owned recordings, the movie industry preexisted videocassettes and DVDs, and is likely to outlive them even if p2p networks were to eliminate that market entirely, which is doubtful.

The harder and more interesting question is whether cheap high-quality digital video-capture and editing technologies combined with p2p networks for efficient distribution could make film a more diverse medium than it is now. The potential hypothetical promise of p2p networks like BitTorrent is that they could offer very robust and efficient distribution networks for films outside the mainstream industry. Unlike garage bands and small-scale music productions, however, this promise is as yet speculative. We do not invest in public education for film creation, as we do in the teaching of writing. Most of the raw materials out of which a culture of digital capture and amateur editing could develop are themselves under copyright, a subject we return to when considering the content layer. There are some early efforts, like atomfilms.com, at short movie distribution. The technological capabilities are there. It is possible that if films older than thirty or even fifty years were released into the public domain, they would form the raw material out of which a new cultural production practice would form. If it did, p2p networks would likely play an important role in their distribution. However, for now, although the sound recording and movie industries stand shoulder to shoulder in the lobbying efforts, their circumstances and likely trajectory in relation to file sharing are likely quite different.

The battles over p2p and the DMCA offer some insight into the potential, but also the limits, of tweaking the institutional ecology. The ambition of the industrial cultural producers in both cases was significant. They sought to deploy law to shape emerging technologies and social practices to make sure that the business model they had adopted for the technologies of film and sound recording continued to work in the digital environment. Doing so effectively would require substantial elimination of certain lines of innovation, like certain kinds of decryption and p2p networks. It would require outlawing behavior widely adopted by people around the world—social sharing of most things that they can easily share—which, in the case of music, has been adopted by tens of millions of people around the world. The belief that all this could be changed in a globally interconnected network through the use of law was perhaps naïve. Nonetheless, the legal efforts have had some impact on social practices and on the ready availability of materials for free use. The DMCA may not have made any single copyright protection mechanism hold up to the scrutiny of hackers and crackers around the Internet. However, it has prevented circumvention devices from being integrated into mainstream platforms, like the Windows operating system or some of the main antivirus programs, which would have been "natural" places for them to appear in consumer markets. The p2p litigation did not eliminate the p2p networks, but it does seem to have successfully dampened the social practice of file sharing. One can take quite different views of these effects from a policy perspective. However, it is clear that they are self-conscious efforts to tweak the institutional ecology of the digital environment in order to dampen the most direct threats it poses for the twentieth-century industrial model of cultural production. In the case of the DMCA, this is done at the direct cost of making it substantially harder for users to make creative use of the existing stock of audiovisual materials from the twentieth century—materials that are absolutely central to our cultural self-understanding at the beginning of the twenty-first century. In the case of p2p networks, the cost to nonmarket production is more indirect, and may vary across different cultural forms. The most important long-term effect of the pressure that this litigation has put on technology to develop decentralized search and retrieval systems may, ultimately and ironically, be to improve the efficiency of radically decentralized cultural production and distribution, and make decentralized production more, rather than less, robust to the vicissitudes of institutional ecology.

The Domain Name System: From Public Trust to the Fetishism of Mnemonics

Not all battles over the role of property-like arrangements at the logical layer originate from Hollywood and the recording industry. One of the major battles outside of the ambit of the copyright industries concerned the allocation and ownership of domain names. At stake was the degree to which brand name ownership in the material world could be leveraged into attention on the Internet. Domain names are alphanumeric mnemonics used to represent actual Internet addresses of computers connected to the network. While 130.132.51.8 is hard for human beings to remember, www.yale.edu is easier. The two strings have identical meaning to any computer connected to the Internet—they refer to a server that responds to World Wide Web queries for Yale University's main site. Every computer connected to the Internet has a unique address, either permanent or assigned by a provider for the session. That requires that someone distribute addresses—both numeric and mnemonic. Until 1992, names and numbers were assigned on a purely first-come, first-served basis by Jon Postel, one of the very first developers of the Internet, under U.S. government contract. Postel also ran a computer, called the root server, to which all computers would turn to ask the numeric address of letters.mnemonic.edu, so they could translate what the human operator remembered as the address into one their machine could use. Postel called this system "the Internet Assigned Numbers Authority, IANA," whose motto he set as, "Dedicated to preserving the central coordinating functions of the global Internet for the public good." In 1992, Postel got tired of this coordinating job, and the government contracted it to a private firm called Network Solutions, Inc., or NSI. As the number of applications grew, and as the administration sought to make this system pay for itself, NSI was allowed in 1995 to begin to charge fees for assigning names and numbers. At about the same time, widespread adoption of a graphical browser made using the World Wide Web radically simpler and more intuitive to the uninitiated. These two developments brought together two forces to bear on the domain name issue—each with a very different origin and intent. The first force consisted of the engineers who had created and developed the Internet, led by Postel, who saw the domain name space to be a public trust and resisted its commercialization by NSI. The second force consisted of trademark owners and their lawyers, who suddenly realized the potential for using control over domain names to extend the value of their brand names to a new domain of trade—e-commerce. These two forces placed the U.S. government under pressure to do two things: (1) release the monopoly that NSI—a for-profit corporation—had on the domain name space, and (2) find an efficient means of allowing trademark owners to control the use of alphanumeric strings used in their trademarks as domain names. Postel initially tried to "take back the root" by asking various regional domain name servers to point to his computer, instead of to the one maintained by NSI in Virginia. This caused uproar in the government, and Postel was accused of attacking and hijacking the Internet! His stature and passion, however, placed significant weight on the side of keeping the naming system as an open public trust. That position came to an abrupt end with his death in 1996. By late 1996, a self-appointed International Ad Hoc Committee (IAHC) was formed, with the blessing of the Internet Society (ISOC), a professional membership society for individuals and organizations involved in Internet planning. IAHC's membership was about half intellectual property lawyers and half engineers. In February 1997, IAHC came out with a document called the gTLD-MoU (generic top-level domain name memorandum of understanding). Although the product of a small group, the gTLD-MoU claimed to speak for "The Internet Community." Although it involved no governments, it was deposited "for signature" with the International Telecommunications Union (ITU). Dutifully, some 226 organizations—Internet services companies, telecommunications providers, consulting firms, and a few chapters of the ISOC signed on. Section 2 of the gTLD-MoU, announcing its principles, reveals the driving forces of the project. While it begins with the announcement that the top-level domain space "is a public resource and is subject to the public trust," it quickly commits to the principle that "the current and future Internet name space stakeholders can benefit most from a self-regulatory and market-oriented approach to Internet domain name registration services." This results in two policy principles: (1) commercial competition in domain name registration by releasing the monopoly NSI had, and (2) protecting trademarks in the alphanumeric strings that make up the second-level domain names. The final, internationalizing component of the effort—represented by the interests of the WIPO and ITU bureaucracies—was attained by creating a Council of Registrars as a Swiss corporation, and creating special relationships with the ITU and the WIPO.

None of this institutional edifice could be built without the U.S. government. In early 1998, the administration responded to this ferment with a green paper, seeking the creation of a private, nonprofit corporation registered in the United States to take on management of the domain name issue. By its own terms, the green paper responded to concerns of the domain name registration monopoly and of trademark issues in domain names, first and foremost, and to some extent to increasing clamor from abroad for a voice in Internet governance. Despite a cool response from the European Union, the U.S. government proceeded to finalize a white paper and authorize the creation of its preferred model—the private, nonprofit corporation. Thus was born the Internet Corporation for Assigned Names and Numbers (ICANN) as a private, nonprofit California corporation. Over time, it succeeded in large measure in loosening NSI's monopoly on domain name registration. Its efforts on the trademark side effectively created a global preemptive property right. Following an invitation in the U.S. government's white paper for ICANN to study the proper approach to trademark enforcement in the domain name space, ICANN and WIPO initiated a process that began in July 1998 and ended in April 1999. As Froomkin describes his experience as a public-interest expert in this process, the process feigned transparency and open discourse, but was in actuality an opaque staff-driven drafting effort.[22] The result was a very strong global property right available to trademark owners in the alphanumeric strings that make up domain names. This was supported by binding arbitration. Because it controlled the root server, ICANN could enforce its arbitration decisions worldwide. If ICANN decides that, say, the McDonald's fast-food corporation and not a hypothetical farmer named Old McDonald owned www.mcdonalds.com, all computers in the world would be referred to the corporate site, not the personal one. Not entirely satisfied with the degree to which the ICANN-WIPO process protected their trademarks, some of the major trademark owners lobbied the U.S. Congress to pass an even stricter law. This law would make it easier for the owners of commercial brand names to obtain domain names that include their brand, whether or not there was any probability that users would actually confuse sites like the hypothetical Old McDonald's with that of the fast-food chain.

The degree to which the increased appropriation of the domain name space is important is a function of the extent to which the cultural practice of using human memory to find information will continue to be widespread. The underlying assumption of the value of trademarked alphanumeric strings as second-level domain names is that users will approach electronic commerce by typing in "www.brandname.com" as their standard way of relating to information on the Net. This is far from obviously the most efficient solution. In physical space, where collecting comparative information on price, quality, and so on is very costly, brand names serve an important informational role. In cyberspace, where software can compare prices, and product-review services that link to vendors are easy to set up and cheap to implement, the brand name becomes an encumbrance on good information, not its facilitator. If users are limited, for instance, to hunting around as to whether information they seek is on www.brandname.com, www.brand_name.com, or www.brand.net, name recognition from the real world becomes a bottleneck to e-commerce. And this is precisely the reason why owners of established marks sought to assure early adoption of trademarks in domain names—it assures users that they can, in fact, find their accustomed products on the Web without having to go through search algorithms that might expose them to comparison with pesky start-up competitors. As search engines become better and more tightly integrated into the basic browser functionality, the idea that a user who wants to buy from Delta Airlines would simply type "www.delta.com," as opposed to plugging "delta airlines" into an integrated search toolbar and getting the airline as a first hit becomes quaint. However, quaint inefficient cultural practices can persist. And if this indeed is one that will persist, then the contours of the property right matter. As the law has developed over the past few years, ownership of a trademark that includes a certain alphanumeric string almost always gives the owner of the trademark a preemptive right in using the letters and numbers incorporated in that mark as a domain name.

Domain name disputes have fallen into three main categories. There are cases of simple arbitrage. Individuals who predicted that having a domain name with the brand name in it would be valuable, registered such domain names aplenty, and waited for the flat-footed brand name owners to pay them to hand over the domain. There is nothing more inefficient about this form of arbitrage than any other. The arbitrageurs "reserved" commercially valuable names so they could be auctioned, rather than taken up by someone who might have a non-negotiable interest in the name—for example, some-one whose personal name it was. These arbitrageurs were nonetheless branded pirates and hijackers, and the consistent result of all the cases on domain names has been that the corporate owners of brand names receive the domain names associated with their brands without having to pay the arbitrageurs. Indeed, the arbitrageurs were subject to damage judgments. A second kind of case involved bona fide holders of domain names that made sense for them, but were nonetheless shared with a famous brand name. One child nicknamed "Pokey" registered "pokey.org," and his battle to keep that name against a toy manufacturer that sold a toy called "pokey" became a poster child for this type of case. Results have been more mixed in this case, depending on how sympathetic the early registrant was. The third type of case—and in many senses, most important from the perspective of free-dom to participate not merely as a consumer in the networked environment, but as a producer—involves those who use brand names to draw attention to the fact that they are attacking the owner of the brand. One well-known example occurred when Verizon Wireless was launched. The same hacker magazine involved in the DeCSS case, *2600*, purchased the domain name "verizonreallysucks.com" to poke fun at Verizon. In response to a letter re-quiring that they give up the domain name, the magazine purchased the domain name "VerizonShouldSpendMoreTimeFixingItsNetworkAndLess MoneyOnLawyers.com." These types of cases have again met with varying degrees of sympathy from courts and arbitrators under the ICANN process, although it is fairly obvious that using a brand name in order to mock and criticize its owner and the cultural meaning it tries to attach to its mark is at the very core of fair use, cultural criticism, and free expression.

The point here is not to argue for one type of answer or another in terms of trademark law, constitutional law, or the logic of ICANN. It is to identify points of pressure where the drive to create proprietary rights is creating points of control over the flow of information and the freedom to make meaning in the networked environment. The domain name issue was seen by many as momentous when it was new. ICANN has drawn a variety of both yearnings and fears as a potential source of democratic governance for the Internet or a platform for U.S. hegemony. I suspect that neither of these will turn out to be true. The importance of property rights in domain names is directly based on the search practices of users. Search engines, directories, review sites, and referrals through links play a large role in enabling users to find information they are interested in. Control over the domain name space is unlikely to provide a real bottleneck that will prevent both commercial competitors and individual speakers from drawing attention to their competition or criticism. However, the battle is indicative of the efforts to use proprietary rights in a particular element of the institutional ecology of the logical layer—trademarks in domain names—to tilt the environment in favor of the owners of famous brand names, and against individuals, noncommercial actors, and smaller, less-known competitors.

The Browser Wars

A much more fundamental battle over the logical layer has occurred in the browser wars. Here, the "institutional" component is not formal institutions, like laws or regulations, but technical practice institutions—the standards for Web site design. Unlike on the network protocol side, the device side of the logical layer—the software running personal computers—was thoroughly property-based by the mid-1990s. Microsoft's dominance in desktop operating systems was well established, and there was strong presence of other software publishers in consumer applications, pulling the logical layer toward a proprietary model. In 1995, Microsoft came to perceive the Internet and particularly the World Wide Web as a threat to its control over the desktop. The user-side Web browser threatened to make the desktop a more open environment that would undermine its monopoly. Since that time, the two pulls—the openness of the nonproprietary network and the closed nature of the desktop—have engaged in a fairly energetic tug-of-war over the digital environment. This push-me-pull-you game is played out both in the domain of market share, where Microsoft has been immensely successful, and in the domain of standard setting, where it has been only moderately successful. In market share, the story is well known and has been well documented in the Microsoft antitrust litigation. Part of the reason that it is so hard for a new operating system to compete with Microsoft's is that application developers write first, and sometimes only, for the already-dominant operating system. A firm investing millions of dollars in developing a new piece of photo-editing software will usually choose to write it so that it works with the operating system that has two hundred million users, not the one that has only fifteen million users. Microsoft feared that Netscape's browser, dominant in the mid-1990s, would come to be a universal translator among applications—that developers could write their applications to run on the browser, and the browser would handle translation across different operating systems. If that were to happen, Microsoft's operating system would have to compete on intrinsic quality. Windows would lose the boost of the felicitous feedback effect, where more users mean more applications, and this greater number of applications in turn draws more new users, and so forth. To prevent this eventuality, Microsoft engaged in a series of practices, ultimately found to have violated the antitrust laws, aimed at getting a dominant majority of Internet users to adopt Microsoft's Internet Explorer (IE). Illegal or not, these practices succeeded in making IE the dominant browser, overtaking the original market leader, Netscape, within a short number of years. By the time the antitrust case was completed, Netscape had turned browser development over to the open-source development community, but under licensing conditions sufficiently vague so that the project generated little early engagement. Only around 2001–2002, did the Mozilla browser development project get sufficient independence and security for developers to begin to contribute energetically. It was only in late 2004, early 2005, that Mozilla Firefox became the first major release of a free software browser that showed promise of capturing some user-share back from IE.

Microsoft's dominance over the operating system and browser has not, as a practical matter, resulted in tight control over the information flow and use on the Internet. This is so for three reasons. First, the TCP/IP protocol is more fundamental to Internet communications. It allows any application or content to run across the network, as long as it knows how to translate itself into very simple packets with standard addressing information. To prevent applications from doing this over basic TCP/IP would make the Microsoft operating system substantially crippling to many applications developers, which brings us to the second reason. Microsoft's dominance depends to a great extent on the vastly greater library of applications available to run on Windows. To make this library possible, Microsoft makes available a wide range of application program interfaces that developers can use without seeking Microsoft's permission. As a strategic decision about what enhances its core dominance, Microsoft may tilt the application development arena in its favor, but not enough to make it too hard for most applications to be implemented on a Windows platform. While not nearly as open as a genuinely open-source platform, Windows is also a far cry from a completely controlled platform, whose owner seeks to control all applications that are permitted to be developed for, and all uses that can be made of, its platform. Third, while IE controls much of the browser market share, Microsoft has not succeeded in dominating the standards for Web authoring. Web browser standard setting happens on the turf of the mythic creator of the Web— Tim Berners Lee. Lee chairs the W3C, a nonprofit organization that sets the standard ways in which Web pages are authored so that they have a predictable appearance on the browser's screen. Microsoft has, over the years, introduced various proprietary extensions that are not part of the Web standard, and has persuaded many Web authors to optimize their Web sites to IE. If it succeeds, it will have wrested practical control over standard setting from the W3C. However, as of this writing, Web pages generally continue to be authored using mostly standard, open extensions, and anyone browsing the Internet with a free software browser, like any of the Mozilla family, will be able to read and interact with most Web sites, including the major e-commerce sites, without encountering nonstandard interfaces optimized for IE. At a minimum, these sites are able to query the browser as to whether or not it is IE, and serve it with either the open standard or the proprietary standard version accordingly.

Free Software

The role of Mozilla in the browser wars points to the much more substantial and general role of the free software movement and the open-source development community as major sources of openness, and as a backstop against appropriation of the logical layer. In some of the most fundamental uses of the Internet—Web-server software, Web-scripting software, and e-mail servers—free or open-source software has a dominant user share. In others, like the operating system, it offers a robust alternative sufficiently significant to prevent enclosure of an entire component of the logical layer. Because of its licensing structure and the fact that the technical specifications are open for inspection and use by anyone, free software offers the most completely open, commons-based institutional and organizational arrangement for any resource or capability in the digital environment. Any resource in the logical layer that is the product of a free software development project is institutionally designed to be available for nonmarket, nonproprietary strategies of use. The same openness, however, makes free software resistant to control. If one tries to implement a constraining implementation of a certain function—for example, an audio driver that will not allow music to be played without proper authorization from a copyright holder—the openness of the code for inspection will allow users to identify what, and how, the software is constraining. The same institutional framework will allow any developer to "fix" the problem and change the way the software behaves. This is how free and open-source software is developed to begin with. One cannot limit access to the software—for purposes of inspection and modification—to developers whose behavior can be controlled by contract or property and still have the software be "open source" or free. As long as free software can provide a fully implemented alternative to the computing functionalities users want, perfect enclosure of the logical layer is impossible. This openness is a boon for those who wish the network to develop in response to a wide range of motivations and practices. However, it presents a serious problem for anyone who seeks to constrain the range of uses made of the Internet. And, just as they did in the context of trusted systems, the incumbent industrial culture producers—Hollywood and the recording industry—would, in fact, like to control how the Internet is used and how software behaves.

Software Patents

Throughout most of its history, software has been protected primarily by copyright, if at all. Beginning in the early 1980s, and culminating formally in the late 1990s, the Federal Circuit, the appellate court that oversees the U.S. patent law, made clear that software was patentable. The result has been that software has increasingly become the subject of patent rights. There is now pressure for the European Union to pass a similar reform, and to internationalize the patentability of software more generally. There are a variety of policy questions surrounding the advisability of software patents. Software development is a highly incremental process. This means that patents tend to impose a burden on a substantial amount of future innovation, and to reward innovation steps whose qualitative improvement over past contributions may be too small to justify the discontinuity represented by a patent grant. Moreover, innovation in the software business has flourished without patents, and there is no obvious reason to implement a new exclusive right in a market that seems to have been enormously innovative without it. Most important, software components interact with each other constantly. Sometimes interoperating with a certain program may be absolutely necessary to perform a function, not because the software is so good, but because it has become the standard. The patent then may extend to the very functionality, whereas a copyright would have extended only to the particular code by which it was achieved. The primary fear is that patents over standards could become major bottlenecks.

From the perspective of the battle over the institutional ecology, free software and open-source development stand to lose the most from software patents. A patent holder may charge a firm that develops dependent software in order to capture rents. However, there is no obvious party to charge for free software development. Even if the patent owner has a very open licensing policy—say, licensing the patent nonexclusively to anyone without discrimination for $10,000—most free software developers will not be able to play. IBM and Red Hat may pay for licenses, but the individual contributor hacking away at his or her computer, will not be able to. The basic driver of free software innovation is easy ubiquitous access to the state of the art, coupled with diverse motivations and talents brought to bear on a particular design problem. If working on a problem requires a patent license, and if any new development must not only write new source code, but also avoid replicating a broad scope patent or else pay a large fee, then the conditions for free software development are thoroughly undermined. Free software is responsible for some of the most basic and widely used innovations and utilities on the Internet today. Software more generally is heavily populated by service firms that do not functionally rely on exclusive rights, copyrights, or patents. Neither free software nor service-based software development need patents, and both, particularly free and open-source software, stand to be stifled significantly by widespread software patenting. As seen in the case of the browser war, in the case of Gnutella, and the much more widely used basic utilities of the Web—Apache server software, a number of free e-mail servers, and the Perl scripting language—free and open-source software developers provide central chunks of the logical layer. They do so in a way that leaves that layer open for anyone to use and build upon. The drive to increase the degree of exclusivity available for software by adopting patents over and above copyright threatens the continued vitality of this development methodology. In particular, it threatens to take certain discrete application areas that may require access to patented standard elements or protocols out of the domain of what can be done by free software. As such, it poses a significant threat to the availability of an open logical layer for at least some forms of network use.

THE CONTENT LAYER

The last set of resources necessary for information production and exchange is the universe of existing information, knowledge, and culture. The battle over the scope, breadth, extent, and enforcement of copyright, patent, trademarks, and a variety of exotic rights like trespass to chattels or the right to link has been the subject of a large legal literature. Instead of covering the entire range of enclosure efforts of the past decade or more, I offer a set of brief descriptions of the choices being made in this domain. The intention is not to criticize or judge the intrinsic logic of any of these legal changes, but merely to illustrate how all these toggles of institutional ecology are being set in favor of proprietary strategies, at the expense of nonproprietary producers.

Copyright

The first domain in which we have seen a systematic preference for commercial producers that rely on property over commons-based producers is in copyright. This preference arises from a combination of expansive interpretations of what rights include, a niggardly interpretive attitude toward users' privileges, especially fair use, and increased criminalization. These have made copyright law significantly more industrial-production friendly than it was in the past or than it need be from the perspective of optimizing creativity or welfare in the networked information economy, rather than rent-extraction by incumbents.

Right to Read. Jessica Litman early diagnosed an emerging new "right to read."[23] The basic right of copyright, to control copying, was never seen to include the right to control who reads an existing copy, when, and how many times. Once a user bought a copy, he or she could read it many times, lend it to a friend, or leave it on the park bench or in the library for anyone else to read. This provided a coarse valve to limit the deadweight loss associated with appropriating a public good like information. As a happenstance of computer technology, reading on a screen involves making a temporary copy of a file onto the temporary memory of the computer. An early decision of the Ninth Circuit Court of Appeals, *MAI Systems*, treated RAM (random-access memory) copies of this sort as "copies" for purposes of copyright.[24] This position, while weakly defended, was not later challenged or rejected by other courts. Its result is that every act of reading on a screen involves "making a copy" within the meaning of the Copyright Act. As a practical matter, this interpretation expands the formal rights of copyright holders to cover any and all computer-mediated uses of their works, because no use can be made with a computer without at least formally implicating the right to copy. More important than the formal legal right, however, this universal baseline claim to a right to control even simple reading of one's copyrighted work marked a change in attitude. Justified later through various claims—such as the efficiency of private ordering or of price discrimination—it came to stand for a fairly broad proposition: Owners should have the right to control all valuable uses of their works. Combined with the possibility and existence of technical controls on actual use and the DMCA's prohibition on circumventing those controls, this means that copyright law has shifted. It existed throughout most of its history as a regulatory provision that reserved certain uses of works for exclusive control by authors, but left other, not explicitly constrained uses free. It has now become a law that gives rights holders the exclusive right to control any computer-mediated use of their works, and captures in its regulatory scope all uses that were excluded from control in prior media.

Fair Use Narrowed.   Fair use in copyright was always a judicially created concept with a large degree of uncertainty in its application. This uncertainty, coupled with a broader interpretation of what counts as a commercial use, a restrictive judicial view of what counts as fair, and increased criminalization have narrowed its practical scope.

First, it is important to recognize that the theoretical availability of the fair-use doctrine does not, as a practical matter, help most productions. This is due to a combination of two factors: (1) fair-use doctrine is highly fact specific and uncertain in application, and (2) the Copyright Act provides large fixed statutory damages, even if there is no actual damage to the copy-right owner. Lessig demonstrated this effect most clearly by working through an example of a documentary film.[25] A film will not be distributed without liability insurance. Insurance, in turn, will not be issued without formal clearance, or permission, from the owner of each copyrighted work, any portion of which is included in the film, even if the amount used is trivially small and insignificant to the documentary. A five-second snippet of a tele-vision program that happened to play on a television set in the background of a sequence captured in documentary film can therefore prevent distri-bution of the film, unless the filmmaker can persuade the owner of that program to grant rights to use the materials. Copyright owners in such television programs may demand thousands of dollars for even such a min-imal and incidental use of "their" images. This is not because a court would ultimately find that using the image as is, with the tiny fraction of the television program in the background, was not covered by fair use. It prob-ably would be a fair use. It is because insurance companies and distributors would refuse to incur the risk of litigation.

Second, in the past few years, even this uncertain scope has been con-stricted by expanding the definitions of what counts as interference with a market and what counts as a commercial use. Consider the *Free Republic* case. In that case, a political Web site offered a forum for users to post stories from various newspapers as grist for a political discussion of their contents or their slant. The court held that because newspapers may one day sell access to archived articles, and because some users may read some articles on the Web forum instead of searching and retrieving them from the news-papers' archive, the use interfered with a potential market. Moreover, because Free Republic received donations from users (although it did not require them) and exchanged advertising arrangements with other political sites, the court treated the site as a "commercial user," and its use of newspaper articles to facilitate political discussion of them "a commercial use." These factors enabled the court to hold that posting an article from a medium—daily newspapers—whose existence does not depend on copyright, in a way that may one day come to have an effect on uncertain future revenues, which in any case would be marginal to the business model of the newspapers, was not a fair use even when done for purposes of political commentary.

Criminalization.   Copyright enforcement has also been substantially crimi-nalized in the past few years. Beginning with the No Electronic Theft Act

(NET Act) in 1997 and later incorporated into the DMCA, criminal copyright has recently become much more expansive than it was until a few years ago. Prior to passage of the NET Act, only commercial pirates—those that slavishly made thousands of copies of video or audiocassettes and sold them for profit—would have qualified as criminal violators of copyright. Criminal liability has now been expanded to cover private copying and free sharing of copyrighted materials whose cumulative nominal price (irrespective of actual displaced demand) is quite low. As criminal copyright law is currently written, many of the tens of millions using p2p networks are felons. It is one thing when the recording industry labels tens of millions of individuals in a society "pirates" in a rhetorical effort to conform social norms to its members' business model. It is quite another when the state brands them felons and fines or imprisons them. Litman has offered the most plausible explanation of this phenomenon.[26] As the network makes low-cost production and exchange of information and culture easier, the large-scale commercial producers are faced with a new source of competition—volunteers, people who provide information and culture for free. As the universe of people who can threaten the industry has grown to encompass more or less the entire universe of potential customers, the plausibility of using civil actions to force individuals to buy rather than share information goods decreases. Suing all of one's intended customers is not a sustainable business model. In the interest of maintaining the business model that relies on control over information goods and their sale as products, the copyright industry has instead enlisted criminal enforcement by the state to prevent the emergence of such a system of free exchange. These changes in formal law have, in what is perhaps a more important development, been coupled with changes in the Justice Department's enforcement policy, leading to a substantial increase in the shadow of criminal enforcement in this area.[27]

Term Extension. The change in copyright law that received the most widespread public attention was the extension of copyright term in the Sonny Bono Copyright Term Extension Act of 1998. The statute became cause celebre in the early 2000s because it was the basis of a major public campaign and constitutional challenge in the case of *Eldred v. Ashcroft*.[28] The actual marginal burden of this statute on use of existing materials could be seen as relatively small. The length of copyright protection was already very long— seventy-five years for corporate-owned materials, life of the author plus fifty for materials initially owned by human authors. The Sonny Bono Copyright

Term Extension Act increased these two numbers to ninety-five and life plus seventy, respectively. The major implication, however, was that the Act showed that retroactive extension was always available. As materials that were still valuable in the stocks of Disney, in particular, came close to the public domain, their lives would be extended indefinitely. The legal challenge to the statute brought to public light the fact that, as a practical matter, almost the entire stock of twentieth-century culture and beyond would stay privately owned, and its copyright would be renewed indefinitely. For video and sound recordings, this meant that almost the entire universe of materials would never become part of the public domain; would never be available for free use as inputs into nonproprietary production. The U.S. Supreme Court upheld the retroactive extension. The inordinately long term of protection in the United States, initially passed under the pretext of "harmonizing" the length of protection in the United States and in Europe, is now being used as an excuse to "harmonize" the length of protection for various kinds of materials—like sound recordings—that actually have shorter terms of protection in Europe or other countries, like Australia. At stake in all these battles is the question of when, if ever, will Errol Flynn's or Mickey Mouse's movies, or Elvis's music, become part of the public domain? When will these be available for individual users on the same terms that Shakespeare or Mozart are available? The implication of *Eldred* is that they may never join the public domain, unless the politics of term-extension legislation change.

No de Minimis Digital Sampling.   A narrower, but revealing change is the recent elimination of digital sampling from the universe of *ex ante* permissible actions, even when all that is taken is a tiny snippet. The case is recent and has not been generalized by other courts as of this writing. However, it offers insight into the mind-set of judges who are confronted with digital opportunities, and who in good faith continue to see the stakes as involving purely the organization of a commercial industry, rather than defining the comparative scope of commercial industry and nonmarket commons-based creativity. Courts seem blind to the effects of their decisions on the institutional ecology within which nonproprietary, individual, and social creation must live. In *Bridgeport Music, Inc.*, the Sixth Circuit was presented with the following problem: The defendant had created a rap song.[29] In making it, he had digitally copied a two-second guitar riff from a digital recording of a 1970s song, and then looped and inserted it in various places to create a completely different musical effect than the original. The district court had decided that the amount borrowed was so small as to make the borrowing de minimis—too little for the law to be concerned with. The Court of Appeals, however, decided that it would be too burdensome for courts to have to decide, on a case-by-case basis, how much was too little for law to be concerned with. Moreover, it would create too much uncertainty for recording companies; it is, as the court put it, "cheaper to license than to litigate."[30] The court therefore held that any digital sampling, no matter how trivial, could be the basis of a copyright suit. Such a bright-line rule that makes all direct copying of digital bits, no matter how small, an infringement, makes digital sound recordings legally unavailable for noncommercial, individually creative mixing. There are now computer programs, like Garage Band, that allow individual users to cut and mix existing materials to create their own music. These may not result in great musical compositions. But they may. That, in any event, is not their point. They allow users to have a very different relationship to recorded music than merely passively listening to finished, unalterable musical pieces. By imagining that the only parties affected by copyright coverage of sampling are recording artists who have contracts with recording studios and seek to sell CDs, and can therefore afford to pay licensing fees for every two-second riff they borrow, the court effectively outlawed an entire model of user creativity. Given how easy it is to cut, paste, loop, slow down, and speed up short snippets, and how creatively exhilarating it is for users—young and old—to tinker with creating musical compositions with instruments they do not know how to play, it is likely that the opinion has rendered illegal a practice that will continue, at least for the time being. Whether the social practice will ultimately cause the law to change or vice versa is more difficult to predict.

Contractual Enclosure: Click-Wrap Licenses and the Uniform Computer Information Transactions Act (UCITA)

Practically all academic commentators on copyright law—whether critics or proponents of this provision or that—understand copyright to be a public policy accommodation between the goal of providing incentives to creators and the goal of providing efficiently priced access to both users and downstream creators. Ideally, it takes into consideration the social costs and benefits of one settlement or another, and seeks to implement an optimal trade-off. Beginning in the 1980s, software and other digital goods were sold with "shrink-wrap licenses." These were licenses to use the software, which purported to apply to mass-market buyers because the buyer would be deemed to have accepted the contract by opening the packaging of the software. These practices later transmuted online into click-wrap licenses familiar to most anyone who has installed software and had to click "I Agree" once or more before the software would install. Contracts are not bound by the balance struck in public law. Licensors can demand, and licensees can agree to, almost any terms. Among the terms most commonly inserted in such licenses that restrict the rights of users are prohibitions on reverse engineering, and restrictions on the use of raw data in compilations, even though copyright law itself does not recognize rights in data. As Mark Lemley showed, most courts prior to the mid-1990s did not enforce such terms.[31] Some courts refused to enforce shrink-wrap licenses in mass-market transactions by relying on state contract law, finding an absence of sufficient consent or an unenforceable contract of adhesion. Others relied on federal preemption, stating that to the extent state contract law purported to enforce a contract that prohibited fair use or otherwise protected material in the public domain—like the raw information contained in a report—it was preempted by federal copyright law that chose to leave this material in the public domain, freely usable by all. In 1996, in *ProCD v. Zeidenberg*, the Seventh Circuit held otherwise, arguing that private ordering would be more efficient than a single public determination of what the right balance was.[32]

The following few years saw substantial academic debate as to the desirability of contractual opt-outs from the public policy settlement. More important, the five years that followed saw a concerted effort to introduce a new part to the Uniform Commercial Code (UCC)—a model commercial law that, though nonbinding, is almost universally adopted at the state level in the United States, with some modifications. The proposed new UCC Article 2B was to eliminate the state law concerns by formally endorsing the use of standard shrink-wrap licenses. The proposed article generated substantial academic and political heat, ultimately being dropped by the American Law Institute, one of the main sponsors of the UCC. A model law did ultimately pass under the name of the Uniform Computer Information Transactions Act (UCITA), as part of a less universally adopted model law effort. Only two states adopted the law—Virginia and Maryland. A number of other states then passed anti-UCITA laws, which gave their residents a safe harbor from having UCITA applied to their click-wrap transactions.

The reason that *ProCD* and UCITA generated so much debate was the concern that click-wrap licenses were operating in an inefficient market, and that they were, as a practical matter, displacing the policy balance represented by copyright law. Mass-market transactions do not represent a genuine negotiated agreement, in the individualized case, as to what the efficient contours of permissions are for the given user and the given information product. They are, rather, generalized judgments by the vendor as to what terms are most attractive for it that the market will bear. Unlike rival economic goods, information goods sold at a positive price in reliance on copyright are, by definition, priced above marginal cost. The information itself is non-rival. Its marginal cost is zero. Any transaction priced above the cost of communication is evidence of some market power in the hands of the provider, used to price based on value and elasticity of demand, not on marginal cost. Moreover, the vast majority of users are unlikely to pay close attention to license details they consider to be boilerplate. This means there is likely significant information shortfall on the part of consumers as to the content of the licenses, and the sensitivity of demand to overreaching contract terms is likely low. This is not because consumers are stupid or slothful, but because the probability that either they would be able to negotiate out from under a standard provision, or a court would enforce against them a truly abusive provision is too low to justify investing in reading and arguing about contracts for all but their largest purchases. In combination, these considerations make it difficult to claim as a general matter that privately set licensing terms would be more efficient than the publicly set background rules of copyright law.[33] The combination of mass-market contracts enforced by technical controls over use of digital materials, which in turn are protected by the DMCA, threatens to displace the statutorily defined public domain with a privately defined realm of permissible use.[34] This privately defined settlement would be arrived at in non-negotiated mass-market transactions, in the presence of significant information asymmetries between consumers and vendors, and in the presence of systematic market power of at least some degree.

Trademark Dilution

As discussed in chapter 8, the centrality of commercial interaction to social existence in early-twenty-first-century America means that much of our core iconography is commercial in origin and owned as a trademark. Mickey, Barbie, Playboy, or Coke are important signifiers of meaning in contemporary culture. Using iconography is a central means of creating rich, culturally situated expressions of one's understanding of the world. Yet, as Boyle has pointed out, now that we treat flag burning as a constitutionally protected expression, trademark law has made commercial icons the sole remaining venerable objects in our law. Trademark law permits the owners of culturally significant images to control their use, to squelch criticism, and to define exclusively the meaning that the symbols they own carry.

Three factors make trademark protection today more of a concern as a source of enclosure than it might have been in the past. First is the introduction of the federal Anti-Dilution Act of 1995. Second is the emergence of the brand as the product, as opposed to a signifier for the product. Third is the substantial reduction in search and other information costs created by the Net. Together, these three factors mean that owned symbols are becoming increasingly important as cultural signifiers, are being enclosed much more extensively than before precisely as cultural signifiers, and with less justification beyond the fact that trademarks, like all exclusive rights, are economically valuable to their owners.

In 1995, Congress passed the first federal Anti-Dilution Act. Though treated as a trademark protection law, and codifying doctrines that arose in trademark common law, antidilution is a fundamentally different economic right than trademark protection. Traditional trademark protection is focused on preventing consumer confusion. It is intended to assure that consumers can cheaply tell the difference between one product and another, and to give producers incentives to create consistent quality products that can be associated with their trademark. Trademark law traditionally reflected these interests. Likelihood of consumer confusion was the sine qua non of trademark infringement. If I wanted to buy a Coca-Cola, I did not want to have to make sure I was not buying a different dark beverage in a red can called Coca-Gola. Infringement actions were mostly limited to suits among competitors in similar relevant markets, where confusion could occur. So, while trademark law restricted how certain symbols could be used, it was so only as among competitors, and only as to the commercial, not cultural, meaning of their trademark. The antidilution law changes the most relevant factors. It is intended to protect famous brand names, irrespective of a likelihood of confusion, from being diluted by use by others. The association between a particular corporation and a symbol is protected for its value to that corporation, irrespective of the use. It no longer regulates solely competitors to the benefit of competition. It prohibits many more possible uses of the symbol than was the case under traditional trademark law. It applies even to noncommercial users where there is no possibility of confusion. The emergence of this antidilution theory of exclusivity is particularly important as brands have become the product itself, rather than a marker for the product. Nike and Calvin Klein are examples: The product sold in these cases is not a better shoe or shirt—the product sold is the brand. And the brand is associated with a cultural and social meaning that is developed purposefully by the owner of the brand so that people will want to buy it. This development explains why dilution has become such a desirable exclusive right for those who own it. It also explains the cost of denying to anyone the right to use the symbol, now a signifier of general social meaning, in ways that do not confuse consumers in the traditional trademark sense, but provide cultural criticism of the message signified.

Ironically, the increase in the power of trademark owners to control uses of their trademark comes at a time when its functional importance as a mechanism for reducing search costs is declining. Traditional trademark's most important justification was that it reduced information collection costs and thereby facilitated welfare-enhancing trade. In the context of the Internet, this function is significantly less important. General search costs are lower. Individual items in commerce can provide vastly greater amounts of information about their contents and quality. Users can use machine processing to search and sift through this information and to compare views and reviews of specific items. Trademark has become less, rather than more, functionally important as a mechanism for dealing with search costs. When we move in the next few years to individual-item digital marking, such as with RFID (radio frequency identification) tags, all the relevant information about contents, origin, and manufacture down to the level of the item, as opposed to the product line, will be readily available to consumers in real space, by scanning any given item, even if it is not otherwise marked at all. In this setting, where the information qualities of trademarks will significantly decline, the antidilution law nonetheless assures that owners can control the increasingly important cultural meaning of trademarks. Trademark, including dilution, is subject to a fair use exception like that of copyright. For the same reasons as operated in copyright, however, the presence of such a doctrine only ameliorates, but does not solve, the limits that a broad exclusive right places on the capacity of nonmarket-oriented creative uses of materials—in this case, culturally meaningful symbols.

Database Protection

In 1991, in *Feist Publications, Inc. v. Rural Tel. Serv. Co.*, the Supreme Court held that raw facts in a compilation, or database, were not covered by the Copyright Act. The constitutional clause that grants Congress the power to create exclusive rights for authors, the Court held, required that works protected were original with the author. The creative element of the compilation—its organization or selectivity, for example, if sufficiently creative—could therefore be protected under copyright law. However, the raw facts compiled could not. Copying data from an existing compilation was therefore not "piracy"; it was not unfair or unjust; it was purposefully privileged in order to advance the goals of the constitutional power to make exclusive grants—the advancement of progress and creative uses of the data.[35] A few years later, the European Union passed a Database Directive, which created a discrete and expansive right in raw data compilations.[36] The years since the Court decided *Feist* have seen repeated efforts by the larger players in the database publishing industry to pass similar legislation in the United States that would, as a practical matter, overturn *Feist* and create exclusive private rights in the raw data in compilations. "Harmonization" with Europe has been presented as a major argument in favor of this law. Because the *Feist* Court based its decision on limits to the constitutional power to create exclusive rights in raw information, efforts to protect database providers mostly revolved around an unfair competition law, based in the Commerce Clause, rather than on precisely replicating the European right. In fact, however, the primary draft that has repeatedly been introduced walks, talks, and looks like a property right.

Sustained and careful work, most prominently by Jerome Reichman and Paul Uhlir, has shown that the proposed database right is unnecessary and detrimental, particularly to scientific research.[37] Perhaps no example explains this point better than the "natural experiment" that Boyle has pointed to, and which the United States and Europe have been running over the past decade or so. The United States has formally had no exclusive right in data since 1991. Europe has explicitly had such a right since 1996. One would expect that both the European Union and the United States would look to the comparative effects on the industries in both places when the former decides whether to keep its law, and the latter decides whether to adopt one like it. The evidence is reasonably consistent and persuasive. Following the *Feist* decision, the U.S. database industry continued to grow steadily, without a blip. The "removal" of the property right in data by *Feist* had no effect on growth. Europe at the time had a much smaller database industry than did the United States, as measured by the number of databases and database companies. Maurer, Hugenholz, and Onsrud showed that, following the introduction of the European sui generis right, each country saw a one-time spike in the number of databases and new database companies, but this was followed within a year or two by a decline to the levels seen before the Directive, which have been fairly stagnant since the early 1990s.[38] Another study, more specifically oriented toward the appropriate policy for government-collected data, compared the practices of Europe—where government agencies are required to charge what the market will bear for access to data they collect—and the United States, where the government makes data it collects freely available at the cost of reproduction, as well as for free on the Web. That study found that the secondary uses of data, including commercial- and noncommercial-sector uses—such as, for example, markets in commercial risk management and meteorological services—contributed vastly more to the economy of the United States because of secondary uses of freely accessed government weather data than equivalent market sectors in Europe were able to contribute to their respective economies.[39] The evidence suggests, then, that the artificial imposition of rents for proprietary data is suppressing growth in European market-based commercial services and products that rely on access to data, relative to the steady growth in the parallel U.S. markets, where no such right exists. It is trivial to see that a cost structure that suppresses growth among market-based entities that would at least partially benefit from being able to charge more for their outputs would have an even more deleterious effect on nonmarket information production and exchange activities, which are burdened by the higher costs and gain no benefit from the proprietary rights.

There is, then, mounting evidence that rights in raw data are unnecessary to create a basis for a robust database industry. Database manufacturers rely on relational contracts—subscriptions to continuously updated databases—rather than on property-like rights. The evidence suggests that, in fact, exclusive rights are detrimental to various downstream industries that rely on access to data. Despite these fairly robust observations from a decade of experience, there continues to be a threat that such a law will pass in the U.S. Congress. This continued effort to pass such a law underscores two facts. First, much of the legislation in this area reflects rent seeking, rather than reasoned policy. Second, the deeply held belief that "more property-like rights will lead to more productivity" is hard to shake, even in the teeth of both theoretical analysis and empirical evidence to the contrary.

Linking and Trespass to Chattels:
New Forms of Information Exclusivity

Some litigants have turned to state law remedies to protect their data indirectly, by developing a common-law, trespass-to-server form of action. The primary instance of this trend is *eBay v. Bidder's Edge*, a suit by the leading auction site against an aggregator site. Aggregators collect information about what is being auctioned in multiple locations, and make the information about the items available in one place so that a user can search eBay and other auction sites simultaneously. The eventual bidding itself is done on the site that the item's owner chose to make his or her item available, under the terms required by that site. The court held that the automated information collection process—running a computer program that automatically requests information from the server about what is listed on it, called a spider or a bot—was a "trespass to chattels."[40] This ancient form of action, originally intended to apply to actual taking or destruction of goods, mutated into a prohibition on unlicensed automated searching. The injunction led to Bidder's Edge closing its doors before the Ninth Circuit had an opportunity to review the decision. A common-law decision like *eBay v. Bidder's Edge* creates a common-law exclusive private right in information by the back door. In principle, the information itself is still free of property rights. Reading it mechanically—an absolute necessity given the volume of the information and its storage on magnetic media accessible only by mechanical means—can, however, be prohibited as "trespass." The practical result would be equivalent to some aspects of a federal exclusive private right in raw data, but without the mitigating attributes of any exceptions that would be directly introduced into legislation. It is still too early to tell whether cases such as these ultimately will be considered preempted by federal copyright law,[41] or perhaps would be limited by first amendment law on the model of *New York Times v. Sullivan*.[42]

Beyond the roundabout exclusivity in raw data, trespass to chattels presents one instance of a broader question that is arising in application of both common-law and statutory provisions. At stake is the legal control over information about information, like linking and other statements people make about the availability and valence of some described information. Linking—the mutual pointing of many documents to each other—is the very core idea of the World Wide Web. In a variety of cases, parties have attempted to use law to control the linking practices of others. The basic structure of these cases is that A wants to tell users M and N about information presented by B. The meaning of a link is, after all, "here you can read information presented by someone other than me that I deem interesting or relevant to you, my reader." Someone, usually B, but possibly some other agent C, wants to control what M and N know or do with regard to the information B is presenting. B (or C) then sues A to prevent A from linking to the information on B's site.

The simplest instance of such a case involved a service that Microsoft offered—sidewalk.com—that provided access to, among other things, information on events in various cities. If a user wanted a ticket to the event, the sidewalk site linked that user directly to a page on ticketmaster.com where the user could buy a ticket. Ticketmaster objected to this practice, preferring instead that sidewalk.com link to its home page, in order to expose the users to all the advertising and services Ticketmaster provided, rather than solely to the specific service sought by the user referred by sidewalk .com. At stake in these linking cases is who will control the context in which certain information is presented. If deep linking is prohibited, Ticketmaster will control the context—the other movies or events available to be seen, their relative prominence, reviews, and so forth. The right to control linking then becomes a right to shape the meaning and relevance of one's statements for others. If the choice between Ticketmaster and Microsoft as controllers of the context of information may seem of little normative consequence, it is important to recognize that the right to control linking could easily apply to a local library, or church, or a neighbor as they participate in peer-producing relevance and accreditation of the information to which they link.

The general point is this: On the Internet, there are a variety of ways that some people can let others know about information that exists somewhere on the Web. In doing so, these informers loosen someone else's control over the described information—be it the government, a third party interested in limiting access to the information, or the person offering the information. In a series of instances over the past half decade or more we have seen attempts by people who control certain information to limit the ability of others to challenge that control by providing information about the information. These are not cases in which a person without access to information is seeking affirmative access from the "owner" of information. These are cases where someone who dislikes what another is saying about particular information is seeking the aid of law to control what other parties can say to each other about that information. Understood in these terms, the restrictive nature of these legal moves in terms of how they burden free speech in general, and impede the freedom of anyone, anywhere, to provide information, relevance, and accreditation, becomes clear. The *eBay v. Bidder's Edge* case suggests one particular additional aspect. While much of the political attention focuses on formal "intellectual property"–style statutes passed by Congress, in the past few years we have seen that state law and common-law doctrine are also being drafted to create areas of exclusivity and boundaries on the free use of information. These efforts are often less well informed, and because they were arrived at ad hoc, often without understanding that they are actually forms of regulating information production and exchange, they include none of the balancing privileges or limitations of rights that are so common in the formal statutory frameworks.

International "Harmonization"

One theme that has repeatedly appeared in the discussion of databases, the DMCA, and term extension, is the way in which "harmonization" and internationalization of exclusive rights are used to ratchet up the degree of exclusivity afforded rights holders. It is trite to point out that the most advanced economies in the world today are information and culture exporters. This is true of both the United States and Europe. Some of the cultural export industries—most notably Hollywood, the recording industry, some segments of the software industry, and pharmaceuticals—have business models that rely on the assertion of exclusive rights in information. Both the United States and the European Union, therefore, have spent the past decade and a half pushing for ever-more aggressive and expansive exclusive rights in international agreements and for harmonization of national laws around the world toward the highest degrees of protection. Chapter 9 discusses in some detail why this was not justified as a matter of economic rationality, and why it is deleterious as a matter of justice. Here, I only note the characteristic of internationalization and harmonization as a one-way ratchet toward ever-expanding exclusivity.

Take a simple provision like the term of copyright protection. In the mid-1990s, Europe was providing for many works (but not all) a term of life of the author plus seventy years, while the United States provided exclusivity for the life of the author plus fifty. A central argument for the Sonny Bono

Copyright Term Extension Act of 1998 was to "harmonize" with Europe. In the debates leading up to the law, one legislator actually argued that if our software manufacturers had a shorter term of copyright, they would be disadvantaged relative to the European firms. This argument assumes, of course, that U.S. software firms could stay competitive in the software business by introducing nothing new in software for seventy-five years, and that it would be the loss of revenues from products that had not been sufficiently updated for seventy-five years to warrant new copyright that would place them at a disadvantage. The newly extended period created by the Sonny Bono Copyright Term Extension Act is, however, longer in some cases than the protection afforded in Europe. Sound recordings, for example, are protected for fifty years in Europe. The arguments are now flowing in the opposite direction—harmonization toward the American standard for all kinds of works, for fear that the recordings of Elvis or the Beatles will fall into the European public domain within a few paltry years. "Harmonization" is never invoked to de-escalate exclusivity—for example, as a reason to eliminate the European database right in order to harmonize with the obviously successful American model of no protection, or to shorten the length of protection for sound recordings in the United States.

International agreements also provide a fertile forum for ratcheting up protection. Lobbies achieve a new right in a given jurisdiction—say an extension of term, or a requirement to protect technological protection measures on the model of the DMCA. The host country, usually the United States, the European Union, or both, then present the new right for treaty approval, as the United States did in the context of the WIPO treaties in the mid-1990s. Where this fails, the United States has more recently begun to negotiate bilateral free trade agreements (FTAs) with individual nations. The structure of negotiation is roughly as follows: The United States will say to Thailand, or India, or whoever the trading partner is: If you would like preferential treatment of your core export, say textiles or rice, we would like you to include this provision or that in your domestic copyright or patent law. Once this is agreed to in a number of bilateral FTAs, the major IP exporters can come back to the multilateral negotiations and claim an emerging international practice, which may provide more exclusivity than their then applicable domestic law. With changes to international treaties in hand, domestic resistance to legislation can be overcome, as we saw in the United States when the WIPO treaties were used to push through Congress the DMCA anticircumvention provisions that had failed to pass two years earlier. Any domestic efforts to reverse and limit exclusivity then have to overcome substantial hurdles placed by the international agreements, like the agreement on Trade Related Aspects of Intellectual Property (TRIPS). The difficulty of amending international agreements to permit a nation to decrease the degree of exclusivity it grants copyright or patent holders becomes an important one-way ratchet, preventing de-escalation.

Countervailing Forces

As this very brief overview demonstrates, most of the formal institutional moves at the content layer are pushing toward greater scope and reach for exclusive rights in the universe of existing information, knowledge, and cultural resources. The primary countervailing forces in the content layer are similar to the primary countervailing forces in the logical layer—that is, social and cultural push-back against exclusivity. Recall how central free software and the open, cooperative, nonproprietary standard-setting processes are to the openness of the logical layer. In the content layer, we are seeing the emergence of a culture of free creation and sharing developing as a countervailing force to the increasing exclusivity generated by the public, formal lawmaking system. The Public Library of Science discussed in chapter 9 is an initiative of scientists who, frustrated with the extraordinarily high journal costs for academic journals, have begun to develop systems for scientific publication whose outputs are immediately and freely available everywhere. The Creative Commons is an initiative to develop a series of licenses that allow individuals who create information, knowledge, and culture to attach simple licenses that define what others may, or may not, do with their work. The innovation represented by these licenses relative to the background copyright system is that they make it trivial for people to give others permission to use their creations. Before their introduction, there were no widely available legal forms to make it clear to the world that it is free to use my work, with or without restrictions. More important than the institutional innovation of Creative Commons is its character as a social movement. Under the moniker of the "free culture" movement, it aims to encourage widespread adoption of sharing one's creations with others. What a mature movement like the free software movement, or nascent movements like the free culture movement and the scientists' movement for open publication and open archiving are aimed at is the creation of a legally self-reinforcing domain of open cultural sharing. They do not negate property-like rights in information, knowledge, and culture. Rather, they represent a self-conscious choice by their participants to use copyrights, patents, and similar rights to create a domain of resources that are free to all for common use.

Alongside these institutionally instantiated moves to create a self-reinforcing set of common resources, there is a widespread, global culture of ignoring exclusive rights. It is manifest in the widespread use of file-sharing software to share copyrighted materials. It is manifest in the widespread acclaim that those who crack copy-protection mechanisms receive. This culture has developed a rhetoric of justification that focuses on the overreaching of the copyright industries and on the ways in which the artists themselves are being exploited by rights holders. While clearly illegal in the United States, there are places where courts have sporadically treated participation in these practices as copying for private use, which is exempted in some countries, including a number of European countries. In any event the sheer size of this movement and its apparent refusal to disappear in the face of lawsuits and public debate present a genuine countervailing pressure against the legal tightening of exclusivity. As a practical matter, efforts to impose perfect private ordering and to limit access to the underlying digital bits in movies and songs through technical means have largely failed under the sustained gaze of the community of computer scientists and hackers who have shown its flaws time and again. Moreover, the mechanisms developed in response to a large demand for infringing file-sharing utilities were the very mechanisms that were later available to the Swarthmore students to avoid having the Diebold files removed from the Internet and that are shared by other censorship-resistant publication systems. The tools that challenge the "entertainment-as-finished-good" business model are coming into much wider and unquestionably legitimate use. Litigation may succeed in dampening use of these tools for copying, but also creates a heightened political awareness of information-production regulation. The same students involved in the Diebold case, radicalized by the lawsuit, began a campus "free culture" movement. It is difficult to predict how this new political awareness will play out in a political arena—the making of copyrights, patents, and similar exclusive rights—that for decades has functioned as a technical backwater that could never invoke a major newspaper editorial, and was therefore largely controlled by the industries whose rents it secured.

THE PROBLEM OF SECURITY

This book as a whole is dedicated to the emergence of commons-based information production and its implications for liberal democracies. Of necessity, the emphasis of this chapter too is on institutional design questions that are driven by the conflict between the industrial and networked information economies. Orthogonal to this conflict, but always relevant to it, is the perennial concern of communications policy with security and crime. Throughout much of the 1990s, this concern manifested primarily as a conflict over encryption. The "crypto-wars," as they were called, revolved around the FBI's efforts to force industry to adopt technology that had a backdoor—then called the "Clipper Chip"—that would facilitate wiretapping and investigation. After retarding encryption adoption in the United States for almost a decade, the federal government ultimately decided that trying to hobble security in most American systems (that is, forcing everyone to adopt weaker encryption) in order to assure that the FBI could better investigate the failures of security that would inevitably follow use of such weak encryption was a bad idea. The fact that encryption research and business was moving overseas—giving criminals alternative sources for obtaining excellent encryption tools while the U.S. industry fell behind—did not help the FBI's cause. The same impulse is to some extent at work again, with the added force of the post-9/11 security mind-set.

One concern is that open wireless networks are available for criminals to hide their tracks—the criminal uses someone else's Internet connection using their unencrypted WiFi access point, and when the authorities successfully track the Internet address back to the WiFi router, they find an innocent neighbor rather than the culprit. This concern has led to some proposals that manufacturers of WiFi routers set their defaults so that, out of the box, the router is encrypted. Given how "sticky" defaults are in technology products, this would have enormously deleterious effects on the development of open wireless networks. Another concern is that free and open-source software reveals its design to anyone who wants to read it. This makes it easier to find flaws that could be exploited by attackers and nearly impossible to hide purposefully designed weaknesses, such as susceptibility to wiretapping. A third is that a resilient, encrypted, anonymous peer-to-peer network, like FreeNet or some of the major p2p architectures, offers the criminals or terrorists communications systems that are, for all practical purposes, beyond the control of law enforcement and counterterrorism efforts. To the extent that they take this form, security concerns tend to support the agenda of the proprietary producers.

However, security concerns need not support proprietary architectures and practices. On the wireless front, there is a very wide range of anonymization techniques available for criminals and terrorists who use the Internet to cover their tracks. The marginally greater difficulty that shutting off access to WiFi routers would impose on determined criminals bent on covering their tracks is unlikely to be worth the loss of an entire approach toward constructing an additional last-mile loop for local telecommunications. One of the core concerns of security is the preservation of network capacity as a critical infrastructure. Another is assuring communications for critical security personnel. Open wireless networks that are built from ad hoc, self-configuring mesh networks are the most robust design for a local communications loop currently available. It is practically impossible to disrupt local communications in such a network, because these networks are designed so that each router will automatically look for the next available neighbor with which to make a network. These systems will self-heal in response to any attack on communications infrastructure as a function of their basic normal operational design. They can then be available both for their primary intended critical missions and for first responders as backup data networks, even when main systems have been lost—as they were, in fact, lost in downtown Manhattan after the World Trade Center attack. To imagine that security is enhanced by eliminating the possibility that such a backup local communications network will emerge in exchange for forcing criminals to use more anonymizers and proxy servers instead of a neighbor's WiFi router requires a very narrow view of security. Similarly, the same ease of study that makes flaws in free software observable to potential terrorists or criminals makes them available to the community of developers, who quickly shore up the defenses of the programs. Over the past decade, security flaws in proprietary programs, which are not open to inspection by such large numbers of developers and testers, have been much more common than security breaches in free software. Those who argue that proprietary software is more secure and allows for better surveillance seem to be largely rehearsing the thought process that typified the FBI's position in the Clipper Chip debate.

More fundamentally, the security concerns represent a lack of ease with the great freedom enabled by the networked information environment. Some of the individuals who can now do more alone and in association with others want to do harm to the United States in particular, and to advanced liberal market-based democracies more generally. Others want to trade Nazi memorabilia or child pornography. Just as the Internet makes it harder for authoritarian regimes to control their populations, so too the tremendous openness and freedom of the networked environment requires new ways of protecting open societies from destructive individuals and groups. And yet, particularly in light of the systematic and significant benefits of the networked information economy and its sharing-based open production practices to the core political commitments of liberal democracies, preserving security in these societies by eliminating the technologies that can support improvements in the very freedom being protected is perverse. Given Abu Ghraib and Guantanamo Bay, however, squelching the emergence of an open networked environment and economy hardly seems to be the most glaring of self-defeating moves in the war to protect freedom and human dignity in liberal societies. It is too early to tell whether the security urge will ultimately weigh in on the side of the industrial information economy incumbents, or will instead follow the path of the crypto-wars, and lead security concerns to support the networked information economy's ability to provide survivable, redundant, and effective critical infrastructures and information production and exchange capabilities. If the former, this impulse may well present a formidable obstacle to the emergence of an open networked information environment.

Chapter 12 Conclusion: The Stakes of Information Law and Policy

Complex modern societies have developed in the context of mass media and industrial information economy. Our theories of growth and innovation assume that industrial models of innovation are dominant. Our theories about how effective communications in complex societies are achieved center on market-based, proprietary models, with a professional commercial core and a dispersed, relatively passive periphery. Our conceptions of human agency, collective deliberation, and common culture in these societies are embedded in the experience and practice of capital-intensive information and cultural production practices that emphasize proprietary, market-based models and starkly separate production from consumption. Our institutional frameworks reflect these conceptual models of information production and exchange, and have come, over the past few years, to enforce these conceptions as practiced reality, even when they need not be.

This book began with four economic observations. First, the baseline conception that proprietary strategies are dominant in our information production system is overstated. The education system, from kindergarten to doctoral programs, is thoroughly infused with nonproprietary motivations, social relations, and organizational forms. The arts and sciences are replete with voluntarism and actions oriented primarily toward social-psychological motivations rather than market appropriation. Political and theological discourses are thoroughly based in nonmarket forms and motivations. Perhaps most surprisingly, even industrial research and development, while market oriented, is in most industries not based on proprietary claims of exclusion, but on improved efficiencies and customer relations that can be captured and that drive innovation, without need for proprietary strategies of appropriation. Despite the continued importance of nonproprietary production in information as a practical matter, the conceptual nuance required to acknowledge its importance ran against the grain of the increasingly dominant thesis that property and markets are the roots of all growth and productivity. Partly as a result of the ideological and military conflict with Communism, partly as a result of the theoretical elegance of a simple and tractable solution, policy makers and their advisers came to believe toward the end of the twentieth century that property in information and innovation was like property in wristwatches and automobiles. The more clearly you defined and enforced it, and the closer it was to perfect exclusive rights, the more production you would get. The rising dominance of this conceptual model combined with the rent-seeking lobbying of industrial-model producers to underwrite a fairly rapid and substantial tipping of the institutional ecology of innovation and information production in favor of proprietary models. The U.S. patent system was overhauled in the early 1980s, in ways that strengthened and broadened the reach and scope of exclusivity. Copyright was vastly expanded in the mid-1970s, and again in the latter 1990s. Trademark was vastly expanded in the 1990s. Other associated rights were created and strengthened throughout these years.

The second economic point is that these expansions of rights operate, as a practical matter, as a tax on nonproprietary models of production in favor of the proprietary models. It makes access to information resources more expensive for all, while improving appropriability only for some. Introducing software patents, for example, may help some of the participants in the one-third of the software industry that depends on sales of finished software items. But it clearly raises the costs without increasing benefits for the two-thirds of the industry that is service based and relational. As a practical matter, the substantial increases in the scope and reach of exclusive rights have adversely affected the operating conditions of nonproprietary producers.

Universities have begun to seek patents and pay royalties, impeding the sharing of information that typified past practice. Businesses that do not actually rely on asserting patents for their business model have found themselves amassing large patent portfolios at great expense, simply to fend off the threat of suit by others who would try to hold them up. Older documentary films, like *Eyes on the Prize*, have been hidden from public view for years, because of the cost and complexity of clearing the rights to every piece of footage or trademark that happens to have been captured by the camera. New documentaries require substantially greater funding than would have been necessary to pay for their creation, because of the costs of clearing newly expanded rights.

The third economic observation is that the basic technologies of information processing, storage, and communication have made nonproprietary models more attractive and effective than was ever before possible. Ubiquitous low-cost processors, storage media, and networked connectivity have made it practically feasible for individuals, alone and in cooperation with others, to create and exchange information, knowledge, and culture in patterns of social reciprocity, redistribution, and sharing, rather than proprietary, market-based production. The basic material capital requirements of information production are now in the hands of a billion people around the globe who are connected to each other more or less seamlessly. These material conditions have given individuals a new practical freedom of action. If a person or group wishes to start an information-production project for any reason, that group or person need not raise significant funds to acquire the necessary capital. In the past, the necessity to obtain funds constrained information producers to find a market-based model to sustain the investment, or to obtain government funding. The funding requirements, in turn, subordinated the producers either to the demands of markets, in particular to mass-market appeal, or to the agendas of state bureaucracies. The networked information environment has permitted the emergence to much greater significance of the nonmarket sector, the nonprofit sector, and, most radically, of individuals.

The fourth and final economic observation describes and analyzes the rise of peer production. This cluster of phenomena, from free and open-source software to *Wikipedia* and SETI@Home, presents a stark challenge to conventional thinking about the economics of information production. Indeed, it challenges the economic understanding of the relative roles of market-based and nonmarket production more generally. It is important to see these phenomena not as exceptions, quirks, or ephemeral fads, but as indications of a fundamental fact about transactional forms and their relationship to the technological conditions of production. It is a mistake to think that we have only two basic free transactional forms—property-based markets and hierarchically organized firms. We have three, and the third is social sharing and exchange. It is a widespread phenomenon—we live and practice it every day with our household members, coworkers, and neighbors. We coproduce and exchange economic goods and services. But we do not count these in the economic census. Worse, we do not count them in our institutional design. I suggest that the reason social production has been shunted to the peripheries of the advanced economies is that the core economic activities of the economies of steel and coal required large capital investments. These left markets, firms, or state-run enterprises dominant. As the first stage of the information economy emerged, existing information and human creativity— each a "good" with fundamentally different economic characteristics than coal or steel—became important inputs. The organization of production nevertheless followed an industrial model, because information production and exchange itself still required high capital costs—a mechanical printing press, a broadcast station, or later, an IBM mainframe. The current networked stage of the information economy emerged when the barrier of high capital costs was removed. The total capital cost of communication and creation did not necessarily decline. Capital investment, however, became widely distributed in small dollops, owned by individuals connected in a network. We came to a stage where the core economic activities of the most advanced economies—the production and processing of information—could be achieved by pooling physical capital owned by widely dispersed individuals and groups, who have purchased the capital means for personal, household, and small-business use. Then, human creativity and existing information were left as the main remaining core inputs. Something new and radically different started to happen. People began to apply behaviors they practice in their living rooms or in the elevator—"Here, let me lend you a hand," or "What did you think of last night's speech?"—to production problems that had, throughout the twentieth century, been solved on the model of Ford and General Motors. The rise of peer production is neither mysterious nor fickle when viewed through this lens. It is as rational and efficient given the objectives and material conditions of information production at the turn of the twenty-first century as the assembly line was for the conditions at the turn of the twentieth. The pooling of human creativity and of computation, communication, and storage enables nonmarket motivations and relations to play a much larger role in the production of the information environment than it has been able to for at least decades, perhaps for as long as a century and a half.

A genuine shift in the way we produce the information environment that we occupy as individual agents, as citizens, as culturally embedded creatures, and as social beings goes to the core of our basic liberal commitments. Information and communications are core elements of autonomy and of public political discourse and decision making. Communication is the basic unit of social existence. Culture and knowledge, broadly conceived, form the basic frame of reference through which we come to understand ourselves and others in the world. For any liberal political theory—any theory that begins with a focus on individuals and their freedom to be the authors of their own lives in connection with others—the basic questions of how individuals and communities come to know and evaluate are central to the project of characterizing the normative value of institutional, social, and political systems. Independently, in the context of an information- and innovation-centric economy, the basic components of human development also depend on how we produce information and innovation, and how we disseminate its implementations. The emergence of a substantial role for nonproprietary production offers discrete strategies to improve human development around the globe. Productivity in the information economy can be sustained without the kinds of exclusivity that have made it difficult for knowledge, information, and their beneficial implementations to diffuse beyond the circles of the wealthiest nations and social groups. We can provide a detailed and specific account of why the emergence of nonmarket, nonproprietary production to a more significant role than it had in the industrial information economy could offer improvements in the domains of both freedom and justice, without sacrificing—indeed, while improving—productivity.

From the perspective of individual autonomy, the emergence of the networked information economy offers a series of identifiable improvements in how we perceive the world around us, the extent to which we can affect our perceptions of the world, the range of actions open to us and their possible outcomes, and the range of cooperative enterprises we can seek to enter to pursue our choices. It allows us to do more for and by ourselves. It allows us to form loose associations with others who are interested in a particular outcome they share with us, allowing us to provide and explore many more diverse avenues of learning and speaking than we could achieve by ourselves or in association solely with others who share long-term strong ties. By creating sources of information and communication facilities that no one owns or exclusively controls, the networked information economy removes some of the most basic opportunities for manipulation of those who depend on information and communication by the owners of the basic means of communications and the producers of the core cultural forms. It does not eliminate the possibility that one person will try to act upon another as object. But it removes the structural constraints that make it impossible to communicate at all without being subject to such action by others.

From the perspective of democratic discourse and a participatory republic, the networked information economy offers a genuine reorganization of the public sphere. Except in the very early stages of a small number of today's democracies, modern democracies have largely developed in the context of mass media as the core of their public spheres. A systematic and broad literature has explored the basic limitations of commercial mass media as the core of the public sphere, as well as it advantages. The emergence of a networked public sphere is attenuating, or even solving, the most basic failings of the mass-mediated public sphere. It attenuates the power of the commercial mass-media owners and those who can pay them. It provides an avenue for substantially more diverse and politically mobilized communication than was feasible in a commercial mass media with a small number of speakers and a vast number of passive recipients. The views of many more individuals and communities can be heard. Perhaps most interestingly, the phenomenon of peer production is now finding its way into the public sphere. It is allowing loosely affiliated individuals across the network to fulfill some of the basic and central functions of the mass media. We are seeing the rise of nonmarket, distributed, and collaborative investigative journalism, critical commentary, and platforms for political mobilization and organization. We are seeing the rise of collaborative filtering and accreditation, which allows individuals engaged in public discourse to be their own source of deciding whom to trust and whose words to question.

A common critique of claims that the Internet improves democracy and autonomy is centered on information overload and fragmentation. What we have seen emerging in the networked environment is a combination of self-conscious peer-production efforts and emergent properties of large systems of human beings that have avoided this unhappy fate. We have seen the adoption of a number of practices that have made for a reasonably navigable and coherent information environment without re-creating the mass-media model. There are organized nonmarket projects for producing filtering and accreditation, ranging from the Open Directory Project to mailing lists to like-minded people, like MoveOn.org. There is a widespread cultural practice of mutual pointing and linking; a culture of "Here, see for yourself, I think this is interesting." The basic model of observing the judgments of others as to what is interesting and valuable, coupled with exercising one's own judgment about who shares one's interests and whose judgment seems to be sound has created a pattern of linking and usage of the Web and the Internet that is substantially more ordered than a cacophonous free-for-all, and less hierarchically organized and controlled by few than was the mass-media environment. It turns out that we are not intellectual lemmings. Given freedom to participate in making our own information environment, we neither descend into Babel, nor do we replicate the hierarchies of the mass-mediated public spheres to avoid it.

The concepts of culture and society occupy more tenuous positions in liberal theory than autonomy and democracy. As a consequence, mapping the effects of the changes in information production and exchange on these domains as aspects of liberal societies is more complex. As to culture, the minimum that we can say is that the networked information environment is rendering culture more transparent. We all "occupy" culture; our perceptions, views, and structures of comprehension are all always embedded in culture. And yet there are degrees to which this fact can be rendered more or less opaque to us as inhabitants of a culture. In the networked information environment, as individuals and groups use their newfound autonomy to engage in personal and collective expression through existing cultural forms, these forms become more transparent—both through practice and through critical examination. The mass-media television culture encouraged passive consumption of polished, finished goods. The emergence of what might be thought of as a newly invigorated folk culture—created by and among individuals and groups, rather than by professionals for passive consumption—provides both a wider set of cultural forms and practices and a better-educated or better-practiced community of "readers" of culture. From the perspective of a liberal theory unwilling simply to ignore the fact that culture structures meaning, personal values, and political conceptions, the emergence of a more transparent and participatory cultural production system is a clear improvement over the commercial, professional mass culture of the twentieth century. In the domain of social relations, the degree of autonomy and the loose associations made possible by the Internet, which play such an important role in the gains for autonomy, democracy, and a critical culture, have raised substantial concerns about how the networked environment will contribute to a further erosion of community and solidarity. As with the Babel objection, however, it appears that we are not using the Internet further to fragment our social lives. The Internet is beginning to replace twentieth-century remote media—television and telephone. The new patterns of use that we are observing as a result of this partial displacement suggest that much of network use focuses on enhancing and deepening existing real-world relations, as well as adding new online relations. Some of the time that used to be devoted to passive reception of standardized finished goods through a television is now reoriented toward communicating and making together with others, in both tightly and loosely knit social relations. Moreover, the basic experience of treating others, including strangers, as potential partners in cooperation contributes to a thickening of the sense of possible social bonds beyond merely co-consumers of standardized products. Peer production can provide a new domain of reasonably thick connection with remote others.

The same capabilities to make information and knowledge, to innovate, and to communicate that lie at the core of the gains in freedom in liberal societies also underlie the primary advances I suggest are possible in terms of justice and human development. From the perspective of a liberal conception of justice, the possibility that more of the basic requirements of human welfare and the capabilities necessary to be a productive, self-reliant individual are available outside of the market insulates access to these basic requirements and capabilities from the happenstance of wealth distribution. From a more substantive perspective, information and innovation are central components of all aspects of a rich meaning of human development. Information and innovation are central to human health—in the production and use of both food and medicines. They are central to human learning and the development of the knowledge any individual needs to make life richer. And they are, and have for more than fifty years been known to be, central to growth of material welfare. Along all three of these dimensions, the emergence of a substantial sector of nonmarket production that is not based on exclusivity and does not require exclusion to feed its own engine contributes to global human development. The same economic characteristics that make exclusive rights in information a tool that imposes barriers to access in advanced economies make these rights a form of tax on technological latecomers. What most poor and middle-income countries lack is not human creativity, but access to the basic tools of innovation. The cost of the material requirements of innovation and information production is declining rapidly in many domains, as more can be done with ever-cheaper computers and communications systems. But exclusive rights in existing innovation tools and information resources remain a significant barrier to innovation, education, and the use of information-embedded tools and goods in low- and middle-income countries. As new strategies for the production of information and knowledge are making their outputs available freely for use and continuing innovation by everyone everywhere, the networked information economy can begin to contribute significantly to improvements in human development. We already see free software and free and open Internet standards playing that role in information technology sectors. We are beginning to see it take form in academic publishing, raw information, and educational materials, like multilingual encyclopedias, around the globe. More tentatively, we are beginning to see open commons-based innovation models and peer production emerge in areas of agricultural research and bioagricultural innovation, as well as, even more tentatively, in the area of biomedical research. These are still very early examples of what can be produced by the networked information economy, and how it can contribute, even if only to a limited extent, to the capacity of people around the globe to live a long and healthy, well-educated, and materially adequate life.

If the networked information economy is indeed a significant inflection point for modern societies along all these dimensions, it is so because it upsets the dominance of proprietary, market-based production in the sphere of the production of knowledge, information, and culture. This upset is hardly uncontroversial. It will likely result in significant redistribution of wealth, and no less importantly, power, from previously dominant firms and business models to a mixture of individuals and social groups on the one hand, and on the other hand businesses that reshape their business models to take advantage of, and build tools an platforms for, the newly productive social relations. As a practical matter, the major economic and social changes described here are not deterministically preordained by the internal logic of technological progress. What we see instead is that the happenstance of the fabrication technology of computation, in particular, as well as storage and communications, has created technological conditions conducive to a significant realignment of our information production and exchange system. The actual structure of the markets, technologies, and social practices that have been destabilized by the introduction of computer-communications networks is now the subject of a large-scale and diffuse institutional battle.

We are seeing significant battles over the organization and legal capabilities of the physical components of the digitally networked environment. Will all broadband infrastructures be privately owned? If so, how wide a margin of control will owners have to prefer some messages over others? Will we, to the contrary, permit open wireless networks to emerge as an infrastructure of first and last resort, owned by its users and exclusively controlled by no one? The drives to greater private ownership in wired infrastructure, and the push by Hollywood and the recording industry to require digital devices mechanically to comply with exclusivity-respecting standards are driving the technical and organizational design toward a closed environment that would be more conducive to proprietary strategies. Open wireless networks and the present business model of the large and successful device companies—particularly, personal computers—to use open standards push in the opposite direction. End-user equipment companies are mostly focused on making their products as valuable as possible to their users, and are therefore oriented toward offering general-purpose platforms that can be deployed by their owners as they choose. These then become equally available for market-oriented as for social behaviors, for proprietary consumption as for productive sharing.

At the logical layer, the ethic of open standards in the technical community, the emergence of the free software movement and its apolitical cousin, open-source development practices, on the one hand, and the anti-authoritarian drives behind encryption hacking and some of the peer-to-peer technologies, on the other hand, are pushing toward an open logical layer available for all to use. The efforts of the content industries to make the Internet manageable—most visibly, the DMCA and the continued dominance of Microsoft over the desktop, and the willingness of courts and legislatures to try to stamp out copyright-defeating technologies even when these obviously have significant benefits to users who have no interest in copying the latest song in order not to pay for the CD—are the primary sources of institutional constraint on the freedom to use the logical resources necessary to communicate in the network.

At the content layer—the universe of existing information, knowledge, and culture—we are observing a fairly systematic trend in law, but a growing countertrend in society. In law, we see a continual tightening of the control that the owners of exclusive rights are given. Copyrights are longer, apply to more uses, and are interpreted as reaching into every corner of valuable use. Trademarks are stronger and more aggressive. Patents have expanded to new domains and are given greater leeway. All these changes are skewing the institutional ecology in favor of business models and production practices that are based on exclusive proprietary claims; they are lobbied for by firms that collect large rents if these laws are expanded, followed, and enforced. Social trends in the past few years, however, are pushing in the opposite direction. These are precisely the trends of networked information economy, of nonmarket production, of an increased ethic of sharing, and an increased ambition to participate in communities of practice that produce vast quantities of information, knowledge, and culture for free use, sharing, and follow-on creation by others.

The political and judicial pressures to form an institutional ecology that is decidedly tilted in favor of proprietary business models are running head-on into the emerging social practices described throughout this book. To flourish, a networked information economy rich in social production practices requires a core common infrastructure, a set of resources necessary for information production and exchange that are open for all to use. This requires physical, logical, and content resources from which to make new statements, encode them for communication, and then render and receive them. At present, these resources are available through a mixture of legal and illegal, planned and unplanned sources. Some aspects come from the happenstance of the trajectories of very different industries that have operated under very different regulatory frameworks: telecommunications, personal computers, software, Internet connectivity, public- and private-sector information, and cultural publication. Some come from more or less widespread adoption of practices of questionable legality or outright illegality. Peer-to-peer file sharing includes many instances of outright illegality practiced by tens of millions of Internet users. But simple uses of quotations, clips, and mix-and-match creative practices that may, or, increasingly, may not, fall into the narrowing category of fair use are also priming the pump of nonmarket production. At the same time, we are seeing an ever-more self-conscious adoption of commons-based practices as a modality of information production and exchange. Free software, Creative Commons, the Public Library of Science, the new guidelines of the National Institutes of Health (NIH) on free publication of papers, new open archiving practices, librarian movements, and many other communities of practice are developing what was a contingent fact into a self-conscious social movement. As the domain of existing information and culture comes to be occupied by information and knowledge produced within these free sharing movements and licensed on the model of open-licensing techniques, the problem of the conflict with the proprietary domain will recede. Twentieth-century materials will continue to be a point of friction, but a sufficient quotient of twenty-first-century materials seem now to be increasingly available from sources that are happy to share them with future users and creators. If this social-cultural trend continues over time, access to content resources will present an ever-lower barrier to nonmarket production.

The relationship of institutional ecology to social practice is a complex one. It is hard to predict at this point whether a successful sustained effort on the part of the industrial information economy producers will succeed in flipping even more of the institutional toggles in favor of proprietary production. There is already a more significant social movement than existed in the 1990s in the United States, in Europe, and around the world that is resisting current efforts to further enclose the information environment. This social movement is getting support from large and wealthy industrial players who have reoriented their business model to become the platforms, tool-makers, and service providers for and alongside the emerging nonmarket sector. IBM, Hewlett Packard, and Cisco, for example, might stand shoulder to shoulder with a nongovernment organization (NGO) like Public Knowledge in an effort to block legislation that would require personal computers to comply with standards set by Hollywood for copy protection. When Hollywood sued Grokster, the file-sharing company, and asked the Supreme Court to expand contributory liability of the makers of technologies that are used to infringe copyrights, it found itself arrayed against amicus briefs filed by Intel, the Consumer Electronics Association, and Verizon, SBC, AT&T, MCI, and Sun Microsystems, alongside briefs from the Free Software Foundation, and the Consumer Federation of America, Consumers Union, and Public Knowledge.

Even if laws that favor enclosure do pass in one, or even many jurisdictions, it is not entirely clear that law can unilaterally turn back a trend that combines powerful technological, social, and economic drivers. We have seen even in the area of peer-to-peer networks, where the arguments of the incumbents seemed the most morally compelling and where their legal successes have been the most complete, that stemming the tide of change is difficult—perhaps impossible. Bits are a part of a flow in the networked information environment, and trying to legislate that fact away in order to preserve a business model that sells particular collections of bits as discrete, finished goods may simply prove to be impossible. Nonetheless, legal constraints significantly shape the parameters of what companies and individuals decide to market and use. It is not hard to imagine that, were Napster seen as legal, it would have by now encompassed a much larger portion of the population of Internet users than the number of users who actually now use file-sharing networks. Whether the same moderate levels of success in shaping behavior can be replicated in areas where the claims of the incumbents are much more tenuous, as a matter of both policy and moral claims—such as in the legal protection of anticircumvention devices or the contraction of fair use—is an even harder question. The object of a discussion of the institutional ecology of the networked environment is, in any event, not prognostication. It is to provide a moral framework within which to understand the many and diverse policy battles we have seen over the past decade, and which undoubtedly will continue into the coming decade, that I have written this book.

We are in the midst of a quite basic transformation in how we perceive the world around us, and how we act, alone and in concert with others, to shape our own understanding of the world we occupy and that of others with whom we share it. Patterns of social practice, long suppressed as economic activities in the context of industrial economy, have now emerged to greater importance than they have had in a century and a half. With them, they bring the possibility of genuine gains in the very core of liberal commitments, in both advanced economies and around the globe. The rise of commons-based information production, of individuals and loose associations producing information in nonproprietary forms, presents a genuine discontinuity from the industrial information economy of the twentieth century. It brings with it great promise, and great uncertainty. We have early intimations as to how market-based enterprises can adjust to make room for this newly emerging phenomenon—IBM's adoption of open source, Second Life's adoption of user-created immersive entertainment, or Open Source Technology Group's development of a platform for Slashdot. We also have very clear examples of businesses that have decided to fight the new changes by using every trick in the book, and some, like injecting corrupt files into peer-to-peer networks, that are decidedly not in the book. Law and regulation form one important domain in which these battles over the shape of our emerging information production system are fought. As we observe these battles; as we participate in them as individuals choosing how to behave and what to believe, as citizens, lobbyists, lawyers, or activists; as we act out these legal battles as legislators, judges, or treaty negotiators, it is important that we understand the normative stakes of what we are doing.

We have an opportunity to change the way we create and exchange information, knowledge, and culture. By doing so, we can make the twenty-first century one that offers individuals greater autonomy, political communities greater democracy, and societies greater opportunities for cultural self-reflection and human connection. We can remove some of the transactional barriers to material opportunity, and improve the state of human development everywhere. Perhaps these changes will be the foundation of a true transformation toward more liberal and egalitarian societies. Perhaps they will merely improve, in well-defined but smaller ways, human life along each of these dimensions. That alone is more than enough to justify an embrace of the networked information economy by anyone who values human welfare, development, and freedom.

Notes

CHAPTER 1. Introduction: A Moment of Opportunity and Challenge

1. Barry Wellman et al., "The Social Affordances of the Internet for Networked Individualism," *JCMC* 8, no. 3 (April 2003).
2. Langdon Winner, ed., "Do Artifacts Have Politics?" in *The Whale and The Reactor: A Search for Limits in an Age of High Technology* (Chicago: University of Chicago Press, 1986), 19–39.
3. Harold Innis, *The Bias of Communication* (Toronto: University of Toronto Press, 1951). Innis too is often lumped with McLuhan and Walter Ong as a technological determinist. His work was, however, one of a political economist, and he emphasized the relationship between technology and economic and social organization, much more than the deterministic operation of technology on human cognition and capability.
4. Lawrence Lessig, *Code and Other Laws of Cyberspace* (New York: Basic Books, 1999).
5. Manuel Castells, *The Rise of Networked Society* (Cambridge, MA, and Oxford: Blackwell Publishers, 1996).

PART I. The Networked Information Economy

1. Elizabeth Eisenstein, *Printing Press as an Agent of Change* (Cambridge: Cambridge University Press, 1979).

CHAPTER 2. Some Basic Economics of Information Production and Innovation

1. The full statement was: "[A]ny information obtained, say a new method of production, should, from the welfare point of view, be available free of charge (apart from the costs of transmitting information). This insures optimal utilization of the information but of course provides no incentive for investment in research. In a free enterprise economy, inventive activity is supported by using the invention to create property rights; precisely to the extent that it is successful, there is an underutilization of information." Kenneth Arrow, "Economic Welfare and the Allocation of Resources for Invention," in *Rate and Direction of Inventive Activity: Economic and Social Factors*, ed. Richard R. Nelson (Princeton, NJ: Princeton University Press, 1962), 616–617.

2. Suzanne Scotchmer, "Standing on the Shoulders of Giants: Cumulative Research and the Patent Law," *Journal of Economic Perspectives* 5 (1991): 29–41.

3. *Eldred v. Ashcroft*, 537 U.S. 186 (2003).

4. Adam Jaffe, "The U.S. Patent System in Transition: Policy Innovation and the Innovation Process," *Research Policy* 29 (2000): 531.

5. Josh Lerner, "Patent Protection and Innovation Over 150 Years" (working paper no. 8977, National Bureau of Economic Research, Cambridge, MA, 2002).

6. At most, a "hot news" exception on the model of *International News Service v. Associated Press*, 248 U.S. 215 (1918), might be required. Even that, however, would only be applicable to online editions that are for pay. In paper, habits of reading, accreditation of the original paper, and first-to-market advantages of even a few hours would be enough. Online, where the first-to-market advantage could shrink to seconds, "hot news" protection may be worthwhile. However, almost all papers are available for free and rely solely on advertising. The benefits of reading a copied version are, at that point, practically insignificant to the reader.

7. Wesley Cohen, R. Nelson, and J. Walsh, "Protecting Their Intellectual Assets: Appropriability Conditions and Why U.S. Manufacturing Firms Patent (or Not)" (working paper no. 7552, National Bureau Economic Research, Cambridge, MA, 2000); Richard Levin et al., "Appropriating the Returns from Industrial Research and Development" *Brookings Papers on Economic Activity* 3 (1987): 783; Mansfield et al., "Imitation Costs and Patents: An Empirical Study," *The Economic Journal* 91 (1981): 907.

8. In the 2002 Economic Census, compare NAICS categories 5415 (computer systems and related services) to NAICS 5112 (software publishing). Between the 1997 Economic Census and the 2002 census, this ratio remained stable, at about 36 percent in 1997 and 37 percent in 2002. See 2002 Economic Census, "Industry Series, Information, Software Publishers, and Computer Systems, Design and Related Services" (Washington, DC: U.S. Census Bureau, 2004).

9. Levin et al., "Appropriating the Returns," 794–796 (secrecy, lead time, and learning-curve advantages regarded as more effective than patents by most firms). See also F. M. Scherer, "Learning by Doing and International Trade in Semiconductors" (faculty research working paper series R94-13, John F. Kennedy School of Government, Harvard University, Cambridge, MA, 1994), an empirical study of semiconductor industry suggesting that for industries with steep learning curves, investment in information production is driven by advantages of being first down the learning curve

rather than the expectation of legal rights of exclusion. The absorption effect is described in Wesley M. Cohen and Daniel A. Leventhal, "Innovation and Learning: The Two Faces of R&D," *The Economic Journal* 99 (1989): 569–596. The collaboration effect was initially described in Richard R. Nelson, "The Simple Economics of Basic Scientific Research," *Journal of Political Economy* 67 (June 1959): 297–306. The most extensive work over the past fifteen years, and the source of the term of learning networks, has been from Woody Powell on knowledge and learning networks. Identifying the role of markets made concentrated by the limited ability to use information, rather than through exclusive rights, was made in F. M. Scherer, "Nordhaus's Theory of Optimal Patent Life: A Geometric Reinterpretation," *American Economic Review* 62 (1972): 422–427.

10. Eric von Hippel, *Democratizing Innovation* (Cambridge, MA: MIT Press, 2005).

11. Eben Moglen, "Anarchism Triumphant: Free Software and the Death of Copyright," *First Monday* (1999), http://www.firstmonday.dk/issues/issue4_8/moglen/.

CHAPTER 3. Peer Production and Sharing

1. For an excellent history of the free software movement and of open-source development, see Glyn Moody, *Rebel Code: Inside Linux and the Open Source Revolution* (New York: Perseus Publishing, 2001).

2. Elinor Ostrom, *Governing the Commons: The Evolution of Institutions for Collective Action* (Cambridge: Cambridge University Press, 1990).

3. Josh Lerner and Jean Tirole, "The Scope of Open Source Licensing" (Harvard NOM working paper no. 02–42, table 1, Cambridge, MA, 2002). The figure is computed out of the data reported in this paper for the number of free software development projects that Lerner and Tirole identify as having "restrictive" or "very restrictive" licenses.

4. Netcraft, April 2004 Web Server Survey, http://news.netcraft.com/archives/web_server_survey.html.

5. Clickworkers Results: Crater Marking Activity, July 3, 2001, http://clickworkers.arc.nasa.gov/documents/crater-marking.pdf.

6. B. Kanefsky, N. G. Barlow, and V. C. Gulick, *Can Distributed Volunteers Accomplish Massive Data Analysis Tasks?* http://www.clickworkers.arc.nasa.gov/documents/abstract.pdf.

7. J. Giles, "Special Report: Internet Encyclopedias Go Head to Head," *Nature,* December 14, 2005, available at http://www.nature.com/news/2005/051212/full/438900a.html.

8. http://www.techcentralstation.com/111504A.html.

9. Yochai Benkler, "Coase's Penguin, or Linux and the Nature of the Firm," *Yale Law Journal* 112 (2001): 369.

10. IBM Collaborative User Experience Research Group, History Flows: Results (2003), http://www.research.ibm.com/history/results.htm.

11. For the full argument, see Yochai Benkler, "Some Economics of Wireless Communications," *Harvard Journal of Law and Technology* 16 (2002): 25; and Yochai Benkler, "Overcoming Agoraphobia: Building the Commons of the Digitally Networked Environment," *Harvard Journal of Law and Technology* 11 (1998): 287. For an excellent

overview of the intellectual history of this debate and a contribution to the institutional design necessary to make space for this change, see Kevin Werbach, "Supercommons: Towards a Unified Theory of Wireless Communication," *Texas Law Review* 82 (2004): 863. The policy implications of computationally intensive radios using wide bands were first raised by George Gilder in "The New Rule of the Wireless," *Forbes ASAP*, March 29, 1993, and Paul Baran, "Visions of the 21st Century Communications: Is the Shortage of Radio Spectrum for Broadband Networks of the Future a Self Made Problem?" (keynote talk transcript, 8th Annual Conference on Next Generation Networks, Washington, DC, November 9, 1994). Both statements focused on the potential abundance of spectrum, and how it renders "spectrum management" obsolete. Eli Noam was the first to point out that, even if one did not buy the idea that computationally intensive radios eliminated scarcity, they still rendered spectrum property rights obsolete, and enabled instead a fluid, dynamic, real-time market in spectrum clearance rights. See Eli Noam, "Taking the Next Step Beyond Spectrum Auctions: Open Spectrum Access," *Institute of Electrical and Electronics Engineers Communications Magazine* 33, no. 12 (1995): 66–73; later elaborated in Eli Noam, "Spectrum Auction: Yesterday's Heresy, Today's Orthodoxy, Tomorrow's Anachronism. Taking the Next Step to Open Spectrum Access," *Journal of Law and Economics* 41 (1998): 765, 778–780. The argument that equipment markets based on a spectrum commons, or free access to frequencies, could replace the role planned for markets in spectrum property rights with computationally intensive equipment and sophisticated network sharing protocols, and would likely be more efficient even assuming that scarcity persists, was made in Benkler, "Overcoming Agoraphobia." Lawrence Lessig, *Code and Other Laws of Cyberspace* (New York: Basic Books, 1999) and Lawrence Lessig, *The Future of Ideas: The Fate of the Commons in a Connected World* (New York: Random House, 2001) developed a rationale based on the innovation dynamic in support of the economic value of open wireless networks. David Reed, "Comments for FCC Spectrum Task Force on Spectrum Policy," filed with the Federal Communications Commission July 10, 2002, crystallized the technical underpinnings and limitations of the idea that spectrum can be regarded as property.
12. See Benkler, "Some Economics," 44–47. The term "cooperation gain" was developed by Reed to describe a somewhat broader concept than "diversity gain" is in multiuser information theory.
13. *Spectrum Policy Task Force Report to the Commission* (Federal Communications Commission, Washington, DC, 2002); Michael K. Powell, "Broadband Migration III: New Directions in Wireless Policy" (Remarks at the Silicon Flatiron Telecommunications Program, University of Colorado at Boulder, October 30, 2002).

CHAPTER 4. The Economics of Social Production

1. Richard M. Titmuss, *The Gift Relationship: From Human Blood to Social Policy* (New York: Vintage Books, 1971), 94.
2. Kenneth J. Arrow, "Gifts and Exchanges," *Philosophy & Public Affairs* 1 (1972): 343.

3. Bruno S. Frey, *Not Just for Money: An Economic Theory of Personal Motivation* (Brook-field, VT: Edward Elgar, 1997); Bruno S. Frey, *Inspiring Economics: Human Motivation in Political Economy* (Northampton, MA: Edward Elgar, 2001), 52–72. An excellent survey of this literature is Bruno S. Frey and Reto Jegen, "Motivation Crowding Theory," *Journal of Economic Surveys* 15, no. 5 (2001): 589. For a crystallization of the underlying psychological theory, see Edward L. Deci and Richard M. Ryan, *Intrinsic Motivation and Self-Determination in Human Behavior* (New York: Plenum, 1985).

4. Roland Bénabou and Jean Tirole, "Self-Confidence and Social Interactions" (working paper no. 7585, National Bureau of Economic Research, Cambridge, MA, March 2000).

5. Truman F. Bewley, "A Depressed Labor Market as Explained by Participants," *American Economic Review (Papers and Proceedings)* 85 (1995): 250, provides survey data about managers' beliefs about the effects of incentive contracts; Margit Osterloh and Bruno S. Frey, "Motivation, Knowledge Transfer, and Organizational Form," *Organization Science* 11 (2000): 538, provides evidence that employees with tacit knowledge communicate it to coworkers more efficiently without extrinsic motivations, with the appropriate social motivations, than when money is offered for "teaching" their knowledge; Bruno S. Frey and Felix Oberholzer-Gee, "The Cost of Price Incentives: An Empirical Analysis of Motivation Crowding-Out," *American Economic Review* 87 (1997): 746; and Howard Kunreuther and Douslar Easterling, "Are Risk-Benefit Tradeoffs Possible in Siting Hazardous Facilities?" *American Economic Review (Papers and Proceedings)* 80 (1990): 252–286, describe empirical studies where communities became less willing to accept undesirable public facilities (Not in My Back Yard or NIMBY) when offered compensation, relative to when the arguments made were policy based on the common weal; Uri Gneezy and Aldo Rustichini, "A Fine Is a Price," *Journal of Legal Studies* 29 (2000): 1, found that introducing a fine for tardy pickup of kindergarten kids increased, rather than decreased, the tardiness of parents, and once the sense of social obligation was lost to the sense that it was "merely" a transaction, the parents continued to be late at pickup, even after the fine was removed.

6. James S. Coleman, "Social Capital in the Creation of Human Capital," *American Journal of Sociology* 94, supplement (1988): S95, S108. For important early contributions to this literature, see Mark Granovetter, "The Strength of Weak Ties," *American Journal of Sociology* 78 (1973): 1360; Mark Granovetter, *Getting a Job: A Study of Contacts and Careers* (Cambridge, MA: Harvard University Press, 1974); Yoram Ben-Porath, "The F-Connection: Families, Friends and Firms and the Organization of Exchange," *Population and Development Review* 6 (1980): 1.

7. Nan Lin, *Social Capital: A Theory of Social Structure and Action* (New York: Cambridge University Press, 2001), 150–151.

8. Steve Weber, *The Success of Open Source* (Cambridge, MA: Harvard University Press, 2004).

9. Maurice Godelier, *The Enigma of the Gift*, trans. Nora Scott (Chicago: University of Chicago Press, 1999), 5.

10. Godelier, *The Enigma*, 106.

11. In the legal literature, Robert Ellickson, *Order Without Law: How Neighbors Settle Disputes* (Cambridge, MA: Harvard University Press, 1991), is the locus classicus for showing how social norms can substitute for law. For a bibliography of the social norms literature outside of law, see Richard H. McAdams, "The Origin, Development, and Regulation of Norms," *Michigan Law Review* 96 (1997): 338n1, 339n2. Early contributions were: Edna Ullman-Margalit, *The Emergence of Norms* (Oxford: Clarendon Press, 1977); James Coleman, "Norms as Social Capital," in *Economic Imperialism: The Economic Approach Applied Outside the Field of Economics*, ed. Peter Bernholz and Gerard Radnitsky (New York: Paragon House Publishers, 1987), 133–155; Sally E. Merry, "Rethinking Gossip and Scandal," in *Toward a Theory of Social Control, Fundamentals*, ed. Donald Black (New York: Academic Press, 1984).

12. On policing, see Robert C. Ellickson, "Controlling Chronic Misconduct in City Spaces: Of Panhandlers, Skid Rows, and Public-Space Zoning," *Yale Law Journal* 105 (1996): 1165, 1194–1202; and Dan M. Kahan, "Between Economics and Sociology: The New Path of Deterrence," *Michigan Law Review* 95 (1997): 2477.

13. An early and broad claim in the name of commons in resources for communication and transportation, as well as human community building—like roads, canals, or social-gathering places—is Carol Rose, "The Comedy of the Commons: Custom, Commerce, and Inherently Public Property," *University Chicago Law Review* 53 (1986): 711. Condensing around the work of Elinor Ostrom, a more narrowly defined literature developed over the course of the 1990s: Elinor Ostrom, *Governing the Commons: The Evolution of Institutions for Collective Action* (New York: Cambridge University Press, 1990). Another seminal study was James M. Acheson, *The Lobster Gangs of Maine* (New Hampshire: University Press of New England, 1988). A brief intellectual history of the study of common resource pools and common property regimes can be found in Charlotte Hess and Elinor Ostrom, "Ideas, Artifacts, Facilities, and Content: Information as a Common-Pool Resource," *Law & Contemporary Problems* 66 (2003): 111.

CHAPTER 5. Individual Freedom: Autonomy, Information, and Law

1. Robert Post, "Meiklejohn's Mistake: Individual Autonomy and the Reform of Public Discourse," *University of Colorado Law Review* 64 (1993): 1109, 1130–1132.

2. This conception of property was first introduced and developed systematically by Robert Lee Hale in the 1920s and 1930s, and was more recently integrated with contemporary postmodern critiques of power by Duncan Kennedy, *Sexy Dressing Etc.: Essays on the Power and Politics of Cultural Identity* (Cambridge, MA: Harvard University Press, 1993).

3. White Paper, "Controlling Your Network, A Must for Cable Operators" (1999), http://www.cptech.org/ecom/openaccess/cisco1.html.

4. Data are all based on FCC Report on High Speed Services, Appendix to Fourth 706 Report NOI (Washington, DC: Federal Communications Commission, December 2003).

CHAPTER 6. Political Freedom Part 1: The Trouble with Mass Media

1. Jurgen Habermas, *Between Facts and Norms, Contributions to Discourse Theory of Law and Democracy* (Cambridge, MA: MIT Press, 1996).

2. Elizabeth Eisenstein, *The Printing Press as an Agent of Change* (New York: Cambridge University Press, 1979); Jeremey Popkin, *News and Politics in the Age of Revolution: Jean Luzac's Gazzette de Leyde* (Ithaca, NY: Cornell University Press, 1989).

3. Paul Starr, *The Creation of the Media: Political Origins of Modern Communications* (New York: Basic Books, 2004), 33–46.

4. Starr, *Creation of the Media*, 48–62, 86–87.

5. Starr, *Creation of the Media*, 131–133.

6. Starr, *Creation of the Media*, 135.

7. The following discussion of the birth of radio is adapted from Yochai Benkler, "Overcoming Agoraphobia: Building the Commons of the Digitally Networked Environment," *Harvard Journal of Law and Technology* 11 (Winter 1997–1998): 287. That article provides the detailed support for the description. The major secondary works relied on are Erik Barnouw, *A History of Broadcasting in the United States* (New York: Oxford University Press, 1966–1970); Gleason Archer, *History of Radio to 1926* (New York: Arno Press, 1971); and Philip T. Rosen, *Modern Stentors: Radio Broadcasters and the Federal Government, 1920–1934* (Westport, CT: Greenwood Press, 1980).

8. Robert Waterman McChesney, *Telecommunications, Mass Media, and Democracy: The Battle for the Control of U.S. Broadcasting, 1928–1935* (New York: Oxford University Press, 1993).

9. "Names of U.S. Dead Read on *Nightline*," Associated Press Report, May 1, 2004, http://www.msnbc.msn.com/id/4864247/.

10. The numbers given here are taken from The Center for Responsive Politics, http://www.opensecrets.org/, and are based on information released by the Federal Elections Commission.

11. A careful catalog of these makes up the first part of C. Edwin Baker, *Media, Markets, and Democracy* (New York: Cambridge University Press, 2002).

12. Ben H. Bagdikian, *The Media Monopoly*, 5th ed. (Boston: Beacon Press, 1997), 118.

13. Peter O. Steiner, "Program Patterns and Preferences, and the Workability of Competition in Radio Broadcasting," *The Quarterly Journal of Economics* 66 (1952): 194. The major other contribution in this literature is Jack H. Beebe, "Institutional Structure and Program Choices in Television Markets," *The Quarterly Journal of Economics* 91 (1977): 15. A parallel line of analysis of the relationship between programming and the market structure of broadcasting began with Michael Spence and Bruce Owen, "Television Programmhing, Monopolistic Competition, and Welfare," *The Quarterly Journal of Economics* 91 (1977): 103. For an excellent review of this literature, see Matthew L. Spitzer, "Justifying Minority Preferences in Broadcasting," *South California Law Review* 64 (1991): 293, 304–319.

CHAPTER 7. Political Freedom Part 2: Emergence of the Networked Public Sphere

1. *Reno v. ACLU*, 521 U.S. 844, 852–853, and 896–897 (1997).
2. Elizabeth Jensen, "Sinclair Fires Journalist After Critical Comments," *Los Angeles Times*, October 19, 2004.
3. Jensen, "Sinclair Fires Journalist"; Sheridan Lyons, "Fired Reporter Tells Why He Spoke Out," *Baltimore Sun*, October 29, 2004.
4. The various posts are archived and can be read, chronologically, at http://www.talkingpointsmemo.com/archives/week_2004_10_10.php.
5. Duane D. Stanford, *Atlanta Journal-Constitution*, October 31, 2002, 1A.
6. Katherine Q. Seelye, "The 2002 Campaign: The States; Georgia About to Plunge into Touch-Screen Voting," *New York Times*, October 30, 2002, A22.
7. Edward Walsh, "Election Day to Be Test of Voting Process," *Washington Post*, November 4, 2002, A1.
8. *Washington Post*, December 12, 2002.
9. *Online Policy Group v. Diebold, Inc.*, 337 F. Supp. 2d 1195 (2004).
10. California Secretary of State Voting Systems Panel, Meeting Minutes, November 3, 2003, http://www.ss.ca.gov/elections/vsp_min_110303.pdf.
11. Eli Noam, "Will the Internet Be Bad for Democracy?" (November 2001), http://www.citi.columbia.edu/elinoam/articles/int_bad_dem.htm.
12. Eli Noam, "The Internet Still Wide, Open, and Competitive?" Paper presented at The Telecommunications Policy Research Conference, September 2003, http://www.tprc.org/papers/2003/200/noam_TPRC2003.pdf.
13. Federal Communications Commission, Report on High Speed Services, December 2003.
14. See Eszter Hargittai, "The Changing Online Landscape: From Free-For-All to Commercial Gatekeeping," http://www.eszter.com/research/pubs/hargittai-onlinelandscape.pdf.
15. Derek de Solla Price, "Networks of Scientific Papers," *Science* 149 (1965): 510; Herbert Simon, "On a Class of Skew Distribution Function," *Biometrica* 42 (1955): 425–440, reprinted in Herbert Simon, *Models of Man Social and Rational: Mathematical Essays on Rational Human Behavior in a Social Setting* (New York: Garland, 1957).
16. Albert-László Barabási and Reka Albert, "Emergence of Scaling in Random Networks," *Science* 286 (1999): 509.
17. Bernardo Huberman and Lada Adamic, "Growth Dynamics of the World Wide Web," *Nature* 401 (1999): 131.
18. Albert-László Barabási, *Linked, How Everything Is Connected to Everything Else and What It Means for Business, Science, and Everyday Life* (New York: Penguin, 2003), 56–57. One unpublished quantitative study showed specifically that the skewness holds for political Web sites related to various hot-button political issues in the United States—like abortion, gun control, or the death penalty. A small fraction of the Web sites discussing these issues account for the large majority of links into them. Matthew Hindman, Kostas Tsioutsiouliklis, and Judy Johnson, " 'Googelarchy': How a Few Heavily Linked Sites Dominate Politics on the Web," July 28, 2003, http://

www.scholar.google.com/url?sa=U&q=http://www.princeton.edu/~mhindman/googlearchy—hindman.pdf.

19. Lada Adamic and Bernardo Huberman, "Power Law Distribution of the World Wide Web," *Science* 287 (2000): 2115.

20. Ravi Kumar et al., "Trawling the Web for Emerging Cyber-Communities," *WWW8/Computer Networks* 31, nos. 11–16 (1999): 1481–1493.

21. Gary W. Flake et al., "Self-Organization and Identification of Web Communities," *IEEE Computer* 35, no. 3 (2002): 66–71. Another paper that showed significant internal citations within topics was Soumen Chakrabati et al., "The Structure of Broad Topics on the Web," WWW2002, Honolulu, HI, May 7–11, 2002.

22. Lada Adamic and Natalie Glance, "The Political Blogosphere and the 2004 Election: Divided They Blog," March 1, 2005, http://www.blogpulse.com/papers/2005/AdamicGlanceBlogWWW.pdf.

23. M.E.J. Newman, "The Structure and Function of Complex Networks," *Society for Industrial and Applied Mathematics Review* 45, section 4.2.2 (2003): 167–256; S. N. Dorogovstev and J.F.F. Mendes, *Evolution of Networks: From Biological Nets to the Internet and WWW* (Oxford: Oxford University Press, 2003).

24. This structure was first described by Andrei Broder et al., "Graph Structure of the Web," paper presented at www9 conference (1999), http://www.almaden.ibm.com/webfountain/resources/GraphStructureintheWeb.pdf. It has since been further studied, refined, and substantiated in various studies.

25. Dill et al., "Self-Similarity in the Web" (San Jose, CA: IBM Almaden Research Center, 2001); S. N. Dorogovstev and J.F.F. Mendes, *Evolution of Networks.*

26. Soumen Chakrabarti et al., "The Structure of Broad Topics on the Web," WWW2002, Honolulu, HI, May 7–11, 2002.

27. Daniel W. Drezner and Henry Farrell, "The Power and Politics of Blogs" (July 2004), http://www.danieldrezner.com/research/blogpaperfinal.pdf.

28. D. J. Watts and S. H. Strogatz, "Collective Dynamics of 'Small World' Networks," *Nature* 393 (1998): 440–442; D. J. Watts, *Small Worlds: The Dynamics of Networks Between Order and Randomness* (Princeton, NJ: Princeton University Press, 1999).

29. Clay Shirky, "Power Law, Weblogs, and Inequality" (February 8, 2003), http://www.shirky.com/writings/powerlaw_weblog.htm; Jason Kottke, "Weblogs and Power Laws" (February 9, 2003), http://www.kottke.org/03/02/weblogs-and-power-laws.

30. Ravi Kumar et al., "On the Bursty Evolution of Blogspace," Proceedings of WWW2003, May 20–24, 2003, http://www2003.org/cdrom/papers/refereed/p477/p477-kumar/p477-kumar.htm.

31. Both of these findings are consistent with even more recent work by Hargittai, E., J. Gallo and S. Zehnder, "Mapping the Political Blogosphere: An Analysis of Large-Scale Online Political Discussions," 2005. Poster presented at the International Communication Association meetings, New York.

32. Harvard Kennedy School of Government, Case Program: " 'Big Media' Meets 'Bloggers': Coverage of Trent Lott's Remarks at Strom Thurmond's Birthday Party," http://www.ksg.harvard.edu/presspol/Research_Publications/Case_Studies/1731_0.pdf.

33. Howard Rheingold, *Smart Mobs, The Next Social Revolution* (Cambridge, MA: Perseus Publishing, 2002).

34. Data taken from *CIA World Fact Book* (Washington, DC: Central Intelligence Agency, 2004).

35. Lawrence Solum and Minn Chung, "The Layers Principle: Internet Architecture and the Law" (working paper no. 55, University of San Diego School of Law, Public Law and Legal Theory, June 2003).

36. Amnesty International, People's Republic of China, State Control of the Internet in China (2002).

37. A synthesis of news-based accounts is Babak Rahimi, "Cyberdissent: The Internet in Revolutionary Iran," *Middle East Review of International Affairs* 7, no. 3 (2003).

CHAPTER 8. Cultural Freedom: A Culture Both Plastic and Critical

1. Karl Marx, "Introduction to a Contribution to the Critique of Hegel's Philosophy of Right," *Deutsch-Französicher Jahrbucher* (1844).

2. Bruce A. Ackerman, *Social Justice and the Liberal State* (New Haven, CT, and London: Yale University Press, 1980), 333–335, 141–146.

3. Michael Walzer, *Spheres of Justice: A Defense of Pluralism and Equality* (New York: Basic Books, 1983), 29.

4. Will Kymlicka, *Multicultural Citizenship: A Liberal Theory of Minority Rights* (Oxford: Clarendon Press, 1995), 76, 83.

5. Jurgen Habermas, *Between Facts and Norms, Contributions to a Discourse Theory of Law and Democracy* (Cambridge, MA: MIT Press, 1998), 22–23.

6. Encyclopedia.com is a part of Highbeam Research, Inc., which combines free and pay research services. Bartleby provides searching and access to many reference and high-culture works at no charge, combining it with advertising, a book store, and many links to Amazon.com or to the publishers for purchasing the printed versions of the materials.

7. Jack Balkin, "Digital Speech and Democratic Culture: A Theory of Freedom of Expression for the Information Society," *New York University Law Review* 79 (2004): 1.

CHAPTER 9. Justice and Development

1. Anne Alstott and Bruce Ackerman, *The Stakeholder Society* (New Haven, CT: Yale University Press, 1999).

2. Numbers are all taken from the *2004 Human Development Report* (New York: UN Development Programme, 2004).

3. Amartya Sen, *Development as Freedom* (New York: Knopf, 1999), 46–47.

4. Carol Tenopir and Donald W. King, *Towards Electronic Journals: Realities for Scientists, Librarians, and Publishers* (Washington, DC: Special Libraries Association, 2000), 273.

5. Harold Varmus, *E-Biomed: A Proposal for Electronic Publications in the Biomedical Sciences* (Bethesda, MD: National Institutes of Health, 1999).

6. C. K. Prahald, *The Fortune at the Bottom of the Pyramid: Eradicating Poverty Through Profits* (Upper Saddle River, NJ: Wharton School of Publishing, 2005), 319–357, Section 4, "The ITC e-Choupal Story."

7. For the sources of numbers for the software industry, see chapter 2 in this volume. IBM numbers, in particular, are identified in figure 2.1.

8. These arguments were set out most clearly and early in a public exchange of letters between Representative Villanueva Nunez in Peru and Microsoft's representatives in that country. The exchange can be found on the Web site of the Open Source Initiative, http://www.opensource.org/docs/peru_and_ms.php.

9. A good regional study of the extent and details of educational deprivation is Mahbub ul Haq and Khadija ul Haq, *Human Development in South Asia 1998: The Education Challenge* (Islamabad, Pakistan: Human Development Center).

10. Robert Evenson and D. Gollin, eds., *Crop Variety Improvement and Its Effect on Productivity: The Impact of International Agricultural Research* (New York: CABI Pub., 2002); results summarized in Robert Evenson and D. Gollin, "Assessing the Impact of the Green Revolution, 1960–2000," *Science* 300 (May 2003): 758–762.

11. Jack R. Kloppenburg, Jr., *First the Seed: The Political Economy of Plant Biotechnology 1492–2000* (Cambridge and New York: Cambridge University Press, 1988), table 2.2.

12. USDA National Agriculture Statistics Survey (2004), http://www.usda.gov/nass/aggraphs/fncht3.htm.

13. First Report of the GM Science Review Panel, *An Open Review of the Science Relevant to GM Crops and Food Based on the Interests and Concerns of the Public*, United Kingdom, July 2003.

14. Robert E. Evenson, "GMOs: Prospects for Productivity Increases in Developing Countries," *Journal of Agricultural and Food Industrial Organization* 2 (2004): article 2.

15. Elliot Marshall, "A Deal for the Rice Genome," *Science* 296 (April 2002): 34.

16. Jikun Huang et al., "Plant Biotechnology in China," *Science* 295 (2002): 674.

17. Huang et al., "Plant Biotechnology."

18. Richard Atkinson et al., "Public Sector Collaboration for Agricultural IP Management," *Science* 301 (2003): 174.

19. This table is a slightly expanded version of one originally published in Yochai Benkler, "Commons Based Strategies and the Problems of Patents," *Science* 305 (2004): 1110.

20. Wim Broothaertz et al., "Gene Transfer to Plants by Diverse Species of Bacteria," *Nature* 433 (2005): 629.

21. These numbers and others in this paragraph are taken from the 2004 WHO *World Health Report*, Annex Table 2.

22. National Science Foundation, Division of Science Resource Statistics, *Special Report: National Patterns of Research and Development Resources: 2003 NSF 05–308* (Arlington, VA: NSF, 2005), table 1.

23. The detailed analysis can be found in Amy Kapzcynzki et al., "Addressing Global

Health Inequities: An Open Licensing Paradigm for Public Sector Inventions," *Berkeley Journal of Law and Technology* (Spring 2005).

24. See Jean Lanjouw, "A New Global Patent Regime for Diseases: U.S. and International Legal Issues," *Harvard Journal of Law & Technology* 16 (2002).

25. S. Maurer, A. Sali, and A. Rai, "Finding Cures for Tropical Disease: Is Open Source the Answer?" *Public Library of Science: Medicine* 1, no. 3 (December 2004): e56.

CHAPTER 10. Social Ties: Networking Together

1. Sherry Turkle, "Virtuality and Its Discontents, Searching for Community in Cyberspace," *The American Prospect* 7, no. 24 (1996); Sherry Turkle, *Life on the Screen: Identity in the Age of the Internet* (New York: Simon & Schuster, 1995).

2. Robert Kraut et al., "Internet Paradox, A Social Technology that Reduces Social Involvement and Psychological Well Being," *American Psychologist* 53 (1998): 1017–1031.

3. A fairly typical statement of this view, quoted in a study commissioned by the Kellogg Foundation, was: "TV or other media, such as computers, are no longer a kind of 'electronic hearth,' where a family will gather around and make decisions or have discussions. My position, based on our most recent studies, is that most media in the home are working against bringing families together." Christopher Lee et al., "Evaluating Information and Communications Technology: Perspective for a Balanced Approach," Report to the Kellogg Foundation (December 17, 2001), http://www.si.umich.edu/pne/kellogg/013.html.

4. Norman H. Nie and Lutz Ebring, "Internet and Society, A Preliminary Report," Stanford Institute for the Quantitative Study of Society, February 17, 2000, 15 (Press Release), http://www.pkp.ubc.ca/bctf/Stanford_Report.pdf.

5. Ibid., 42–43, tables CH-WFAM, CH-WFRN.

6. See John Markoff and A. Newer, "Lonelier Crowd Emerges in Internet Study," *New York Times*, February 16, 2000, section A, page 1, column 1.

7. Nie and Ebring, "Internet and Society," 19.

8. Amitai Etzioni, "Debating the Societal Effects of the Internet: Connecting with the World," *Public Perspective* 11 (May/June 2000): 42, also available at http://www.gwu.edu/~ccps/etzioni/A273.html.

9. Manuel Castells, *The Rise of Networked Society* 2d ed. (Malden, MA: Blackwell Publishers, Inc., 2000).

10. Barry Wellman et al., "The Social Affordances of the Internet for Networked Individualism," *Journal of Computer Mediated Communication* 8, no. 3 (April 2003).

11. Robert Kraut et al., "Internet Paradox Revisited," *Journal of Social Issues* 58, no. 1 (2002): 49.

12. Keith Hampton and Barry Wellman, "Neighboring in Netville: How the Internet Supports Community and Social Capital in a Wired Suburb," *City & Community* 2, no. 4 (December 2003): 277.

13. Gustavo S. Mesch and Yael Levanon, "Community Networking and Locally-Based

Social Ties in Two Suburban Localities," *City & Community* 2, no. 4 (December 2003): 335.

14. Useful surveys include: Paul DiMaggio et al., "Social Implications of the Internet," *Annual Review of Sociology* 27 (2001): 307–336; Robyn B. Driskell and Larry Lyon, "Are Virtual Communities True Communities? Examining the Environments and Elements of Community," *City & Community* 1, no. 4 (December 2002): 349; James E. Katz and Ronald E. Rice, *Social Consequences of Internet Use: Access, Involvement, Interaction* (Cambridge, MA: MIT Press, 2002).

15. Barry Wellman, "Computer Networks as Social Networks," *Science* 293, issue 5537 (September 2001): 2031.

16. Jeffery I. Cole et al., "The UCLA Internet Report: Surveying the Digital Future, Year Three" (UCLA Center for Communication Policy, January 2003), 33, 55, 62, http://www.ccp.ucla.edu/pdf/UCLA-Internet-Report-Year-Three.pdf.

17. Pew Internet and Daily Life Project (August 11, 2004), report available at http://www.pewinternet.org/PPF/r/131/report_display.asp.

18. See Barry Wellman, "The Social Affordances of the Internet for Networked Individualism," *Journal of Computer Mediated Communication* 8, no. 3 (April 2003); Gustavo S. Mesch and Yael Levanon, "Community Networking and Locally-Based Social Ties in Two Suburban Localities, *City & Community* 2, no. 4 (December 2003): 335.

19. Barry Wellman, "The Social Affordances of the Internet."

20. A review of Ito's own work and that of other scholars of Japanese techno-youth culture is Mizuko Ito, "Mobile Phones, Japanese Youth, and the Re-Placement of Social Contact," forthcoming in *Mobile Communications: Re-negotiation of the Social Sphere*, ed., Rich Ling and P. Pedersen (New York: Springer, 2005).

21. Dana M. Boyd, "Friendster and Publicly Articulated Social Networking," *Conference on Human Factors and Computing Systems (CHI 2004)* (Vienna: ACM, April 24–29, 2004).

22. James W. Carrey, *Communication as Culture: Essays on Media and Society* (Boston: Unwin Hyman, 1989).

23. Clay Shirky, "A Group Is Its Own Worst Enemy," published first in *Networks, Economics and Culture* mailing list July 1, 2003.

PART III. Policies of Freedom at a Moment of Transformation

1. For a review of the literature and a substantial contribution to it, see James Boyle, "The Second Enclosure Movement and the Construction of the Public Domain," *Law and Contemporary Problems* 66 (Winter-Spring 2003): 33–74.

2. Early versions in the legal literature of the skepticism regarding the growth of exclusive rights were Ralph Brown's work on trademarks, Benjamin Kaplan's caution over the gathering storm that would become the Copyright Act of 1976, and Stephen Breyer's work questioning the economic necessity of copyright in many industries. Until, and including the 1980s, these remained, for the most part, rare voices—joined in the 1980s by David Lange's poetic exhortation for the public domain; Pamela

Samuelson's systematic critique of the application of copyright to computer programs, long before anyone was paying attention; Jessica Litman's early work on the political economy of copyright legislation and the systematic refusal to recognize the public domain as such; and William Fisher's theoretical exploration of fair use. The 1990s saw a significant growth of academic questioning of enclosure: Samuelson continued to press the question of copyright in software and digital materials; Litman added a steady stream of prescient observations as to where the digital copyright was going and how it was going wrong; Peter Jaszi attacked the notion of the romantic author; Ray Patterson developed a user-centric view of copyright; Diane Zimmerman revitalized the debate over the conflict between copyright and the first amendment; James Boyle introduced erudite criticism of the theoretical coherence of the relentless drive to propertization; Niva Elkin Koren explored copyright and democracy; Keith Aoki questioned trademark, patents, and global trade systems; Julie Cohen early explored technical protection systems and privacy; and Eben Moglen began mercilessly to apply the insights of free software to hack at the foundations of intellectual property apologia. Rebecca Eisenberg, and more recently, Arti Rai, questioned the wisdom of patents on research tools to biomedical innovation. In this decade, William Fisher, Larry Lessig, Litman, and Siva Vaidhyanathan have each described the various forms that the enclosure movement has taken and exposed its many limitations. Lessig and Vaidhyanathan, in particular, have begun to explore the relations between the institutional battles and the freedom in the networked environment.

CHAPTER 11. The Battle Over the Institutional Ecology of the Digital Environment

1. Paul Starr, *The Creation of the Media: Political Origins of Modern Communications* (New York: Basic Books, 2004).

2. Ithiel de Sola-Pool, *Technologies of Freedom* (Cambridge, MA: Belknap Press, 1983), 91–100.

3. *Bridgeport Music, Inc. v. Dimension Films*, 2004 U.S. App. LEXIS 26877.

4. Other layer-based abstractions have been proposed, most effectively by Lawrence Solum and Minn Chung, *The Layers Principle: Internet Architecture and the Law*, University of San Diego Public Law Research Paper No. 55. Their model more closely hews to the OSI layers, and is tailored to being more specifically usable for a particular legal principle—never regulate at a level lower than you need to. I seek a higher-level abstraction whose role is not to serve as a tool to constrain specific rules, but as a map for understanding the relationships between diverse institutional elements as they relate to the basic problem of how information is produced and exchanged in society.

5. The first major treatment of this phenomenon was Michael Froomkin, "The Internet as a Source of Regulatory Arbitrage" (1996), http://www.law.miami.edu/froomkin/articles/arbitr.htm.

6. Jonathan Krim, "AOL Blocks Spammers' Web Sites," *Washington Post*, March 20,

2004, p. A01; also available at http://www.washingtonpost.com/ac2/wp-dyn?page name=article&contentId=A9449-2004Mar19&notFound=true.

7. FCC Report on High Speed Services, December 2003 (Appendix to Fourth 706 Report NOI).

8. 216 F.3d 871 (9th Cir. 2000).

9. *National Cable and Telecommunications Association v. Brand X Internet Services* (decided June 27, 2005).

10. *Turner Broad. Sys. v. FCC*, 512 U.S. 622 (1994) and *Turner Broad. Sys. v. FCC*, 520 U.S. 180 (1997).

11. *Chesapeake & Potomac Tel. Co. v. United States*, 42 F.3d 181 (4th Cir. 1994); *Comcast Cablevision of Broward County, Inc. v. Broward County*, 124 F. Supp. 2d 685, 698 (D. Fla., 2000).

12. The locus classicus of the economists' critique was Ronald Coase, "The Federal Communications Commission," *Journal of Law and Economics* 2 (1959): 1. The best worked-out version of how these property rights would look remains Arthur S. De Vany et al., "A Property System for Market Allocation of the Electromagnetic Spectrum: A Legal-Economic-Engineering Study," *Stanford Law Review* 21 (1969): 1499.

13. *City of Abilene, Texas v. Federal Communications Commission*, 164 F3d 49 (1999).

14. *Nixon v. Missouri Municipal League*, 541 U.S. 125 (2004).

15. Bill Number S. 2048, 107th Congress, 2nd Session.

16. *Felten v. Recording Indust. Assoc. of America Inc.*, No. CV- 01-2669 (D.N.J. June 26, 2001).

17. *Metro-Goldwyn-Mayer v. Grokster, Ltd.* (decided June 27, 2005).

18. See Felix Oberholzer and Koleman Strumpf, "The Effect of File Sharing on Record Sales" (working paper), http://www.unc.edu/cigar/papers/FileSharing_March2004 .pdf.

19. Mary Madden and Amanda Lenhart, "Music Downloading, File-Sharing, and Copyright" (Pew, July 2003), http://www.pewinternet.org/pdfs/PIP_Copyright_Memo .pdf/.

20. Lee Rainie and Mary Madden, "The State of Music Downloading and File-Sharing Online" (Pew, April 2004), http://www.pewinternet.org/pdfs/PIP_Filesharing_April_ 04.pdf.

21. See 111 F.Supp.2d at 310, fns. 69–70; *PBS Frontline* report, http://www.pbs.org/ wgbh/pages/frontline/shows/hollywood/business/windows.html.

22. A. M. Froomkin, "Semi-Private International Rulemaking: Lessons Learned from the WIPO Domain Name Process," http://www.personal.law.miami.edu/froomkin/ articles/TPRC99.pdf.

23. Jessica Litman, "The Exclusive Right to Read," *Cardozo Arts and Entertainment Law Journal* 13 (1994): 29.

24. *MAI Systems Corp. v. Peak Computer, Inc.*, 991 F.2d 511 (9th Cir. 1993).

25. Lawrence Lessig, *Free Culture: How Big Media Uses Technology and the Law to Lock Down Culture and Control Creativity* (New York: Penguin Press, 2004).

26. Jessica Litman, "Electronic Commerce and Free Speech," *Journal of Ethics and Information Technology* 1 (1999): 213.

27. See Department of Justice Intellectual Property Policy and Programs, http://www.usdoj.gov/criminal/cybercrime/ippolicy.htm.

28. *Eldred v. Ashcroft*, 537 U.S. 186 (2003).

29. *Bridgeport Music, Inc. v. Dimension Films*, 383 F.3d 390 (6th Cir.2004).

30. 383 F.3d 390, 400.

31. Mark A. Lemley, "Intellectual Property and Shrinkwrap Licenses," *Southern California Law Review* 68 (1995): 1239, 1248–1253.

32. 86 F.3d 1447 (7th Cir. 1996).

33. For a more complete technical explanation, see Yochai Benkler, "An Unhurried View of Private Ordering in Information Transactions," *Vanderbilt Law Review* 53 (2000): 2063.

34. James Boyle, "Cruel, Mean or Lavish? Economic Analysis, Price Discrimination and Digital Intellectual Property," *Vanderbilt Law Review* 53 (2000); Julie E. Cohen, "Copyright and the Jurisprudence of Self-Help," *Berkeley Technology Law Journal* 13 (1998): 1089; Niva Elkin-Koren, "Copyright Policy and the Limits of Freedom of Contract," *Berkeley Technology Law Journal* 12 (1997): 93.

35. *Feist Publications, Inc. v. Rural Telephone Service Co., Inc.*, 499 U.S. 340, 349–350 (1991).

36. Directive No. 96/9/EC on the legal protection of databases, 1996 O.J. (L 77) 20.

37. J. H. Reichman and Paul F. Uhlir, "Database Protection at the Crossroads: Recent Developments and Their Impact on Science and Technology," *Berkeley Technology Law Journal* 14 (1999): 793; Stephen M. Maurer and Suzanne Scotchmer, "Database Protection: Is It Broken and Should We Fix It?" *Science* 284 (1999): 1129.

38. See Stephen M. Maurer, P. Bernt Hugenholtz, and Harlan J. Onsrud, "Europe's Database Experiment," *Science* 294 (2001): 789; Stephen M. Maurer, "Across Two Worlds: Database Protection in the U.S. and Europe," paper prepared for Industry Canada's Conference on Intellectual Property and Innovation in the Knowledge-Based Economy, May 23–24 2001.

39. Peter Weiss, "Borders in Cyberspace: Conflicting Public Sector Information Policies and their Economic Impacts" (U.S. Dept. of Commerce, National Oceanic and Atmospheric Administration, February 2002).

40. *eBay, Inc. v. Bidder's Edge, Inc.*, 2000 U.S. Dist. LEXIS 13326 (N.D.Cal. 2000).

41. The preemption model could be similar to the model followed by the Second Circuit in *NBA v. Motorola*, 105 F.3d 841 (2d Cir. 1997), which restricted state misappropriation claims to narrow bounds delimited by federal policy embedded in the Copyright Act. This might require actual proof that the bots have stopped service, or threaten the service's very existence.

42. *New York Times v. Sullivan*, 376 U.S. 254, 266 (1964).

Index

Amazon.com
Sat 24 May 2008
(mail order)
$29.70 no tax

THE BLACK TATTOO

SAM ENTHOVEN

The Black Tattoo

RAZORBILL

Published by the Penguin Group
Penguin Young Readers Group
345 Hudson Street, New York, New York 10014, U.S.A.
Penguin Group (USA) Inc., 375 Hudson Street, New York, New York 10014, U.S.A.
Penguin Group (Canada), 90 Eglinton Avenue East, Suite 700, Toronto,
Ontario, Canada M4P 2Y3 (a division of Pearson Penguin Canada Inc.)
Penguin Books Ltd, 80 Strand, London WC2R 0RL, England
Penguin Ireland, 25 St Stephen's Green, Dublin 2, Ireland
(a division of Penguin Books Ltd)
Penguin Group (Australia), 250 Camberwell Road, Camberwell,
Victoria 3124, Australia (a division of Pearson Australia Group Pty Ltd)
Penguin Books India Pvt Ltd, 11 Community Centre, Panchsheel Park,
New Delhi – 110 017, India
Penguin Group (NZ), Cnr Airborne and Rosedale Roads, Albany,
Auckland 1310, New Zealand (a division of Pearson New Zealand Ltd)
Penguin Books (South Africa) (Pty) Ltd, 24 Sturdee Avenue, Rosebank,
Johannesburg 2196, South Africa

Penguin Books Ltd, Registered Offices: 80 Strand, London WC2R 0RL, England

10 9 8 7 6 5 4 3 2 1

Copyright 2006 © Sam Enthoven
All rights reserved

Library of Congress Cataloging-in-Publication Data is available

Printed in the United States of America

To Laura
"My heart is in my hand.
. . . *Yuck*."

Do I dare
Disturb the universe?

T. S. Eliot,
"The Love Song of J. Alfred Prufrock"

FRESH BLOOD

LONDON. The West End. A little after four in the morning. At the base of the skyscraper known as Centre Point Tower, in the darkness at the end of a dank concrete walkway, something stirred. The shadows there began to ripple and coalesce. The dark became a man-like shape of pure liquid black. Then the demon emerged, taking its first leisurely step toward the woman who stood there watching it.

"**Jessica**," it said.

Hearing that voice again, and the way the sound of it seemed to take shape inside her head like black flowers blossoming behind her eyelids, it was all Jessica could do to stop her legs from trembling. She'd been so close! Another few minutes and she'd've made it! She gritted her teeth and told herself to concentrate. The demon took another step. It was clear of the shadows now, and the rainy orange streetlight glinted off its inky wet skin. Its face was a blank, but she could feel it looking at her.

"**You should not have come back**," it said.

Slowly Jessica put down the plastic bag full of fourteen years' worth of carefully hoarded tobacco shreds and cigarette ends that she'd been collecting and saving for this moment. She unbuttoned her filthy overcoat.

"Really," she replied. "And what makes you say that?"

"**You must have realized that I can't let you warn them,**" the demon told her. "**You must have known that if I found you you'd be killed, and what knowledge you possess would die with you— but you still came. Why?**"

"Confident," said Jessica, "aren't you?"

Her amber eyes glittered. Her hard brown hands lifted fractionally from her sides.

The demon looked at her.

"**Very well,**" it said. "**Since you insist . . .**"

It took one more step—

—blurred into motion—

—and attacked.

Jessica wasn't as young as she used to be. She'd been expecting the demon's charge, but her reactions had slowed over the years since they'd last fought. When she leaped, with superhuman speed, six feet straight up in the air, flinging herself in a twisting forward roll so tight it left her dizzy, she was, therefore, slightly too late. Her knackered old trainers clipped the demon's back as it flashed past beneath her. She was slightly off balance as her soles smacked back onto the concrete—and the first knife she threw as she landed went wide, spanging off the walkway's railing and spinning off into the night.

Smoothly her right hand whipped back and out again, but the demon had already recovered itself; it swatted her second knife out of the air with something very like contempt. Jessica held her breath as she reached for her third: the blade crossed the space in a flash of silver and struck the demon in the face, right between where its eyes would have been if it had been a person.

But it was not a person. Grimly she watched her knife vanish into the glossy darkness, leaving barely a ripple. The demon didn't even break stride. With the best speed she could muster, Jessica dived to one side. She just had time to notice that the demon had anticipated her . . .

. . . when she felt a blow that took her breath away.

The concrete wall at the end of the walkway was a clear twenty feet behind her; the blow flung her the distance in less than a second, and she smacked into the wall back-first. Helpless with pain, she slid to the floor, waiting for the follow-up that would finish her.

But it didn't come.

When she looked up, the demon was watching her.

"Feeling your age, Jessica?" it inquired.

Jessica didn't answer. Her bones were aching, and she could taste blood in her mouth, warm and coppery. She gritted her teeth and got to her feet, keeping one hand behind her back. *Magic,* she was thinking. All right: she was going to have to use magic.

"I sympathize," said the demon. "Truly, I do. As you see"—it gestured at itself with one ink-black hand—"I've taken what strength I can from my current host. But he, like you, is old now, and weak. He will not sustain me for much longer."

Jessica said nothing. She was concentrating. Behind her, slowly, agonizingly, the air above her palm wobbled, bulged—

then a light appeared. It was a tiny spark at first. The spark glistened and twinkled as she coaxed it into life, gradually becoming a little brighter, a little stronger with each passing moment. It was *herself* that Jessica was pouring into it—all of her determination, her power, and her hatred condensed into a single, glittering point. The spark grew to a sphere, a whirling globe of orange-flecked and sizzling silvery-blue, as the demon continued to speak.

"**What I need,**" it said, "**is a new vessel to work from—*fresh blood*,**" it added, "**as it were. Someone vigorous yet . . . pliable. Someone spirited yet suggestible. In short, someone *young*. Why *did* you come back?**" it asked again, suddenly. "**Was it the girl?**"

Still Jessica did not reply.

"**Well,**" said the demon, "**it doesn't matter.**" It waved wearily at the hand Jessica still held behind her back.

"**All right,**" it said. "**Go on, then. Surprise me.**"

Jessica bowed her head. She brought out her hand and what was inside it—

—and she smiled.

Already, a thin shell of softer blue was forming around the small globe of light that still danced and whirled over her hand. Another second and the shell seemed to harden, then *crush* inward, turning the light of the globe to an angry red, then white.

Then, suddenly, the demon was screaming.

Its head tipped back, the glistening liquid black of its jaws gaping so far they seemed to roll and fold back on themselves. Its body was flailing now, around where the light was hitting it, reaching and flailing as if being blown about in a wind tunnel, and all the time the scream went on and on.

The sound was one Jessica knew well. She had heard it in her dreams every night for fourteen years: a sound like paper tearing in your head; an intaken, wailing, braying sound that shot up in pitch like a rocket—a sound like nothing on Earth.

Her amber eyes flashed as she stared the demon down. Holding the light out in front of her, Jessica walked toward it. It was reaching for her: long, liquid-black fingers were grasping at the light, testing her will, checking her strength, but Jessica fought with all her heart, forcing the demon back, step by step. Without taking her eyes off it, she reached out and picked up her bag.

From her years on the streets, Jessica had learned to make the best use she could of whatever materials came to hand. Manifesting her power externally for any length of time was exhausting, but certain substances (Jessica had discovered) could be induced to hold magic, storing it up and releasing it slowly like a battery does an electric charge.

Tobacco, for example.

She began to pour the bag's contents out on the ground at her feet, a little at a time, as evenly as she could with just one hand. Slowly, steadily, she let the precious stuff fall, shaking it out, forming a line on the concrete between herself and her enemy. Holding the blazing light above her head, she forced herself to turn her back on the demon as she continued to pour. The bag went empty: her collection of shreds and dog ends flared briefly, then blackened as she completed the protective circle. She sat down and crossed her legs.

Suddenly, the demon seemed to realize what she was doing. It sprang toward her in a spreading flood of darkness—swallowing the walls, the rain, the world outside, and everything. Jessica took a deep breath. Forcing herself to blank out everything except the light of her will, forcing herself not to think of what would happen if that light went out . . .

. . . she closed her eyes.

The sound of the door buzzer, long and ugly, ripped Esme out of her sleep. The dream she'd been having was one she had often: a long, slow, freezing kind of dream, full of darkness and falling and cold that squeezed stony fingers round her heart. It was a frightening dream, but in a moment Esme had dismissed it as usual. She opened her eyes.

Her thick black curly hair had swung forward around her face, which meant she was on the ceiling again, where she always seemed to wake up. Parting her hair with her fingers, she floated soundlessly to the cushioned floor of her bedroom and walked the two steps to the intercom by the door. Just as she reached it, it crackled: her father had reached his first.

"Yeah?" he said, his deep voice managing to convey in that one syllable just how unhappy he would be if the person at the door turned out to have woken him up for no reason.

"Raymond?" said the voice from outside.

There was a pause.

"*Nick?*" said Raymond hoarsely—and suddenly, Esme's blood turned to ice.

She pressed the button. "I'll be down in a moment," she said.

Nick was small and thin and dressed in black from head to foot: he wore a black suit, black shoes, a black shirt open at the neck, and black silk gloves on his hands. His beard and mustache were as dark and neat as the rest of him, but there were deep lines of worry at the edges of his glittering blue eyes. He looked older than Esme had been expecting, old and very tired.

"Esme," he said. "Good to see you."

"You too," Esme lied. She and Raymond had been preparing for Nick's return almost the whole of her life. She was nervous.

"Can I get you anything, Nick?" boomed the grinning giant standing by the table. "Cuppa? Something stronger, maybe?"

Raymond, in contrast to Nick, was massive. His nose was squashed flat, his ears were out of shape, and he had no discernible neck of any kind, just an immense black beard with wispy white streaks in it, behind which his great bald clump of a head seemed to join straight onto his shoulders. In the army-issue undershirt he was wearing, his hairy arms looked huge. His meaty red hands, with their swollen knuckles, were resting easily on the back of a chair. But Esme knew from the way his fingers were clenching that Raymond was almost as nervous as she was.

"This isn't a social visit," said Nick.

Esme watched him. Nick took a deep breath and closed his eyes. Before he spoke, his face seemed to sag inwardly.

"I'm afraid," Nick said softly, "that the Scourge has escaped again." He looked up. "We're in trouble."

The grin fell off Raymond's face: a second later, he looked like he'd never smiled in his life. "How?" he said.

"I don't know," said Nick. "I can only assume one of the others must have released it. But one thing's for sure: the Brotherhood's in no shape to handle this as we are. We're . . . going to need some new recruits."

Surprised, Esme and Raymond exchanged a look.

"Have we time?" asked Raymond. He had never been very good at hiding his emotions, and the skepticism on his face was clear to see.

"No," Nick snapped, "I dare say we don't. But we'd be useless against the Scourge right now, and you know it."

Raymond blinked.

"We . . . do have young Esme here," he said carefully. He took a step closer to the other man and tried for a smile. "I'll tell you what: I've never trained anyone like her. You should see the way she—"

"Yes," said Nick, "but in case you haven't noticed, there's only one of her, and that's *not going to be enough!*"

His words echoed around the room. Raymond and Esme looked at each other uncertainly.

"I'm sorry," said Nick, "but we simply must have new recruits—*fresh blood*," he added, "as it were." He looked at Esme. "Will you help me?"

"Sure," said Esme. "No problem."

CHARLIE AND JACK

The West End stank in the heat of summer: the smell came up at Jack in waves from the warm, gum-pocked pavement. A police sign on the corner warned in five different languages that thieves were operating near the cash machines—don't let anyone distract you, it said—but Jack had seen the sign plenty of times before, and besides, he was thinking. Any minute now they'd be at the restaurant. If he was going to get any answers about what was going on, then he'd better bite the bullet and ask now.

"Er . . . Charlie?"

No response. Charlie just kept striding ahead of him.

"Charlie?" Jack repeated. "Charlie, wait!"

Only now, when Jack had shouted, did Charlie stop.

Jack Farrell had known Charlie Farnsworth since they'd been put next to each other on the first day of school; Jack wasn't the kind of person who made friends easily, but he'd been impressed with Charlie straightaway, and they'd been best mates almost ever since. Both boys were now fourteen years old; Charlie was a month older than Jack and an inch and a half taller, and his cheekbones stuck out in a way that Jack's only did if he sucked his cheeks in. Charlie's hair was black as night and just tousled enough, whereas Jack's was blond and fluffy no matter what he did with it. Jack, like Charlie, was wearing black jeans and a blue cotton shirt, unbuttoned and untucked over his white T-shirt—but Jack didn't look . . . well . . . *cool*, like Charlie did. All these things were normal—*typical*, in Jack's opinion—and he'd pretty much learned to get used to them. But there was something else different about Charlie that day: it was obvious. Every step he took seemed to be filled with a kind of rage.

"Listen," said Jack, "you want to tell me what's going on?"

"What d'you mean?"

"Well," said Jack patiently, "what's the deal with having lunch with your dad? We haven't done that since we were kids."

There was a pause.

Suddenly, Charlie took a deep breath and said, "He's left."

Jack looked at Charlie carefully. "What?"

"He's *left*," Charlie repeated, making an exasperated face. "Look, you know how our answering machine's been on all day lately? That's 'cause the day before yesterday, Dad told me and Mum he was *leaving*—then he *left*. Okay?"

The words had come out in a rush. For a long moment after, there was silence between them.

"Oh, mate . . ." said Jack.

"Yeah," said Charlie.

"How did it—?"

"At breakfast," said Charlie. "Saturday morning. He comes

to wake me up just like normal—right? Only his voice is all funny and he's like, 'Come downstairs, there's something we've got to talk about.' So I go downstairs, and Mum's got this . . . expression on her face. . . ."

Jack could see Charlie was having trouble getting the words out—especially since, at that moment, a group of some forty tourists, all wearing identically ludicrous bright yellow fanny packs, were pushing past on either side of them.

"And Dad says . . . well, basically . . . he's going," said Charlie.

"Oh, mate," Jack repeated, uselessly.

"He says he's got this rented flat all sorted out, right? And him and this . . . woman he met through work are going to live over there for a bit while they work out what to do next. Then he packs a bag of stuff, and, well . . . " Charlie blinked. "He's gone."

"Mate, I am *so* sorry," said Jack. It sounded feeble, but what else was there to say?

"Mmm," replied Charlie and grimaced. "Listen," he said, "this is going to be the first time I've seen him since . . . you know."

"Oh, right," said Jack doubtfully.

"Well . . . I'd really appreciate you, you know, coming in with me. Backing me up a little bit." Charlie was looking at him. "What do you say?"

Suddenly, Jack began to feel awkward.

If Charlie had asked him to watch zombie films with him until four in the morning, he would've agreed like a shot, as always. Splattery team death matches on the Internet? Likewise, sure, no problem. This, however . . .

"Please," said Charlie.

Jack looked at him. Charlie was his friend. Of course, there was no choice, really.

"Well . . ." He shrugged. "Okay."

Charlie let out a sigh of relief and put his hand out. They shook.

"Thanks, man."

"Sure."

Charlie's smile faded quickly. "Well," he said, "here goes."

"Charlie," said Mr. Farnsworth, standing up as soon as he saw his son. He took a couple of steps across the room toward him, his arms opening for a hug—then he caught sight of Jack. His eyes widened for a moment: his smile stayed in place, but Jack knew, at that instant, that he shouldn't have come.

"And Jack!" said Mr. Farnsworth, letting his hands fall to his sides. "Good to see you. Come and sit down: the duck's on its way."

They sat. There was a very long silence.

"So . . ." said Mr. Farnsworth. "How are things at home?"

"Not great," said Charlie, "since you ask."

There was more silence for a moment as Mr. Farnsworth waited to hear whether Charlie had anything to add to this. Charlie didn't.

"And . . . how's your mum?"

"How do you think?"

Jack looked up from his plate to sneak a glance at Charlie's dad, but Mr. Farnsworth noticed, so he had to stare quickly down again. Jack heard him take a deep breath.

"Charlie," he began, "I—"

The waiter glided up with the Peking duck.

The small round straw box of pancakes arrived first, together with the dish of hoisin sauce and the plate of spring onions and cucumber. These were followed by the duck itself, which the waiter proceeded to mash into shreds with quick, well-practiced movements. This only took about thirty seconds, but to Jack, with Charlie and Mr. Farnsworth sitting there in silence, it felt like much longer.

"Right," said Mr. Farnsworth brightly, once the waiter had left. He rubbed his hands. "Who's going first?" When nobody answered, he lifted the lid on the pancake box and offered it across the table: "Jack?"

Well, Jack wasn't made of stone. . . .

"Thanks," he said. He took a pancake and spread a thin layer of the rich, sweet plum sauce across it with a teaspoon. Charlie took one too. Jack noticed a quick smile of relief on Mr. Farnsworth's face at this. Obviously he saw it as an encouraging sign.

"So, Jack," said Charlie's dad, turning heavily toward him, "how're things with you? Got any plans for the summer?"

"Er, nothing much," Jack said. He wanted to look at Charlie, to take his cue for how to speak to Mr. Farnsworth from him. Luckily, he had his pancake to work on.

"You still skateboarding much?"

"Dad, that was *years* ago," said Charlie.

"Oh," said Mr. Farnsworth.

By now, Jack's first pancake was ready to eat. He'd laid

out just the right proportions of cucumber, spring onion, and mashed-up duck on top of the sauce, and he'd success-fully rolled the whole thing up into the proper cigar shape. He lifted it to his lips and took a bite: it was delicious.

"That's a very neat job you've done of that," said Mr. Farn-sworth.

"Thanks," managed Jack through his mouthful. "Peking duck's one of my favorites."

Mr. Farnsworth smiled at him. Jack smiled back uncertainly.

Then Charlie threw his pancake down on the table.

"Dad, *why did you do it*?" he asked.

It was hot and bright in the restaurant, especially next to the window where they were sitting. Slowly, Mr. Farnsworth put down his pancake.

"Charlie," he said wearily.

"Yes?"

"Well . . ." prompted Mr. Farnsworth, "don't you think . . . ? You know, with Jack here?"

"Why not?" said Charlie, in a voice that made Jack squirm in his seat. "I want him to hear this too."

Mr. Farnsworth sighed. Then he dabbed at his lips with his napkin, spread it back across his lap, and looked up at Charlie again.

"All right," he said, and he took a deep breath.

"Your mother and I . . ." he began. "Well . . . we've never been really happy."

Now Jack *really* didn't know where to look. He certainly wasn't going to look at Charlie or Mr. Farnsworth, so he was reduced to fidgeting with his pancake. It was ridiculous and horrible at the same time—but suddenly he couldn't help wondering if he just had to sit there, or if it was okay for him to take another bite. Peking duck was his favorite, after all.

"I tried to make it work," said Mr. Farnsworth, staring earnestly at his son. "I tried to keep it going, for as long as I could. But, well . . ." He shrugged. "I'm not getting any younger. And when the chance came up for me to be really *happy*, I had to take it. Do you see?"

Charlie's mouth opened and closed a couple of times before he got his words out. His voice, when it came, sounded high and strangely muffled.

"But you left," he said, "so . . . suddenly."

Mr. Farnsworth sighed again. "Charlie, there's—"

"'Never a good time for something like this.' Yes, you said."

Mr. Farnsworth blinked, surprised.

"Good for who, though?" asked Charlie, his voice getting louder. "Good for who?"

"Charlie—"

"Mum was happy. She thought you were happy. We were happy! And all the time you were . . . making *arrangements*."

"Charlie—"

"Do you have any idea how stupid you've made us feel?"

"Now, Charlie," said Mr. Farnsworth, "you've got a right to be angry. . . ."

Charlie said nothing. Jack looked from his friend's expression to the last of the pancake—the perfect, mouth-size morsel of duck, rich sauce, and crisp, pale green vegetables. Slowly, he put it down.

"But you've got to let me make things right between us," Mr. Farnsworth was saying. "Charlie, you've got to understand that nothing's really changed between me and you, *nothing*. And if you'll just—"

"And I want *you* to understand," Charlie cut in, in a voice that made his father stop dead, "that I am never, *ever* going to forgive you for this. Do you understand that? *Never.*"

He paused.

"Come on, Jack, we're going."

He stood up. Hurriedly, Jack stood up too.

"Charlie, wait," said Mr. Farnsworth. "Please?"

But Charlie didn't wait. And Jack, of course, had to follow. When Jack looked back, Mr. Farnsworth was sitting absolutely still at the table, staring straight ahead. Then the door swung shut behind them, and they were gone.

"Er . . . Charlie?" said Jack.

Charlie didn't even turn, just kept stomping straight ahead, head down. Jack sighed.

For a good two minutes they strode on together without speaking, and before long they were coming out into Cambridge Circus. The big crossroads was packed as always, full of shuddering red buses, gaggles of tourists, brightness, noise, and heat. Looming over it all was the Palace Theatre.

The Palace Theatre is one of the most impressive buildings in the West End—a grand and ostentatious mass of stripy pink brick festooned with turrets, glittering windows, and fat stone cherubs. Jack was looking up at it, distracted, when—

WHUMP! A passerby barged into Charlie's shoulder, sending him staggering sideways.

"Hey!" Charlie shouted.

The man, who'd continued on his way as if nothing had happened, stopped and turned.

He was dressed in black from head to foot: black suit, black shoes, a black shirt, and black silk gloves on his hands.

"I'm sorry," he said. "Did I knock into you?"

"Why don't you watch where you're going?" said Charlie.

The man's eyes narrowed a little. "I've told you I'm sorry," he said.

"Yeah?" replied Charlie. "Well, sorry's not good enough!"

Jack held his breath.

The man raised an eyebrow. His face seemed to take on an odd, calculating sort of expression. There was a long, slow moment of silence, then—

"Suit yourself," said the black-clad man, and in another second he'd vanished into the crowd.

"Jesus," said Charlie. "Some people. Come on, I need to get some cash."

Jack followed without arguing.

The queue for the cash machine was seventeen people long. A very smelly, very dirty young man with sunken-in cheeks and a filthy blue sleeping bag slung over one shoulder was squatting in the alcove at the side of the machine.

"Spare any change, lads?" he asked when they eventually got to the front.

"Piss off," Charlie replied. He shoved his card into the machine and jabbed at the numbers.

Jack sighed again. It was going to be a long afternoon.

"'Scuse me," said a voice.

The boys looked round.

"'Scuse me," said the sleeping-bag man again. "It's just . . . I think you've dropped a fiver." He pointed at the ground next to him. The boys looked. It was true: lying on the pavement not two inches from the man's bare and astonishingly dirty feet was a crumpled green five-pound note.

"Er . . . cheers," muttered Charlie. He bent down to pick up the money, and then everything happened very fast.

The man shot out an arm, yanked Charlie's card out of the machine, leaped to his feet, and ran off down the street, shoving tourists aside as he went.

"What?" said Charlie. "He's got my card!" He ran off after him.

Jack watched Charlie haring up the road. The thief, it seemed to Jack, was impossibly far ahead. But then something amazing happened. The thief stopped running.

He'd stopped dead, in fact, in the middle of the pavement, right in front of another pedestrian.

It wasn't, was it? The black-clad man! And as, panting heavily, Jack arrived at the scene, he could hear the man speaking, slowly and carefully.

"**Give it to me,**" the black-clad man was saying, holding out a gloved hand. "**Give me what you've stolen. Now.**"

His voice was strange: it seemed to echo in Jack's head, making small flowering explosions go off behind his eyeballs.

For another moment, the thief just stared as if mesmerized. Then his hand was coming out.

No way!

"**Now go**," said the man, and the thief ran off, even faster than he'd been going before.

Jack gaped.

Charlie gaped too.

The black-clad man just smiled and handed the card back to Charlie.

"Whoa," said Charlie, looking at the card in his hand. "I mean . . . thanks," he added quickly.

The man shrugged, but he kept looking at Charlie with the same calculating, almost greedy expression that Jack had noticed before.

"Uh . . . listen," Charlie began, "I'm sorry about before."

"Think nothing of it," said the man. "You look like you're having a rough day. I'm Nick."

"Charlie."

"I'm Jack," said Jack—but suddenly, it seemed, no one was listening.

"I, uh, really appreciate you, y'know, getting my card back," said Charlie. "Is there anything I can do to, ah, thank you?"

"Well," said Nick, "there is one thing. I'd like you—both of you," he corrected himself, "to come with me and take a small test. It won't take more than a few moments of your time, and it's something you might find . . . interesting."

"What kind of test?" asked Charlie.

"Actually," said Nick, "words don't really help. It's something you have to see for yourself. But I rather think," he added, smiling at Charlie again, "that you're exactly the person I've been looking for. What do you say?"

Cynical, Jack crooked an eyebrow. But then—

"Sure," said Charlie, "why not?"

"Splendid. Well, follow me," said Nick, and with that, he set off across the road.

Charlie turned, but before he could follow this total stranger that he'd just randomly decided to go off with, Jack grabbed him.

"Charlie!"

"What?" asked Charlie, shaking Jack's hand off and scowling.

For a moment, Jack just stared at him.

Jack and Charlie were teenagers now. Maybe there was some point after which "talking to strangers" was okay, some point at which the rules changed and you were less likely to get kidnapped, murdered, or whatever.

Jack sighed. Of course there wasn't.

"Charlie, what are you doing?" he asked, gesturing and trying for a smile. "That guy could be anybody!"

"So?" Charlie asked.

Jack blinked.

"You coming?" Charlie asked. "Or what?"

Without waiting for a reply, he set off after Nick, leaving Jack staring at his back.

Well, thought Jack, there it was. With Charlie in this kind of a mood, there was no telling what he was going to do— or what kind of trouble he was going to get into. And just as before, when they'd been standing outside the restaurant, there was no choice for Jack, not really. Sighing uselessly, he set off after his friend.

They were heading back toward Cambridge Circus, back the way they'd come, but then Nick turned left, taking Charlie down a side street. When Jack caught up with them, they were standing outside an old and solid-looking black back door that looked strangely small in the mountain of red brick that surrounded it. Nick smiled thinly at the boys and pressed the buzzer. Jack looked up at the Palace Theatre again.

It was odd how different the back looked from the front. There were no fancy windows and statues here, just a vast Victorian clod of red brick with a cast-iron fire escape sticking out the top. The afternoon sun was very bright, so Jack looked down—and that was when he glimpsed something strange.

There was a weird kind of shadow on the back of Nick's neck: weirder still, it was *moving*. Curves and spikes of inky darkness were drifting across the man's skin. Jack blinked.

But when he opened his eyes again, whatever he'd seen was gone. Except for the glossy comma of Nick's long black ponytail, the back of his neck was bare.

Jack shook his head to clear it. *Should've brought my sunglasses*, he told himself.

"Yeah?" grunted a voice from the intercom.

"It's me," said Nick.

The door buzzed. The black-clad man pushed it open, and he gestured the boys inside.

THE TEST

Nick led them up a spiral staircase to a set of double doors. Jack had been feeling more uneasy with every step—but then the doors opened, and he suddenly found he was looking at the most beautiful girl he'd ever seen in his life.

She was dressed in a red hooded top and green combat trousers. Her thick black curly hair was tied back tightly in a bunch, leaving dark little wisps at her temples. Her face was angular and fiercely elegant, her skin was the warm color of milky tea, and her eyes were the most extraordinary shade of amber. They flicked from Jack to Charlie, and the fine black curves of her eyebrows arched at Nick in a quizzical expression: evidently, she wasn't too impressed by what she'd seen. As far as Jack was now concerned, however, following Nick didn't seem like quite such a bad idea.

"Esme," said Nick, "I'd like you to meet Charlie . . ."

"Hi," said Charlie.

". . . and, I'm sorry, what was your name again?"

"Jack," said Jack, annoyed.

"And this is Raymond," Nick said, joining the large and

---

frankly terrifying-looking hairy man who was standing by the long conference table in the center of the room. "There. Now the introductions are out of the way, perhaps we can get started."

"Hold on," said Raymond. "*These* are the new recruits you wanted? Two kids you just found on the street?"

"That," said Nick crisply, "is precisely what we're about to find out."

Esme frowned at the boys, shrugged, then closed the doors, leaving Jack and Charlie just standing there.

The room they were in was very big. The wide walls sloped inward toward a high, arched ceiling and were covered with a pattern of regularly spaced, strange-looking blotchlike things. The only light in the room came from a great round window at the far end, so Jack was having trouble making out the details.

"My colleagues and I," said Nick, leaning back against the table, "belong to a small yet ancient organization known as the Brotherhood of Sleep. We're . . . jailers," he said. "Of a kind anyway; our prisoner is a demon. We call it the Scourge."

At that, Jack gave up looking around and stared openly at Nick instead.

"I'm sorry," said Charlie, "but I don't think I heard you right. Did you just say 'demon'?"

"That's right," said Nick. "A demon. A being of pure liquid darkness, bent on a path of destruction."

Jack raised his eyebrows.

"Many thousands of years ago," said Nick, "the Scourge was defeated by a powerful curse. The curse kept the demon imprisoned where it could do no harm, and the Brotherhood's task was to make sure that it stayed that way. However, as the centuries passed, our order became complacent: our numbers thinned, and those who remained grew . . . weak. One day, over a decade ago now, one of our members betrayed us."

Nick walked slowly around the table until he stood at the far end, resting his black-gloved hands on the chair at its head.

"Hungry for power, the man—Felix, his name was—allowed the Scourge to possess him. The demon took him over and became very strong: we only just managed to recapture it. In the battle another member of our group—Esme's mother, Belinda—was killed."

Jack looked at Esme, but she showed no reaction. Her strange amber eyes were bright as she concentrated on what was being said. (She was, Jack decided, really very pretty indeed, actually.)

"In the years since that night, I've traveled the world," said Nick, "searching for new recruits to bring the Brotherhood back up to strength—without success," he added, with a wan smile at Charlie, "until today. But now, with the Brotherhood still in tatters, I find we have been betrayed again."

He sighed (a bit dramatically, Jack thought).

"The Scourge has been unleashed once more," said Nick. "For thousands of years it has been biding its time, waiting for the moment to come when it can put its terrible plans into action. Now, I fear, it will succeed. Unless we have your help."

Nick paused.

"I need the three of you," he said, looking at Esme, then Jack, then back at Charlie again, "to take a small test. This test will decide which of you is going to become the Brotherhood's next leader."

"But Nick!" Raymond spluttered. "You didn't mention this was about who's going to be leader!"

"Frankly, Raymond," said Nick, "I'd've thought it was obvious. You and I no longer have the strength to do what must be done: it is time to pass the burden to the next generation. The one who performs best in the test will take on as much of my own power as I am able to give, becoming the new leader of the group."

"But . . . that should be Esme, shouldn't it?" Raymond asked. "She's been training all her life."

"So you keep telling me," said Nick. Then, seeing Raymond's and Esme's shocked expressions, he sighed.

"Look," he told them, "I know this might seem strange to you. But the Brotherhood needs reinforcements and time is short. You've always trusted me before, Raymond: trust me now. *Trust me*," Nick repeated. "That's all I ask."

Raymond and Esme looked at each other but said nothing: already, Nick had gone back to concentrating on Charlie.

"Now, what you're being offered here," he went on, staring at Charlie intently, "is something in the way of a proper adventure. A chance to battle an ancient evil and—quite possibly—save the world. And all I need from you, at this stage, is a simple yes or no. So . . . what's your answer?"

There was a pause.

Jack had loved fantasy, science fiction, and horror all his life—the films, the games, and the books. He'd heard worse stories, and, frankly, he'd heard better ones, but no one had ever expected him to believe one was actually *true* before. He was so nonplussed, he wasn't sure how to react, so he turned and looked at Charlie.

To his amazement, Charlie wasn't even smiling: he was looking at Nick with fixed attention—giving every appearance of having listened seriously to every word Nick had said. Jack waited for him to say no. He waited for Charlie to burst out laughing—for him to do anything, in fact, except what he did, which was shrug and say—

"All right. Sure."

"Splendid," said Nick, already setting off back round the table toward them.

Jack stared at his friend.

"Wait!" he said, his voice coming out (infuriatingly) as a kind of squeak. "Er . . . what sort of 'test' are we talking about here?" he asked, in the gruffest voice he could manage.

"I'll show you," said Nick.

Slowly, grimacing with pain, he began to pull off his gloves, one finger at a time. Then, when the gloves were off, he turned his hands and held them out in front of him, palms out. There was a sharp intake of breath from everyone in the room.

The skin of Nick's hands was horribly burned all over. The palms were two masses of thick scar tissue—red, inflamed, and glistening.

"Could the three of you stand in a line, please?" asked Nick politely. "This won't take long."

Suddenly, Jack was standing with Charlie on his left and Esme on his right. Their faces were grim: to Jack's mounting dismay, everyone apart from him seemed to be taking this seriously. He looked at Nick, who had closed his eyes, concentrating—and Jack's stare widened even further.

Something was happening. Something weird.

The air in front of Nick's dreadful scarred hands began to wobble and shake. The effect was a bit like heat haze, but it only lasted for a moment, because just then a shadowy shape appeared, a shape that instantly began to thicken and stretch. In another moment something long and silvery had formed in Nick's hands, which were closing around it. Then, before Jack's brain really had time to register what it had seen, Nick was holding what appeared to be some sort of long metal bar, horizontally, so it stuck out to either side of him. The bar's length stretched along all three of them—Esme and Charlie too.

"Now," said Nick, "take hold of the staff."

Esme went first, taking her end of the object with both hands. Charlie took hold of his end too. *All right*, thought Jack, and followed their example. The object was smooth and cool in his hands—solid and real in every respect, save for the fact that it had just appeared out of thin air.

"Ready?" Nick whispered. His horrible burned hands were clamped on either side of Jack's. "Go," he croaked.

Jack felt a sudden pain, like red-hot scissors stabbing into his hands.

Before he could stop himself, he'd let go.

Nick's eyes snapped open.

"S-sorry," Jack stammered. "Wasn't ready."

"On three this time," said Nick, through his teeth. "Hold on for as long as you can." He closed his eyes once more.

"One . . . two . . . *three*."

And it started again.

The pain was astonishing. It felt as though the skin of Jack's hands was being peeled off with red-hot pincers, like his palms were being devoured by ants. Jack resisted as long as he could—which was about two seconds—then he let go with a gasp.

This time, however, Nick did not stop the test.

Jack glanced down at his hands. They were completely unharmed. They weren't even tingling. Jack turned to Charlie, fully expecting his friend to have let go too.

But he had not.

Charlie's hands were clenched tight around the staff, the bones in his knuckles standing out white under the skin. His eyes were squeezed shut, and the muscles around his mouth were bunched into knots from the way he was clamping his jaws closed—but he wasn't letting go. And that, really, was when Jack began to get scared.

He looked from Charlie to the girl on his right, Esme. Her

eyes were closed too, but she appeared much more relaxed than Charlie. Her face was a mask of concentration and control, and Jack could see that she wouldn't be letting go of the staff anytime soon. What scared him was that he knew Charlie wouldn't either.

In the breathless hush of the big, dimly lit room, Jack suddenly became aware of a low, electrical humming sound. In front of him, under the hands of Nick and Charlie and Esme, Jack saw the blue-black surface of the staff give off a gunmetal glint—then begin, imperceptibly at first, to glow. Slowly, Charlie's lips parted and curled back, his face scrunching up even harder.

What is he thinking? Jack wondered.

In Charlie's mind, there was a soft, velvety rush of darkness.

When it lifted, he was at home, back in the kitchen, with his dad.

The scene was exactly the same as the morning when his dad had told him he was leaving, only the light was a bit strange and flickery. Charlie's dad's eyes too were different somehow. Darker. Almost black.

"**Listen to me carefully, Charlie,**" said Charlie's dad. "**It's time you heard the truth.**" The voice was a little deeper, a little louder than normal, and each word seemed to set off small flowering splashes behind Charlie's eyes.

"**You know what it means,**" his dad began, "**about me leaving?**"

Charlie said nothing, just listened.

"**It means that everything you know is a lie.**"

A shrill, cold sensation was filling up in Charlie's stomach. He stared, frozen.

"I don't expect you to understand this—you're young, after all," said his father. "But I think even *you* can get it, if I say that a lot of the time when you were growing up—for a lot of the time when we were together as a family—I was . . . wishing I was somewhere else."

He paused, giving Charlie a few moments to let this sink in.

"But—" said Charlie.

"Ah," said his dad, holding up a hand, "don't tell me. You're going to say that you had no idea. That you thought I seemed happy. Yes?"

Charlie said nothing.

"You know the answer to this one, Charlie," said his father.

"Oh no . . ." said Charlie. The cold feeling in his belly was getting stronger.

"I did it for *you*," said his dad slowly. "For fourteen years, fourteen years of living a lie, I kept the whole miserable thing going—for you. Now."

He smiled, the lips drawing back from his teeth.

"Parts of our time together as a family have been . . . nice. And I love you, Charlie. You're my son."

"Oh, Dad . . . please . . ."

"But the fact remains that every good memory you have, each and every good time you thought we had, has now changed."

He paused.

"From now on, whenever you think back to time you spent with me—whenever you look back to your childhood and anything good in it—you'll be wondering . . ."

He leaned forward, his eyes flashing darkly, the blackness in them widening.

"**Were we happy?**" asked his father.

"Oh no," Charlie whispered.

"**Were we really as happy as you remember?**"

"Please, Dad . . . no . . ."

"**Or was one of us just . . . pretending?**"

Charlie's hands were black shapes, clenched tight against the brightening orange-yellow of the staff. His head hung low, his shoulders were hunched—and Jack watched helplessly as, right in front of him, his friend started to moan to himself.

It was a quiet sound at first, a sound that Jack had never heard a person make before: a low, weird, keening kind of sound. Charlie's mouth was barely open. He was swaying slightly, as if the sound itself were making him move, as if the sound were a separate creature somehow, something that had been waiting and growing deep inside him, waiting for its chance to come out.

"Ohhhhhh-ho," said Charlie. "Oh, Dad."

His face was red and sticky-looking, his tears glittering in the light from the magical staff. Jack stared, fascinated.

"Ohhhhhh, Dad," moaned Charlie, louder now. "Oh no."

He took one more rasping breath, threw back his shoulders, and tipped his head back—

—and *howled*.

It was a terrible sound, an indescribable sound—a dry, scratching, inhuman sound, like grinding glass and tearing paper. It went on and on, getting louder and louder. Jack wanted to shut his eyes but he couldn't, he couldn't look away, and now, suddenly, the staff was blazing white, and the humming was filling the room, almost loud enough to drown out the terrible, maiming sound that was coming from Charlie's mouth.

Esme's lips were pressed tight together now, turning pale with tension and effort.

"It's not right," said someone suddenly. It was Raymond. "Nick, this isn't right! It shouldn't be like this!"

"Let it out," said a voice in Charlie's head. "Let it all out, open your heart, and LET ME IN. *YES!*"

And suddenly, everything happened at once.

Esme let go with a shout.

There was a thunderous, echoing CRACK.

And the staff, or whatever it was, vanished.

For a long moment, there was silence. Nick, still holding out his horribly scarred hands, stood swaying on his feet, blinking.

"What?" he said, looking at his surroundings and the people staring at him, as if taking them in for the first time.

"Where am—? Wait," said Nick. "This is . . ." Then he looked down at his hands. His face went suddenly white with horror, and his mouth fell open.

"Oh no," he said. "Oh, God. This is—wait! No! You can't! *The*—"

But before he could finish whatever he'd been going to say, his eyes rolled back, his knees buckled beneath him, and he sank, insensible, to the floor. Esme and Raymond rushed to his side.

Charlie, meanwhile, was looking at his hands.

The skin, from palms to fingertips, was completely, utterly black: an inky, glistening, polished-ebony black. As he watched, the darkness bunched and wriggled for a moment—then it shot straight up his arms, disappearing under the sleeves of his shirt. Slowly, Charlie let his hands fall to his sides.

"Charlie?" said a voice. It was Jack. "Charlie, what's happened?"

For a moment, Charlie didn't answer. His eyes, though red from crying, were shining strangely. He blinked, looked at Jack, and smiled.

"It's all right, mate," he said slowly. "It's all going to be all right."

Esme—who'd been holding Nick's wrist—looked at Raymond. There was a long silence. Then she said, "He's dead."

"Three o'clock tomorrow," barked Raymond to Charlie, as he bundled the boys through the door.

"But what about that guy?" spluttered Jack. "He's, you know . . . dead!"

"Not your problem, mate," said Raymond. "Three o'clock *sharp*," he emphasized, still looking at Charlie.

"What about me?" asked Jack, before the door closed.

Raymond paused.

"I don't know," he said, his eyes narrowing at Jack. "What about you?"

"He comes or I don't," said Charlie.

"Suit yourself." The big man turned and was gone.

Jack and Charlie stared at the door for a moment, even though it had slammed shut. They looked at each other, then they looked out at the street.

The sky was empty of clouds, and the afternoon sun was still hot and strong, making the pavement blaze uncomfortably. Traffic was heavy in both directions, and another long snake of sweaty-looking tourists was crawling its way west on the opposite side of the street.

Charlie turned to Jack. "It's too hot for the Tube," he said. "Let's get a bus."

"Oh," said Jack, surprised. "Er, okay." They set off, and soon they were safely wobbling their way north, back toward where they both lived.

They were sitting on the top deck of the bus, at the front, where they always sat, like everything was perfectly normal. It was almost as if—Jack thought—the whole episode had been some kind of dream. When he found that he couldn't stand it any longer, Jack spoke.

"Charlie, are you all right?"

"Huh?" said Charlie, drumming his hands on his knees.

"Are you *all right*?" Jack repeated.

"I'm fine, mate!" said Charlie. "Better than fine: I'm terrific. Fantastic. Amazing!"

Jack looked at him. Charlie's eyes were shining: his grin was huge. He certainly looked well enough.

"What about your hands?" Jack asked.

"What? Oh," said Charlie. He stopped drumming and showed them to Jack. "Look, they're fine too. Not a scratch!"

It was true. Charlie's hands looked perfectly normal; there were no outward signs of his ordeal. There was no sign in Charlie of anything that had happened, in fact, from the scene in the restaurant to . . . whatever the Hell had just taken place upstairs at the theater.

"So," said Jack. "Let me get this straight."

Charlie looked at him and grinned some more.

"Demons are real," Jack started.

"Apparently," said Charlie.

"And there's one on the loose. A bad one."

"'Liquid darkness, bent on destruction,' yadda yadda yadda," said Charlie.

"And *you*," said Jack, grinning back despite himself, "are now the new leader of an ancient brotherhood whose sole sworn purpose is to fight this . . .'scourge'—and bring it back under control."

"That's about the size of it, yeah," said Charlie. His grin widened. "Pretty cool, huh?"

Jack was doing his best: really, he was, and Charlie's enthusiasm, as always, was infectious. But a large part of his brain just couldn't help having doubts, and he knew that he had to say something.

"What about that guy, though?" Jack asked. "The one who just, like, *died* right in front of us?"

Charlie's grin vanished. "Jack, don't get boring on me, all right?"

Stung to the quick, Jack closed his mouth and fell silent.

Being called boring—especially by Charlie—was Jack's

Achilles' heel. The idea that he was boring scared Jack, because secretly, he was worried it might be true. Jack admired Charlie's ability to throw himself into things. It was part of the reason they got on.

Perhaps seeing the effect that his words had had, Charlie smiled again.

"Mate, this is what we've been waiting for," he breathed. "The chance to have a real adventure! Don't you see? Heh," he added, chuckling to himself, "and what about that Esme, eh?"

"What about her?" asked Jack, as casually as he could.

"Come on, man," said Charlie. "You were there."

Jack squirmed for a second as Charlie grinned in his face, and finally admitted, "She's all right."

"All right?" Charlie echoed with disbelief. "She's better than all right, mate. She's *gorgeous*. And did you see the way she looked at me?"

Jack hadn't, but his lack of reply didn't seem to stop Charlie.

"Oh yes," Charlie pronounced sagely. "Very promising, I'd say."

There was a pause.

"So," said Jack, giving up trying to sort it all out in his head. "This 'power' the guy gave you. You're, what, some kind of superhero now?"

"I guess we'll find out tomorrow," said Charlie gleefully.

"You going to start wearing your pants outside your trousers, then?" asked Jack. "Do you think we should get you a cape?"

"Tchah, *right*," said Charlie, looking out of the window again.

DARKNESS

People are used to seeing the homeless in the West End, and as the day passed and Jessica sat motionless in her circle, few people noticed her and none cared. That night, when the Scourge came to her for the second time, it just stood there at first, testing the protective ring of magic-charged tobacco and cigarette ends with long, wet, ink-black fingers.

"Do you believe in God, Jessica?" it asked.

Jessica had now been sitting cross-legged on the damp concrete walkway, without changing her position, for a full twenty-four hours. She did not dignify this with a reply.

"I've met him, you know," the demon told her conversationally. "Your 'God.' He's rather different from how you imagine him, I should think. Still, I'm looking forward to seeing him again. I want to tell him exactly what I think of him."

Jessica didn't answer.

"It was clever of you to suspect Nick all this time," said the Scourge, unperturbed. "No one else guessed he would never complete the ritual to reimprison me. Even he thought he was strong enough to resist—right up to the end."

Surprised despite herself, Jessica looked up.

"Yes," the Scourge told her, "Nick's dead. And I have found a worthy vessel at last."

Jessica said nothing.

"He's perfect," said the demon. "Young, hotheaded, and with a pain and fury inside him that is most"—it gave a liquid shudder—"invigorating. When the time comes for him to understand what I can offer him, there's no chance whatever he'll refuse me. You see, I'm not just going to make him into a god." It leaned closer. "I'm going to make him *stronger* than God."

The Scourge took a step toward her.

"I'm going to take your life, Jessica," it said. "I'm going to suck out your essence, to your last breath; I'm going to do the same to each of your little band until I've had my satisfaction from every one of you. And then, *then*, with this boy as my puppet, I'm going to open the Fracture, and—"

"And what?" Jessica interrupted, making a face. "What is your 'sinister master plan to conquer the world,' exactly? I wish you'd tell me straight, instead of all this posing."

"My dear woman," said the Scourge slowly, "I may still be stuck here in this ludicrous little science project, but I assure you, my horizons are somewhat wider. When I go back to Hell I'm going to wake the Dragon—and the Dragon is going to destroy *every-thing*. Well?" it asked. "What do you think of that?"

"Would you be quiet, please?" said Jessica. "I'm trying to concentrate here."

The demon froze.

"It's started, Jessica," it told her quietly. "There's nothing anyone can do to prevent it."

Jessica just closed her eyes again.

Esme was far too angry to sleep—and whenever she couldn't sleep, she trained. At this moment, she was using her makiwara boards.

The makiwara boards were the only pieces of actual training equipment that Raymond had ever allowed her to own or use. Five solid oak blocks screwed to the wall in the shape of a cross at the far end of her training room, their purpose was brutally simple. With her fists, her feet, her knees, her elbows—with every striking point of her body from the top of her forehead to the backs of her heels—she was hitting the blocks as fast, as hard, and as often as she could.

Students of martial arts have used makiwara boards—or their equivalents—for centuries. They are used to toughen the skin, to deaden and finally kill the nerve endings in the student's striking points—to make the student's body as resilient, as hard, as the wood. The purpose of makiwara training is also mental: thanks to her years with the blocks, Esme had learned to control her pain and not let it affect her.

She had been hitting the boards for about an hour. Standing behind her, Raymond noted wearily that each of the five dark oak surfaces now carried a telltale dark smudge of red.

"Esme?"

She ignored him, continuing to smash at the boards.

Raymond stood behind her, watching her, watching the way the muscles in her back bunched and moved as she worked: graceful, efficient—lethal. It was odd, he thought, how being so proud of someone could hurt you so much at the same time.

"I'm sorry, petal," he said quietly. "I . . ." He looked at his feet. "I didn't know the test would be like that."

"Don't make excuses," said Esme, without looking—without stopping. WHAM. CRACK. *CRUNCH.* A knee strike, an elbow smash, and a straight punch followed each other into the boards. Under the last, one of them splintered. "That's what you've always told me, right? No excuses."

There was nothing to say. Raymond looked at her helplessly. Should he tell her how astonished he still was by Nick's last actions? How bitterly disappointed he was too that after all these years, all the hard work he and Esme had put in, Nick should give the job of new leader to a novice? No. That was all just doubt. Nick had told them to trust him, and with the Scourge on the loose, doubt was a luxury. Still . . .

"Esme, I want to tell you something."

He looked back down at his feet and took a deep breath.

"I don't pretend to know a lot about magic," he said carefully. "That side of things is best left to those who have the gift, and that's fine with me, as you know. But in my time, I've met some very powerful people. I saw Nick in action in the early days. Your mum too. And I—" He stopped suddenly and took another deep breath.

"Well. Here's what I wanted to say."

He looked at her hard.

"There's something a bit special about you," he said. "I know it."

He paused.

"Now, if this 'Charlie' is the new leader, well, that's it, that's how it is. But I'm telling you, there's no chance we can recapture the Scourge without your help—no chance at all. This is still what we've been working and training for," he told her fervently. "This is still your moment to break out and spread your wings: your moment to shine. So . . . will you stop that now and get some rest? Please?"

He waited, trying not to let his smile waver.

After a long moment, Esme let her hands fall to her sides. Already the blood on her knuckles was drying up and vanishing: the physical damage she'd inflicted on herself was melting magically away, just as it always did—leaving only what was inside. Turning, she stood toe-to-toe with Raymond, her chin about level with his chest. Then suddenly, she stepped forward and wrapped her arms round his waist, as far as they would go.

Raymond gave a deep sigh and put his own arms around Esme's small, strong body, patting her gently with his big hands.

"G'night, Dad," said Esme, her voice muffled.

"G'night, petal," said Raymond. As soon as he felt her arms relinquish him, he released her and turned to go.

Felix Middleton, the man who'd first betrayed the Brotherhood, stood in his flat and waited. The Alembic House apartment was one of the finest and most expensive in the whole city, and Felix didn't like it. He didn't really care for its stunningly opulent furniture, its thick dark rugs and carpets. The panoramic view of the Thames and half of London, even lit up (as it was then) with all the glories of the city's nighttime lights, did little for him. From where he was standing, the wide picture window held two images: the city and a reflection of himself, standing in his room, alone. Felix wasn't relaxed. He wasn't happy or sad—but he was calm. After all, he had done all he could.

The logistics of arranging his not-inconsiderable personal fortune so that, on his death, one girl could have access to all of it, instantly, without fear of interference from governments, tax departments, or any other hindrances, had been no simple matter. But Felix was not a simple man. In the fourteen years since he had set himself on his path, Felix had cut a swath across the financial markets of the world, a trail of conquest no less devastating for its having been so quiet. But when the Scourge came for him now, as he fully expected it would, would that be the end of it? Would he have . . . atoned?

Felix allowed himself a bitter smile. Of course not.

He had done it, the unthinkable. By releasing the Scourge he'd unleashed a terror in the world, a terror that could be slowed but never put down. He had also destroyed a family. For him there could be no redemption, no forgiveness. He could only do what he could, use what he was good at as best he could, and never make another mistake, ever, ever again.

And he had made no more mistakes. His life was empty,

dry as sand, but he had made no more mistakes. He could take what comfort he could from that.

He gazed at the reflection in the window: the dim green of the glass-shaded lamps, the winged silhouettes of the dark leather chairs, and all the other expensive trappings. He gazed at them and past them, at the city beyond, until the ice cubes melted in his glass and, finally, in one corner of the room behind him, a patch of shadow began to move by itself. He fixed his eyes on the reflection of that piece of the dark as it bulged, swam, and took shape.

"At last," he said.

Felix gulped the remains of his drink: the fiery liquid slid down inside him as he put down his glass. Still smiling a bitter, grim smile, he now turned to face his nightmare.

"For nearly fifteen years, I've dreamed of you," he told it. "Every night the same dream. And every morning I've woken up knowing that I'm never, ever going to be free of you, and what I—*we*—did. So come on." Felix beckoned. "Come on and get it over with. Because frankly, I've got nothing left to lose."

"**No**," said the Scourge.

Felix frowned at the demon uncertainly. This wasn't how the moment was supposed to go. "No . . . what?" he asked.

"**No, I'm not going to kill you yet**," the Scourge replied, "**and no, you still have something to lose.**"

Felix looked at the demon: its man-shaped body of liquid black and the shiny black blank of its face. "You're not talking about . . . Esme?" he asked.

The demon just waited.

"But I'm nothing to her," said Felix, smiling bitterly. "Less than nothing, I should think. Why, all she knows is that I released you, and through me you . . ." He trailed off suddenly and shuddered.

"Precisely," said the demon. It paused.

"Felix," it asked slowly, "**have you ever wondered about Esme? About her power, her strength, her speed? Have you ever asked yourself where they came from?**"

Felix turned pale. "No. Never. Why?"

"**Felix, Felix,**" the demon admonished. "**You never could lie to me.**"

There was silence between them for a moment.

"Oh, God," said Felix. "Oh please, no. No."

"**This is one secret you don't get to carry to your grave, I'm afraid. She'll never take my word for it alone.**"

"But . . . please," said Felix. "Why can't you just—?"

"**Quiet.**"

And there was quiet.

Presently, the demon stopped what it was doing and froze, crouched over Felix's body.

It was good enough. Felix wouldn't be telling any tales until the time was right. The demon stood up, took two steps, then vanished.

In his house, in his room, in his fitful sleep, Charlie twisted on the bed. Darkness spread through his veins like strong wine.

SKILLS

Charlie answered the door in his sunglasses. Once Jack was safely inside, however, he took them off—and Jack had his first shock.

"I know," said Charlie, looking away before Jack could even think of what to say. Charlie's eyes were red and puffy, with thick dark blue smudges underneath them. He looked awful.

"Mum was up most of the night again," he said. "She's asleep now, so we'll have to be quiet."

"Oh, mate," said Jack stupidly.

"Anyway," said Charlie, and a glint appeared in his eyes, "listen, before we go, I want to show you something. What do you know about tattoos?"

"Er . . ." said Jack—but Charlie had already got his T-shirt up round his neck.

"What do you think," he asked, "of this?"

He turned his back, and Jack had a second shock.

"Eh?" said Charlie, when Jack didn't answer at first, then again: "Eh?" He stretched out his arms.

"Blimey," said Jack finally.

From shoulder to shoulder and right down Charlie's back, almost as far as the waistband of his jeans, was a huge black tattoo.

Jack stared.

It was an odd sort of pattern. The tattoo's broad, curving shapes reminded Jack of certain tribal designs, Celtic or Native American ones, but it wasn't quite like anything he'd ever seen before. The shapes seemed to radiate out from Charlie's spine, scything across his back like a crest of broad feathers or a set of great curved sword blades. The shapes were black against Charlie's pale skin—completely, utterly black—and each and every one of them ended in a perfect, razor-sharp point. Charlie clenched his arms, and the black shapes seemed to bunch and shift of their own accord as his muscles moved underneath them.

Even apart from the fact that it had just appeared on Charlie's back, the tattoo made Jack uneasy. Still, he thought, with a twinge of envy, it was certainly impressive. In fact, no denying it, it was most definitely . . .

"*Cool*," he breathed.

"Huh. Yeah," said Charlie, turning casually. "Got the surprise of my life when I caught sight of it in the mirror this morning."

"Does it hurt?"

"Naaah," said Charlie. "Not really."

"And that's the . . . thing? From yesterday?"

"Well, I don't think Mum drew it on me in the night."

"Wow," said Jack. He meant it.

"Come on," said Charlie, pulling his T-shirt down and getting into a short-sleeved shirt. He left it unbuttoned and untucked, hanging over the waistband of his black jeans, showing his black T-shirt underneath. He stuck his shades back on and turned to Jack.

"Let's go," he said.

"Yeah?" Esme's voice was cool and level through the speaker.

"It's me," barked Charlie.

"You're early." It was a statement, nothing accusatory, but Charlie said, "Well, I'm here. You letting me in or what?"

The girl didn't answer, but the lock on the door at the back of the theater buzzed loudly. Charlie pushed it open, then they were through.

"Raymond's not back yet," said Esme. "We'll have to wait." Then she just stood there, arms crossed, looking at the boys. An awkward silence began to develop.

Jack looked around the room. It was the same room they'd been taken to the day before, but this was the first chance he'd really had to get a proper look at it.

"That, er, pattern," he said, pointing at the regularly spaced blotch things he'd noticed previously. "It's . . . well, what is it?"

"Butterflies," said Esme, as if it were obvious.

"Oh, right," said Jack. "They're . . . nice."

Esme looked at him. "Thanks," she said. "I did them myself."

"Really?" asked Jack. "Mind if I . . . ?"

Esme shrugged. Jack walked over to the nearest wall.

Each butterfly was about thirty centimeters across and painted with incredible accuracy. The wings of the one that had first caught Jack's eye were quite beautiful: a powdery, electric-blue color on a background of deepest black. Its neighbor was different, orange and black this time, with wider, more elongated wings. In fact, although it was hard to see far along the wall with the light so low, it suddenly occurred to Jack that—

"Are they all different?"

"Yep," said Esme.

"I didn't know there were that many kinds," said Jack.

"Well, there are. Nobody really knows how many."

"How many have you got here?"

"Five thousand, four hundred and seventy-two," Esme replied flatly.

"Wow!" said Jack.

It came out much more loudly than he'd meant; both Esme and Charlie were now staring at him. Charlie rolled his eyes and gave Jack an exasperated look.

"Er . . . how long did that take you?" Jack mumbled.

"Seven years," said Esme (making Jack stare at her). "On a good day, I can do three." She gestured toward a shadowy point some distance away in the corner of the ceiling. "I haven't quite finished yet, though."

The boys looked up. The arched ceiling had to be a good sixty or seventy feet high, surely taller than the tallest stepladder, and yet it too was entirely covered in row upon row of painted butterflies—all except for a large empty patch at one end. *How on Earth . . . ?* Jack looked back down at Esme, but then the double doors opened and Raymond strode in.

"Right," said the big man. "Esme, Charlie—walk to the center of the room, turn, and face each other. It's time to see what Wonder Boy here can do."

Charlie blinked but did as he was told. Esme followed. Jack watched.

The butterfly room was cool and dark after the heat of the day outside. The sun through the great round window cast a long oval of creamy light across the hard matting of the floor. The conference table had been shifted out of the way, propped against the wall at the far end; there was nothing in the center of the room but the big padded floor, the pool of light, and Charlie and Esme, standing in the shadows to either side of it, some three yards apart. Charlie had taken off his button-down shirt so was now dressed in just his black T-shirt and jeans. He was smiling. Esme too was dressed lightly, in a fitted camouflage-green T-shirt and loose combat trousers, her hair tied back in a thick, tight bunch: her face was expressionless. Raymond stayed by the door, obviously keeping well back from whatever was about to happen, and Jack took his cue from him. The whole scene was beginning to remind Jack of pretty much every martial arts beat-'em-up game he'd ever played in his life. This was not a happy realization for him.

"Brotherhood members have different talents," said Raymond. "Our first job, Charlie, is to find out where yours lie, so let's start you off with a little sparring match. Esme?"

She turned. Raymond smiled, making his beard bristle alarmingly.

"Go easy on the lad to start with," he said. "We wouldn't want to hurt him"—his smile widened—"much."

Esme didn't smile back, just turned to face Charlie and dropped into a shallow crouch, one foot slightly ahead of the other. Her honey-brown arms were held loosely at her sides. Her hands were open, relaxed. Charlie, still grinning, if a little dubious, did his best to follow her example.

"Ready?" called Raymond. "Fight."

There was a blur, then—

"*GAHH!*"

It was Charlie who made this noise, as all the air exploded out of his body.

Jack gaped.

Charlie was now sitting on the floor, with his back against the wall, some ten yards behind where he'd been standing. His legs were sticking out in front of him, and he was gasping like a stranded fish as he tried to get his breath back. Esme's expression and demeanor had not changed in the slightest. She looked exactly the same as she had a moment ago, only now she was standing in the middle of the room, where Charlie had been.

Whatever had just happened had been so fast, Jack hadn't even seen it.

"Get up, you big jessie," said Raymond. "She barely touched you."

Blinking, then scowling as he realized he was being insulted, Charlie did as he was told—staring at Esme.

"Walk back to the center," said Raymond. "Esme, step back a little if you please. All right, face each other again."

He waited until Charlie and Esme were back in their original positions. Charlie's panting breaths sounded loud in the silence.

"Now," said Raymond. "Did you notice something there, Charlie?"

Charlie looked at Raymond. "How d'you mean?" he managed.

"That little side kick to the ribs," prompted Raymond. "Did it get your attention?"

Charlie scowled again.

"Good. Charlie, Nick must have picked you for a reason. As I believe I mentioned, we're here to see what you can do. If you don't concentrate, you're wasting our time. Plus, Esme'll clump you again. It's as simple as that."

There was a pause. Charlie stared at Raymond, then turned and raised his eyebrows at Jack, who shrugged back, helplessly.

"CONCENTRATE!" barked the big man, making them both jump.

Charlie shrugged and turned to face Esme, who was still regarding him calmly.

"Now, ready?" said Raymond.

Jack leaned forward, willing his eyes to catch something of what was going on this time. Esme and Charlie dropped into their crouches, just as before. Charlie frowned.

"Fight!" barked Raymond.

Jack stared, and time went slack.

Instantly, on the word of command from Raymond,

Esme had leaped forward, pirouetting in the air as she hurtled toward Charlie, the spin bringing her right heel out and round for a kick that should have taken Charlie's head off.

But it missed him. Without the slightest sign of effort apart from his continued look of hunched concentration, Charlie simply leaned back out of the way, just far enough for Esme's foot to flash harmlessly past, scant millimeters in front of his nose.

Esme dropped smoothly onto her left foot and sank, still spinning, converting the momentum of her first attack into a low, scything sweep at Charlie's feet, but this time Charlie hopped into the air like a kangaroo, and Esme failed to reach her target again.

Jack stared and kept staring as the fight continued. It was like nothing he'd ever seen. No, scratch that: he *had* seen what he was seeing, thousands of times—only that had been in films or in games, and not right in front of him when one of the people involved was his best mate.

Esme was moving so fast he could hardly see her—faster than he'd ever seen a person move before—and her skills were extraordinary. But the thing was, as quickly, smoothly, and gracefully as Esme attacked, daisy-chaining her moves into a constant, blurring barrage of fists and feet—Charlie was faster.

Every blow Esme launched at him, every hammering punch or slashing kick, somehow failed to land. Charlie had no finesse. He had no skill. Even Jack could see that the way Charlie fought was closer to the playground style of flapping your arms wildly in front of you than anything in the work of, say, Jet Li or Yuen Wo Ping. But the fact remained, it was working: he was holding her off. Charlie's face was a blank, a mask. His feet (when they were on the ground) moved slowly, almost mechanically, as he stepped back under the force of Esme's onslaught. But then suddenly—

Whoosh—SMACK!

It was over.

In a move that took a whole second after it had happened for Jack to work it out, Esme simply flipped through the air over Charlie, lashing out as she landed with a vicious high kick with her right leg. Charlie turned to follow her—just in time to receive the sole of her foot squarely in the middle of his face. His legs went out from under him and the back of his head struck the floor. He actually slid for a clear six yards before coming to a stop.

Esme jogged a couple of steps lightly on the spot, her hands dangling loosely at her sides again.

Suddenly, Jack remembered to breathe. His eyes were out on stalks.

Charlie reached a hand to his face and groaned.

"You okay there, son?" called Raymond, not sounding too bothered either way.

"My dose hurds," was the muffled reply from the floor.

"You poor dear," said Raymond. "Sit up, let's 'ave a look at you."

Charlie sat up, gingerly feeling his face, a stunned look in his eyes. His nose was a weird putty-gray color, almost as flat as Raymond's, and the blood was running from it freely. Jack was about to go and help him, but before he'd even completed the thought, he felt a massive and steely grip on his arm. Raymond had grabbed him without even looking.

"Take your hand away," said Raymond to Charlie.

Charlie looked at him.

"Take your hand off your nose," Raymond repeated, none too patiently, "and close your eyes."

Frowning uncertainly, Charlie did as he was told.

"Now . . . concentrate."

There was absolute silence in the room now. Wondering what was supposed to happen next, Jack looked at Raymond. The big man still had Jack's arm in a viselike grip, but all his attention was focused on Charlie.

"Stop the pain," said Raymond, almost whispering. "And *make it better.*"

Frowning, Jack looked over at Charlie, and his eyes went wide again.

No way!

Charlie's nose appeared to be *straightening itself.* The tip came out slowly at first, almost as if Charlie were pushing it out with his tongue, but the shape of it was re-forming and the color was going back to normal. In another moment Charlie opened his eyes, crossing them as he stared at his good-as-new nose. Then he wiped off the last of the blood in a long streak along his arm—and he smiled.

"No *way,*" said Jack, aloud this time.

"Haaaaaaaaaaaah," said Charlie.

"Get up," said Raymond.

Charlie did, still smiling.

Without looking at Jack, Raymond let go of his arm.

"Right," he said quietly. "Now, before Esme beat you again, what did I say?"

Charlie's smile faded. "You . . . said I should concentrate."

"After that," said Raymond.

"That I was wasting your time?"

"After that too."

Charlie frowned back at him, trying to figure out whether this was a trick question. "After?" he said.

"That's right," said Raymond. "*After* I told you to concentrate, *before* Esme beat you, what did I say?"

There was a long and heavy silence.

It was Jack who took a deep breath, then said, "'Fight'?"

Raymond turned on him with blazing eyes.

"Sorry," said Jack.

Raymond turned back to Charlie, who was trying for an 'isn't he ridiculous?' type of smile, in the hope of breaking the ice with him.

"Stop bloody grinning!" barked Raymond.

The grin vanished.

"Your friend here," said Raymond quietly again, "would appear to have been listening more carefully than you were." He turned to Jack and acknowledged him with a polite nod. Jack just stared at him.

"'Fight,'" Raymond went on, turning to face Charlie again.

"That's what I said. Now, which part of that didn't you understand?"

"What?" asked Charlie.

"God save us," said Raymond, looking up at the roof. "'Fight,'" he repeated, staring hard at Charlie. "'Come to blows,'" he added. "'Exchange a dose of fisticuffs.' *'Engage in single combat,'* for crying out loud."

"I don't understand," said Charlie.

"No," said Raymond. "You don't." He sighed. "Do it again," he said. "Face each other. Get ready."

Frowning, Charlie did as he was told. Esme stepped back to make way for him: she rolled her shoulders a little—Jack heard a soft *pop* from the muscles in her neck—then she dropped back into her crouch, waiting.

"Now," said Raymond. "We'll start again. Only for heaven's sake, I want you to lay one on her this time."

Charlie stared at him blankly.

"Hit her!" said Raymond exasperatedly. "If you can," he added, when Esme raised her eyebrows at him. "Ready?"

Jack blinked a couple of times to clear his eyes and leaned forward to watch. Charlie was scowling.

"Right. *Fight.*"

Charlie pulled back his right arm and let fly.

No chance. Warding Charlie's fist off easily with her left hand, Esme stepped toward him, into the blow. Her whole body weight, therefore, plus whatever forward momentum Charlie had put into his punch, was concentrated in the heel of her right hand as it struck the point of Charlie's chin, palm open, hard.

The force of the blow lifted Charlie off his feet. He sailed a clear ten yards back through the air and hit the wall again, with a solid, sickening crack.

"Tch*uhh*," he said, or something like it, as he came to rest on the floor.

There was a pause.

"God's teeth," said Raymond. "What d'you call that?"

"But . . ." began Charlie, simultaneously holding his chin with one hand and rubbing the back of his skull with the other. "I . . . *can't*," he said, his voice coming out in a kind of whine.

"No," said Raymond, "if that's the best you can do, then maybe you're right. My gran could punch better than that—mind you," he broke off, turning to Jack with a wink, "she was a terror, that one."

Jack just stared at him.

"Come on, man: on your feet. I can see we're gonna have our work cut out with you. Have you no backbone at all?" he added, when Charlie didn't move straightaway.

Charlie picked himself up once more. His face was turning red. "Just how the *Hell*," he began, his voice going high and strangely quavery, "am I supposed to—?"

"I told you," said Raymond. "Concentrate."

Charlie stared at him, speechless.

"Now, again," said Raymond. "Face each other."

This time, however, Charlie didn't move.

Raymond grinned. "Face each other," he repeated.

Still Charlie didn't move. All the color seemed to have

drained out of his face. His mouth had hardened into a thin, bloodless line. He blinked once, but still kept staring at Raymond.

Uh-oh, thought Jack.

"Ready?" said Raymond, with elaborate sarcasm.

Esme looked at Raymond. Raymond's grin just widened. She shrugged and turned back to face her opponent, dropping into her crouch again.

Jack watched, holding his breath.

"Fight," said Raymond.

Esme leaped, sweeping her right leg up for a kick—

—but then something strange happened.

About two centimeters from the side of Charlie's head, her foot simply stopped in midair. For a moment Esme just hung there, off the ground, frozen except for the frown of incomprehension beginning to dawn across her face. Then, quietly—distantly at first, but quickly getting louder—a rumbling sound began to echo around the room.

Charlie had turned to face her. His arms were coming up either side of him, and as he raised his hands toward the hovering girl his face twisted slowly into a mask of sudden and absolute fury.

Esme sank to her feet. Her hands too were coming up as if to protect herself. Her eyes were wide. Her legs were bending as if she were pushing against some terrible weight. The air in front of her seemed to be shivering—rippling.

And now, slowly, Esme's feet were beginning to slide back across the floor.

Jack stared.

Charlie leaned forward, eyes bright with rage, his fingers clawed and stiffening. The weird shivering in the air around Esme's outstretched hands was spreading, turning a heavy bruise-black, stretching and folding back around her. The rumbling got louder: the beginnings of a grimace of pain appeared on Esme's lips, then—

"STOP!" roared Raymond.

Charlie turned, arms still outstretched—

Released, Esme dropped to the ground with a thump—

Something hot and electrical rushed past Jack, almost knocking him down. Then—

Silence.

Charlie's arms dropped to his sides. He was breathing hard.

"W—" said Raymond, then cleared his throat. The big man looked pale and shaken. "Well," he said. "That's certainly . . . more like it. You okay, Esme?"

She nodded. Lying where she'd fallen, propped up on her elbows, Esme stared up at Charlie for another moment before flipping smoothly to her feet.

"You're . . . obviously a lot stronger than I thought," Raymond told Charlie. "I can understand what Nick saw in you."

Esme's face fell.

"Your control could use a lot of work, though," Raymond announced. "And Esme'll need to put you through your paces till you learn some technique. Kicking and punching," he added. "Yeah, 'specially punching." He smirked. "You punch like a girl."

At this, Esme managed a thin smile.

Jack looked from her to Raymond and finally to his best mate, who apparently really *was* some kind of superhero. He noticed a hollow feeling in the pit of his stomach, and it took him a moment to work out what it was.

Jack was scared, he realized: scared of what was happening and scared of where it all might go.

Charlie just grinned to himself.

"So," he said. "Tell me about this demon."

KNOWLEDGE
AND POWER

"The Scourge isn't an easy thing to describe," said Raymond.

They'd set up the conference table again, and he, Esme, Charlie, and Jack were sitting around one end of it. The afternoon sunlight was streaming in through the butterfly room's big round window, making the dust motes sparkle in the air.

"Try," said Charlie.

"It's not . . . physical, like you or me," said Raymond, giving Charlie a look. "The Scourge doesn't have a fixed size or weight or shape. It's intangible: a thing of chaos and magic. That's one of the reasons it's so dangerous."

The boys looked at him blankly.

"The laws of physics—gravity and so on?" Raymond shook his head. "They don't apply to the Scourge. I've seen it be in two places at once, and it can travel big distances apparently instantly. It never gets old. It never gets tired, and we don't think it can be killed."

The boys' mouths started to open.

"However," Raymond went on, holding up a hand to forestall them, "it does have one important weakness. It's this."

He leaned forward, putting his beefy hands on the table.

"The Scourge seems to need a host body," he said. "Like a home base to come back to. A person," he emphasized. "Someone who'll let the demon live inside them and work its will through them."

He gave the boys a moment for what he was telling them to sink in.

"Do you mean it's . . . kind of like a parasite?" Jack asked.

"A little, I guess—yeah," said Raymond, nodding. "One thing, though: it seems like once it's got itself established in someone, the Scourge can also project itself out of them somehow. It can take a piece of itself and send it out into the world—like a ghost or a double or . . . a shadow. That part of it can go wherever the Scourge likes: it can speak and find out stuff; it has physical strength and it can fight. But for . . . certain things, the Scourge has to stay completely in its host. Or . . . that's what I think, at any rate."

"You think?" Charlie echoed, raising his eyebrows. "You mean you don't know for sure? Why not?"

"Because until fourteen years ago," Raymond replied bleakly, "the Scourge had never escaped before."

Jack frowned. "But . . . what about the Brotherhood?" he asked.

"Yeah! Didn't they know anything?" asked Charlie.

Raymond sighed.

"Look," he said, "there are two things you need to know about the Brotherhood. The first is that it's very old. The earliest written account we have is from Anglo-Saxon times, around fifteen hundred years ago, but the secret was passed down by word of mouth before then, and there's no way of knowing for how long. Nick always believed the Brotherhood began much earlier: centuries, even millennia earlier. And as to how it began—and who it was who first imprisoned the Scourge? Well . . ." He shook his head. "Nobody knows."

The boys gave him a skeptical look.

"The other thing about the Brotherhood," Raymond went on, regardless, "is that it's secret—perhaps the most closely guarded secret in the world. There are other groups that have powers. There are other groups that use magic or have dealings with what you might call 'the supernatural'—but there's nothing else out there like the Brotherhood. And no one outside this room—apart from two others who I'll come to in a moment—has the faintest idea we exist."

"Why?" asked Jack.

"Yeah," said Charlie. "If the Scourge is so dangerous, why don't more people know about it?"

"Think about it," Raymond replied. "The Brotherhood was founded with a single purpose: to keep the Scourge imprisoned. Everything we do or have done, for thousands of years, comes—or came, I guess I have to say now—down to that. The order's members, right down to Nick's father, Jeremy, believed that the more people who knew about the Scourge, the more likely it would be that someone would make a mistake—that the Scourge would be released and that the Brotherhood would fail in its purpose. And . . . well, when you think of all that's happened, who knows?" Raymond's face turned sad. "Maybe they were right."

"How did you get involved in all this?" Jack asked.

Raymond looked at him. "Nick chose me." He smiled wryly. "Against his dad's wishes, I might add. Nick chose us all: picked us out for our different skills. There was me, two sisters—Belinda and Jessica—and another feller called Felix. Four disciples, one master."

"Five's not really much of a brotherhood," Charlie commented.

"Believe me," Raymond replied, "even five was a lot more than there had been. By the time Nick's dad got round to telling him about the Scourge, there was no one else left who knew the secret but him. When Nick announced he was going to find some new recruits, they had a row so big that they even stopped speaking to each other—right up until Jeremy's death. But Nick did his best to make the Brotherhood strong again: if it wasn't for Nick, none of us would be here." He paused.

For a second—that was all, before Raymond's self-discipline took over—Jack had a glimpse of just how much the big man wished his old leader were there with them now. Frankly, this didn't make Jack feel any better about things.

"Now, our job, as I say," Raymond went on, "was to keep the Scourge from escaping."

"Escaping from what?" asked Charlie instantly.

"A tree."

"A tree?" said Charlie, looking from Raymond to Esme incredulously. "A *tree*?"

"The Scourge was imprisoned in the roots of a tree," said Esme.

"That's right," said Raymond. "A big oak, it was, in . . ." He hesitated, looking suddenly secretive. "Well, you don't need to know where now."

"But this tree," said Charlie, obviously having difficulty with the concept (and Jack couldn't blame him: he was too). "Was there something special about it? I mean, how did you actually know it had a demon inside it?"

Raymond ran a hand over his shiny bald scalp and frowned, remembering.

"Again," he said, "it's . . . hard to explain. You could sort of . . . feel it."

He stopped and thought some more.

"When you were out looking after the tree," he said, "pruning or what have you, you'd sometimes catch yourself . . . thinking things. Unless you were awake to it, you might not even've noticed you were doing it, but you'd find yourself getting . . . ideas."

"What ideas?"

"One time," said Raymond, "and I'm not proud of this—I caught myself thinking about the rest of the group. I started thinking about magic, about how rubbish I was at it compared to Belinda and Jessica and Nick—and I found myself wondering if the others thought . . ."—he frowned—"*less of me* for it."

He looked up at the boys.

"That's what it does, the Scourge," he said. "It manipulates you. It looks all through you for weaknesses—all your little hurts and resentments—and it exploits them. I think that's what happened to Felix," he added. "I think that's how the Scourge escaped."

"Nope," said Charlie, making an 'over my head' gesture. "You've lost me."

"How?" asked Jack. "How did it escape?"

Raymond sat back on his chair and looked into the past.

"Felix was jealous, that was his problem," he said. "He always took things personally. He saw coming second-best as a slur on his spirit—second in magic, in combat, in anything. And when Belinda and I fell in love," he added and paused. "Well, I think that's what pushed him over the edge."

"What happened?" asked Jack.

"Felix went to the tree and let the Scourge possess him," said Raymond. "There was a fight: the rest of us managed to force the demon out of him, and Nick recaptured it in his staff. But Belinda, my wife, was . . ." He trailed off. "Well, she died. Esme was only a baby at the time."

Quietly, without fuss, Esme touched Raymond's hand with one of hers. Jack was looking at them, but Esme noticed, so he stared down at his lap.

"Ever since then, we've trained," said Esme, taking up the story. "Every day since then I've worked and waited, perfecting my skills in case the Scourge ever escaped again. And now," she added, and her amber eyes glittered, "now, my chance has come."

Jack looked at Esme—at the way she held herself, the set

of her mouth and the cold hard glow of her strange amber eyes. At that moment, the gulf between him and her seemed so wide as to be uncrossable. What must it be like for her, living like this? Really, he knew, he could have no idea. To dedicate your whole life to one purpose, to spend every single day training and preparing . . . Sometimes, in the past, Jack had imagined himself doing something similar. Sometimes he'd even liked the idea. Just then, however, he knew that imagining was going to be as close as he was ever going to get. And to be honest, he wasn't very sorry about it.

"What about the other one?" asked Charlie suddenly.

Everyone looked at him blankly.

"The other Brotherhood person. You know . . . what's-er-name?" Charlie snapped his fingers. "Jessica?"

"Oh," said Raymond, surprised. "Well, Jessica and Nick had a row."

"What about?" asked Charlie.

"After . . . what happened," Raymond said, "Nick had . . . doubts. He must've felt guilty for what happened to Belinda: maybe he wished he'd done like his dad had said and never brought the rest of us into this thing in the first place. At any rate, he made a decision. He announced he was going to find a new place to keep the Scourge: another tree, but somewhere secret, where supposedly none of us would know about it. Now . . ."

He leaned forward in his seat, which creaked dangerously under his bulk.

"Jessica disagreed with him," he said. "She reckoned no one

should be trusted with the Scourge alone—none of us, not even Nick. And when Nick set out on his own anyway, Jessica stormed out too. She left the Brotherhood, left all of us. And no one's heard hide nor hair of her in what must be—"

"So," Charlie interrupted, "two suspects."

Everyone stared at him again.

He scowled. "Come on, people, *keep up*. Whoever let the Scourge out this time had to be one of the Brotherhood; otherwise how would they have known about the demon in the first place? Right?"

No one replied. Jack wasn't even sure he understood the question.

"Look," said Charlie with a sigh, "I assume we all agree it wasn't *Nick* who was possessed—right?"

Jack blinked—but Charlie was already pressing on.

"Well, if it wasn't *Nick*," he announced, as if to a room full of idiots, "and it wasn't you two," he added, looking at Raymond and Esme, "then who else is left? Jessica and Felix! Come on, it's not exactly complicated."

Jack winced inwardly. Charlie *was* making a kind of sense, he supposed, but he didn't have to be so smug about it.

"So," Charlie repeated, "which of those two d'you think's the baddie? Felix or Jessica?"

"Felix," said Raymond firmly. "He was the one who let it out last time, so—"

"I think Jessica," said Charlie, interrupting again. "Especially if you've no idea of where she is. That's right," he added, "isn't it?"

"What is?"

"That you've no idea where Jessica is," Charlie repeated sweetly. "Bit suspicious, that, don't you think?"

Raymond opened his mouth—and closed it again, annoyed.

"I'm afraid that's true," said Esme for him.

"*So*," said Charlie again, grinning triumphantly, "how do we find her? How do we find this . . . Jessica?"

Raymond looked Charlie dead in the eye. "I'm open to suggestions," he said.

It wasn't the answer Charlie had been expecting. His grin became uncertain, then faded. An uncomfortable silence was just starting to develop, when Jack spoke.

"Er . . . can I ask something?"

In fact, Jack had a whole bunch of questions. How come Charlie was suddenly able to move at lightning speed and make magic powers come out of his hands? (He was still getting his head round that one, frankly.) And the enormous tattoo that had appeared on Charlie's back: was that some mark of the Brotherhood or what? But if Charlie wasn't going to ask about these things himself, Jack certainly wasn't going to do it for him. Not if it meant risking looking like any more of a spare part than he did already in front of Raymond and (especially) Esme.

Everyone was looking at him, and he could feel his face going red. Jack took a deep breath and said: "Um . . . what does the demon want?"

Charlie made a snorting sound in his nose.

"Actually," said Esme, "that's a good question."

"There's a place," said Raymond, "not far from here. We call it the Fracture."

"It's a weak spot in the fabric of reality," said Esme. "A magical gateway: a door. The Scourge wants to open the Fracture and escape back to where it came from."

"And where's that?" asked Charlie, with a skeptical expression—and to be fair, even Jack wasn't sure how much more of this stuff he could take.

Esme and Raymond looked at each other.

"The Brotherhood's earliest accounts speak of the Scourge as having come from a 'dark place,'" said Raymond. "An ancient place: a dimension of chaos and violence. This place, apparently, is where our universe began and it's where—the record says—it will end. The last time we fought, the Scourge spoke of the place by name."

"What place?" asked Charlie, becoming exasperated. "What are you talking about? What name?"

Raymond looked at him. "Hell," he replied.

For a long moment, there was silence.

"When you say 'Hell,'" said Charlie slowly, "you don't mean the real thing: fire and brimstone, eternal torment and damnation, that sort of Hell. *Hell* . . . do you?"

"That's the one," said Esme dryly.

"*Cool*," said Charlie.

Esme blinked.

"What happens if the Scourge goes back to Hell?" asked Jack.

"It could form an army of demons and invade the Earth," Esme put in. "That's what we've always thought—right?"

"We don't know for certain what the Scourge's intentions are," said Raymond, acknowledging her with a nod. "But if it's been imprisoned here all this time just to keep it *away* from Hell, well, you can bet whatever it wants to do can't be good."

Jack frowned again.

"But . . . Hell!" said Charlie. "Has anyone been there? I mean," he grinned, "what's the place look like?"

"I'm sorry?" asked Esme.

"This gateway," said Charlie impatiently. "Has anyone ever opened it and, you know, had a peek?"

"Listen, son," said Raymond, "maybe you don't under-stand—"

"We think only the Scourge has the power to open the Fracture," Esme explained.

"But even if anyone else could open it," said Raymond, his voice getting louder, "do you seriously think they *would?* This is Hell we're talking about! If the Fracture were to be opened . . . why, who *knows* what might happen?"

"Not *you*," snapped Charlie with sudden venom. "That's for sure." He looked at Raymond and shook his head in disbelief. "I can't believe you people!" he said. "Do you really mean to tell me that you've taken all this stuff, all this weirdness, on *trust*, without asking any of these questions before?"

"Yes," said Raymond flatly. "We trusted Nick completely."

"But now Nick's dead. And *you*, it seems, don't have the first clue about what's really going on!"

Jack was staring at Charlie now. Tact had never really been Charlie's strongest point, but the way he was acting was getting weirder and weirder. How did he manage to be so *certain* all the time? Where was all this confidence coming from?

"Where is it?" Charlie was asking. "This . . . 'Fracture,' I mean."

There was a pause. Esme and Raymond exchanged another look.

Raymond grimaced, then shrugged. "It's . . . a pub," he admitted.

Both Jack and Charlie gaped at him.

"But it's no kind of pub I'd be seen in, that's for sure," Raymond added quickly. "The Light of the Moon, they call it now. It's all chrome and steel and stripped pine floorboards, and about as much atmosphere as the *real* bloody moon." He shuddered. "Horrible."

"A pub," said Charlie.

"Yes."

"The gateway to Hell is in a London pub," said Charlie. "That's what you're saying."

"Yes," said Esme.

"And that's what this demon wants to do: to open the gateway to Hell."

"That's what we think. Yes," said Esme.

"O-*kay*," said Charlie. "Now we're getting somewhere."

Everyone fell silent. Charlie rubbed a hand across his brow, back and forth. His eyes were open, looking down. No one spoke.

"Well," said Charlie finally, looking up, "it's pretty obvious, isn't it?"

He began to grin wildly.

"What's obvious?" said Raymond.

"What we *do*," said Charlie. "It's simple! We wait at the Fracture for the Scourge to make its move, and then, when it comes, we *kick its arse!*"

There was another pause.

"You're going to kick its arse," echoed Raymond, looking hard at Charlie. "You," he emphasized, even more heavily.

"I said *we're* going to kick its arse, actually," Charlie replied, his smile vanishing as quickly as it had come, "but if it comes down to it, then yeah, that's *exactly* what I'm going to do. I'm going to wait for it to come, I'm going to square up to it, and then I'm going to kick its—"

And at that precise moment, a phone rang.

It was a mobile phone. For a dreadful second, Jack thought it might be his, but it was Charlie's. Everyone watched as Charlie fished his mobile out of his pocket, looked at the screen, and scowled. It was no use—the thing still kept ringing. He pressed the button and held it to his ear.

"Mum," he said, "this really isn't a good time."

Mrs. Farnsworth's voice was only audible as a sort of distant quacking. Everyone was pretending not to listen, but of course, they all were.

"Look, Mum, can I call you back in a minute?" tried Charlie. "Me and Jack are sort of in the middle of something here."

Listening, he frowned.

"Well, no, I'm not at Jack's *house*. And what do you think you're doing *checking* on me anyw—?"

Charlie sighed again and put a hand up to his brow.

"I'm with some friends of ours," he said. "Round their place. I'm in the West End, if you must know—"

Quack quack.

"Friends from school. Well, not school. I—"

Mrs. Farnsworth kept talking, and a horrible expression appeared on Charlie's face.

"No!" he said. "God! No! Look, I'm not with *Dad*. All right? Of course I'd tell you if I was with Dad!"

The silence in the room became even more awkward.

"What are you talking about, 'behind your back'? I *wouldn't*—"

Suddenly, Charlie just looked dreadfully, horribly tired.

"But Mum, I—"

Still the voice kept going.

"All right," said Charlie quietly. "All *right*. I'll be there as soon as I can. Yeah. You too. Yeah. See you later. Bye."

He pressed the button to end the call and looked up—just as everyone else looked away, pretending they hadn't been watching him.

"Listen," he said. "Me and Jack've got to go."

Jack was on the point of saying something about this, but the look on Charlie's face silenced him.

"All right," said Raymond. "On you go, then."

"We don't know whether anything would've happened tonight anyway," said Esme.

"But I want you here bright and early tomorrow!" called Raymond. But on 'tomorrow' the double doors of the butterfly room had already slammed shut. Charlie and Jack were gone.

"Well!" said Raymond after a moment. "A right little know-it-all, isn't he? Anyone'd think he was the one who'd trained all his life, instead of—"

"Yeah," said Esme glumly.

Raymond bit his lip.

"All right," she went on, once she'd had a moment to concentrate. "I'll take first shift at the Fracture, I guess. You go see if you can't track down Felix and Jessica."

Hearing the uncertainty in her voice, Raymond lifted his eyebrows at her.

"I know!" said Esme. "I just . . ." She paused, shaking her head to herself. "I guess I always thought that when the time came it would all be clearer somehow. This . . . " She shrugged helplessly. "This isn't happening at all how I expected."

"Me neither, petal," said Raymond grimly. "Me neither."

The train journey back to North London passed in silence. Charlie just sat there, staring ahead into space; he only looked up when other passengers jostled his legs, and the jostlers looked away quickly, perhaps sensing, like Jack, the fury that surrounded him like a storm cloud. The silence kept up as they left the station. The sky was starting to turn a darker, deeper blue as sunset approached, but Charlie just kept stumping on ahead, head down, and Jack found he was having to walk quite quickly to keep up with him. Only when they were almost as far as the front door of Jack's house did Charlie finally stop and turn.

"Well," he said, still not looking at Jack, not really, "I guess I'll see you tomorrow."

"I'll go across the park with you," said Jack.

Charlie looked at him.

"I need the exercise," added Jack as casually as he could. Lame as this was, it was the best excuse he could come up with. He had to get Charlie to talk to him, and keeping him company across the park might be the only way.

Charlie shrugged—then made a face. "I tell you," he said, "I don't. Esme gave me a real going-over." Slowly, creakily, he rolled his shoulders, trying to loosen them a bit.

"What about all that healing-yourself business?" Jack asked. "I thought you were supposed to be invincible now or something."

"Not invincible enough, apparently," Charlie replied, and smiled.

Jack smiled back.

"Come on, let's go."

They set off.

Their silence was more companionable now, but Jack was still finding it hard to ask what he wanted. In the end, he just blurted it out:

"Charlie, are you . . . okay?"

Charlie looked at Jack but didn't stop walking. "Yeah," he said. "Why wouldn't I be?"

"But isn't it . . . weird?"

"What, the superpowers thing?"

"Well, yeah!" said Jack. "Come *on*."

Charlie made a dismissive gesture with one hand. "It's not that weird, you know."

"No?"

"No," said Charlie, frowning now.

He thought for a moment.

"It's like . . . once you're into it—once you can do the stuff, you just . . . do it," he said. "You know? You just get on with it, and it all just feels right. Everything's straightforward. Clear. Simple. Until your mum rings up and tells you you've got to go home for *dinner*."

They crossed the road and went through the gate into the park. Jack said nothing.

"I swear," said Charlie, "you should've heard her. Nothing I could've said would've made any difference. Straightaway she's like, 'You're with your father, aren't you? You're seeing him behind my back!'"

"Oh, mate."

"Straight up," said Charlie. "I couldn't believe it."

Five or six older boys were playing football on the big stretch of grass to Charlie and Jack's right. At the end of the path, the church spire was already lit up for the night with its lights: it stuck out of the ground and into the evening sky like a giant, pale spike of bone.

"It's going to get worse, isn't it?" said Charlie. "This thing with my folks, I mean. Mum's going flaky on me. And Dad . . . well."

He stopped and turned to Jack. "You saw him in the restaurant. He just sat there looking all surprised, like he hadn't expected I'd be angry with him. Like I was just supposed to say, 'Yeah, sure, split up with Mum and go live with someone else, I don't mind!' Honestly, he doesn't have a *clue*."

Past Charlie's shoulders, Jack could see the footballers coming closer: one of them was lining up a shot at the goal— or the space between the two piles of jackets on the ground anyway.

"Saving the world's *easy*," Charlie was saying. "I'd rather fight a demon, you know? Better that than have to go through all this—"

Jack watched as the footballer took his shot: he knew, with a sudden and absolute certainty, where the ball was going to end up. And sure enough—

CLUMP!

It caught Charlie square on the back of the head, knocking him forward with the force of the blow.

Suddenly, all six footballers were laughing.

"Sorry, mate!" called the one who had kicked the ball, smiling broadly as his friends caught up with him. They all looked about sixteen or seventeen years old—certainly a lot bigger and stronger than Charlie and Jack. One of them was laughing so hard he was making little snorting noises through his nose.

Jack had seen these guys before. Year after year they spent the whole summer kicking their football around, and they never once seemed to get bored with it. Jack looked from them to his friend. Charlie was just standing there stiffly—head still forward from where the ball had knocked him.

"You all right?" called the lead footballer. The others were still sniggering.

Now, slowly, Charlie turned. "Who kicked it?" he asked. "You?"

"That's right," said the guy. His smile was cocky, not apologetic at all—and certainly not apologetic enough for Charlie.

"Come on," said Jack quietly, "let's leave it." But he knew he was wasting his breath.

"Why don't you watch what you're doing?" said Charlie. "You stupid sod!"

For a whole second the six lads stared at him. Then they burst out laughing again, all except for the one who'd kicked the ball, who just frowned.

"Listen, mate," he said, "I've told you I'm sorry."

"And I'm telling you, *mate*," said Charlie, "sorry's not good enough. Get on your knees. Right now."

Now everyone was staring at Charlie, even Jack.

"What?" said the lead footballer, grinning with disbelief.

"On. Your. *Knees*," said Charlie, and at the sound of his voice, the boy fell as if he'd been shot.

From where Jack was standing, he could see the back of Charlie's neck. He frowned. Weird black shapes were appearing under his friend's skin. Needle-sharp points of some inky-black substance were trickling up from under the collar of Charlie's T-shirt, widening into curved slivers of pure liquid darkness as they crawled up around his throat. Now the shapes were creeping down out of Charlie's sleeves, sliding past his elbows and down his forearms with an oil-dark, liquid eagerness.

Jack recognized the shapes: the curves, the hooks, the spikes. He'd seen them that morning on Charlie's back.

It was the black tattoo.

It was *moving*.

"**Now**," said Charlie, barely speaking above the level of a whisper, but something in his voice made strange explosions go off behind Jack's eyeballs.

"**Wet yourself.**"

The eyes of the hapless footballer fell closed. A blissful expression crossed his face: there was a moment of silence, then a soft, trickling sound, and now everyone was staring at the dark stain that was spreading down one leg of his shorts.

"Euugh! Gross!" said someone.

The footballer woke up and looked down at his crotch, a look of total horror beginning to form on his face.

Charlie just grinned and turned his back. The moment was gone. The strange shapes of the black tattoo had vanished back to wherever they had come from. Jack blinked.

"Come on, man," said Charlie to Jack. "Let's go."

No one tried to stop them.

"Er . . . Charlie?" asked Jack, once they'd safely gone a few hundred yards farther down the path.

"Yeah?"

"Do you think it's safe? Using your . . . powers like that?"

Charlie smirked. "Who are they going to tell?"

In another moment, it seemed, they were standing outside the gate.

"Take care, mate," said Charlie, turning to go.

"Yeah," said Jack, to his friend's retreating back. "You too."

JESSICA

The demon didn't even bother to visit Jessica on the third night. By the fourth, she knew she was finished.

The Scourge just stood there at first, a scarecrow figure of rippling shadows. Its arms hung loosely at its sides; its long, liquid fingers twitched lazily.

"Humans," it told her, "**with your little concerns: your tiresome and selfish preoccupations. I'd always thought demons were bad enough, but really—you people are something else.**"

"Don't you ever shut up?" Jessica asked, and closed her eyes.

She reached past the pain in her body. She reached past the terrible exhaustion in her head, the mental fatigue from keeping her circle going for so long—going further inside herself, further still. In her lap, her brown hands opened slowly. With a soft hiss, a thin blue spark appeared over her palms. She poured herself into it, and the spark began to grow.

"**Think of it,**" said the Scourge, "**what it'll be like when I succeed. Think of the peace: the pure emptiness. The silence. All Creation finally consigned to the Void. All the noise, waste, and pointlessness** wiped clean in an instant, when this *witless boy* helps me wake the Dragon, and at last we finish what it began. . . ."

While the demon spoke, the spark had swelled to the size of a marble. The magical bolt was spinning, picking up speed, its surface becoming a rushing blur of scorching white and deepest midnight blue. Jessica sent more of herself into it, reaching down inside for everything that she had left. Now the bolt was the size of a squash ball and beginning to crackle and spit in the dark, stifling air of the tattered circle. Jessica was as ready as she'd ever be. Slowly, savagely . . . she smiled.

"It's a shame, in a way, that you won't be there to see what I mean," the Scourge was saying, "to see what your flyspeck of a 'brotherhood' has been supposedly preventing all these years, because—"

"Here's an idea," Jessica interrupted. "How about you stop talking and come and get me if you can, eh? Or are you planning on *boring* me to death?"

The Scourge looked at her. "I've kept you here long enough for my purposes," it said. "You were a useful false trail for the others while you lasted, but now I'm almost ready to make my move. In fact, there's just one more trick to play. Funny," it added, "isn't it, Jessica? All these years hunting me, preparing to face me, and that's all you were—a distraction. Still . . ." The demon shrugged, its shoulders and neck dripping together in long, tarlike strings. "If you're ready to die, I'll be happy to oblige you."

"Do your worst," she told it.

"As you wish."

Jack had been watching Charlie and Esme train all day. While Raymond kept watch at the Fracture, Esme had been putting Charlie through his paces on martial arts, acrobatics, weapons training, flying—the lot. Each new and amazing skill that Esme introduced to Charlie he seemed to master almost instantly, and without any particular effort. By the time evening was coming round, Jack was thoroughly, utterly *fed up*.

He'd asked questions, made comments, and tried to keep his end up—and Esme had been polite enough to respond, even when (as seemed painfully obvious to Jack) his remarks had come less from any wish to share wisdom or advice than the simple desire to remind her that he was still there. But the fact of the situation was, he knew, that both she and Charlie were far too engrossed in what they were doing to take any real interest in him. After all (as he asked himself), why should they?

They were superhuman: Jack wasn't. They were powerful and important: Jack wasn't. Charlie and Esme were getting ready to fight the forces of evil: Jack's job, apparently, was to sit there and watch. It was as simple—as *typical*—as that.

So the afternoon had passed. Jack was just letting out something like his three hundred and seventy-fifth sigh of the day . . .

. . . when everything started to go wrong.

"Oh!" said Charlie suddenly. He broke out of the complicated silat arm-trap-and-sweep combination he'd been working through with Esme up by the butterfly room's ceiling and dropped to the floor. His eyes were closed.

"What?" asked Jack, without much interest.

"It's . . . the demon," said Charlie. His eyelids were fluttering strangely.

"What about it?" asked Jack.

"I think I know where it is," said Charlie, frowning.

"How?" asked Esme, landing in front of him.

Charlie's eyes flicked open. "No time to argue: I can *feel it*, all right? It's at Centre Point Tower right now! You take Jack. Let's go!"

Esme stared at Charlie, but already she was looking at his back: in another second Charlie was out the door.

"Well, okay," she said, turning to Jack. "Come on."

Jack followed her out onto the landing—just in time to see Charlie throw open the door that led to the fire escape.

Jack saw him stand there for a moment. In front of him, beyond the black iron railing, was the West End—its roofs, the traffic, the lights, and the empty air. Charlie spread his arms, leaped, and plummeted from sight.

Jack hadn't had time to shout, or even move. He'd barely had time to register what was going on—namely that his best mate had just jumped off a tall building. Suddenly, Esme had taken his arm in a surprisingly viselike grip.

"Ready?" she asked.

Her face beside him in the half-light was hard, fierce looking.

"What?" Jack managed. "Now, wait. Hold on a second. Just—no! I can't fly! You can't carry me! And I am *not* just going to—*WhAAAAAAAAAAAAAAAAAAAAAAAGH!*"

His third step had been into nothing: his feet had left the ground.

He was flying.

The streetlights slid by in an orange blur below him. Jack saw what the roofs of red London double-decker buses look like from above, and the tops of trees seemed to skim his feet. He was still screaming, but his scream was lost in the roar of the exhaust-filled summer air whipping past him, turning hot on his face as they picked up speed. In front of him Jack could see Charlie's silhouette just ahead, blasting through the evening sky, his arms spread wide—and Jack suddenly found he had an enormous grin on his face.

It was only a moment. It would stay with Jack forever—

But then the huge, ribbed spine shape of an ugly skyscraper reared up in front of them. Charlie lurched out of sight. The earth was rushing up toward him—and they'd landed.

There was a woman sitting on the ground, holding her hand out. There was something in her hand, something blue and white and impossibly bright at first, but quickly darkening, weakening, as the strange and horrible creature she was being attacked by surrounded and began to swamp her.

Jack stared, trying to take it all in. *That*, he thought numbly, *must be the Scourge.*

At that moment, the demon was a shapeless splatter of darkness, gathering and battening and convulsing round the woman like something between a giant black cobweb and a bat's wing. Esme had let go of Jack's arm now and was rising in the air again, standing between him and the demon, ready to fight.

But Charlie got there first.

"HEY!" he called.

Abruptly the demon seemed to suck back into itself: now it was like a stick figure made of darkness. In a movement so dazzlingly fast that you could barely see it, it leaped straight up the side of the building, vanishing into its shadowy concrete alcoves, and Charlie—

"No! WAIT!" yelled Esme.

—leaped after it.

Jack watched with his mouth hanging open, seeing his friend haring up the wall of the big skyscraper, planting each foot as if he were running on the ground. It wasn't exactly "in a single bound," but Charlie was clearly well capable in the "leaping tall buildings" department. In another second, Jack's superhero mate had disappeared from view.

Jack looked down. The bolt of electric-blue something-or-other flickered out and disappeared, and the woman who'd been holding it sank back, unconscious. Esme only just caught her before her head hit the ground. Then, at last, there was a pause.

"Is she okay?" Jack asked, pointing.

It had been the first thing to come into his head, and he knew it was a stupid question as soon as he said it. Of course she wasn't okay. The expression on her face was calm, peaceful even, but as Esme took hold under her arms the woman's head lolled limply.

"Get her feet," said Esme. "One. Two. *Three.*"

They swung her up off the ground. She was horribly light—in fact, she hardly seemed to weigh anything at all. Plus, Jack couldn't help noticing, she was . . . well, a bum. A homeless person. And to be honest, she didn't smell too good.

"Head toward the church," said Esme.

Across the street from the towering skyscraper a small old church was standing there looking stranded and abandoned. They shuffled hurriedly toward it, Jack struggling to keep up. Esme took them down a narrow alley at the side of the church and out into its tiny graveyard. They'd been lucky so far: no one else had been there to witness Charlie's lunatic charge after the demon, but it wouldn't hurt to keep away from any curious eyes on the street.

"Okay, put her down here," said Esme, stopping beside an ancient stone slab set into the grass. "You stay here with her," she told Jack.

"Wait!" said Jack. "Who is she?"

"It's my aunt," said Esme, softly. "It's Jessica."

Jack blinked.

"Listen," said Esme. She gestured at the unconscious woman lying on the grass between them. "Take care of her, okay?"

"Sure," said Jack, in the gruffest voice he could manage.

Esme gave him a wan smile. Then, with a graceful gesture, she let her hands fall to her sides, palms spread: she was already lifting into the air again. Jack blinked again—and she was gone.

"Be careful!" he shouted—and then felt very silly indeed.

He looked around himself, at the graveyard and the woman who was still lying on the ground.

"Right," he said. Then again: "Right."

Some time passed—Jack wasn't sure how much. It was only a few minutes, probably, but however long it was, it wasn't enough for him to get used to Jessica's smell. The combination of unwashed human being and (odd but true) *boiled cabbages* emerging from the unconscious body next to him was surprisingly powerful, even in the open air. It was getting dark too. The evening sun was setting fast, and what little light penetrated the graveyard from the streetlamps outside came through only as a thin kind of orange-blue haze. Plus, Jack had left his shirt behind at the theater and had only come out in a T-shirt. He was getting cold and hungry too. All in all, in his opinion, it was a pretty typical sort of situation.

He didn't get to be able to fly or do kung fu or chase demons up the sides of tall buildings—no, of course he didn't. *His* job, apparently, was to stand around waiting with smelly, trampy ladies in graveyards in the dark, while all the important stuff happened somewhere else. Typical.

"Ohhhh," said Jessica suddenly, making Jack jump. She sat up and, opening a pair of eyes that were every bit as astonishingly amber as Esme's, gave Jack a level look.

"Who are you?" she asked.

"I'm, er . . . Jack," said Jack.

Jessica just kept looking at him. Clearly, that answer alone wasn't going to be enough for her.

"I . . ." began Jack, then tried again. "We—I mean, the others—well, we, ah . . . rescued you, I suppose."

"You're from the Brotherhood?"

Jack nodded.

"Damn."

It wasn't quite the reply Jack had been expecting. He waited, watching Jessica look around at the graveyard, its empty spaces and its cold gray slabs.

"Listen," she said suddenly, "what was your name again?"

"Jack," said Jack.

The amber eyes narrowed at him. "I don't like our position here, Jack." Jessica gestured at the old black stone of the back of the church. "If the Scourge comes back, we'll be better off over there, with the wall behind us." She looked at him again. "Can you help me?"

Jack's brain was still coping with the possibility she'd mentioned of the demon's return. "Er . . ." he said.

"I've been sitting cross-legged on a cold concrete walkway for seventy-two hours straight," said Jessica. "My legs went numb after the first four."

Jack blinked.

"You're going to have to carry me," Jessica added, seeing that she wasn't getting her point across.

"Right," said Jack, standing up. "Of course. Right."

Jack was fourteen years old and of an average height for his age. His mother was always telling him that he was about to grow in huge spurts, but it hadn't happened yet: Jessica was taller than him, if only by an inch or two. He looked down at her, at the thin brown skin of her hands and face, and her narrow bony wrists jutting out of her filthy old overcoat.

"What?" she asked him.

"Nothing," said Jack.

"Come on, then." She beckoned.

Jack did as he was told. Jessica's hands in his felt dry, waxy, and horribly delicate, like he could crush them by mistake if he wasn't careful.

"Now, up we go."

He did his best.

"Wah!"

But her legs wouldn't support her: Jessica slid out of his grip and sat back down on the edge of a gravestone, hard.

"Oooh," she said, grimacing with pain.

"Sorry!" said Jack. "Sorry! Sorry!"

"Don't you get taught anything anymore?" she asked. "Telekinesis? Levitation?"

"No," said Jack. "I mean—well, not *me*." He broke off. Jessica was staring at him again now. "I'm just . . . kind of tagging along," he said miserably. "I don't have any . . . you know . . . powers."

"Wonderful," said Jessica. "Oh, that's just wonderful."

Seeing Jack's expression, she softened a little.

"Look," she said. "Here's what you do. You just crouch down in front of me here, with your back to me. . . . Yup, that's right. Now, let me get a grip on you."

Quickly, she slid her arms around Jack's neck. Jack did his best not to flinch.

"Right. Now stand up."

He did, taking Jessica with him. She was now hanging off his back. Her head was perched next to his, on his right shoulder. Her breath was warm and nasty, and her hair was itchy on his cheek.

"Reach up and grab my elbows," said Jessica. "Right. Now put me down over there."

Jessica weighed next to nothing, and her body was so swaddled in clothes that Jack couldn't really feel her at all. It was okay, he supposed. Weird but okay. Apart from the smell, obviously.

"Listen," she said, once he'd set her down, "I don't think we have much time."

"Why?" asked Jack. "What do you mean?"

"I know what the Scourge is going to do," Jessica told him. She paused and shook her head. "This thing—it's bigger than the Brotherhood. It's bigger than you or me—it's bigger than anything! Now, I've sent for help, and for what it's worth, help's on its way. But someone's going to have to follow the Scourge to Hell and stop this before it's too late. I just wish I could figure out *who.*"

She sat back against the black stone walls of the church and sighed.

"The Brotherhood's finished," she said. "Raymond, the rest of us—and that *idiot,* Nick—we're useless. Worse than useless. Maybe we always were."

She looked up—and froze.

"Oh no," she whispered, making Jack stare at her again. Then, "Look, quick. Help me up."

Jack looked in the direction Jessica was looking and blinked.

A patch of shadow in the darkness at the far end of the graveyard was behaving . . . oddly. As he watched, the darkness seemed to wobble and shake. It *bulged*, taking on a strange kind of shape—and then a figure was standing there at the end of the graveyard. A weird stick figure made out of liquid darkness—completely, utterly black.

"Help me up, Jack," Jessica repeated.

It was the Scourge. It had obviously doubled back somehow and had come back to finish Jessica off. There was no sign of Charlie or Esme. And now—as Jack continued to stare at it—the demon began to walk toward them.

"Jack, *help me up*, dammit!"

"Right," said Jack. "Right."

"Get behind me," Jessica told him.

She was only standing with an immense effort of will. Taking a deep breath, refusing to let her legs buckle beneath her, Jessica looked away from the demon that had come to kill her and down at the boy instead.

"Okay," she said. "It looks like this is it."

She smiled sadly.

"I'm sorry, Jack," she said. "You shouldn't have got into this. None of us should."

She turned, took another deep breath, then, with more

venom than Jack had ever heard in a person's voice before, she said:

"I hope you choke, you piece of—"

And suddenly, the Scourge was on her.

It leaped, crashing into Jessica, instantly knocking her flat. For a second or two Jessica and the demon wrestled with each other before the Scourge pinned down her arms and brought the blank black shape of its liquid face right up to hers. Jessica fought as hard as she could: she wriggled and snarled, but as Jack stared, utterly helpless, a strange haze of light began to emerge from Jessica's face, a smoky gray light that crossed the space between her and the demon—crossed it and was instantly *absorbed*. Suddenly, Jessica gave a long, gasping sigh—impossibly long, as though all the breath were being sucked out of her body.

The demon was sucking out her life, Jack realized. The Scourge was sucking out Jessica's life, right in front of him! Before he could even think about what to do to stop it, Jessica shuddered and went rigid. The dreadful noise stopped; there was a long, frozen moment—then Jessica went limp and fell back.

The demon lifted its eyeless, blank black face from what it had been doing.

And it looked at Jack.

Now it was getting up.

And now it was *coming for him*!

What? said Jack's brain. *No way!* This was totally unfair! *His* job wasn't dealing with demons! *His* job was sitting and watching! Numb with fear, Jack backed away, tripped over a gravestone, and fell over. In a kind of ecstasy of panic, unable to take his eyes away from the demon, he kicked out frantically with his feet, trying to push himself away back across the ground. But it still kept coming. The ink-black figure kept walking toward him, a step at a time. Closer it came, closer still, until suddenly—

"HEY!" said a voice. "HEY, YOU!"

Jack looked up. Standing behind the demon . . . was Charlie.

With a soft thump, twin balls of flaming orange light appeared in his hands.

"EAT *THIS*!" Charlie yelled, and flung them, catching the demon square in the middle. Suddenly, to Jack's utter amazement, the demon's body was a mass of flames.

And then the Scourge began to scream.

It was like the screech of brakes, like paper tearing slowly in your head. The black shape of the demon turned fluid, shooting out in all directions and snapping back in an effort to escape the magical fire, and the flames made great *whoomph*ing sounds in the air as the Scourge flung itself about. The screaming kept going, on the same dreadful single note. The demon flapped wildly, pounding on the ground. The flames seemed to tear upward, straight through the demon's body, then—

WHUMP!

They vanished, leaving nothing but a few twinkling blue sparks floating in the empty air.

Silence.

"HAH!" yelled Charlie. "HAAAAAAH!"

Esme elbowed past him and leaned down over Jack.

"Are you okay?" she asked.

Jack looked up at her, at her lovely face staring down at him in concern.

"Yeah," he said. "I'm fine."

She smiled at him!

"But I think it got Jessica," he said, watching her smile vanish with an ache in his heart as she caught sight of Jessica's lifeless body.

Esme felt for a pulse.

"Is she—?" said Jack.

"Yeah," said Esme miserably. "She's gone."

"I got it, though!" said Charlie, dancing on the spot. "I *got* it! *The Scourge is dead!*"

Swords and Pigeons

They were back at the theater. At last, the doors opened. It was Esme.

"You can come in now," she said.

Jack looked at Charlie. They'd been waiting outside in the passage for almost twenty minutes while Esme gave her report to Raymond about what had happened with Jessica. Still, for a moment Charlie stayed where he was, leaning against the wall. Eventually, making it perfectly clear that it was in his own time and not because anyone had asked him to, Charlie detached himself and made for the door. Esme stood aside to let him through. Jack sighed, followed him, caught sight of the room beyond—and blinked.

The room they were standing in now wasn't quite as big as the butterfly room, but it was still impressive. A large, coal-fired forge, presently unlit, with a wide, blackened metal flue poking out of the top of it and leading up through the ceiling, dominated the center of the space. The forge was surrounded by workbenches, racks of tools, and several large pieces of machinery, one of which Raymond was standing over and adjusting. He had his back to them, and as the boys came in he didn't turn round.

"This is the armory," said Esme. This didn't really need explaining, Jack felt, because the walls of the room were entirely covered in weapons.

There were axes: single- and double-headed, from small throwable hatchets and tomahawks to a five-foot-tall thing with giant gleaming steel half-moons that could probably chop Jack in half just by him looking at it. There were throwing stars, glaives, and knives of every description—some sheathed, some hanging in their cases with their blades exposed. Most of all, there were swords.

There were foils, with long blades stretching to points so sharp you could hardly see them. There were cutlasses and scimitars—curved and wicked looking. Every edged or stabbing weapon Jack had ever seen or heard about seemed to be represented somewhere—and a fairly high proportion that he hadn't.

"Nice collection," said Charlie, pretending not to be impressed. "Where'd you get 'em all?"

"One or two of the older pieces belonged to the Brotherhood," said Esme. "But most of them Raymond made himself."

"Come 'ere," growled Raymond without turning around. "I've got something to show you."

Winding their way between the long workbenches, the boys went over to take a look. On the table beside Raymond lay a long bundle of thick black canvas, which the big man proceeded to unwrap.

"This," he said to Charlie, as the contents were revealed, "is what I've been working on for you."

It was a sword. A big one. It had no grip, no handle yet: the long, gently curved, dull-blue-colored blade stopped abruptly, revealing the short, rough oblong of the naked tang beyond that. But it was already an impressive-looking weapon. It was shaped like a katana, a Japanese sword, the ones samurai warriors used. Even unfinished, the sword looked beautifully proportioned and elegantly, utterly deadly.

"*Cool*," breathed Charlie, and reached out to touch it—but he suddenly found he'd grasped a pair of goggles instead.

"Put 'em on," grunted Raymond.

"Jack?" called Esme.

Jack turned as Esme tossed another pair of goggles to him: he caught them—just—and smiled at her. She didn't smile back, just pulled her own pair down over her eyes and walked over to join the boys in watching what Raymond was about to do.

The big man flicked a switch. A low electrical hum sprang up from the machine, rising to a whine as it gathered speed. The machine had a small wheel, not much bigger than Jack's fist, and it was this that was being spun by the motor.

"Watch this, now," said Raymond, lowering his goggles. He took Charlie's unfinished sword and pressed it, gently but firmly, against the wheel's surface.

The wheel screamed, and an instant shower of sparks sent

bright blue splashes across Jack's retinas, even behind the dark goggles. The sparks sprayed a clear two feet ahead of the wheel as Raymond ground the long blade twice, once for each side of the sword's traditional single edge. His strokes were smooth and easy looking, following the curve with a steadiness born of years of practice. Then he turned the sword over and started again, grinding twice more.

Jack frowned, looking at the sword as best he could through the gusting sparks: was he imagining it, or was the sword actually getting smaller?

Raymond turned the sword over and ground it yet again. And again.

Now Jack was sure of it: the sword *was* getting smaller. And then the realization hit him: Raymond wasn't sharpening the blade. He was destroying it. He was destroying Charlie's sword!

The wheel ground and shrieked as it bit into the steel. Fat sparks flew as Raymond pressed at the remains of the sword mercilessly. Jack watched where the sparks fell, watched their glow fade from white to orange and finally to black on the pitted surface of Raymond's workbench. The long, curved blade became a stumpy blunt nub. Then Raymond tossed the last bit of it aside, laid his goggles down carefully, and switched off his machine.

As the whine of the machine dropped back down to silence, Raymond unhooked a dustpan and brush from under the workbench. He swept at where the sparks had landed, collecting the filings into a neat pile before transferring them to a nearby bucket. Then he picked up the bucket and set off for the door at the far end of the room, before the boys had time to do anything other than stare.

"What the Hell did you do that for?" spluttered Charlie finally.

"Just watch," said Esme quietly.

They followed Raymond into a storeroom of some kind. Long metal shelves lined the walls to either side. Raymond reached up to the top right-hand shelf and brought down a small sack of something, which he proceeded to pour into the bucket, mixing it in well with what remained of Charlie's sword.

"Mind how you go," he said to Jack, surprising him. "There's no railing or nothing, so don't be getting too close to the edge now." Then he opened another door, which took them out onto a roof.

The night air was cool, and the sky was stained a weird kind of violet by the orange color of the London streetlights. The roof at the back of the theater was wide and flat, and at its center stood a big square crate made out of roughly nailed wooden slats. The crate was almost as tall as Jack was, and there were fluttering and cooing noises coming from inside it. Jack could hear the noises even under the sound of the West End traffic, which was surprisingly loud now that they were outside, even up where they were.

Raymond had turned his back again and was sprinkling great handfuls from the bucket over the top of the crate, provoking a frenzy of flapping and cooing from inside it.

There was a pause.

"Erm . . . what are you doing?" asked Jack.

"Feeding these pigeons," said Raymond.

"We can see that," snapped Charlie. "What we want to know is, why're you feeding them bits of sword?"

"They haven't eaten since I caught them," said Raymond. "They're hungry." Then he went back to the feeding—smiling and making absurd little kissing noises at the pigeons, while the boys kept staring at him

The boys looked at each other. Then they looked at Raymond again. Presently, he turned around and looked at Charlie.

"I've been making swords," he said, "for thirty years now, near enough. I'm going to tell you how it's done."

Charlie stared at him, then shrugged. "All right," he said.

"Find yourself a nice bit of metal," Raymond began. "I'm simplifying, obviously. Then you heat it up in a forge. Around fourteen hundred degrees is best, I find, but 'bloody hot' will do for a rough description. With me so far?"

"'Bloody hot,'" said Charlie. "Right."

"Then you take a big hammer and you beat it. Hard. And when it's the shape you want, you quench it."

"You *what* it?"

"You stick it in something to cool it down," muttered Jack.

"That's right," said Raymond, nodding to Jack.

"Next," he went on, "I *grind* it. I keep grinding, till there's nothing left but filings. Then I sweep the filings up, I mix 'em with seed, and I feed 'em to some pigeons."

"Why?" said Charlie.

Raymond's beard bristled as he grinned. "Because the next day, when nature's, ah, 'taken its course,' as it were, I can collect what's under the pigeon coop, melt it down, and then start the whole thing again."

"*What?*"

"The Saxons were where I heard it first," said Raymond blithely. "They used chickens. But the Arabs, Toledo—most everyone was at it at some time or another. Some Eastern swordsmiths even used ostriches, if you believe the stories."

"What are you talking about?" Charlie asked.

Raymond frowned. "The droppings," he said, as if it were obvious. "The feces. The birds' mess—the poo."

The boys just stared at him.

Raymond sighed.

"Let me ask you something," he said. "What does bird poo smell of?"

"Ammonia," said Jack, surprising himself.

"Right!" said Raymond. "That's because it's full of nitrogen. Well, feed the filings to your birds—with a nice bit of seed, of course—and when they, ah, come out, the nitrogen will've reacted with the metal, hardening it. Melt down the result, beat it into the shape you want, and you end up with a sword that's smaller, sure, but it'll be unbreakable, near enough. Do the whole thing three or four times and it'll be stronger still. Now . . ."

He paused.

"I make good swords, some of the strongest, hardest, toughest swords in the world. I'm not one to boast. Other people's swords may be nicer to look at. But my swords, you can trust your life to 'em. Which, after all, is what a sword is for."

"Good swords," said Charlie. "Right. What's your *point*?"

"By the time I'm done with a sword," said Raymond, looking hard at Charlie, "it's been heated red hot, smashed flat with hammers, ground down to nothing, crapped out by pigeons, heated red hot, smashed flat with hammers—et cetera, et cetera, *et cetera*. Seven times is my record."

"Seven?" echoed Esme with sudden interest.

"Never mind that now," said Raymond. "My point is," he went on, turning back to Charlie, "*you*'ve had your powers since . . . when? *The day before yesterday.*"

Charlie frowned at him, not understanding.

"Why did you chase the demon, Charlie?" asked Raymond patiently.

"What?"

"Why did you chase the Scourge by yourself instead of waiting for backup?"

For another long moment Charlie just looked at him.

Then he scowled.

"All right," he said. "Well, I don't know if Esme mentioned this to you, but it was going *quite quickly.* If I'd waited, we'd've lost it."

"No," said Raymond quietly. "If you'd waited, you could've helped get Jessica back here. Instead of which, you took off, forcing Esme to follow you, and Jessica—and Jack—were left unprotected."

"I didn't *force* Esme to—" Charlie began.

"The day before yesterday, Charlie," Raymond repeated. "Understand? Esme's been training her whole life. You're not qualified to make those decisions. She is."

"But—"

"Plus, of course," Raymond went on, ignoring him, "you lost it anyway."

Charlie's scowl deepened.

"You lost it," said Raymond. "Yes or no?"

"All right!" said Charlie. "All right! Yes, I lost it!"

He paused.

"I followed it across the rooftops," he said. He turned to Jack. "You should've seen me, mate, it was amazing!"

Jack looked at him.

"But then it . . . vanished suddenly," Charlie went on. "It happened when we were back near the theater. And that's where . . ." He trailed off.

"That's where Esme caught up with you," said Raymond.

"That's right," said Charlie.

Raymond looked into the pigeon coop at its cooing, fluttering occupants for a whole minute. Then, obviously satisfied by what he saw, he put down the bucket.

"Let me ask you another question," he said wearily.

Charlie just looked at him.

"If Esme hadn't decided—"

"Raymond," said Esme softly from the doorway. "Don't you think—?"

"No, petal, this is important," said Raymond. "He may

be new to all this, but he's got to realize what's at stake." The big man turned his gaze back onto Charlie. "If Esme hadn't decided that the first priority was to get back to Jessica, what do you think would've happened?"

Charlie scowled but didn't answer.

"Shall I tell you?" Raymond asked. "Your friend here"—he gestured at Jack without looking at him—"would be dead. And it would be your fault, just like it's your fault that Jessica's dead."

Raymond kept looking at Charlie.

"What do you say to that? Eh?"

Jack too looked at Charlie. Charlie's mouth had turned into a hard white line. When he spoke, it was quietly.

"Look," he said slowly. "In case it slipped your mind, that demon of yours, the one that you've been making all this fuss over—is *gone*. I killed it." He paused. "Now, I'm sorry about . . . what's-er-name, Jessica. But we know now for sure that what happened to her isn't going to happen to anyone else, ever, because it's *over*. And I won."

Raymond said nothing.

"I'm the boss," said Charlie, looking slowly around the room. "I *rule*," he added, as if extra emphasis were needed. "So . . ." He shrugged. "What's next?"

There was another long silence—broken only by the sudden sound of Charlie's phone, ringing again.

Charlie sucked his teeth, pulled out the phone, looked at the screen, and scowled.

"You'd best run along home to your mum, son," said Raymond quietly. "It's late."

For a moment, Charlie just stared at him. Then he stamped his foot.

"I don't *believe* this!" he shouted. "What's wrong with you people?"

No one answered.

"Come on, Jack, we're going," said Charlie. In another moment he was heading back for the door. He waved a hand and it swung open for him: it flew round on its hinges and smacked into the wall, hard.

Jack set off after him quickly, but before leaving the roof he cast one quick look back. Both Esme and Raymond were standing perfectly still, apparently lost in thought, with the great wooden coop standing between them. Then the door swung shut.

There was a pause.

"So," said Raymond. "What do you think?"

"I'm going to get my paints," said Esme, and set off, not looking at Raymond.

Raymond followed her through the storeroom and then through the armory. Then, when Esme turned left, heading for her room, he crossed the landing and opened the doors to the butterfly room. He walked over to the long conference table and sat down. Presently, Esme returned: in one hand she was carrying a paint-spattered tray that held a small jug of water and a large palette spotted with a variety of colors—blues, mostly. In the other, she held a clutch of fine, red-handled paintbrushes. Raymond sat scratching his beard as, still not looking at him, Esme walked past the long table and off toward the shadowy far corner of the room, the place where the pattern ran out. She stopped walking, closed her eyes—

—and lifted off the ground, floating smoothly up toward the high ceiling.

Her thick black curly hair was tied back in its customary tight bunch, and she was wearing a thin scarf of some dark material to catch any splashes. Quickly, easily, she let the rest of her body swing upward until she was lying flat in the air, facing the ceiling, with the tray resting on her belly. She chose a brush, dipped it in the water, and dabbed at the thick black poster paint she was using for the outline of tonight's butterfly. When it was the consistency she wanted, she set to work.

All this while, Raymond said nothing. Esme was concentrating on her butterfly. Raymond waited.

Finally, Esme said, "I don't know."

Still, Raymond just waited.

"All my life . . ." said Esme, working the fine brush around the butterfly's outline with a rock-steady hand. Only when it was roughed in to her satisfaction did she turn to look at the man at the table below her. "You know?"

"Mm," said Raymond.

"I don't—" began Esme, then frowned.

"I *didn't*," she corrected herself, "think I'd feel like *that* when it was dead."

Raymond looked up at her. "Like what?" he asked.

"Like nothing," said Esme.

Raymond waited.

Esme dropped the first brush into the water jug and chose another. Frowning, she began filling in the butterfly's outline, laying the paint on thick.

"Maybe we've been wrong all this time to think the Scourge couldn't be killed," she said. "Maybe Charlie really *is* that strong. I mean, the Scourge *died*—or it certainly looked that way: I watched it die; it was screaming. But I . . ."

She sighed and shook her head.

"I should have *felt something*. Not . . . happy or anything. You know I wasn't expecting that. But there should have been something—shouldn't there?"

She looked down at Raymond.

"Mm," he said again.

She turned back to the butterfly—and blinked. There was nothing there now but a great butterfly-shaped splat of darkness: not a glimmer of the ceiling's original cream showed through. The thing she was going to say was growing inside her, pushing to get out, so she gave up what she was doing and looked down at Raymond again.

"I just can't believe it's dead," she said.

She waited, holding her gaze on him until he looked up at her again.

"Not like that," she added.

"No," said Raymond finally. "Me neither."

"I think you'd better find Felix," Esme said.

"Yeah," said Raymond. "I think you're right."

THE CHANCE

Charlie and Jack were walking back across the park toward Charlie's house. There were no lights in the park, and when Charlie left the path, his steps becoming suddenly inaudible on the grass, the silence settled around the boys like a cloak. Charlie stopped by the lake that ran along the park's south side. Jack caught up and stood beside him, and they looked out at the water: it was as black as ink, and Jack could hear it whispering to itself.

"So," said Charlie suddenly, his voice sounding bright and crass in the quiet. "That was a pretty classy bit of rescuing, eh?"

"Yep," said Jack. "Just in the nick of time too. I think this superhero business is starting to suit you."

"*So*," repeated Charlie, with sudden savagery, "why the Hell didn't you stick up for me back there?"

Jack stared at him, astonished. "What?"

"For Christ's sake, Jack, I saved your life tonight! You might at least've said something to back me up with Raymond—but instead you're all, 'Stick it in something to cool it down.'" Charlie's voice had gone high and singsong as he threw Jack's words back at him. He sounded nothing like Jack whatsoever.

"Well?" he asked.

"Well what?" asked Jack, unable to fathom where all this was coming from.

"Why didn't you say anything?"

Jack looked at Charlie. Charlie's face was in darkness. Jack thought for a moment, then said quietly, "Do you think it would've helped?"

"I mean," he went on, when Charlie didn't reply, "it's not like you or the others have ever really listened to me before. Right?"

There was a long pause.

Charlie sighed.

"I'm sorry, man," he said. "I didn't mean to have a go at you. I just . . ."

He turned to face Jack suddenly.

"You know," he announced, "you're my *best mate*."

"What?" said Jack again.

"You're the only one: the *only one* who I know'll stick by me, no matter what. Like at the restaurant," Charlie went on, speaking so fast he was almost babbling. "You know, when you came in with me. I don't think I could've said what I did to Dad if you hadn't been there. In fact, maybe I'd never've been able to tell him how angry I was if it wasn't for . . . well, if it wasn't for you."

Jack squirmed a bit. Charlie had never spoken to him like this: it was weird.

"Er . . . sure," he managed. "No problem."

"I can't tell you how happy I am that you're with me on this, man."

"No worries, mate," said Jack, frowning. "You know, whatever." He shrugged.

Apparently satisfied, Charlie turned to look out at the lake again.

"What do you think's wrong with them?" he asked after a moment. "Esme and Raymond, I mean.

"I mean . . . you *saw* me. Right?" he added, before Jack had time even to think, let alone reply. "I killed the demon! I made fireballs come out of my hands and I burned it to death! Right?"

"Mm," said Jack. "About that. How did you *do* that?"

"Oh," said Charlie with a dismissive *fff*ing sound, "that sort of stuff, I don't even have to think. It's just . . . you know, simple."

"Yeah," said Jack uneasily. "But it sounds like sometimes you sort of *have* to think too. Don't you?"

"What d'you mean?" Charlie shot back, instantly defensive.

"Well," prompted Jack carefully, "they didn't sound too happy with you just now."

"But that's just what I'm saying!" said Charlie. "I mean, I know it must've been a shock for them, all this. Me passing the test and not Esme. Me coming along out of the blue and just whacking this demon when everyone else has been running scared of it for years. I can see that'd be hard to take, 'specially for Esme, with her mum and everything."

"Hm," said Jack.

"But, you know, they've just got to deal with it! Right? Like tonight, f'rinstance. I mean, I didn't want them to make a big thing out of it, right? Of course not. Not my style. But still, you know, job well done, credit where credit's due—and what do I get? A bollocking!"

Charlie looked out at the lake again.

"Jack, can I ask you something?" he asked suddenly.

"Sure," said Jack. "'Course."

"Do you ever wish that the world just . . . didn't exist?"

Jack stared at him again. "How d'you mean?"

"Well . . . all this *stuff*," said Charlie. "The Scourge. The Brotherhood. My *folks* . . ."

The list was an odd one and Jack might have smiled if it weren't for what Charlie said next.

"Don't you think it'd be simpler if . . . none of it was here anymore?"

"Sorry?" said Jack.

"Wouldn't it be better if there was *nothing*?" Charlie asked, turning to face him. "Don't you ever feel like it'd be better if one day everything, the whole universe, just came to an end—pop!—like that?"

Jack looked at him. He didn't really know what to say.

"Sometimes," said Charlie, frowning, "I just feel like . . . I don't know. . . ."

He bunched his fists.

"Like I want to reach out and smash everything," he said. "Like I want to rip everything up. Tear it to shreds, burn it all down and dance in the ashes. Do you ever feel like that?"

Jack looked at Charlie carefully.

"Not really, mate, to be honest," he said. "No."

Charlie sighed. "Ah, forget it." He grimaced. "Listen, it's late. Mum'll be having kittens. I reckon I'd better just head home by myself."

"Sure?"

"Sure."

Jack looked at his superhero friend and attempted a smile.

"'Faster than a speeding penguin,'" he told him.

"Yeah, right," said Charlie, attempting a smile back. "See you."

"See you."

They parted.

Later, Jack would look back at this moment and wonder if he could have done things differently. By this point Charlie was already helpless under the Scourge's influence, but even so, if Jack had said something, if he'd obeyed his instincts telling him that something was badly wrong with his friend and stayed with him until they'd talked things out somehow, then maybe the rest of what was to come might not have happened the way it did.

Now it was too late.

BUTTERFLIES

Esme was most of the way through her third butterfly of the night. Her eyes were tired, and her eyelids were beginning to droop—but as soon as she heard the noise, she was wide awake.

She slid to the ground soundlessly, placing the tray of paints and brushes on the floor. At that moment, the only light in the butterfly room came from the single lamp she'd left glowing in the center of the long table. Crouching well back in the shadows at the far end of the hall, she watched as the double doors swung open, and a dark figure strode in.

"Esme?" said Charlie. "It's me."

"Oh, hi, Charlie," said Esme, stepping slowly out into the light.

Charlie gestured behind himself vaguely: "The, ah, door to the roof was open. Mind if I . . . ?"

"Sure," said Esme. "Come in."

They stood at opposite ends of the table. Charlie put his hands on the back of the chair in front of him.

"Been painting, I see," he began.

"Yeah," said Esme. "There hasn't been much time the last

couple of days, so I had a bit of catching up to do." She smiled at him politely. The grin he gave back was very eager.

"Butterflies, eh?" he said.

"Yes."

There was a pause.

"What made you choose them?" asked Charlie. "Butter-flies, I mean."

Esme, surprised, looked at him for a moment, then shrugged.

"It's partly because there are so many kinds," she said. "Also, they're hard to paint: getting the colors right used to be pretty tough, especially when I was starting out."

"But the main reason," Charlie interrupted, "is that they're like *you*." He grinned. "Aren't they?"

Esme frowned at him. "What do you mean?"

"You've been waiting your whole life to fight the Scourge," said Charlie, his eyes never leaving hers for an instant. "Every day you've been training, preparing, perfecting your skills: you said so yourself."

"Yeah," said Esme. "So?"

"Well, you're like them, aren't you?" said Charlie delight-edly, gesturing at the walls. "You're there in your cocoon, waiting to come out. Waiting and waiting—waiting all your life for the moment when you can spread your wings and fly."

For a second, Esme just stared at him.

"What on Earth are you talking about?" she said. "I . . . just like butterflies, that's all." To her horror, however, she could feel her cheeks beginning to go red.

The thing was, though she'd've died before admitting it . . . Charlie wasn't entirely wrong. The life cycle of caterpillar to cocoon to butterfly had fascinated Esme ever since Raymond had first explained it to her. It was the reason she had started painting butterflies in the first place, seven long years before. And Charlie knew. He was grinning at her now smugly, pleased with himself for making her lie like that. He *knew*.

"They're beautiful," he said—looking at her.

"Thanks," said Esme, infuriated.

"How many was it again?"

"Five thousand, four hundred and seventy-five," said Esme, "now."

"Wow," said Charlie softly.

Esme took a breath. "Charlie, don't take this the wrong way, but . . . do you mind if I ask what you're doing here?"

Charlie's grin grew wider.

"Do you like surprises?" he asked.

Esme frowned at him again.

"I don't know," she replied. "It depends."

"Because I had this idea," said Charlie. "A surprise for you. As soon as I thought of it I came straight over."

"That's . . . nice," said Esme.

"Just you wait," said Charlie, still smiling. His fingers clasped and unclasped on the back of the chair.

"You know," he said, "I was thinking. It's all happened very fast, this whole thing."

"Uh-huh."

"And the way things've been going, you and me haven't

really had much of a chance to . . . get to know each other."

"No," said Esme. "I suppose that's true."

"Well, I don't know about Raymond," said Charlie quickly, "but I think you and me could . . . get on. You know?"

Esme looked at him.

"I want us to be friends," said Charlie. He shrugged—a study in elaborate casualness. "What do you say?"

His stare was very intense. Esme found herself looking away.

"Sure," she said, shrugging carefully back.

"Great!" said Charlie, delighted. "Great! Well! About that surprise I mentioned . . ."

"Oh yes."

"It's the classic. You know—you've got to close your eyes. No peeking!"

Esme just looked at him. "What?"

"Come on," said Charlie. "Just close your eyes for a moment."

"Charlie—"

"You'll love it! I promise!"

"Well . . ."

It was odd, but Esme really didn't want to. Still, what could she do? Pursing her lips, she did as she was asked and closed her eyes.

"Now," she heard Charlie say, "just give me a second here."

She heard him take a breath and hold it. Then the air in the room seemed to be heating up.

She could feel it from where she was standing. It was as if the atmosphere were thickening or swelling somehow. There was a weird smell, like ozone or hot metal, and the air was crackling with something like electricity: it made her scalp tingle. Esme tried opening her eyes but found, with a shock, that she couldn't. Then—

"*Ffffff*," said Charlie suddenly, as he let out a great breath—and as quickly as it had come, the weird feeling in the air vanished.

"You can open them now," he said.

Esme did and looked around, but the only difference she could see was that Charlie's big, satisfied grin was even bigger and more self-satisfied than before.

"What?" she asked uncertainly. "What am I looking for?"

"Just a second," said Charlie. His eyes were darting little looks around the walls, as if he were searching for something. Then—

"There!" he said, pointing, almost jumping up and down, he was so excited.

Esme looked, and her breath caught in her chest.

On the ceiling above her, one of her butterflies, the one she'd just been painting—was moving.

It was nothing more than a tremble at first. Very faint. But in another moment the unfinished butterfly, one set of markings on the lower part of its right wing still not properly inked in, was twitching convulsively. Its small black body was straining and pulling. One thick powdery wing came free, then another, and then the butterfly was flapping its wings experimentally, each flapping movement revealing the wing-shaped gaps in the surface of the paint underneath. Now, suddenly, the movements were spreading, being followed and imitated all across the ceiling and down the walls. All over the room, all Esme's butterflies, all seven years' worth of them, were rippling and twitching, jerking and straining—and coming free. She looked back at the first one, the unfinished one, just in time to see it tense itself, then leap away from the ceiling. It plummeted like a stone, and Esme thought for a second that it would hit the ground—but then, as if with a heart-stopping effort, the oversized butterfly flapped its wings once, twice—and bobbed back up into the air.

And *then*—

—suddenly—

—they *all* took off.

"WHEEEEEEEEEEEEEE-HEEEEE!" screamed Charlie, disappearing from view in a blizzard of fluttering wings. The air was thick with them now, thick with the butterflies and the soft clattering sounds they made as they flew—a sound like the slow, soft crumpling of a million sheets of paper. They followed each other, swinging round the room in a great arc, a seething, shivering, whirling mass of blurring bright painted colors.

Charlie danced on the spot, still screaming and waving his arms in the air as the butterflies dived and swooped all around him.

Esme, however, stood still.

For a second, as the air cleared between them, Charlie saw her. Still grinning, he called out to her.

"What do you think? Huh? How about this?"

He made a casual gesture in the air with one hand, and

suddenly tens, hundreds of the painted creatures were landing on her shoulders, on the skin of her bare arms.

Esme watched one on her hand. She recognized it: it was
an early one. Her brushstrokes had none of the finesse she'd
developed later. Without legs or antennae, it bumped against
her blindly, each contact shaking tiny flakes of paint dust
from its dark wings.

"They're alive," she said slowly. "They're really alive."

"Yep," said Charlie.

"You can do this?" asked Esme. "You can bring things to life?"

"Looks that way to me," said Charlie, smirking. He too
was covered in the oversize butterflies now, all over his arms
and his hair. Behind him, the rest of the great flock suddenly
changed direction at once, sweeping the other way around the
sides of the room.

"And you've done this," said Esme, "just to impress me?"

Charlie looked at her.

"It's a present!" he reminded her. "Why? Don't you like it?"

"Do you have any idea what you're doing?" asked Esme.
The butterflies leaped off her as she rounded on him, her
hands shaking with sudden rage. "Stop it!"

Charlie stared, his face slack with surprise. "What?"

"Stop it!" shouted Esme. "Turn them back!"

"Why?"

"Do it NOW!"

"All right!" said Charlie. "All right!"

He blinked.

For a second, the butterflies froze in the air.

Then they fell.

Each one shattered into powder as it touched the ground. In a moment, the floor was a mass of tiny flakes of paint. The walls were covered in butterfly-shaped silhouettes. These things were all that remained of Esme's seven years of work.

From opposite ends of the table, Esme and Charlie stared at each other.

"Don't ever," said Esme, "*ever* do anything like that again."

He stared at her for a moment. Then he scowled.

"I'll do what I like!" he said.

"No, Charlie," said Esme quietly. "You won't."

Something in her voice made Charlie stop dead.

He looked at her and grinned uncertainly.

"Come on," he said. "I don't want to fight you, Esme."

Esme just looked at him.

"I mean, it was a present—right?" Charlie's grin was wide again now, as if he were sure she'd still come round. "I didn't mean anything by it. I just wanted us to be friends."

"Well, that wasn't the way to go about it."

The silence between them then lasted for a long time. At last, Charlie's smile went hollow—and faded.

"Fine," he said suddenly. He looked up and shrugged. "*Fine*. Well . . . *bye*, then."

He turned. Already the double doors were opening to receive him.

"Charlie?"

He didn't answer.

"Charlie! Wait!" she called.

But the doors clicked shut. He hadn't looked back.

Esme was still staring when a loud, ugly buzz from the intercom broke the silence. She went over to the door and pressed the button. "Yeah?"

"It's me," said Raymond. "Can you come down here and give me a hand a second?"

"What is it?"

"I've found Felix."

Raymond had only really wanted Esme to talk to: even with Felix's unconscious body over his shoulder in a fireman's lift, he still climbed the stairs to the headquarters two at a time.

"He was in a private clinic out in the suburbs," he explained. "He was checked in there by his housekeepers two days ago; that's why we couldn't find him till now."

"Is he . . . ?"

"Dead?" asked Raymond. "No. It's the Scourge's doing, that's for sure, but it's some sort of coma, like—*blimey*," he added, as Esme opened the doors to the butterfly room and he caught sight of the scene beyond.

"Yeah," said Esme grimly. While Raymond laid Felix down on the table, she quickly told him what had just taken place.

"But how?" Raymond asked. "I mean, I don't think even Nick had that much power."

Esme was pacing the floor. "What worries me is the way Charlie was afterwards," she said. "The way he left seemed awfully, I don't know . . . final." But then, noticing Raymond's look of dawning horror, she stopped. "What?" she asked.

For another moment Raymond just stood there by Felix's unconscious body, frozen by what had just occurred to him.

"Esme," he said—and gulped. "I've never seen anything like this." He gestured woodenly at the remains of the butterflies. "I mean, bringing things to life! Nobody in the Brotherhood's ever done anything remotely like this. Ever!"

"So?"

"Well, what if . . . ?" Raymond began—and fell silent.

Esme stared at him. "Wait a second," she said, "let me get this straight. Jessica wasn't the host, and neither was Felix—not if he's been in a coma for two days."

"Right."

"But the only other person who the host could have been is—"

"Nick!" Raymond finished for her.

"What about the test, though?" Esme asked. "Choosing a new leader?"

Raymond shook his head. "Nick wasn't looking for a new leader. He wasn't even looking for new recruits: the Scourge was controlling him! What it wanted was a new *host*!" He paused. "And it found one."

They looked at each other.

"Oh no . . ." Esme whispered.

SORRY'S NOT
GOOD ENOUGH

It was the same night: it was stiflingly hot, and Jack was having bad dreams when the knocking sound got loud enough to wake him. He sat up in bed suddenly. Still wrapped up in his dream, it took him a while to realize that the knocking wasn't in his head, it was coming from the window.

Jack's curtains were thin. Normally, the orange of the street-light outside came through them quite strongly. At that moment, however, a large black shadow was blotting out most of the light.

Jack got up and pulled the curtains open. Jack's room was three floors up off the ground, but there, waiting outside as if he were standing on solid ground, was Charlie.

He was smiling. His arms were out at his sides; ink-black tattoo shapes were dripping down them, coiling restlessly under his skin.

Jack opened the window. "Charlie, what the hell are you doing here?"

Charlie just smiled. "Nice to see you too," he said.

"What time is it?" asked Jack. When Charlie didn't answer, he looked back at the glowing red digits of the clock on his bedside table.

"Jesus, Charlie! It's four in the morning!"

"Yeah?" said Charlie. "I didn't check. You were certainly out for the count."

"Yeah, well, that's because it's *four in the morning*," Jack repeated, since the information clearly hadn't got through the first time.

"Jack," said Charlie, "we've got to go somewhere."

Jack looked at him. "What?"

"You and me," said Charlie. "You see, I've just had the most amazing idea. But I want you to come with me."

"Come with you where?"

"To the demon world," said Charlie. "I want you to come with me to Hell."

There was a pause.

Jack looked at Charlie carefully for a moment. Then he put both hands on the windowsill and leaned forward, looking out and down. Charlie slid back in the air a few inches to make room. Jack looked past his friend's feet, at the ground below, then he looked up at him again.

"You're steady as a rock," he said. "Getting pretty good at this flying thing now, eh?"

"Jack," said Charlie, "help me on this. I don't want to do it alone."

"Do what?"

"Open the Fracture."

"Ah," said Jack.

"Raymond'll never let me do anything," Charlie spat. "And Esme . . ." His expression turned hurt and puzzled looking. "Well, I don't think me and her are ever going to get on, man. That's all."

"What are you talking about, Charlie?"

"A real adventure," said Charlie. "Don't you see?"

His eyes took on a weird gleaming quality that Jack didn't like one bit.

"You and me," said Charlie, "we don't need the Brotherhood. We're better at fighting demons than they ever were. And now we've got the chance to go somewhere *no one's ever been*. So how about it? What do you say?" Charlie had got so excited that he'd actually started bobbing slightly in the air. Now, however, as he leaned forward for Jack's answer, the bobbing subsided until he hung still once more.

Jack looked at him.

"Give me a minute," he said. "I'll get some trousers on."

Jack changed out of his pajamas quickly. He was thinking quickly too, and his thoughts went something like this:

There was no point in saying no. That was obvious. Whatever Charlie was intending to do, he was almost certainly still going to do it whether Jack came with him or not. But if Jack did go with him, then there might be a chance to warn the others or stop him somehow before it was too late.

In moments, he was ready. He was dressed lightly: black jeans, black T-shirt, and his favorite trainers. In his back pocket, he also had his phone, with Esme and Raymond's number already programmed into it.

"Okay," he told Charlie. "I'll meet you outside."

Charlie shook his head. "No good, mate," he said. "Your folks are downstairs, asleep in front of the telly. You might wake 'em when you go past." He held his arms out. "Give me your hands," he said.

"Okay," said Jack. "But listen, erm . . ."

"What?" said Charlie with a flash of impatience.

Jack was thinking about his parents—two lumpish shapes sprawled across the sofa in the light of the TV screen, their heads lolling. He almost smiled. They'd be snoring. They'd be stiff in the morning too: his dad was always particularly bad when they'd spent the night on the sofa.

Should he tell them he was going? *Yeah, right,* he thought: what would he say? Besides, if he managed to warn Esme and Raymond in time, then maybe he'd be back in his bed before his folks even woke up. But Jack sighed: somewhere in his heart, he knew already that that probably wasn't how the night was going to end up. Not with his luck.

Typical.

Grimly, he swung his legs up onto the windowsill, took hold of Charlie's hands, and stepped out into thin air.

"Let's go," said Charlie.

"All right," said Jack. And they were off.

Jack's home, his street, shrank below his feet and vanished into the night. There was a rush of hot air, a sensation like huge black wings closing around them both—then they were stepping out of the shadows onto Charing Cross Road, in London's West End.

From the front, the Light of the Moon looked a bit like a cinema. The entrance was a sort of wide stone porch, supported by three fairly ridiculous-looking cream-colored pillars. The doors themselves consisted of six panels of thick sheet glass, with large and ugly vertical brass handles stuck onto them. The darkness beyond the glass was total: everyone who worked or drank there was long gone—but the street itself still had a few stragglers passing by. The boys waited until no one was looking. Charlie put his hand on one of the heavy locks, Jack heard a soft *click*, then Charlie was pushing through into the dark, empty space of the pub that was a gateway to Hell.

Jack sighed and—a little unsteadily—followed Charlie in. The light from the street quickly shrank into the enveloping darkness of the empty pub. The sensation that they weren't supposed to be there was, Jack found, very strong.

"Charlie?" he asked, in that ridiculous hoarse whisper you use when you want to be heard but don't at the same time.

"Over here," came the reply, in Charlie's normal speaking voice. "Come in. Mind the steps."

By the light of the street behind him, Jack could just make out a wide flight of steps, and he followed them down until his trainers made squeaking contact with the bare floorboards.

"Charlie, how about a bit of light?" he asked, in his best casual voice.

"Sure."

Whump! A ball of light appeared over the open palm of Charlie's hand. Charlie grinned.

Jack looked at the glowing fireball, still trying not to boggle too much. Then he looked around himself.

The light of Charlie's fireball thing showed a space that was surprisingly big, maybe even as big as the butterfly room. To Jack's left, a long chrome bar top spanned about two-thirds of the length of the room, and there was a partitioned-off section of tables and sofas along to his right. Charlie stood in the middle of the wide, largely bare open area that took up most of the room. The whole place stank of stale cigarettes and booze. But what Jack really noticed was the high ceiling, which, in the flickering yellow-orange light of Charlie's fireball, seemed very far away.

Jack looked back down at Charlie, who was doing something weird—well, even more weird anyway. He was hunched over, his head sticking out forward as if he were sniffing for something. His hands were groping about in the air. The fireball thing hung over him, following him smoothly as he moved.

"Charlie, what are you—?"

"Here," said Charlie suddenly, turning to Jack with a huge grin. "Here. Feel."

Jack shrugged and walked over, his trainers squeaking loudly as he crossed the bare wood of the floor.

"Put your hand where mine is," said Charlie.

Jack gave him a sideways look but did as he said, putting his arm out.

"Can you feel it?" asked Charlie, still grinning wildly.

Jack felt about a bit. "I can feel . . . a draft," he said.

"It's not a draft," said Charlie. "See? If I stand in front of it. Here. Or here. Where could it be coming from?" His smile got even wider. "It's not a draft."

Jack frowned. It certainly was very odd. There was a cold space in the air, just above waist level, like putting your hand in a fridge. It was a very small and very defined sort of space: if he moved his arm so much as a few centimeters anywhere around it, the sensation vanished. He'd read stories about supposedly haunted houses that had "cold spots." He wondered whether that was anything to do with this.

"This is it, man," said Charlie, so excited he was practically vibrating. "The Fracture. The gateway to Hell."

"Mm," said Jack, straightening up and looking at his friend. He took a deep breath. "Listen," he said, "are you sure about this? I mean, really?"

"I've never been more sure of anything," said Charlie, "in my entire life."

"But—"

"I can feel it," said Charlie. His face glowed weirdly in the light of the fireball that was still hanging in the air above him. "In my heart," he said, "in my head—and in my blood." He closed his eyes, sniffed in a great lungful of air, and his eyelids fluttered.

Jack frowned at him. "Er, right," he said. "But don't you think, you know, that we should maybe call the others?"

"No," snapped Charlie, his eyes flicking open. "No others."

The two boys looked at each other.

"Don't you get it?" asked Charlie, with a smile that was

blatantly false. "The others don't want us. They don't want us to do this."

"But Charlie—"

"Come on, Jack!" Charlie's voice turned desperate. "There's nothing for us here. Nothing! And what we've got—right?— what we've got is a chance to leave it all behind." He stared at Jack, eyes wide.

"Come *on*, man," he repeated. "People never get the chance to do something like this. Not for real. The others had it, but they blew it. We're not going to make the same mistake."

Jack said nothing.

"All right?" said Charlie.

"I guess," said Jack.

"Cool. Now take a step back. I've got to do something here."

Jack did as he was told.

Charlie turned his back on him. He spread his arms, and the ink-black shapes of the tattoo slid down under his skin like they were being poured there.

Jack watched the tattoo. In seconds, Charlie's skin was a mass of black shapes—twisting, curling, and caressing.

Then the whole room started to hum.

It was a sound that seemed to come from everywhere. The air in the room seemed to be tightening around Jack like polyethylene. Charlie's outstretched arms began to make strange, jerky coaxing gestures—and an eggshell-thin line of light began to form in the space in the air in front of him.

It was just a crack at first. But as Charlie jerked and

weaved—as if he were a puppet being pulled by invisible strings—the line was widening and filling the room with an unearthly red glow.

Slowly, carefully, Jack eased his phone out of his jeans pocket.

Not taking his eyes off Charlie, he pressed the buttons that would bring up and dial the number he wanted.

After three long rings, Raymond answered. "Yeah?"

His voice sounded tiny and far away.

"It's Jack," whispered Jack.

"Hello?" said the big man. "Who's there?"

"It's *Jack*."

"Jack? I can't—"

"I'm at the Fracture," said Jack. "Charlie's—*hkh*—"

And a blow struck all the air out of his body, immediately followed by a stunning impact from behind that almost made him black out.

When his vision cleared, he was staring into Charlie's face, down Charlie's arm. Charlie's hand was locked round his throat.

Charlie's eyes were full of blood. His face was like a mask: the black shapes of the tattoo seethed and boiled under his skin, wriggling like eels. The corners of his mouth lifted in a strange grin, before the mouth opened, and a horrible voice said:

"**No, no, *no*. That's quite out of the question, I'm afraid.**"

Jack forced himself to look down, away from the eyes, and saw (past his own dangling feet) that he was now some distance off the ground, pinned to the wall over the bar, on the other side of the room from where he had been standing before. He guessed Charlie must have grabbed him and just flown through the air with him until they'd hit the nearest wall. He looked back up at Charlie as, slowly, Charlie's head tipped to one side. The burning blood-filled eyes glanced at the phone in Jack's hand—

—and it tore from his grasp, shattering somewhere out of sight.

Silhouetted against the low, red glow of the Fracture, Charlie's face turned sad.

"You called them, Jack," he said, in his own voice—slowly, as if he couldn't believe what he was saying. "Why would you do that? Why would you . . . *betray* me like that?"

Jack said nothing. It was hard to speak when someone had you by the throat. He grabbed Charlie's arm with both his hands, but he might as well have been squeezing an iron bar. The grip tightened, cutting off Jack's breath, and in another second Jack's vision was closing in: great swaths of velvety black were swishing in from all around, surrounding Charlie's face until it was all that he could see.

He was losing consciousness, he realized.

Charlie was strangling him.

Jack felt a pressure on the inside of his skull, a squeezing in his heart, a tearing, thickening, swelling in his blood as it pounded in his ears—and he suddenly felt very stupid indeed. Now, at last, it was obvious: everything, from meeting Nick for the first time, all the way up until this moment, had been nothing more than a trick. Nick hadn't passed on any powers to Charlie: he'd passed on *the Scourge*. It was *Charlie* who was the Scourge's host body. It was *Charlie* who'd been harboring the demon inside him all this time. And though Jack had *known* there was something wrong with Charlie all along, he'd done and said nothing. He'd been so stupid! Stupid, stupid, stupid, *stupid*—

WHAM!

He glimpsed something slam into the side of Charlie's head.

The grip on his throat was suddenly released.

And Jack fell to the ground, hard.

He sat there in a crumpled heap, gasping for air.

"Esme," he heard Charlie say, surprised.

"Yeah," said Esme, and her amber eyes flashed fiercely. "Me."

Jack looked up. Esme was standing off to his right, on the steps that led down from the pub's entrance: Jack had never been so glad to see anyone in his life. Opposite her, to Jack's left, on another flight of wide steps that were the mirror image of the first, stood Charlie. Across some twenty yards of bare, polished floorboards, Charlie and Esme faced each other.

"I should have known about you," said Esme quietly. Her hands hung loosely at her sides. She shifted her weight from one trainered foot to the other slowly. "I should've spotted you from the start."

"Oh yeah?" said Charlie. "And why's that?"

"It's all come pretty easy for you, hasn't it?" said Esme. "Didn't it ever occur to you to wonder why?"

"What are you talking about?"

Esme shook her head, smiling.

"You're nothing more than an *accident*, Charlie," she said. "The wrong person, in the wrong place, at the wrong time." She leaned forward a little, staring at him hard to push home every word. "The Scourge needed a puppet. Someone who was easy to push around. You—with your little tantrums—fit the bill perfectly. That's why you were chosen, Charlie. Not for any other reason. And certainly not—God forbid—because you had any *talent*."

"Is that right?" asked Charlie.

"It's like you said, Charlie," Esme told him. "I've been waiting for this moment my whole life. Ever since the thing that you let inside you took my mother from me. You?" she added, and shrugged. "You're here by *mistake*."

And she lunged.

She leaped straight off the steps, hurling herself through the air toward Charlie.

Charlie too leaped toward her, a fraction of a second later.

Jack saw a blur of limbs.

There was a resounding and sickening *crack*.

Then the two of them landed again, on the opposite sides to where they'd been standing before.

Charlie looked shocked: his eyes were wide and staring, and his left arm cradled his right, which was sticking out at an alarming angle.

Esme's mouth was twisted in a sneer of rage: her killing hands twitched at her sides. She leaped again.

Charlie flung up his arms to ward her off.

And then the fight really began.

It was almost too fast for Jack to watch. He could see Charlie doing his best to block her, but Esme was too quick: for every blurring blow of foot or fist that landed relatively harmlessly on Charlie's shins or forearms, there seemed to be twice as many that cracked into a rib, hammered at his face, or smashed the air out of his belly, leaving him gasping. Esme spun on the spot and drove her trainered foot squarely into Charlie's midriff, doubling him over, taking him off his feet and hurling him through the air, straight back into the stairs he'd started off on. As the rest of his body hit the steps, his head snapped back, cracking against an edge. Charlie's hands fell to his sides, his eyes rolled up in his head, and he lay there unconscious.

Snarling, Esme leaped again, straight up this time, ready to stamp Charlie, when she landed, right through the floor.

Charlie was out for the count, defenseless.

Jack held his breath. But suddenly—

—at the moment of impact—

—Esme stopped.

Jack stared.

Esme began to struggle, but she was stuck fast. Hands like steel pincers gripped her waist: Charlie's hands.

Instead of dodging or rolling Charlie had simply caught her.

His face just inches from hers, Charlie's eyes flicked open, filling with blood. The black tattoo shivered, then rippled through his whole body.

And the thing inside him smiled.

Still grasping Esme, Charlie swung upright. Now he was hovering off the ground. Esme stared back in horror as Charlie continued to grin at her. Then Charlie began, slowly at first, to spin.

He spun once. Esme's hands began to pluck uselessly at his.

He spun twice. Esme's legs were already beginning to trail out behind her as the terrible momentum took hold.

He spun a third time, still grinning at her.

And then he let go.

Like a stone from a sling, Esme was flung across the room. She crashed to the floor in a pile of tables and chairs.

Charlie's awful smile remained frozen in place. Slowly, easily, he looked around the room—

—and the furniture, the bottles, the glasses, everything in the pub that wasn't screwed to the ground rattled in its place for a moment, then lifted into the air. The cloud of objects began to move, picking up speed, converging on Esme.

She sat up, blinked—and sprang to her feet as the blizzard of objects came whistling toward her. Instantly Esme became a blur of flailing limbs—ducking, twisting, and blocking as she used every ounce, every minute of her years of training and preparation to defend herself. When the first bar stool hit her she was ready, warding it off with a combination of a backward roll and a scything kick that sent it winging away into a corner: it smashed into the wall leaving a large hole in the plaster. The second and third met similar fates. Then the first table caught her in the small of the back.

Jack heard her gasp.

She missed a step.

And now, suddenly, she was down. The stools and tables and bottles and chairs kept coming, smashing into her, sending her sliding across the polished wooden floor under a burgeoning mound of twisting, twitching furniture. At the wall, not five yards along from where Jack was lying, she stopped.

The furniture stopped moving. She was trapped.

Charlie's smile widened further, in a ghastly grin that showed all his teeth. Then—

"LEAVE HER ALONE!"

In a blinding white burst, all the lights of the pub went on at once.

There, at the top of the steps above Esme, stood Raymond.

"KHENTIMENTU THE SCOURGE!" he roared. "TO ROOTS THAT BIND AND TO THORNS THAT CATCH I CONSIGN YOU!"

Charlie froze.

"By the light of the world," said Raymond, quieter now. "By the strength of my will and the curse that first stilled you, I command that you return to your prison. *Get you hence, and trouble us no more!*"

Charlie—or the thing that was wearing him—smiled again.

"**Do you know,**" said Charlie's mouth, though the voice that came out of it was nothing like Charlie's now, "**what it's *like* to be imprisoned for nine thousand years?**"

Charlie's eyes, as the Scourge glanced around the room, were completely black, like marbles: Jack looked at them and shuddered.

"**Just try and imagine it,**" said the demon. "**Nine thousand years, a day at a time. You can't do it,**" it said. "**Can you?**"

"Kh-Khentimentu the Scourge," began Raymond again, less confidently this time.

"**Quiet,**" said the Scourge, and there was quiet. "**I've been planning my revenge for longer than you could possibly comprehend. *You*—**" it paused, and the eyes in Charlie's face seemed to bore into Raymond's, "**are my finishing touch. When you're gone, your little 'Brotherhood' will have ceased to exist.**"

"Yeah?" blustered Raymond. "What about Esme?"

The demon smirked.

"**It's already too late for her.**" Charlie looked down at Esme, who was still trapped under the pile of furniture.

"**It's *always* been too late for her,**" said his mouth. "**Just ask Felix.**"

"What are you talking about?" began Raymond, then stopped. He turned pale.

"**That's right,**" said the Scourge, grinning delightedly. "**Haven't you ever had your doubts about where her powers come from? Her strength? Her speed? Her *spirit*? Well, now, at last, you can begin to understand. Now, when it's too late.**"

"No," said Raymond quietly. "Ah, no. Surely not." He looked at Esme.

"**You're going to die now, Raymond,**" said the demon. "**You are harmless and weak, and you pose me no threat, but vengeance** is vengeance and I will not be denied. If you have anything left to say, say it now."

Raymond looked at Esme.

"Listen to me carefully, petal," he said quickly. "Remember what I told you about your mother, all right? *Remember your mother.*"

"Dad," said Esme, "I—"

Raymond shook his head. "Look in my room," he said. "There's something for you. I was going to give it to you for your birthday, but that doesn't matter now: when you're ready, when you know what to do, you *use* it. All right?"

"Dad, I don't—"

"There's *more to life than this*, petal," said Raymond urgently. "Don't ever forget that. And don't ever forget . . . well, that I love you."

"Oh no," said Esme. "Oh, God. *Dad!*"

"All right," said the big man, straightening up and pushing his chest out. "All right, you bastard: do your worst."

The demon spread Charlie's arms. Its smile faded. The air in the room heated up suddenly, crackling and popping in Jack's ears with an awful electricity. A blast of pressure blew out all the lights of the pub, leaving it in darkness once more except for the dull red glow of the Fracture.

Then there was silence.

Raymond was gone. There wasn't even a body. It was as if he'd never existed.

Charlie's hands fell to his sides. The light from the Fracture was brightening now: it was widening, opening, the red glow changing quickly to orange, then yellow, then a freezing, icy white. Charlie looked down at his hands. His face was blank.

"You're dead," said Esme, sitting up. "I'm coming after you, and when I find you . . . you're *dead!*" Her voice cracked as she said it.

Charlie turned. The tattoo had subsided. The demon inside him had let go for the moment, and it was Charlie the boy who was looking at Esme now. A pang crossed his face, and his jaw began to tremble.

"I . . . didn't . . ." he said.

Esme just looked at him.

"I . . . what . . . ?" said Charlie. He looked back down at his hands.

"Oh no," he said. "Oh, God."

He turned to look at the blinding white gap in the air that had appeared, silently, behind him. It was now wide enough to step through.

And suddenly, watching him, Jack knew what he had to do.

There's nothing for us here. That was what Charlie had said. It wasn't true—of course it wasn't. But Charlie had let himself forget: the thing that had used him had made him forget. Jack got to his feet.

Charlie looked at him: a begging, pleading look that twisted in Jack's heart like a knife.

And instantly, the black shapes were swarming up Charlie's neck again. Charlie's face went slack as the demon took control once more, ensuring that its victory wouldn't slip away at this, its most triumphant moment. Charlie turned away woodenly, facing the Fracture. He stepped forward—

—and vanished.

Not pausing to think too much, Jack ran. The Fracture was already closing. He could hear a screaming sound as the freezing white space loomed up in front of him, a screaming he suddenly (with an odd sort of clarity) was able to identify as coming from Esme, begging him not to do what he was about to do.

But it was too late. He had done it already.

The light had him now. The shouts behind him were getting fainter, and soon there was nothing but light.

Right, thought Jack, waiting for the next bit. *Here we go, then.*

He was on his way.

On his way to Hell.

END OF

BOOK ONE

"If someone comes at you with a sword, run if you can. Kung fu doesn't always work."

Bruce Lee

BOOK TWO

THE PIGEON SWORD

WELCOME TO HELL

Some time later, Charlie opened his eyes. The first thing he saw was the demon.

It was the same black figure he'd chased over the rooftops. The same one that had pretended to die when he'd struck it with magical fireballs—a slim, narrow, but man-shaped thing made out of absolute darkness, its face a shiny black blank. It was looking at him.

"**Good**," said the Scourge. "**You're awake.**"

"Er . . . yeah," said Charlie.

"**Did you sleep well?**" The voice came directly into Charlie's head, with a sensation like icy fingertips behind his eyes. Before answering, Charlie sat up. The tattoo was still there in the skin of his arms, but it wasn't moving now; it was still. The room he was in didn't appear to have any walls or ceiling or even a floor that he could see. There was himself, the bed, and the demon: everything else was just featureless white.

"I don't know," he said. "How long was I out for?"

"**There's . . . something I want to show you**," said the Scourge gently, ignoring the question. "**It's a sight that I promise you'll never** forget as long as you live." With a smooth, liquid movement, it stood up and offered an ink-black hand. "**What do you say?**"

Charlie looked at the Scourge's hand.

"All right," he said, and took it.

The demon's touch was cool but firm. Charlie felt a rush of hot air, a sensation like huge black wings closing around him, then—

"**There,**" said the Scourge. "**Open your eyes.**" Because as soon as Charlie had glimpsed what was there, he'd closed them tight before he could stop himself. The demon lifted one of its arms in a wide, sweeping gesture.

"**Welcome to Hell,**" it said.

Charlie looked down at his feet. He was standing, unsupported, on a lip of black stone barely as wide as his trainers. Above him and around him there was nothing but starless sky, warm and thick and strangely still. And in front of him . . .

In front of him, and below him, stretching as far as he could see in any direction, was Hell.

"Buh—buh—" Charlie gibbered.

"**Take your time,**" the Scourge advised. "**Take it in slowly.**"

Charlie did his best, but it was difficult.

It's one of the strangest things about the human mind that, when it sees something really impressive—the Grand Canyon, for instance—the first reaction, often, is simply to dismiss it. "Naaah," says your brain, "it's a *backdrop*. Painted scenery. Special effects. It's not really there." You have to stand and look for quite a long time sometimes, just to let the realization sink in that what you are looking at *is* actually there.

That what you are looking at really is many millions of times bigger than you. And *it* doesn't care whether you believe in it or not.

"This place is known as the Needle," said the Scourge conversationally. "It's the highest point of the palace and, therefore, the whole of the realm."

Charlie didn't reply. He was too busy staring.

It was like standing on the summit of a mountain, he decided. Only instead of being made out of rock, the crags and peaks below him were actually buildings. Keeps, turrets, and towers of all shapes and sizes, from slender spires to things like giant cathedrals, all seemed to be jutting nonchalantly from the palace's gargantuan tapering sides. From the foot of it, miles below him, five vast and arrow-straight white-lit lines struck out into the landscape as far as his eyes could see. These lines were linked by smaller curved paths that split the land into a series of roughly concentric rings, broken up into sections by the five great roads. Charlie's attention was immediately caught by a country-size chunk that was the only bit of Hell so far that was anything like what he'd been expecting: the whole section appeared to be made out of flames. The flames were a beautiful rushing red and orange and yellow, and they slid up the walls of the pit that contained them and slipped back down again, heaving and subsiding like coastal sea on a stormy day. At every seventh great convulsion the waves of fire leaped even higher, sending a great gout of flame bursting up into the night sky before it crashed back into itself, leaving blossoming purple flashes on Charlie's retinas as he stood watching, spellbound.

"**It could all be yours,**" said the Scourge quietly.

"What could?"

"**All this,**" said the Scourge, gesturing again. "**All Hell.**"

Charlie stopped looking at the sea of fire and turned to look at the demon.

"What are you talking about?" he asked.

"**Here,**" said the Scourge. "**I'll show you.**" Without further warning, it grabbed Charlie's hand—and they stepped off the edge.

Charlie's heart rose in his chest and his breath caught in his lungs as, for a full ten seconds, they plummeted straight down. Past his feet, the sheer black stone blocks of the tower they'd been standing on blurred past with sickening speed. His eyes were streaming, but when he looked ahead he could see the spiked roof of the next-tallest turret rushing up to meet him and—apparently—impale him. A scream pushed its way out of his throat. But it wasn't fear.

It was joy.

"HAAAAAAAAAAAAAAAAAAAAAH!" screamed Charlie, or something like it, as, with a pressure that made his insides feel like they were being squeezed flat, he and the demon suddenly leveled out and swooped round the turret. For a wonderful fraction of a second, Charlie actually felt his foot brush the edge of the roof—then they were diving, swimming through the air. The Scourge swung him out to their left, taking him in a wide circle, as the spectacularly fanged and spiked and crenellated and twisted towers of the palace rose to meet them, and pass beneath their feet.

"These are the High Reaches," said the demon, and Charlie heard its voice perfectly clearly even over the din of the rushing air. "From here all Hell's affairs are managed and directed."

They were now level with the highest windows of the palace. What Charlie saw didn't make a lot of sense to him. Up where he was, the turrets all seemed very small—individual structures separated from each other by the yawning spaces below—and they were all different from each other. He glimpsed windows of all shapes and sizes, and all were brightly lit, but he and the Scourge were flying too fast for him to be able to make out any more than a blur.

"This actually isn't the best way to see the palace," said the demon. "To appreciate it fully, one really needs to get away from it a little."

And with that, the roofs dropped away beneath them, and he and the Scourge swung out over the clear skies of Hell.

The night sky was a deep and tender purple-blue, warm and clear apart from occasional tiny wisps of strange cotton wool–like clouds that tickled past them as they continued their strange descent. Charlie gave himself up, letting the demon take him where it would, until the rushing air on his face slowed to a breeze—then, suddenly, they stopped.

Perfectly still, floating in the air, they turned round to face back the way they'd come.

"There," said the Scourge. "Impressive, don't you think?"

And Charlie had to admit, the Scourge was right.

The palace was unquestionably the biggest thing in the whole landscape. It was so big that if he hadn't been told what it was, Charlie wouldn't have been sure it really qualified as a single building. From where he was, hanging suspended high in the air, still holding the demon's hand, Charlie saw his earlier impression confirmed: the palace *was* more like a mountain than a building, with hundreds, maybe thousands of individual structures seemingly growing out of it in an astonishing profusion, a bewildering and chaotic array. The harder Charlie looked, the more detail there was to find.

So he stopped himself.

A small, thin stream of cloud drifted past: Charlie felt the moisture of it on his face and stuck out his tongue to taste it on his lips. It was salty, like tears.

"So this is Hell," he said, as casually as he could.

The Scourge didn't answer.

"Listen," said Charlie, his voice sounding high and strange in his ears. "Before we go any further, you're going to have to clear a few things up for me."

He took a deep breath.

"First of all, and I'm sorry if this comes out sounding a bit stupid, but—are we dead?"

"No," said the Scourge. "**Not dead. On the contrary: for the first time, I think, you are truly *alive*.**"

"Sure, whatever," said Charlie, "but . . . well, you know, isn't Hell supposed to be where you go *after* you're dead? I mean, normally?"

The demon thought about this for a moment.

"Mm," it said finally. "**You are referring, perhaps, to some sort of belief system in the place where you come from.**"

"Sorry?"

"What do your people believe?" asked the Scourge patiently. **"What do your people think happens after death?"**

"Oh," said Charlie, surprised. He had to think for a moment.

"Well, some of them," he began. "Not *me*, obviously, but some of them believe that, you know, when you die, there's a couple of possible things that could happen. If you've been good, if you've led a good life, then you go to, er . . . Heaven."

He broke off and looked at the demon, to see if he was getting this across properly. It was impossible to tell.

"It's supposed to be a nice place," said Charlie, doing his best. "You know, eternal happiness. That sort of thing."

"I see," said the Scourge.

"And if you've been *bad*," said Charlie, "then you go to this other place. A *bad* place, where bad things happen to you. Fire. Brimstone. Eternal torment or whatever. And that's Hell."

"That is what you believe?" asked the Scourge, with a smile in its voice.

"Not me," said Charlie quickly. "Just, you know—some people."

Slowly at first, but with gathering speed, something strange was happening to the demon: it was trembling. In another moment, it was quaking all over, big shudders running all over its liquid black body.

"What?" asked Charlie. "What is it?"

But then he realized what it was. The Scourge was laughing.

"I'm sorry, Charlie," it said, once it had managed to get itself back under control a little. "But that's very funny."

"Why?" asked Charlie, annoyed.

"I knew your people were primitive, but really," it said, "that's—"

"*What*?" said Charlie.

The Scourge stopped laughing and looked at him.

There was a pause.

"In backward, *unenlightened* societies," it said slowly, "it is possible to control people by means of what they believe. This belief system of yours: it's a perfect example."

"Oh yeah? And why's that?"

"Think about how it works," said the Scourge. "If you're *good*, if you do what you're told, then when you die you'll go to . . . where was it?"

"Heaven," said Charlie.

"Yes," said the demon. "But if you're *bad*, if you don't do exactly what everyone says is the right thing to do, or behave as you're told to behave, then—"

"You'll go to Hell," finished Charlie.

"Exactly. Charlie," said the Scourge, "you must understand that beliefs like those you've described are for the *weak*. They make you easy to control, and they can be comforting too: it's so much simpler to make decisions about how to live your life when all the guidelines are set out in front of you. Look at me."

Obediently, Charlie turned to look at the Scourge's face. In the blank shiny blackness that he found there, his own reflection stared back at him.

"The only way to make a decision is of your own free will. You yourself must weigh up the consequences for and against and make your choice accordingly, without anyone else telling you what is right and what is wrong. That is what free will is all about."

Charlie didn't answer; he just stared at himself, reflected in the demon's face.

"There is something," the Scourge began, "that I need you to help me to do. It will not be easy, but the rewards will be great."

"What is it?" asked Charlie.

"I will tell you," said the demon, "but not just yet. I have something else to ask of you first."

"And what's that?"

"Charlie," said the Scourge, "I want you to trust me."

Charlie stared.

"Trust you?" he echoed. "*Trust* you? Well, let me think about that for a second. *No.*"

"No?" said the Scourge, surprised.

"Come on!" said Charlie. "What do you think I am— stupid? It's all very well, you coming on like 'the Snowman' and giving me the guided tour *now*. A little late, though, don't you think?"

"Charlie—"

"You tricked me! You made me think I had superpowers, when all the time you were possessing me! Taking me over! *Using* me so you could get what you want! And *then* you . . ." He remembered the moment he'd realized what the demon had done through him. He remembered Esme's face as she'd vowed her revenge. He shuddered.

"Give me one good reason," he said.

"Because I'm offering you the choice," the Scourge replied.

Charlie stared again. "What?"

"You know what I can do, Charlie," said the demon simply. "You know the power I can wield over you. And yet you see that I do not use it."

"So?"

"I think that by the time you have seen what I plan to do," the Scourge explained, "you will want to do it every bit as much as I do. And we can work so much better, I think," it added, "as a team."

It paused.

"Let me be your guide," it said. "Let me show you what I'm planning. Trust me that much at least."

"And if I decide I don't want to help you with whatever you're doing, then what?" asked Charlie. "You'll let me go home?"

"Back to your world?" asked the Scourge, surprised again. "Back to your family, or what's left of it?"

"Hey!" said Charlie.

"I'm sorry," said the demon, "but it seems hard to believe that you'd want to return, with things as they are right now."

"That's not the point!" said Charlie—loudly, because the Scourge had reminded him of something he didn't want to think about.

"Of course," said the Scourge soothingly, "you are free to choose. You have my word." It looked at him, waiting.

Charlie thought about it.

He looked down at Hell, far below him, laid out under his feet as if just for him. He looked at the palace and the surrounding fantastical landscape that spread to the horizon in every direction. No one on Earth had been where he was. No one on Earth had seen what he was seeing. Looking around, Charlie suddenly had a very powerful impression that the whole world—the whole universe, maybe—revolved around where he was standing (or floating, to be strictly accurate).

Then he thought about a Chinese restaurant in London's West End and the last time that he'd seen his father. He thought about the abandoned meal and the things that they'd said to each other—things, in his opinion, that could never be taken back. He thought about his mother, who was probably still waiting for him at home and wondering already where he was. He thought about the hateful mess his father had made of their lives by leaving them the way he had—and he briefly considered whether, frankly, he could really be bothered with any of it.

Stay or go back. Those were his choices.

No contest.

"Okay," said Charlie. "Show me."

FRESH MEAT

Jack woke with a jolt, looked up—and stared.

He was in a throne room of some kind—that was the first thing he noticed: an immense, cavernous, dome-shaped space with a raised circular dais at its center. Jack was kneeling on a narrow strip of bloodred carpet, and to either side, forming the rest of the floor of the room, was a huge and glittering gray-blue expanse of . . . what? Jack frowned as he realized that the floor was *moving*—bulging and rippling like an oily sea. But then he looked up and found himself staring even harder.

Just next to the throne, dipping slightly in the air as it made a small movement of its tail, was what appeared to be . . . a shark.

The shark was very big—thirty feet long at least. Its torpedo-like body was crisscrossed with a network of horrible puckered scars; its blank gray eyes glinted at Jack like gun barrels—and it was floating in the air, just hovering there, as if this were the most natural thing in the world.

The shark—and the throne room—were already, frankly, just a little bit more than Jack felt able to cope with at this point. But as if these things weren't enough on their own, there was the throne itself and the strange figure that sat on it.

He looked like a man—or most of him did. His gleaming white three-piece suit was immaculate and well cut; his jet-black hair was elegantly tousled, and his goatee beard and narrow sideburns were so neat they looked like they had actually been sharpened. But there were also, Jack noticed, several weird things about him, too. The skin of the man (if *man* was the right word) was unmistakably red. His hands, which were folded in his lap, were actually more like hooves, with stubby black spur things instead of thumbs. And the worst thing—the thing that made Jack actually shiver as he looked at him—was his eyes.

They were golden, with black vertical slits in them instead of pupils. They were not human eyes, and the look they were giving him was not a friendly look: the expression on the man's face was the kind you might give to a really large spider that you've just found in your bath. "Who are you?" he said.

"J—" said Jack, then found his voice. "Jack Farrell," he said. "Sir."

The man arched his perfect black eyebrows. "That's not much of a name."

Jack found he didn't really have anything to say to that, so there was a pause.

"Are you . . . the Devil?" Jack asked finally.

The man frowned. "I've never heard that word before. Say it again."

"The Devil."

"No. The name means nothing to me. I may add it to my collection, though." The man sat up straight on his throne, and his chest swelled as he prepared to speak.

"I am Ebisu Eller-Kong Hacha'Fravashi," he said. "God of Rulers, God of the Dead, God of Darkness, God of Gods. I am the Voice of the Void, whose breath is the wind and whose rage makes all worlds tremble. I am Lord of Crossing-Places, King of All Tears, and the Suzerain Absolute of the Dominions of Hell."

"Er . . . pleased to meet you," said Jack.

"You will address me as 'Emperor,'" said the man on the throne. Beside him, the shark's mouth hinged open in a wide and meaningful grin—and Jack decided that now wasn't a good time to argue.

"Pleased to meet you," Jack repeated, "Emperor."

"This," said the Emperor, gesturing at the giant flying shark with one cloven red hand, "is Lord Slint. You find his presence . . . off-putting?"

"A little bit," Jack admitted, "yes."

The Emperor smiled. "You may leave us, Slint," he said. And as soon as the words were spoken, the shark lunged.

Jack ducked—he couldn't help himself—but the shark, all thirty feet of it, had already passed over him and away, making for the giant doors that stood behind where Jack was kneeling. They were a hundred meters off, maybe more. In the second or two it took to cross the distance, Jack watched the shark's easy, undulating movement and the sinuous way it slipped through the doors and out of sight.

"Now," said the Emperor, leaning forward on his throne. "We have a rather pressing matter to discuss, do we not?"

"We do?" queried Jack. "Er, Emperor?" he added.

"Indeed we do."

There was another pause.

"Come now," said the Emperor, when Jack continued to stare at him. "You have just made use of the same crossing-place that the Scourge employed to return from your world. It may interest you to know that the Scourge's reappearance has come as something of a surprise to me. Khentimentu's banishment was long ago considered purely a matter of myth among my people: the Scourge's very existence was cause for conjecture, right up until its return. And the discovery that its incarceration took place in a world of which all records appear to have been lost is of no small interest to me also."

Jack just kept looking at the Emperor, waiting for whatever he was going to say next.

The Emperor sighed. "It appears I must be blunt." The golden stare narrowed and sharpened. "*Why are you here?*"

"Oh," said Jack. "I'm, ah, here for my friend. Emperor," he added, as the man on the throne continued to stare at him.

"You don't mean the Scourge's *vessel*," said the Emperor, with an expression of distaste. "Do you?"

"His name's Charlie," said Jack. "Emperor," he added again (getting a bit tired of doing it, to be honest).

"And what, may I ask, do you propose to do when you find this 'Charlie'?"

"Well, I want to rescue him," said Jack, feeling his ability to deal with this whole situation finally begin to leak out of his ears. "You know, take him back home."

"Let me get this quite clear," said the Emperor, sitting back. "You've come, alone, unaided, into my kingdom, to find your . . . 'friend,' release him from the Scourge's influence, and bring him back with you to wherever you came from?"

"That's about the size of it," said Jack. "Yeah."

For another long moment, Jack and the Emperor just looked at each other.

"Your story is ridiculous," said the Emperor finally. "And this encounter has already taken up more of my time than I am prepared to waste."

He drew himself up, staring down at Jack.

"You will be taken to Slint's gladiator pits," he announced. "There you will be pitted against the finest fighters of all my dominions, and we shall see how well you fare. If your performance proves diverting, I may perhaps grant you a boon, such as a privileged position from which to watch the invasion and conquest of your world. But it is my suspicion," the Emperor added, "that you will fail and die. Goodbye."

Like most of the rest of the conversation, this last bit had pretty much gone over Jack's head. At any rate, the Emperor sat back on his throne, and Jack suddenly found that he did not have time to think about it any further.

The surrounding stuff from the floor of the throne room—the stuff that he'd noticed moving earlier—was now flooding out over the sides of the carpet and *running up Jack's legs.* In another second, Jack's whole body was covered in a weird, clammy, grayish-blue jellylike substance that clung to him all over, locking him in position: any effort to struggle produced no result whatsoever. He was helpless as the jelly stuff ran up his neck, quickly spreading all over his head and then—revoltingly—his face. There was a squeezing sensation. A moment of unbelievable tension, then—

Darkness.

Presently, Jack opened his eyes again and sat up.

The room he was in now looked very small after the throne room: more like a cell, really. The floor was bare earth, reddish and dusty. The walls were smooth yellow stone, forming the room into a perfect square of maybe fifteen feet by fifteen, with no door, no apparent way in or out, except through the ceiling, which, Jack suddenly realized, wasn't there. The walls simply stopped, some thirty feet above him. Obviously his cell was only a part of some much larger room—and that, for the time being, was all Jack really cared about in that direction.

Not wanting to stand up just yet, Jack crawled over to one of the walls and sat there, with his back to it, his arms huddled round his legs.

He was frightened. Terrified, in fact. Large parts of his brain were wibbling and gibbering to themselves, quietly yet with gusto. Single words like *Hell* and *shark* played leapfrog in his head, amongst the more prosaic ones like *Help!, No!* or *AAAAAAAAAAARRGH!*

There were, he decided after a moment, two main approaches to this thing.

The first, the obvious one, was to give up: to burst into tears, scream himself hoarse, or start banging his head against the wall. All these options were certainly tempting. There was a strong swelling sensation in his chest and stomach and a hot wetness behind his eyes that wouldn't need a lot of encouragement. He was alone, in Hell. Approach one was very attractive indeed.

But then there was approach two, which went something like this.

Whatever was going to happen was obviously going to happen whether he liked it or not. (*Easy*, he told himself, as he started to panic again. *Easy. Come on, think it through.*) Well, if that were true, there was a *possibility*, however remote it might turn out to be, that he might—at some future moment—find some way of making things *less* unremittingly awful for himself. Opportunities might come (he told himself): chances might present themselves—and it would be a lot easier to spot these and take advantage of them if he *didn't* let himself go completely off his chump and start gurning like a man whose nostril hairs were on fire. He was in Hell, he told himself. All right, that much was obvious. But what that meant, what that would actually involve, was yet to become clear. Besides, there was something else about this situation, he saw: something familiar and, oddly, rather comforting.

Here he was, on his own in, apparently, an ultimately horrible position. And why was that?

Because, simply, that was the way things always seemed to turn out for him.

It was an extreme example, the scenery was different and so forth, but the fact was that, really, when it came to the sort of luck Jack had come to expect in his life, this was nothing more or less than *business as usual.*

What this *was,* in fact, he thought, as he flexed his legs and (using the wall for support) pushed himself upright, was absolutely, devastatingly . . .

"Typical," he finished aloud.

"Hello?" said a voice, making Jack nearly jump out of his skin. "You awake in there? You hear me?" The voice was high and scratchy, like sharp stones grating against each other.

"Y-yes," croaked Jack. Then he tried again. "Yes!"

"Shhh! Not so loud!" hissed the voice. "What's your name?"

"Jack," said Jack.

For a moment, there was silence. Then, "Hur," said the voice.

"What?" asked Jack.

"Hur, hur, hur."

Jack frowned.

"Hur, hur, hur, hur," he heard. "Hee hee hee HEE!"

"What's so funny?" asked Jack, an irritating whining note coming out with the question before he could stop it. The scratchy laughter ceased abruptly.

"Thass not your name," said the voice.

Jack stood in silence, staring at the wall in the direction the voice was coming from.

"*Fresh meat,*" said the voice. "Thass your name."

HOME

Esme lay on the floor of the Light of the Moon, in darkness, remembering.

"You lost," said Raymond.

Esme lay flat on her back. What had just happened had happened so fast that she hadn't even broken her fall properly: her head still rang from the impact as she'd hit the floor, and her vision was full of darkness. In the middle of it, she could see the big man standing over her. His face was flushed and sweaty but he was grinning from ear to ear, delighted.

"You lost," he repeated. "How?"

Grimly, biting back frustration, Esme closed her eyes. The last move, the kick—that was where she'd overextended herself and left herself vulnerable, obviously. But how? How had it been possible? Concentrating, she played the fight back in her head.

This latest bout had begun much like all their others. Throughout the opening exchange, she'd pulled back before committing herself to every attack she'd started. This was for the simple reason that each time she'd started a move, Raymond had already been moving to anticipate her, just as he always did. But this time, Esme had tried something new.

Gradually, as the bout continued, she'd allowed a little desperation to come through into the way she was responding. To a spectator, the two of them would have been moving almost too fast to watch—but as the fight went on, Raymond would have noticed (she hoped) a little raggedness, a little roughness in her usual glassy-smooth technique. In due course, her strategy had been rewarded: the big man had apparently become more confident, letting himself come a little further into her striking range than he usually did. So Esme had launched her main attack.

She'd begun the move in textbook style, leaping off her left foot into a spinning midkick with her right. If it had all gone according to plan, Raymond should have lowered his hands to protect himself, at which point Esme could have completed the feint by folding her right leg into a further 180-degree spin, letting her left foot scythe up over Raymond's guard to take the big man up under the chin.

Pretending to attack with one foot only to surprise one's opponent with the other was a classic move. It had taken Esme many months of hard training to master it, but she had pulled this one off, she knew, flawlessly. There was no way, therefore, that Raymond could have anticipated what she was going to do.

And yet, he had read the feint for what it was.

He had not reacted to the approach of her right foot in the least—just stayed absolutely still.

And when Esme was fully committed to the follow-up—when she was in the air, well and truly past the point when she could pull back on the kick or prevent what was about to happen—Raymond had stepped *toward* her. His hands were in exactly the right place to catch her left foot effortlessly as it passed its target. Keeping an easy grip around her ankle, transferring his weight smoothly, he too had spun, once—

—and released her, letting her own momentum hurl her halfway across the room, to land in an undignified heap on the butterfly room's hard, matted floor.

"You *knew*," Esme spluttered up at him, furious.

"About the kick?" Raymond pretended to think for a moment, then grinned again. "Yup."

"How?"

Raymond's bushy beard bristled as his smile widened further.

"I'll tell you what it wasn't, if that's any help," he said. "It wasn't magic. I didn't read your mind or anything like that." He leaned over her. "And I hope you're not going to tell me about *strength*. Are you?"

"No," said Esme sulkily.

"Well?" Raymond held out a beefy hand to help her up. "How do you think I knew?"

Esme looked at his hand, made a contemptuous sucking noise with her tongue against her teeth, and got to her feet by herself.

"I failed," she said. "I wasn't good enough, that's all. Something in the execution must've told you what I was planning. I need more practice. Obviously."

"No, petal," said Raymond, shaking his head. "You're wrong there. For what it's worth, it was beautifully done."

"Oh yeah?" Esme stared at him, exasperated. "If it was *that* beautifully done, how come I didn't *get* you with it, then?"

Raymond's smile faded. He sighed.

"Petal," he began, "just answer me this one question. Who do you think taught you about feints and combinations? Who do you think taught you all about putting your opponent off guard? About anticipation? About control?"

"You!" snapped Esme, not seeing what he was getting at. "It was you, of course."

"So," said Raymond, putting his beefy hands out to his sides in a small shrug. "How did you think you were going to take me by surprise?"

Esme froze.

"Eh?" added the big man.

There was a long pause.

"I . . ." began Esme, then fell silent.

"You've been a pleasure to teach, petal," said Raymond quietly. "I've never met anyone to touch you for dedication, concentration, or focus.

"But right now," he added, "everything you've got comes from *me*."

"So how am I supposed to *beat* you?" asked Esme.

Six years later, lying on the floor again, she realized she'd spoken aloud.

For a long time, she just lay there. The light from the

Fracture had vanished when it had closed. Every lightbulb in the Light of the Moon had exploded in the battle that had just taken place. Esme lay on the ground, in the darkness, alone. After a while, though, as if from far away, she began to be aware of the pain of her injuries as they started to heal themselves. It was the pain, really, that brought the facts of the situation home to her.

The Scourge had escaped.

Raymond was dead.

She, strangely, was alive.

Slowly, carefully, Esme freed herself from the pile of objects that had held her trapped and stood up. Then, because no better ideas seemed to occur to her, she started walking, a step at a time.

She went up the stairs. She went out of the door, out of the pub, out into the warm, sickly air of the London summer night—and she set off back toward the theater.

Her insides felt like they were filled with broken things. Shattered clockwork, jagged glass: the wreckage moved and ground and ripped at her with every small step that she took, and something cold and dark was in the place where her heart had been. But she kept walking. And soon, almost before she'd expected it, she was home. She climbed the stairs up to the Brotherhood's headquarters, and to her it was as if she were walking into a dream.

It was no different, she realized. Her home still looked and smelled and felt exactly the same as it always had, in all the years of her life that she had shared it with Raymond. It seemed inconceivable to her that it could still be the same, when the man at its heart, the man who had made it what it had been to her, was gone. It was incredible. Enormous. She felt like she was balancing on the edge of the world and could fall off it into nothingness at any second. The nothingness feeling was too much. It was going to swallow her. So she got enough of a grip on herself to make a decision.

It was now nearly five in the morning. On a normal day, in a couple of hours, she would be waking up.

She would act as if it were a normal day.

First, she set off toward the bathroom. She stripped, got under the shower, and turned the hot tap on full blast. Hard jets of scalding water drove at her skin like needles, but Esme hardly felt them. She stood under the shower numbly till she'd had enough, then she switched it off and got out.

Next she combed her hair—then pulled it back, hard, and tied it in place with six ordinary rubber bands, just like normal. She hung up her dressing gown on the back of her bedroom door and changed into the gear she always wore for her morning workout—a clean pair of loose white cotton trousers with a thick elasticized waistband and her second-favorite red hooded top. Then she headed down to the butterfly room.

Esme opened the doors and flicked on the lights. Then she paused.

The room was empty.

Felix—the man who was supposed to be lying on the table in a coma—wasn't there.

He'd gone.

Strange.

Esme frowned for a moment but decided she couldn't deal with that right now. Setting all thoughts of Felix aside for the time being, she concentrated on preparing herself for her morning workout. She fetched a broom and, mechanically, trying to ignore the gaping butterfly-shaped holes in the paint on the walls, she swept her dojo clean. Then she got started.

Ever since that day six years ago, the day of her failure with the feinting kick, Raymond had let her set her own training regime, contenting himself only with a few judicious suggestions once in a while. For six years now, therefore, Esme had always started the day in the same way, with her own combination of yoga, Pilates, and tai chi. After about thirty minutes, when her circulation was up to speed, she moved onto some gymnastics: slow handstands to begin with, followed by rolls, cartwheels, and finally some combination handsprings from one end of the room to the other. Next she turned to the makiwara boards. After perhaps an hour, when she had built up the speed and power behind her attacks until she was outpacing her body's magical ability to repair itself—when all five of the dark oak surfaces carried their telltale smudges of red and the muscles of her body ached with strain—she stopped and picked up her sword.

It was a bokken, a heavy, Japanese-style training sword, a rounded, gently curved black pole exactly two feet eight inches long, also made out of solid oak. Raymond had given it to Esme for her sixth birthday, when the sword was not much smaller than her: back then, she'd been unable to lift it for more than a few minutes at a time. Now, for the next part of her morning regime, Esme assumed a horse stance (feet parallel and apart, with her legs well bent) and held the sword out in front of her. Though she had built up her strength until she could stand like that for much longer, nowadays she was content to keep the horse stance for just another hour. This, she had found, was long enough for the energy of her workout to spread around her body and for her mind to settle. Standing alone in the butterfly room, Esme waited for the spreading warmth, the sensation of being alive and awake, the relaxed-yet-focused singing of her blood in her veins that time in this stance usually gave her.

It wouldn't come.

It was a mess, she decided, after a time. Her whole life was a mess. Her whole life she had trained, her whole life she had waited for the chance to defeat the Scourge—and she had failed. The Scourge had escaped to Hell. She had failed, and Raymond had died.

Esme felt sick inside: sick and empty and confused and hopeless. She didn't know what to do. And the longer she stood there, hoping for some peace and calm to return to her through the act of going through her daily routine, the more hopeless she felt.

Still, she stood there.

Still, she waited.

And suddenly, the doors to the butterfly room burst open.

Kicked in by heavy boots, the doors swung round on their hinges and smacked into the walls. Ten—no, fifteen—men, all dressed identically in black, with gas masks covering their faces, poured in and fanned out, the noise of their combat boots on the floor resounding round the room. Seeing Esme, they froze, and there was a lot of ostentatious ratcheting, racking, and clicking from the several varieties of guns that the men appeared to be carrying, as they pointed them all at her.

"Freeze!" barked the leader, dropping into a firing crouch and leveling a fat-barreled black pistol at Esme. "Stay where you are!" he added, in case she hadn't known what he'd meant.

There was a pause.

Esme looked at the group with a strange kind of detachment. Everything was unreal to her after Raymond's death: for a moment, she had the urge to laugh. Slowly, not breaking her stance, she took one hand off the sword and pulled her hood back.

"Hello," she said evenly. "Who are you?"

"Oh," said the man, lowering his gun. "You're a girl."

Esme's eyebrows flew upward. *Now* she was surprised. "And?" she inquired.

"It's all right!" called the man. "Weapons down, gentlemen: she's a girl." Instantly, the rest of the group flicked the safeties on their MP5s back on and snapped to attention.

"All units, this is Number Two," said the man, holding one hand to his ear. "We have a civilian in the main room of the top floor. Lone female, young, apparently harmless. Testing for possible contamination now."

Esme glanced around at the rest of the men, noting their positions. Holding her stance, keeping both her hands on her practice sword, she looked back at the man who had spoken.

"What do you mean," she asked, "'possible contamination'?"

"We are sorry, mademoiselle," said a second man, stepping forward. (He spoke slowly and calmly, with a pronounced French accent.) "We believe you may 'ave been in contact with something rather dangerous."

"Really," said Esme, still not moving in the slightest. "And who are you people, if you don't mind me asking?"

"We are the Sons of the Scorpion Flail," the French-accented man replied, "a secret international rapid-reaction force, sworn to protect the world from supernatural—"

"What have I told you, Number Three?" the first man interrupted, rounding on his comrade. "For the last time, what is our first rule of engagement?"

There was another pause.

"But she is 'ere, sir," said Number 3, gesturing awkwardly at Esme. "She must be part of zis 'Brotherhood' the informant mentioned, so I see no reason for—"

"Our first rule, Number Three," the man repeated.

Number 3's shoulders slumped. "'Operational information may be divulged to civilians on a need-to-know basis only,'" he quoted miserably. "Sir."

"Thank you, Number Three," said Number 2. "So, enough talk. Number Nine? Number Twelve? Give her the test." Obediently, two men began to advance on Esme from either side.

"What test?" Esme asked.

"A blood test," Number 3 told her quickly. "It will

determine in moments whether we 'ave anything to fear from you. And we would feel better," he added, "if you would lower your weapon."

"I'm afraid," said Esme quietly, "that that's just not going to be possible."

Halfway across the floor toward her, Number 9 and Number 12 stopped and turned to look at their leaders.

"Drop the stick, honey," said Number 2. "We're not fooling around here."

Looking at the men, in their black gear and gas masks, something inside Esme came awake with a *whoosh*: a soaring, sizzling, sparkling sensation that flushed through all her senses and left her tingling.

"No," she said.

"Sweetheart," said Number 2, "you have no idea who you're dealing with. We're the Sons of the Scorpion Flail. We travel the world, looking for evil, and wherever we find it, we kick its butt. Now, I'm telling you, girl, drop that thing and take the test; otherwise I'm going to have to get nasty."

"No," Esme repeated, with a predatory smile. She was going to enjoy this now.

"I'm going to count to three," Number 2 announced brilliantly. "ONE!"

If shouting was supposed to make Esme flinch, it didn't work.

"TWO! Look," said Number 2, when Esme still didn't move, "you want to do this the hard way? Fine! You asked for it. *THR—*"

That was as far as he got before Esme's bokken smacked into his face.

It had happened so fast that no one had seen it, but the faceplate of the man's gas mask now had a jagged spiderweb crack. Esme deliberately hadn't thrown the practice weapon hard enough to do more than give Number 2 a surprise, but he staggered backward, holding his hands up to his face. In the sudden silence as the rest of the men stared at him, the clatter the bokken made falling to the floor seemed very loud indeed.

"Whuh. What?" said Number 2. "T-uh. Take her down!"

Number 9 and Number 12 looked at each other. Then they lunged.

Number 9 got his hand on the girl first. His black-gloved fist closed around her left elbow, and for a fraction of a second he felt pleased with himself.

The feeling didn't last.

Esme's first move was minimal, a single small step, turning on the balls of her feet—but Number 9 suddenly found himself off balance, stumbling toward her. To his further surprise (it was supposed to be *him* grabbing *her*, after all), Esme took hold of his wrist with both her hands—and now she had control of his arm.

Esme could have broken Number 9's arm in a number of different places. She could have hurt him so badly that he never did anything with the arm again—but instead, she contented herself with a simple but well-executed aikido move. Number 9 was a good foot and a half taller than Esme, but her utter command of her weight and balance made this no problem: she flipped him, straight into Number 12, his partner, and the two Sons of the Scorpion Flail crashed to the ground, astonished, in a tangle of black-clad limbs and military equipment.

The third man to reach her didn't fare any better: a bare heel on the end of a whiplash kick exploded under his armored ribs, and, still reaching for the girl, he found himself lifted off his feet, climbing into the air, flying back over the heads of his fellows.

A scything low sweep cut a fourth man's legs from under him.

A snapping back-smash with the point of her right elbow dropped a fifth without Esme even needing to look.

Then, while the rest of her attackers piled at the place where she'd just been standing, Esme sprang into the air, flipped over once in a tight forward roll, and came down in a crouch beside where her practice sword had landed.

Perhaps a whole second had passed. The man she'd kicked, Number 24, was just hitting the wall: surprisingly high up, he slid to the floor with a crash. At any rate, by the time the rest of the group turned round, Esme had retrieved her bokken.

The remainder of the fight happened very quickly indeed.

She struck at knees, and elbows, and necks and ribs and ankles. She struck the breath from lungs and the strength from bodies. She kicked, she flipped, she swept, sliced, and smashed—and all with a fierce and easy joy, because it was what she was good at, what she did best. The heavy black weapon blurred in her hands and—silent and unconscious or howling and clasping themselves—the men toppled helplessly around her.

Suddenly, it was over. In her right hand she still held her bokken. In her left, she held the group's leader by the collar.

She had him off balance: she was supporting his entire weight easily with one hand—if she let go of him, he would fall flat on his back. Tucking the bokken's tip under the black rubber edge of his shattered mask, she ripped it neatly off his face and looked at him.

The man looked to be about forty years old. He hadn't exactly been handsome to begin with, and his face was now disfigured by terror: his piglike eyes glittered at her from under their beetling black brows, and his mouth was opening and closing like a ventriloquist's dummy's. Number 2 was plainly frightened out of his wits—by her. He was frightened of Esme. The sensation was strange to her, and a little uncomfortable.

"You're . . . not . . . *human*," the man gibbered.

Esme just looked at him. Hurting the man suddenly didn't hold quite the same attraction for her as it had a few moments ago—and now, to be honest, she didn't really know what to do instead.

"You're not human!" Number 2 repeated. He cast a wild-eyed glance at what remained of his troops and heard the moans and whimpers of those who were conscious. "We need backup," he added to himself. "We need more men. My—yes!" He put a hand up to his headset. "All units, this is Number Two! We are under attack! Repeat! We are under attack! All units converge on the first-floor main room! Get me backup—now!"

Esme's eyes narrowed. She dropped the man (he hit the ground with a thump) and took an uncertain step backward. "How many of you are there?" she asked.

"Hundreds!" said Number 2, crawling back from her. "Thousands! Keep away from me!"

"We 'ave another twenty men," said a voice from behind her. "Mademoiselle? Please listen to me."

She turned round and saw Number 3, the French-accented man. Like the rest of the group, he'd been wearing body armor: nonetheless, Esme was reasonably certain that she had cracked at least two of his ribs, and he could only be sitting up with great difficulty. Strangely, this didn't seem to have affected how polite he was being.

"We were told of this," he said. "An ancient evil, and a secret Brotherhood pledged to stop that evil from being released. It seems the informant spoke the truth."

He paused, and all Esme could hear was the sound of heavy boots pounding up the stairs and outside the doors, onto the landing.

"When the others come, do not fight them," said Number 3. "If you fight, they will shoot you: it is useless. We are 'ere to 'elp you!" he added desperately. "And all I ask in return is that you trust me."

"Why?" asked Esme.

Number 3 pulled off his mask. His jet-black hair was

cropped short, and running just above his right eyebrow half-way down his cheek was a long, angry scar. The eye crossed by the scar was a pale grayish-blue color, but the other, Number 3's left, was a deep, warm brown with flecks of gold in it. He was looking at her and—strangely—smiling.

"Jessica sent for us," he said.

Esme stared at him. But then the doors burst open, and more men filled the room.

"Fire at will!" shrieked Number 2.

"Non!" yelled Number 3. But the guns were already coming up: black-gloved fingers were tightening on the triggers.

And now, Esme saw, these people were shooting at her.

Time went slack.

Esme watched the flowering muzzle-flash of the guns with a weird kind of breathless concentration. The clattering bubble-wrap pops of the MP5s seemed to have slowed to rhythmic gluey thumping in her ears. She could see the spreading black stream of bullets stitching the air; their trails sticking out of the barrels like stair-rods, like banners that would unroll and say BANG. She caught a long glimpse of them all, the men firing their guns, and—*There's something a bit special about you. It's always been too late for her*—strange words seemed to be echoing in her ears.

She dropped the sword. Faster than time—faster than the world—but with an easy grace that felt as natural to her as breathing, she leaped.

And by the time the first bullets reached the place where she'd been standing—

—Esme wasn't there.

Rising now, her arms out to either side of her, Esme swung her legs up, flipping backward this time. As she reached the height of the butterfly room's great round window, she was in position: with perfect precision, the bare soles of her feet struck the exact center of the circle.

Then the world sped up around her once more.

Metal struts buckled and split: glass exploded, and cool air hit her like a shock wave. Ignoring the bullets buzzing around her, Esme completed her back flip, coming upright, outside now, high above Cambridge Circus. Her thoughts were now utterly focused on the one place in London she had left to go.

Turning toward the Thames, gathering her strength, she flung herself out into the air.

SPECTATORS

Charlie and the Scourge were standing at the foot of a small mountain of bloodred cushions. At the top of them, a tall man with red skin and a white suit was lounging about as if he owned the place. Which, as it turned out, he did.

God of Rulers, God of the Dead. The Voice of the Void . . . the demon who stood beside them was saying. Or at least, Charlie supposed that it was this demon: it was always hard to tell when someone was speaking to you without their mouth moving. It (Charlie had decided to think of this demon as an "it") was about six feet tall, dressed in long robes, and was floating about thirty centimeters off the ground. Its head was squat and heavy, ridged with thick bones, and appeared to be much too big for its delicate body. It also had what Charlie could only describe as a *really* disgusting monster-type mouth; the four yellow inch-long hooks that crossed in front of its gob instead of lips had spread wide open as soon as Charlie and the Scourge appeared, exposing a truly revolting wet pink hole within. This demon, Charlie decided, was quite staggeringly ugly. Which, now that he came to think of it, was pretty much exactly what he'd been expecting demons to look like.

"His name is Gukumat," the Scourge murmured. "He has the power to replicate himself, and his consciousness is collective: each one of him is linked to the others. At this moment, hundreds, perhaps thousands, more of him are currently engaged in the upkeep and administration of every part of Hell and its dominions. Overminister Gukumat is a powerful ally indeed. And a useful friend."

Lord of Crossing-Places, Gukumat droned on pompously, in a weird, lots-of-people-talking-at-once voice that made the words appear directly inside Charlie's head. *King of All Tears, and Suzerain Absolute of the Dominions of Hell.*

The Emperor gave a vague wave of one cloven hand.

Sire, said Gukumat, turning slowly toward him, *allow me to present Khentimentu the Scourge.*

The Scourge made a low bow. Taking his cue, Charlie bowed too—though it hadn't escaped his notice that he hadn't yet been introduced.

There was a pause.

"I wonder, Khentimentu," said the Emperor, "is it *normal* for you to go around like this?"

"Like what, my lord?"

"Outside your vessel," said the Emperor, gesturing at Charlie with distaste. "I mean, it's almost as if"—he smirked—"as if you're not fully dressed!"

"I'm Charlie," said Charlie brightly, stepping forward.

"Well," said the Emperor, looking at the Scourge again and

ignoring Charlie utterly, "your personal habits are your own affair."

Charlie blinked.

"Gukumat!" barked the Emperor suddenly.

Yes, Excellency?

"What do you have for me and my guests?"

Jocasta is fighting the Ogdru Sisters in the pit, was the reply.

The Emperor gave a wide smile. "Gukumat," he said, "you know what I like."

There was a low rumble of shifting stone, then a crack of blazing white light opened out across the darkened room. Still dimly realizing that the Emperor had insulted him, Charlie turned, just as the whole of the wall behind him seemed to come away from the ceiling and slide downward. The air was suddenly filled by a sound unlike anything Charlie had ever heard in his life. It was quiet at first, like the distant hiss of a gas tap—but as the wall opened further the noise became louder, gradually resolving into a terrible boiling mixture of sounds: baying, barking, howling, jeering, rumbling, crashing, and screaming. Charlie stared out of the enormous hole where the wall had been, at what lay beyond it, stared—and gaped.

"Welcome to the royal box," said the Emperor.

Outside and far below them was the wide, blinding-white sandy-floored ring of an arena. The noise Charlie was hearing, he realized, was a crowd noise, coming from the unbelievable mass of spectators that rose, tier upon dazzlingly huge tier, around the arena's massive black walls. There were hundreds of thousands of demons out there, all apparently

different. There were things out there that defied belief: creatures that Charlie couldn't have begun to describe. For the
time being, however, strangely enough, Charlie wasn't really
looking at the audience. Like the rest of the spectators, his
attention was inexorably drawn to what was taking place on
the arena's floor.

Spread in an even circle around the ring was a pack of a
dozen or so of what Charlie immediately identified as velo-
ciraptors, or something very like them. They had the same
long, muscular bodies, the same loping movements, the same
beautifully balanced proportions of crouching torso and elegant, sinewy tail. Their eyes were quick and their claws were
sharp, and the only thing that was different about them was
the scythelike talons that protruded from the front of each of
their hind feet: apparently made of some kind of metal, the
talons glittered and flashed, occasionally sending bright little
reflections scurrying over the black stone of the arena walls.

Their opponent was something Charlie had never seen
before. It looked a bit like a rhinoceros: it had a similar sort of
humped, armored body—only instead of four legs it had six.
The creature's head was wide and flat: its brow and the length
of its snout were protected by a triangular plate of thick,
heavy bone. The skin that covered this part of the creature's
face was a raw-looking pink, covered in whorls and wrinkles.
Also, the creature was *huge*: its length covered more than a
third of the diameter of the ring, and the tip of its ridged back
actually reached *above* the line of massive stones at the arena's edge. The monster shook its heavy head and bellowed at

the nearest of the raptors, exposing a variety of businesslike teeth, and the raptors took a careful skip back out of snapping distance.

The big beast was breathing hard: the thick gray hide of its sides pumped in and out, tightening and slackening. Charlie noticed four wide gashes just behind the heavy bulk of its front left shoulder. The wounds were red, raw, and shining. As the terrible noise of the crowd fell suddenly to an expectant rumble, one of the raptors opened its wide mouth and squealed something, provoking a high, scratching cackle of unmistakable laughter from the rest of the pack. They bobbed on their taloned feet, enjoying the moment.

Jocasta's been wounded, said Gukumat, *but the two sides are still quite perfectly matched. The Ogdru Sisters have pack tactics and youth, but Jocasta has strength, experience, and . . . well.* The tall demon lifted a long, robed arm and pointed at the arena. *See for yourself.*

The audience gave a great roar of delight as six raptors suddenly and simultaneously leaped to the attack. At the same moment, the creature that Gukumat had referred to as Jocasta reared up into the air and—with a speed and accuracy that Charlie would never have believed possible from one so bulky—caught two of the raptors in her claws. In another second, the great beast slammed back down, pinning them to the floor with her full weight. The other four scratched uselessly on the big creature's armored sides and then fell back. The two that had been unlucky jerked on the ground as Jocasta took her weight off them—then lay still.

The remaining raptors abruptly abandoned the outflanking maneuver they'd been planning and slunk back to the shadows at the edge of the ring to rethink their tactics. Jocasta just bellowed at them contemptuously.

"What do you do for entertainment in your world?" asked the Emperor abruptly.

"Sorry?" said Charlie. The suddenness of the question had startled him—but the Emperor did not repeat himself. He just continued to stare at Charlie with his weird golden eyes.

"Oh," said Charlie. "Well, we have films. You know, stories. Games. Music. Stuff like that."

"I'm not talking about those things," said the Emperor dismissively. "Don't you have anything *physical*? Anything . . ." He gestured toward the arena, just as one of the raptors leaped into the air, its steel-shod talons flashing, only to catch Jocasta's double-spiked tail in the chest. The unconscious raptor was flung against the nearest wall-slab, where it slid down and landed in the shadows in a wet heap. The crowd went wild. "Like this?" finished the Emperor with a smile.

"Not really," said Charlie, doing his best. "Well, we have, er, *sport*, I guess. We compete against each other in running or swimming—or football."

"Football?" echoed the Emperor. In the arena, Jocasta had caught two more of the raptors in her front paws and was busily engaged in smashing them against each other. Again and again.

"Yeah," said Charlie awkwardly. "You've got, er, eleven guys on each side, they're on this big field, and they're only allowed to touch the ball with their feet. Right? And you've got a net at each end. That's the goal: whoever kicks the ball in there gets a goal, and whichever side gets the most goals . . . wins." Seeing that the Emperor's attention was elsewhere, he turned. Two lucky members of the raptor flock had got a hold under Jocasta's armor: they dug their talons in, hard. The big beast's mouth hinged open in a grimace of agony.

"But is there violence?" asked the Emperor. "Does anyone get hurt? Or die?"

"No," said Charlie uncertainly.

"Then what's the point of it? This . . . 'football'?" The Emperor made little quote marks in the air with his cloven hands.

"How d'you mean?"

"I mean," said the Emperor, rolling his eyes, "that this game you're describing is a test of strength. The best team wins, yes?"

"Er, yeah."

"Well, what greater test of strength could there be than *fighting*?"

Charlie stared. "But—"

"No physical trial could be more testing than fighting for your life. None. Therefore, any other physical trial is inferior. Correct?"

Now Charlie just gaped.

"So, if no one gets hurt," said the Emperor slowly, as if he were talking to a moron, "what's the *point*?"

Out on the arena floor, the fight was reaching some kind

of a climax. Jocasta, her face a mask of pain and rage, was swinging her great body from side to side, trying to dislodge the raptors. But they clung on stubbornly. Seeing their chance, the rest of the flock leaped to the attack. Another fell prey to a swipe of her tail—but the others were climbing all over Jocasta now, stabbing and slashing with their great steel claws, leaving raw red welts as they went. The crowd was screaming its approval.

"But . . . watching things kill each other—that's just wrong!" said Charlie.

Jocasta rolled, howling, onto her back, squashing all but four of the raptors, who managed to leap clear in time. But they came back as soon as she righted herself, clinging on even tighter than before, tearing and ripping at her in an ecstasy of fury—and the big beast was starting to weaken. The Emperor yawned.

"They're in pain!" said Charlie, his voice going high and reedy, which only made him more indignant. He felt the Scourge lay a restraining hand on his arm, but he wrenched it away and jabbed at the arena. "They're dying!" he said. "And for you it's supposed to be what—*fun*?"

Slowly, the Emperor turned to Charlie and raised an eyebrow.

"All right," he said. "First, I don't find it fun. Rather the opposite. I usually find the whole thing to be quite *dull*, if the truth be told. You see, it's always been this way, ever since the time of the ancestors."

He smiled slowly, at the Scourge first, then at Gukumat.

"It may shock these two veterans to hear it," he said, "but I think the Old Ones were wiser than they let on. We demons are a disparate lot and prone to violence, so making that violence a part of our culture—*officially*, as it were—was undoubtedly a very shrewd and clever idea. That's why I allowed it to continue, even after—your world presently excepted—we succeeded in conquering the universe.

"Second," the Emperor went on, "there *is* something in it for the combatants, if they win. Which reminds me—Gukumat? What is the Ogdru Sisters' favor?"

Charlie turned to face the arena again, and his eyes went wide. The fight was over. Jocasta lay on her side, a great pool of liquid spreading from the terrible wounds that the raptors had inflicted on her. Her eyes were open and apparently lifeless. The three remaining raptors were standing side by side, facing up toward the royal box, their front claws clasped in a gesture of what appeared to Charlie, astonishingly, to be supplication.

Nothing of great import or interest, my lord, said the tall demon. *I was going to grant their request without troubling you with it.*

"Please, Overminister, for the benefit of our guests: do tell us."

Well, Sire, said Gukumat. *It* is *rather amusing, I suppose. They wish to start a small . . . business.*

"Business? What sort of business?"

There is a settlement, near the borders of the Plains of Flame. "Gehenna," they call it. There's not much there, no facilities to

speak of, but the Ogdrus believe that the place has some poten-
tial as . . . well, a tourist destination.

"Really?" asked the Emperor, wrinkling his nose. "But all that brimstone and so on! A bit sulphurous, I'd've thought. Wouldn't you?"

Indubitably, Sire. But as my lord knows, with the High Reaches demons one can never predict what fads and foibles may catch on next. The Ogdrus propose to start what they call, I believe, a "health spa."

"A health spa?" echoed the Emperor with distaste. "Guku-mat, you amaze me."

Shall I grant their request?

"Fine," said the Emperor, suddenly losing interest. He turned back to Charlie. "You see? The winner is granted a boon from me." He leaned forward on his mountain of cush-ions.

"This is how things work here in Hell," he said. "If you want something, you have to fight for it. Kill or be killed." He yawned again. "You follow?"

Charlie nodded numbly, though he didn't—not in the least.

"You may clear the arena, Gukumat."

At your command, Sire.

Gukumat bowed.

The arena floor seemed to ripple—

—and the remaining raptors, plus the body of their oppo-nent, suddenly vanished. In another moment, the stains of the battle were gone too. It was as if none of it had happened.

"Now," said the Emperor, settling back once more. "I've got something rather special lined up next, I believe. Gukumat?"

Sire?

"Is it time?"

Time for what, Sire?

"The boy," said the Emperor, annoyed. "Is he in position?"

Yes, my lord.

"Splendid." The Emperor looked down at Charlie, smiling again. "Here's something that might interest you." He gestured lazily at the next gladiator as he stumbled uncertainly out into the center of the arena. "This little chap arrived just after you did. Said he was a friend of yours. Now, what was his name?" He looked up at the ceiling as if trying to remember.

"Oh, God," whispered Charlie. "Jack."

"Oh yes," said the Emperor. "That was it. Jack. Gukumat?" he barked. "Open the other gates. Let's see what the little fellow is made of."

His grin widened.

"Quite literally, I should imagine," he added.

"GLADIATOR JACK"

Jack had been waiting in his cell when the jelly stuff came for him again. It had appeared from nowhere, swallowed him as before—and deposited him, this time in some sort of short passageway.

He was standing in front of a blank wall of cool, slate-gray stone. The passageway was empty and, apart from his breathing, entirely silent. Also, he had a knife in his hand.

The knife's blade was very short, an elongated half oval of glinting blue-gray metal. The black stuff the handle was made of was smooth and vaguely rubbery: against its dark surface Jack's knuckles looked whiter than he was expecting, until he noticed how tightly he was holding it.

His having a knife wasn't, he realized, particularly good news. He had not missed the Emperor's earlier words about gladiator pits. The knife meant, in all probability, that Jack was going to be expected to fight with it—and knife-fighting was not, as it happened, something that he had ever done before. Forcing his hands to relax, Jack tried a couple of jabbing and stabbing movements in the air and only succeeded in making himself feel very silly indeed. No, he decided: this whole situation was really getting worse and worse all the time.

That was when, with a low rumbling sound, the wall lifted to reveal what was beyond.

Gladiator Jack, step forward into the arena, please, said a voice in his head. The voice sounded bored and unfriendly, but suddenly, Jack wasn't really listening to it.

Step forward, gladiator. In accordance with the rules of the pit, if you do not step forward, you will be disemboweled, slowly and carefully. You have four seconds to comply.

Three.

Two.

One.

Jack blinked and stepped out.

Thank you. Please proceed toward the center of the arena and await the start of the bout.

Numbly, on legs that felt distant and rubbery, like they belonged to someone else, Jack did as he was told.

The arena was the size of a football pitch—bigger, probably—and surrounded all the way round by huge black slabs of rock, identical to the one that was rumbling down behind him, cutting off the only exit.

And above the slabs was the audience. Each and every row was filled to bursting by thousands—hundreds of thousands—of monsters. They were all looking at him. They were all screaming, howling, and jeering at him. The noise alone was incredible enough; the overall effect of the scene, Jack found, was really very alarming indeed.

As Gladiator Jack's opponent in this next bout, intoned the voice in his head (the crowd quieted a little, so Jack knew that the voice wasn't talking to just him anymore), *we present to you an undisputed master of the pit—the most feared fighter of our time. No quarter has he asked or given in a career that has now spanned some fifteen years.*

Terrific, thought Jack limply. *Oh, terrific.*

His speed is unmatched, the voice went on. *His cruelty is unparalleled. His name alone strikes ice-cold terror deep in the hearts of all who hear it. Fight fans, we present to you the Black Prince himself: LEO THE UNSPEAKABLE!*

Well, thought Jack, the name wasn't exactly the scariest he'd ever heard.

But now, on the opposite side of the ring from where Jack had come in, another of the black slabs was lifting.

It came slowly at first. Extending two long black—what? legs? feelers?—out into the blazing light, the thing seemed to test the ground, flexing. Then it took a whole step and moved into view.

It was a giant spider, and quite the most vile creature that Jack had ever seen in his life. Its body, slung at the center of its arched, oddly delicate-looking legs, was a good twenty feet long by itself, massively bloated and covered all over with spines like large screwdrivers. Its fangs glistened with slime, and its rows of eyes regarded Jack greedily.

BEGIN! barked the voice, and as Jack watched, the spider bounced once in a preparatory way, then began to scuttle toward him, its long legs striking eagerly at the sandy ground.

Jack was still staring at the spider, rigid with horror, when it *leaped,* knocking Jack flat on his back.

And now it was standing over him! It was bending down at him, blotting out the sky, and the distant roaring of the crowd was reaching a fever pitch. Jack's nostrils were filled with the spider's damp, musty smell. Layers of wet fangs split open like terrible flowers in front of him. There was nothing else in the world, nothing else to see but the dark maw and dripping fangs reaching toward him. And then—

"Stab me," said a voice.

There was a pause.

Jack had been screaming a bit. He screamed once more, but without quite so much conviction this time.

"Stab me," the voice repeated.

Jack stared. The dreadful mouth was still there, but it hadn't moved.

"Can you hear me?" asked the voice. The words were appearing in Jack's head, much as others had done before, but the effect was strangely soothing, as if soft, cool fingers were stroking his mind.

"Can you *hear* me?" the voice asked again.

"Y-yes?" said Jack aloud.

"Good," said the voice. "We don't have much time. Listen carefully."

As far as Jack was concerned, this instruction wasn't going to pose any problems. He had never listened more carefully to anything in his entire life, ever.

"The tip of your knife," said the voice, "is only a short

distance from my abdomen. If you drive your hand upward, right now, then you will stab me."

Jack did nothing, just gaped.

"Is there a problem?" asked the voice. "Can you move?"

"Er, yes," said Jack. "It's just—you *want* me to stab you?"

"Of course not. But it will be better for you if you are seen to put up a struggle, yes? So do it. Do it now."

Drawing on all his strength, Jack gripped the knife and jerked it upward. The spider had him pinned down; he couldn't see what effect the blow had had, but he felt something warm and slimy drip down and over his hand.

"Like—like that?" he asked.

"That's the best you can manage?" asked the voice.

"Yes," said Jack.

"Then it'll have to do. *YEEEEEEEEEEEEEE!*"

With a noise like hideously amplified chalk on a blackboard, the spider reared up over him, screeching. Jack watched the spider's massive black underside in awe as its legs twitched and shook, giving every impression of terrible agony. He could hear the crowd roaring and baying and clamoring, and for a moment he felt a strange kind of exhilaration.

Then the jaws came down. They closed around his neck.

And the spider bit him.

Jack could feel the spider's fangs in his neck, and a weird, wet, itchy dripping sensation as his blood began to well out around the punctures. But almost as soon as he had identified it, the feeling was gone. Jack wanted to scream some more—and why not? The situation certainly merited it—but he found he couldn't open his mouth. The blood seemed to be clogging in his veins, the breath was sticking in his chest, and Jack's vision was fading, filling with purple splashes that swam and spread, turning everything dark.

"There," said the spider. "Before you lose consciousness, I want you to know that—well, this isn't personal. I don't know you, I've never seen you before, and in any other circumstances it's quite possible that we might have become friends. I just want you to know," the spider repeated, "that I find that thought very distressing."

Oh, great, thought Jack weakly. *Thanks a bunch.*

"Goodbye, Jack," said the spider's voice. "Go with my blessing."

Then the purple patches spread to cover everything.

Well, Jack thought, *that's the last time I try and rescue anybody.*

Typical, he just had time to add. *This whole thing. It's absolutely bloody TYP—*

Then everything went black.

"Well," said the Emperor, looking down at Charlie. "That wasn't too exciting, was it? Really," he added, "was that the best you people can do?"

Charlie said nothing.

"I mean," the Emperor went on, gesturing out at the arena floor, "we've had shorter bouts, of course we have. But they've always been a bit more interesting than *that*."

The Emperor was looking at Charlie carefully, studying his reaction. A small smile played across his lips.

Charlie didn't move.

"*Wait, Charlie*," the Scourge told him firmly, speaking directly into his mind so the Emperor wouldn't hear. "**Our time will come, but only if you *wait*.**"

"You may leave us, Khentimentu," said the Emperor, still smiling. "Now."

"**Thank you, Sire,**" the Scourge replied. "**Come, Charlie.**"

They vanished.

When Charlie and the Scourge had gone, the Emperor relaxed on his mountain of cushions and munched meditatively on a sweetmeat.

Gukumat, at his side, bowed once more.

Shall I dispose of the small human in the usual way?

"No!" said the Emperor. "Heavens, no! What possible use could we have for a puny little blood-sack like that? I won't have my powers diluted, you know."

Indeed not, Sire, the Overminister replied. *How foolish of me.*

"Still," said the Emperor slowly.

Sire?

"Send him to Godfrey."

As you wish, my lord.

As soon as the command was given, it was done.

The Emperor settled back. Already the next combatants were entering the pit.

"He killed him," Charlie was saying. His eyes were unfocused: he was white and shaking. "He killed Jack!"

He and the Scourge were standing on the Needle again—the highest point of Hell, the place the demon had taken Charlie to first.

"Charlie—"

"Jack's dead!" said Charlie. "Jack followed me here, and now he's—"

"Charlie, listen to me," said the Scourge gently. "What do you want to do?"

Staring at the Scourge, Charlie thought about it.

He thought about staying up with Jack until four in the morning, watching zombie movies when they were supposed to be asleep.

He thought about the time in the Chinese restaurant with his dad: how he'd known Jack would come in with him and back him up, almost without having to ask him. Jack had always come with him, in all the time Charlie'd known him—even here, to Hell.

Jack's music taste was thoroughly dubious. His clothes were all bought by his mum. But Jack was Charlie's friend. And now he was gone. He was gone, and the Emperor had smiled.

Charlie drew one hand across his nose, wiping away the tears and snot onto the leg of his black jeans. He blinked.

"The Emperor," he said slowly, figuring it out. "I want to kill the Emperor."

"I do too," said the Scourge.

They looked at each other.

"Killing him," said Charlie. "That's what you—?"

"If we kill the Emperor," said the Scourge, "we can take his place on the throne. And then all his power—all Hell itself—will be ours, to do with as we wish."

"Can we do it?" asked Charlie. "Do you think it's possible?"

"As I said," the Scourge replied, "it won't be easy. But our chances will be greatly improved, I believe, if we work together."

Charlie sniffed again and looked out at the view. All around them, Hell glittered like dewdrops on a spiderweb. Already, the warm breeze was drying his tears to a crust.

"All right," he said. "Let's do it."

"Good," said the Scourge. "Very good."

ORIGINS

Holding steady in the air seven floors up outside Alembic House, Esme reached out one hand and knocked.

After a long pause, the curtains on the other side of the window slid open by perhaps a foot, and a white-faced, stunned-looking Felix loomed up out of the shadows of the room beyond.

"We have to talk," Esme mouthed through the glass.

Floating smoothly some two feet away from the wall, she slid through the air round the corner and came upon a small balcony, accessible from an open French window. Felix was waiting for her there. Esme spread her arms, drifted up over the balustrade, and touched down, her bare feet cold on the stone. Then she looked at him.

"Hi," said Felix, attempting a smile.

"Hello," said Esme.

"Are you up early? Or late?" Felix asked, once he'd closed the window. "I was just, ah, having a drink. The president of Paraguay has sent me some rather wonderful brandy. I don't suppose you'd—?"

Esme shook her head.

"Quite right!" said Felix awkwardly. "Very well, then. Do come through."

Silently, Esme followed him into the sitting room. The thick curtains were drawn tight: only one or two shafts of daylight betrayed the fact that it was early morning.

"All right," said Felix. "What can I do for you?"

"What do you know about a group called the Sons of the Scorpion Flail?" Esme asked bluntly.

Felix blinked. "Well," he said, "officially, they don't exist, of course. Off the record, I've heard . . . rumors. They started out as a branch of the Freemasons, would you believe. They've been peddling their supernatural cloak-and-dagger act all over the world for more than three hundred years. Why do you ask?"

"They've taken over the theater," Esme told him.

"Esme," said Felix slowly, looking at her, "would you mind telling me what's going on? The Scourge attacked me, and the next thing I knew I was lying on a table in the butterfly room. No one was around, so I called my driver and now—"

"The Scourge has escaped to Hell," Esme interrupted. "Raymond is dead."

"Oh, Esme," said Felix, shocked. "I'm so sorry."

Esme just shook her head. She wasn't interested in sympathy.

"Just before the Scourge killed him," she began, then stopped. The word *killed* seemed to have a physical shape: it left a tingling mark on her tongue. "It said something. It said that it's too late for me. It said that it's always been too late for me and that I should 'just ask Felix.' What do you think it meant?"

She looked at him. He had gone very still.

"It killed them all, Felix," she said, when he didn't answer. "Nick, Jessica, Raymond—everyone. But you woke up and went home like nothing had happened. It left you alive, Felix. Why?"

For another long moment there was silence.

"What did Raymond tell you," Felix asked, turning his glass in his hands, "about why I let out the Scourge?"

"He said that you did it for power," Esme answered. "He said you released the Scourge because the others in the Brotherhood were always better at stuff than you: you did it because you were jealous."

"Jealous?" echoed Felix with a sad smile. "Well, that's true in a way, I suppose. But I didn't release the Scourge just for power."

"No? Why, then?"

Felix took a deep breath. "I suppose it's time you heard the truth." Gesturing at another chair, he sat down and took a sip of his brandy.

Esme crossed her arms and just waited.

"A long time ago," said Felix slowly, "I . . . met someone." He looked up at Esme. "She was beautiful, clever, and thoroughly wonderful, and I loved her with an intensity that I scarcely would've believed possible. There was, however, one problem." He paused. "She was in love with somebody else."

Esme just looked at him.

"We worked together, she and I," said Felix, "so I was lucky enough to see her every day. I told myself I'd learn to be content with that. Perhaps I even believed it. But as time dragged past and my feelings didn't change, I began to become sick."

Felix sipped again.

"The color drained out of my life," he said. "My love was eating me up inside like a disease: sometimes I thought I could feel it killing me. And then, one day, one horrible day, I thought of something I could do about it."

"What?"

"Magic," said Felix simply.

Esme stared at him.

"Nick taught us to use our power in different ways," Felix explained. "Disguise was one. My attempts were always short-lived—partial, at best—but the potential of it began to obsess me. You see, with enough power, it seemed to me, a person could make themselves resemble *anyone*. You could even make yourself look so much like someone else that *nobody would know the difference.*

"Of course," he added, "I knew I couldn't do it alone. As you say, I just wasn't strong enough. But it occurred to me that I knew someone who might be."

"Who?" Esme asked.

"One night," said Felix, "that was all I wanted: one night with the woman I loved. And I realized that there was a way I could be granted that." He looked at Esme, hard. "For a price."

There was a pause.

"You don't—" said Esme.

Then, "No. You're not seriously telling me that's what you—"

Her brain was reeling. She could hardly get the words out.

"I mean, that's why you did it? *That's* why you let out the Scourge? So it could help you *pretend to be my dad* and . . ." She made a face. "With my *mother*?"

"I loved her," said Felix solemnly, "more than my own life. More than life itself—more than anything. And if I could have her love, even just once—"

"Even though she thought you were someone else?"

"Even though it was a lie," said Felix. "You're still young. You don't underst—"

"I understand pretty well. That's the weirdest, most disgusting, pathetic—"

"Call me names, if you like," said Felix. "You'll find it doesn't help. Believe me."

"But . . . you released the Scourge!" Esme spluttered. "You betrayed the Brotherhood! For—"

"Look," said Felix. "You know that phrase 'madly in love'? Have you ever thought about what that means? As long as I got what I wanted, I didn't care what happened! As long as I got," he repeated slowly and sadly, "what I wanted."

There was another pause. A long one this time.

"So, all right," said Esme, grimacing. "That's why you let out the Scourge. But that's got nothing to do with *me*, has it? What did the Scourge mean when it said it was 'too late' for me? That's what I'm asking."

"And that—I'm afraid—is what I'm telling you."

"Felix," said Esme, "I'm getting fed up now. Why don't you just tell me what you mean?"

Felix took a big swig of his brandy and swallowed hard.

"When I let the demon out," he said heavily, "it didn't make the break for the Fracture straightaway. The Scourge was weak to begin with: weak enough for me to think I could control it. It took over nine months before I found out how wrong I was. What a horrible mistake I'd made."

"Wait a second," said Esme. "Nine months? *Nine months* went past between you releasing the Scourge and it . . . ?"

Then suddenly, she felt a great rushing sound, like black wings closing around her. The world went dark, and all she could hear were voices.

There's something a bit special about you, said one.

It's always been too late for her, said another.

And then, with dreadful inevitability, something inside her clicked and fell into place.

"No," she said. "No. It *can't* be."

"Esme, I was afraid of this," said Felix. "For nearly fifteen years I've been hoping and praying it's not true. But I think . . ." He bit his lip. "I think the reason the Scourge left me alive is that it wants me to tell you."

He took a deep breath.

"What if Raymond wasn't really your father?" he asked. "I mean, think of your powers," he went on, leaning forward on his chair again. "Your flying. Your speed. Esme, I believe you were conceived while I was *possessed*. What if all your gifts don't come from your mother, or—or from me, but from . . . ?"

But to Esme, his mouth was moving but no sound was coming out. The only thing she could hear were the voices:

Something a bit special . . .

It's too late for her.

You're not human!

It's always *been too late for her. Just ask Felix.*

A strange pressure seemed to be building in the room: a dreadful focusing, as tremendous forces shifted and stirred.

"No," said Esme, breathing hard. Then she screamed it aloud. "NO!"

The voices, the black-wings sensation, and the pressure in the room all suddenly receded—and she could see Felix again, staring up at her, white-faced.

"You're wrong!" Esme told him. "Okay? You're just wrong, that's all."

There was silence.

Sleep, Esme told herself. Suddenly, she had to get some sleep.

"Look, do you have a spare room?" she asked.

"Seven of them," said Felix miserably.

"One without windows," Esme told him. "Sometimes when I have dreams I get . . . restless."

"Certainly," said Felix. "Whatever you want. Anything that's in my power to give, it's yours for the asking."

For another long moment Esme looked down at the little businessman.

An idea occurred to her.

"You know," she said, "actually, there is one thing."

"Yes?"

"It'll be simple," she told him. "You almost did it before. In fact," she went on, her skin beginning to tingle, "if my mother hadn't stopped you, you'd have done it already, instead of leaving it for the next sucker to do."

"Sorry?" said Felix. "I'm afraid I don't understand."

"They say that whoever the Scourge possesses can never really be freed," she told him. "Would you say that's true?"

"Certainly," said Felix. "In all the years since, there hasn't been a day that's gone past when I haven't felt its influence inside me. And as for the nights . . ." He shuddered.

"You're going to help me open the Fracture, Felix," said Esme.

Watching him gape at her, she smiled.

"I'm going after them," she told him slowly. "I'm going after the Scourge. To Hell."

TYPICAL

Blank.

There was nothing: no time, no sensation. There wasn't even enough of him to *tell* that there was no time and no sensation. Not, that is, until—

WHAM!

"Can you hear me, small human?" asked a high, elderly voice. "Hello in there? Hello?"

"What," asked Jack, none too politely, "do you want?"

"I have a couple of questions to ask. Are you ready?"

Jack said nothing.

"Splendid," said the voice anyway. "Well, it's like this. Since, as I think you'll agree, your last body was, let's say . . . somewhat underwhelming, I've decided to create you a new one. Before I begin, it seems only fair to ask if you have any preferences."

For a long moment, Jack thought about this.

"Sorry?" he asked finally.

"Now, I'm going to make some suggestions," said the voice,

"and all you have to do is tell me yes or no. All right? Let's start slowly. How about a tail?"

Jack said nothing.

"You can't go wrong with a tail," said the voice with sudden enthusiasm. "Extra balance in a fight. Prehensile, if you like. Or with spikes, a poisonous sting—whatever you like!"

"No," said Jack, with difficulty. "No tail."

"Claws, then," said the voice. "Retractable. Unbreakable. Good for climbing, hunting, or . . . hm . . . *close* work."

"No," said Jack. "No claws."

"As you wish," said the voice. "I think we can assume, however, that at the very least you'll be wanting a thicker *hide*. Hmmm. Bony plates on the shoulders, maybe."

"No."

"A thick, horny ridge on the head, strong enough to take a direct hit."

"No," said Jack firmly. "No horny ridge. No claws. No tail. Nothing! For Christ's sake, why can't you just leave me *alone*?"

There was an icy pause.

"Fine," snapped the voice. "See if I care!"

Then the darkness took him again.

"There," said the voice, sometime later.

Is he awake? asked another—one Jack remembered from the arena.

"He can hear us. It'll be a minute or two before he can respond."

Gladiator Jack, the second voice announced. *In accordance with the wishes of his most merciful Eminence the Emperor Ebisu Eller-Kong Hacha'Frav—*

With a soft click, the speech stopped dead.

"Enough of that for the time being, I think. Just open your eyes, please, and take everything in. Slowly."

Blearily, Jack did as he was told.

He was lying on a long, low couch in what appeared to be an ordinary hospital room. Beside him stood what looked, to Jack's eyes at least, like a man. The man looked old—his cheeks were sunken in, and his beard, though neatly trimmed, was shot with gray. He was wearing a rumpled tweed suit with patches on the elbows, a red woolen tie, and, Jack noticed, a gray woolly V-neck jumper.

"How do you do?" said the man. "I'm God."

Jack just looked at him.

Something of an awkward pause began to develop. The man frowned.

"You know," he began tetchily, "in most cultures, the polite response to being told someone's name is to reply with your own."

Jack blinked. "All right," he said. "I'm Jack."

"Yes," said the man. "I knew that, naturally. But I think it's important to observe the formalities, don't you? I mean, where would one be, otherwise?"

Jack blinked a couple more times. It didn't help.

"Am I . . . dead?" he managed finally.

"No. At least, not at the moment. I should've thought that was pretty obvious, to be honest."

"But you're God," said Jack, doing his best. "*The* God."

"Well!" The man's eyes twinkled. "That rather depends, doesn't it?"

"On what?"

"On which one of your lot's *funny books* you happen to prefer."

Jack stared at him.

The man made a *tsk*ing sound. "I should've known this'd be difficult," he said, and sighed again heavily.

"All right," he began. "If you're talking about belief in one all-powerful being who created the world, blah blah, then yes, technically I suppose you could say I'm 'the' God. After all," he explained, "it was me who created you."

"You . . . created me," echoed Jack, suddenly finding it hard to keep the sarcasm out of his voice.

"Not you personally," said the man. "Well," he added, "apart from just now. But I was there at the beginning: I caused it, you see."

"The beginning of what? Caused *what*?"

"Your world," said the man, grinning from ear to ear.

"It was a pet project of mine," he went on, while Jack gaped at him some more. "You know, like planting a tree. You put all the elements in place, all the things an organism needs to grow and flourish, and, well, you sit back and see what happens!"

"So what happened?" asked Jack.

"How d'you mean?"

"Well, assuming I believe you," said Jack.

"I can assure you," the man broke in, suddenly scowling, "it's never made the slightest difference to me whether you people believe in me or not."

Jack blinked. He'd clearly hit some kind of nerve there. *Whatever.* "What happened to you?" he persevered. "Why did you leave? And what are you doing here?" he added, his head beginning to hurt.

"Here in Hell, do you mean?"

"Well, yeah."

"My dear child," said the man. "Delighted as I am to be able to have at least a *semi*decent conversation with one of you at last, I must point out that this moment has been an extortionately long time in coming. As a species you really developed very slowly indeed, and the truth is . . . well, I got bored."

"Bored?"

"Life goes on, you know. I believe even *your* lot say that. And when the chance at the librarianship came up here, well, I took it. Much more interesting crowd, you see." He shrugged. "I'm sorry, but there it is. Now, how about taking a look at your new body, eh?"

Jack turned and looked down at the white sheet that came up to his neck. Parts of an earlier conversation about tails, claws, and so forth were coming back to him, and the religious implications of what he had heard suddenly didn't seem all that important anymore.

"Go on," said the man. "Take a look!"

Scared of what he might find, Jack yanked off the sheet. And saw—

"The same," said Jack. "It's the same."

"Mm." The man smiled a secretive little smile. "Looks that way, doesn't it? But I couldn't resist the idea of making just a couple of improvements. Tweaking you a bit here and there. You're a very old design, after all."

Jack was about to reply to this, when there was a soft *click* in his head, then—

May I remind you, Godfrey, that tampering with or inhibiting my telepathic transmissions is an offense punishable by—

"What's that?" asked "God." He winked at Jack, startling him. "What's that you say? I'm sorry, Gukumat, you're breaking up!"

I am not a fool, Godfrey. You would be ill advised to take me for one.

God just smirked. The voice behind Jack's eyeballs let out an icy sigh.

Is the gladiator ready to return to his cell?

"Oh yes," said God. "Quite ready. But Gukumat, could I ask you, please, not to bother me with things like this again? The Halls of Ages don't run themselves, you know."

Gladiator Jack, please be ready for transportation in three.

From nowhere, instantly, the jelly stuff had reappeared. It was slipping up under Jack's back.

Two.

The slime was encasing him, covering his whole body, sliding up over his face.

One.

Here we go again, Jack thought.

Zero.

And he was in his cell.

Jack sighed.

Then, very slowly and carefully, he began to feel himself all over.

It was a long process, and a strange one. After a while, he concluded that he certainly *felt* normal enough.

Finally, Jack settled down on the sandy floor as best he could. He lay curled up on his side, with his arm under his head: just then, that was enough. It had been a long day; he'd apparently come back from the dead, and any place to grab some kip was going to be fine by him.

Presently, he slept.

THE PITS

Jack was woken by a low grinding sound. He looked around and saw that one of the walls of his cell was moving—lifting, slowly and smoothly. The wall didn't stop at the ground, Jack saw: it continued straight down into it for a surprisingly long way. The yellow stone surface rumbled upward for about five seconds, then a gap appeared: a doorway.

Well, thought Jack, standing up, *after what I've had so far, what's the worst that can happen?*

He shuddered and told himself not to be so stupid.

Outside, across a thin strip of sandy floor, there was another cell, identical to his own—but Jack wasn't thinking about the cells anymore. He was thinking about their occupants: specifically, the coiled, sinewy shape on the floor of the cell that, as he continued to stare, suddenly *un*coiled itself a little, rose into the air, and looked right back at him.

"Fresh meat!" it exclaimed in a familiar scratchy voice.

The creature's face was wide and rubbery, with goggling bloodshot eyes. The rest of it reminded Jack, bizarrely, of a picture he'd seen once of the world's longest-ever tapeworm. The color was the same, a smeared mixture of rancid off-white and intestinal brown. Also, though Jack had never actually *smelled* a tapeworm, this thing was giving a pretty convincing impression of what that might be like—and a tapeworm not too long removed from its natural habitat, at that. Effortlessly, the beast nosed its way into Jack's cell: in a moment, its body had made a complete loop all around him—and still, Jack couldn't help noticing, a disconcerting amount of the rest of the creature's length remained behind it, on the floor of its own cell, its coils piled up, moist and glistening.

"Hello, fresh meat," it said, leering right in Jack's face— and the dizzying stench that came with the words almost buckled Jack's knees. "MMM-hmmm," it added, obviously liking what it saw. "Nice fresh thing. Nice fresh thing for Shargle!"

"Shargle!" barked a voice from outside, making Jack and the creature both jump. "Where are you? Get out here!"

A flash of annoyance crossed the hideous face, and the eyes turned in the direction of the passage outside.

"*Now*, Shargle. Or do you want me to tie your heads together again?"

"No, Inanna!" squeaked a voice from outside. "Not the tying! Not together! Not again!"

Jack stared. *Heads?* he thought dimly.

"I'm warning you, Shargle. My name's coming up, I can feel it, and I won't have my chances ruined just 'cause a long streak of pus like you won't come out of his cell!"

The worm creature made a furious hissing sound, then, with a sudden twisting movement, unwrapped itself from around Jack and backed out through the doorway.

"And whatever else is in there, you'd better follow him or I'll skewer you myself. Move!"

Jack obeyed without question. Still reeling from the smell, he stumbled out after Shargle. And his eyes went wide.

There were several reasons for this.

First, now that he was outside, he could see that his initial guess about his cell being just a part of something much larger had been dead right. He was surrounded by other doorways, leading to cells just like his own, stretching to either side as far as his eyes could see.

Second, he wasn't the only one coming out. Other creatures were too—all gradually forming up outside in the sandy passageway in an enormous and unruly line. He only had time for a quick glance each way, but what he saw was enough to make him feel very nervous indeed.

Third, well . . . when he looked up at what was standing in front of him, he couldn't *help* but stare.

Whoever she was, she was a good nine feet tall and unmistakably female. Her bulging torso was encased in some sort of black armored corset, a mass of straps, buckles, and—also unmistakably—weapons. She was festooned with swords and knives of every description, all arranged within easy reach of her hands. The hands themselves looked big enough to crush Jack's skull. She was completely bald, with some kind of tribal tattoo on her scalp. She had six silver rings in each ear and a silver spike through her bottom lip. Her arms were bare; muscles like bowling balls twitched and rippled all over her, and, oh yeah, she was *blue*.

She was looking at him.

"Inanna," she boomed.

"Er, sorry?" said Jack.

"Name's Inanna," the giant repeated. "And you are . . . ?"

"Jack."

"Bit small for this job, aren't you?"

"Um," said Jack. "Er . . ." But that was as far as he got. Quietly at first, a strange hissing sound began to fill the air. Somewhere, a long way away, a gong had been struck. Inanna shrugged, turned, and followed the line of monsters, who had begun to shuffle away along the sandy floor of the passage ahead.

"Move, fresh meat!" hissed Shargle into both his ears at once.

Flinching, Jack glanced round to find not one but two faces now leering into his.

Shargle has a head at both ends, thought Jack numbly— and, a moment later, an uncomfortable realization occurred to him as to why the creature's breath was so bad.

He started walking quickly.

Supplicants, boomed Gukumat's voice, *you have been summoned at the behest of Ebisu Eller-Kong Hacha'Fravashi, God of Rulers, God of the Dead, God of Darkness, God of Gods—*

"Yadda yadda yadda yadda," Jack heard Inanna mutter. "Come on."

This food you receive now is his gift to you, you penitents and seekers of boons. When you have taken your bowl, you may proceed to the dining hall.

"I take the bowl this time," hissed one of Shargle's heads suddenly. "*I* take the bowl."

"Uh-uh," spat the other quickly, rearing up to face its twin. "No way!"

"Yes!" squeaked the first. "*My* turn to do the eating! *You* do the other this time! MY TURN, MY TURN!"

Up ahead, something was making its way down the line—something unlike anything Jack had ever seen before. It basically consisted of six pale and disconcertingly human-looking legs, joined at the waist (knees pointing outward) to form a sort of arch shape. The place where the legs joined was wide and flat and held a tray on which were piled four tottering stacks of shiny black bowls: a pair of arms that sprouted from each side of the creature was busily handing them out. The legs walked with a rippling, spidery movement as the creature made its way down the row. Jack accepted his bowl, trying not to stare too much.

He could hear a long, low, rasping sound, a sound a little—no, a lot—like cheering. He kept walking, and the passage opened out into a space that took his breath away.

At the center of the dining hall was a vast and blazing bonfire. The floor of the hall sloped down gently toward it, and long curving tables of shiny black stone surrounded the fire in five concentric rings. Across the vast room from where Jack was standing, two more lines of gladiators were pouring out from other passageways beyond. But this wasn't where the cheering, which had seemed to double in strength when he emerged into the hall—was coming from. Jack looked up. The hall was like a massive chimney of black rock: being in it was like standing at the bottom of a dormant volcano. All around the wall of the room (though high enough to be well out of reach of any of the ground level's occupants) was some sort of observation deck. This upper level too was teeming with demons—some of them surprisingly smartly dressed, compared to the gladiators, but all of them cheering and yelling and waving and baying and barking and shrieking. Another packed observation deck was visible above it, and another above that. The walls stretched higher than Jack could see, and it was all he could do to tear his eyes from the sight and follow Inanna down one of the wide aisles to a table.

Presently, he sat down—and took a look at his dining companions.

Directly opposite him, in between a giant octopus and a thing like a big black praying mantis, sat a creature that looked, Jack thought, strangely normal. Mind you, he realized, his definition of "normal" had been pushed in some surprising new directions lately. The creature was a man, or at least he looked like one: he had only one head and a body not unlike Jack's own. The man's eyes were a bit blank and fishy looking, but he was looking at Jack interestedly enough, and—slowly, as if it were an effort for him—he smiled. Jack decided to take this as an encouraging sign.

"Er, hi!" he shouted. There had to be thousands of gladia-tors all around him, and most of them seemed to be banging their bowls on the table. "I'm Jack. What's your name?"

The man's grin got wider, but that was his only response.

Now, suddenly, Jack became aware that Shargle's heads had stopped squabbling with each other and were looking at him. The octopus and the mantis thing were too. Jack looked at the man again, and at that moment—

SPLOT!

The man's eyeballs dropped out of his face and fell into the bowl in front of him.

Empty eye sockets gaped at Jack like small wet mouths.

"Whee!" said the man. Then, louder, "*WHEEEEEEEEEE!*"

Then something nasty happened to his face.

It was as if his head were a balloon, and all the air had sud-denly been let out of it. The dome of his narrow skull seemed to sag inward, provoking a considerable outpouring of greenish-gray goo that followed the eyeballs out of the sock-ets and into the bowl, joining them there. The mouth kept screaming and grinning until the head collapsed utterly, at which point the scream subsided into a choked, wet gurgle. The empty skin of the man's face sat between his shoulders for a moment—shivered—then *melted*, as the whole of what Jack could see of his body (shoulders, everything) suddenly turned liquid and slid out of sight.

Then there was a pause.

The giant octopus could barely contain its hilarity. Its great bulbous sack of a head was quaking and rippling, its tentacles draped over each other and twitching in helpless little paroxysms. The big black mantis creature was rocking itself back and forth so hard that it almost toppled over backward.

"HAAAAAAH!" said Shargle. "HAAAH HAA HAA HAA! Didn't you like that, fresh meat? That was *you*—see? Jagmat pretended to be *you*!"

Jack said nothing. He waited as, gradually, the laughter subsided.

"That's very clever," said Jack slowly. "Oh yeah, I'm *really* impressed."

At his words, the thing sitting opposite seemed to re-form itself. What was in the bowl turned pink and slid back with a hiss, and in another moment the creature had reared up in its true form, a frozen man-sized explosion of pink custardlike stuff. It wobbled and shook. Big bubbles formed and popped on its skin, belching out words.

"Fresh meat!" it burped. "Fresh meat! Fresh meat!"

"Whatever," said Jack—and sighed. *Yep*, he thought. *Gang up on the new guy.* In some ways, when it came down to it, Hell was really pretty predictable. He turned away to look at Inanna and found to his surprise that she was smiling. The smile vanished as soon as she saw him looking. Still, Jack couldn't help but feel a small glow of triumph. Maybe—just maybe—he was getting the hang of things.

"Chinj!" yelled someone off to Jack's right, interrupting his thoughts. In another second, the cry was taken up by the whole room. "CHINJ! CHINNNNNNNNNNNNJ!"

Jack, and everyone, looked up.

High up in the vaults of the gigantic dining hall, something was happening. Jack couldn't really see what was going on at first: it looked to him as if the shadows up there had somehow come to life. A strange rattling, clattering sound was gradually making itself audible, and as the great black mass of shapes sank toward the light of the fire, Jack saw what was causing it. The air of the hall was packed with a flock of small, black, birdlike creatures.

"CHINNNNNNNNJ!" howled the mass of gladiators. "CHIIIIIIIIIIIIIIIINNNNNNNNNJ!"

Jack watched the twisting, skittering flight of the creatures as they continued their descent toward the waiting hordes below. Lower they came, circling wildly. Now, one by one, individuals were breaking away from the group, plummeting like falling rocks to land on the tables below.

Patience! said Gukumat's voice in Jack's head. *Your patience, please! There are enough Chinj for each and every one of you. You'll all receive your share in good time!*

The first "Chinj" to land on Jack's table was having a hard time dodging the various limbs and appendages that whipped out to grab at it. Jack realized it was coming in his direction.

In the context of what Jack had seen of Hell's inhabitants so far, the Chinj was surprisingly pretty. Its daintily folded leathery black wings were batlike, but it was bigger than any bat Jack had ever seen or heard of, and much more solid looking: its glossy, fat little body reminded him of those large furry microphones on sticks that you sometimes see when people are being interviewed on TV. The creature had a button nose and a small, perfectly heart-shaped mouth. Its large furry ears looked endearingly ridiculous. Its big dark eyes were wide and trusting, and—as, with soft thumps that rapidly became a thunderous rumble, more and more of its fellows landed on the tables around it—it walked straight up to where Jack was sitting, looked up at him, and smiled warmly.

"Good evening," it said, not taking its big black bush-baby eyes off Jack for a moment—even as impatience and outrage finally overcame the blancmange monster opposite and the Chinj had to dodge a slicing grab from a quivering pink pseudopod. Calmly refolding its umbrellalike wings, the Chinj came back to earth just behind Jack's bowl.

"You're new to all this, aren't you?" it said in its clear, musical voice, and its eyes took on a winsomely sympathetic expression. "I can tell."

"Er, yeah," said Jack.

"It's no problem," said the Chinj. "There's nothing to it, I assure you. Perhaps," it added, taking a step toward him, "you'd be so good as to put out your hand."

"Why?" asked Jack. He'd just caught sight of what was going on around the rest of the table and was a bit distracted.

"No, look at me," commanded the creature, then smiled coyly as Jack did as he was told. "You're much nicer than the others," it said, still looking up at him through long, furry eyelashes. "I know we're going to get on famously, if you'll only just trust me. Put out your hand."

"Well, okay," said Jack, then, "What? OW!"

With a movement that had been too fast for his eye to catch, the little creature had ducked forward and fixed its fangs into his thumb, hard. The Chinj's jaws tightened: Jack felt the liquid slither of its tiny tongue and the unmistakable beginnings of a powerful sucking action. It was drinking his blood! He struggled to escape, but the chair he was sitting on had somehow changed shape, and more of that hateful jelly stuff he'd first encountered in the Emperor's throne room now had his body and both his arms in an inescapable grip. Plus, weird things—as in, even *more* weird things—were now going on all around him.

All over the room, and to the obvious delight of the howling company of assembled demons, the small winged creatures were *being sick*. To either side of Jack, a neat line of Chinj stretched all along the table, and every single one (except his own, obviously) stood bent, heads over the bowls, quietly but comprehensively regurgitating as if their lives depended on it. It was this that had distracted Jack earlier.

"What are you doing?" he yelled weakly at the Chinj that was sucking his blood. In actual fact, the pain had lessened after the initial bite, and the sensation of having his blood drained was really not much worse than getting an injection at the doctor's, but still some yelling was in order. "Get off me!"

It did. As suddenly as it had bitten him, the bat thing relinquished its grip and sat up. A tiny blob of ruby-red blood dripped from its mouth and hit the shiny black surface of the table. Now it too took up its position behind Jack's bowl—but all its earlier grace was gone. It moved uncertainly, with shuffling steps, and it was beginning to look unmistakably ill.

"There," it wheezed. "Sorry." Its small bulging chest pumped in and out, and words were clearly a struggle. "Had to—take a sample," it gasped, "before—I—'scuse me."

It broke off, bowed over the edge of the bowl—and let fly.

The way the little creature was being sick wasn't at all like the way that people do it. When human beings "blow chunks," "shout soup," or "do a Technicolor yawn," it comes out a bit at a time. The way the Chinj was doing it (or *were* doing it—for they were all at it) was in a constant stream, its mouth wide, its head back, projecting a pouring torrent into Jack's bowl like water out of a high-pressure hose. The small creature looked perfectly serene, its eyes closed. The stuff coming out of its mouth was pale pink, the consistency of smooth porridge, and—unlike what you'd normally expect from the contents of someone's stomach—it smelled surprisingly sweet.

Now, one by one, all over the room, the bat things were straightening up, their job done. Presently, Jack's Chinj too suddenly stopped—the torrent cutting out as quickly as it had started. A little stiffly, it drew itself up to its full height (its eyes were about level with Jack's chin) and passed a dainty wingtip across its lips.

"There," it said, its large, dark eyes shining with obvious pride. Its furry body had shrunk considerably, and it was huddling its leathery wings around itself as though to keep warm. "Enjoy your meal, sir," it said.

"Oh," said Jack, realizing. "Er, thanks."

The creature smiled and unfurled its wings, ready to take off—but then it stopped, looked up and down the table, and made a beckoning gesture with one of its tiny front claws. Much to his own surprise, Jack found himself leaning closer to hear what the small creature had to say.

"We're not supposed to know about things like this," said the Chinj, in a voice that lost none of its conspiratorial quality for the creature's having to speak quite loudly to make itself heard over the surrounding din. "But between you and me, sir, I think your number's up." It smiled up at him delightedly. "I think you're going to be in the games this time! Isn't that exciting?"

"Yeah?" said Jack.

"You're a very lucky fellow," enthused the Chinj. "I *do* so hope it goes well for you. Now, have you got your boon all worked out?"

"My what?"

"Your boon. Your favor to ask of the Emperor. You know," it prompted, its eyes flashing joshingly, "if you win!"

"Oh," said Jack. "Right. Yeah."

"The best of luck, sir!" squeaked the creature.

"Thanks," Jack repeated.

"And may I just say how *delicious* you are," the Chinj added, glancing up at Jack coyly. "I do so hope we'll meet again soon."

"Sure," said Jack. "Likewise, I guess."

"Well, must dash," said the Chinj, unfurling its wings and

shaking itself a little, preparatory to liftoff. "Goodbye—and good luck!"

"Thanks," said Jack. "See you."

But the Chinj had already leaped into the air and was arrowing its way back up to wherever it had come from. In another second, it had vanished from sight.

Jack's arms (and most of the rest of his body, in fact) were still firmly held by the jelly chair. When he looked round, he could see that all the gladiators were similarly restrained. The jelly chairs of the blancmange monster and the octopus were having serious difficulty keeping their charges in check, so impatient were they to get at their bowls. But then the massive echoing hiss of the gong came again.

Jack's arms were released.

And as each and every gladiator except Jack lunged forward and tucked straight into their dinner, all the cheering and baying and yelling cut out completely, and the massive room went suddenly, eerily quiet.

Jack looked around.

Inanna had taken her bowl up in both her skull-crushing hands and was gulping the contents: the impressively large blob of her Adam's apple pulsed up and down on her thick blue neck. Shargle's heads butted and hissed at each other, making disgusting gurgling and bubbling noises whenever one of them managed to stick itself under the surface and slurp at the substance within. Jack's eyes returned to what was sitting on the table right in front of him. His own bowl of Chinj chunder.

He looked at the weird pink goo and the faint wreaths of

fragrant steam that still rose from its depths and found to his horror that his stomach was rumbling. With a sense of resignation, he reached for the bowl with both hands.

It felt warm.

It smelled sweet and creamy.

So he held his breath, lifted the bowl to his lips—

—and took the first sip.

A shiver ran down his back, part revulsion and part something else.

Pleasure.

The stuff tasted absolutely *delicious*. Like cauliflower soup, only sweeter. Milky, with a hint of coconut—only the consistency was quite thick, more like a puree than a liquid. As he took a gulp, then another and another, the stuff ran over his tongue with a weird, oaty, floury texture, and little clumps and threads of it clung to his teeth.

He was drinking *sick*: a part of him knew this, a large part. But the stuff was warm and nourishing, and it was making him feel better than he'd felt in a long time. The warmth of the stuff spread down his insides, making him tingle all over. He found himself tipping the bowl back, getting it all down, and as the flow slowed to a dribble, he ended up shaking the bowl to dislodge the last few drips. He wished he could have had more.

But suddenly, the gong was sounding again.

Pray silence, the voice intoned sonorously, *for the keeper of the pits. The invincible. The awesome . . . LORD SLINT!*

Something large and heavy shifted in the massive bonfire at the hall's center, releasing a shower of upward sparks, and the room was suddenly bathed in an unearthly glow. Jack looked up. High up on the wall on one side of the great hall, between two of the observation decks, a bright rosette of light unfurled as a circular tunnel opened. The light that came from within was blindingly bright, but as suddenly as it had appeared, it was blotted out: the immense and sinuous shape of the giant flying shark slid through it and out into the air beyond.

Tremble, supplicants, Gukumat announced, *as you discover whom among you is to meet their doom at tomorrow's games, and what form that doom is to take.*

The giant shark made a swishing circuit of the hall, just above the heads of the crowd on one of the observation decks, eliciting an appreciative chorus of oohs and aahs. The jelly chair tightened around Jack again, as if anticipating trouble— and that was when he realized that the shark was not alone.

It was surrounded by something that looked, at first, like a strange kind of golden cloud. As, in wide, lazy circles, the shark descended through the air, Jack saw that the cloud was made up of a shoal of tiny creatures a little like, well, fish. They looked like angelfish, with the same strange, flat, almost triangular bodies and the same long, elegant whiskers pointing and trail-ing above and below. Their colors were very beautiful: alter-nating vertical stripes of glossy black and glittering gold that caught the light of the great fire and flashed it back and forth until the walls of the great hall shone with spots of light like a gigantic mirror-ball effect. There must have been hundreds of them, glittering and shimmering and whisking through the air around their master's every movement like a golden, hazy halo.

And each one, Jack could see, held something in its mouth.

Plink!

Something had dropped and landed in the bowl of one of the gladiators further up Jack's table.

Plink!

Another of the silvery objects flashed down through the air, to land in the bowl of the black mantis creature. They were falling all over the room now, like the first spots of a strange, tinkling rain—and the watching demons on the observation decks were howling and cheering again.

"Who'd you get, Qat? Who'd you get?" chorused both Shargle's heads at once.

The mantis clicked its slimy black jaws together and reached one of its alarmingly large claws into the bowl. It pulled out a small shiny disc with a word printed into the center. The word was like no word Jack had ever seen; it seemed to swim before his eyes for a second before it resolved itself into what, he guessed, was a name: something like—

"Svatog?" barked Shargle. "*Svatog?* Haaaah! He'll make mincemeat out of you!"

"Arse!" belched the blancmange firmly. "Qat's got what it takes, ain't you, Qat?"

The coin things were falling thick and fast now, and the air of the great hall sang with the high ringing sound of their impacts. The shark continued to circle overhead, and the babbling of the gladiators was reaching a crescendo again. So far, to Jack's relief, no coin had yet landed in his bowl. He turned to look at Inanna—and had a surprise.

She too was staring up at what was going on. But her whole posture had changed completely. Just then, Jack thought, she looked for all the world like a kid in class with her hand up, begging for the chance to answer some question that the teacher has asked. The whole of her massive blue body seemed to be straining upward: her whole being seemed to be begging the golden shoal that spiraled and glittered above them, begging them to notice her.

She wants it, thought Jack, her earlier words coming back to him. *She* wants *the chance to fight. But then—*

Plink!

A coin dropped into Shargle's bowl. And then—

Plink!

Something flashed past Jack's eyes.

Jack knew what it was, with a terrible certainty, without having to look. And when he did look, he wasn't wrong.

There it was, still shivering to a stop at the bottom of his bowl: Jack's own coin. The Chinj had been right. His number *was* up. And in the center of the coin was a word.

"HAAAAAAAAAAAAAAAAAAAAH!!" yelled both Shargle's heads at once.

"Fresh meat and Shargle," Jack heard—barked, burped, and burbled by a multitude of mouths as word spread up and down the table. "Fresh meat and Shargle!" "Fresh meat and Shargle!"

"HEEEEEEEEEEE hee hee hee hee!" croaked Shargle, oily tears coursing down all four of his brown cheeks. "OOOOOh ho. No, that's too good. Hoo-HOO!"

The sound of the coins falling from above was drowned

out now as, for a moment, it felt like every single demon in the room was laughing at Jack.

"Oh, fresh meat!" Shargle crowed, wiping his eyes on his coils. "You won't *believe* what's in store for you. Just you wait! Why, I'll—"

But anything else the worm would have said was suddenly cut off by a terrible bellow from Inanna.

"NO!" she screamed suddenly. "NOOOOOOOOOO!"

As the whole of the room fell instantly, horribly silent, Jack looked up just in time to see the great shark, with three sinuous flicks of its body, rushing through the air back up to where it had come from. The golden shoal of fish things, their task completed, wasn't far behind. Already they too were vanishing back into the rose-shaped opening high above, right behind their master.

"NOOOOOOO!" shrieked Inanna again, her voice suddenly cracking with a despair that was terrible to hear. "Choose me!" she implored, straining up as her jelly chair struggled to hold her back. "CHOOSE ME!"

But the golden cloud was gone. The bright light of the wall's opening was blotted out as it closed. No more coin things were going to be dropped that night, even Jack could tell that. Now there was absolute silence in the room, as every single one of the thousands of gladiators waited to see what she'd do next.

Inanna closed her eyes, and for another moment her whole body was limp. Then she flung back her arms and exploded up out of her chair and onto her feet.

"It's a FIX!" she roared. "A FIX, I tell you!"

Jelly stuff was spreading and tightening around her, struggling to get her under control. Nonetheless, her words had already had their effect. A nasty murmur of agreement had spread around the hall of gladiators.

"Fix!" echoed the blancmange monster as the octopus began slamming its tentacles on the table.

"FIX!" roared the vast mass of demons with one voice. "FIX! *FIX!*"

Jack felt the jelly stuff that held him tightening the hardest it had yet, pressing and crushing in on him. The whole floor of the dining hall seemed to have gone soft and wet, as more and more of the stuff rushed to contain what was starting to look like a full-scale riot.

SILENCE! Gukumat's voice thundered in Jack's head, ringing in his brain and making big ugly blue flashes in front of his eyes. And indeed, the room did seem to be getting quieter, as each and every creature in it suddenly found itself locked in its own personal struggle with what held it.

You will all return to your cells, said the voice.

"Yeah?" someone yelled back. "And who's going to make us?"

You misunderstand, said Gukumat. *That was not a request.*

And at that moment, the pressure on Jack's body reached a climactic, terrible intensity. He felt like his brain was threatening to squeeze out of his eye sockets, much as the blancmange creature's had done earlier when it was trying to frighten him. He felt a hideous, bulging, *ripping* sensation—

—then darkness.

WEAPONS

The Scourge stopped walking and looked around. Apart from the way they'd come, three more vast corridors led away from the crossroads: ahead, left, and right.

The floor of the room they were standing in was marble, the center inlaid with a subtly repeating pattern of black and white tiles—but Charlie wasn't looking at the floor. The high ceilings were covered in lurid paintings depicting scenes from demon history in full and revolting detail—but Charlie wasn't looking at these, or at the giant fluted stone pillars that flanked the corridors either. He was looking at the Scourge.

"**Up one more floor, I think,**" it said.

"We've been up about twelve already," Charlie pointed out.

"**Seven, actually.**" The demon turned to him and held out its hands. "**Ready?**"

"Of course I'm ready."

"**Well then,**" said the Scourge—and with that, they lifted smoothly into the air.

Charlie watched the pattern on the floor shrink beneath his feet and scowled.

"Look," he said, as yet another colossal balcony hove into view all around them, "are you going to tell me what we're looking for or what?"

They swung away to one side, lifting effortlessly over the balcony's wrought-stone parapet.

"Weapons," the Scourge replied, as they came to rest soundlessly on one of the huge marble slabs that made up the floor on this level. "To kill the Emperor, we're going to need weapons—though it seems a little unfair to call them that. We're looking for Ashmon and Heshmim—"

"Ash-what and Hesh-who?"

"My familiars," finished the demon.

The Scourge turned and set off toward the nearest of the pillars, which seemed to continue exactly from where the ones on the floor below had stopped. It bent to examine the large blank slab of polished black rock that was attached to the pillar's base. Charlie heard a soft *flump!* Then the surface of the slab began to fill up from right to left with line upon line of intricate, inch-high letters. The letters were red and seemed to flicker like tiny flames.

"Hey," said Charlie, coming over for a look. "That's kind of cool. What's it say?"

The letters vanished.

"It *says*," said the Scourge, "that if you can be patient for just a little longer, we are almost there. This way, I think," it added, and set off down the corridor.

"We are now," the Scourge announced, "in a part of the palace known as the Halls of Ages. To my knowledge, the Emperors of Hell have never once thrown anything away: the Halls of Ages are where everything is kept."

"Sounds like my house," said Charlie.

"This whole section of the palace is a network of halls and corridors like these. To either side of us are rooms containing all manner of wonders—an incalculably valuable physical record of the whole of Hell's history."

"Which is why no one comes up here," said Charlie.

"Precisely," said the demon. "Ah," it added, suddenly coming to a stop at the foot of yet another enormous pillar, which looked exactly the same as the others. "I believe we've arrived."

"Yeah?"

"Oh yes," said the Scourge, with a small shudder of pleasure, "most definitely." It made a gesture in front of the column, and a section of solid fluted marble wobbled for a moment, then vanished, to reveal a surprisingly ordinary-looking door, with a small brass doorknob.

"After you, Charlie," said the Scourge.

"All right," said Charlie dubiously. He grasped the cool metal, turned it, and the door swung open to reveal a small dusty room. At its center stood a solid-looking dark wooden desk, on which stood the green-shaded brass reading lamp that was the room's only light. Sitting at this desk, still holding the book he'd been reading, was a startled-looking elderly man in a rumpled tweed suit with patches on the elbows.

"Kh-Khentimentu," the man stammered out finally.

"Godfrey!" said the Scourge. "**So good to see you.**"

"L-Likewise!" lied Godfrey, standing up.

"**Charlie, Godfrey.**"

"Hi," said Charlie.

"Oh!" Godfrey looked at the Scourge. "He isn't another . . . is he?"

"**Another what, Godfrey?**"

"You know," said Godfrey, with a coy smile. "Human."

"**He is human,**" said the Scourge. "**Yes.**"

"Oh, but—fascinating! Really?"

"**Really.**" The Scourge sighed. "**Godfrey, time *is* rather against us. Ashmon and Heshmim—are they here?**"

"Right," said Godfrey, suddenly nervous again. "Yes. Yes, of course." He got up and went over to the wall of small dark wooden drawers that lined the room from floor to ceiling. He reached into one, extracted something, and put it on the desk in front of Charlie.

"There we are," he said. "All present and correct."

"**At last,**" said the Scourge in a quiet, breathy voice. "**Go on, Charlie. Pick them up.**"

Charlie frowned. The two objects on the table were cylindrical and of equal size: two batons of perfect black, each maybe eight inches long and an inch and a half in diameter. Frankly, they didn't look very impressive. Still, Charlie shrugged and did as he was told, picking up one in each hand.

Instantly, he froze, horrified. At the first contact with his skin, the two strange objects seemed to melt, becoming oily and greasy in his hands. They were *warm* too, a sudden animal warmth that Charlie didn't like one bit. He made to drop them—and nothing happened! He shook his hands, palm down, over the surface of the desk, only to find that the two black objects clung to him obstinately. In another second they had lost their shape completely, running out and around his palms, a sudden oily welter of hot wet blackness that strung in ropy strands between his fingers, gluing them together. Now the stuff was running up his arms, two humped mounds of inky black, slithering round his shoulders, wriggling down his back, and playing in his hair.

"What the *Hell*?" he said.

"I present to you," said the Scourge, "**Ashmon and Heshmim. Ashmon and Heshmim? This is Charlie.**" At the demon's words, the two blacknesses suddenly sucked back into themselves, and all that was left were two small ferretlike creatures. They sat on Charlie's hands, staring at him intently with sharp, shining eyes.

"**Heshmim will defend you,**" said the Scourge. "**At a thought from you—or before you even think it—Heshmim will transform himself into shields or armor strong enough to repel almost any attack. Heshmim will also clothe you, with better than any of the rough garments you brought with you from your world.**

"**Ashmon,**" the Scourge went on, "**is for attack. He will assume the shape and properties of any weapon you can imagine.**"

"Not in here, though," put in Godfrey quickly. "Yes, practice with them *later*."

"**You will find, Charlie,**" said the Scourge, "**that a steady purpose and a strong will are not all that are required to rule. Sometimes—**"

Hiss, flick, WHAM!

An object like a three-foot-long black javelin had struck, quivering, in the wall behind Godfrey, some three millimeters to the right of his left ear. The javelin thing remained in the wall for another moment, then melted as Ashmon reassumed his ferret shape and scampered back to his place on Charlie's right hand.

"Eep," said Godfrey.

"Sometimes," said the Scourge, "you have to *act*."

"Coooooool," said Charlie.

"You may go out into the passage and get used to each other. Godfrey and I have to talk."

"Sure," said Charlie. He was up and out of the door in about a nanosecond.

The demon and the librarian turned to face each other.

"So," said God. "How've you, ah—been?"

"Much better, thank you," said the Scourge. "Now."

"It's, er, nice to see you!" said the librarian with obvious effort.

"Really?"

"Yes," said God. "Yes, of course it is! Er, why wouldn't it be?"

"I didn't think you would've expected to see me again," said the Scourge slowly. "My return from exile on that little . . . experiment of yours must be something of a shock to you, I would imagine."

"Wh-what do you mean?" asked God.

The demon didn't answer.

"N-now hold on just a second!" said God, stammering again. "You know perfectly well that I had nothing to do with what happened to you—nothing whatsoever! You were exiled on Earth because no one knew the place existed, but it might just as well have been anywhere! You were bound by a power far greater than mine, as you well know, so *how* you could even *think* that I—"

"Godfrey," said the Scourge, "**shut up.**"

God did as he was told.

The Scourge planted its liquid hands on the desk: they pooled there, at the end of its arms, glinting green in the light from the lamp. "**If I knew for certain,**" it began, leaning over the man in the chair. "**If I had so much as a shred of proof, Godfrey, that you had anything to do with my imprisonment on that world you created**—do you know what I'd do to you?"

God looked up at it.

"N-no," he said.

"**No,**" echoed the Scourge. "**You don't. But believe me, it would be far from pleasant. After all, I've had a very long time to work it out.**"

There was a pause.

"So," said God. "What are your, ah, plans?"

"**You know my plans,**" the Scourge replied. "**They have not changed.**"

"Oh," said God. "Oh dear."

"**With that human boy as my vessel,**" said the Scourge, gesturing out toward the passageway, "**I will kill the current Emperor and take my rightful place on the throne. Then, Godfrey, I will do what I originally set out to do.**"

"But surely," said God, "you *can't* still want to—?"

"I will awaken the Dragon," the Scourge told him, "and the Dragon will destroy the universe. All Creation shall be returned to the Void, and pure emptiness will reign once more.

"And this time," it added, standing up, "nothing is going to stop me."

THE PATH
OF VENGEANCE

Esme had lived above the theater her whole life. She knew every inch of it, every creak in every floorboard. The Sons of the Scorpion Flail had set sentries in case she came back, but they might as well not have bothered: Esme moved through the passageways like a ghost, in silence and darkness.

Look in my room, Raymond's voice echoed. *There's something for you.*

Part of Esme had been expecting that Raymond's room might have changed somehow. But of course it looked exactly the same.

It was full of him. Full of memories. There was his regimental photo from his SAS days, taken so long ago now that the Raymond in that picture was almost unrecognizable. Above that were his certificates from his years of brutal budo training with the Tokyo Riot Police. In the corner by the wardrobe, his outsized practice armor stood like the abandoned carapace of some giant insect that had molted and moved on.

She found what she was looking for easily enough, under the bed.

It was a rectangular narrow flight case—black, with steel-reinforced corners. The case was four feet long, a foot wide, and six inches deep.

When you're ready, when you know what to do, you use *it.*

Esme flipped the catches. As she lifted the lid, she was holding her breath. For a moment, she stared at what she saw, eyes wide, drinking it in. Then, still hardly daring to breathe, Esme reached into the case and lifted out what it contained. A strange sensation of pleasure spread up her arms and shivered through her whole body as she felt its weight.

At first glance, it looked a lot like her training sword—her bokken. The scabbard was made of the same plain, dark wood, and the overall dimensions of the sword were exactly the same too. But there was something unusual, she noticed, about the sword's tsuba. The disc of metal, which divides the handle from the blade and prevents your opponent's blade from simply sliding down yours and wounding your sword hand, was thicker than usual: a flat but solid-looking gold-colored lump, four inches in diameter at its widest points, cast roughly, but clearly, into the unmistakable shape of . . .

"A butterfly," said Esme aloud—and for a moment, then, she almost lost it.

Don't be soft, said Raymond's voice in her head. *Put it on.*

With a hard sniff, Esme slung the sword across her back. She adjusted the strap until it fit snugly and the grip lay close to her right hand. Then, reaching up without looking, Esme released the small catch that held the guard against the scabbard. It gave out a soft but deeply satisfying *click*.

In a fluid movement, she drew the sword. The soft hiss as it slid from the sheath was followed by a high, singing hum as the blade reverberated.

"Oh," she said. "Oh, Dad. It's beautiful."

Turning her wrists, she let the light from Raymond's bedside lamp play along the sword's edge. The warm glare traced the length of the blade from guard to tip: two feet eight inches of cold curved steel.

It was a pigeon sword—forged by Raymond's own peculiar process. For extra strength, it had been ground down and reshaped—*Seven times is my record*, she remembered him saying. It was the life's work of a master swordsmith, and it had been created just for her.

She let the sword dip once, twice in the air, in tiny, controlled chopping movements. The weapon, as Raymond had no doubt planned, was fractionally lighter than her training sword: it felt absolutely right in her hands.

"How do I look?" Esme asked aloud.

Deadly, Raymond's voice replied fervently. *Bloody* deadly.

The tears were coming freely now, but she smiled.

Less than two minutes later, she was back on the theater's roof. She unhooked the latch on the pigeon coop and flung it open. Esme stood there and watched the birds go: an explosion of wings, clattering off into the London night. Then, when she was ready—when she'd fully accepted that she (like the birds) might never come back—she followed them, dropping away into the dark.

By the time the Sons of the Scorpion Flail even got the door to the roof open, she was long gone.

"Esme, listen to me," Felix was saying presently, as they approached the ludicrous cream-colored pillars outside the Light of the Moon, the pub that was a gateway to Hell. "I've got to say, I'm really, *really* not sure about this. I mean, quite apart from the whole idea of you going on your own, I . . ." He winced inwardly, hearing the sound of his own voice. "Well, I don't know what it is you think *I* can do."

Esme wasn't even looking at him. She had her hands on the heavy padlock that held the pub's wide glass doors locked tight. There was a soft click. The padlock fell open.

"You're right about my never being really freed," Felix went on, "but if you think there's enough of the Scourge left inside me to help you open the Fracture, then—"

"Come on," Esme said, and set off into the darkness beyond.

Felix sighed heavily, and followed.

The pub had closed only a few hours before, and it stank, but it wasn't this that was making Felix uncomfortable. He was remembering the horror of the last time he had come here. The night when—through him—the Scourge had almost triumphed; the night when the woman he loved had died. Even in the dark, his footsteps led him unerringly on. Felix felt sick in his heart.

"Here," said Esme.

Felix put out a hand, and icy cold slid down his arm. There it was: the same cold space in the air, just above waist level. Beside him, he heard Esme take a deep breath.

"Ready?" she asked.

"Not really," said Felix. "No."

"Well, we're doing it anyway. *Go.*"

They both closed their eyes.

For six long seconds, nothing happened. Felix felt a stir of hope and relief. Perhaps the dreadful power that had taken him over all those years ago was really gone: perhaps there was nothing of it left inside him. "There," he was about to say. "Now let's go home."

But then, quietly at first, the whole room started to hum.

It was a sound that seemed to come from everywhere. The air thickened, tightening around them like polyethylene; then an eggshell-thin line of ruby-red light was appearing just in front of where he and Esme were standing. The crack in the air began to widen, revealing the freezing whiteness beyond. And in another moment . . .

It was done. The Fracture was open. All too easy.

Esme opened her eyes. Then she looked down at her hands.

"Esme?" said Felix.

"What?"

"The Fracture," said Felix, gesturing. "I didn't do any-thing."

"What do you mean?" Esme asked him. "It's open, isn't it? Maybe you did it without realizing."

"No," he replied. "I'm sure I—well, I think you did it by yourself."

They looked at each other.

"Esme," he began, "I—"

Esme cut him off. "Felix, if you're going to start telling me all that stuff about all my power coming from the Scourge again, then I don't want to hear it. All right? I know you don't want me to go. But I have a job to do."

She adjusted the strap that held the pigeon sword on her back. She checked the elastic bands holding her hair in place: they hadn't moved. She squared her shoulders and turned to face the gateway to Hell.

"Esme, wait!" said Felix.

"Goodbye, Felix," she told him. Already she was moving. She took one more deep breath, and she—

"FREEZE!" yelled another voice—one that definitely didn't belong to Felix.

She turned. The Fracture had lit up the whole room, which was now filling up with some forty armed men. It was the Sons of the Scorpion Flail. At last, it seemed, they had caught up with her. Esme blinked, and her chest and belly lit up with the bright red spots of laser sights as the men took aim.

"Wait, mademoiselle!" Number 3, the scar-faced man she'd spoken to before, was standing at the top of the steps: his mask was still off and his eyes were wild. "We can 'elp you!" he shouted again.

Esme just smiled grimly. No one could help her. She turned her back—on the men, on Felix, and on the world. She stepped into the freezing white light, feeling it take her—

—and she vanished.

"I am Ebisu Eller-Kong Hacha'Fravashi," the Emperor announced, sitting up on his throne. "God of Rulers, God of the Dead, God of Darkness, God of Gods. I am the Voice of the Void, whose breath is the wind and whose rage makes all worlds tremble. I am the Lord of Crossing-Places, the King of All Tears, and the Suzerain Absolute of the Dominions of Hell."

"Esme," said Esme. She was standing in the throne room, in almost the exact spot where Jack had stood when he'd arrived. "So," she added, "you're in charge here."

The Emperor's gaze narrowed and sharpened. "Yes," he said dryly. "I am in charge here. And what brings you to Hell, if you please?"

"I've come for the Scourge," said Esme.

"Really?" said the Emperor without much interest. "Why?"

"I'm going to recapture it and put it back in its prison," said Esme.

The Emperor's eyes went wide.

"Oh, but how *fascinating*!" he said, clapping his cloven hands.

"I'm glad that makes you happy," said Esme. "Now tell me, please. Where's the Scourge?"

"I'm afraid," said the Emperor, slowly and with relish, "that if you want a favor from me, you'll have to fight for it."

Esme looked at him. "What?"

"I won't let you see the Scourge without my permission. And if you want my permission . . ." The Emperor trailed off, smiling delightedly.

Esme blinked, then took a step toward the throne. "Fine," she said. "I'm ready."

"We shall see," was the reply.

Suddenly, Esme found she couldn't move. Some kind of jelly stuff seemed to have slithered up over the sides of the red carpet and trapped her feet. Already it was climbing up the legs of her combat pants. In another second it had pinned her arms to her sides and was slopping up over her shoulders.

"You will be taken to the gladiator pits," said the Emperor, sitting back on his throne, "together with the rest of the sup-plicants."

"I confess," he added, as the stuff covered her completely, then stiffened, ready for transport, "I can't wait to see you in action."

He gestured with his cloven hands. Esme disappeared.

Alone on his throne, the Emperor smiled. Really, the next day's action in the pits might prove the most diverting in a very long time.

AKACHAṢH

"Ah, *what?*" said Jack.

The jelly stuff had left him, but he wasn't at all where he'd been expecting to be. Instead of standing in the stone passageway again, he'd appeared in the auditorium's stands.

The banks of seats were filling up rapidly with other spectators: wherever Jack looked, sticky columns of jelly stuff were shimmering into being, then vanishing to reveal demons underneath. Dimly, Jack realized that he was going to need to find a place to sit down. But before he could search for any place other than where he was, which was practically next to the blancmangelike shape-shifting monster he'd met the night before, it was too late. It had noticed him.

"Hey!" it belched. "Wotsyerface!"

"Oh . . . hi," said Jack.

"Whatcha waiting for? Siddahhn. It ain't the royal box, but it's all we got, so . . ." The thing made a lashing gesture with one clammy pink flipper.

Reluctantly, Jack did as he was told.

"Jagmat," belched the blancmange monster.

"Jack," said Jack, hoping the creature had actually been telling him its name.

"Ehhh," it said, "about last night. You know, when I did all that . . ." Here the creature broke off, abruptly doing a sped-up version of the trick it had performed when they'd first met. It was every bit as disgusting as the first time, and Jack hadn't really needed reminding.

"Yeah?" he asked.

"Just a bit of fun, y'know. Someone always pulls some stunt on the fresh meat. S'traditional. Didnmeanuffinbyit."

"That's all right," said Jack distractedly. His attention had been caught by another demon settling itself down beside him: a flat-headed, oily-looking eel-like creature, about two meters long and as thick as Jack's leg. It nodded at Jack politely.

"Er, Jagmat?" Jack asked.

"Yep?"

"What's going on? I mean, I thought I was going to be fighting Shargle today. Not that I'm disappointed or anything," he added quickly.

"Big fight this time," was the reply.

"Yeah?" asked Jack. The auditorium was crowding up quickly, and before long he found himself pressed up a lot closer to his neighbors than he'd've liked.

"*Oh* yeah. The program's been all switched around. Even Inanna got a last-minute call-up."

"Really?"

"I reckon we're looking," the blancmange monster added, leaning even closer to Jack, "at an Akachash."

"A what?" said Jack. The word had left little moist pink spatters on his chin when Jagmat had said it. But the blancmange monster didn't answer.

Loyal subjects of the Emperor Hacha'Fravashi! boomed Gukumat's voice. A thrill went around the arena. *It gives me great pleasure to announce for you now that the next bout—*

"Whaddatellyou?" belched Jagmat.

—is an AKACHASH!

Instantly, Jack found he was standing up. He'd had no choice in the matter—the place was now so packed with demons that he couldn't have remained seated if he'd tried. Jack was in a bubble of sound, a cocoon of noise. All around him was hooting, roaring, baying, barking. His ears were battered with it.

SEVEN GO IN! roared the voice in his head, making stars blossom in front of Jack's eyes.

"ONE COMES OUT!" roared the crowd in answer, in a horrible clashing battery of tongues.

SILENCE! boomed the voice suddenly. As one, the crowd sat down.

First gladiator, the voice announced, as one of the arena's massive entrance slabs began to rise, *undefeated in seventeen straight bouts, with claws of steel and the cold of the Void itself in his heart—SVATOG THE CANCELER!*

"YAAAAAAAAAAGH!" yelled Jagmat. His whole wet pink amoeba body sprang into a glistening mass of thrashing tentacles, each one with a shrieking mouth at the end of it.

"Whoa," said Jack.

'Svatog the Canceler' shambled into the arena and stood there, blinking. He was a good size for a demon, perhaps eighteen feet tall. From the waist down, his body was glossy and black, a little like a horse's: his powerful-looking springy back legs ended in two great hooves that actually *smoked* (Jack couldn't help but notice) where they touched the ground. But it was Svatog's arms that tended to catch your eye first: they were *huge*. Forming a great horseshoe-shaped expanse of hulking muscle, they were so long that Svatog could comfortably lay each entire, massive, three-fingered hand out flat on the hot sand to either side of him. By contrast, Svatog's head looked almost comically small, not so much perched between his shoulders as set into his chest. He looked mean, Jack thought—mean and stupid.

"That's Svatog," Jagmat confided. "He's my mate, and he's going to KICK *AAAAAAAAAAARRRRRRRRRRRSSSSSSE!*" The blancmange monster suddenly leaped up again on the last word, his voice rising to a roar. The demon in the ring apparently heard him, for Svatog's eyes narrowed, and one of his great arms suddenly lifted to point in their direction.

SHHINNNG!

Jack and Jagmat found themselves looking down two great yard-long spikes of gleaming steel that seemed to have sprung from the spaces between the Svatog's fingers.

"YOU THE BOSS!" shrieked Jagmat. "YOU THE BOSS!"

Svatog winked slowly and retracted his claws. As his arm

sank back down to his side, the wide slash of his mouth burst open in a wet and toothless smile.

Second gladiator, said the voice, *a firm favorite among fight fans in the years that she has graced the pits—GLADRASH THE BLUNT!*

From somewhere beyond the great raised entrance stone came a deep, rhythmic rumbling sound. Suddenly, to the accompaniment of a howl of ecstasy from her fans, Svatog's first opponent came rocketing out of the gate and into the arena, like—

You have to be joking, thought Jack.

—well, like a bull at a bullfight.

Gladrash the Blunt looked a lot like a bull: a heaving great brown-black mass of meat and muscle, with wild white rolling eyes and mountainous haunches that humped and sank as her hooves pummeled the ground. The main thing about Gladrash the Blunt that was different, however, from any bull Jack had ever seen, was her size: Gladrash the Blunt was big. Very big. About the size of a bus, in fact.

At the sound of their heroine's name, a whole section of the audience suddenly erupted in cheers and screams of delight. Svatog's smile vanished, his eyes narrowing into a gormless but vivid scowl as the great cow shot out of her gate and trampled past him, kicking up dust. Gladrash skidded to a halt on the opposite side of the ring, snorting as she pawed at the sand with one plate-size front hoof. Jack just stared.

Third gladiator, said the voice, *TUNKU THE SNOOL!*

Another entrance slab ground upward, and the audience

fell suddenly quiet. When Jack saw what came out next, he understood why. It looked like nothing more than a large floating jellyfish: as it drifted out into the arena, its dimpled tentacles trailed delicately in the air beneath it.

"But that's ridiculous," said Jack, echoing the sentiments of most of the crowd. "What chance has that third one got? That Svatog guy'll just *step* on it."

"Wait and see, kid," muttered Jagmat. "Believe me, just 'cos Tunku's invertebrate that doesn't mean he hasn't got it where it counts."

Fourth gladiator, said the voice, *RIPITITH GUNCH!*

The figure that strode out into the ring now was broadly human looking, if a bit on the tall side. Ripitith Gunch was wrapped in a long black cloak that covered him all over, even down to his feet. The skin of his face was deathly pale, and his head was thin and strangely elongated, culminating in a great foot-long shock of blinding white hair that stuck straight out of his head like a crown of spikes. The crowd started booing.

"Cheat!" shrieked the eel thing. "CHEAT!"

"I hate that guy," said Jagmat, getting an acknowledging wild-eyed nod from the eel.

"Why?" asked Jack.

"All that transfiguration crap, 'stead of a straight fight," snorted the blancmange. "Cowardly, I'd call it."

"'Sright!" yapped the eel thing.

"I see," said Jack—though he obviously didn't.

"No, no, *no*," snapped the Emperor, up in the royal box. "I asked for the *pickled* spleens today, not the sugared ones! I *specifically* asked for the *pickled* ones!"

"A thousand apologies, Your Excellency," gasped the small lizardlike creature beside him, shuddering beneath a silver tray that was bigger than itself. Charlie looked on in disgust.

"I would have Lord Slint chew your legs off," said the Emperor, "if I didn't think such a puny job might hurt his feelings." He sat up and beckoned to Gukumat. "Where *is* Lord Slint, by the way?"

He is preparing to make his entrance, Sire.

"Good, good." Scowling, the Emperor turned to the lizard creature, who was still trembling at the corner of the dais. "Are you still here?"

"S-Sire?"

"Didn't I just tell you what I want? Or are you waiting for me to have you *skinned*?"

"In-indeed, Sire," stammered the lizard. "I shall fetch them at once."

"Leave the tray," said the Emperor.

"As you wish, Sire," the lizard replied, grunting with effort as he set the tray and the greenish-gray pyramid of its contents down within his master's reach. "I live to serve you," it squeaked, bowing low once more before scuttling from the room.

"I think you'll find this quite interesting, Charlie," said the Emperor, selecting a sweetmeat and turning to Charlie with a wide grin.

"I can't wait," Charlie replied, doing his best.

Fifth gladiator, Gukumat's announcing voice boomed out, *fresh in from the twelfth-segment stench pits—the GRAKU-LOUS SLOAT!*

A gasp of delighted disgust rose up from the crowd as they saw what came into the ring next. Charlie barely suppressed a shudder. It was something between a centipede and a hedge-hog. Some forty feet long, its cockroach-brown segmented body marched forward on a selection of disgusting, crab-like pincers, and a ridge of shuddering black spines ran in a line down the center of its back. Emerging into the white-hot light of the ring, the hideous creature suddenly reared up on its hind legs, exposing a flat, disc-shaped head and two evil yellow eyes. Its mouth, a mass of dripping mandibles, hinged open to let out a terrible gurgling hiss. The creature eyed its opponents, then shook itself contemptuously, as if shrugging them all off.

"Ah, the Sloat," said the Emperor, chewing luxuriously. "I think we're going to see great things from him."

Sixth gladiator, boomed Gukumat's announcing voice: *a longtime supplicant, first-time entrant, give a warm demon wel-come to . . . INANNA TWELVE-SWORDS!*

The rest of the audience fell quiet, content to gaze curi-ously as the big blue swordswoman strode into the ring—but the section of the auditorium where the uncalled gladiators were sitting erupted with cheers. Charlie watched the new-est entrant. The dark blue, leather-clad figure was well built, muscular, and bristling with weaponry, but to his eyes she didn't look like much, not next to more imposing contestants like Gladrash, Svatog, or the Sloat.

"Remember what I said, Gukumat," said the Emperor, in an uneasy tone that made Charlie turn and look at him. "No surprise results."

Do not disturb yourself, Majesty. Lord Slint has been alerted to your feelings on this matter. It has all been taken care of.

"Good." The Emperor and the Overminister exchanged a look, then, still grinning widely, Hacha'Fravashi turned to look at Charlie. "I've another surprise for you," he said.

"Yeah?"

"A new acquisition for the gladiator pits," said the Emperor airily, though the golden slits of his eyes never left Charlie's for an instant. "She arrived yesterday. Another acquaintance of yours."

"Acquaintance?" echoed Charlie.

Still grinning, the Emperor settled back in his seat. Raising one immaculately suited arm, he pointed at the ring. Charlie looked—and his eyes went wide.

Seventh and final gladiator, boomed the voice, *a surprise late entry! Newly arrived from the as-yet-unclaimed planet of Earth, and perhaps the best opposition that world has to offer, show your appreciation for Miss ESME LEVERTON!*

FAVORS

Jack's mouth fell open.

It was her. His head filled with questions like, How did she open the Fracture? What was she doing there? Had she come to rescue them? But as he watched her walking out calmly onto the white sand of the arena floor in her red top with the hood up, the main thing Jack thought was—

Oh no.

Suddenly, he realized that everyone was looking at him. He had said the words aloud.

"Friendayours?" belched Jagmat, nudging him. The eyes— and other organs of attention—of the entire row seemed to swing round and focus on Jack as they waited for his answer. Jack felt the blood climbing up his neck and into his face.

"Yeah," he managed.

"Well, no offense, mate," said Jagmat, "but I hope she's better than you."

"**She came**," said the Scourge.

"Surprised?" said the Emperor.

"Yes," said Charlie, fighting to keep his expression blank. "Yes I am. Has she . . . said what she wants?"

"I'll be hearing her request officially in a moment," said the Emperor. He smiled. "But I think you already know what it is."

"She's come for us," said Charlie.

The Emperor's smile only widened.

"**She will have to survive the Akachash first**," said the Scourge.

As referee for this fight, said Gukumat, *O loyal subjects, we present to you none other than the keeper of the pits himself: the Clashing Jaws, the Potentate of Pain, the Undisputed Master of the Ring . . . LORD SLINT!*

A hatch screwed open in the wall just below the royal box, and the great shape of the flying shark emerged into view, blotting out half the scene below. With a single lazy swish of his horribly scarred tail, Lord Slint propelled himself down through the air toward the ecstatic crowds. As the seven gladiators waited, with varying degrees of self-restraint, the shark made three wide, lazy circuits over the audience, provoking a Mexican wave effect as he did so.

Svatog, Gladrash, and Gunch, Gukumat went on, *your requests are already known to the Emperor. Tunku: you do not wish your request known unless you win. As for you other three,*

His Highness the Emperor will now hear your supplications. Fifth gladiator, what is your boon?

The Sloat gave a great shudder. Rearing up on its hind legs once more, its disgusting brown jaws hinged open, its unspeakable poison-tipped mandibles mashing together as it ground out a single word: "FLESH."

A thrill shook through the crowd.

Inanna Twelve-Swords, state your request. Briefly, please, the voice added as Inanna strode forward, her great black-leather-clad torso bulging as she took a deep breath before she spoke.

"Demons of Hell," she shouted, "I have waited a long time for my chance in this ring, and this is the favor that I ask. I come from a far corner of the Demon Empire, a world called Bethesda. We are a peaceful people. A hardworking people. But the tithes and taxes we have been forced to pay lately are more than we can bear. Now, I'm going to give you," she went on, raking the other gladiators with a piercing glare, "a display of fighting you have never seen. And in return, I ask only that the Emperor and his Overminister relax the *grossly* unfair—"

Thank you, sixth gladiator.

"—and cruel demands they have—"

Thank you, sixth gladiator, the voice repeated, losing patience.

"—seen fit to inflict on a planet that never did them any harm!"

That will be all!

"MY PEOPLE ARE STARVING!" boomed Inanna in a voice that echoed round the great stadium even despite the booing and jeering of the crowd. "ALL I WANT IS THAT YOU PUT RIGHT WHAT YOU HAVE DONE!"

Sixth gladiator, said the voice.

The sand of the arena floor went dark around Inanna as Lord Slint settled, gently, in the air just over her head. Big as she was, Inanna would go down the great shark's gullet in not much more than a single mouthful. Looking up, she fell silent and her face turned grim.

You will hold your peace, or the consequences will be swift and painful, Gukumat told her, in a voice that only she could hear. Inanna scowled for a moment, then nodded curtly.

Seventh gladiator, you may speak, said Gukumat, in his announcer's voice again.

All eyes in the ring turned to Esme.

Esme just stood there at first, staring up at the royal box.

Speak, Gukumat repeated. *The Emperor is listening.*

Never taking her eyes off the distant bulk of the royal box, Esme took a step forward. She pulled back her hood, opened her mouth, and, in a quiet voice that everyone there heard quite distinctly, said, "It doesn't have to be this way."

In the royal box, the Emperor smiled. Then he got out of his seat.

Sire, Gukumat muttered, *keep back from the window. It's not safe!*

But the Emperor had already brushed the Overminister aside. He walked straight up to the great sandy sill and spread out his hands on it luxuriously. He leaned out into the open air and replied, "Oh yes? And why is that?"

Now the silence in the arena was intense. To the absolute and certain knowledge of every demon there present, the Emperor had never answered a gladiator directly in this way. Never.

"You could just give me what I want," said Esme.

"Which is what again? Remind me."

"The Scourge," said Esme, the steel in her voice sending a cold chill down Charlie's back. "Let me fight the Scourge."

A buzz of fevered speculation spread round the audience, quelling itself quickly when the Emperor opened his mouth to answer.

"I *shall* let you fight the Scourge," he said grandly. "*If* you win."

"I have no quarrel with you or these others here," said Esme, casting a glance around the ring at the six other gladiators. The Sloat rippled its legs listlessly, but the other, more experienced fighters did not react. "But for them, and for you, this is the last chance. Give me the Scourge."

In the rows around the royal box, a bit of guffawing and tittering broke out among the more aristocratic demons.

"I told you," said the Emperor, pretending to be surprised. "*If* you win!"

"Then everyone in this ring," said Esme simply, "is going to die."

For a moment, there was shocked silence.

Then, suddenly, the whole arena was laughing. Svatog even

joined in, the great foghorn grunts of his glee bouncing off the great black walls and echoing round the pit.

Esme's expression didn't change in the slightest—and the Emperor, despite himself, found his own smile beginning to fade.

"We'll see." He spun on his heel and went back to his royal seat. "She has courage, I'll give her that," he said, frowning as he settled himself. "Gukumat, I grow weary of preliminaries. Let's get this under way."

With pleasure, Your Magnificence, Gukumat replied with a bow.

GLADIATORS, his voice boomed in the heads of everyone present, *TAKE YOUR POSITIONS!*

Every demon in the audience began to stamp the ground in time. The rhythm was slow, unhurried, and merciless at first.

Crash. Crash. CRASH-CRASH-CRASH!

Crash. Crash. CRASH-CRASH-CRASH!

But it quickly got louder and faster, reaching an ecstasy of noise and thunder, and now, suddenly, the whole crowd was up for it, ready for the blood, ready for the carnage, ready to scream and howl and roar their guts out at the terrible battle that was about to take place on the shining white sand of the arena floor below. The noise of the crowd was like a solid thing, pressing on Jack until he was dizzy with it.

And, said Gukumat, pausing fractionally.

BEGIN!

THE FIGHT

As soon as the command was given, the cheering died away to an excited murmur.

Esme unstrapped the pigeon sword from her back: now she held it by her hip, in her left hand, her fingers loosely encircling the top of the dark wooden scabbard. She let her right hand fall easily to her side again: she bounced a couple of jogging steps on the spot, to ease a little of the tension in her legs—then she was ready.

Ninety-nine times out of a hundred, Raymond had always told her, *a fight'll be decided in the first few seconds.*

Esme glanced round the ring. Her attention was caught by Inanna, the tall blue woman: for a moment, they looked at each other—then Esme let her eyes flick onward as she waited to see which of her opponents was going to make the first move.

It didn't take much longer to find out.

To the delight of the crowd, Svatog the Canceler—standing some twelve yards off to Esme's right—was the first to lose his patience. With a heave of his arms, he lifted both his feet off the ground and *slammed* them down, hard enough to make the earth tremble under Esme's trainers. Turning toward Esme and flinging his arms wide (the gleaming steel claws sprang out to either side), he pushed out his great black chest—

—and screamed.

The sound was incredible. Like the blast of a steam engine, the acrid gust of his roar blew out at Esme with the force of a thirty-mile-an-hour wind. His squinty eyes bulged with rage and the roar continued, on and on, until it seemed it would never stop. Svatog's smoking hooves smacked into the ground, a step toward Esme, and another step. The crowd roared with him, waiting for blood, waiting to see the small human girl torn to shreds whenever Svatog chose to bring those clawed arms of his together.

Esme stood still.

Jack, frozen in his seat by helpless horror, glimpsed a blur of movement.

A glint of something flashing in the light.

Then, suddenly, the scream stopped.

The audience too fell silent. Why had Svatog gone quiet? Why was he just standing there like that? And *why* did the girl now have her *back* to him?

For a long, slow moment, nothing happened. Then, with a terrible, echoing hiss, something burst. The sand at Svatog's feet turned suddenly black. The eighteen-foot-tall demon sank to his knees, then fell on his face—hitting the arena floor with a ringing *smack*.

"What?" said Jack.

"Holy crap!" belched Jagmat.

One gladiator down, five to go.

The crowd erupted.

Esme just stood there, with the pigeon sword out in front of her. Outwardly she was perfectly composed—but inwardly her highly trained fighter's mind was working at full speed, alert to every detail of what would happen next.

Because then the battle really began.

Without warning, drawing one of her own curved swords, Inanna leaped sideways—and struck. For a second, as the wide blade bit into the fluttering black of his cloak, it looked like the bout was already all over for Inanna's neighbor, Ripi-tith Gunch.

But something strange was happening. The fourth gladiator's cloak was moving, shifting—changing. For one more long second, his narrow face seemed to hang in the air, his cruel mouth opening in a hideous grin.

Then the place where he'd been standing simply burst apart, into a boiling, tearing, chittering brown cloud of . . .

What?

Screaming with frustration, Inanna threw one of her arms up to cover her face as a swarm of locusts suddenly engulfed her. The swarm blasted past her in a tornado of beige insectile wings that seethed in the air and left a long black shadow on the arena floor, as her opponent—transfigured—sped out of her reach.

Meanwhile, with a bellowing scream, Gladrash the Blunt set off on a galloping circuit of the ring. The giant cow had not yet reached top speed by the time she reached Esme, but the thundering hooves would certainly have squashed her flat if she hadn't been watching. A leap, straight up into the air, tucking her legs under her into a smooth flip—and Gladrash's charge passed through empty space. Still, the giant cow kept on, kicking up dust, thundering toward her next opponent—Inanna.

The Sloat's legs gave a convulsive ripple, and it advanced away from the shadows at the arena's edge. Hissing nastily and grinning through its mandibles, it brought its face low onto the blinding white of the sandy floor, arching its long body up and over behind its head. The ridge of foot-long spines along its back began to quiver. As Esme dropped to her feet, the Sloat took a deep breath that made the membranous sacs on either side of its mouth bulge with effort—

—and it fired the spines straight at Esme.

Ripitith Gunch, rematerializing in the center of his cloud of locusts just behind Esme, with his long knife drawn and ready, transfigured himself back again suddenly as he realized his surprise attack was mistimed. As a flock of bats this time, he poured, shrieking, across the ring again, but not before several of his flock had been brought down, caught in midair, to expire, convulsing on the sand as the poison of the Sloat's stings worked its own awful magic. Gunch took himself in his bat-flock form to the far end of the ring, gathering the elements of himself into a shivering black column before he rematerialized fully. He looked down. There were three or four gaping holes in his cloak. He tutted and tossed the frayed edge of the cloak over one shoulder. Then, suddenly, he stiffened. His eyes bulged. His cold blood seemed to thicken and congeal in his veins. For a second more, he stood there shuddering—then he too fell facedown dead on the sand.

Two down, four to go. The crowd was in raptures. Tunku the Snool showed no reaction at all. The long, thin tentacle that had touched the transfiguration master on the back of the neck retracted up toward the floating watery sac of Tunku's jellyfish body, its poison exhausted. But there were plenty more where that one came from. Tunku the Snool sank back into the shadows, waiting.

And meanwhile, Esme was fighting for her life.

The Sloat's volley of poison-tipped spines was spread too wide: there had been no time to jump or dodge. Dropping the scabbard, Esme had taken the pigeon sword in both hands and—with a speed born of instinct as much as her years of training—she was knocking the spines away out of the air. The pigeon sword flickered in her hands. The air in front of her was a silvery blur, and the stings were clattering against the massive stone slabs to either side of the ring. But they were coming too fast, even for her.

Esme stepped back and, with a desperate outward blow of the pigeon sword, caught a low incoming spine and turned it aside. But now the sword was too far away from her body to catch the next one in time. She dropped flat onto her back. Twisting, she brought her right foot up for a kick that caught the last spine in midair, smacking it away.

But then, with a dreadful hiss, the Sloat charged.

Its dripping mandibles clashed shut in a blow that would have severed both Esme's legs at the thigh if she hadn't been fast enough: at the last possible moment, she flipped backward and up onto her feet, bringing her sword up in front of her with a desperate lurch. Confronted by the flashing blade, the Sloat reared up, hissing, giving Esme the precious seconds she needed to back out of striking distance.

Esme cursed herself inwardly. She'd been lucky: concentrating on an opponent's attack rather than the opponent was an amateur's mistake. Now too there were just too many factors, too many thoughts tearing at her concentration, demanding attention. She was watching the Sloat—but what about the other gladiators? She could track Gladrash by the sound of her hooves: the giant cow creature was making wild circuits of the ring, charging at whoever or whatever was in her way. But as to where any of Esme's other opponents were, why, one could be right *behind*—

Hold on: she'd had an idea. The corners of Esme's mouth twitched and lifted in the tiniest ghost of a smile. Then she attacked.

The gleaming blade of the pigeon sword hissed in the air. The Sloat ducked its broad, flat head, and Esme's stinging cross-body slash passed it harmlessly—millimeters from contact. Surprised, the foul beast danced back, its legs rippling. Holding the pigeon sword's long grip near the pommel for extra extension, Esme swung again, slashing downward. The Sloat counterattacked, snapping out at Esme's legs with its pincers—but they closed on nothing. Esme had sprung into another tight roll in the air, forward this time, whipping her feet round until they landed—

—hard—

—down on the top of the Sloat's head, driving it into the ground with a two-footed stomp that had her full weight behind it.

There was a gratifyingly nasty popping sound. The crowd roared its approval. Esme jumped clear, and both combatants staggered back from each other.

The Sloat backed away dazedly. One of its great mandibles was hanging off by a grisly flap.

Esme straightened up, breathing hard. The last move had taken a lot out of her, and she could see that while she'd wounded the Sloat, it wasn't seriously weakened. All she'd really done was annoy it. However, it was now quite close to the ring's edge—its hindquarters were plunged in shadow, some three yards from the black stone wall. It might be enough.

Suddenly, in a frenzy, the Sloat lunged, driving its wounded head straight into Esme's body, knocking her flat on her back. With two ringing *thunks*, the Sloat jabbed each of its front pincers into the sand on either side of her.

Esme was trapped.

The monstrous creature regarded her unblinkingly. Fat milky droplets of putrescent slime were dripping from its ruined mouth, sizzling and spitting as they hit the sand, and the broken mandible dangled horribly. Still, the Sloat *hissed*, a deep hiss of contentment and delight. It reared up, looked down at Esme one last time.

And it saw she was smiling.

The crowd was in a frenzy now—roaring, screaming,

baying, barking. But under that, suddenly, the Sloat could hear another sound. A rhythmic, walloping, thundering sound, getting closer and closer. Now the smile on the small human morsel's lips had widened into a vicious, wicked grin: the Sloat's insect brain lit up with a flash of realization—

And then, with a terrible bellow of joy, Gladrash struck.

The Sloat reared up as the giant cow trampled it, its whole body an explosion of pain. Esme flung herself to comparative safety, the horrible *smutch* as the great hooves hit home still echoing in her ears. The Sloat's armored sides simply burst, spreading the creature's innards in a wide, wet circle, staining the sand. The Sloat's head and forequarters, comparatively unscathed, plucked at the arena floor weakly as what remained of the creature tried to pull itself toward her, staring at her wildly. It knew: it *knew* she'd tricked it.

But Esme had already turned her back on it—and in another moment, it was dead.

Strike three.

Esme allowed herself a deep breath. Then she was taking in the situation.

The giant cow's eyes were wild and bloodshot, and she was definitely favoring her front hoof. Ignoring the howls of her fans in the crowd, Gladrash lowered her wide black head, bellowing, as she charged again—at Inanna this time.

Esme watched.

The big blue swordswoman stood her ground as the giant cow thundered closer and closer. At the last possible second—when it looked to Esme like Inanna might let

Gladrash trample her too—she leaped to one side, bringing the curved blade of her scimitar round and down in a crashing blow that sent the giant cow almost to her knees.

Gladrash staggered on past Inanna and ran straight into the arena wall beyond. Her supporters—a whole section of the audience—let out a short gasping sigh and sank to their seats in horror. Gladrash the Blunt tottered back from the wall, swinging round to face her opponent, shaking her horned head as if trying to clear it.

Then she froze and fell and lay still.

Strike four.

Scowling, Inanna turned, with her back now to the line of shadow at the arena's sides. That was when Esme saw Tunku the Snool. The jellyfish slid from the darkness, tentacles outstretched. Almost before Esme knew what she was doing, the pigeon sword was out of her hand. It flew across the ring—

—passed straight over Inanna's shoulder—

—and nailed the third gladiator to the sheer black stone of the arena wall.

For a second, the crowd fell silent. Tunku the Snool just hung there, spitted. Its tentacles quivered for a moment, then dropped.

Strike five.

Suddenly, the whole crowd was up out of its seats again, screaming and howling and crying with delight. No one could remember an Akachash as good as this. No one.

Looking carefully at Esme, Inanna walked slowly over to the arena's edge, only taking her eye off the girl for a moment when she reached up to yank the pigeon sword out of the wall. As, with a soft *splotch*, the jellyfish demon slid to the arena floor behind her, Inanna took the weapon and hefted it, testing its balance. In her hands, the pigeon sword was like a toy. Then, with a snapping motion of her wrist that was almost too fast to follow, Inanna flung the sword back at Esme.

Esme put up a hand, and the pigeon sword's hilt slapped into it effortlessly. Then, as the crowd fell expectantly silent again, the last two gladiators eyed each other.

"I don't want to fight you," said Esme.

Inanna gave her a pitying look, then—*SHINNNG!*—drew her other scimitar. Now both her hands held the huge, curved blades. Slowly, deliberately, she took a step toward Esme.

"I mean, you've got a good reason to be here too, right?" Esme looked away from Inanna and called up toward the royal box. "Give us both what we want. This finishes now!"

Of course, there was no answer.

Some of the crowd started jeering and booing.

"Get on with it!" someone bellowed.

Slowly, the audience started their stamping, rhythmic crashing noise again, the sound that Esme had heard just before the start of the fight.

Crash. Crash. CRASH-CRASH-CRASH!

Crash. Crash. CRASH-CRASH-CRASH!

Inanna flexed her wrists, letting her scimitars spin and twist around her. The wide, curved blades glimmered and flashed as she sped them up, letting them cross and recross in front of her, a glittering whirlwind of razor-edged steel. She took another step toward her opponent: only a few more and she would be in striking range.

Esme didn't move.

"What's wrong?" asked the Emperor, up in the royal box. "Why isn't she defending herself? What's she doing?"

No one answered.

"Gukumat, if Inanna *wins*," the Emperor went on, his voice rising to an anxious whine, "I will be most displeased. Do you understand?"

The crashing got louder as the audience settled themselves back in their seats contentedly. What was coming next ought to be pretty good.

Jack, alone in the noise of the crowd, felt sick.

Wearily, grimly, Esme brought the pigeon sword up to a ready position. She sighed.

"All right, then," she said.

Inanna didn't answer, just lunged.

And in less than two seconds—

—two blurring, *lurching* seconds—

—it was over.

"I'm sorry," said Esme quietly.

Inanna froze, and the audience's rhythmic thumping died away in confusion as they saw her swords drop from her hands. She looked down from her opponent to the wound that had appeared down the length of her chest—a long, diagonal slash that stretched from her left shoulder down to her right hip. Then, still disbelieving, she looked back up at the girl who had just defeated her.

Inanna had waited a long time for her chance in the ring—her chance to ask the Emperor's favor. Now both were gone, in three moves.

The first had been a simple step back—the girl had been more ready than Inanna had realized. The blow itself had come in the second move. Esme had timed her attack exquisitely, reading the pattern in the swirling blur of Inanna's swords and striking at the exact point when her foe was unprotected—pulling herself clear (the third move) before the whirling blades could close around her and do any damage. It was, Inanna had to admit, beautifully done—and, strangely, she was glad.

Entertainment—that's what the crowd had wanted. They'd wanted her and Esme to get into some long and complicated battle—maybe even bantering with each other a little while they fought, trading witty insults as well as injuries: that sort of thing would have gone down well, for sure. Well, she was happy not to have given them the satisfaction.

Inanna's great knees buckled under her, and her head went light.

"I'm sorry," said Esme again.

Inanna just smiled. Then she died.

For a long second, Esme looked down at her opponent. She sniffed and, still holding the pigeon sword lightly with one hand, wiped a long brown arm across her brow. Then she glared up at the royal box.

"There," she said. "Are you satisfied? Is *that*," she added, gesturing at Inanna's fallen body with the sword, "what you wanted?"

"Marvelous," said the Emperor, relief at the outcome only adding to his delight. "Quite marvelous." He turned to Charlie. "And what was it again, in comparison, that you said you had in *your* world?"

Charlie looked at him blankly.

"Ah yes," sneered the Emperor. "Football."

My lord . . . ? asked Overminister Gukumat quietly.

"Oh yes," said the Emperor. "I think so, don't you? Definitely."

Congratulations, Gladiator Esme, said the Overminister's announcing voice. *His Highness the Emperor Hacha'Fravashi salutes a well-fought bout and has indicated that he may, in this instance, grant you one boon. What is your favor to be?*

"Riches!" cawed a scrawny, alligatorlike creature in the audience, jumping up and down. "Riches! Riches!"

"I told you what I want," said Esme.

Say it again, gladiator, the voice murmured in her head. *The audience wants to hear you.*

"The Scourge!" said Esme, exasperated. "Bring me the Scourge!"

Gladiator Esme has stated her boon, Gukumat announced grandly. *In view of her spectacular performance—*

Some of the slower members of the audience, who had blinked or otherwise failed to catch the last part of the battle (which was most of them), let out a great and disappointed *boo* at this.

—and her status as undisputed champion of this Akachash,

His Excellency the Emperor, in his infinite generosity, has decided to accede to her request.

"We shall have to face her, Charlie," said the Scourge, in a voice only Charlie could hear. "I'm afraid I see no other choice. Are you ready?"

"All right," said Charlie, taking a deep breath. "Yeah. Okay. We'll do it."

"No," said the Emperor, "you won't."

THE CHALLENGE

Loyal subjects, said the Overminister, once Inanna's body too had disappeared like the others, *it gives me great pleasure to announce that, while the Akachash itself is over, Miss Esme Leverton has been granted permission for one more, final battle.*

Esme, standing in the center of the ring now, was concentrating on preparing herself. She retrieved the pigeon sword's scabbard and slotted it home. She reached up and felt the elastic bands that were holding her hair back: they hadn't moved. She straightened her spine and squared her shoulders; she jogged a couple of bouncing steps on the spot. She was tired. But now she was ready.

Gladiator Esme has come to Hell with one single purpose in mind—to wreak her vengeance on the one who is about to step into the ring.

A delighted anticipatory murmur spread through the crowd. In the royal box, Charlie stood up; the Scourge did too—

—then vanished, bursting suddenly into a whirling haze of powder-black vapor, which gathered around Charlie like his own personal storm cloud. The Scourge settled on him, taking hold: instantly, the curving hooks and spikes of the black tattoo began to boil and wriggle under Charlie's skin.

Most loyal subjects, Gukumat intoned, *I present to you a demon whose very name is the stuff of legend. Put your appendages together, my brethren, for the Prince of Darkness! The Sultan of Sorrows! The Dragon's Awakener, returned at last— KHENTIMENTU THE SCOURGE!*

Charlie stepped up to the window of the royal box and dove off.

Liquid darkness unfurled about him like a pair of enormous black wings. As the crowd roared its approval, Charlie descended through the air with regal grace and landed in the center of the arena. The darkness billowed, gathering itself around him into a sizzling, rippling tornado of black, then evaporated.

"Hi, Esme," he said.

"Charlie," Esme replied.

"You shouldn't have come."

Esme's lip curled. "Really."

Charlie sighed. "Look," he said, "you don't understand. Me and the Scourge—we're partners now. And we've got things to do here, important things."

Esme shook her head. "I'm going to give you one more chance," she said, taking a deliberate step toward him. "If you've got any vestige of self-respect, any shred of guts or decency, then you'll take it."

"What?"

"Concentrate," said Esme. "You can force the demon out. Make it let go of you. If you want."

Charlie didn't answer.

"Partners," Esme echoed, exasperated. "Look around you! And what about the announcement just now? I didn't hear *your* name—did you? Just the Scourge's!" She took another step toward him. "Charlie, if you don't help me now, then that's the way it's always going to be. You're a puppet," she added. "Nothing more. Is that really what you want?"

"No," said Charlie, frowning.

"Well, then . . ."

Esme held out her hand.

Watching in the crowd, Jack held his breath.

"No," said Charlie again, his frown getting deeper.

Esme looked at him, waiting.

"**No**," the word came out of his mouth again, and the black liquid patterns boiled and slithered in the skin of his arms.

Esme let her hand fall to her side.

"No," said Charlie once more, quietly. He shook his head. "This is too important. And what we have, the Scourge and me—it's not how you think."

"Then I'm sorry," said Esme, "but that makes you my enemy."

Crash. Crash. CRASH-CRASH-CRASH!

Crash. Crash. CRASH-CRASH-CRASH!

The crowd stamped out their excitement. Jack stared at Charlie and Esme—stared down at the two figures until they shimmered in front of his smarting eyes against the blazing white of the arena floor. Again he was surrounded by the cocoon of noise: it pressed and pushed and battered at him as the demons around him howled out for blood.

But the command to begin never came.

"What is it?" he asked, turning to Jagmat, as the crowd noise died away confusedly. "What's going on?"

Jagmat shrugged—an impressive and slightly alarming sight. "It's a private duel," he belched. "There'll be terms."

"What?"

"See for yourself," said Jagmat, gesturing with a wet pink flipper.

For a second more, Charlie and Esme looked at each other. Then they both vanished.

This duel, Gukumat announced, to boos and wails from the audience, *will be held in private, and at a later date. And now, on with the show!*

And that, it appeared, was that.

"What's wrong, sir?" asked Jack's Chinj later as, grimly, Jack sipped at his dinner. "You seem a little preoccupied, if you don't mind my saying so."

"He's scared!" shrieked one of Shargle's heads delightedly, seizing the opportunity to spread some misery now that it had lost the evening's battle over which end of the worm got to do the eating and which the . . . other function. "What's gonna happen tomorrow, fresh meat?" it crowed. "Maybe you die nasty! Maybe you don't come back!"

Jack ignored the worm utterly.

"It's my friends," he admitted to the small bat creature. "I'm worried about them."

"The two other visitors?" said the Chinj. "Esme and Charlie?"

Jack almost choked on his mouthful. "Yes!" he said. "Do you know something? What's happened to them? Nobody here knows anything!" he added, nodding at the serried ranks of guzzling demons that surrounded him.

"Well, of course they don't," said the Chinj primly. "They're gladiators."

"But you do?"

The small creature gave a secretive smile. "Finish your gruel," it ordered, "or I'm not saying a word."

Obediently, Jack raised the bowl of still-steaming goo to his lips and took another gulp.

"Tonight," whispered the Chinj conspiratorially. "It's happening tonight! Isn't that exciting?"

Jack put down the bowl. The Chinj was staring at him with wide eyes.

"I mean, can you *imagine*, sir?" it asked. "A real grudge duel, outside of the pits! A fight to the death, in the Emperor's own chambers no less! I'd give anything to be there, wouldn't you? It'll be thrilling!" it added, with an ecstatic little shiver of its wings.

So, thought Jack, it was true, then. The last little hope that maybe they weren't going to fight, the last ridiculous chance he'd been clinging to, winked out inside him and died. Jack gave the Chinj a long look.

"My friends are going to kill each other," he said slowly. "*Thrilling* isn't really the word I'd use to describe it."

THE EMPEROR

Charlie lifted his arm, and living darkness poured down over his hands. His fingers vanished under the velvety warmth, closing together and extending—and now Charlie held in his hands an exact replica of the pigeon sword. The long, curved blade glinted in the light, its tip lining up between his eyes and his opponent's.

"All right," he said. "Let's do this."

Charlie and Esme were standing in the Emperor's throne room, facing each other along the narrow strip of bloodred carpet that led up to the throne itself. The great domed ceiling loomed above them. All around them, the rippling jelly stuff that made up the rest of the room's floor heaved and subsided like an oily sea. Past Esme, the Emperor was lolling on his throne, grinning. For a second, Charlie looked at him.

Esme was standing between him and the throne—literally. The only way to get to the Emperor—the only way to avenge Jack and carry out the Scourge's plan—was through her. Charlie didn't want to hurt her. He didn't want to kill her. But Esme had followed him here. She had got in his way. And now there was no choice.

Esme's amber eyes remained fixed on his, her expression neutral. She held the pigeon sword by its dark wooden scabbard in her left hand, loosely, up near the hilt; her right hand was stuck nonchalantly in the pocket of her combats.

"You haven't drawn your sword," Charlie pointed out.

"Full marks for observation," she replied.

Charlie sighed. "Look," he said. Already he was angry with her. "Do you want to do this or what?"

Instead of answering, Esme gestured at him with the pigeon sword's pommel.

"That thing in your hand," she said. "You ever used one before?"

"Esme," said Charlie wearily, "just draw your sword."

"You think you're a match for me?"

"Draw your sword!" Charlie repeated.

"Or what?" said Esme. "What do you think you're going to do?"

"Fine," said Charlie, running the hand that wasn't holding the sword through his hair angrily. *"Fine."*

He set his feet a little apart, spreading his weight.

"Ready or not, then," he said, with a smile that showed his teeth, "here I come."

He took his sword in both hands, leaped into the air, and flew at her.

SHINNNG! *WHUD!*

Warding Charlie's blade off easily with her still-scabbarded sword, Esme had stepped toward him. Her whole body weight, therefore, plus whatever forward momentum Charlie had put into his attack, was concentrated in the heel of her right hand as it struck the point of Charlie's chin, palm open, hard. She'd hit him that way before—in exactly the same place, in fact—one of the very first times they'd fought.

Charlie's head snapped back. The force of the blow lifted him off his feet. He sailed a clear ten yards back through the air—and crashed, eyes wide with surprise and shock, on his back.

"You're an idiot, Charlie," she told him.

Still without drawing her weapon, Esme advanced on him. Her amber eyes flashed down at him fiercely.

Charlie got to his knees, then his feet, pointing his sword toward her, frowning uncertainly as she approached.

"I gave you a chance to start making up for what you've done," Esme said. "You rejected it. If it wasn't for that, I might almost be feeling sorry for you right now. As it is, I'm just sick of the sight of you. You're an *amateur*," she spat, knocking his blade almost out of his hand with the still-scabbarded pigeon sword. "An *accident*," she added, dealing Charlie's blade another smacking blow. "And this—"

SHANG!

"—has gone on—"

SHING!

"—long *enough*."

Charlie was holding his sword high up in front of his chest, expecting her to hit it again. He was completely unable to defend himself, then, when Esme took her sword by its grip and lunged, low and hard.

The steel-capped tip of the pigeon sword's scabbard crashed into his stomach. Doubled up around her blow, Charlie flew back again, the breath driven out of him in a long and undignified gasp. When he next looked up at her, he was grimacing with pain.

The black tattoo—its curves, its hooks, its spikes—was spreading under his skin, pouring down his arms like oil, running up into his face.

"When you're ready," Esme told him.

Bristling with rage, Charlie got up and started toward her.

Esme's thoughts went something like this.

All she needed, she knew, was an opening, a chance to strike at Charlie before the Scourge could take over and protect him. To get it, she planned to needle Charlie, probing mercilessly at his swollen pride until she provoked him into an error big enough to give her the opportunity she wanted. Then she would take her chance and . . .

And what? Kill him?

Esme frowned, not moving, as she watched him getting closer and closer.

The only way to get at the Scourge, she told herself—the only way to do what she'd spent her whole life training to do—was through the boy. She knew this. And the boy was an idiot. He was stupid and selfish and seemingly entirely lacking in self-control.

But—and this was the problem, now that it came down to it—did being an idiot mean that Charlie deserved to *die*?

Suddenly, when he was still outside normal striking

distance, Charlie made a snapping motion with the wrist of his right hand and flung something at her.

It wasn't the sword—at least, not anymore. In the fractions of a second that it took to cross the space between them, the weapon in Charlie's hand had somehow lost its shape, the glinting steel vanishing and stretching and liquifying. Whatever it was now, it was long and black, and it hissed through the air with something like eagerness. Esme stepped smoothly aside, expecting the weapon to pass her, but it turned to follow her—

—and caught round her neck! It wrapped right round her throat, then constricted, its coils tightening and crushing inward round her neck like a snake's coils on its prey. Excruciating pain flashed and fizzed through her whole body like a thousand-volt dose of electricity. Instantly, Esme drew the pigeon sword and severed the whatever-it-was just inches in front of her chin. Dropping the scabbard, she reached up with her left hand, grabbed the wriggling black tentacle thing that still clung to her neck, and flung it away. Spreading her arms, she leaped backward, out of Charlie's reach.

Something was wrong with the places where the weapon had touched her—badly wrong. The skin of her neck when she felt it had that deadened, bulbous feeling that comes just before blistering. Where she'd touched it, her fingers were numb, cold, as if they were frostbitten. Holding the pigeon sword up in front of her, she stepped back, stepped back from Charlie for the first time—and stared.

Leaving no mark, the ink-black severed part of the weapon

slid across the carpet in a liquid blob. Just before reaching Charlie it transformed, becoming a strange kind of ferretlike creature, scampering back up Charlie's leg before vanishing into the blackness that now bulged and rippled all over his body.

Charlie smiled.

"Cute," said Esme, through her teeth. "Very cute."

Still smiling, a smile that was horrible with the way the tattoo was now swarming up into his face, Charlie started to walk toward her again.

"That's quite some toy you've got there," Esme told him. "Something the Scourge gave you, maybe? Like it knew you couldn't do anything to me with an actual *sword*?"

Charlie shook his head as if to clear it but kept walking.

Well, there was no way she could risk another blow like that. So, no mercy, then. No more games.

Without any further warning, she attacked.

With an echoing *crack*, Charlie found himself parrying a sizzling slash that—if he had stopped to think instead of instinctively lifting one demon-reinforced arm to block it— would certainly have ended the fight there and then.

Esme frowned.

CHING! CHING! CHING! CHING! CHING!

Esme launched a stinging succession of lightning blows, but Charlie's reinforced arms seemed to move by themselves as they caught and blocked them.

She feinted and spun, shaping for a wide cross-body slash but suddenly converting it into a roundhouse kick that struck

Charlie hard in the ribs. He staggered back. But not as far as she'd hoped. He was protected, shielded—*armored* somehow—by the same liquid stuff as his weapons.

So Esme did the feinting kick.

She began the move in textbook style, leaping off her left foot into a spinning midkick with her right. With utter predictability, Charlie lowered his hands to protect himself, at which point Esme folded her right leg into a further 180-degree spin, letting her left foot scythe up over Charlie's guard, striking him in the face.

Bingo. Charlie flew back a good ten feet—

—twenty—

—and smacked into the nearest wall. He sank to his haunches, propped there, his head lolling. There. Now, before things got any worse, it was time to finish it.

Esme leaped, flinging herself through the air toward her enemy. She let out a scream, raising her sword over her head with both hands as the bloodred strip of the throne room floor slid past underneath her. She brought the pigeon sword out and down, concentrating all her speed and strength into the two feet eight inches of hissing steel and the enemy that would die at its edge.

The curves and hooks of the black tattoo seemed to bunch in Charlie's face. Charlie's still-open eyes rolled up in his head, showing only the whites. Charlie's hands came up. The palms slapped together.

And the blow stopped, two inches short.

He had caught her blade between his hands.

"**There**," said the Scourge, through Charlie's mouth. Eyes filled with darkness locked on Esme's. "**That's enough.**"

Charlie's body swung upright, the steely grip on the sword never loosening for a moment. The pigeon sword's point was now just an inch from Charlie's right eye, but Esme found herself forced to step back or lose her grip on her weapon completely.

"**Again**," said the demon inside him, "**it comes down to this.**"

Esme gave an extra wrench on the pigeon sword. The blade was pressed flat between his palms with a superhuman strength. Apart from flexing the sword slightly, her efforts had no effect whatsoever. Esme pulled and twisted as hard as she could, but the sword might as well have been trapped in stone.

"**Give the weapon to me**," the Scourge told her.

"No!"

"**Give it to me**," said the demon quietly. "**Now.**"

"Never!"

The air between them began to flare and smoke as the demon's magic coursed out and around her—a bulging, crackling field of power. Her hands were still clasped around the pigeon sword's hilt, clinging desperately to Raymond's last gift to her, but the air around her was closing in, clamping down all around at her. Suddenly, she felt her feet lifting off the ground. She felt her grip beginning to weaken, her strength giving out, and then, horribly, it was over. Her fingers left the sword. Now she was flying through the air, flung back and upward by the Scourge's power from one side of the throne room to the other, and in the long slow moment, the moment before she hit the opposite wall, she realized what it was that had defeated her.

Herself.

WHAM!

The impact stunned her. She slid to the ground, her legs folding under her, and the world turned black in front of her eyes.

There was a sound in her head like the sea, whispering in her ears. For a whole second she felt like drifting away on it. But she shook her head, hard. Tasting blood in her mouth, warm and coppery, she opened her eyes, and looked up.

"**You are beaten**," said the Scourge, through Charlie's mouth. The demon was standing over her. The pigeon sword was at her throat.

"**And you know how**," it told her. "**You know how, in fact, every time you fight me, you're going to lose. Look**," it said, making a small gesture in the air with the hand that wasn't holding the sword. "**Look at yourself**."

Esme didn't want to. She knew what she'd see. But she looked. And she saw.

There was a pool of darkness, quivering, under the skin of her palms. In another second, it was moving, spreading: the long, graceful curves and the scalpel-point hooks were already beginning to form.

"**You're *marked*, Esme**," said the Scourge. "**You've always been marked. You just never knew yourself before**."

The black tattoo was swarming up her arms. She could feel

it under her skin, all over her body. It had been waiting inside her all her life, and now she could feel it moving.

There's something a bit special about you, echoed Raymond's voice in her head.

You're not human! echoed another.

It's already too late for her, echoed the Scourge's. *It's always been too late for her. Just ask Felix.*

"No," she whispered.

"**There,**" said the Scourge, watching her reaction. "**I believe you're beginning to understand.**"

Esme stared up at the thing behind the boy's face, stared up at it helplessly.

"**All your power,**" the Scourge told her, "**your speed, your flying, your strength—all of it comes from *me*.**"

The demon regarded her carefully.

"**You are fighting yourself,**" it said. "**How can you expect to win,**" it asked, and there was an odd note of kindness in its voice, "**if you are fighting yourself?**"

Esme lay there in Charlie's shadow. Her mind was swarming with darkness: her whole body felt *thick* with it, so that she could hardly breathe. She could recognize the power of the demon inside her. And for the first time, in perhaps the whole of her life, she began to be scared.

"**The night you were conceived, I could have made my escape,**" said the Scourge. The point of the pigeon sword rested on the carpet now, with Charlie's hands on the pommel. The demon spoke slowly, taking its time. "**Felix had released me, and in return I had granted him his wish of that one night with your**" mother. At long last, I was free to do as I pleased. But instead . . ." It paused. "I stayed."

Esme stared up wordlessly.

"For nine months I waited," the Scourge went on. "And even after you were born I remained. Watching you through his eyes. Seeing you grow. Wondering about what you might become. Why do you think that was? I'll tell you." The demon leaned over her.

"I stayed because I could not help myself." The eyes stared down at hers.

"My child," it whispered.

Esme felt the dark inside her quicken at the words—and shuddered.

"You've ruined my life," she said softly, almost disbelievingly. "Before I was even born, you ruined my life."

The boy with the demon inside him, the great dome of the throne room beyond him—all of it was turning blurry and dark.

Remember your mother. . . .

"But I swear," she said, "I'll make you pay for what you've done."

She stared up at the demon, her amber eyes flashing fiercely.

"I'll have my revenge," she hissed. "I *will* have my revenge. I *swear* it."

Her breath choked in her throat.

She fell back.

And for Esme, everything went black.

"Bravo!" said a voice, and the throne room resounded with slow, ironic handclaps. "Bravo!" said the Emperor again.

With regal slowness, he stood up from his throne.

"That went even better than I'd hoped!" he said. "The battle. The great revelation. Truly, that was all most amusing. But now, I think, it's time to proceed to more important matters." He waved one cloven red hand, and his Overminister shimmered into view beside him. "Gukumat?"

Sire?

"Bring the boy. You know, the other one. Let's have all three of these tiresome earthlings in one place. It's time to get this whole thing wrapped up."

At your command, Sire.

The air in front of the throne seemed to bulge for a moment—then Jack appeared.

For a second, as the jelly stuff slithered off him and slipped over the sides of the carpet to join the rest of the pool, Jack just stared at Esme's limp body. Then he ran to her and knelt by her side.

"You've killed her," he said, looking up at Charlie.

The Scourge made Charlie's head swivel toward Jack. It looked at him.

"No," it said, "I have not. And this state she is in now is not of my doing. Believe me," it added, "I have no wish to harm her."

"Khentimentu," the Emperor interrupted. "Let's start with you."

Charlie's head swiveled to face the throne.

"I've let you have your fun for long enough," the Emperor announced. "It's time to add this girl's powers—and yours—to my own. Gukumat?" he added. "Put Miss Leverton into the pool."

There was a pause.

"*What?*" said Jack.

"**I can't let you do that,**" said the Scourge.

"Come, come, Khentimentu," said the Emperor, smiling again. "You didn't seriously think I'd allow you to run around Hell making plans behind my back, did you?"

He gestured at Esme.

"You and that girl are connected by a special bond, as you've just proved. By adding her essence to my collection," he went on, indicating the slowly rippling pool of jellylike matter that rose and fell all around them, "I will take your powers and add them to my own, just as I have with any other demon who poses a threat to me, and any gladiator who showed any promise." He smiled.

"Hold on," said Jack. "You mean *that's* where the jelly stuff comes from? It's all"—he grimaced, staring around at the oily liquid, hardly believing it—"*dead demons*?"

"Even in death, my subjects continue to serve me," said the Emperor, his golden eyes glinting. "Oh." He frowned, pointing at Jack. "Except for *you*, of course. You're no use to anyone, alive or dead, quite frankly."

Jack blinked.

"**Your powers are a sham, Hacha'Fravashi,**" said the Scourge, squaring Charlie's shoulders. "**You are weak and decadent, and you do not have the strength to stop me from fulfilling my destiny.**"

"Which is what again?" asked the Emperor, raising his eyebrows. "Remind me."

"**I will awaken the Dragon,**" said the Scourge. "**Its breath will be destruction. Its fury will cleanse the firmament. Its gaping jaws will swallow us, every one, and at last all Creation shall—**"

"Oh yes," said the Emperor, pretending to stifle a yawn. "Boring."

Then he struck.

His handsome face sharpened into a scowl of pure rage, and his right arm flashed across his chest in a vicious back-hand slap. At the same moment, a kind of undersea explosion lit up the surface of the throne room floor, and something like a ripple in the air passed between the Emperor and his victims. Though they were twenty feet apart, Charlie's body suddenly bent double, as if something large and heavy had smashed into his midriff. Flung back across the throne room, he hit the wall again, a full thirty feet up off the ground this time. Then he slid to the floor in a helpless heap and lay there, unconscious once more.

Jack just gaped.

Standing where Charlie had been was a man-shaped blob of blackness. The Scourge sank to the floor, shuddering with pain, looking at itself as if in sheer disbelief at what had just happened.

With a single blow, the Emperor had completely separated the Scourge from its host body.

"There," said the Emperor, lifting into the air. He floated smoothly over and touched down on the carpet in front of the Scourge. "Perhaps now you'll realize how much trouble you're really in." He looked down at the demon at his feet. "How's it feel," he asked, "being forced outside your vessel? I imagine you must be feeling a bit . . . exposed. Defenseless, even."

On the word *defenseless*, the Emperor leaned over the Scourge, staring down hard, his golden eyes livid with super-human concentration. The jelly stuff around him lit up again—and suddenly the Scourge was writhing in soundless, convulsive agony. The Scourge lost its man shape, turning into nothing more than a splatter of black, jerking and flap-ping on the carpet in front of the Emperor's spotless white shoes. Just as suddenly, the Emperor stopped what he was doing and stood upright again.

"Gukumat, did you hear me or not?" he snapped. "Put the girl into the pool!"

Obediently, Gukumat floated over, reaching toward Esme with long, elegant fingers.

"No!" said Jack, his voice coming out in a kind of squeak. "I mean, leave her alone!" he added, as gruffly as he could manage.

Now everyone in the room was looking at him.

"Yes," said the Emperor, regarding Jack with obvious dis-taste. "I suppose we'll have to do something about you too. Lord Slint!" he called, looking round. "Where *is* he? Ah, there you are. If you'd be so kind . . ." He gestured vaguely in Jack's direction.

Jack turned, just as the giant flying shark slithered in through the throne room's double doors. He caught a pinkish-gray glimpse of a widening mouth.

"Oh, *shi*—" Jack just had time to say as he was lifted off the ground.

And then, with a great sweep of his tail, Lord Slint swam away through the air, powering his way up toward the vaults of the throne room's roof, where he could devour his freshly plucked morsel in peace. Jack hadn't even had time to scream.

In the shadows over by the wall, Charlie stirred. Across the throne room, the Emperor and the Scourge faced each other.

"Now," said the Emperor. "Time to have some *real* fun." And he lashed out with his power again.

The world spun crazily. The walls of the throne room slid past at hideous speed—but Jack's thoughts, strangely, were quite clear.

The shark hadn't bitten him seriously yet: for the time being, it was only carrying him, but Jack wasn't really thinking about that. What he was thinking, in between things like *AAAARGH!* and *SHARK!*, went something like this:

How come *he* didn't get to have superpowers that made him be able to do cool things?

How come *he* didn't get to face his enemies on equal terms? Or have sword fights or do kung fu?

And this! said his brain, with mounting indignation. Look at this latest situation! He'd thought having to go to Hell was bad. Getting bitten by a giant spider—well, at the time, that had seemed about as low as you could get. But oh no, *his* luck had to go one better, didn't it?

This whole situation, Jack was deciding—not just this latest development but pretty much everything, stretching back in an unbroken line for what seemed like most of his life—was infuriatingly, excruciatingly, incandescent-apoplexy-inducingly UNFAIR.

What this was, Jack decided, what this whole situation *was*, really, when you came down to it, he thought, the realization hitting him with almost as much force as the shark had—

—was *typical*.

Jack's mind lit up with a freezing-white blast of clarity.

And now, suddenly, he was angry. Very angry indeed.

In his hand, much to his astonishment, was his knife. He must have got it out before the shark had grabbed him. His arm was free, trailing below the giant flying shark's lower jaw. So Jack reached up with the knife—and he struck.

The first blow almost jarred the knife's handle from his grasp as it hit Lord Slint's hard snout. Jack took a stronger grip.

"NO!" he shouted as he stabbed down again.

"NO. NO. NO!" he shouted, stabbing down on each word, oblivious to the soft *thunk*s of the puncturing sounds echoing in his ears.

"I'm NOT!" he yelled.

"GETTING!"

"BLOODY!"

"KILLED!"

"AGAIN!"

On the last stab, Jack heard a soft and unforgettably revolting *smutch* as his knife hit home. Then several surprising things happened at once.

Lord Slint's gray-pink mouth hinged open in a grimace of sudden and terrible agony. He stopped swimming. His marblelike eyes rolled back in his head.

And slowly, but with gathering speed, Jack and the giant shark demon began to fall.

"Oh no," said Jack, feeling gravity take hold.

"Oh *no!*" he repeated with feeling, as he kicked himself loose from the shark's vile mouth.

And then, suddenly, they landed.

"It is *you* who are weak," the Emperor had been saying. "*You* who are overconfident." On each "you" he flashed his power out again, making the Scourge jerk helplessly where it lay.

"Now . . ." He paused, raising his hands for the killer blow. "Now it's game over."

Then he froze.

Wham! With a sudden and stunning impact, Jack struck the soft carpet—just a few scant inches from the jelly stuff.

Ker-*splash!*

Lord Slint, in comparison, wasn't so lucky.

Whether the giant flying shark was alive or dead before he hit the pool, it's hard to say. Lord Slint did not have time to struggle or fight before the seething jelly stuff picked him clean. In another second, even his great skeleton was gone, and there was nothing left of his carcass but an evaporating stain on the surface. But Jack wasn't looking at that.

"*Huk*," said the Emperor—and stood there rigid, his golden eyes bulging out with shock.

There was a long, slow moment of silence in the room.

The Emperor had been poised to destroy the Scourge—poised to wreak final destruction on this mythical creature and add its powers to his own—when, quite by accident, he'd been distracted. As the small gladiator—this "Jack"—had fallen from the roof, followed by Lord Slint, the Emperor had paused in what he'd been doing, to watch. In that moment, while his attention was elsewhere, something extraordinary had happened.

Ebisu Eller-Kong Hacha'Fravashi, Suzerain Absolute of the Dominions of Hell, looked down at his chest. Specifically, he looked down at the long spike of cold steel that had suddenly appeared there. Already the area around the wound was filling up with blood, a spreading stain of bright red, made brighter still by the shining whiteness of the suit he was wearing.

"What?" asked the Emperor. "How . . . ?"

In answer, Charlie put his head up from behind the Emperor's shoulder, clenched his neck in the crook of his arm to get a better grip—

—then rammed the pigeon sword home, further still.

"YES," hissed the Scourge, rising up weakly from the floor.

"*No!*" gasped Jack, watching from where he'd landed. What Jack saw on Charlie's face at that moment appalled and horrified him. This time, unlike before, there was no sign of the black tattoo. This time, Charlie's killing rage was nothing but his own. And there wasn't just rage on his face: the fury was matched in equal measure by a savage kind of glee. It was obvious to Jack—it was written, truly, all over his friend's face—that for the first time, Charlie was enjoying this new power he had found, unaided: the power to kill.

"It's not fair!" the Emperor whined, drips of bright blood coming out with the words, making even more of a mess of his suit. "It's . . . not . . . *fair!*"

"**You are weak, Hacha'Fravashi,**" the Scourge repeated, putting its face right up to its enemy's. "**Weak and decadent. You, and those before you since I was banished, have turned from the one true path. With Gukumat's help, I will awaken the Dragon. The whole universe will be brought to an end, and at last all Creation will be returned to the purity of the Void. And** *you,*" the Scourge finished, "**you and everyone else no longer have the power to stop me.**"

As if in answer to the Scourge's words, the Emperor's golden eyes rolled up in his head. His whole body went suddenly rigid in a last paroxysm of agony—then limp.

Into the pool, said Gukumat.

"**Yes, into the pool,**" echoed the Scourge, its husky whisper a shred of the commanding voice it had always used before. "**Do it, Charlie. Do it now.**"

Slowly, wordlessly, Charlie let the pigeon sword's point tip forward, further and further, until finally the weight of the Emperor's body made it slip off the end—flopping into the jelly stuff with a splash.

It hissed delightedly as it received him. The surface seethed and boiled. There was a loud electrical sizzling sound. Then silence.

Ebisu Eller-Kong Hacha'Fravashi was gone.

The Emperor is dead, said the Overminister in his strange, multitudinous voice. *Long live the Emperor.*

Charlie looked up. Slowly, as if his mind were coming back from some place far away, his eyes regained their focus.

"Huh?" he said.

All hail to Charlie Farnsworth, Gukumat intoned. *God of Rulers, God of the Dead, God of Darkness, God of Gods. The Voice of the Void, whose breath is the wind and whose rage makes all worlds tremble. Lord of Crossing-Places, King of All Tears, and the Suzerain Absolute of the Dominions of Hell.*

"**Hail**," the Scourge answered, bowing deeply.

Jack just stared.

But then, slowly—

—warily—

—Charlie started to smile.

TRUST ME

"Not being funny or anything," Charlie was saying, sometime later, "but—when I thought you were dead? It really . . . sucked."

Jack looked at him.

"Being on the receiving end wasn't all that great either," he replied. "But, you know, thanks."

There was a pause.

Behind Jack, the blazing light of the Fracture beckoned and shrieked. In front of him stood Charlie, smiling in a way that Jack suddenly found completely and utterly exasperating. Past Charlie's shoulder he could see the Scourge, making a great show of conversing with Gukumat but doubtless listening to every word he and Charlie said.

Suddenly, he didn't care.

"At the risk of stating the completely bloody obvious," he began, "this is a staggeringly bad idea. Don't you think? I mean, for one thing, what the Hell am I going to tell your folks?"

"Huh?" said Charlie.

"Your parents," Jack prompted. "Remember them? Come on, man, they're going to be frantic!"

Charlie's face darkened. "Tell 'em whatever you like," he growled.

"Sure," said Jack. "I'll tell them that you've gone off to become Emperor of Hell—"

Acting *Emperor of Hell*, said an officious voice, and Jack realized that Gukumat was looking at them. *He has not yet been crowned.*

"Whatever," Jack muttered. He looked back at Charlie.

"Come on," he told him. "Come back with us."

"I want to stay, Jack," said Charlie, shaking his head. "I'm telling you, there's nothing for me"—he gestured at the Fracture—"over there."

"Oh yeah?" said Jack. "And what's for you here?"

"Anything I want," said Charlie simply, and smiled.

Jack looked at that smile.

"Well," he said, "I suppose this is it, then."

"Yeah. I guess it is."

There was another pause.

"Listen," said Jack. "You're not going to get into anything *evil* here, are you?" He was trying to keep the tone of his voice light and joshing, but the effect sounded pathetic, even to him.

"Trust me," said Charlie, smiling.

Yeah, thought Jack sadly. *Right.*

"Well," he said, "good luck."

"Yeah," said Charlie, sticking out a hand. "You too."

They shook.

"But I think you're making a big mistake," Jack told him.

Charlie tore his hand out of Jack's and stalked off, scowling. Jack sighed.

"Mr. Farrell," said a voice.

Jack whirled round, and there—its ink-black face mirroring his own—stood the Scourge.

"What I'm going to say is quite obvious," it said, "but I thought I'd make it clear to avoid any . . . misunderstandings."

Jack just looked at it.

"I have been merciful with you this time. If our paths cross again, I can't guarantee I may be so again. I would earnestly advise you, therefore, not to interfere in the future."

"Is that right?" said Jack, doing his best. "Well, I guess that depends on what happens between you and my friend over there, doesn't it?" He gave the Scourge his most threatening look—and saw from his reflection that it wasn't very impressive.

"You humans," said the Scourge. "So melodramatic. And so dreadfully, *dreadfully* predictable. You have been warned, Jack Farrell."

It turned and drifted smoothly away.

"Yeah," said Jack to its retreating back, "what*ever!*" But it didn't turn round.

Jack sighed again and put his hands on the bar at one end of the ordinary-looking hospital trolley that was standing beside him with Esme laid out on it.

Esme's face was completely blank, utterly, horribly lifeless except for the rhythmic rise and fall of her breathing. There was nothing anyone could do, God had said. Physically, there was nothing wrong with her—and it wasn't magic either. Her unconsciousness was somehow self-induced, self-inflicted: she could wake up at any time, or she might never wake up at all. Personally, Jack had his doubts about this analysis, but his opinion, as usual, didn't seem to count for much.

He looked back at Charlie, who immediately looked away, pretending not to have been watching him.

Jack sniffed. If he was going, it was time to go.

He turned his back, took a deep breath, and started pushing the trolley.

Its wheels squeaked, with a low keening sound almost like a human voice. The squeaking stayed audible for a surprisingly long time as the boy and the girl passed into the crackling whiteness of the Fracture—

—and vanished.

Charlie watched them go. Then he turned away.

END OF

BOOK TWO

"There is nothing else involved. You either do it or you don't. There is only one purpose in attacking the enemy—to cut him down with finality."

Miyamoto Musashi,
from The Book of Five Rings,
as interpreted by
Hanshi Stephen Kaufman

BOOK
THREE

THE MASTER OF NONE

THE CATCH

Charlie Farnsworth stood on the edge of the Needle and looked out over Hell.

The gargantuan mountainlike shape of the palace seemed to swell out beneath his feet. Beyond, the glory of Hell's fantastic landscape seemed barely contained by its purple-blue horizon. Everything Charlie could see—the sea of fire, the five great roads, all of it—now, supposedly, belonged to him. But Charlie still wasn't happy.

"What did Gukumat mean?" he asked the ink-black figure standing beside him. "What was that about my just being 'acting' Emperor of Hell, exactly?"

"It is just as the Overminister said, Charlie," the Scourge replied carefully. "You have killed Hacha'Fravashi. You have taken his place on the throne. But you have not yet been crowned Emperor."

"So? What's the holdup? Why can't you just crown me and get on with it?"

"I'm afraid," said the Scourge, "that it's not quite as simple as that."

"Why?" asked Charlie, rounding on the demon. "*Why* isn't it as simple as that, exactly? You promised me if I killed the Emperor we could rule Hell together. You *promised*! And now what're you doing? Backing out on me! Using me again, to get what you want!"

Inwardly, the Scourge sighed.

"**We can both have what we want,**" it told Charlie slowly. "**You can still become Emperor, and the demons will follow you until the end of the universe.**" It paused. "**There is, however, a catch.**"

"I *knew* it!" Charlie stamped his foot.

"**There is something you have to do first,**" said the Scourge.

"Oh yeah? And what's that?"

"**You must make a decision, once and for all.**"

"What decision?"

"**If you truly wish to become Emperor of Hell—**"

"Yes?" said Charlie. "Yes?"

"**—then you can never go back to your world.**"

There was a pause.

"That's it?" asked Charlie. "That's the catch?"

"**That is the catch,**" said the Scourge. "**Understand me, Charlie: after this, there is no turning back. If you want to become Emperor, I can make it so. The price, however, is that you must give up your past life and all it entails: friends, family—everything. You must choose, Charlie,**" it emphasized. "**Them or us. One or the other. Forever.**"

Charlie blinked.

"**You will, I'm sure, want to make a last visit to your home world before you decide,**" said the Scourge. "**This has already been arranged for you.**"

"Wow," said Charlie, pouting. "You've really got this all figured out, haven't you?"

"Time is short," the Scourge snarled. "If you want to become Emperor, you must learn to expect some decisions to be made for you. That is the way for those who rule. If you find this *objectionable*, perhaps it would be better if—"

"No!" said Charlie quickly. "No, that's okay."

It was the first time the demon had lost its temper with him like that. He was surprised and, he realized, more than a little frightened.

"You can have one night," said the Scourge. "One night in your world—we can't spare you for longer than that. You can then choose to return here or stay, as you wish—though if you choose to stay on Earth, you will naturally have to give up your powers. At any rate," it added, "the choice will be yours." It paused. "What do you say?"

Charlie looked up at the demon standing beside him, this magical being that had come into his life and changed it utterly. Reflected in liquid darkness, his own eyes blinked back at him nervously.

Them or us, he thought. *One or the other. Forever.*

"Sure," Charlie heard himself say. "One night on Earth. Why not?"

"Very well," said the Scourge. "Gukumat?"

At his master's command, the Overminister shimmered into view.

"Prepare the Fracture."

As you wish, my lords, said Gukumat, bowing. *As you wish.*

INTRUDERS

London. The West End. 10:24 p.m.

"That's it," the enormous security guard announced. "I'm going to have to ask you to leave."

Number 3 looked up at the man, who stood a good foot taller than him (and a good two feet wider). The single button that the bouncer had managed to do up on his jacket was showing serious strain from the job of holding back his massive chest.

"Come on, mate," said the bouncer, "let's have you outside. You don't want any trouble, believe me."

Number 3 sighed, reached up, and pushed his mirrored sunglasses a little way down his nose. Thanks to a scuffle with a vampire some years ago, his right eye was false, but his left one was looking up at the bouncer—hard.

"Listen, please," Number 3 told him. He crooked a finger, and the other man bent obligingly forward. Number 3 rewarded him by opening his coat a little and giving him a brief glance at the small but efficient-looking 9mm machine pistol currently strapped under his left armpit. The bouncer's eyes went wide.

"I represent an organization called the Sons of the Scorpion Flail," said Number 3. He spoke quietly, with a pronounced French accent. "You 'ave not 'eard of us, and I would advise you now to forget you ever did. But call your boss, call the police, call the prime minister if you like: they will all tell you the same sing. Leave me alone, please. *Now.*"

For another long second Number 3 and the bouncer looked at each other, as the pub's denizens went about their business around them.

Number 3 disliked this place. He never drank, so he supposed he wasn't really qualified to comment, but even if he did drink, it wouldn't be in the Light of the Moon. Night after night, the pub was packed with beery civilians, until the overworked bar staff could hardly keep up. All that meant to Number 3, however, was that Number 2 had made a serious operational error in not closing the place down. Because this pub, though it looked no different from the many other places just like it in London's West End, had a secret.

The tiny speaker embedded in his sunglasses crackled for a second. Without breaking off his staring match with the bouncer, the Son pushed the shades back into position.

"Three 'ere," he said.

"We're reading activity in the Fracture," said a voice in his ear.

Despite his years of experience, Number 3 felt his heart rate beginning to speed up.

"Copy," he said. "Go away, please," he told the bouncer. "Sank you." He turned and focused his eyes on a spot at the far end of the room. Smoothly, the lenses of his shades switched down through the ultraviolet and thermal levels to a deeper, more sinister spectrum that reduced everyone and everything in the room to pale green smudges—everything except that spot, which, as Number 3 watched, began to whiten and swell outward.

The Light of the Moon looked like a bad West End pub. It sounded and *smelled* like a bad West End pub. But as well as being a pub, it was something else: it was a gateway to Hell. And the gateway was opening.

Number 3 watched as the spot in the air that marked the Fracture went greenish-white, then began to send out lazy little tendrils of magical power—power that only Number 3, at that moment, with his special lenses, was able to see. Slowly, he let his right hand creep up and under his coat, toward where his weapons were waiting. Then, abruptly, his view was blocked by a hulking shadow, and his wrist was caught in a strong grip.

"Oi! Just stop right there."

"Let go of me, please," said Number 3 politely.

"I don't care who you think you are," said the bouncer, "but I'm not letting you get your popgun out in here. There are people about. See?"

"Let go *now*, please," said Number 3. "I 'ave no wish to 'urt you."

Past the bouncer, a burst of whiteness filled Number 3's vision: for a moment, the bones of the bouncer's rib cage stood out like an X-ray against the light before the lenses' protective layers reacted and dimmed down the transmission to a dull glow.

"Listen, mate," said the bouncer, "you don't—OW!"

Number 3 was already moving. In less than a second he had shifted his weight, breaking the bouncer's grip, spinning the man round, and driving the arm that had held his up the man's broad back in a vicious and immobilizing half nelson. With his left hand (Number 3 could shoot just as well with his left), he yanked out a second, identical machine-pistol, already drawing a bead on the thing that had emerged from the Fracture, tracking its flapping, desperate flight across the room.

But already, Number 3 knew, he was too late.

The intruder shot past, right over the oblivious pub-goers' heads, and up over the wide steps. It burst straight through one of the big plate-glass doors and out into the London night, leaving nothing but tinkling splinters behind it.

Shoving his gun back into its holster, the Son of the Scorpion Flail applied a nerve-pinch to a certain spot: the bouncer slumped to the floor without protesting. The drinkers nearest the shattered door were only now just starting to scream.

"*Merde*," said Number 3, with feeling.

Whatever it was that had just come through from Hell— he'd lost it.

Alembic House. Same night. 3:47 a.m.

Felix sat up in bed, coming awake instantly in the darkness. He was breathing hard, he was sweating, and as he felt for the lamp on his antique bedside table, his hand was shaking helplessly.

He'd been dreaming. It was a long, slow, freezing kind of

dream, full of darkness and falling and cold that squeezed stony fingers round his heart. It was a frightening dream. It was also a dream that Felix had had before: he knew what it was, and he knew what caused it.

He was being summoned. The darkness still inside him from all those years ago was calling him again, and he knew he was powerless to resist. Felix sat up, sighing as he put on his glasses.

And some time later, he was across the street from the Light of the Moon, standing in the shadows, watching the two men who were now guarding the door.

"This is crazy," Number 12 was saying.

His partner, Number 9, just sighed. This was the fourth time his fellow sentry had made this observation that night, and they'd only been on duty outside the Light of the Moon for about an hour and a half.

"I'm serious," Number 12 went on. "If Number Three couldn't do anything, then what good can *we* do? Next time something comes through, it's gonna take more than the two of us to stop it."

"Orders are orders," said Number 9 primly.

Number 12 scowled. Since Number 9's recent promotion up the ranks and into single figures, he was really becoming insufferable: all the years they'd worked together, and now it was "Orders are orders." Suddenly, Number 12 decided that hinting at what he wanted to know wasn't going to be enough: he'd have to ask his partner out straight.

"It's tonight, isn't it?" he said. "That's why they won't

send more of us. They're bringing Project Justice in tonight."

"What do you know about Project Justice?" asked Number 9.

"Come on," said Number 12, enjoying the chance to scoff. "You don't think I've heard the rumors? They've done it: the Star Chamber finally pulled off the deal with the Russians. And now, if this Fracture thing really goes where they say it goes, then *we* can go in with a nuke!"

"Why don't you shut up?" suggested Number 9. "Before I—"

A simultaneous crackle in the men's ears cut him off.

"Nine here," said Number 9. The signal was faint and full of interference. Both men cupped their hands to their earpieces in an effort to make it clearer.

"Repeat, please," said Number 9, in a voice loud enough to get both Sons of the Scorpion Flail noticed if anyone had happened to be passing at that moment. "You're breaking up! Hello?"

Silence.

"I think," began Number 12, "he said there was movement round the back."

"I know what he said!" snapped Number 9. Actually, this was a lie: he was glad Number 12 had been there to make sense of the message, though he would never have told him so to his face.

"Well?" asked Number 12, looking at him.

"All right," said Number 9. "Let's check it out. But remember, look casual, okay?"

Number 12 sighed again, but he followed Number 9's lead. The two men set off.

Felix watched them go. It would take the Sons at least two

minutes to get round the block to reach the rear door of the pub and the same again to get back: more than enough time. As he crossed the road, he smiled. That had been the first time he'd used magic since . . .

His smile faded. He'd enjoyed himself for a moment there, but when he remembered the last time, his expression turned grim once more.

Noting the broad wooden board that had been chained over the shattered pane of glass, Felix put his hands round the padlock that held the doors shut and concentrated: it fell open with a soft click. Felix straightened up, brushed his lapels, did up the button on the jacket of his impeccably expensive suit, and stepped through.

The darkness inside him, a darkness blacker than that of the empty pub around him, was stirring: Felix could feel it. Unbidden, his feet took him to the spot at the end of the room, and his hands began the gestures by themselves. He watched, with a strange sort of detachment, as the Fracture's dull red glow widened to a fierce, freezing whiteness.

Then he was there, in Hell. He was standing in a broad, tall, blood-colored dome-shaped room, with a round, raised dais at its center. On the dais was a throne. On the throne, sitting comfortably, was what had woken him.

"**Good evening, Felix,**" said the Scourge. "**Thank you for coming.**"

"You say that like I had a choice," Felix replied.

"**My dear fellow, do let's be civil. After all, we've known each other quite a long time.**"

"You destroyed my life," said Felix. "And now the only person left that I care about in the world is lying in a coma, because of you."

"You destroyed your own life," the Scourge replied evenly, "when you made your bargain with me. Everything that has happened to you, you've brought upon yourself. Don't tell me all this time you've been pretending otherwise, *please*."

"All right," said Felix, after a moment. "Then how about you tell me what I'm doing here?"

"I think you know the answer to that," said the Scourge. "You're here to die."

Felix and the demon looked at each other. Once again, the Scourge was right about him: Felix had known this was the end. He'd known since he'd woken up.

"But first," the Scourge went on, "there's something you're going to do for me."

The demon settled back on the throne, and there was a short pause before it spoke again.

"It's about Esme," it said. "You're going to give her a message."

The Palace Theatre. Same night. 4:49 a.m.

Darkness. Freezing, black, bottomless. The darkness slid past her, through her, taking her down, and a soft voice said—

We're the same.

What?

We're the same, it repeated, you and me. In fact, there is no "you and me." I'm you. You're me. You've always been me. And the only reason I'm speaking to you like this is that you just won't admit it yet.

Black water. Cold, darkness, and falling. There was a pause, then the voice spoke again.

You know what I can offer you.

Esme said nothing.

You can feel it, said the voice. In your body, your blood: strength without limit. Power beyond imagining. And all you have to do is accept me.

Open your heart, the voice told her, and Esme couldn't help but listen. Open your heart, and LET ME IN . . . YES!

Then, suddenly, urgently, as if its owner were standing right next to her, another voice said, *Remember your mother.*

Esme's eyes fluttered, then opened.

She was wearing nothing but a long white cotton T-shirt, she realized: one of hers, an old one, one she never usually wore. Also, she saw, she was strapped to the bed. Three thick brown padded leather straps stretched from one side to the other: one across her legs just above her knees, one across her hips (with loops for her wrists), and another across her chest. The buckles on the straps were done up quite tightly, so Esme closed her eyes, reached inside herself, and concentrated. The air in the room turned thick for a moment. There was a soft clinking sound as the straps fell loose. Then Esme sat up.

There was a door at the foot of the bed, with a thin crack of light beneath it. Hugging herself because the floor was cold under her feet, she walked over to it. She waited for a moment, listening, then she turned the handle. A young man was standing outside, dressed in black from head to toe, with a gun on his belt. On seeing Esme, he turned pale.

"Oh," he said. "You're . . . uh—"

"Where is it?" asked Esme. Her voice came out in a kind of croak.

"I'm—I'm sorry?"

"Where *is* it?" Esme repeated, already losing patience.

"Where's what?" asked the man, genuinely puzzled.

Esme frowned. She let her head fall to one side: a thick clump of her wild black hair swung down over one eye while the other fixed him unblinkingly.

"Listen," said the man, suddenly having trouble getting his words out. "I've, ah, got to call someone. If you just stay right there, then—"

Esme's arm shot out and she caught the man's hand when it had barely moved toward his hip. He found himself being pulled toward the girl as her hand crushed, mercilessly, on his. His vision was turning dark, but he could still see her face and her burning amber eyes.

"**Where. Is. It?**" asked Esme, and her voice seemed to blossom like black flowers in his head.

"I don't—I don't—" said the man, the last vestiges of his training making him reach, with his other hand, for his gun.

Esme sighed—and the man flew back, smashing into the wall and landing in a heap on the floor.

Esme looked down at the prone body for a moment. Then, still dressed only in her long T-shirt, she stepped over the guard and set off down the corridor.

The next few minutes—

"Freeze, or I'll—*AAAGH!*"

—passed in a sort—

"I repeat, subject is . . . NO! *PLEASE!*"

—of blur. Esme was beginning to recognize her surroundings, but the loud alarm sounds were unfamiliar and, she found, quite irritating. Plus, there were all these *people*. At one point, on the landing outside the butterfly room, twenty-two more of the black-clad men fanned out and surrounded her. They were wearing gas masks and body armor. They were shouting. Their guns made a lot of clicking noises as they pointed them at her. It was all, she found, very irritating indeed.

A burst of harsh light blasted in around the edges of the butterfly room's double doors, and Number 2 looked up just as, with a heavy *crump*, the doors buckled inward.

He stood up, facing the doors, nodding to the two men he had stationed to either side, who took up position, waiting.

The doors opened, and Esme came in.

Her wild black hair stood out all around her. Her hands, as she stepped over the unconscious body of one of the men who had tried to get in her way, opened and closed on the empty air by her sides. Her amber eyes flicked once around the room, taking in her old dojo and the way that now it seemed to be filled with men and machinery. Then they fixed on Number 2.

"So," said the Sons' leader unhappily. "You're, er, awake, then."

Esme just looked at him.

"Now," Number 2 went on quickly. "There's no need to get, er, overexcited. For the last day or so you've been in . . . well, some kind of a coma. We had no idea when, or if, you'd wake up, but we thought—for your own protection, of course—that it might be best to put you in . . . well, in restraints. I can see that that might not have been quite the right thing to do, and I apologize, truly, so please, there's no reason for any violence. All right?"

Still Esme said nothing.

"This," said Number 2, gesturing at the oblong metal box behind him and the racks of improvised laboratory equipment that surrounded it, "is a, ah, rather dangerous piece of equipment."

Esme raised an eyebrow.

"All right," said Number 2. "I'll tell you. It's a bomb. It's rather a powerful one. We are, at present, engaged in quite a delicate stage of its preparation. So, you know, perhaps if you'd be good enough to wait outside or in your room for another twenty minutes or so, then we'd be able to discuss things a little more—"

Esme brushed the cloud of words aside. "Where is it?" she asked.

Number 2 frowned. "I'm sorry," he said slowly. "I'm not sure if I under—"

"WHERE IS IT?" wailed Esme suddenly, as the sadness clawed at her.

Number 2 stared. Some sort of horrible change had come over the girl. Her face was stricken with grief. "I'm afraid I don't understand what you're talking about," he finished uncertainly.

"Look," said Esme, trying again. She looked down at her

feet. Her hair swung down over her face again, and her eyes were going a bit watery. She bunched her fists and straightened up. "It was taken from me, all right? The Scourge took it, and I've got to have it back." She opened her hands and held them out, empty, trying to show how important it was.

"It's all I've got—you see?" she explained. "It's all I've got left from . . . from Raymond." Her voice had gone wobbly again. The men were just looking at her blankly. She felt a stab of impatience. "I'm going to ask you again," she said. "Then I'm going to get angry. Where is it?"

Suddenly, the air in the room was heating up—the pressure building. Number 2's eyes narrowed, and he nodded to the two men standing behind her.

Instantly, before Esme could react, they fired.

The glowing tips of the Tasers hit home at her back, on either side of her spine. Esme's body began to convulse, and the bursts of bright current began to run in weird blue splashes down her T-shirt and her bare brown legs. The men kept their fingers pressed on the triggers of their specially adapted weapons. But Esme was still asking.

"WHERE IS IT?" she cried, and again. "*WHERE IS IT? WHAT HAVE THEY DONE WITH MY SWORD?*"

The equipment rattled on the shelves.

Everyone winced.

Then, suddenly, she fell.

"Tranquilizer," barked Number 2. There was a long, soft hiss as the injection was applied to the girl's neck. It was a large dose. It would have to be.

FRIENDS

Jack was in a foul mood.

When he'd come back from Hell the day before, stepping out of the Fracture wheeling the trolley with Esme's lifeless body in front of him, he hadn't exactly known what to expect. Not flags and a brass band to welcome him or anything, of course not: the most he'd hoped for, he supposed, was a chance to get Esme back to the Brotherhood's headquarters before he decided what his next move should be. But no. Oh no. As had been the case, it seemed, with so much in Jack's life, things had naturally turned out worse.

What he'd got instead was a surprise encounter with a bunch of black-clad men in gas masks, all of whom seemed to be pointing guns at him. They'd whisked Esme off to who-knows-where before Jack barely had time to protest, and any attempts he'd made since to ask after her—let alone get to see her—had been met with total indifference from his captors. The men had proceeded to spend most of the next twenty-four hours grilling Jack for his story, making him go over it again and again while at the same time clearly not believing a word of it. They'd refused to explain who they were or what they were doing there. They'd refused to let him call his parents, and they had locked him in one of the rooms at the theater.

And as if all of that weren't enough by itself, he felt sick.

He'd first noticed the feeling just a couple of hours after his return from Hell: it hadn't been too bad at first—just a light, nagging sensation in the pit of his stomach, particularly whenever he looked at food. Over the following twenty-four hours, however, the feeling had got steadily worse. There was a feverish sort of tingle in his shoulders and under his arms. His mouth tasted furry and his stomach kept gurgling and twisting itself up, like he'd swallowed a snake and it was eating him alive down there, eating him from the inside.

Typical, he thought. What a time to get ill. How absolutely bloody typ—

He froze, staring.

A patch of shadow in the corner of the room was moving, rippling—solidifying, as he watched, into a manlike shape of purest liquid black. The darkness vanished, and a figure stepped out of the shadows.

"Charlie," said Jack.

"Hey," said Charlie. He had a sword strapped to his back, and he looked very pleased with himself. "Got a minute?" he asked.

"I suppose so," said Jack dryly. "I'm not exactly in the middle of anything here."

"Cool." Charlie grinned again and reached out a hand.

There was a sensation of huge black wings closing around them. Then Jack and Charlie were standing in the open night air.

Jack looked around himself. They had reappeared on some kind of rooftop: a high one too—he could tell because of the breeze.

"Where are we?" he asked.

"We're on the roof of Centre Point Tower," said Charlie.

Jack walked to the edge. Of course Charlie was right.

Built in the 1960s out of ribbed concrete and glass, Centre Point Tower used to be one of the tallest buildings in London. It's still one of the ugliest. Nonetheless, Jack had to admit, there was a pretty good view from the roof. London's streets were spread out all around him like the glittering threads of a spiderweb, the Thames cutting through them like a slash of darkness.

"Well?" Jack prompted, still in no mood to mess around.

"Well what?" asked Charlie, who was now sitting cross-legged on the concrete.

"You want to tell me what this is all about?" asked Jack. "I thought you were staying in Hell with the Scourge." It was difficult to keep the bitterness out of his voice—and to be honest, he wasn't trying very hard.

"I'm just . . . visiting," was Charlie's faint reply.

"Really!" said Jack, with heavy sarcasm. "Staying long?"

"Just tonight," said Charlie, attempting to make it sound casual and once again failing pathetically. "Just tonight," he repeated, and he let out a single hollow laugh. "Huh."

Jack looked at him. "What?" he asked.

At last, Charlie looked up. His eyes glinted.

"This is it, Jack," he said. "This is my last visit. After tonight, if I go back to Hell, I can't ever come back here again."

Jack blinked.

"How come?" he asked.

Charlie sighed. "I'm just too important," he replied, "apparently."

Jack rolled his eyes in disbelief.

"I guess it's kind of like with the prime minister or the queen or something," Charlie explained blithely. "Every move I make'll be planned in advance, and they simply can't put the arrangements in place to guarantee my safety with the way things are over here. You know how it is."

"Oh, *sure*," said Jack. "Sure, I know how it is." But the sarcasm flew over Charlie's head—again. Jack sighed. "So?"

Charlie looked surprised. "So what?"

"So, are you going to do it?" asked Jack, losing patience. "Are you seriously telling me you're going to stay in Hell for good?" He paused. "Or—or what?"

Charlie looked down at his lap again before answering, and his hair swung forward over his eyes.

"I dunno," he said distantly.

"Maybe," he added.

"Yeah," he finished. Then he flicked his hair back, shrugged at Jack, and smiled.

For another long moment, Jack stared at Charlie, getting what he wanted to say in the right order. It was difficult.

"Do you know?" he began finally. "There's something I've been thinking about you for a while now. I think it's time I told you, because you really ought to know."

"What's that?" asked Charlie.

"You're a complete and utter *git*," said Jack.

Charlie stared at him.

"What do you want me to tell you?" asked Jack. "Am I supposed to beg you not to go? 'Don't go, *mate*—I'll miss you.' Would you like that?"

Charlie shook his head. "Jack—"

"No, really," said Jack, hitting his stride now. "I want to know. Would it make any difference if I told you again how stupid you're being? I mean," he asked, "what about your parents?"

"It'll be dealt with," said Charlie. "I've got a plan."

"Ooh, a *plan*," echoed Jack, with utter contempt. "Well, hooray for that."

He sighed. His anger was cooling now. Truth be told, Jack wasn't very good at being angry, even when he had a right to be. Being angry was too much bother: he could never manage it for long.

"So what's the deal here?" he asked wearily. "What exactly has the Scourge promised you?"

Charlie perked up visibly.

"Well, it's like this," he said. "I can't tell you very much, it's kind of a secret, but me and Khentimentu are going to perform this ceremony."

"What ceremony?"

"There's this old temple kind of thing, in the deepest part of the palace. No one's even been down there for thousands of years."

"Uh-huh," said Jack, already not liking the sound of this at all.

"When everything's all set up, we're going to do this, like, ritual. It's called 'waking the Dragon.' And after that, every demon in Hell will do whatever I say."

"But this ritual," said Jack. "What does it involve? What happens?"

Charlie shrugged and grinned. "What do I care? I mean, it's just some public-relations thing, right? Me and the Scourge do a bit of hocus-pocus, some bogus religious cere- mony, then all the demons'll follow me forever!"

"That's it?" asked Jack. "You're sure that's all it is? I mean, how do you know?"

"I know," said Charlie heavily, "because the Scourge told me."

"The Scourge told you," echoed Jack. "It actually said to you, 'This dragon business means nothing.'"

"Yes!"

"Those exact words."

"Yes!"

Jack waited.

"Well," said Charlie, "no. But I promise you, Jack, it's no big deal."

The two boys looked at each other.

"All right?" prompted Charlie.

"Not really," said Jack. "There's obviously more to it than that. Something's happening, and you don't know what. And," he added, seeing Charlie shaking his head again, "I don't trust the Scourge."

"Well, I do," said Charlie. "I *do* trust the Scourge!"

The boys looked at each other. There was a pause.

"Look," said Charlie, shuffling himself a little closer toward Jack across the gritty concrete. "You don't know what it's like. I've tried to tell you, but you just won't believe me."

Jack looked at him.

"Meeting the Scourge is the best thing that ever happened to me," said Charlie. "Do you understand? Since that day I took the test, it's like every part of my life—every step, every breath—is magical and important and *real*. Now, I'm asking you, man, what is there here that could possibly be better than that? Go on," he prompted, when Jack didn't answer straightaway. "Tell me."

Jack still didn't answer. Charlie smiled.

"When's term start again?" he asked. "A couple of weeks' time? So are you seriously telling me I should come back to school, on top of everything else, when I could be, like, ruling the universe?"

Still Jack said nothing.

"That's the choice," said Charlie. "I can rule in Hell—or come back here and be . . . *ordinary*." He snorted. "As for my parents . . ." He smiled bitterly. "Well, like I said, I've got a plan. The whole thing's going to blow over. Pretty soon, no one'll even remember I've gone. So there's nothing for me here," said Charlie, edging closer to Jack. "You see? Nothing. Except you."

There was another long pause.

"You know," said Charlie, "you could always come and visit me. I'll always make time for you, mate. You know that, right?"

"Come on, man," he added when Jack still didn't reply. "Say something!"

For another long, slow moment, there was silence between them. Then Jack did say something.

"You're an idiot, Charlie."

Charlie blinked.

"I can't believe you can't see how stupid you're being," said Jack. "And it just makes me sad, because whatever I say, whatever I do, you're just going to go ahead and do this stupid, *stupid* thing, and there's nothing I can do to stop you."

He looked at Charlie.

"That's right, isn't it?" he asked. "There's nothing I can do?"

"No," said Charlie thickly. "There isn't."

"Then," said Jack, standing up with an effort, because he was fed up and sad and sick and his feet had gone to sleep, "you might as well take me back to the theater."

Charlie sniffed.

"You go," he said, still sitting, his face obscured by his hair. "I've got stuff to do."

"You're going to make me walk?" asked Jack.

"No. You don't understand. You're going back. You'll be there in less than a second. Don't worry about it."

"Oh," said Jack, doing his best not to. "Okay."

"Goodbye, Jack," said Charlie. "I'm sorry it has to be like this."

"Bye, Charlie," said Jack. "I'm sor—"

He felt a rush of blackness, then he was back in the locked room.

"—ry too," he said to the empty air. And that was when it occurred to him that he could have asked Charlie to put him wherever he liked. *Typical.*

On the roof of Centre Point Tower, Charlie sat cross-legged for perhaps another minute and a half. On his shoulders, two ink-black shapes suddenly hunched outward, then Ashmon and Heshmim ran down his arms and nibbled at his fingers with their sharp little teeth. Charlie stroked their shiny black bodies absently for a while.

Well, he thought, *that* hadn't exactly gone as well as he'd hoped.

Them or us. One or the other. Forever.

Frankly, the choice didn't seem like such a big deal. At any rate, if the world was going to persuade him to stay, it would have to work pretty hard to impress him now.

Charlie stood up. His familiars vanished into a cloak of darkness, and as the cloak spread billowing about him, he walked to the edge of the roof. For a moment, he looked out over the city. Then he stepped off, plunging into the night.

THE LAST NIGHT

Number 27 was thinking of pastries. Specifically, he was thinking of mille-feuille, his favorite pastry, and just how delicious it was. He was beginning to doze off, when a single red light on his control panel suddenly started to wink.

Instantly he was awake, reaching for the radio on his desk with one hand even as the other was punching the relevant display up onto his monitors.

"Two here," said the radio.

"Sir," said Number 27, "we have a problem."

At that moment, every one of the newly installed speakers dotted all over the top floors of the building let out a dreadful rising shriek. The intruder alarms had kicked in.

"Monitors?" barked the radio.

"Sorry sir?" said Number 27.

"Anything on the *monitors*?" repeated Number 2.

"Nothing sir," said Number 27. "Except—wait."

"Yes?"

"There's something coming up the stairs. No . . . No, not coming *up* the stairs."

There was a pause.

"What?" asked Number 2.

Number 27 just sat back and rubbed his eyes. But when he looked again, he could see that what was happening was, unfortunately, still happening.

"Twenty-seven, I'm waiting."

"It's going *through* them, sir," said Number 27. "Whatever it is, it's coming through the walls!"

"Put the whole team on full alert."

Number 27 didn't need telling twice.

On the landing outside the butterfly room, Charlie paused, frowning. He'd set off the intruder alarm almost a minute ago now, and still no one had appeared to try and stop him. What sort of response time did they call this? Tutting exaggeratedly, he set off for Esme's room. Rather than have to bother with all the stairs and corners, he went straight through the walls.

Charlie had been doing this a lot lately, back in the palace in Hell. The novelty of the sensation—the sudden damp feeling of the cold, old stone as it passed through him even as he passed through it—had worn off quite quickly. Scaring the pants off the people in the rooms beyond, though: that, he found, was the fun bit.

There had to be about twenty of these goons camped out in each room, packed like sardines in their little rows of sleeping bags. The effect of his appearance on them as he rose up through the floor, letting his cloak ripple about him and fill the room with a flood of crackling darkness, was, Charlie found, very satisfactory indeed. Grinning to himself, he slid through the ceiling, leaving chaos and screams in his wake. Once inside Esme's room, however, he stopped and frowned again.

He looked around the room, pointlessly checking all its cushion-covered surfaces. It was dark in there, but that wasn't a problem for him. The problem was, the room was empty.

Hmm.

He opened the door and stepped out onto the landing outside, just as some five or six Sons of the Scorpion Flail finally got there to intercept him. He was greeted by a chorus of ratcheting safety catches, orders for him to freeze, and so forth. It was so like something off the telly, it was really very funny.

"You," said Charlie to the one standing nearest him, who hadn't even managed to get his gas mask on properly yet. "Where is she?"

"Er, wh-who?" stammered Number 16.

"The girl, stupid," said Charlie, reaching into the man's mind when he didn't answer straightaway. "Thank you," he added, when he'd got what he wanted, and with (though he said it himself) a pretty credible burst of manic baddie cackling, he whirled his cloak about himself and vanished, reappearing at Esme's bedside.

He looked down at her.

She looked awful.

It wasn't just that she was tied to the bed with a frankly

bewildering array of straps, buckles, and (now) chains holding her in place. It wasn't even that she was attached to an intravenous drip full of (Charlie noted with a superhuman glance) enough tranquilizers to stun a whale. Her eyes were scrunched up like she was in pain. Her arms were covered in long clawed scratches that she'd obviously done herself. Her hands, strapped down to either side of her, were bunched into small fists. She was pale and sick looking and desperately, desperately sad.

For the first time in a while, Charlie felt a pang of something a little like regret.

But it was okay, he told himself, because that was why he'd come.

He'd been in the room perhaps three seconds at most. The ceiling and the walls rang with the impact of boots as the Sons ran down to catch up with him: it was time to do what he'd come to do. He reached up and took off the pigeon sword, sliding the strap from his shoulders. Gently, carefully, he laid it by Esme's right side and closed her fingers around the hilt. Her hand was warm, and he held it for a fraction of a second longer than he needed to.

"There you go," he said quietly.

Instantly, Esme stirred. Her eyelids fluttered—and Charlie stood back, watching her uncertainly. Suddenly, he realized, she was holding the sword for herself, clasping it to her chest in both hands now, until her knuckles bulged white against the dark wood of its scabbard.

The Sons were battering at the door. Great heavy blows

threatened to knock it off its hinges—yet the small and uncontrollable shiver that Charlie gave as he watched Esme begin to wake was nothing to do with them.

The door burst open—

—but Charlie was gone.

For a long, delicious moment, Charlie soared through the orange-tinged sky over the West End. His cloak of liquid darkness rippled about him, and he laughed with delight as the wind of his passing grew hot on his face.

He vanished again and reappeared standing in his room.

It was his bedroom, in the house in Stoke Newington—the place where he'd grown up. All his stuff—his games, his comics, his film collection—was all exactly as he'd left it. After everything that had happened, Charlie found this inexplicably annoying.

How lame and paltry it all looked now, especially with the thin layer of dust that had already started to form over all of it. When he'd thought about this moment before, he'd imagined he'd be tempted to take something as a keepsake, despite the risk that it might be noticed. Now he was here, he wasn't tempted in the least. There was nothing worth coming back for, nothing compared to what was waiting for him in Hell. Sneering, he sank through the floor.

He appeared in his parents' room, by their big four-poster bed. Like Esme's room had been, it was empty. Charlie frowned and sank through another floor, ending up in the passage that led to the sitting room. Now, at last, he could see light, escaping round the gaps at the edges of the door. He stood outside in the passage for a moment. Then he took a deep breath, held it, and slid through.

The wood of the door was old and hard and had what must have been about forty different layers of paint on it. The way his eyes were now, he could even see the little lines that his parents had marked off on the doorway over the years, to show how much he'd grown.

He'd found her. His mum was asleep on the sofa. Charlie just stood there and looked at her.

She didn't look good either. She was pale, her lipstick was smeared, her mouth was open, and her head was lying at an angle that would obviously give her a very sore neck in the morning. The floor surrounding the sofa was covered in scrunched-up tissues; there was an empty glass and a half-drunk bottle of white wine on the table in front of her, and the TV had been left switched on, though very quietly. Across the floor stretched a long cord that led to the telephone, which lay at her side on the cushions, under her hand.

She'd fallen asleep waiting for it to ring: waiting for him, Charlie, to call.

Charlie felt bad then. For a long second the bad feeling ran all the way through him like a slow electric charge, and all he could do was stand there.

But then, after a moment, another urge took hold of him, the urge to get out. He had a way to fix everything, quickly and—he reckoned—cleanly. He was going to leave the whole mess, everything, behind him. He could do that. He was going to do that. He *had* to do that.

"Bye, Mum," he said quietly. Then he vanished again.

This time, he reappeared outside Blackhorse Road Underground station.

His father had moved into a flat near here with his new . . . "girlfriend," as Charlie supposed he had to call her (he grimaced). This was where his dad had been living since leaving Charlie's mum. Charlie could remember the address all right: the problem was that since he'd never been there before, he didn't know how to find his way there. Tutting slightly, because it was annoying that even a superhuman like himself still had to stop for directions, Charlie looked closely at the local map that was outside the station. There. That was where it was. Moments later, he was outside the building.

Floating smoothly upward through the summer night air, he began to look in through the windows. On the south-facing side, the side where he'd materialized, all of them were dark except one. Luckily (or unluckily), that turned out to be the one he'd been looking for. Six floors up off the ground, Charlie froze.

They were standing in the middle of the kitchen: his dad and the woman Charlie hardly knew. They were hugging each other.

It wasn't the kind of hug he'd ever seen his dad and his mum give each other: Charlie knew that straightaway. His dad's face was pressed deep into the side of the woman's neck. The woman was running her hands very slowly across Charlie's dad's back, high up, up near his shoulders.

The kitchen looked bright and new and amazingly clean, as if it had never been used before. The glare of the bare strip light on the kitchen's ceiling gave the place a harsh, antiseptic appearance. Outside, staring in from the darkness, watching them, Charlie felt his stomach knotting into icy twists of loathing and disgust.

Charlie remembered what his dad had told him that time in the Chinese restaurant: *When the chance came up for me to be really happy, I had to take it.* He smiled fiercely. Maybe the two people he was looking at thought they were happy now. Maybe they were even right. But it wasn't going to last. Soon they'd be sorry. When they found out about what he was about to do, they'd be sorry for the rest of their lives. And that, Charlie decided, was fine by him.

"God, Sandra," said Mr. Farnsworth finally, lifting his head to look at her. His eyes were red and puffy. "What if he's done something stupid? What am I going to do? I just wish he'd call."

"I know," said the woman doggedly. "I know."

But Charlie didn't hear this. He was long gone.

This time, he reappeared on Hungerford Bridge.

Of all London's bridges across the Thames, this was Charlie's favorite. From Hungerford Bridge you can see most of the city's landmarks, and the looping golden-yellow lights on either side of the river at that point are really quite lovely. Charlie looked down at the black, silent Thames moving below him, cold and deep and merciless, and for a second he felt that the bridge—the whole city with him on it—was moving, and that the river itself was still. Then he pulled himself together. Dawn was on its way now. If he was going to finish what he'd come to do, he had to act fast. He took a step back from the railing and began to use his magic.

Even at that time of night, there were still a few people on the bridge. His first priority, therefore, was to prevent anyone from seeing him and what he was about to do. Charlie frowned, and the space around him began to shimmer: for the next few minutes, until he was ready, the eyes of anybody who looked would simply slide past him as if he weren't there. Now he was free to get on with the real business at hand.

The air started to thicken and go hot as Charlie coaxed it into giving him what he wanted.

The trunk came first—an ugly, solid clump that he massaged into shape with a grimace of disgust, smoothing it with his fingers. With quick, careful movements, he extended the arms and legs, focusing his concentration on the bones, the sinews, and the blood vessels as they whispered into being behind the delicate layers of the skin. Next, still frowning, he looked at the gap between the shoulders—and it began to glisten and bulge. In another moment it was inflating: swelling as it filled with bone and blood and, finally, brain. Still Charlie concentrated, smoothing and whittling and working at the surfaces until at last his hands fell to his sides, and he stood back and looked at his handiwork.

He gripped the railing, suddenly dizzy. His stomach felt watery, his temples twitched, and his whole body ached with a kind of shock at what he had just pulled out of himself.

But there. It was done. It would do.

Floating in front of him, standing stiff like a mannequin, pinned in the air by Charlie's power, was a replica of himself. Charlie hadn't bothered to copy all his moles and freckles and so forth, but apart from those, the replica was exact in every detail: hair, blood type, fingerprints, even his teeth, in case Charlie's dental records were used to identify him.

It felt quite strange, looking at himself like this. For a moment he almost felt sorry for this body of his and what was going to happen to it on its journey down into the cold and the dark. But then he remembered.

He'd come there to kill himself. And it was time to finish the job.

Charlie transferred his watch to the body's wrist. He took out his mobile phone and stuck it into the back pocket of the identical black jeans the body was wearing. He gave the new version of himself a last, critical look—then pitched himself up, over the railing, and into the river. There was a soft splash from below, and his body vanished, to be washed up some-where downstream.

The Emperor was dead. Long live the Emperor.

It was done. His last links to the world he'd grown up in were severed. There was nothing else to keep him there, so he closed his eyes, opened them again, and then he was standing in front of the Fracture.

There were some more of the goons from earlier, shouting and firing guns at him, but he paid them no mind. He just stepped through, back into the quiet, seething whiteness that seemed to reach out and beckon him in. In another moment, he was back in the throne room.

"Sorry I'm late," he said.

The Scourge stood up, walked quickly down the steps of the dais, and took Charlie's hands in two of its own. Its touch was smooth and cool.

"I'm so glad to see you," it said. **"I can't tell you how glad. We have big things to accomplish, you and I."**

"Yeah," said Charlie, and smiled.

He felt great. All the pent-up frustrations of his life were falling away: he could feel them streaming off him like water when you climb out of a swimming pool. All the tension and the rage and the fear and the hurt were slipping away until all that was left was himself and the demon and their future together. He felt strong and fit and full of excitement: he felt better than he'd ever felt in his life.

"Let's do it," he said. "Let's go to work."

And inwardly, triumphantly, the Scourge smiled.

Arm in arm, the boy and the demon walked out of the throne room.

Charlie didn't look back.

PERSONAL DEMONS

When the dreadful noise of the intruder alarms finally stopped, Jack noticed a tapping sound—coming, he realized, from the window.

"*What?*" said Jack aloud. What the Hell was it now? Scowling, he stood up and yanked open the curtains.

There, on his windowsill, sat a small, batlike creature.

It was Jack's Chinj.

It was looking at him.

Jack stared. He hadn't been expecting to see the Chinj again: certainly not here, on Earth, in London's West End, on the windowsill of the Palace Theatre. The small creature's smile of delight widened to a look of near-ecstasy as Jack opened the window.

"Sir!" it breathed. "I can't tell you how glad I am to see you!"

"Er, hi," said Jack. There was a pause. "Um, if you don't mind my asking, what are you actually *doing* here?"

"Why, sir," said the Chinj, obviously hurt but trying not to show it. "You can't seriously be suggesting that I should have abandoned my sacred duty to you simply because you decided to leave our realm? But of course," it joshed, nudging Jack's arm with one leathery wing and looking up at him slyly, "you are joking with me."

"What do you mean," asked Jack, grim-faced, "'*our*' realm?"

"Why, our *home*," said the Chinj, its jaunty expression beginning to slip.

"The pits," it added, seeing that its point wasn't getting across.

"Hell," prompted the Chinj finally, giving Jack a puzzled look. "Sir."

Jack stared at the Chinj. Then he rubbed a hand over his eyes.

"Listen," he said, "I think there's been some kind of mistake. *This*"—he pointed past the Chinj and out at the London night—"is my home, where *my* kind come from. I know we met there and everything, but I'm not actually from Hell. I mean . . ." He tried a smile. It didn't come out very well. "I'm not actually a demon or anything. Okay?"

The Chinj frowned.

"Yes, you are, sir," it said. "Or part demon anyway."

"Er, no," said Jack. "I'm not."

"Of course you are."

"*No*," said Jack, quite firmly now. "I'm *not*."

"Sir," began the Chinj, holding up one tiny finger. "If I might point out, I *have* been performing most of your digestive functions for you for some time now."

"*What?*" said Jack.

"And I think I can claim to know what I'm talking about. Yes, sir, you *are* a demon. At any rate, you certainly need to feed like one."

"Look," said Jack, "I'm not going to argue about this. It's nice to see you again and everything, but if you don't mind,

I'm having a miserable night and I really, really want to go back to bed. I'm sorry about your wasted journey. But, you know, good night."

He reached for the window, ready to close it again.

"You are sick?" asked the Chinj quickly.

Jack froze.

"You have aches and pains in your limbs? Your stomach keeps rumbling?"

Jack said nothing.

"You are always hungry, yes?" the Chinj went on. "But there is nothing to eat here that seems to satisfy you?"

"Yes," said Jack quietly.

"Well," said the creature, unable to keep the note of triumph out of its voice, "why do you think that is?"

There was another pause.

"I'm just ill," said Jack, with a sudden and horrible uncertainty. "Upset stomach. You know, something I ate, that's all."

But the Chinj was shaking its head.

"Oh, sir," it said sadly. "I had no idea."

"No idea what?"

"That you didn't know," said the Chinj. "It must come as a bit of a shock." It reached out a leathery black wing and touched Jack softly on the arm. "It's all right, sir. I'm here now. And I'll take care of you. Always."

Jack stared at the Chinj, too stunned to be angry anymore. He looked into its wide, dark eyes. The Chinj felt sorry for him, he realized. This threw Jack completely.

"If I may say so," said the small creature quietly, "you

really don't look at all well. Little wonder," it added, "when you haven't fed properly in so long. If I might suggest . . . ?"

Smiling kindly, the Chinj gestured with its eyes to a place on the floor somewhere behind where Jack was standing.

Jack turned and looked. All he could see in the direction the Chinj was indicating was a small bright blue plastic bucketlike object, an empty wastepaper bin, sitting in the corner of the room. He looked back at the Chinj.

And it was then, with a falling sensation in his heart, that Jack realized what the creature meant to do.

His stomach let out a growl so astonishingly loud that Jack was suddenly scared that it might alert the guards outside. The growl went on for what seemed like an eternity, a long, gurgling ripple of deep sound that finally tailed off into a high, soft series of murmurs. Obviously, there was no choice. Jack bent down and, with shaking hands, picked up the empty bin. When he turned back, the Chinj was already in position, its wings folded neatly behind its furry back to keep them out of the way. As Jack did his best to hold the blue plastic bin steady in front of it, he watched as a momentary spasm of something like pain crossed the face of the small creature.

Then it opened its mouth and let fly.

Jack closed his eyes. He didn't want to watch any more. Hearing the thick splatter as the stuff hit the plastic bottom of the bin—feeling the occasional droplets that splashed back up onto his hands in tiny, warm spots—these sensations were enough for him. When at last the Chinj had fulfilled its sacred duty, the edges of the bin were heavy in his hands and the smell was thick and strong in his nostrils.

"There," said the Chinj, with quiet pride.

Jack opened his eyes and looked down. He looked at the porridgey stuff lurking darkly in the shadows at the bottom of the bin. To his horror, he found that he had never wanted anything so much in his entire life. His whole body was gripped with a deep, physical need that was so strong it shocked him.

Nervelessly, he lifted the edge of the bin to his lips, staring with a strange fascination at the reluctant, bulging way the stuff crept up the side as he tipped it up toward his eager, suddenly slavering mouth.

"There," murmured the Chinj again soothingly. "Long swallows, sir. Nice and steady, that's the way."

And time went slack.

Charlie and the Scourge reappeared in darkness. They were traveling downward and at tremendous speed, but even with Charlie's eyes as superhumanly powerful as they were now, he could see nothing anywhere, in any direction. He could smell nothing, feel nothing. Apart from the demon's cool liquid hand holding his, there was only darkness.

"Okay," said Charlie. "How about you tell me where we actually *are*? And, like, what we're actually doing here?"

"**We have now passed beyond Hell's foundations,**" the Scourge answered. "**We are reaching the heart of Creation: the sleeping place,**" it said and paused, "**of the Dragon.**"

Charlie considered this for a moment.

"And this," he said, "means what to me, exactly?"

"It means everything, Charlie," the Scourge replied. "This place is where it all began, and this is the place it will end. The being that sleeps here created it all. And from here too Creation will be unmade."

There was a pause while Charlie gave this his best shot.

No, he decided, he still wasn't getting it.

"So, this Dragon, it's . . . what? Another God?" he asked.

"That would be one name for it," the Scourge replied, "yes. But it would be better to leave the old stories of your world behind. The truth of the matter is this: the Dragon created everything. Then it slept."

"'On the seventh day He rested,'" quoted Charlie mechanically.

"Well," the Scourge admitted, "that part of your folklore is surprisingly accurate. But that's where the resemblance ends. After creating the universe, the Dragon slept, but it did not wake up."

"It didn't?" asked Charlie, doing his best to get his head round it.

"No," said the Scourge. "It has been asleep since time began."

Charlie was going to say something about this.

But then a thousand voices spoke in unison, and all thought ran out of his head.

Only one for whom the Void is pure in his heart, said the voices, *can awaken the Maker of All.*

The words had come like a series of explosions behind Charlie's eyeballs. He was stunned by them. Even so, it occurred to Charlie that—was it possible?—he recognized who was speaking.

Charlie Farnsworth, said Gukumat, *are you that one?*

There was a long silence. Charlie looked in vain to where the Scourge's face should have been, but all around him there was still nothing but darkness.

"Is this the, er . . . ?" he whispered. "Do I—?"

"**Say yes, Charlie,**" said the Scourge.

"Yes!"

"'**The Void is pure in my heart.**'"

"The Void is pure in my heart!"

Approach, boomed Gukumat's voices, in the same eerie, thunderous unison.

And instantly, the darkness blazed into light.

"I know why the Scourge was exiled," Felix began. "I know why it was imprisoned."

Felix had returned from Hell. He'd had no choice in the matter. And now he was delivering the Scourge's message.

Esme stood in the butterfly room's ruined doorway. She was dressed in black—black combats and a black hooded top with the sleeves pulled well down—and she held the pigeon sword clasped to her chest.

The rest of the room was filled with men with guns. Their last attempt to keep Esme sedated had ended badly: there had been a number of casualties, and now the Sons of the Scorpion Flail had decided on a policy of keeping a discreet and careful distance. They looked nervous. But Felix only had eyes for her.

"Go on," said Esme quietly.

"Well," said Felix, "we in the Brotherhood always believed that if the Scourge were ever allowed to escape and make its way back to Hell, it would form an army of demons and lead it back to conquer the Earth." He shrugged. "We were wrong."

"Tell me, Felix," said Esme.

"All our religions are false," Felix said. At this, a couple of the Sons began to shift awkwardly. Felix ignored them and pressed on.

"There's no benevolent Creator watching over us all. There's no divine justice, no grand master plan. There's just this . . . *being* that made the universe and has been asleep ever since. The demons call it the Dragon."

He took a step closer toward her.

"I've seen it," he said. "The Scourge took me to the lowest part of Hell, far below where the demons live, and showed me where it sleeps."

His voice dropped almost to a whisper.

"It's huge, Esme. You can't imagine how big it is: the brain just can't take it in. All of Hell is built on its back, and I don't think it's even noticed. And now the Scourge is going to wake it up."

"So?" said Number 2.

Felix gritted his teeth.

"The sole purpose of the Scourge's existence," he explained, "is to wake the Dragon. For the whole of its life—longer than we can possibly imagine—it's been trying to do this one thing. Once, before, it almost succeeded: instead, the Scourge was sent into exile—imprisoned, here on Earth. But ever since then it's been biding its time, waiting for another chance. And now, thanks to this boy, Charlie, that chance has finally come."

"The chance for what?" asked Number 3 quietly.

Felix didn't want to say it. It felt too much like another betrayal.

He took a deep breath.

"The Scourge hates all living things," he said. "Even—it seems—itself. The Scourge will use Charlie to help it wake the Dragon, and if the Scourge succeeds, if the Dragon wakes . . . the universe will come to an end."

He paused.

"The whole of Creation will be wiped out: *everything will cease to exist.* Instead, there will be only Void: nothingness. 'Purity,' the Scourge calls it. Forever."

There. He had said it. Immediately, the thing inside him woke up and began its work. Felix could feel it. There was no turning back now.

It was an odd sensation. When the Scourge had told him what was going to happen to him, he'd been expecting to panic when the time came. Now that it was here—now he could see it happening and feel the slow seeping cold moving all the way through him—he felt strangely calm. He looked down at his hands. Already they were becoming translucent. Another moment, and a dull metallic line began to make itself visible through the flesh of his wrists. The line was the other side of the handcuffs the Sons had put him in when they'd found him as he stepped back through the Fracture.

When he'd returned from Hell, Felix had brought his death with him. Now he was fading away. Literally.

"My message is this," he said. "The only thing that can stop the Scourge from waking the Dragon—the only thing that can stop the universe from being destroyed—is you, Esme. This is what I was summoned to tell you. Either you return to Hell and face the Scourge again, or, well . . ." He shrugged miserably. "You get the picture."

The handcuffs fell to the floor with a dull clank.

"That's it," he said. "That's the end of the message. I don't know what the Scourge wants with you: it's obviously a trap. But as you can see," he said, holding his hands up in front of his face, "I had no choice."

His hands were completely transparent now. Through the thin misty shapes that were all that remained of them, Felix and Esme looked at each other.

"I'm sorry, Esme," said Felix, keeping his gaze on her thirstily for as long as he could. Esme was, after all, the only person he cared about in the whole world—even though she was the one person who could never have cared about him. He didn't mind, he realized. He loved her anyway, just the same: he *loved* her, he told himself, and the realization cast a last wisp of warmth through the freezing, creeping cold inside him.

Esme stared back at him. Her eyes were bright.

Then suddenly, silently, Felix disappeared.

The Brotherhood of Sleep was finished: the last surviving member of the generation that had let the Scourge escape was gone, and the demon's vengeance on its jailers was complete.

Almost.

"Jack," Esme whispered.

"What?" said Number 2.

"Jack," she told him. "I need Jack."

THE MISSION

"So . . ." said Jack to Esme later. "What's the plan again?"

They were standing in the Light of the Moon. It was late in the evening of the following day. Number 2 had finally bowed to Number 3's repeated requests and closed the pub down: the place was deserted apart from Jack, Esme, and the Sons of the Scorpion Flail, who were busily checking their equipment.

The Sons looked tense. Fair enough, Jack decided: when he'd made his first trip to Hell, he'd done it without thinking. These guys, by contrast, had had a whole day to worry about what they were getting themselves into.

Esme adjusted the strap of the pigeon sword on her back and gave him a tired look.

"Jack," she said, "we've been through all this. Until we go in, we don't know what we're dealing with. I've got to tackle the Scourge—we know that much. You've got to do whatever you can with Charlie." She sighed. "That's all we can say for sure at this point."

"But what about these Sons guys?" Jack asked quietly, taking a step closer to her. "D'you really trust them? After they, like, chained you up and everything?"

Esme bit her lip.

"I was dangerous," she said. "They didn't know what I might do." She shivered. "*I* don't know what I might do. Besides," she added, banishing the thought quickly, "Jessica sent for them. They can't be completely useless—can they?"

"I suppose we need all the help we can get," said Jack dryly.

"Not all the help," Esme replied, looking around. "Too many and I'll have to be watching their backs, as well as yours and mine."

There was a pause.

"So," said Jack. "That's it, then."

"What is?"

"The plan." Jack tried a grin. "The plan is there is no plan."

"That's about the size of it," said Esme, with, Jack was glad to notice, a grim but definite smile. "Yeah."

"Business as usual, eh?" Jack quipped. His own smile faded. "Listen, there's, er, something I've got to tell you. It's about Charlie."

"What about him?" Esme asked.

Jack took a deep breath. "Esme," he said, "you can't kill him."

"Now, I know how it is," he went on quickly. "If it's a straight choice, Charlie or, like, saving the universe, then I guess you've got to do what you've got to do. But before things get that far, I just wanted to say . . . well . . ."

He looked at Esme.

"Charlie's an idiot," he told her. "I know he's an idiot. He's stubborn, impatient, arrogant, pigheaded, and, you know, sometimes he's a bit of a knob. But"—he shrugged helplessly—"he's my friend. He's got into this thing and it's gone over his head: he doesn't know what he's doing. And I want you to know that . . . well, whatever happens, I still think there's a chance we can save him. Okay?"

There was another pause.

Jack didn't claim to know very much about girls. He couldn't figure out what Esme was thinking. Her expression at that moment was, to him, unreadable.

"Jack," she said, "I don't know if we'll get the chance later, but . . ." She trailed off and looked down at her feet.

"What?" asked Jack.

"Well," said Esme, "I just wanted to thank you."

Jack stared at her.

"What for?"

Esme looked up at him, and Jack found himself transfixed by her amber eyes. Suddenly, he noticed a strange kind of tightening in his chest. His right kneecap, of all things, seemed to be twitching uncontrollably by itself: he hoped she didn't notice it. She really was, he decided again, very pretty indeed, actually.

"You brought me back," she said.

"Back?"

"Back from Hell," Esme prompted, smiling now. "When I was unconscious. That was you, right?"

"Oh," said Jack. "Er, yeah."

"Well, you know . . . thanks," Esme told him.

"'S'allright," Jack managed.

"I'm glad you're coming with me," said Esme.

And suddenly, she was giving him a hug! Esme was giving *him*—Jack!—a *hug*, and a stray hair from her elastic bands was tickling him on the nose! But just as suddenly as the hug had begun, it was over. Esme stood back.

"Good luck," she told him, looking into his eyes again. "And try to stay out of trouble, all right?"

"You too," said Jack. His ears were going red.

Esme smiled bleakly and turned away.

"Last check, gentlemen," said Number 2, and instantly the big pub was echoing with the nervous clicking and clinking of equipment—guns, ammo, who knew what else?—being rechecked for what must have been about the seventeenth time. Jack heard a flapping sound, then the Chinj swooped down to land on Jack's shoulder. Looking around, Jack caught its eye. The creature had arched one bushy eyebrow: it was smiling and giving Jack what looked suspiciously to him like a saucy look. Jack scowled. Then he noticed that the fiddling sounds of the Sons and their gear had stopped abruptly.

"What, may I ask," said Number 2, marching up to Jack in the sudden silence and pointing at the Chinj, "is *that*?"

Jack sighed. "It's a Chinj," he said gamely.

"How do you do?" asked the Chinj.

"What," said Number 2, still managing not to shout, "is it doing here?"

"He's not very polite, is he?" said the Chinj.

"It's kind of a long story," said Jack quickly, "and I figured it would only hold things up if I mentioned it before. The main thing is, it's coming with us."

"It most certainly is not!"

"And since it actually comes from Hell, it might be able to, I don't know, show us around a bit," Jack finished.

"I think you'll find I can really be quite helpful," put in the Chinj with a winning smile, doing its best.

For a moment, Number 2 just stared. His face was going a strange gray-red color, and Jack could see some goodish-sized veins standing out on his neck.

"I am *not*," began Number 2, "going on this mission with—"

"Hey," said Esme, walking up to Number 2 and looking up at him, right in the eye. "Me and Jack and . . ." She paused. "His, ah, friend here are going on this trip no matter what. As for you and your men . . ." She raked the room with a piercing gaze. "I still haven't decided yet whether I want *any* of you to come along—at all."

Number 2 stared at her and gaped.

"B-but," he spluttered. "But . . ."

Esme's amber eyes narrowed. Her hard hands lifted fractionally from her sides.

"Problem?" she asked.

Number 2 fell silent.

"Thought not," said Esme. "I'll let you take"—she considered—"three men. And you'd better stay out of our way. Now if you'll excuse us, we have a job to do."

She stalked off, over toward the cold spot in the air that marked the Fracture, leaving Number 2 standing there seething.

"Civilians," he said finally, and shook his head. He looked at his men and clicked his fingers: "Number Three? Number Nine? Number . . . Twelve? You're all with me. The rest of you, guard the Fracture till we come back." His face darkened. "*If* we come back."

"Sir! Yes, sir!" barked the Sons—while the ones he'd called stepped forward.

"All set, Number Nine?" asked Number 2, with a significant look at the enormous pack the younger Son was carrying. "Everything five-by-five?"

"Yes, sir!" Number 9 snapped back proudly. The mysterious black rectangle on his back was so large that it stuck out all round his head, making his face look almost comically small. "Cocked and locked and ready to rock! Sir!"

Jack winced.

"Good man," said Number 2. "Suit up, gentlemen. It's time to hit the road."

Four black gas masks were pulled into place with a simultaneous whisper. Looking at the effect, Jack had to admit it was a good one. With the simple addition of this one prop, the Sons had ceased to look quite so terrified and had become— well, if not actually terrifying, they certainly looked a lot more formidable than they had before.

Gesturing at the Fracture, Number 2 turned to Esme. "After you, Miss Leverton."

Esme didn't bother to acknowledge this. She didn't even turn round. She just lifted her hands, and immediately the patch of air in front of her took on its glowing sheen.

Jack sighed. *Well*, he thought, *here we go ag—*

"This is it, gentlemen," said Number 2, interrupting. "This is what we've been training for. You," he added, turning to his men—and conspicuously ignoring Jack, "have been picked for this mission for one simple reason: you're the best. You hear me?"

"Sir! Yes, Sir!" barked the three Sons, their voices now muffled by their gas masks.

"Make me proud," said Number 2.

Wallies, thought Jack conclusively.

The Fracture began to open, and the dull red gave way to crisp, whispering white. Number 2 took a step forward, so he stood shoulder to shoulder with Esme.

"Let's do it," he said.

They stepped into the light and vanished. The three other Sons went after.

"Here we go, sir," murmured the Chinj in Jack's ear. "Home sweet home."

"Sure," said Jack, not looking at it. *Right*. He stepped into the whiteness, feeling it take him.

When he opened his eyes, he was in the throne room.

"And Mr. Farrell!" said a voice. *"What a surprise."*

A glance around the great red room was all it took. Jack saw that the Sons had already been unmasked and were now struggling in the grip of the same jelly stuff he'd encountered on his first trip to Hell.

The Scourge stood up from its throne.

"Overminister," it said, "if you'd be so good, I'd like these people transported to the gladiator pits." It glanced at Jack. "That's where they belong, after all."

My pleasure, Sire, Gukumat replied.

"Esme, you're coming with me. Take my hand, please."

And that, really, was when Jack began to be scared.

Esme was standing before the throne. Her arm was lifting as if it were being pulled by invisible strings. As Esme put herself into the hands of her enemy, all Jack could do was watch in horror. Then, together, they disappeared.

Jack sighed bitterly. More jelly stuff was already climbing his legs, running up his back, surrounding him all over from head to toe. He felt an all-too-familiar squeezing sensation—a moment of unbelievable tension—then Gukumat, the Sons, and the throne room all vanished, and Jack found he was back in his cell.

The Chinj wasn't with him, he realized. It was the first time Jack had thought of the little creature since they'd stepped through the Fracture, and for a moment he felt a little guilty: he hoped it had got away all right. To be honest, though, as he reflected, looking around himself, he had enough problems to be getting on with on his own.

The cell was exactly the same. He was surrounded by the same sandy-colored walls, the same ceiling—or lack of one;

there was the same floor. It was almost as if he'd never left.

"Can anyone hear me?" he shouted quickly before his voice betrayed him. "Hello? Is anyone there?"

For a long moment there was silence. Then—and the sound was like two pieces of sandpaper rubbing together—Jack heard laughter.

"Well, well, well," said a voice. "If it isn't fresh meat."

Jack did not reply.

"How are you, fresh meat?" asked Shargle. "Did you miss me? I sure missed you."

Jack walked over to the nearest wall and leaned against it. Then he let his legs sag and his back slide down it, until he was sitting on the floor in the corner. *Oh, perfect*, he thought, this was just perfect. Of all the demons in Hell he could've had for a next-door neighbor, it had to be this one. How completely, utterly—

"I knew you'd come back," the worm hissed through the wall. "I've been waiting. And we're going to have fun, you an' me. I know it."

Well, thought Jack, that was that. His second trip to Hell had already gone about as well as his first. He sighed, rested his head on his hands, and waited for whatever was going to go wrong next.

BLOOD

"I'm glad you decided to come," said the Scourge.

"You didn't exactly leave me much of a choice," Esme replied.

"Perhaps not. But before that, before Felix passed on my message, you had already made another choice, had you not?"

Esme could feel warm air slipping by on the bare skin of her face. Although the darkness surrounding her was total, she knew they were traveling downward, and at great speed. The Scourge's hand was still holding hers; it was cool and smooth and nothing like a human hand at all.

"What are you talking about?" she asked.

"When we last fought, when I showed you what you are, you reacted strangely," said the Scourge. "For a while, I was even afraid that you might not recover. Your attempt to deny the truth about yourself might easily have destroyed you utterly. Instead, you woke up—and that is a choice, of a kind. The question is, Why?"

"Why do you think?" asked Esme through her teeth.

"I was hoping," said the Scourge, "it was because you've accepted the situation: you've understood what you are at last, and you've realized it's pointless to resist me."

"Guess again."

"But in fact," the Scourge went on wearily, "you've only come back because you still think you can defeat me."

"Bingo," said Esme.

"Oh dear," said the Scourge. "How tiresomely human of you. Well, we shall see."

A glimmer of light appeared far below them, quickly growing to a chilly white glow as they continued their plummeting descent. Esme now saw they were traveling at blurring speed down an arterial red–colored tunnel. The tunnel was becoming narrower and narrower, until there was barely enough room to pass without touching its moist-looking sides. Then it opened out suddenly into a space so vast that for a moment it took Esme's breath away.

Beneath Esme's feet, to begin with, was nothing more than a kind of steamy red mist: wherever the floor was, it was too far away to see, and the same was true of the walls. The ceiling, the only part of the room she could make out so far, seemed to stretch out forever in any direction she looked. It was made of the same wet-looking fleshy red stuff as the tunnel. All across it ran a series of meandering raised strips, like gigantic dark blue pipes of some kind. What Esme was seeing wasn't making a whole lot of sense to her, so as she and the demon hurtled on downward, she waited as calmly as she could for whatever the Scourge was going to show her next. But when at last the floor of the vast room *did* finally loom into view, Esme found herself staring again.

From here—from the altitude she was at now—the raised bluish pipe things didn't look like pipes anymore. They were more like blood vessels. *Veins*, she realized. Vast as it was, the room looked like it was alive. And gigantic. Bigger than anything she could possibly have imagined.

"**The heart of the Dragon,**" said the Scourge.

For the past few minutes, Esme had noticed an odd sensation inside herself. It was a kind of quickening: a shivering sense of electric anticipation, spreading through her whole being, sending rushes of goose bumps up her arms and the back of her neck. It wasn't fear or nerves—she'd learned to control those. It was something else. Something—

"Yes!" said the Scourge delightedly. "**You feel it. I knew you would.**"

"Feel what?" said Esme, and scowled at her own stubbornness forcing her into so weak a lie.

"**Don't you know what that is? That sensation?**"

"No."

"**I'll tell you. It is the demon in you.**"

"Yeah, right."

"**This place,**" said the Scourge, gesturing grandly with its free hand, "**is where our power comes from. This is where our people began: the first people, the rulers of Creation, and the ones who will bring it to its conclusion. All that is strong and good in you—all that is demon—has its origin in here. That is why you're feeling what you feel now.**"

"Why don't you just cut the nonsense," Esme suggested,

"and show me whatever it is you want to show me?"

"**All in good time,**" said the Scourge.

Far below, the veins on the floor of the chamber were getting bigger—bunching and bulging and knotting together. Before much longer, Esme could see what they were leading to: a plateau, huge and roughly circular, that swelled out of the surrounding meaty red flesh like some bulbous growth or excrescence. As they got closer, Esme began to make out more details.

Every inch of the plateau's fleshy red surface was covered, it seemed to her, by thousands of tall figures—each one of them apparently identical. Each and every one of them was dressed in flowing robes and floating off the ground. Each and every one of them had conjured a magical globe of light and was holding it, patiently, suspended over their long fingers to show the way.

Gukumat: all of the army of strange floating figures were Gukumat. As Esme and the Scourge made their final approach to the plateau, the Overminister's multiple bodies parted simultaneously, drifting back with a rustle of silk to form a place for the two of them to land. Trying hard not to boggle too obviously, Esme touched down, only a yard or so away from the boy the Scourge had brought her to see.

"**Charlie,**" said the Scourge. "**How are you?**"

"Oh, hi," said Charlie vaguely. "Yeah, I'm okay. How are you?"

Charlie was standing in front of a strange hump in the plateau's surface: a thick cylinder about the size of a petrol drum, made of meat. It was gnarled and twisted by the bone structure and blood vessels behind its fleshy exterior: like the plateau and everything else since the tunnel, it didn't look built, it looked *grown*.

Strangely, Charlie didn't seem to recognize Esme or even know she was there. After answering the Scourge, Charlie's eyes had gone blank: he just stood there, frozen, like a shop-window dummy waiting to be positioned, while the black tattoo writhed listlessly under his skin. Esme frowned.

"I now have complete control of his mind," the Scourge explained. "He will respond only to the stimuli I choose for him. He can't hear or see or sense anything other than what I allow him to. Including, of course, you."

"Nice," said Esme. "How did you manage that?"

"He wants to become Emperor of Hell," said the Scourge, with a smirk in its voice. "The fool wants it so much that he has abandoned everything from his life before he met me and put himself entirely into my hands. In short," it added, "he trusts me."

Esme looked at Charlie. She waved a hand in front of his eyes and only succeeded in making herself feel very silly indeed.

"All right," she said. "Well, what are you going to make him do?"

"We're going to wake the Dragon," said the Scourge. "This heart chamber, when the Dragon wakes, will be flooded for an instant with its lifeblood. In that instant, the Dragon will unmake what it created, and the purity of the Void will be complete once more."

Esme smiled mirthlessly. "That's a Hell of a story."

"Indeed," the Scourge replied. "It is, nonetheless, true."

Esme thought for a moment. The air in the chamber was moist and still. She was conscious of the vastness of the space around her and of Gukumat's eyes on her: all of them.

"Let's say I believe you," she began.

"I assure you," said the Scourge, "if you don't, then by the time you realize your mistake, it will already be too late."

"Sure. But this 'waking the Dragon' business," Esme went on slowly. "Can anyone do it, or is it just you?"

"Only I have the power to awaken the Dragon," said the Scourge, with quiet pride. "It is my greatest gift: the purpose of my life and the cause of my years of exile."

"But you can't do it *alone*," Esme pursued. "Can you? You have to have a puppet—some sucker to be your hands and do your dirty work for you. Am I right?"

"I cannot do it without a willing host body," the Scourge replied. "That is correct."

Esme thought some more. "Well," she said—

—and drew her weapon. The pigeon sword whispered through the air and stopped, millimeters from Charlie's throat.

"What if I just kill him?" she asked.

There was a pause.

No one had tried to stop her. Neither the Scourge nor Gukumat had moved in the slightest—and as for Charlie, Esme doubted whether he'd even noticed how close to death he was. Esme kept her blade at his throat. Her eyes became rooted to the rhythmic pulse of the artery in Charlie's neck.

She could strike him dead in a heartbeat. But she did not.

"You can't," said the Scourge gently. "Can you?"

The point of the blade shook fractionally as, for a second, Esme tried to force herself. Then, slowly, she took the sword away from Charlie's neck.

"Now you see how weak your humanity has made you," said the Scourge. It turned to the nearest Overminister. "Let us begin."

At once, Gukumat's voices rose in unison.

Blood will decide it. Blood will begin it. Seal your intention with blood.

Charlie blinked, and his eyes came into focus. He was still looking at the Scourge.

"What happens now?" he whispered.

Esme shook her head. It was pathetic.

"You must cut yourself, Charlie," the Scourge explained.

"You want me to *what*?"

"Cut yourself. Let a few drops of your blood fall onto the altar. This will"—it paused—"prove your determination to rule. Your left thumb would be a good place."

The Scourge made a small gesture, and an ink-black shape hunched out on Charlie's right shoulder: Ashmon scampered down his arm, and by the time the ferret creature reached his hand, it had become a scalpel-like knife. Surprised, Charlie looked down at the knife, then he looked back up at the Scourge.

"You, er . . ." he said. "You really want me to . . . ?"

"Trust me," said the Scourge.

"Well," said Charlie, "okay."

He wiped his left thumb on the leg of his black jeans, then brought it up toward the knife. The short, gleaming blade was now just a millimeter or two away from his skin.

Suddenly, weirdly, Charlie found that he was thinking of his body—falling into the river, dropping away endlessly into the cold and the wet and the dark. Then Charlie thought of his mother, still waiting for him at home. There was an odd feeling in his stomach—something warm and bright—and he realized that a big part of him didn't really want to do this. So, quickly, before he could think too much—

—he did it anyway.

The knife was so sharp that it didn't even hurt at first. It was only when he pushed the blade upward, opening the wound, that it started to sting. Charlie bit his lip and held his hand out over the cylinder thing. With a clicking sound that was surprisingly loud in the silence, fat droplets of dark blood fell onto its surface. The droplets began to form a pool.

Then it started.

With a sudden gurgling sound, the pool of blood simply vanished, sucked away out of sight. Surprised, Charlie took a step back—or rather, he tried to and found that he couldn't: his feet seemed to have disappeared into the ground.

There was a strange rustling, whispering, stretching-splitting-crackling sound, as unseen tendrils of flesh and sinew began to grow and thicken all around him. Something big was emerging from the floor behind him, a rearing shape like a shadow made of flesh, molding itself around Charlie's body. When the stuff reached his elbows, caressing him encouragingly, he flinched: but then, as he was gently but firmly pulled back into the chair—the throne of blood and bone that had been prepared for him—he smiled uncertainly. Seated now, his hands resting on great red swelling pillows of sticky meat, he rode the throne upward, grinning like an idiot, and all Esme could do was watch.

"CHARLIE!" she yelled. "*CHARLIE!*"

Of course, Charlie didn't answer. The Scourge took her hand. There was a sensation like huge black wings closing around her.

Then Esme opened her eyes, and she was somewhere else.

She was sitting on the edge of a bed. It was an ordinary single bed, but it looked quite strange to her just then, because apart from the bed there was nothing else in the room except whiteness—blank, bright, and surrounding—and the Scourge, standing before her.

"There," it said. "Now, for the first time, I think I see why living things are so strangely attached to their short and pointless little lives."

Esme just looked at it. "Excuse me?" she said.

"I have been waiting for that moment," said the Scourge slowly, "for longer than you could possibly imagine. It has been my one purpose in life, and my lifetime has lasted many thousands of times longer than the longest of humankind."

"Yes?" Esme managed. "So?"

"Through years of exile and imprisonment, I have been waiting to finish my task. And now—now, when the end is in sight—I find, to my astonishment, that I am thinking of renouncing it. Do you understand me?"

"Not really," said Esme. "No."

"Of course you don't." The Scourge shook its head. "How could you? How could you possibly grasp the enormity of what—"

"Okay, look," Esme interrupted, pointing at her face. "See? I'm bored now. Why don't we just fight and get this over with?"

"Because," said the Scourge, "I think . . ." It paused.

"I love you."

Esme stared at it with wide eyes.

"*What?*"

"You heard me."

"Yeah, I heard you," Esme spluttered, "but I don't know what the Hell you think you mean. What—what are you talking about?"

"You are my child!" said the Scourge, with sudden fervor. "Crippled, twisted, stunted by your humanity—but my child, a child of mine nonetheless."

It stood closer to her, leaning over her.

"I can help you," it murmured. "I can help you to become whatever it is in you to become. You are unique, my poor one. Since time began, there has been nothing to compare with you. And with me at your side you can—"

"All right, that's *enough*," said Esme. She shuddered.

The Scourge took a step back.

"I told Felix you could stop me," it said, sounding strangely . . .

hurt all of a sudden, Esme realized. "I didn't lie: here are my terms. If you will agree to stay with me here in Hell, I will stop the ritual. I'll release the boy. I'll abandon the very purpose of my existence, and the Dragon's sleep will remain unbroken."

Esme just stared.

"You are my daughter," the Scourge told her. "We belong together. If you can accept that, then the universe will be spared. If not, well . . ."

The Scourge shrugged.

"Think about what I've said. But don't take too long to decide."

It vanished, and Esme was left in the freezing whiteness, alone.

THE GATHERING

This is ridiculous, thought Jack, finally slumping on the sandy floor.

How the Hell was he supposed to rescue Charlie when he was trapped in a cell?

Come to that, how the Hell could Jack possibly find Charlie, even if he were able to get out? Thanks to the teleporting properties of the jelly stuff, Jack knew next to nothing about Hell's geography: he wouldn't've known where to begin to look.

Face it, he thought, if saving the universe was something someone like *him* was capable of doing, then everyone would be at it. It was as simple—as typical—as that.

It was at that moment that he heard a soft rumbling and creaking sound. The large stone wall was lifting again.

Jack sat up. The outside of his cell was in shadow: beyond the wall he could see nothing but darkness. He stood, walked over, and, gingerly, put his head out.

That was when Shargle grabbed him.

Thick coils of muscle dropped around him and tightened.

Jack struggled, but he couldn't move: his arms were crushing against his ribs, and one of Shargle's unspeakable heads was looming toward him, eyes glinting gray-blue in the dark.

"Hello, fresh meat," said the worm, grinning delightedly. "Remember me?"

"Of course I remember you, Shargle," said Jack, with exasperated effort. "But what the Hell do you want?"

"I'll tell you what I want," said Shargle, leaning closer. "I want to see your insides. Yes! Your nasty little innards, squeezing out of you! Fresh meat, you owe me a death!"

"What are you talking about?"

"You were promised to us!" whined Shargle's other head, rearing out of the darkness to Jack's left. "You're ours! It said so on the coin!"

"So?"

"Everyone's always so *mean* to Shargle," said the first head, pouting.

"Name-calling!" said the second.

"Hitting us!"

"Tying us together!" The heads looked at each other, shuddered in sympathy, then smiled. "But now," both of them chorused, "now, at last, *Shargle* can be mean to *you*!"

Heaven's sake, thought Jack. "Shargle," he began, "this really isn't a good time—"

"For us," announced Shargle's first head, "any time is a good time."

"But the universe is about to end!" Jack gasped, doing his best. "The Dragon is about to wake up!"

For a moment, all four of Shargle's eyes widened in surprise—then scowled.

"'The Dragon,'" one head snorted. "*That* old story!"

"No one believes in the Dragon anymore!"

"Now beg us for mercy!"

"Yes, beg." The worm's coils wrenched tighter.

"Whine! Cringe! Squeal!"

And now Jack could feel his bones grinding together. Great gouting blue fireworks were going off behind his eyeballs; his head felt ominously tight, like a tube of toothpaste being squeezed without the cap being taken off, and when he tried to breathe all there was was the nauseating stench of the worm. As Shargle's heads leaned toward him, the revolting wet brown holes of his mouths opening wider and wider, Jack's vision seemed to shrink down until he could see nothing else, but then . . .

Then, suddenly, there was a burst of light, and a thunderous, echoing voice said,

CITIZENS OF HELL, YOUR ATTENTION PLEASE: THIS IS OVERMINISTER GUKUMAT. YOU ARE SUMMONED, ONE AND ALL, TO AN ANCIENT CEREMONY. PREPARE FOR TRANSPORTATION, EACH AND EVERY ONE OF YOU, IN THREE—

There was a rising hum in the air: jelly stuff winked into being and began, instantly, to spread.

TWO, boomed the voice.

"EEEEEAAAAAAAAAAAAGHlllp!" Shargle shrieked out his frustration from both of his heads but was abruptly cut off as the shimmering substance swallowed him.

ONE.

The jelly stuff stiffened, went thick.

And for a moment, everything was black.

Shargle and Jack had been transported together: Jack was still wrapped in the worm's coils. Shargle's grip had loosened—a little, not much—but the weird thing was that Jack couldn't feel the ground. He seemed to be floating.

"Where are we?" Jack managed. "What's happened?"

"Jack?" said a voice with a French accent he recognized. "Jack? It is you?"

"Number Three!" said Jack. "Where are you? Oh, *Shargle,*" he added, struggling in the dark, "for God's sake, why can't you just get off me?"

"No!" squeaked Shargle nervously. "Shan't! No! Fresh meat can just—"

ATTENTION, SCUM OF THE GLADIATOR PITS!

Everyone fell silent.

You are here, said the voice, *not because we wish it but because the ritual demands that all demons in Hell be witness to the Dragon's awakening. You should see your presence here for what it is—an unspeakable honor for ones such as yourselves—and act accordingly.*

"Arse," belched another familiar voice.

You have been brought into the presence of the most holy and omnipotent DRAGON, Gukumat went on. *The Eater of Worlds: Alpha and Omega—the Creator and Destroyer of*

All. Look on your god, you supplicant scum. Look on your god and TREMBLE!

"Gah!" said Jack—and everyone else—as the darkness suddenly flooded with light. Jack's seared retinas took several moments to adjust. But the next thing he said was, "Whoa." The word didn't cover it. No words did. So for a while, Jack just stared.

Jack and Shargle were being held in a bubblelike field of what was, presumably, magic of some kind. As well as Jack and the worm, the bubble was big enough to hold all four Sons of the Scorpion Flail and a large pulsating blob that Jack was able to recognize—to his surprise—as Jagmat. Jagmat, Jack, Shargle, Number 3, Number 2, Number 9, and Number 12 were all floating around in the bubble like snow in a recently shaken snow globe. The Sons looked scared. They had a right to be. But Jack wasn't paying attention to his companions. The surface of the strange magical bubble thing that was now imprisoning them was transparent: Jack was looking out of the bubble at what was beyond.

He gaped.

The bubble was suspended from the ceiling of a gigantic red chamber—so big that Jack wasn't even sure it qualified as a single room. Other bubbles just like it, containing various numbers of unhappy gladiators, were strung around the ceiling in a vast, necklacelike ring.

Waiting below them, on the floor of the chamber, was what had to be every single demon in Hell. The entire demon population was laid out below Jack in a huge, dark, crawling circle. There were creatures down there that defied description. But he wasn't looking at these either.

In the center of the chamber was an enormous plateau, made out of the same bulging fleshy red stuff as the ceiling and floor. All across it stood a mass of identical white-robed figures. And in the center of that—at the center of everything—were two who Jack knew well: Charlie, seated on a throne of meat, and the Scourge, standing beside him.

DEMONS OF HELL! boomed Gukumat's multitudinous voice. *This is a day that has been long in coming! Only once before, since the beginning of Creation—only once, since the most holy Dragon first fell into its ancient slumber—has the whole mass of our people been gathered together as we are at this moment. And WHAT A SIGHT WE ARE!*

The gladiators' bubbles actually shuddered in the air at this; the giant chamber rang with the sound as all the demons on the ground roared their approval.

SINCE TIME BEGAN, IT IS WE WHO HAVE HAD POWER IN THE UNIVERSE!

The crowd was in ecstasy.

IT IS FOR US THAT THE PLANETS TREMBLE IN THEIR ORBITS!

Delirium. Pandemonium.

AND IT IS WE, said Gukumat, *BY DIVINE RIGHT, WHO WILL BRING ALL CREATION TO AN END!*

Strangely, on this line, the riotous applause from Hell's assembled population seemed to die down a little.

"Jack?" asked Number 2 suddenly. His face was pale, his

eyes were bright, and his voice was high and tight sounding. "Could you possibly tell us what's going on here, please?"

"Quiet," said Jack.

For too long, Gukumat went on, *the universe has been allowed to continue, filling the Great Darkness with its chatter and its noise. For too long we, the true guardians of Creation, have allowed it to wallow in its trivial and pointless pursuits. My brothers,* said the voice, *it is time to bring history to a close. It is time to awaken the Great Swallower and let darkness reign supreme once more! It is TIME,* the voice screamed, *reaching a pitch of feverish intensity, FOR A RETURN TO THE PURITY OF THE VOID!*

On uttering this, Gukumat raised every single one of his sticklike arms, ready to greet the rapturous thunder of acclaim that the Overminister was naturally expecting.

He didn't get it. Instead, the vast crowd murmured and blustered in confusion.

Gukumat's thousands of hands dropped to his thousands of sides. His thousands of shining robes flashed white as he turned his backs on the crowd—and bowed once, inward, low.

My demon brethren, he said, *there is one here who will explain what you are about to witness much better than I ever could. It is, therefore, my peculiar honor to present to you your one true Emperor. The Voice of the Void, whose breath is the wind and whose rage makes all worlds tremble. The Lord of Crossing-Places, King of All Tears, and the Suzerain Absolute of the Dominions of Hell. Demons, I give you—*

"Get *on* with it!" belched Jagmat.

—KHENTIMENTU THE SCOURGE!!!

Breaking scuffles on the ground suddenly became good-size riots: the crowds of demons were jostling for position, trying to get a look at what was going on.

Helpless, Jack just watched.

"But what about *me*?" whined Charlie suddenly.

The Scourge had been just about to speak. Now, distracted, it turned to look at the boy on the red throne. Charlie was scowling and tugging, weakly but insistently, at the demon's liquid-black arm.

"Hey!" said Charlie. "Aren't you listening? What about *me*? I mean—I'm going to be the Emperor, right? Not you."

"We're coming to you, Charlie," said the Scourge soothingly. **"In fact, I was just about to mention you."**

"No tricks," said Charlie. "*I'm* going to be Emperor. I am! Right? You promised."

"Indeed I did, Charlie," said the Scourge, resting a cool, liquid hand on the boy's cheek. **"Indeed I did."**

Charlie felt a soft pressure in his brain—a pushing sensation so slight that he barely noticed it.

And instantly his ears rang with an echoing storm of noise.

It was the crowd!

And they were chanting something! A rhythmic chant, two simple syllables, making the vast room reverberate as they repeated them again and again. What were they saying? It was hard to make it out. It wasn't—was it? Yes!

CHAR-LEE! they roared. CHAR-LEE! CHAR-LEE! CHAR-LEE!

"Your true Emperor, who will lead all Hell into a new era of peace and prosperity!" said the Scourge, the chant already collapsing into a surge of delirious noise. "CHARLIE FARNSWORTH!"

And the crowd went wild!

Charlie smiled, tears coming to his eyes and running down his face. He raised an arm, acknowledging the wave of respect, admiration, and, yes, love *that was coming at him then, a wave that threatened to lift him up and sweep him away on a tide of unspeakable happiness. They loved him! They really loved him! And what was even better, of course, the best thing of all, was that they'd* always *love him—forever and ever! Unlike, say, his dad for instance* (he grimaced), *the demons would never leave or decide they preferred someone else. They would never get tired or fed up or sad or change in any way whatsoever: they would love him unconditionally, forever. And Charlie and the demons would be happy together! Safe and happy until the end of time! Safe and happy and—*

The Scourge looked at the boy on the throne. Charlie's eyes were open, but they were glazed, their attention turned inward, lost in the trivial yet apparently necessary delusion that had taken perhaps two seconds to construct and position in the child's primitive mind.

You don't deserve the universe, thought the Scourge, disgusted. **None of you do.**

It turned to face the assembled masses.

"My fellow demons," it said, **"the time has come."**

"Shargle, get off me!" said Jack for what felt like the millionth time as he continued to struggle in the worm's quivering coils.

"The Dragon!" shrieked one head.

"It's real!" shrieked another. "The Scourge'll wake it up! We're doomed!"

"Shargle, give it a rest, will yer?" belched Jagmat, rippling a frill of his blancmangelike body to propel himself through the magic-charged air toward Jack.

"Whotsyerface!" he boomed, dealing the still-trussed Jack a blow on the shoulder with a burly pink pseudopod that sent him careening helplessly into the magic bubble's wall. The wall bulged, fizzed, but—luckily, in view of the vertiginous drop onto the waiting horde below—held.

"Jagmat," Jack managed. "Hi."

"Ain't that your friend down there?" Jagmat remarked, pointing at the distant figure of Charlie with a tentacle.

"Yeah," said Jack. "I'm afraid so."

"Him'n the Scourge ain't gonna do what I fink they're gonna do, are they?" Jagmat asked. His tone was light, but Jack could hear the seriousness underlying the question.

"Yeah," said Jack. "I think they are."

"Well, holy crap!" belched Jagmat, swelling up and turning pale. "We're in some trouble here and no mistake!"

But Jack didn't reply. He was distracted. At the top of the bubble something weird—as in, even more weird—was happening. A strange black spot had materialized in the air. For a moment, Jack thought he was imagining it, but the spot was getting bigger—until suddenly, before Jack's astonished eyes, a *face* had appeared: a tiny face, just hanging there.

It was the Chinj.

"There you are, sir!" it said. Its dainty features creased into a delicate grimace. "Erm, I'll be right with you."

For a moment, the extraordinary spectacle outside the bubble was forgotten. Jack, Jagmat, Shargle, Number 3, and the rest of the Sons all just stared as the strange hole in the air suddenly widened to a kind of doorway.

Beyond the doorway was darkness: it clearly led to some-where else. And it was big enough for a person to get through easily.

With a flutter of its wide black wings, the Chinj emerged into the bubble with them.

"What?" began Jack, his head beginning to hurt. "How did you—?"

"I'm afraid explanations will have to wait, sir," said the Chinj firmly. "Suffice it to say, I had help. Now . . ." It ges-tured behind itself. "This mini-Fracture will take us to a secure location in the Dragon's lymphatic system."

"Sorry?" said Jack.

"We should be far enough away for Gukumat not to be able to find us. However," the Chinj pursued grimly, "this Fracture is, I'm afraid, only temporary. If you wish to escape from your imprisonment here, you need to come with me. Right," it added, "now."

"Where're you going?" To Jack's surprise, it was one of Shargle's heads that had spoken.

The Chinj frowned. "It's no concern of yours, gladiator," it said primly. "But Jack and I are going to the Parliament."

"Parliament?" echoed Jack.

"It's our only hope," the Chinj announced. "We must speak with the Grand Cabal."

"No!" shrieked Shargle, unwinding his coils from round Jack at last and propelling himself to the furthest side of the bubble. "Not the Cabal! Not the Parliament! Not that!"

"I 'ate to admit it," belched Jagmat quietly, "but the worm's got a point: fink I'd rather take my chances with the Dragon."

"There's no time to argue," said the Chinj, turning to Jack. "Sir, if you want to help Miss Esme—if you want to stand any chance of preventing the Scourge from awakening the Dragon—then you simply must come with me this instant. I promise you," the Chinj added quietly, looking deep into Jack's eyes. "There's no other way."

"All right," said Jack. He turned to look at the Sons.

Even with his previous experience of Hell, Jack was finding the current situation alarming enough; the effect it was having on the Sons was clearly nothing short of catastrophic. The four grown men were floating and tangling and clinging helplessly to one another, a confused huddle of limbs, military equipment, and miserable scared faces.

"Come on," Jack told them. "Let's go."

"I am with you," said Number 3 after a moment, detaching himself and swimming over toward him through the magic-charged air.

"No *way*!" Number 2 spluttered, staring after him. "No way! There's no possibility on Earth that I'm following a kid and a . . ." Words failed him. "A *thing* into who-knows-what just because they say so. We're all staying here to, uh, assess the situation." He recovered himself. "That's an order."

"Sir," began Number 3, "with respect, we are not 'on Earth' any longer." He gestured outside the bubble, at the scene below. "We are out of our depth here: far out of our depth. Jack and his friend seem to know what zey are doing. I believe we should—"

"Three, I forbid you to follow them." Number 2 crossed his arms. "That's final."

"Look," said Jack, with sudden fury. "I don't know what you people have come here for. It's obviously some big secret, since you haven't told me what it is. Frankly, I couldn't care less. But I'll tell you why I'm here." He paused. "I'm here to help my friends and—it sounds like—save the universe. And I could do with a little help. Now, are you coming with me or what? Because if you're not, then you can just get stuffed!"

Get stuffed? echoed Jack's brain jeeringly. It was typical, really, just typical that he hadn't even managed to swear properly. Still, he'd said his piece: it was up to them now.

"Hell, I'll go," said Number 12, with a nervous glance at Shargle and Jagmat. "Anywhere's gotta be better than here— right?"

"Roger that," said Number 9.

The Chinj was looking at the portal, the edges of which

were vibrating and quivering ominously. "Sir," it said warningly.

"Just coming," said Jack.

"Well, I'm not!" said Number 2. "And you can't make me! There's no way you can—AAAGH!"

Number 12 and Number 9 had grabbed his shoulders roughly and thrown him. Helplessly, he slid through the magic-charged air. The Chinj fluttered daintily aside as Number 2 approached the mini-Fracture and plunged through it before he could stop himself.

The other Sons followed. Then Jack. Then the Chinj.

"Nutters," belched Jagmat.

But they'd vanished.

BLACK WINGS

For a long time Esme sat where the Scourge had left her, staring into whiteness, alone.

Then, a strange dark spot materialized in the air. The spot widened—and a small old man appeared.

The man was wearing a rumpled tweed suit with patches on the elbows and a large leather flying cap with big earflaps. He also wore fingerless gloves made out of purple wool, and he was rubbing his hands vigorously, producing an odd soft scrunching sound in the silence of the weird white room.

"I can't stand this place," he said, looking around.

"Sorry?" asked Esme.

"This *place*," snapped the man, who clearly hated repeating himself. "I can't stand it! Why the Scourge insists on taking people here, I simply can't imagine." He paused, looking nervously from side to side. "It's definitely gone. Hasn't it?"

"What's gone?"

"The Scourge!"

"Oh. Yes. Yes, it's gone."

"Well, that's something, at any rate. Oooh, it's cold in here." The man went back to rubbing his hands for another moment or two. Then, suddenly, as if noticing her for the first time, he looked up at Esme. "How do you do?" he said, beaming delightedly. "I'm God."

Esme's eyes narrowed. "Hi," she said carefully.

"I've been meaning to speak to you for quite a while, actually," said God. "I've helped your friend, and now it's your turn, but . . . well, it's much too cold for me in here." He gestured behind him at the extraordinary hole in the air, which was now wide enough for them both to pass through. "Why don't we step into my office," he asked, "as it were?"

Esme looked at him.

"I'm sorry," she said, feeling very strange, "but really, I have to stay here."

God's hand fell to his sides. "Don't tell me," he said. "You've got to save the universe."

"Well, yeah," said Esme, surprised.

"Well, believe me," said God, "you certainly won't be able to do that alone, so please, why don't you stop wasting my time and—*unkh*!"

He made the last noise because Esme's hand was suddenly around his throat. Pulling God toward her easily, Esme showed him she was serious for a moment: his eyes bugged outward and his little arms flapped in the air in a very satisfactory manner. Then she relaxed her grip enough to let him breathe.

"You know," she said, "I'm not feeling very patient or

polite right now. In fact, I'm not in a good mood at all. So how about you just tell me what you want?"

"It's not what *I* want," said God, with obvious difficulty. "It's what *you* want. What I can offer you."

"And what's that?"

"Knowledge," said God.

Esme just looked at him.

"I'm the archivist here," God explained. "I have records of everything that has happened—and I do mean everything—since time began. If there's anything you want to know—anything at all—then I can help you!"

Esme frowned. "You can tell me how to beat the Scourge?"

"Maybe."

"Maybe's no use to me."

"Maybe's all I've got," snapped God.

Esme stared at him, surprised again: he was annoyed at her, she realized, not because she had him by the throat but because she'd disrespected his job and what he knew.

"All right," she said, and released him.

"*Thank* you," said God. "Now, shall we?" He held out a hand.

Esme took it uncertainly, and they stepped through the hole in the air, out into whatever was beyond.

Esme blinked: the whiteness of the strange room had vanished, and it took a moment for her eyes to adjust. They were hovering, she realized, in midair, in the center of a tall, chimneylike structure. The chimney was very wide, and its walls were made of thousands of huge slabs of black rock, fitted one on top of the other. High above, Esme saw a tiny pinprick of gray light. Darkness yawned below her feet.

"We are now," God announced proudly, "in the central shaft of the palace. It stretches all the way from the Needle, at its summit, right down to the Dragon's heart—a distance of some seventy thousand—"

BOOM! He was interrupted by a sudden deep burst of noise coming up from somewhere below them. A jarring series of rippling shock waves shook the rocks, massive as they were, in their places.

"Ah," said God, as loose dust and soot fell pattering around them. "Oh dear."

"You want to tell me what that was?" asked Esme.

"It's the Dragon," said God, as if it was obvious. "The Dragon's juices have been released, and they are now eating away at the foundations of the palace. Soon all Hell—and all its inhabitants—will be digested, converted into raw energy so that the Great Swallower can wake itself up. The Scourge must be further along with the ritual than I thought. We'd better hurry."

"Hurry where?" asked Esme.

"That way," said God, jabbing one mauve-gloved finger upward. "And quickly, if you please. As fast as you can."

Esme pursed her lips but did as she was asked. The massive slabs of black rock in the chimney sides began to blur together as she picked up speed. After a few seconds, she turned to look at her companion.

"Is this right?" she enquired. "We keep going like this?"

"No," said God, shaking his head. "Stop a minute. Please, just stop."

Puzzled, Esme did. Soon they were perfectly still once more, hanging in midair over the yawning chasm below.

"I thought," said God, with elaborate sarcasm, "that you were supposed to be *fast*."

"Sorry?" said Esme.

"You're kin to Khentimentu!" said God, as if he were talking to a moron. "When it comes to speed, in all Hell's long history there's never been a demon to match the Scourge. And here you are," he added, "toddling along like we've got all the time in the universe!"

"You want me to go faster?" Esme asked. "Is that what you're saying?"

"If it's not too much trouble," said God, with a sneer.

For another long moment, Esme just looked at him. Then, "Fine," she said—

—and took off at high speed straightaway. The old man's fingers tightened around hers in an effort not to be left behind. She forged on, blasting her way upward, until noise of the air resistance building up in front of her began to roar in her ears.

"There!" she shouted. "How about that?"

But to her surprise, God was shaking his head again.

Incredulous, Esme slowed to a stop once more, just as—

BAKHOOM! Another great shudder of noise from below rippled the very air around them. When the walls stopped shaking, Esme saw that God was almost incandescent with impatience.

"Didn't you hear me?" he asked. He gestured round them. "Didn't you hear that? We have places to go! Things to do! And all you do is dawdle!"

"I wouldn't call that dawdling," said Esme.

"I've known Chinj who could fly faster than you're going," God spat. Then he sighed. "I thought you had a real chance against the Scourge. I thought you might have what it takes." He looked her up and down, then shook his head. "Obviously, I was mistaken."

"Look," said Esme, feeling herself losing patience again. "I don't know what it is you want from me exactly, but I'll tell you: it's not possible to fly any faster than that."

"Oh, great!" said God. "Perfect! Now we're going to get into an argument about what's 'possible'! And what a wonderful time and place for it, I might add!"

Esme stared at him.

"Don't you know anything?" said God. "The Scourge can be faster than *light*. The molecules simply part around it: the very fabric of reality would get out of Khentimentu's way if that were its wish. And here's *you*, arguing with *me* about what's possible."

"Hang on," said Esme. "You're saying I can be as fast as the Scourge?"

"Hallelujah," said God theatrically. "I do believe the penny is starting to drop."

"Faster than light?" echoed Esme.

"And things like walls won't stop you either," said God. "Now, are you going to get a move on or aren't you?"

Esme bit her lip and thought about it.

"All right," she said. "I suppose I could try. But there's just one thing. If I can really be as fast as you say, how will we know where we're going?"

"My dear girl," said God. "You just keep to your side of things, and I'll worry about mine. All right? I just need you to get up to speed."

Esme shrugged. "Okay, then. Let's go."

"And put your back into it this time!" squeaked God.

But suddenly, they were going so fast that the wind whipped the words from his mouth.

Still frowning, Esme took herself up to what she'd considered up till then to be her top speed and stayed there. Words echoed and spun in her head.

The Scourge could move faster than light.

There's something a bit special about you.

Strength without limit. Power beyond imagining—

Was it true? she wondered. Was it really true that all along she had only been using a fraction of her potential? Perhaps it was. But if she did let her power out, if she did use her potential, wasn't that . . . well, dangerous? If her power came from the Scourge, then perhaps she wouldn't be able to control it. Perhaps it might make her evil: perhaps it might mean that the Scourge could control her. Even now, with so much at stake, that was too much of a risk. It was just too dangerous—wasn't it?

But . . .

A real chance against the Scourge.

You still think you can defeat me.

You're not human!

Remember your mother.

Esme concentrated. She felt the air resistance on her face like a weight, pressing at her all over, but she forced herself to ignore it. She ignored the strange old man with his hand in hers, she ignored the walls of the great chimney flashing past—she ignored everything, in fact, and turned her attention inward, forcing herself to concentrate only on each moment and the moment that followed it, one at a time. She closed her eyes, feeling the tension of the air, its reluctance to let her pass.

And she let her mind find a way through it.

Suddenly, every molecule in her body began to dance and tremble. It was a little like the sensation she'd felt in the heart chamber, only this time it was stronger. She could feel, inside herself, the power that had waited all her life as it began to wake, uncurl itself, take hold.

Now Esme let it happen.

"Yes!" shrieked God. "Yes! *Yes!*"

But Esme didn't hear him. All she could hear was the rushing scream of the air as it grew red-hot—then white-hot—then, finally, as it gave up its resistance and let her through.

There was silence.

Black wings closed around them both.

And when Esme opened her eyes, she was somewhere else.

"Not bad!" said God, grinning at her slyly. "Not bad at all. For a beginner."

Esme didn't reply.

"Set us down over there," God suggested, gesturing past the large stone balustrade that had appeared around them. "Go on. Take a moment to get your bearings."

She did as God said, slipping smoothly through the air, over the balustrade, bringing them both to rest, gently, on the cool marble floor that lay beyond it.

Blinking a bit, Esme looked around herself.

"Welcome," God announced, "to the Halls of Ages! The single greatest repository of history in the universe!"

A deep rumble from below them greeted his words, and God suddenly turned rather pale.

"Whatever you've brought me here to see," said Esme, "you'd better show it to me right now."

"Yes," said God, grimacing. "I think you may be right. This way, please." And with that he scuttled away, down one of the vast, arched corridors that led away ahead of them.

Esme sighed, but she set off after him.

THE PLUNGE

Number 2 picked himself up from where he'd landed, brushing nonexistent dust off his uniform with great care, while the other Sons and Jack watched him apprehensively.

"The device," he said finally, snapping his fingers.

Number 9 frowned. "Sir?"

"The *pack*, soldier!" growled Number 2. "Give it to me! On the double!"

"Sir! Yes, sir!" said Number 9.

"Now," said Number 2, when the giant black pack's mysterious weight was settled on his back to his satisfaction, "I want you all to listen to me very carefully."

He looked at his men one at a time, conspicuously ignoring Jack and the Chinj.

"In view of current, uh, circumstances"—he eyed the narrow, moist, pink-walled tunnel they'd appeared in with distaste—"I'm going to pass over what happened just now and pretend that it never took place. But I will say this." He fixed each member of his team with a glittering glance. "If any one of you punks even thinks about pulling a stunt like that again, you'll have me to answer to. And believe me, when I'm done, Hell's gonna look like the teddy bears' picnic. Clear?"

"Sir. Yes, sir," said the other Sons.

"I am ranking officer here," said Number 2, with great emphasis. "I'm in charge. That means no one decides what we're going to do except *me*. Understand?"

"Sir, yes, sir."

Number 2 sighed, turned, and looked at the Chinj, who was now perched on Jack's shoulder. "So, uh, where to next?" he muttered.

"That way," said the Chinj, stifling a smirk and pointing down the tunnel with one wing. "In my opinion," it added politely.

"This way, people!" Number 2 announced loudly, gesturing in the direction the Chinj had just indicated. "Come on, let's move with a purpose."

They set off.

The tunnel was quite narrow, so the group had to walk in single file.

The floor sank slightly with every step, a little—but not quite—like wet sand. Jack, touching one of the walls briefly with one hand, couldn't help noticing that as well as being rather slimy, it was also unnervingly warm to the touch.

"The passage," he whispered to the Chinj. "It's almost like . . . like it's alive."

"It is," the Chinj replied.

S
A
M

E
N
T
H
O
V
E
N

Jack turned to the creature perched on his shoulder and gave it a level look.

"Okay," he said, "you're definitely going to have to explain that one."

"With pleasure." The Chinj cleared its throat. "Over the millennia since the universe began," it announced, "Hell has vastly outgrown its original size. Its foundations, nonetheless, were built upon a system of living tissue."

"What living tissue?" asked Jack. "Not . . ." He thought about it for a moment. "Not the Dragon?"

"That's right," said the Chinj encouragingly.

"So Hell is part of the Dragon?" asked Jack, doing his best.

"A very small part, yes. A bit like a mole, or a . . ." The small creature paused, obviously struggling to find the right word. "A growth."

"Wait a second," said Jack. "Are you seriously trying to tell me that the whole of Hell is just, like, a spot on the Dragon's *bum*?"

"I beg your pardon, sir," said the Chinj icily, "but the heartland of the Demon Empire is rather more significant than a—what did you call it? A 'spot.' And as to which part of the Dragon's anatomy Hell is situated upon, why, that's one of the fundamental mysteries of the universe. The greatest Chinj theologians have debated that very point for—"

"But Hell grew out of the Dragon," pressed Jack, interrupting, "and this Dragon is so big that it didn't even notice—right? That's what you believe?"

"It's what I know."

"How do you know?"

"Because I'm part of it too."

"You're *what*?" said Jack.

The Chinj sighed. "Look," it said. "In your body you've got all sorts of . . . pathways. You have a nervous system, blood vessels, digestion—right?"

"O-kay," said Jack slowly.

"Well!" The Chinj gestured at the pinkish-red walls around them and at the sloping floor that was becoming increasingly warm and moist and squelchy the further down-ward they progressed. "That's what we've got here! Now, when we first met and I took that sample of your blood, I noticed that it contains a number of specialized cells that ferry essen-tial supplies around your body—oxygen, that sort of thing. Correct?"

"I guess."

"Well, that's what we Chinj do for the Dragon," said the creature.

"Sorry," said Jack. "You've lost me."

"But it's simple, sir!" squeaked the Chinj exasperatedly. "Think about it: think about us and what we actually do. We carry essential nutrients to the various parts of the demon population. We feed the body politic! In essence, there's no difference between we Chinj and your blood cells—it's simply a matter of scale."

Jack gave this his best shot—and failed.

"No, I'm not getting this at all," he said. "How come you're awake and the Dragon isn't? How come, if you're part of the Dragon, it was okay for you to leave and come to Earth to get me?" *And how come I'm even* asking *questions like this?* he added, though not aloud.

"I told you," the Chinj replied. "If you stayed away, I'd just have to come back here every day. And to answer your other question: well, your body keeps going when you're asleep, doesn't it?"

"Yeah, but—"

"You remain alive even when you're not awake, don't you?"

"It's not the same thing. We're talking about being asleep since *time began.*"

"That's true," said the Chinj, "but the Great Depositories—the stores of eternal nourishment to which all Chinj must return to replenish themselves—are bigger than you can possibly imagine. They're a long way off running out yet. Perhaps," it added, with a mischievous nudge of one leathery elbow, "one day, if we survive this, I may even show them to you. But there, now: I'm talking about secrets that even demons do not know."

"Really?" asked Jack, frowning. "The demons don't even know this stuff?"

"Of course not," said the Chinj, shocked. "Why, none but the Chinj may know the secrets of the gruel. In fact," it went on, its small furry face taking on an unmistakably guilty expression, "strictly speaking, it's only the Chinj themselves who are allowed to enter these tunnels. On pain of death, actually."

Jack gave the Chinj another long look.

"Well, I'm sure it won't happen in this case," said the

Chinj, a little too enthusiastically for Jack's liking. "I mean, these are rather particular circumstances, don't you think?"

"Hmm," said Jack. "Who's in charge down here?"

"The Grand Cabal," said the Chinj loftily. "The Parliament"—it paused—"of the Chinj."

"Oh!" said Jack. "Just you Chinj, then."

"Naturally."

Jack let out a sigh. "Phew. That's all right, then. I thought for a second you were telling me we were in trouble here."

The Chinj flared its tiny nostrils and shot Jack a look of surprising venom.

"Do *not*," it said, "underestimate the power of the Grand Cabal. We Chinj have guarded our secrets for longer than you could ever understand. Why do you think the demons are afraid to come down here? Because only a fool would risk the wrath of the Parliament of Chinj."

"Sure," said Jack distractedly. "Right."

He was concentrating on the floor. The passage was now so steep that he was finding it hard to keep his footing—and the Sons were having the same problem. He looked ahead, just in time to see Number 2—

"*Gah!*"

—slip, and bring the full weight of the pack down with him as he fell. *Wham!*

"I'm all right!" he said, flinging off the helping hands of Number 3. He shuffled around to face Jack and the Chinj; Jack struggled to wipe the smile off his face in time, but he wasn't quite fast enough.

"Mind telling me how much more of this stuff there is to deal with?" Number 2 growled.

"These passageways are not usually navigated on foot," the Chinj replied sniffily.

"Is it going to get much steeper?"

"Yes," said the Chinj. "I'm afraid so."

"Terrific," said Number 2. "So how do you suggest we continue? Besides on our arses, I mean."

"That," said the Chinj, drawing itself up to its full height on Jack's shoulder, "is *your* problem."

For a long moment, the man and the Chinj looked at each other.

"Let's keep going," said Jack quietly.

"What did you say?" asked Number 2, his eyes flashing dangerously.

"I said, let's keep going. We can't solve anything by standing about here."

"You know," said Number 2, "I think I've had just about enough of you. You're not here to give orders. In fact," he added, "why *are* you here? I wish someone would tell me why we've got to have a *kid* along, because I'd really like to—"

"Jack is right," said Number 3, from up ahead. He shrugged. "Let's go."

For a second, Number 2 seemed so enraged that Jack thought his eyeballs were going to pop right out of his head. This was no figure of speech: Jack had seen it happen to someone once before, after all. But when Number 2 had got himself and the pack turned back round again, all he said was, "All right. Let's keep it moving. But watch your step now."

They continued in silence down the passageway.

Now Jack found himself having to turn his feet sideways to stop himself from slipping completely: the sides of his trainers seemed to bite a little way into the soft pink surface of the wall, giving him a precious bit of extra traction, but soon just trying to stay upright became a hard enough task, even without the effort to keep going. The walls were close enough for him to support himself with his hands: the passage was now so narrow that Jack could barely see past the struggling figure of Number 2 and his pack.

Jack was looking at the pack, still trying to guess what it might contain, when, suddenly, Number 2 lost his footing again. His big boots slid out from under him. The pack hit the floor, and in another second he was plunging down the tunnel.

Number 3 didn't stand a chance: Number 2 scythed helplessly into him, then the pair of them vanished from sight.

Jack looked behind him at the two remaining Sons—Number 9 and Number 12. Both were wearing identical horrified grimaces on their faces.

"Great!" said Number 12. "Now what're we going to do?"

"We go after them," said Number 9. "Obviously."

"Wait!" said Jack. He turned to the Chinj. "What's down there? Is it safe?"

The Chinj shook its head. "I—I couldn't say. I've always flown this way before. Perhaps the impact might—"

"Look, we've got to go after them!" Number 9 repeated. "We've got to. Right?"

"I think the landing should be soft enough," said the Chinj. "I'm just worried that all this noise might—"

"'Kay," said Number 9. "Let's go." He shoved past Jack. He reached his hands out to either side of him and took as good a grip of the slippery pink walls as he could. Then he swung himself once and set off.

Jack and Number 12 exchanged a look. Sheepishly, the last Son squeezed past Jack, shrugged, sat down, and gingerly pushed himself off, following his comrades out of view almost instantly.

There was a pause.

"Humans," said the Chinj. "So impetuous. As bad as demons, really."

"I guess we're going to have to follow them," said Jack.

"I see no other option," the Chinj replied. "They'll definitely get into trouble without us."

"Why? What's down the end of this thing?"

"It's not what's down there," said the Chinj. "It's what all their noise is going to bring. Look," it added distractedly, frowning and gesturing with one wing, "you'd better go."

Jack looked down the tunnel.

"Oh, Hell," he said, but he sat down.

"Piece of advice, sir," said the Chinj into his ear from behind him. "There's a bit of a drop at the end. My guess is that you'll minimize any injuries you sustain if you keep as relaxed as possible. All right?"

"What?" said Jack.

But with a sudden leaping movement, the Chinj had knocked Jack's hand away from the wall. Jack scrabbled to get his grip back, but already, inexorably, he had begun to slide.

"Good luck, sir!" Jack heard the Chinj call after him. "And remember! Do try to relax!"

Jack picked up speed quickly. Once he'd forced himself to take his hands in from the sides and fold them in his lap, he began to go faster still. The tunnel was now almost vertical: the walls were accelerating to a smooth pink blur—and Jack found, to his surprise, that he was enjoying himself.

It was better than any water chute he'd ever been on. Still the tunnel continued, an apparently endless tube of glistening fleshy red. The only sound was the soft hissing from where his jeans and T-shirt were still making contact with the sides—and soon even that had faded away, because the chute was now so steep that he was barely touching them. There was a long, drawn-out moment of absolute silence, a silence in which Jack had time to reflect that whatever was at the bottom of this thing had better be *unbelievably* soft, when, suddenly, without warning, the pink walls of the tunnel abruptly vanished, to be replaced by . . . nothing.

AAAAAAAAAAAAAGH! said his brain, not unreasonably. Darkness and emptiness gaped around him. The trickles and droplets of thin, clear slime that had eased his descent seemed to thicken in the air, drifting up past his face as he fell. His arms began to paddle and flap. He waited, plummeting for long, aching moments, and then—

WHUDGE!

He hit something.

There was a thrashing of darkness, warm and wet. It streamed past every inch of Jack's body. Gradually, he felt himself slow, then stop falling—and then, of course, he had another problem. He couldn't breathe. His chest was going tight and his ears were beginning to sing. The thick, squidgy liquid seemed reluctant to let him through. Jack struggled and kicked, struggled and kicked. Then, suddenly, he caught a glimmer of light. He flung himself upward. Strong hands had grabbed him. The dreadful slime burst over his head— and he was out.

He gasped, sucking in a great glob of gunge with his first breath, which made him start coughing all the air out again.

"There," said Number 3's voice. "Just breathe. You are safe."

Jack hacked and spluttered some more. "Blimey!" he managed finally. Then he fell silent, looking at Number 3's face, which loomed palely at him out of the surrounding darkness. Jack saw the expression there change from concern to relief. Number 3 was actually glad he was all right: Jack found that oddly touching.

"Did, er . . ." he said, once he'd got himself together. "Did everyone make it all right?"

"They are all 'ere," said Number 3, gesturing with his torch.

For a second Jack didn't recognize them, covered as they were in the same tarlike substance he could feel dripping from his own ears, hair, and everywhere else. The other

Sons were all taking a moment. Number 2, who'd presumably had an especially difficult time, what with the pack, simply sat, breathing hard, with his oil-black legs sticking out in front of him.

The floor was strange. It crackled and crunched like shingle when Jack moved. He reached underneath himself and picked up a bit of it. Whatever the object was, it was too big to be a pebble. It felt hollow and delicate, and it was an odd shape: his probing fingers suddenly slipped into two little holes in the thing, and Jack hurriedly shook the object off with a shudder he couldn't explain.

"Is anyone hurt?" he asked quickly.

Hearing him, Number 2 looked up and took a deep breath.

"Everyone okay?" he barked. "Everyone still five-by-five?"

"I don't know about anyone else," said a voice in the darkness, "but—far as I'm concerned? This mission sucks."

"You shut your mouth, Number Nine," said Number 2.

"I'm Number Twelve, sir," said the voice. "*He's* Number Nine."

"I don't care what your number is, soldier," Number 2 snapped back. "I'm telling you, if you don't shut your mouth, you'll . . . you'll be sorry!"

"Um, where's the Chinj?" Jack asked.

No one answered.

Well, Jack thought, the Chinj could look after itself. It would be back soon enough—he hoped. He sighed. Suddenly he decided he'd had enough of the darkness.

"Do any of you have anything stronger than these

torches?" he asked, doing his best to ignore the way his voice was echoing. "What about a flare or something?"

There was a rustling sound, and torch beams danced overhead as the Sons checked their pouches and pockets. "I've got one," said Number 9.

"Well, don't keep us in suspense, soldier," said Number 2. "Light it up!"

There was a soft *flump*! Then the room was bathed in red light.

And Jack's mouth fell open.

At the center of the room, lapping sluggishly at the shore of crunchy stuff, was a lake of what appeared to be oil of some kind. It was completely black, except for where it reflected the burning red of the flare, and the ripples moved eerily slowly across its surface. But it wasn't this that Jack was looking at, really. What he was looking at was the roof.

The room was big: a gigantic hemisphere of shining black rock, arching overhead. He could see at least a dozen tunnel openings, high up the sides. Between these, the ceiling was entirely covered by a carpet of dangling, leathery black egg-like objects, packed together very tightly. As the flare continued to burn, Jack stared at them—stared until the light began to flicker, then went out, and the darkness was filled with the big blue splashes on his retinas.

At the last moment, some of the egg things had started moving.

There was another soft *flump* and another. As two more flares lit up the room, Jack saw that his earlier impression had been right. The strange dangling objects *were* moving, in a rippling motion that quickly spread across the whole of the ceiling.

"What on Earth?" began Number 2 as a soft, high-pitched squeaking began to fill the air.

"Put out the light," said Jack. Realizing he was whispering, he said it again, as loud as he could. "PUT OUT THE LIGHT!"

The two men holding the flares looked at him for a moment.

Then the ceiling seemed simply to drop.

"GET 'EM OFF! GET OFF ME! *AAAAAAAGH!*" someone screamed, as everything vanished in a welter of wings and fangs. Long, clever fingers were clutching at Jack's neck, feverishly groping for something; whatever it was, they obviously found it, because Jack felt a sudden nervous pressure that made his whole body go limp and floppy. Curled up on the floor, in the last, wild second before losing consciousness, Jack glimpsed the "pebble" he'd picked up earlier. The strange holes his fingers had got stuck in *looked back*, and he realized that it was a skull.

His head filled with darkness. It was as if a second passageway had opened up beneath him and he was plunging again, as helplessly as before.

This time, however, it was bottomless.

THE STAFF

"Right," said God. He pulled his gloves off and dropped them on the table, next to the brass lamp with its green glass shade. Then he held his hands out and closed his eyes.

The air in front of God's hands began to wobble and shake. The effect was a bit like heat haze, but it only lasted for a moment, because just then a shadowy shape appeared, a shape that instantly began to thicken and stretch. The shape was long and silvery: a small flash of light trickled along its length as it materialized.

Esme looked at the magical staff that had formed in God's hands. Her throat seemed to have gone strangely dry.

God opened one eye. "You've seen one before."

"Yes," said Esme. Nick's "test" suddenly seemed a long time ago. "But—"

"In here," said God, "is the answer you're looking for." He closed his eye again. "For what it's worth."

Esme took a deep breath. "All right," she said. "I'm ready."

"We'll see," said God.

Esme put her hands out: already her fingers were curling around the magical staff. Slowly, carefully, she let them curl a little further, and a little further still, until she could almost feel the cool of its metal on her skin. Then she closed her fists on it.

It was like being hit by a wave of cold water. The shock of the first images almost stopped her heart in her chest.

Death.

The images flickered and spun.

Death.

The images wouldn't stop coming.

Death.

And before she knew she was doing it, she'd let go of the staff, gasping.

"*God*," she said. "That was—"

"Yes," he replied. "That was your mother."

"I don't . . ." Esme was breathing hard. "Why are you showing me this?"

"Because, even though she failed, it's the last time the Scourge came close to being defeated," said God. "Because it's time you knew the truth—and the truth, I'm afraid, always hurts. Now, have you seen enough? Do you understand what you have to do?"

Esme stared at him. Her head was full of what she'd just seen, the glimpses of it. Still, she took another deep breath, forcing herself back under control.

"Show me the rest," she said.

God looked at her, blinked, and bit his lip.

"Actually," he said, "I'd rather not."

"I'm sorry?"

God pouted. His eyes, Esme noticed, were shining strangely.

"If you must know," he said, "I find it all rather upsetting. It upsets me," he repeated, "personally. All right? So if it's all the same to you, I think I'd really prefer it if—"

"Show me," said Esme quietly. "Now."

"Oh, all *right*," said God—and sniffed heavily. "Hold out your hands, then."

Esme did. She closed her eyes. She took hold of the staff, and as the magical vision took her up like a wave, she held on tightly.

And this time, she saw everything.

A young woman was lying on a concrete floor.

Her skin was very dark, her orange caftan was very bright, and her strong brown feet were bare in a pair of knackered old sandals. Her hair fizzed out all around her face like a black halo. Her amber eyes were dim with pain, and thick blood was running from her nose and mouth. The young man kneeling beside her pulled down his sleeve and dabbed at her uselessly.

"She's bleeding internally!" he said, panicking. "I can't stop it!"

"Belinda," said Nick, standing over the woman, still dressed in his customary black. "I—"

The woman scowled and deliberately looked away from

Nick, turning her gaze instead on the kneeling man. A hand reached up and pulled him toward her with a fierce, feverish strength that surprised him.

"Raymond," she whispered.

"I'm here, petal," breathed the big man.

"You," said the woman, with difficulty. "Not Jessica. Not Nick. *You*." She took a breath. "Teach her," she said. "Look—" The word rattled to nothing. "Look after her." She was breathing fast now, the breaths coming in little shallow gulps that made it hard for her to form the words. "Tell her I l—"

She tried again.

"Tell her I l—"

It wouldn't come out.

"I'll tell her, love, I swear it!" said Raymond. "I'll tell her every day!"

And when the woman heard this, she smiled. Slowly, she drew her hand down the big man's rough, wet cheek—and the quick breaths suddenly ceased.

Then she died.

"There," said God, as the magical staff wobbled and disappeared. Tears dribbled freely down his wrinkled face. "*Now* are you satisfied?"

Esme just looked at him. She felt numb inside—cold. Still, she had enough strength left to ask the first question that had to be asked.

"How do you know all of this?" she said.

"What?" God sniffed. "You think I *faked* it?"

"What proof," asked Esme, with infinite patience, "can you give me that all that really happened?"

For a moment, God stared at her as though dumbfounded.

"Hell's teeth!" he shouted, stamping his foot and gesturing at his face. "Look what that did to me! Are you made of *stone*?"

But Esme just stared back at him, waiting. Her own tears were long dry now. A ball of something hard and bright and cold and heavy had formed inside her; she could feel it, the shape of it, tight against her ribs when she breathed. Her expression as she stared at the old man then did not waver in the slightest. She met God's eyes: met them until he had to look away.

He sighed. "Look, I told you," he said. "I'm the archivist of Hell. I'm your *god*: I know everything, that's how I got this job."

Esme was still staring at him. Still waiting.

"All right!" said God, throwing his hands up. "I don't have any proof!" He thought of something and, smiling a thin smile, he added, "You're just going to have to take it on faith."

There was a long pause.

"Okay," said Esme. "Then I've got a few more questions I'd like to ask."

"Shoot," said God.

Esme took a deep breath, because for a moment, to her surprise, it seemed that the tears might come back. But then she said it.

"They didn't stand a chance, did they?"

God looked up. "Who? The Brotherhood?"

"Everybody," said Esme. "If it hadn't been Felix who let the Scourge out, it would've been someone else."

"Yes," said God. "I'm afraid that's probably true."

"So why was the Scourge imprisoned on Earth?" asked Esme. "Why put it among people, when it was obvious that one day someone would let it escape?"

God sighed. "Nobody knew or cared about my little planet." He shrugged. "It seemed the safest place. But the fact is, wherever Khentimentu was imprisoned, it was only ever going to be a matter of time before it got out." He smiled mirthlessly. "That's the problem with dealing with something that can't be killed."

"But why put it among people?" Esme repeated. "I mean, how could you do that to them?"

"It wasn't *my* decision!" God bit his lip. "Besides," he huffed, "I've helped you now. Haven't I?"

Esme sighed.

"All right, then," she said slowly. "Well, what about how to defeat the Scourge?"

God stared at her. "I thought *that* was pretty obvious," he said. "Didn't you? I'm certainly not going to show you the vision again."

"I don't want you to," said Esme, her patience beginning to wear thin. "I just want you to tell me something I can use, like you promised."

"But I showed you!" said God, exasperated.

"Showed me what?" said Esme, her voice rising despite herself.

"The answer!"

"What answer? Why can't you just tell me?"

"DUH!" said God. "What's wrong with you people? Did you all turn stupid after I created you? The only way to defeat the Scourge—the only way to make the magic strong enough to trap Khentimentu in the staff—is through—"

"Yes?" said Esme.

"Through . . . well . . ." God trailed off suddenly.

"*Yes?*"

"Through sacrifice," he finished.

There was a pause.

"What?" asked Esme.

"I think that someone has to die," said God. He looked up and, seeing Esme's expression, added: "I'm sorry, but there it is." Then he looked down at his feet.

There was another, longer pause, as Esme considered this.

She'd known, she supposed. At least, she always should've known.

What else was there for her, anyway? She was neither one thing nor the other, not demon and not human: she belonged nowhere.

This was her job. One job she'd trained her whole life to do: one chance to have her revenge.

Boom! The room shook, and a million glass bottles rattled in the boxes on the walls.

"You, er . . ." God looked guiltily at his feet again. "You don't have much time."

Esme squared her shoulders.

"All right," she said. "I'll do it."

TO THE DEATH

"There," said the Scourge, turning to the nearest Gukumat. "I believe we are ready to proceed. Is everything in place?"

The Overminister bowed. *Yes, Sire. It's just—*

"What is it?" The Scourge was suddenly aware of all of Gukumat's eyes looking in its direction.

Gukumat bowed again and folded his long-fingered hands in front of his robes in an awkward, self-effacing gesture. *One hates to question Your Worship at a time like this,* he said, *but the situation being what it is, one can't help but feel a little . . . concerned.*

"Say what you mean, Gukumat," said the Scourge, beginning to understand why Hacha'Fravashi had disliked him so much.

Very well, Sire. It's the boy. Gukumat gestured toward Charlie, who was still sitting bolt upright, a blissful smile on his face. *Are you quite sure he's . . . safe?*

"The boy is in my power," said the Scourge, as patiently as it could. "He is, I assure you, perfectly 'safe.'"

Your Worship's words are most reassuring, said the Overminister.

However, the fact remains that when he realizes what is to become of him, he—

"Charlie is not your concern, Gukumat," snapped the Scourge. Then, in a more conciliatory tone, it added, "Please, leave him to me. Now, is everything ready for the next stage?"

For perhaps three whole hundredths of a second, Gukumat thought about this.

At that moment, the Overminister was engaged in a number of simultaneous activities. The Carnotaur—arguably the most dangerous of the gladiators—had lost what little patience its pea-size brain possessed and was busily attempting to break out of its magical bonds. A detachment of twelve clones was subduing it with fire lances while another fifteen were combining their powers to shore up the bubblelike wall of its makeshift prison. At that very instant too some seven thousand other Gukumats were also engaged throughout the vast heart chamber in similar containment activities with Hell's increasingly unruly populace. Demons were an impatient breed and not given to waiting in one place for long: there had already been casualties. However, these were well within acceptable limits. In fact, as the Overminister had discovered, having Hell's entire population in one place actually made it a lot easier to deal with—logistically speaking, at least.

It is, Sire, he answered.

"Splendid," said the Scourge. "Then—"

A ripple went through the humid air, a soft susurrus of power that set the silken robes of the surrounding Gukumats rustling. The Scourge paused, distracted. Some twenty feet away across the wet pink fleshy floor, a patch of space seemed to bulge suddenly, condensing, taking shape.

Then Esme appeared.

She stood with her hands at her sides, the hilt of the pigeon sword jutting over her shoulder. The nearest Gukumats opened their hooked jaws and hissed at her, but they might as well not have been there. Her eyes were closed, but as soon as the haze of molecular disturbance in the air had dispersed around her, she opened them and looked at the Scourge, hard.

The Scourge folded its liquid-black arms. Though it showed no outward sign of it, it was smiling.

"So," it said. "You've taken the first step. You're beginning to realize what you can become. My congratulations: you're clearly a fast learner."

Esme said nothing.

"Am I to understand that this means you have decided to accept my offer?"

Esme looked around herself slowly. She looked at the gladiators, trapped high above in their bubbles of magic. She looked at Charlie, frozen, staring, on his throne of meat. She looked at the massed ranks of the Gukumats and the clamoring horde of demons spread across the landscape far below.

"You've been busy," she said.

"We have," agreed the Scourge. It gestured in Charlie's direction with long, inky fingers. "The boy is about to complete the ritual," it said. "You're just in time."

"How does it work?" said Esme. "If you don't mind my asking?"

"Not at all!" said the Scourge. "It's like this: before awakening fully, the Dragon must first be convinced that the universe is ready for its own annihilation. Do you understand me so far?"

Esme grimaced but nodded.

"Well," said the Scourge, "the reason I need Charlie is that he's going to play the part of the universe's *representative*."

Esme frowned.

"In just a few moments now, Charlie will be offered a choice. He will be granted a glimpse of the whole of Creation, and the Dragon will ask Charlie, as the universe's spokesman, what he, Charlie, wishes should be done with it. In that instant, the fate of us all will rest solely in Charlie's hands."

"And?"

"Naturally, Charlie will be so obsessed with his own little preoccupations that he won't have the wit to understand what is being offered. With—I assure you—only the slightest of nudges from me, he will answer the Dragon's question in exactly the way I want him to. Then, at last, the awakening will be unstoppable."

"By *mistake*?" said Esme, incredulous. "You're saying that Charlie's going to cause the destruction of the universe by *mistake*?"

"You could call it a mistake on his part, perhaps," said the Scourge. "There will, I promise, be no mistake on mine.

"So," it added, after a moment, "what do you say?"

There was a pause.

"Let me get this straight," said Esme. "If I agree to what you said, then you're going to stop all this?"

Abruptly, every single one of the Gukumats seemed to stiffen.

"You're going to abandon the idea of waking the Dragon," Esme went on, "and never even think about ending the universe again, *ever*. Right?"

"**That was my offer,**" the Scourge replied. "**Yes.**"

A ripple of consternation spread through the ranks of Gukumats.

My lord! the Overminister began. *I—!*

"I don't believe you," said Esme.

There was another pause.

"**What?**" said the Scourge.

"It's quite simple," Esme began. "If I really believed that taking up your offer—that acting"—she wrinkled her nose—"as your 'daughter' was actually going to stop you from doing what you're doing, then believe me, I'd agree like a shot."

She smiled fiercely.

"I'm not going to lie to you: I wouldn't like it. In fact, the idea of having to call you 'Daddy' is just about the single most repulsive thing I can think of. But if it was really a straight choice between that and letting you kill everyone, then repulsive or not, there'd be no contest, obviously. *However*," she added, continuing to stare at the Scourge, trying to gauge what effect her words were having (its liquid-black face remained smooth and impassive, just as it always did), "that's not really the situation here—is it?"

No one answered.

"You know," said Esme, taking her time, "there's one thing about this that makes me very angry indeed."

Neither Gukumat nor the Scourge spoke.

"It's not the blackmail," said Esme, "the 'love me or else!' thing—though to be sure that certainly is pretty irritating.

"It's not even," she added, "the fact you've murdered my family and put a blight on my entire life.

"It's the fact," she went on, the cold, tight sensation in her chest brightening, hardening, "that you've asked me to *trust you afterwards.*"

She glared at the demon.

"Do you really expect me to believe anything you say, after all you've done?" she asked. "Do you really expect me to believe that you can keep a promise, after the lies you've told and the lives you've ruined?"

"**I gave you my word**—" said the Scourge.

"Yeah, and maybe you even believed it," said Esme. "But the point is, *I don't.* And if you thought I was going to, you're obviously a lot stupider than I imagined."

"**You reject my offer, then?**" asked the Scourge.

"You're damn right I reject your offer."

Esme's hard brown hands lifted fractionally from her sides. Her amber eyes glittered as she faced her enemy, and the Gukumats around her all backed away—away from the girl and the way that she smiled.

"No tricks," said Esme. "No more lies. You and me are going to fight this out to the finish. Right now."

THE GRAND CABAL

Jack came to, or thought he did—it was so dark it was hard to tell—to the sound of voices.

"Didn't even get a shot off," said one.

"Twelve," began Number 3 wearily.

"Hello?" croaked Jack.

"Jack!" said Number 3, relieved. "You are all right over there?"

"Um, yes. I think so." In actual fact, Jack wasn't at all sure. He could wriggle his fingers and toes, but everything else seemed to be stuck. Even turning his head was apparently impossible: he pushed, quite hard in fact, but the only result was a soft, resinous creaking sound from whatever held him. His whole body was throbbing, as if a great weight were pressing on it.

"Well? What the Hell is this place, kid?" burst out Number 2, to Jack's annoyance. "Just where the Hell are we now?"

"Where the Hell do you think?" said Jack grimly. "We're in Hell."

"But what's going to happen to us? Why's it so dark?"

"Because in Hell," muttered Jack, "no matter how bad things get, you know they can always get worse."

"Listen to the smallest of you!" said an unfamiliar voice suddenly. "He shows wisdom! It's a pity that he didn't show this wisdom earlier—before you all committed the crimes that will result in your death!"

There was an answering chittering sound that came from all around them: a sound, Jack realized, like laughter.

"Bring lights for the soup-suckers!" said the voice. "It's time for them to see who they've offended!"

There was a soft *flump*; then there was light. The cave they were in was not big by Hell's standards, perhaps fifty or sixty feet high—but Jack and the Sons were *stuck to the ceiling*. Directly below them was another pool of mysterious liquid, this one pale and frothy looking, the color of sour milk. Ranged around the pool, clinging to the floor and walls of the cave staring up at them with a million shiny black bush-baby eyes that glinted in the light, were more Chinj than Jack could ever have guessed existed. The ranks of leathery-winged bodies stretched as far as Jack's eyes could see.

"*Gluttons!*" screeched the voice. "Soup-slurpers! Vulgarians! See the grisly fate that awaits you—you and all who trespass in the sacred byways of the Chinj!"

Jack looked for where the voice was coming from: its origin wasn't hard to find. On the far shore of the frothy sour-milk stuff, three long steps had been cut roughly into the sheer black walls of the cave. At the center of the top step, flanked by a squadron of fierce and, with their graying fur, oddly venerable-looking bat creatures, stood a lone, pale figure.

This elder Chinj was almost white with age. Its wings were ragged, peppered with holes. The fur all over its body had fallen out in places, and great ugly patches of its gray and wrinkled skin had been left exposed to the elements. Its ears, by contrast, were crested with large and luxuriant snow-white tufts of hair, growing straight out of the tips as well as, Jack noticed, from the insides. A thick milky cataract dulled one of the Chinj's eyes, but the other blazed up at them with a hatred that was astonishing to see.

"You who have feasted on our holy works!" the Chinj shrieked. "You who have suckled at our treats! You, who've grown fat on the fruits of our toils and yet now have violated our most sacred trust!"

There was a chorus of angry squeaks from the rest of the flock.

"Gruel gobblers!" howled the elder Chinj. "Chunder-munchers! Let the trials," it screamed, "commence!"

It was at this point, unfortunately, that Number 2 burst out laughing. Soon, the walls of the cave were ringing with it—hard, brash gales of laughter that were made all the more ugly by the obvious edge of hysteria to them.

To Jack's surprise, the elder Chinj just waited until the laughter died away.

"You find us amusing?" it asked quietly.

Number 2 made a snorting sound in his nose. "What is all this?" he said.

The elder Chinj's stare did not waver. "I'm quite certain that you don't need reminding," it said. "But just for the record, I will state your crime. You were caught trespassing in the nursery pits, where none but the Chinj may go."

"And this means what to me, exactly?" said Number 2.

"There is but one penalty for this offense," said the elder Chinj, drawing itself up to its full height, which, it had to be said, wasn't very high. "Death," it announced.

The word spread around the cave like an echo, carried by the squeaking voices from a million furry throats.

"Death!" the flock chanted in time: "Death! Death!"— and now it was Number 2's turn to wait until the noise died down.

"Cut us loose, short stuff," said Number 2. "Don't mess with us: you might get stepped on."

Number 12, glued in place beside him, guffawed loudly. Jack gritted his teeth.

"Yes," said the elder Chinj, with dignity. "I will cut you loose. I think first, however, it's time for a little demonstration of who, exactly, is 'messing' with who." It turned to the squadron of thickset Chinj standing on the step below it. "Start with the one to the noisy one's left," it said, indicating Number 12 with a skeletal front paw.

As one, the squadron leaped into the air. In seconds the creatures were swarming all over him, until it seemed the Son had simply vanished under a mass of leathery bodies—but then, suddenly, and with an eerie precision, the Chinj stopped what they were doing and flapped back down to their places on the steps. In another moment, an excited, barely maintained silence had returned to the cave.

Jack waited, holding his breath.

"Are you ready, soup-sucker?" asked the elder Chinj quietly. "Are you ready for your death?"

"You know what?" Number 12 asked back, with a smug glance at his colleagues. "I've had just about enough of this. Why don't you just cut me loose and—"

There was a soft ripping noise, and before Jack knew what had happened, Number 12 had fallen into the pool.

There was a long moment, then the hapless Son bobbed to the surface, coughing and spluttering. Whatever the milky stuff was, he was covered in it from head to foot. Thick curds of it clung to him all over: he looked like he'd been sprayed with cottage cheese.

Quietly at first, the Chinj were chanting again: a single word, getting louder all the time. "Death," they said. "Death. Death. *Death. Death.* DEATH. DEATH. *DEATH!*"

Number 12 was looking down at his hands, frowning at something. The white stuff that covered him was beginning to take on a strange, pinkish quality. The pink turned to soft red as it started to happen.

Jack's eyes went wide.

No, he thought.

Oh, God. Yes! It was true!

Suddenly, unstoppably, Number 12 was being *dissolved*.

With horrible speed, his hands seemed to melt—to shrink and then vanish into fat pinkish-red droplets that fell to the surface of the frothing, milky pool. Now his whole body was disappearing, and the skin on his skull was sizzling away to reveal the raw, wet bone underneath. As Jack stared down, unable to look away from the hideous spectacle, Number 12 helplessly turned his now-empty eye sockets upward at Number 2.

His lipless jaws had just hung open to scream when he sank from sight.

The chanting of the Chinj broke down into a feverish chorus of cackling and cheering. All that remained of Number 12 was a spreading, pinkish stain. In another moment that too had gone, and the elder Chinj raised a front paw for silence.

Jack gaped.

"You see?" crowed the chief Chinj, once relative silence had returned to the cave. "You see who you have offended?"

"Wh-what?" stuttered Number 2. "What have you done with my man?"

"You have blundered," said the elder Chinj, "into the belly of the beast. You and your comrades will be made useful for perhaps the first time in your guzzling little lives: you shall be broken down!" it announced, hopping from one long three-toed foot to the other. "You shall be dissolved in the holy juices of the Dragon! Your bodies shall be among the first to become fuel for the Awakening—an unmerited honor for the likes of you, I might add! So, prepare yourself, soup-sucker!" it finished, leering toothlessly. *"You're next!"*

The flock was already all over Number 2. He'd all but disappeared under a blur of leathery black bodies, but his screams were still as clear as anything.

"Wait!" he screeched. "God! No! For the love of Christ, please, *wait!*"

Smiling broadly, the old bat creature made a signal with one wizened forepaw. Instantly, the flock drew back.

"This isn't . . ." began Number 2, then tried again. "This isn't right!"

"'Not right'?" scoffed the elder Chinj, its eyes bulging. "Are you in our sacred chambers or not?"

"But we didn't know about the—the sacred places," Number 2 wailed. "It wasn't our idea to come here!"

Er, hang on, thought Jack.

"Really," said the elder Chinj. "Then whose was it, may I ask?"

"Number Two," hissed Jack. "Shut up!"

"We were led here!" said Number 2, his voice reaching a sort of ecstasy of whining. "We were led here by a *Chinj*!"

The word echoed around the cave. Bat creature looked at bat creature in stunned dismay, dismay that turned to outrage, outrage that echoed from a million furry throats in a rising, chattering tide.

"Who," managed the elder Chinj, its forepaws actually quivering with fury. "*Who did this?*"

"Me," said a voice from the far end of the cave. "I did it," said Jack's Chinj.

The whole room went instantly quiet.

The elder Chinj turned. Its good eye took on a laserlike intensity that would have reduced even a full-size demon to jelly. However, Jack's Chinj stood firm, meeting its ruler's gaze with a look that managed to be defiant yet respectful at the same time.

"What is your designation, young Chinj?" asked the eldest bat creature grimly.

Jack's Chinj stood to attention. "Second division, third under-Chinj, rating B-thirty-seven-stroke-six! Sir!" it recited, then bowed deeply.

"Chinj B-thirty-seven-stroke-six," said the elder Chinj, acknowledging the bow with a curt nod, "you have been accused of leading these creatures into our most sacred places. This constitutes high treason, the most heinous crime it is within the power of our people to commit. I will ask again—and I want you to think carefully before you answer. *Did you lead them here?*"

The silence and tension in the room were palpable: the air was thick with them—or maybe it was the smell that was all that was left of Number 12; Jack didn't really want to think about which.

"I want to tell you why," said the Chinj.

In the tension-filled hush the elder Chinj looked around the cave. "Go on," it said.

"I did this," said Jack's Chinj. "I broke the most important rule of our people because I believed it was the right thing to do." It paused. "Every Chinj here knows what I'm talking about. You've all, every one of you, known it for ages."

"Reach your point, young Chinj," cautioned the elder. "Our patience grows thin."

"The Dragon is about to awake," said Jack's Chinj.

A small murmur spread through the flock at its words—though what sort of emotion the reaction represented it was impossible at that moment for Jack to tell.

"As you say," said the elder Chinj carefully. "We know this. What's your point?"

"My point, Sire," said Jack's Chinj, "is that this cannot be allowed to happen."

The murmur rose to a rumble of dissent, and Jack's Chinj had to struggle to make itself heard.

"I brought these people here because I believe they can stop the awakening! We should help them, not kill them!" These last words were lost under a sudden tumult of squeaking and flapping from the flock.

"QUIET!" roared the elder Chinj. "I MUST HAVE QUIET!"

It thumped its stick on the platform until the hubbub died down a little.

"You astonish me, young Chinj," it said. "You seem to forget: we *are* the Dragon. It lives through us. Its wakening and final triumph should be our ultimate goal! I mean . . ." The elder Chinj looked incredulously around at its flock. "Don't the rest of you *want* the Dragon to wake up?"

Jack was working out what all the fuss was about. While it was true that some of the Chinj supported the elder, it was obvious that at least an equal number of the creatures weren't at all so certain. Squabbles were breaking out all over the cave, and the air was filled with anxious screeching and cackling as the flock began to fight.

"Listen to me!" shouted Jack's Chinj. "If the Dragon wakes, it'll mean the end of *everything*. The end of the demons! The end of the universe! The end of *us*!"

"This is heresy!" roared the elder Chinj. "All our lives we have suffered the indignity of serving the demons! Now at last the time of judgment is at hand! We shall take our rightful places at the cornerstone of Creation and plunge gladly into the Great Void from whence we came!"

"I don't *want* the Great Void," snapped Jack's Chinj, to a dangerous chatter of agreement from the flock. "I like being alive!"

"You call what we do *life*?" replied the elder. "All we do is feed the soup-suckers!"

"I like being alive!" repeated Jack's Chinj stubbornly. "The Dragon's awakening can't be allowed!"

"It is *right*! It is fate! It is how the universe was ordained!"

"RUBBISH!" screamed Jack's Chinj.

Anything further in this exchange was drowned out utterly as the whole of the gigantic flock of bat creatures finally flew into confusion.

In all this, it seemed, Jack and the rest of the Sons had been temporarily forgotten.

Quickly, Jack tried his bonds—not too hard, obviously. He was still stuck fast. So were the three remaining Sons. All the men were doing was staring helplessly. The Sons were going to be no use at all. So, of course, it was down to Jack. *Typical.*

He took a deep breath, then shouted at the top of his lungs. "HEY!"

He was bigger than the Chinj. He was definitely noisier. A good third of the flock suddenly stopped arguing and looked up at him. The others were still at it, so he tried again. "HEY! HEY, *YOU*! *HEY!*"

The noise died down a bit more. Now even the elder Chinj was looking in his direction.

"Listen," said Jack. "I've got a proposition for you."

"I don't believe this," said Number 9, later. He and Number 3 were making an inventory of whatever equipment had survived their journey.

Number 3 didn't answer. After a last vain attempt to clear the black slime out of the barrel of one of the two rocket launchers the team had brought with them, he tossed it aside with a scowl.

"I don't believe that kid!" said Number 9. "Where'd he learn to bargain like that? I mean, that was beautiful! Number Two gets left here with the pack, so Project Justice is still game on—and it's all down to Jack! Who'd've guessed it?"

Suddenly, Number 3 stopped what he was doing and straightened up, his expression darkening.

"Number Three?"

"I told you," Jack was saying to the elder Chinj. "You've got my promise."

"And what use is that? The word of a *soup-sucker.*"

"And you've got a *hostage*," Jack finished through gritted teeth.

"The Grand Cabal finds your terms to be acceptable," said the large Chinj standing to the elder's right. It turned to the elder. "May I remind you, my lord, that the Parliament has made its decision. The Chinj peoples have spoken—and you, I'm afraid, must abide by their wishes. Your truculence is unseemly."

"But this is *wrong*, my brother," said the elder Chinj. "You cannot expect me to stand idly by and watch the long-awaited awakening being jeopardized."

"Look," Jack interrupted. "This is a no-lose situation for you. If we do stop the awakening, then you've still got your consolation prize: you've got my promise that I'll come back, and I've left you Number Two as security."

"Believe me, young human," hissed the elder Chinj, "your agony shall give me considerable pleasure."

"Fine, dissolve me, whatever, I don't care—but you never know," Jack went on. "If we fail, then you get your awakening thingamajig anyway. So you'll still be happy. All right?"

"Hmph," said the elder Chinj.

"Now if you'll excuse me," said Jack, "I've got to go and help someone save the universe. Before it's too late," he added grimly.

"We too must make our preparations," replied the Chief Grand Cabal SpokesChinj. "We shall meet again."

"Count on it," said Jack.

He watched as the council head and the elder Chinj leaped into the air and flapped off back down the tunnel. His own Chinj stood by him, also watching them go. Then it looked up at Jack.

"Sir," it began.

"Jack," said Jack. "Call me Jack."

"Jack, then," said the Chinj. "I must say, I don't think I understand you very well. Not at all, to tell the truth."

Jack looked at the bat creature. "It's pretty simple," he said. "I figured either you Chinj get me, or the universe comes to an end. I'm stuffed either way, so what difference does it make how it happens?"

"Well," said the Chinj, "I suppose if you put it like that . . ."

It paused.

"Do you know, sir?" it said—and by the time Jack had thought to correct it it had already gone on—"I think that there may be more demon—more *gladiator*—in you than you suspect."

They looked at each other. The Chinj was smiling. After a moment, Jack found that he was too.

"Come on," he said. "Let's go find the others. I want to introduce you to an interesting human invention."

"Oh yes?" asked the Chinj, polite but dubious. "And what's that?"

"Guns," said Jack, and smirked darkly to himself. "Lots of guns."

He set off down the tunnel.

The Chinj shrugged its small shoulders and set off after him.

The Last Battle

For another moment, the Scourge stared at Esme.

"**You still think you can win?**" it asked. "**Even after your failures before?**"

"Stop talking and find out," was Esme's reply.

"**As you wish.**" The Scourge unfolded its liquid-black arms.

It took two steps, blurred into motion, and before Esme had time to realize what was happening she felt a blow that took her breath away.

It was like being swatted with an oil tanker. She was hurled back a clear forty feet straight through the air, landing with an impact that drove the air from her lungs. In front of her eyes, the air shimmered, shook, and the Scourge reappeared again. Now cool liquid fingers held Esme by the throat. Looking down the shining black surface of the Scourge's arm, she caught her own startled expression reflected in its face. Carelessly, easily, it jerked her into the air. Feeling her trainered feet leaving the sticky pink ground, Esme looked downward.

She was dangling over the edge of the plateau.

"Now," said the Scourge, its voice completely casual, "**are you beginning to realize what a mistake you've made? Or do you need me to show you some more? Hmm?**"

Esme felt the dreadful grip loosen on her neck. Her windpipe released, she gasped for air. "You're—" she managed. "You're—"

"Yes," said the Scourge, enjoying the moment. "**My strength has returned. I'm now quite capable of defeating you without the boy. So** *you*," it went on, the grip going tight again, "**have lost what little chance you had. Haven't you?**"

Esme closed her eyes. Her head was pounding, her vision was closing in: dark shadows were swallowing everything. As the seconds stretched out, Esme knew she couldn't wait: whatever she was going to do, she would have to do it now. Forcing herself, she reached down inside herself. She felt a shifting sensation—

—then the Scourge's grip was gone, and she could breathe again. She staggered, looking around herself. She had reappeared on the other side of the platform, away from the edge. She could see the Gukumats, backing away all around her. She could see Charlie still sitting frozen on his throne. And as the air bulged and shook and a liquid-black shadow materialized in front of her, she could see the Scourge.

"Good," it said. "**You're learning. It's a shame, really, that this thing between us has to come to an end. But it** *is* **going to end. Now.**"

And with another blur of movement that was faster than the eye could catch, it launched its attack.

Esme caught the first blow on her forearm, blocking it without thinking. Another blow instantly came lashing at her face and she swerved back to dodge it, swinging her elbows round and together to block the demon's follow-up to her body. Every blow that followed she managed to block, but every block she managed still *hurt*—and step by driving step, she knew, the Scourge was forcing her back across the plateau, away from the center, back toward the edge once again. Esme tried a leap—

—and a muscular piston of darkness shot out from the liquid-black body, catching her by the waist and dragging her back down easily, even as a clubbing roundhouse punch swung in toward the right side of her head to punish her. She caught the blow again on the outside of her forearm: the impact drove a flare of pain right through her shoulders.

But then, with her left, she struck.

It was a solid blow: though it only traveled about a foot or so, it carried all her weight and strength behind it.

It landed smack in the center of the Scourge's face.

For a moment, Esme could actually feel the darkness spreading around her fist, taking her in. She pulled, and a tiny ripple of black spread around the spot where she'd struck, but her fist was now trapped—stuck fast.

The Scourge's body began to shiver and shift. When the darkness resettled, an ink-black hand was on the point of her elbow, and the place where she'd struck had become another hand, gripping her at the wrist.

Esme's arm was straight out. She had time to realize what was about to happen—when the demon retaliated.

With a soft *crack!* the Scourge broke her arm once, snapping it back at the elbow by simply pushing against the joint.

With a rippling *pop!* it took her trapped wrist and twisted it, a full one hundred and eighty degrees.

It jabbed on her hand, shoving the bones back. By now, Esme's mouth was opening to scream. So then, only then—it released her.

Esme fell on her back, paralyzed by pain, her arm flopping weakly by her side. The sharpened fractures had punched straight through the skin of her elbow, and the bone was sticking out by a clear inch. She stared at the wound. Then she looked up. The Scourge was towering over her.

There was a pause.

"**Hurts, does it?**" it enquired.

Esme stared back, blinking, eyes wide with pain—but, determined not to give the demon the satisfaction, she said nothing.

"**These fighting skills of yours,**" it said, raising an admonishing finger, "**they might work on Charlie, but they're not going to be of any use on me. Not now.**"

Esme concentrated, concentrated on using her power to heal herself, but it was hard. The pain was incredible; it blanked out everything—everything except the Scourge's voice.

"**'Ninety-nine times out of a hundred,'**" it was saying, "**'a fight'll be decided in the first few seconds'—isn't that what Raymond used to tell his students?**"

Esme closed her eyes, and with a terrible, twisting *push*, the bones in her arm began slowly to move back to their positions.

"He was wrong, of course. Fights are more usually won—and lost—before they even begin. For instance, I would say that it's always a good idea to make sure you know *how* to win before you *can* win, yes? Otherwise," the Scourge added, turning its back on her and walking a few steps away, "you're going to lose. Painfully."

It was done. Blood still ran from the wound, but the bones themselves were back in place, the fractures healed, the torn muscles beginning to mend. Sour adrenaline flushed through Esme's body, making every part of her feel heavy. But her arm and her fingers were working. She got to her feet.

"What's next?" the Scourge asked. "What would you like to try now?"

Esme was thinking. She hadn't bargained on the Scourge being so powerful outside Charlie: in this respect, it was true, she had miscalculated. Despair was clawing at her heart, a sense of doom and failure that a less disciplined fighter might have allowed to overwhelm her. Shoving the feeling aside, forcing herself to concentrate, Esme accepted the mistake and began to consider what it was she could actually *do* about it.

There was only one answer. Esme shut her eyes—and reappeared somewhere else. It didn't occur to her that the skill was coming to her more easily each time she used it: there wasn't time. She reached up, drew the pigeon sword, and, at a speed that hurt to watch, she charged, now—

—at Charlie.

With the fight going the way it was, there was no other option. Mercy was a luxury she could no longer afford. She would find a way to make her peace with what she was about to do later, when the stakes weren't so high. It was, after all, a straight choice now: Charlie or the universe.

One of them had to die.

Charlie's eyes were glazed: he was utterly oblivious. Before the Gukumats could stop her, Esme had blasted past them like a thunderbolt. She raised her arms for the killing stroke. The girl and the sword become one long, glittering streak in the air.

With a ringing *crack* and an impact that traveled up Esme's arms and shook her to the core, her stroke was parried, stopped dead in midflight, less than a foot from the target.

"No, no, *no*," said the Scourge. "**That's quite out of the question, I'm afraid.**"

For a moment, Esme froze.

The demon had caught her easily: it had simply appeared at the last moment between her and Charlie and had met the edge of the pigeon sword with a swordlike object of its own. The shape mirrored that of her own weapon—it had the same graceful curve and proportions of the classical Japanese katana. But it, like the Scourge, was still a glossy ink black. As she watched, with a last oily shimmer the darkness of the blade seemed to ripple away: it was only then that the cold steel was revealed beneath.

"**Swords, is it, next?**" asked the Scourge, without much interest. "**Very well. If you insist.**"

It took a step toward her, its liquid feet pooling on the soft pink floor, and Esme sprang back into a guard position, watching carefully, waiting. With a rustle of silk, the Guku-mats formed two rows, a long line of space to either side of the combatants.

"**Ready?**" asked the Scourge.

Esme said nothing.

"**Then let's begin.**"

Instantly, the space between them turned to a scissoring blur of steel.

It was impossible for a bystander to tell where one attack ended and another began. One by one, all the gladiators that were trapped in the bubbles above gradually stopped trying to escape and stared instead at the dreadful combat that was taking place below them. All Hell seemed to fall silent, except for the stinging hiss of sword on sword.

Esme was fighting on instinct—instinct and her years of training. If she'd stopped to think out each move, she'd've been lost, instantly. As it was, the battle was all going her opponent's way, because all she could do was react. Each swirling, whistling block and parry sent little ripples of fatigue up her arms. Each deft dodge, left, right, up, down, back—sometimes the Scourge came so close that she could actually feel the air move as her opponent's blade slid past her face—left her a little slower, a little more tired.

Obviously, she realized, she was going to lose.

It wasn't a question of pessimism. The Scourge was keeping pace with her easily: though it seemed to take every ounce of her speed and strength to meet those of her enemy, every attack *she* launched was parried and riposted smoothly and, apparently, without effort. As she began to tire—as the speeding blades slowed until the sharper-eyed bystanders found themselves actually able to tell the swords apart from each other—it seemed the Scourge was even slowing down with her.

"**Really,**" it said, meeting a lunge from Esme with a twisting movement that all but jerked the pigeon sword from her fingers. It followed it up with a vicious slash at her legs that Esme had to jump to avoid. "**Is this the best you can do?**"

In reply, Esme spun on her feet. Leaning forward into the stroke, she dropped her hands: she brought the sword round in a blow at the demon's waist that would have sliced a man in two.

The blade did pass straight through the demon, right where a man's waist would be. But the ink-black body simply sealed itself up after it, and, with a movement that was almost too quick for Esme to catch, the Scourge repaid her for her trouble with a straight-arm punch in the face with the pommel of its sword. She blinked and shook her head, momentarily stunned.

That was when the Scourge struck again, stabbing Esme through the shoulder of her sword arm.

The pigeon sword fell from her fingers.

Not bothering to remove its own weapon from her body, the Scourge advanced toward Esme; as she staggered back, shuddering at the pain, it put one glistening foot on Raymond's last gift where it lay and snapped the pigeon sword cleanly, up near the butterfly-shaped guard. Then it stopped and looked at her.

"I'm sorry if this offends you," it said, "but I must be honest: I'm beginning to lose interest."

With another ripple, the steely glint of the Scourge's weapon vanished, swallowed under glossy darkness, and the part of the thing that had impaled Esme suddenly changed shape. Widening and twisting in the wound in her shoulder, the demon lifted Esme upward until she was teetering on tiptoe, and though her jaw was set and her lips bitten shut against crying out, tears were running down her face.

"You're better than this," said the Scourge, bringing its own face up to hers. "Aren't you?"

With a soft, sucking sound, the darkness retracted. Esme dropped to the ground like a sack of potatoes, next to her shattered sword.

"Surely we've passed the point where physical violence is going to solve anything, don't you think?" the Scourge asked. "Punching. Kicking. Going at each other with pointy objects. It's all so *limited.*

"Come on," it added, leaning over her. "Why don't you show me what you can *really* do?"

But then . . .

AWAKENING

For Charlie, now, there was silence: absolute silence except for the low thump of his own blood pumping in his ears. Seated on his throne, he looked down at his arms, at the black tattoo shapes still swarming and pulsing there—and then he looked out at his kingdom.

He saw the ranks of Gukumats, stretching in every direction. Beyond that, he saw the vast serried legions of the demon peoples—the whole gross, adoring mass of his subjects, screaming and cheering from all around him. The view changed: for a second, all Hell seemed to expand and bulge—and now, suddenly, he could see further still.

Darkness slid through him like icy water, glimmering and glittering with tiny points of light that Charlie was suddenly able to identify as . . . *stars*. Planets and galaxies swam past like beautiful jellyfish, twinkling in the surrounding blue-blackness of space, close enough to reach out and touch. Black holes opened in front of him like flowers. Suns—whole solar systems—blazed into being, then shrank and winked out as he watched.

At the same time, the noise in his head was changing. The sound of his own pulse in his ears had gone, mixing with the crowd noise, mutating and modulating downward into something darker, thicker, deeper. It was all around him: throbbing and seething, and all the time it was getting louder and louder.

Ba-BOOM!

Ba-BOOM!

Ba-BOOM!

Ba-BOOM!

It was inescapable, dreadful, unspeakable, the noise. It was as if every creature in the universe were banging on a drum and screaming at him at the same time. The noise assaulted him on every level, getting more and more irritating the more irritated he got.

And suddenly, Charlie found himself wishing he could do something about it.

Here he was, at what should have been the proudest moment of his entire life, and what happened? There was all this noise, interrupting.

All there ever was for him was noise and interruptions.

Whenever things went well for him, there was always something going on to spoil it. Esme and Jack were a prime example: they could've left him to get on with stuff, they could've trusted him a little—but no! Of course, they'd had to interfere.

His *dad* too, instead of messing everything up, could've—

Surrounded by light and life, sitting on his throne in the center of the universe, Charlie blinked.

Dad, he thought.

He thought of his mother's expression at the breakfast table that morning when his father had told them he was leaving.

He thought of his dad sitting alone in a Chinese restaurant and how Charlie had told him he was *"never going to forgive him. Never."*

He frowned.

Well, he told himself, he didn't care about that—not anymore. He'd taken steps. He'd left all that behind. And there—it occurred to him—was the answer.

The universe shimmered and roared around him, waiting for whatever Charlie was going to think next.

This, he thought—the noise, the lights, the stuff going on around him now—was all no different. His days of weakness, of being at the mercy of events, were gone. He alone—he, Charlie—had the power; he was in complete control of his destiny. Nothing was going to get in his way or hurt him anymore in any way whatsoever—he wouldn't allow it. He could just decide, and whatever he wanted would be so.

Well, the noise and the lights were getting to him.

He'd had as much as he was prepared to take.

So he decided.

Let it out, a voice echoed in Charlie's head. *Let it all out, open your heart, and LET ME IN. YES!*

It would all . . . just have . . . to **STOP.**

As soon as he'd completed the thought, he felt something move inside himself. The thing that had been waiting inside him, waiting for this moment for longer than Charlie could possibly have imagined, suddenly seemed to give a great, convulsive LEAP.

In front of his eyes, the vision was sucking back into itself like someone had pressed rewind. The black holes slammed shut, the suns brightened and went out again, and the planets and galaxies were flung past him and back into their appointed places. The view shrank and collapsed.

Then he was back on his throne, and at last the horrible noise was dying down.

Charlie let out a big sigh, glad it was all over. He had an odd taste at the back of his mouth—a strange, coppery taste that he couldn't identify at first—and to be honest, he was feeling a bit weird. He made to lift his hands to rub his eyes and found to his surprise that he couldn't: his arms seemed to be stuck to the throne somehow, as if they'd been glued there.

Odder still, the black tattoo seemed to have vanished: of the great swirling pattern of curving blades and hooks, there was now no sign whatsoever. All there was was his own bare skin and the nasty taste that stayed in his mouth no matter how many times he swallowed.

Blood, he realized suddenly. It was blood.

Something's wrong here, he thought, beginning to panic: something was definitely wrong. Everything looked different. The Gukumats weren't looking at him—no one was. And underneath him, behind his back, the throne was moving again. With a speed that was shocking to Charlie, he saw that it was growing again. Tonguelike petals of moist-looking meat were curling upward in front of him, closing inward, blotting out the scene outside. Charlie gave a last, great effort to escape his throne: his left arm came slightly free of its armrest—

—and his eyes widened in horror.

The movement had released a pool of dark red liquid. Two thick dribbles of his blood just had time to run over the edge of the armrest before thin tendrils of pink shot out, lassoing his arm and yanking it back into position.

The throne went back to what it had been doing. It went about its work with redoubled strength now, battening down hungrily until Charlie's flesh quivered with each terrible *suck*. The realization, when it came to Charlie, was sudden and devastating.

The charade was over. The throne was killing him.

And now, at long last, Charlie began to get an inkling of just what an idiot he'd been.

MAGIC

Suddenly, a great thunderclap rang out. Rolling around and back from the distant walls, it was loud enough to silence the entire hordes of Hell. Everyone—Esme included—looked at the throne. In this sense, Charlie had finally got his wish, but the petals of meat had already closed, blocking him from sight.

In the silence, a strange, rushing, gurgling sound became audible, getting nearer and nearer until it seemed to be coming from all around. Closer it came, an encroaching silvery tinkling hiss, quickly growing to the thunderous roar of an approaching torrent.

Abruptly, a frothy, milk-colored liquid burst in from all sides of the room. The back rows of the assembled demons were caught completely by surprise, dissolving to nothing where they stood.

The Dragon's juices had reached the heart chamber. It was the demons' turn to be broken down into energy for the awakening. Already the flood of pale fluid was darkening into a nutrient-rich, bloodred broth.

There was a moment of horror, then the screaming started.

"Oh *crap!*" barked Jagmat, high up above proceedings, still trapped in his magical bubble. Suddenly this didn't seem such a bad place to be, not compared to what was happening to the rank-and-file demons on the ground. As one, in a blind panic, the population had lunged for the center of the room, trying to get as far away from the surrounding tide of juices as they could, trampling anyone and everything in their path in a headlong charge of storming feet, tentacles, pseudopods, fins, coils, and whatever else they used to get around. It wasn't going to do them any good: the climb to the top of the central plateau was all but impossible, as it was protected by magical barriers that Gukumat had constructed for the very purpose of preventing any escape. Jagmat stared downward, horrified, as the foremost of the demon hordes scrabbled frantically up the sides of the central platform, only to fall back and vanish into the teeming, howling mass that followed them.

The walls, the floor, the entirety of the chamber gave a long, rippling shudder. All over the room, gigantic veins and blood vessels began to twitch and convulse as each and every part of the heart chamber began, slowly, to come to life.

The air was hot with carnage. Esme stood there, stunned by it, hardly able to make sense of it all—

—and in that moment, the Scourge *laughed*.

It was a dreadful sound, like no laugh Esme had ever heard. It was husky, like dry bones scraping together, yet it was also high and screeching, like the brakes on a bus full of screaming children just before it plummets over a cliff. It echoed through the surrounding noise, chilling her to the quick, and in another moment the Overminister—all seven thousand of him—joined in.

They were enjoying this, the Scourge and Gukumat. They were enjoying their moment, savoring a triumph that, for them, had been a long time coming.

Esme set her jaw, shaking off the last of the pain of the Scourge's stab wound. It hadn't healed up properly yet, but she wasn't thinking about that. The shoulder would work: that was all that mattered.

She stood up.

The Scourge saw her and, with an effort, managed to stop laughing.

"**There**," it said, gesturing behind itself at the throne at the center of the plateau, which was still sealing and tightening—slowly—around its victim. "**If you're planning any last-minute heroics, Esme, I should tell you, there's no longer any point. Charlie has served his purpose. The Dragon is waking.**"

"We're not dead yet," said Esme. "That means there's still a chance."

The Scourge looked at her, then shrugged, the movement making its shoulders and neck drip together in long, tarlike strings.

"**If you could get to the throne in the next few moments, you could still rescue Charlie, I suppose. Perhaps you might even convince the Dragon to return to its slumber—though it would certainly want your life in Charlie's place.**"

"Fine. Whatever it takes."

"Still," said the Scourge, "two further problems remain for you. First, you don't have much time."

"And second?"

"Second, I won't let you."

"Then I guess I'd better pull out all the stops," said Esme.

She could feel it now, feel it inside herself. This was the last battle. This was what she'd been waiting her whole life to do.

Magic. She would have to use magic.

Already the power was rippling through her, coursing in her veins until the very ends of her hair crackled with it. And now, for the first time, she recognized what it was and where it came from.

Remember what I told you about your mother, said Raymond's voice in her head. *Remember your mother. And don't ever forget . . . well, that I love you.*

It was Raymond who had brought her up, Raymond who had trained her. *Raymond* had made her what she was, not the Scourge. And *her mother's blood* ran in her veins, every bit as strong as anything else that was there.

Almost without realizing she was doing it, Esme lowered her hands to her sides. She lifted, rocking forward slightly, until only the tips of her toes remained in contact with the fleshy red ground below her. She closed her eyes.

"At last," said the Scourge. "At long last, the moment of tr—"

In that second, before the demon could finish what it was saying, Esme struck.

The air over her hands heated up, rippled, and burst into light. Her feet left the ground and she rose into the air, but she had eyes for nothing but the face of her enemy. Bringing her hands up, concentrating her hatred and determination, summoning every ounce—every drop—of the unstoppable, bottomless desire for revenge that seemed at that moment to consume her entire being, Esme flung her magic at the Scourge.

Jagmat, high above, glimpsed a smoking streak run a line between the girl and the demon. It left a black scorch mark on the fleshy red ground, and for a second, as whatever it was struck the Scourge's outstretched palms, it seemed that nothing else was going to happen. Then—

KER-BLAM!

Spreading from the line, widening and swallowing all in its path, a sudden, shatteringly bright light expanded, searing every sense in Jagmat's jellylike body. The magical bubble that held him rattled and shook; he and Shargle bounced around inside it like dice in a cup; and when Jagmat next was able to see what was happening, he saw that the Scourge had vanished and a great ring of the Gukumats—hundreds of them—had been flung back from the blast. There was a wide, clear space around where the girl and the demon had been standing, swept clean in a spreading wave as if from an explosion. Those Gukumats at the edge had been knocked straight over the precipice. The robes of many that remained were on fire; shrieking, they thrashed and slapped at themselves as they tried to put out the flames, and some just lay where they'd been flung.

"Whoa," said Jagmat, with his usual understatement. Then, "I wonder which ones were lookin' after the—*AAAAAGH!!*"

Abruptly, as soon as he'd articulated the thought, the walls of his bubblelike magical prison simply flickered out of existence, and the hapless demon found himself plunging toward the ground.

And then all Hell broke loose.

Howling with a mixture of terror and sudden delight, the wave of rank-and-file demons that at that moment had been scrabbling up toward the central platform suddenly found that their way was no longer blocked by the Overminister's magic. They poured in a black screaming rush over the edge, overwhelming the first line of Gukumats before they had time to put up any resistance.

Those Gukumats behind the outside lines were no luckier: the ring of glowing bubbles holding the gladiators had failed, and now the air was filled by a sudden plummeting deluge of grudge-filled and angry fighting demons. The Carnotaur, in particular, was not satisfied with the score or so of flattened Gukumats that cushioned its landing: it had disliked the Overminister for a long time, and now, it had decided— unsheathing its claws, glands seeping acid from every pore— that some serious payback was due.

Gukumat had a full-scale rebellion on his hands. And suddenly, for the first time in its millennia-long life, his hivelike mind found itself uncomfortably uncertain of what the outcome was going to be.

Slowly, in the weird calm at the center of all this chaos, Esme came down to earth. She was breathing hard, but she forced herself back under control. There was no sign of the

Scourge. Ignoring the fierce battle that was beginning to rage around her, she looked all over the place, checking the smoking heaps of lifeless Gukumat bodies that seemed to have piled up at the edge of the blast.

She had never used her power like that. She had never known it could be used like that, or how powerful she really was. Truth to tell, she had scared herself more than a little, but she forced herself not to think about that now. The Scourge wasn't dead—it couldn't be dead. All she had done, she knew, was strike the first blow—and she wasn't sure if she had the strength to strike a second.

Well, now was her chance. She closed her eyes and took a deep breath. She was just on the point of disappearing, ready to find Charlie and see what she could do to stop what was happening, when she felt, without looking, the air in front of her face as it rippled and went hot.

The blow came instantaneously.

Her eyes flew open, and she watched with a sort of detached weariness as she was thrown back another twenty feet. She hit the ground hard, and by the time she'd skidded to a halt, the Scourge was standing over her again.

"**Not bad**," it said. A stinging slap to her face made Esme's world explode into stars. "**Not bad at all**," it added, swinging at her again.

But when it struck this time, the blow landed on thin air. The Scourge froze, staring, but Esme had vanished. And when it heard her voice again, she was behind it.

"Khentimentu the Scourge," said Esme quickly, wiping the

blood from her mouth in a long streak down her arm. "To roots that bind and thorns that catch I consign you."

The demon shook a little—wobbled—but stood firm. It turned to face her. So Esme said it again.

"Khentimentu the Scourge," she said. "To roots that bind and thorns that catch I *consign* you."

"You still don't understand, do you?" it said. "Those words have no power over me, not from you. You can't banish me. You *are* me. All that you can do—all that you've learned—comes from me!"

"That's not true," said Esme. "My mother defeated you before, and I can defeat you now: Khentimentu the Scourge, to roots that bind and thorns that catch I—"

"No," said the demon, wrapping one liquid-black hand around her throat, "you *can't.*"

And once more, it started to squeeze.

THE END

"Now, are you absolutely sure that you've got me all right?" It was something like the seventeenth time Jack had asked this question, he knew. A part of him even suspected that the Chinj might be becoming a little impatient with him, but he didn't really care. At that moment, he was being carried, bodily, high over a horde of demons that—when they weren't being horrifyingly dissolved by a rising tide of juices—were busily engaged in massacring each other in a variety of creative and enthusiastic ways. Given the situation, the question of whether the flock of batlike creatures had a firm grip on him or not was one that he needed to hear the answer to, he found, both urgently and often.

"You are not . . . as heavy . . . as the other humans," said the nearest Chinj into his ear, with some difficulty. "I suppose . . . we should be thankful . . . for that."

Jack was surrounded by them. If anyone down below had chanced to look up (which, thankfully, they were all too busy to do) they would have been hard-pressed to make Jack out amongst the rattling, clattering flock. The Chinj had carried him a long way already. The glimpses that Jack caught in between the heaving, flapping, furry bodies were enough to tell him that they need only go a little further.

The radio in his ear crackled suddenly.

"Jack?"

"Yep."

"They cannot take me any further; I am dropping now," said Number 3.

"Are you on target?" he asked. "Are you close enough to the center?"

"Can't see. No time. They're—"

The signal dissolved into a burst of static, or possibly the clattering of wings.

"Number Three!" said Jack. "Number Three, can you hear me?"

The radio crackled again, but there was no answer.

"Good luck!" called Jack—immediately feeling very silly indeed. If the Chinj had dropped Number 3 into the mass of demons, then he was going to need a lot more than luck.

But suddenly, it was his turn.

"We are close to the center," said the voice in his ear. "Going down now. Do not . . . forget your promise to us . . . small human."

The landing, when it came, was surprisingly gentle. In less than a second, it seemed to Jack, he was standing on his own two feet on the eerily squishy arterial-red ground, and the fluttering black flock was opening around him, peeling away in a great spreading tornado of dark furry bodies and leathery wings.

Now, finally, he could take in the scene.

An explosion off to his right was the first thing that attracted his attention. A blast wave full of something wet and sticky passed over him, and when his vision cleared, he glimpsed Number 3 backing away from the crowd toward the center of the plateau, covering his escape with a hail of fire from his MP5.

Jack couldn't see what was following him, not at first. For a moment it seemed as though the mass of demons—still fighting one another—were going to leave him be. But then the crowds parted—the impromptu barricade of prone and still faintly smoking Gukumat bodies was roughly shoved aside—and Jack realized that Number 3 was in trouble.

The demon that was after him wasn't especially big, but it looked strong. Its squat, barrel-like body was covered in a gray-green scaly armor of some kind: it swatted at Number 3's bullets with its long-fingered razor-clawed hands as though the gunfire were a cloud of mosquitoes. It rattled forward on its stumpy legs with a terrible eagerness: its small head, not much bigger than a pair of fists held side by side, was split up the center by a disgusting vertical maw of hooks and thrashing tentacles, and its long bony arms grasped out for the Son as he backed away.

Jack watched, frozen, as Number 3's first gun ran dry. The creature lunged—and the Son leaped to one side, drawing a heavy Sig Sauer automatic pistol from his hip and shooting several fat bullets into the creature's face at almost point-blank range. The demon staggered back a yard or two, physically driven back by the force of the shots—but Jack could see, with a terrible detached certainty, that it was stunned rather than actually hurt.

With a smooth movement, Number 3 pulled the rocket launcher that was strapped to his back round to a firing position. He raised the long, tube-shaped weapon up onto his shoulder and, without even appearing to take aim, let rip.

The rocket hit the demon in the chest, lifting the hapless creature off its feet and carrying it bodily right over the improvised barricade and over the battle raging below, until it vanished from sight.

"Number Three!" yelled Jack, screaming to make himself heard over the dreadful wave of noise that seemed to assault his ears from every direction.

The Son didn't hear him.

Jack thought about yelling again. Then he stopped himself.

Number 3 couldn't help him. There was no one who could help him. Somehow, his desperate plan had worked, and he was through to the center of the room, alone. There was no telling how long he'd be left that way. He had a job to do, and here was the chance to do it.

He turned and faced the killing throne.

"Oh no," gasped Esme, catching sight of Jack as he started off up the steps. "Oh, God, no—Jack!"

The steps were steep: slippery and disgustingly warm to the touch, they pulsed with dreadful life under Jack's bare feet—but he kept going. The vile meaty purple petal things that now surrounded the throne almost refused to move aside for him. He had to dig his fingers into their slimy rough edges and yank at them, hard, before they'd get out of his way. It was like trying to unwrap a giant artichoke: no matter how many of the tonguelike objects he managed to pry away, there always seemed to be another one underneath. The noise of the battle sank to a dull roar behind him, muffled by all the layers. Then, suddenly, the last one parted, and he saw what was waiting for him in the center.

He didn't recognize Charlie at first. Or rather, he knew it was Charlie, but what sat in the throne as the tentacles caressed and sucked at him looked like a mannequin—a model of Charlie, not the real thing. His face was drawn, his cheeks shrunken. His arms and hands were skin and bones, and his eyes, shut tight, looked like peeled hard-boiled eggs in their sockets.

Then Charlie opened them and looked at him.

"Oh, Charlie," said Jack. "You *berk* . . ."

"Jack," croaked Charlie, stretching toward his friend with two fingertips—all he was able to move. "Jack . . ."

"Well, okay," said Jack, with a confidence he didn't remotely feel, "let's get you out of this thing at least." And he strode toward the throne. Trying not to flinch too much, he grasped one of the slimy, pinkish-gray tentacle things that was sucking at his friend's arm and yanked it away. The tentacle wriggled and thrashed, its nasty leechlike mouth parts opening and shutting convulsively on thin air. Charlie shuddered.

"Don't," he said.

Jack stared at him. "What?"

"Don't."

"What the Hell do you mean? Do you want to get out of this mess or what?"

"The Dragon," croaked Charlie. "It's—"

But something strange was happening. All over Charlie's body, the sucking writhing tentacle things were letting go, releasing him. Charlie slumped in the throne, unable to move, his blood still dripping listlessly from a hundred different wounds—but the thing that had done this to him was changing, shifting before Jack's eyes.

Suddenly, it seemed to Jack that the throne—the tongues, the tentacles, everything—was looking at him. It was all pointed in his direction. And then, in a voice from the bottom of a pit . . . something began to speak.

"You," it said. The voice was like the Scourge's, only older. Deeper. Stronger.

"You," it repeated. The voice didn't seem to be coming from any particular place, but Jack heard it with every fiber of his being.

"You have forced your way into my throne room. You seek to deprive me of my rightful victim. Explain yourself."

"Er," said Jack. "Um . . ."

"Do you wish to stop the awakening?" prompted the voice.

"Er, well, yeah," said Jack, grabbing at this chance and hardly believing that it was being offered. "Yes, actually," he said, putting more effort into his voice this time. "I want to stop the awakening. Yes."

"This child has paid for the awakening with his life. The price for preventing it will be the same. Do you, then, offer your life?"

"Er, what?" asked Jack.

"Blood will awaken me," explained the Dragon patiently. **"Blood will send me back to my slumbers. All dealings with me must be sealed with blood. Do you, then,"** it repeated, **"offer your life?"**

Jack stared.

Then he scowled.

For Heaven's sake! he thought (only he didn't use the word *heaven*). If this didn't just beat everything. Here he was, with the existence of the universe now—apparently—depending on him. Against all the odds, he had got his chance: he could save Charlie, he could save the day—but of course, it had to hinge on him volunteering to die. How completely, *utterly*—

"All right," he said, stepping up. "Okay. I'll do it."

"Do what?" boomed the voice.

Jack scowled again. "I'll 'offer my life' or whatever! Come on, let's get on with this!"

"Then take the boy's place on the throne."

"Right," said Jack.

The tentacle things didn't resist him now. They fell away easily. What resisted him was Charlie.

"No!" said Charlie, plucking weakly at Jack's arms as Jack lifted him out of the throne—and dumped him, none too ceremoniously, on the fleshy red floor.

"Shut up," said Jack, "and listen to me. You have a job to do, and it's time for you to do it."

Charlie stared at him, stunned by the strength in Jack's voice. For the first time ever, Jack realized, Charlie was actually taking him seriously.

Jack sighed.

"You've got to go out there," he said, gesturing past the purplish, tonguelike layers of the walls, "and you've got to help Esme."

Still Charlie stared.

"You've got to do what you first said you were going to do. Remember? You've got to help her defeat the Scourge. You've got to do it," said Jack, staring right back into his eyes. "For me."

There was another pause.

"Oh, mate," said Charlie. "I'm so sorry. I—"

"Save it," said Jack, sitting down on the throne. "Just go. Let me get on with this."

He closed his eyes, not wanting to look at Charlie anymore. This whole situation was, after all, entirely Charlie's fault.

To his credit, Charlie didn't try to say anything else. And when Jack opened his eyes, Charlie was gone.

Right, thought Jack, and waited for the next bit.

It wasn't long coming.

"Khentimentu the Scourge," said Charlie, from Esme's side. "To roots that bind and thorns that catch I *consign* you."

The demon froze. "**You!**" it said.

"Hi, Charlie," said Esme.

"Hi, Esme."

"Glad you could make it."

"Don't thank me," said Charlie. "Thank Jack."

Esme looked at him and nodded slowly. "Well," she said. "Let's make sure he didn't waste the effort."

"Ready when you are."

"On three, then," said Esme. "*One.*"

The air in front of Charlie and Esme suddenly wobbled and shook; then a long, glistening, stafflike object was forming between them, stretching across in front of them, under their hands.

"**Charlie?**" asked the demon, and for the first time in its long life, it suddenly sounded uncertain. "**Charlie, let me explain.**"

"Two."

"**You can still be Emperor. I can still give you everything you wanted! Charlie, *you'll be sorry!***"

"I already am," said Charlie, then closed his eyes.

"Three," said Esme. The magical staff was fully formed now: a last gunmetal glint passed down its length, then it was ready for the job it had to do.

"**KHENTIMENTU THE SCOURGE!**" said Esme and Charlie

both at once, and their combined voice was so loud that all Hell suddenly found that it had stopped what it was doing and now had no choice but to listen to the boy and the half-demon girl and hear what they had to say next.

The Scourge trembled.

"TO ROOTS THAT BIND—"

The words echoed around the heart chamber. The magical staff glowed blinding white.

"—AND THORNS THAT CATCH—"

Now the demon was screaming—a terrible sound, a sound like tearing in your head, a maiming scream that went on and on.

"WE *CONSIGN* YOU!" roared Esme and Charlie at once. *"GET YOU HENCE, AND TROUBLE US NO MORE!"*

And with a final, piteous shriek, the liquid darkness that was Khentimentu the Scourge was sucked, helplessly, toward the burning magical staff that Charlie and Esme held in their hands. It swirled around them, a nimbus of pure black, rushing and hurtling and twisting and rippling.

Then, with a final clap of thunder—

—it was gone.

Exhausted, Esme sank to the floor.

They'd done it! They'd trapped the Scourge in the staff! Now if Esme could only get the demon back to Earth and reimprison it, she would have succeeded at last where Nick had failed. Hardly believing it, she turned to smile at Charlie.

But he wasn't there.

"Been here—*ow*," Jack said aloud, as the Dragon began to suck out his life. "Done this," he added, doing his best to put a brave face on things—though to be honest, at that moment, he wasn't sure why he was bothering.

"You are . . . very strange," said the Dragon suddenly.

For a moment, Jack was too surprised to speak, but it didn't take him long to recover himself.

"No," he replied. "I'm normal. It's *you* who's strange."

"What . . . do you mean?"

"I mean," said Jack, with an effort, "this business of you creating the universe and falling asleep, then waking up and destroying it."

"Yes?"

"Well, what kind of a routine is that? If all you were ever going to do was sleep through the whole thing, why bother creating the universe in the first place? It just . . ." Jack shook his head. "It doesn't make any sense!"

Suddenly, to Jack's surprise, the sucking sensation stopped. The throne still held him tight: the tentacle things still gripped his arms—but the blood was no longer being leeched out of his body.

"Your question is a fair one," the Dragon said, considering. **"You're about to die, so I shall let you in on a secret."**

Jack held his breath.

"*I have not been asleep.*"

"So?" asked Jack, annoyed. "What've you been doing all this time? Pretending?"

"My slumber was a convenient fiction," said the Dragon

smugly. **"It was necessary, to preserve the conditions of my experiment."**

"What experiment?" asked Jack.

"When I created your universe," the Dragon announced, **"I also created its nemesis: an immortal being that thrived on the worst in people—a being that, if it were given the chance, would have the power to bring my Creation to an end."**

"The Scourge," said Jack.

"The central question of my experiment, then, was this," the Dragon went on. **"Could the other sentient creatures work together to prevent this catastrophe from occurring? Or would they be so wrapped up in their own concerns that they would allow themselves to be destroyed?"**

"I don't understand," said Jack.

"That question has now been answered," said the Dragon, regardless. **"The Scourge succeeded. The awakening was not prevented."** It paused. **"You failed."**

Jack thought about this, following through the implications of what he'd just heard.

It took several seconds, but when he finally got his head round it, he felt an emotion that was so strong he couldn't actually identify it at first.

"Hang on," he said. "Let me get this straight. This whole thing—the whole history of the universe—was just some kind of . . . test?"

The Dragon did not reply.

"But that's insane!" said Jack, with rising fury. "Are you seriously telling me, after everything that's happened, that it's all been, like, a game for you?"

"Not a game," the Dragon replied. **"An *experiment*. And now the experiment is over."**

"But—I don't *believe* this!" said Jack. "All this effort, all this pain and suffering, and it's just so you can prove some *point*?"

"That is correct," said the Dragon simply.

"Well," said Jack. There was, he found, only one more thing to be said.

"You SELFISH GIT!"

"*What?*" said the Dragon, astonished. **"*What* did you just say?"**

"I think you heard me," said Jack, disgusted. "Well, I've got a question for you too. Where do you get off playing with people's lives like that? What gives you the right? *Who*," he added, reaching a pitch of righteous rage, "*do you think you are?*"

"I am THE DRAGON," roared the Dragon. **"I am your Creator. It is an unspeakable, immeasurable honor,"** it went on, **"for an insignificant speck such as yourself to have the opportunity to converse with one such as me. You are here as a penitent, offering your pitiful life in exchange for a stay of execution for your universe. I would think, therefore, that a little *respect* is—"**

"Hang on," said Jack suddenly. "Say that again."

"I said," said the Dragon, **"I am the Dragon. Your Cr—"**

"No, after that."

"After what?"

"After all that crap you just said," said Jack, another ugly thought beginning to occur to him. "What do you mean, *my* universe?"

"I'm sorry?" asked the Dragon.

"You said, 'your universe,'" pursued Jack doggedly. "What exactly did you mean by that? Are there others? And come to think of it, what do you mean by 'one such as me'?"

"You must have misheard me."

"No," said Jack. "Your voice is pretty loud, and I'm quite sure you distinctly said—"

"It is not for one such as you to question the utterances of the Dragon!"

"Just tell me this," said Jack quickly. "If you created us—the universe, everything—then who created *you*?"

"No one!" said the Dragon. **"I created myself."**

"Nope. Sorry," said Jack. "I don't believe you." He shook his head, actually smiling to himself now. "Blimey!" he said. "You gods—you're all the same. You must just think we're all stupid!"

"Wh-what do you mean?"

"I mean, look at what you do, going around 'creating' things. Why do you do it?"

"My motivations are like me: infinite and mysterious. A puny mortal could not—"

"Oh, *save* it," said Jack. "Please, just give it a rest, will you? If you don't have the guts to tell me yourself, then I'll tell you what *I* think—all right?"

"**Very well,**" snorted the Dragon. "**Amuse me!**"

Jack took a deep breath.

"I don't think," he began, "that when you—and people like you—go and start something like this, you do it with some grand master plan in mind. You do it," he said, "because you're bored. That's my guess.

"Yeah," Jack went on, liking his idea more and more the more he examined it. "You do it because you think it'll be fun. You do it because it might be interesting. You do it," he finished, "because you've got *nothing else to do!*"

There was a long silence.

"Am I right?" asked Jack. "Or what?"

"**That's . . .**" said the Dragon—and paused. "**Actually,**" it conceded, "**that's rather acute of you. Intriguing. Go on.**"

"Well!" said Jack. "In that case, it follows that you don't actually want *my* universe to end. Do you? I mean, if that happens, then you'll have to find something else to play with!"

The Dragon did not answer.

"In fact, I reckon you'd be pretty pleased if you didn't really have to destroy us. In *fact*," Jack added, hardly believing in his own audacity, "you don't really want to kill *me* at all either!"

There were another few seconds of silence—seconds that felt, to Jack, very long indeed.

Then Charlie shoved his way into the throne room. Esme appeared beside him.

"Jack!" they shouted. "Jack! *No!*" And they set about trying to rescue him.

Charlie—Jack was surprised (and at the same time kind of pleased) to notice—was crying: his eyes were red and puffy, and guilty tears were pouring down his cheeks. Even Esme looked worried—but she was the first to catch Jack's eye and interpret the few frantic and secretive gestures he could manage, glued as he was to the throne.

"It's all right, mate! I'm coming! We'll just get you out of— ow! What?" sputtered Charlie, when Esme grabbed him and roughly pulled him a couple of steps back. "What are you—?"

"Wait," said Esme.

There was a rumbling from all around them, and a whispering, crackling, rustling sound as the fleshy walls began to shrink back.

"**I have decided,**" the Dragon's voice announced, "**that on this occasion the universe shall be spared. I have also decided**"—Jack held his breath—"**to allow this boy to live.**"

"**I like you,**" it added, in a quieter voice that Jack knew only he could hear. "**You're *interesting*. However, your enquiring nature has made you most impertinent. If your universe had more like you in it, then I might have to destroy it for my own peace of mind. Do I make myself clear?**"

"No problem," said Jack fervently.

"**The Dragon has spoken,**" said the voice. "**Be sure of what you want of me, foolish mortals, before you disturb my ancient slumber again.**"

Not wanting to push his luck any further than he had already, Jack kept his mouth shut.

Then, for a long moment, he thought about it.

He thought about God, and the god who'd created God, and the god who'd created the god who created God, and so on. He thought about what it all might mean for himself and his life and his place in existence. He thought, in that moment, about the meaning of it all—and wondered, briefly, whether there actually *was* one. But then the throne released him.

And *then* Esme threw her arms around him.

And suddenly, Jack found that, actually, he didn't really care.

"So," said the elder Chinj, much later, "you have fulfilled your promise. You have returned to throw yourself upon our mercy— to prostrate yourself," it added, "before the righteous wrath of the Grand Cabal. I confess, small human, I am surprised."

"Yeah, well," said Jack. "A promise is a promise."

"And let me remind you," said the elder Chinj, "and all those here present, of what that promise consisted!"

"*Get on with it!*" squeaked a voice from the back row of the flock, to a dangerous chatter of agreement.

"You have agreed, in accordance with our most holy laws," intoned the elder Chinj, scowling furiously, "to pay for your heinous crimes. You have promised," it added, "to make good your gross violation of our most sacred byways. YOU HAVE SAID," it shrieked, reaching a fever pitch of ferocity, "THAT WE CAN DO WHATEVER WE LIKE WITH YOU!"

"That's right," said Jack, when the flock had quieted down enough for him to make himself heard. "I did."

"Well," said the elder Chinj, suddenly going quiet. "The Parliament of Chinj, in its infinite wisdom, has decided to be—*muhnuhmuful*."

It coughed, covering its mouth with one withered paw.

"I'm sorry?" said Jack. "I didn't quite catch that."

"We've . . . decided to be . . . *mmmuhful*," said the elder Chinj, with obvious reluctance.

"I'm really sorry," said Jack politely. "But I still didn't—"

"We're going to let you live!" snapped the elder Chinj. "All right? Satisfied?" It turned and stumped its way out of the cave, which, by now, was ringing with cheers.

"There," said Number 3, from beside where Jack was standing. "At last. It is all over."

"I couldn't have put it better myself," said a voice—and they all turned.

There, some twenty yards down the passageway, standing beside a large, but still pack-size, technological-looking metal shape—

—was Number 2.

"It's no good trying to stop me!" he screamed (though in fact, as yet, no one had). "The countdown has begun. In thirty seconds, all that's going to be left of this place is a mushroom cloud the size of New York!"

In the silence that greeted this announcement, Number 3 sighed.

"Number Two," he began.

"No, wait a second," Jack interrupted. "You mean, that thing in the pack was . . . a bomb? A nuclear *bomb*?"

Number 2 grinned widely, and his eyes glittered: "Project Justice," he said, with a gesture at the device. "As soon as the gateway to Hell was discovered, I gave the order myself. The first away-team to make the trip was to go in with tactical nuclear capability. That way, if Hell's inhabitants proved hostile, we could strike decisively while we had the chance—eliminating a potential threat at its source, and saving the human race!"

"You . . . plank!" Jack spluttered. "You stupid, half-witted—"

"Number Two," said Number 3 again. His voice was quiet, but something in its tone made Jack stop talking suddenly. "This is unnecessary."

"Don't you try and tell me what's unnecessary, Number Three," said Number 2. "You know your orders, and the situation's been clear ever since we got here. This whole place is a threat to our world and our way of life, and the only chance we've got is to strike first and strike hard. So, listen, any last words you got? You'd better say them now, because in"—he consulted the readout on the device—"less than eighteen seconds, you'll have missed your chance. Permanently."

"Would someone mind telling me what's going on here?" asked Esme. She pointed at Number 2. "This man's not really going to do what he says he's going to do, is he?"

"*Non*," said Number 3. "He is not."

"Watch me," said Number 2. "Here we go! Two! One! MOMMYYYYYYYYYYY!" he screamed, crouching and covering his ears while everyone—Number 3, Number 9, Jack, Charlie, Esme, and the numberless Chinj—just stared at him.

Beside him, the machine beeped twice, then fell silent.

After another few seconds, Number 2 opened his eyes.

"Number Two," said Number 3, "for some time now it 'as been my belief that your judgment as a Son of the Scorpion Flail 'as been less than . . . reliable."

Number 2 stared at him, eyes wide.

"I must say," Number 3 went on, "my observations of your performance on zis mission 'ave certainly borne out my suspicions. Wi' zis in mind, I took the decision to remove Project Justice's security key." He held up the object: it dangled from his gloved hand. "A fact you would 'ave noticed if you 'ad checked for its presence before attempting to detonate the device."

"You . . ." said Number 2. "Wait a second. What the Hell *is* this?"

"Number Two," Number 3 continued, "you are 'ereby relieved of command, and your membership of the Sons of the Scorpion Flail is rescinded pending a full enquiry."

"Yeah? Well, I've got news for you, *pal*," said Number 2, standing up. "You don't have the authority. Only Number One himself has the power to fire me—and his true identity's so top secret that nobody even knows what he looks like!"

Number 3 allowed himself a small smile. "That is not," he said, "ze case at all, I am afraid."

"What do you mean?"

"Well," the man Number 2 had always thought of as his subordinate pointed out, "*you* know what I look like, do you not?"

For another moment, there was silence.

Number 2 turned sheet-white. "Y-you don't mean . . ." he stammered. "No, I don't believe it. You mean, all this time—all these years—*you* . . . were . . ."

Still Number 3—or Number 1, to give him his proper designation—said nothing.

"What the Hell's going on?" whispered Jack.

"W-well, IT MAKES NO DIFFERENCE!" shrieked Number 2, whipping out his own Sig Sauer and pointing it at his superior officer. "See? Who's in charge now, huh? *Who's in charge now?*" In three quick steps he moved away from the machine, the fat black hole at the end of the gun's barrel looming ever closer in Jack's vision.

"I'm going to count to three!" said Number 2. "If you haven't given me that security key and got down on your knees by then, I swear to God I'm going to shoot you in the face."

"And what difference will that make if you're just going to blow us all up anyway?" asked Jack brightly.

"SHUT UP!" screamed Number 2. "Just *SHUT UP!* ONE!" He pressed the barrel up against Number 1's forehead.

"Two!"

Nobody moved.

"Thr—*uhn!*" Number 2 grunted, as the large rock that had been dropped from above landed on his head and he fell to the ground.

"There," said Jack's Chinj, fluttering into view and finding a perch on the back of its prone victim. It looked up at the others. "I *did* enjoy that," it said—and winked.

INTERLUDE

Mr. and Mrs. Farnsworth were standing side by side.

Mr. Farnsworth was pale: his jaw was clenched, and his lips were pressed together in a bloodless line. Mrs. Farnsworth's eyes were wide and red, and she was blinking a lot: her knuckles were white where she gripped her handbag.

The two of them were standing in the morgue of Charing Cross police station in London's West End, in front of a mortuary slab. They'd come to identify a body that had recently been found floating in the Thames.

However, except for a rumpled white sheet, the slab in front of them was empty.

"But . . . I don't understand it!" said the attendant. "It was here! It was here not thirty seconds ago, when I went to open the door for you! And now it's—"

"It's what?" asked Mr. Farnsworth, with heavy emphasis.

"Gone!" said the attendant. He got a grip on himself.

"I'm so, *so* sorry," he said. "I've been helping people to identify bodies for over fifteen years, and I assure you, nothing like this has ever happened before. It's extraordinary! It was here not two minutes ago, and now it's just . . . vanished!"

"Not 'it,'" said Mr. Farnsworth.

"Pardon?"

"Not 'it!'" Mr. Farnsworth repeated, his voice rising dangerously. "Stop saying '*it*'! That's our *son* you might be talking about, you bl—!"

At that exact moment, a phone rang.

It was a mobile phone. There was an embarrassed pause, as first the attendant and then Mr. Farnsworth huffed, sighed, patted their pockets, checked their phones—and frowned.

Blinking, Mrs. Farnsworth took her mobile from her bag. She looked at the screen, pressed the button, and, numbly, held it up to her ear.

"Mum?" said Charlie. "Mum? It's me."

THE TREE

"Here," said Esme. "This one."

"What, really?" asked Charlie, surprised. "But it's just like the others!"

"That's the whole point," said Jack, "I imagine."

"Looks safe enough," acknowledged Number 1. He looked at Esme. "We do this now?" he asked.

Esme said nothing. She took the staff—which had grown strangely dull and rusty looking, like an elderly scaffolding pole—and strode ahead of them into the undergrowth surrounding the large and gnarled-looking oak tree that stood a little way up the small slope beside the battered tarmac path. Pausing only to look around to make sure no one happened to be watching, Number 1 and the boys set off after her.

They were in a certain park, in London. It was early autumn now, but the sky was a pleasingly clear pale blue and the sun was warm on Jack's back, casting long shadows on the ground in front of him as he followed the others into the shrubbery. It was a good day to be in a park. A five-a-side football match with jumpers for goalposts was going on some three or four hundred yards away. People were flying kites, walking dogs, throwing Frisbees and doing other park-type things. No one saw the little group disappearing off the path—or if they did, they didn't think anything of it. In another moment, Jack was sloshing through the piles of leaves as the air around him (under the shade of the tree) turned dark.

"Looks old," he said, looking up at it.

"Yeah," said Esme. "No one knows how old." Her face turned sad. "At least," she added, "not anymore."

"Well," said Charlie. "What happens next? How does it work?"

Esme didn't answer. She was circling the tree, the leaves making soft scrunching sounds under her trainers. The trunk of the tree was wide and solid looking, covered in bulbous lumps like petrified cauliflowers, or possibly, Jack thought, brains.

"Here," said Esme finally, taking up a spot some four or five feet away to Jack's right. With a sudden smooth movement, she lifted the staff and struck it into the ground. For a fraction of a second, Jack actually thought he could feel an impact tremor vibrating up through the soles of his trainers. But then he told himself he must be imagining things.

Esme tested the staff, which was now sticking straight up into the air, but it remained where it was.

"All right," she said. "We need to get around the tree. If we stretch out, I think we should be able to hold hands."

Before he could do anything about it, Jack found himself

holding hands with Charlie and Number 1, having missed his chance. With hideous predictability, he'd ended up on the opposite side from Esme and the staff—out of sight of whatever was about to happen. *Typical.* He sighed.

"Ready?" he heard Esme ask.

"Er . . . sure," he said hurriedly.

"Then we'll begin." Esme took a deep breath.

Jack suddenly noticed that all around them, all the noises of the park—the people, the traffic from the road beyond, even the birds—seemed to have gone strangely silent.

"**Khentimentu the Scourge,**" said Esme quietly, and her voice seemed to set off small flowering explosions behind Jack's eyeballs. "**To roots that bind and thorns that catch, I consign you.**"

Number 1's and Charlie's hands grew warm in Jack's own. He was standing very close to the tree, facing inward, and his nostrils were filled with the dark, earthy, wet smell of the leaves and the mossy bark of the tree in front of him. The smells were strong, sweet, and—suddenly—almost overwhelming.

"**By the light of the world,**" said Esme in the same clear voice. "**By the strength of my will and the curse that first stilled you, I command that you return to your prison. Get you hence,**" she finished, "**and trouble us no more.**"

From far away at first, but coming quickly closer, Jack felt a low, bubbling, sizzling sensation. It traveled up his arms and rushed through his veins, a tide of something hot and dark. It was like being hit by a wave of warm oil, but oil that was somehow alive, scrabbling and rippling and seething all through him in a frantic last effort to take hold. Jack held on tight to the hands that held his. The circle remained unbroken, and . . .

And then, as quickly as it had come, the sensation vanished.

For another long second the four of them stood there like that. Then . . .

"There," said Esme.

Charlie let go first, Number 1 a moment after that, and Jack found himself standing in front of what still looked like an ordinary tree, with his hands tingling.

He walked round to join the others, noticing as he did so that the staff that Esme had been carrying had now vanished.

"Is that it?" he asked.

"Yes," said Esme. "Yes it is."

"And is it . . . safe?" asked Charlie.

"As safe as it can be," said Esme. "Yes."

"Only we know ze secret," said Number 1. He looked around the little group, unsmiling. "Only one of us, or someone that we tell, will be able to release ze demon."

"Yeah, like *that's* going to happen," said Charlie, and shuddered.

For a moment, there was silence among them.

Jack was looking at Esme. Suddenly, she just looked incredibly, utterly tired. Come to think of it, he felt the same way.

"So," said Charlie, with a casual tone that was blatantly false. "What's next?"

Jack had to admit, it was a good question.

To his surprise, it was Esme who broke the silence.

"I've been fighting the Scourge," she said, "my whole life. There's nothing I've done—not one single thing—that hasn't been totally taken up with that."

Jack looked at her. He hadn't thought of this, but it was true. All the time he'd spent in Hell, all the time since this whole thing had started, only really amounted to a few days in real time. Esme had been fighting since before she was born.

Suddenly, she smiled.

"I'm going to learn how to live," she said. "That's what I'm going to do next. And maybe you'd all better do the same." She turned to Charlie. "Especially you."

"Yeah," said Charlie, looking at his feet. "I guess."

"I've got to go," said Esme, coming toward Jack and giving him a quick hug that was over before he'd even realized that that was what she was going to do. With her hands on his shoulders, she looked into his eyes. "See you round?" she asked.

Jack was blushing furiously, but he managed not to look away. "Er, sure," he managed, then immediately felt very silly indeed.

"Bye now," said Esme to the others.

Then she vanished.

"I too must go," said Number 1. Ignoring Charlie, he looked at Jack. "It 'as been a pleasure," he said.

"Thanks," said Jack, surprised.

Smiling at Jack, Number 1 nodded once—and walked away.

Then Charlie and Jack looked at each other.

"Well," said Charlie finally, "apart from thinking of something to tell my folks, I guess that's it."

"Yeah," said Jack. He felt strangely empty. Almost . . . disappointed, somehow.

"You taking the Tube?" asked Charlie.

"Sure."

"It's not quite as quick as dematerializing, but it gets there in the end."

"Fine."

"Let's go, then."

The two boys emerged onto the path and set off toward the nearest Underground station.

They didn't look back.

EPILOGUE

Three weeks later, Jack was back at school. He was sitting by the window, in a double history class.

Jack hated double history. He'd spent the first ten minutes of the class drawing little dashes around the edge of his history folder for every single minute there was left. Next, he'd started crossing them out as they passed. In about five minutes' time, he knew, he was going to be exactly an eighth of the way through the double class, and that wasn't anything like far enough for him.

He was in a foul mood. And really, he thought, who could blame him? Being forced to sit through the best part of two hours' tiresome waffling about Tudors and Stuarts seemed like a pretty poor reward for recently saving the universe. Plus, naturally, there was the fact that nobody knew about it: there was nobody he could tell. He wouldn't have known where to begin even if there *were* anyone he could tell. *You* try explaining to someone that you know Hell exists because you've been there, that you've met God (and God's god) and that the universe only continues to keep going because of decisions and actions that *you* made. See how far it gets you.

At first, Jack had been pleased to be back. His parents had been so wildly (and guilt-inducingly) relieved to see him that they'd accepted his story about running away with Charlie and spending a few nights in a hotel, almost without question. To his further surprise (perhaps it was something to do with his meeting with the Dragon), he'd found he was able to eat proper food again rather than Chinj vomit, which had obviously been a plus too.

But then—very soon after, in fact—the problems had set in.

He felt . . . detached from things. It felt to him as though a sheet of clear plastic lay between him and the world. He found he was wandering around in a sort of daze, going about the daily stuff of his average-fourteen-year-old's life like a robot, or maybe a puppet. And slowly, grimly, he'd begun to realize why.

No one has adventures every day.

This, he realized, was what was "typical." Not the fact that everything that could possibly go wrong for him always seemed to do so—he wasn't sure he really believed that anymore. What was typical, what was really typical, was the universal truth that no matter what amazing things you've done, what incredible adventures you've had, you've still got to come back to reality afterward. You've got to go to the toilet, you've got to do the washing up—you've got to go to double history, even when, if it wasn't for you, the Tudors and Stuarts would have become even more pointless and irrelevant than (it seemed to Jack) they are already. And this, Jack decided, was even worse.

There. Five minutes gone. He could now cross off an entire chunk of the dashes around his history folder. Hell, he thought, he might even color them in—anything to help pass the time.

His reverie was interrupted by a soft tapping at the window beside him.

Jack looked up. On the other side of the glass, standing on the windowsill, was a large, furry, batlike creature wearing a pair of wraparound sunglasses. It was waving at him.

Very slowly, Jack looked around the room. Mr. Hildegast was still droning on. Everyone else in the room still looked bored beyond belief. No one appeared to have noticed the Chinj's appearance.

He looked back at the Chinj, which was making a series of pointing and jabbing gestures with its small front paws, its wings flapping dangerously.

The meaning was obvious. Jack nodded once. The Chinj grinned, bowed, and dropped out of sight.

Jack turned and put his hand up.

"Ah, Mr. Farrell!" Mr. Hildegast beamed at him. "Do you have a question?"

"I'm sorry, sir," said Jack. "But I was wondering if I could be excused."

Mr. Hildegast's expression turned sour and thunderous. "Mr. Farrell! Are you seriously suggesting," he asked, and his voice held the beginnings of what Jack grimly realized was going to be one of his drearily predictable climaxes of indignation, "that I should let you disrupt my class—that I should let you *disturb your colleagues*—just because of your bladder? You should have gone before you came in!"

A few appreciative titters spread around the room at this, and Jack was aware of everyone looking at him.

He didn't care.

"Sorry, sir," he said, "but I'm . . . not well. I think it's something I ate. And I really need to be excused, right now."

The tittering went up a notch.

"Heaven's sake, man," said Mr. Hildegast, "why didn't you say so? Go! Go quickly!"

"Thank you, sir," said Jack, and the laughter of the rest of the class followed him out down the passageway, until the door to the classroom banged shut behind him.

He made it to the toilets, got into the cubicle at the end that had the window, opened it, and sat down.

"All right," he said, "this had better be important."

"I'm very happy to see you, sir!" squeaked the Chinj, bobbing up and down on its long toes as it clung to the cubicle's tiny windowsill.

"You too," said Jack. And it was true: it was good to see the small bat creature. "Nice sunglasses," he added.

"Thank you," said the Chinj modestly. "Miss Esme gave them to me."

"They look good on you."

"You're too kind."

"And how is Miss Esme?" Jack asked, a little pointedly. He hadn't heard from Esme since the business at the tree. He'd tried ringing the number at the theater, but it always seemed to be busy—and he'd begun to feel more than a little hurt.

"She's well," said the Chinj judiciously, "but she's been a bit busy. In fact, that's rather what I wanted to talk to you about."

"Oh yes?"

"There's a problem," said the Chinj, "at the Fracture."

Jack's expression turned grim. "What sort of problem?"

"Well, it's like this," the Chinj began. "Thanks largely to your efforts, Hell's been going through some rather big changes lately. For one thing, ever since . . . what happened, the new Emperor and I have—"

"New Emperor?" echoed Jack. "Who?"

"I was coming to that," said the Chinj. "As I was saying, the new Emperor and I have been approached by a number of parties who've been enquiring about the possibility of . . . well, *emigrating*, as it were."

Jack looked at the Chinj. "What are you talking about?" he asked.

"There are some demons," the Chinj replied patiently, "who want to come and live here, in your world."

"*Here?*" asked Jack, incredulous. "Why?"

"I honestly couldn't tell you," said the Chinj. "I mean, I was prepared to travel back and forth for you, of course, but I really can't see what merits the place has to offer by itself. To be honest, it seems rather"—it grimaced daintily—"well, boring, actually. No offense," it added quickly.

"None taken," said Jack.

"But these demons just won't listen to reason. We've been positively *flooded* with enquiries about the Fracture. One enterprising lot even set up a company, offering the chance for rank-and-file demons to book holiday tours—"

"*What?*"

"Though I'm sure I need hardly tell you," the Chinj went on hurriedly, "all requests to use the Fracture have been vehemently denied. It's under constant guard in case anyone is foolish enough to attempt to go through without permission."

"So?" asked Jack. "What's the problem?"

"The problem," said the Chinj, "is that the Emperor himself has expressed an interest in visiting."

"Oh yes?"

"In fact," the Chinj admitted, "he's already come through."

"Is that right?"

"Actually, there's a rather heated scene going on as we speak. It's becoming difficult to prevent other humans who don't . . . 'know the score,' as it were, from seeing things that they probably shouldn't."

"I can imagine," said Jack distractedly. Much as he was enjoying talking to the Chinj, he was uncomfortably aware of how much time was passing. Soon, no doubt, he was going to have to go back to his double history class and pretend that nothing had happened. "So," he asked, "what does this have to do with me?"

The Chinj hopped awkwardly from one foot to the other.

"The Emperor has asked for you personally," it said. "In fact, his Royal Highness has indicated that he will tear every part of the Light of the Moon into tiny pieces with his tentacles unless you come and explain to everyone how he once fooled you into thinking he was a human."

"Jagmat," said Jack, realizing. "*Jagmat*'s the new Emperor?"

"I believe," the Chinj went on, with obvious exasperation, "he thinks that this will somehow convince Esme and the Sons to let him take a look around. At any rate, you'd better come and talk to him."

"Well, fancy that," said Jack, pleased for the blancmange-like demon.

The Chinj looked at him doubtfully.

"How soon can you get away from this place?" it asked.

Jack looked up at the small creature, seeing his own reflection in the lenses of its sunglasses.

He didn't reply straightaway. A part of him was telling him that he ought to say no, that he should probably go back to double history and get on with the rest of his life.

But the other part of him was already working out how he could escape.

"Tell them I'm on my way," he said.

And then, for the first time in quite a while—

—he smiled.

ACKNOWLEDGMENTS

I am particularly grateful to the following people for their help with this book.

First, and most important, to my lovely girlfriend Laura, and my stalwart flatmate Simon, for putting up with me and for giving *Black Tat* merciless critical savagings whenever it needed them, which was often. To my brother Jack: when it comes to draft-readers, I'm really very lucky. For fight scene advice, "Sifu" Sid and "Swordmistress" Suze: any technical errors I've made in the fights in this story certainly aren't for want of effort on their part. To Kelly and Lucy at RHCB and Liesa and Eloise at Razorbill, for their sensitive and eagle-eyed editorial input. To Maggie, for waving her wand and changing my life. To the staff (past and present) of Blackwell's bookshop on London's Charing Cross Road, for their support and encouragement. To Douglas Hill—grandmaster of SF thrills for young people—for being an inspiration. To James Long and his fine novel *Silence and Shadows* for the idea behind the pigeon sword (and to Simon M. for knowing how much it would appeal to me!). Finally, to my friend Antonia, for being *Black Tat*'s number one fan when there was no number two. In June 2003 I'd all but given up on this book: if it wasn't for her insisting she find out how the story ends, then you wouldn't be reading this now. Thank you. Thank you all.

Musically, *The Black Tattoo* was written under the combined influence of a lot of brutal drum-and-bass abuse (old-fashioned to some, but it still does the job for me) and the soundtracks to many of my favorite films (you've read the book, you can probably guess which ones I mean!).

"Write the exact book that you yourself would be thrilled to read," Lee Child once said. That's still the best piece of writing advice I've ever heard.

All best wishes to you,

Sam, 12th Jan. 2006

www.theblacktattoo.com

Password: "Fetid"